Family Maps
of
Jones County, Mississippi
Deluxe Edition

With Homesteads, Roads, Waterways, Towns, Cemeteries, Railroads, and More

Family Maps
of
Jones County, Mississippi
Deluxe Edition

With Homesteads, Roads, Waterways, Towns, Cemeteries, Railroads, and More

by Gregory A. Boyd, J.D.

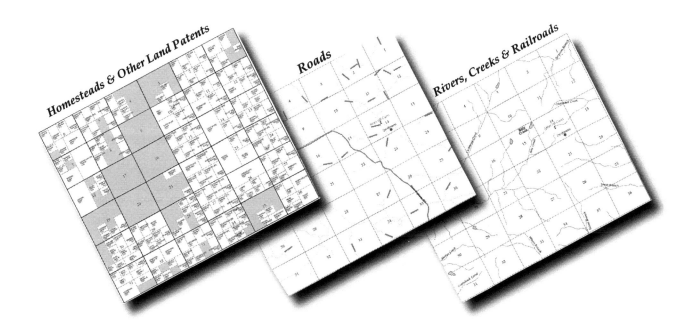

Featuring 3 *Maps Per Township...*

Arphax Publishing Co.
www.arphax.com

Family Maps of Jones County, Mississippi, Deluxe Edition: With Homesteads, Roads, Waterways, Towns, Cemeteries, Railroads, and More.
by Gregory A. Boyd, J.D.

ISBN 1-4203-1500-5

Published by Arphax Publishing Co., 2210 Research Park Blvd., Norman, Oklahoma, USA 73069
www.arphax.com

First Edition

ATTENTION HISTORICAL & GENEALOGICAL SOCIETIES, UNIVERSITIES, COLLEGES, CORPORATIONS, FAMILY REUNION COORDINATORS, AND PROFESSIONAL ORGANIZATIONS: Quantity discounts are available on bulk purchases of this book. For information, please contact Arphax Publishing Co., at the address listed above, or at (405) 366-6181, or visit our web-site at www.arphax.com and contact us through the "Bulk Sales" link.

—LEGAL—

This book is dedicated to my wonderful family:

Vicki, Jordan, & Amy Boyd

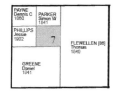

Contents

Preface..1
How to Use this Book - A Graphical Summary..2
How to Use This Book..3

- Part I -

The Big Picture

Map **A** - Where Jones County, Mississippi Lies Within the State 11
Map **B** - Jones County, Mississippi and Surrounding Counties 12
Map **C** - Congressional Townships of Jones County, Mississippi 13
Map **D** - Cities & Towns of Jones County, Mississippi 14
Map **E** - Cemeteries of Jones County, Mississippi 16
Surnames in Jones County, Mississippi Patents 18
Surname/Township Index 21

- Part II -

Township Map Groups

(each Map Group contains a Patent Index, Patent Map, Road Map, & Historical Map)

Map Group **1** - Township 10-N Range 14-W...42
Map Group **2** - Township 10-N Range 13-W...46
Map Group **3** - Township 10-N Range 12-W...52
Map Group **4** - Township 10-N Range 11-W...58
Map Group **5** - Township 10-N Range 10-W...64
Map Group **6** - Township 9-N Range 14-W...70
Map Group **7** - Township 9-N Range 13-W...76
Map Group **8** - Township 9-N Range 12-W...88
Map Group **9** - Township 9-N Range 11-W...100
Map Group **10** - Township 9-N Range 10-W...112
Map Group **11** - Township 8-N Range 14-W...122
Map Group **12** - Township 8-N Range 13-W...128
Map Group **13** - Township 8-N Range 12-W...138
Map Group **14** - Township 8-N Range 11-W...148
Map Group **15** - Township 8-N Range 10-W...158
Map Group **16** - Township 7-N Range 14-W...168
Map Group **17** - Township 7-N Range 13-W...174
Map Group **18** - Township 7-N Range 12-W...184
Map Group **19** - Township 7-N Range 11-W...194

Map Group **20** - Township 7-N Range 10-W 206
Map Group **21** - Township 6-N Range 14-W 216
Map Group **22** - Township 6-N Range 13-W 222
Map Group **23** - Township 6-N Range 12-W 232
Map Group **24** - Township 6-N Range 11-W 244
Map Group **25** - Township 6-N Range 10-W 256

Appendices

Appendix A - Congressional Authority for Land Patents 268
Appendix B - Section Parts (Aliquot Parts) 269
Appendix C - Multi-Patentee Groups in Jones County 273

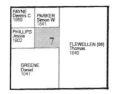

Preface

The quest for the discovery of my ancestors' origins, migrations, beliefs, and life-ways has brought me rewards that I could never have imagined. The *Family Maps* series of books is my first effort to share with historical and genealogical researchers, some of the tools that I have developed to achieve my research goals. I firmly believe that this effort will allow many people to reap the same sorts of treasures that I have.

Our Federal government's General Land Office of the Bureau of Land Management (the "GLO") has given genealogists and historians an incredible gift by virtue of its enormous database housed on its web-site at glorecords.blm.gov. Here, you can search for and find millions of parcels of land purchased by our ancestors in about thirty states.

This GLO web-site is one of the best FREE on-line tools available to family researchers. But, it is not for the faint of heart, nor is it for those unwilling or unable to to sift through and analyze the thousands of records that exist for most counties.

My immediate goal with this series is to spare you the hundreds of hours of work that it would take you to map the Land Patents for this county. Every Jones County homestead or land patent that I have gleaned from public GLO databases is mapped here. Consequently, I can usually show you in an instant, where your ancestor's land is located, as well as the names of nearby land-owners.

Originally, that was my primary goal. But after speaking to other genealogists, it became clear that there was much more that they wanted. Taking their advice set me back almost a full year, but I think you will agree it was worth the wait. Because now, you can learn so much more.

Now, this book answers these sorts of questions:

- Are there any variant spellings for surnames that I have missed in searching GLO records?
- Where is my family's traditional home-place?
- What cemeteries are near Grandma's house?
- My Granddad used to swim in such-and-such-Creek—where is that?
- How close is this little community to that one?
- Are there any other people with the same surname who bought land in the county?
- How about cousins and in-laws—did they buy land in the area?

And these are just for starters!

The rules for using the *Family Maps* books are simple, but the strategies for success are many. Some techniques are apparent on first use, but many are gained with time and experience. Please take the time to notice the roads, cemeteries, creek-names, family names, and unique first-names throughout the whole county. You cannot imagine what YOU might be the first to discover.

I hope to learn that many of you have answered age-old research questions within these pages or that you have discovered relationships previously not even considered. When these sorts of things happen to you, will you please let me hear about it? I would like nothing better. My contact information can always be found at www.arphax.com.

One more thing: please read the "How To Use This Book" chapter; it starts on the next page. This will give you the very best chance to find the treasures that lie within these pages.

My family and I wish you the very best of luck, both in life, and in your research.   Greg Boyd

How to Use This Book - A Graphical Summary

Part I
"The Big Picture"

Map A ▸ *Counties in the State*
Map B ▸ *Surrounding Counties*
Map C ▸ *Congressional Townships (Map Groups) in the County*
Map D ▸ *Cities & Towns in the County*
Map E ▸ *Cemeteries in the County*
Surnames in the County ▸ *Number of Land-Parcels for Each Surname*
Surname/Township Index ▸ *Directs you to Township Map Groups in Part II*

The Surname/Township Index can direct you to any number of **Township Map Groups**

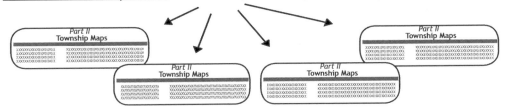

Part II
Township Map Groups
(1 for each Township in the County)

Each Township Map Group contains all four of of the following tools . . .

Land Patent Index ▸ *Every-name Index of Patents Mapped in this Township*
Land Patent Map ▸ *Map of Patents as listed in above Index*
Road Map ▸ *Map of Roads, City-centers, and Cemeteries in the Township*
Historical Map ▸ *Map of Railroads, Lakes, Rivers, Creeks, City-Centers, and Cemeteries*

Appendices

Appendix A ▸ *Congressional Authority enabling Patents within our Maps*
Appendix B ▸ *Section-Parts / Aliquot Parts (a comprehensive list)*
Appendix C ▸ *Multi-patentee Groups (Individuals within Buying Groups)*

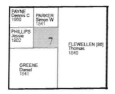

How to Use This Book

The two "Parts" of this *Family Maps* volume seek to answer two different types of questions. Part I deals with broad questions like: what counties surround Jones County, are there any ASHCRAFTs in Jones County, and if so, in which Townships or Maps can I find them? Ultimately, though, Part I should point you to a particular Township Map Group in Part II.

Part II concerns itself with details like: where exactly is this family's land, who else bought land in the area, and what roads and streams run through the land, or are located nearby. The Chart on the opposite page, and the remainder of this chapter attempt to convey to you the particulars of these two "parts", as well as how best to use them to achieve your research goals.

Part I
"The Big Picture"

Within Part I, you will find five "Big Picture" maps and two county-wide surname tools.

These include:

• Map A - Where Jones County lies within the state
• Map B - Counties that surround Jones County
• Map C - Congressional Townships of Jones County (+ Map Group Numbers)
• Map D - Cities & Towns of Jones County (with Index)
• Map E - Cemeteries of Jones County (with Index)
• Surnames in Jones County Patents (with Parcel-counts for each surname)
• Surname/Township Index (with Parcel-counts for each surname by Township)

The five "Big-Picture" Maps are fairly self-

explanatory, yet should not be overlooked. This is particularly true of Maps "C", "D", and "E", all of which show Jones County and its Congressional Townships (and their assigned Map Group Numbers).

Let me briefly explain this concept of Map Group Numbers. These are a device completely of our own invention. They were created to help you quickly locate maps without having to remember the full legal name of the various Congressional Townships. It is simply easier to remember "Map Group 1" than a legal name like: "Township 9-North Range 6-West, 5th Principal Meridian." But the fact is that the TRUE legal name for these Townships IS terribly important. These are the designations that others will be familiar with and you will need to accurately record them in your notes. This is why both Map Group numbers AND legal descriptions of Townships are almost always displayed together.

Map "C" will be your first intoduction to "Map Group Numbers", and that is all it contains: legal Township descriptions and their assigned Map Group Numbers. Once you get further into your research, and more immersed in the details, you will likely want to refer back to Map "C" from time to time, in order to regain your bearings on just where in the county you are researching.

Remember, township boundaries are a completely artificial device, created to standardize land descriptions. But do not let them become a boundary in your mind when choosing which townships to research. Your relative's in-laws, children, cousins, siblings, and mamas and papas, might just as easily have lived in the township next to the one your grandfather lived in—rather than in the one where he actually lived. So Map "C" can be your guide to which other Townships/ Map Groups you likewise ought to analyze.

Of course, the same holds true for County lines; this is the purpose behind Map "B". It shows you surrounding counties that you may want to consider for further reserarch.

Map "D", the Cities and Towns map, is the first map with an index. Map "E" is the second (Cemeteries). Both, Maps "D" and "E" give you broad views of City (or Cemetery) locations in the County. But they go much further by pointing you toward pertinent Township Map Groups so you can locate the patents, roads, and waterways located near a particular city or cemetery.

Once you are familiar with these *Family Maps* volumes and the county you are researching, the "Surnames In Jones County" chapter (or its sister chapter in other volumes) is where you'll likely start your future research sessions. Here, you can quickly scan its few pages and see if anyone in the county possesses the surnames you are researching. The "Surnames in Jones County" list shows only two things: surnames and the number of parcels of land we have located for that surname in Jones County. But whether or not you immediately locate the surnames you are researching, please do not go any further without taking a few moments to scan ALL the surnames in these very few pages.

You cannot imagine how many lost ancestors are waiting to be found by someone willing to take just a little longer to scan the "Surnames In Jones County" list. Misspellings and typographical errors abound in most any index of this sort. Don't miss out on finding your Kinard that was written Rynard or Cox that was written Lox. If it looks funny or wrong, it very often is. And one of those little errors may well be your relative.

Now, armed with a surname and the knowledge that it has one or more entries in this book, you are ready for the "Surname/Township Index." Unlike the "Surnames In Jones County", which has only one line per Surname, the "Surname/Township Index" contains one line-item for each Township Map Group in which each surname is found. In other words, each line represents a different Township Map Group that you will need to review.

Specifically, each line of the Surname/Township

Index contains the following four columns of information:

1. Surname
2. Township Map Group Number (these Map Groups are found in Part II)
3. Parcels of Land (number of them with the given Surname within the Township)
4. Meridian/Township/Range (the legal description for this Township Map Group)

The key column here is that of the Township Map Group Number. While you should definitely record the Meridian, Township, and Range, you can do that later. Right now, you need to dig a little deeper. That Map Group Number tells you where in Part II that you need to start digging.

But before you leave the "Surname/Township Index", do the same thing that you did with the "Surnames in Jones County" list: take a moment to scan the pages of the Index and see if there are similarly spelled or misspelled surnames that deserve your attention. Here again, is an easy opportunity to discover grossly misspelled family names with very little effort. Now you are ready to turn to . . .

Part II
"Township Map Groups"

You will normally arrive here in Part II after being directed to do so by one or more "Map Group Numbers" in the Surname/Township Index of Part I.

Each Map Group represents a set of four tools dedicated to a single Congressional Township that is either wholly or partially within the county. If you are trying to learn all that you can about a particular family or their land, then these tools should usually be viewed in the order they are presented.

These four tools include:

1. a Land Patent Index
2. a Land Patent Map
3. a Road Map, and
4. an Historical Map

As I mentioned earlier, each grouping of this sort is assigned a Map Group Number. So, let's now move on to a discussion of the four tools that make up one of these Township Map Groups.

Land Patent Index

Each Township Map Group's Index begins with a title, something along these lines:

MAP GROUP 1: Index to Land Patents
Township 16-North Range 5-West (2ⁿᵈ PM)

The Index contains seven (7) columns. They are:

1. ID (a unique ID number for this Individual and a corresponding Parcel of land in this Township)
2. Individual in Patent (name)
3. Sec. (Section), and
4. Sec. Part (Section Part, or Aliquot Part)
5. Date Issued (Patent)
6. Other Counties (often means multiple counties were mentioned in GLO records, or the section lies within multiple counties).
7. For More Info . . . (points to other places within this index or elsewhere in the book where you can find more information)

While most of the seven columns are self-explanatory, I will take a few moments to explain the "Sec. Part." and "For More Info" columns.

The "Sec. Part" column refers to what surveryors and other land professionals refer to as an Aliquot Part. The origins and use of such a term mean little to a non-surveyor, and I have chosen to simply call these sub-sections of land what they are: a "Section Part". No matter what we call them, what we are referring to are things like a quarter-section or half-section or quarter-quarter-section. See Appendix "B" for most of the "Section Parts" you will come across (and many you will not) and what size land-parcel they represent.

The "For More Info" column of the Index may seem like a small appendage to each line, but please

recognize quickly that this is not so. And to understand the various items you might find here, you need to become familiar with the Legend that appears at the top of each Land Patent Index.

Here is a sample of the Legend . . .

LEGEND

```
              "For More Info . . . " column

A = Authority (Legislative Act, See Appendix "A")
B = Block or Lot (location in Section unknown)
C = Cancelled Patent
F = Fractional Section
G = Group (Multi-Patentee Patent, see Appendix "C")
V = Overlaps another Parcel
R = Re-Issued (Parcel patented more than once)
```

Most parcels of land will have only one or two of these items in their "For More Info" columns, but when that is not the case, there is often some valuable information to be gained from further investigation. Below, I will explain what each of these items means to you you as a researcher.

A = Authority
(Legislative Act, See Appendix "A")
All Federal Land Patents were issued because some branch of our government (usually the U.S. Congress) passed a law making such a transfer of title possible. And therefore every patent within these pages will have an "A" item next to it in the index. The number after the "A" indicates which item in Appendix "A" holds the citation to the particular law which authorized the transfer of land to the public. As it stands, most of the Public Land data compiled and released by our government, and which serves as the basis for the patents mapped here, concerns itself with "Cash Sale" homesteads. So in some Counties, the law which authorized cash sales will be the primary, if not the only, entry in the Appendix.

B = Block or Lot (location in Section unknown)
A "B" designation in the Index is a tip-off that the EXACT location of the patent within the map is not apparent from the legal description. This Patent will nonetheless be noted within the proper

Section along with any other Lots purchased in the Section. Given the scope of this project (many states and many Counties are being mapped), trying to locate all relevant plats for Lots (if they even exist) and accurately mapping them would have taken one person several lifetimes. But since our primary goal from the onset has been to establish relationships between neighbors and families, very little is lost to this goal since we can still observe who all lived in which Section.

C = Cancelled Patent

A Cancelled Patent is just that: cancelled. Whether the original Patentee forfeited his or her patent due to fraud, a technicality, non-payment, or whatever, the fact remains that it is significant to know who received patents for what parcels and when. A cancellation may be evidence that the Patentee never physically re-located to the land, but does not in itself prove that point. Further evidence would be required to prove that. *See also*, Re-issued Patents, *below*.

F = Fractional Section

A Fractional Section is one that contains less than 640 acres, almost always because of a body of water. The exact size and shape of land-parcels contained in such sections may not be ascertainable, but we map them nonetheless. Just keep in mind that we are not mapping an actual parcel to scale in such instances. Another point to consider is that we have located some fractional sections that are not so designated by the Bureau of Land Management in their data. This means that not all fractional sections have been so identified in our indexes.

G = Group
(Multi-Patentee Patent, see Appendix "C")

A "G" designation means that the Patent was issued to a GROUP of people (Multi-patentees). The "G" will always be followed by a number. Some such groups were quite large and it was impractical if not impossible to display each individual in our maps without unduly affecting readability. EACH person in the group is named in the Index, but they won't all be found on the Map. You will find the name of the first person in such a Group

on the map with the Group number next to it, enclosed in [square brackets].

To find all the members of the Group you can either scan the Index for all people with the same Group Number or you can simply refer to Appendix "C" where all members of the Group are listed next to their number.

O = Overlaps another Parcel

An Overlap is one where PART of a parcel of land gets issued on more than one patent. For genealogical purposes, both transfers of title are important and both Patentees are mapped. If the ENTIRE parcel of land is re-issued, that is what we call it, a Re-Issued Patent (*see below*). The number after the "O" indicates the ID for the overlapping Patent(s) contained within the same Index. Like Re-Issued and Cancelled Patents, Overlaps may cause a map-reader to be confused at first, but for genealogical purposes, all of these parties' relationships to the underlying land is important, and therefore, we map them.

R = Re-Issued (Parcel patented more than once)

The label, "Re-issued Patent" describes Patents which were issued more than once for land with the EXACT SAME LEGAL DESCRIPTION. Whether the original patent was cancelled or not, there were a good many parcels which were patented more than once. The number after the "R" indicates the ID for the other Patent contained within the same Index that was for the same land. A quick glance at the map itself within the relevant Section will be the quickest way to find the other Patentee to whom the Parcel was transferred. They should both be mapped in the same general area.

I have gone to some length describing all sorts of anomalies either in the underlying data or in their representation on the maps and indexes in this book. Most of this will bore the most ardent researcher, but I do this with all due respect to those researchers who will inevitably (and rightfully) ask: *"Why isn't so-and-so's name on the exact spot that the index says it should be?"*

In most cases it will be due to the existence of a Multi-Patentee Patent, a Re-issued Patent, a Cancelled Patent, or Overlapping Parcels named in separate Patents. I don't pretend that this discussion will answer every question along these lines, but I hope it will at least convince you of the complexity of the subject.

Not to despair, this book's companion web-site will offer a way to further explain "odd-ball" or errant data. Each book (County) will have its own web-page or pages to discuss such situations. You can go to www.arphax.com to find the relevant web-page for Jones County.

Land Patent Map

On the first two-page spread following each Township's Index to Land Patents, you'll find the corresponding Land Patent Map. And here lies the real heart of our work. For the first time anywhere, researchers will be able to observe and analyze, on a grand scale, most of the original land-owners for an area AND see them mapped in proximity to each one another.

We encourage you to make vigorous use of the accompanying Index described above, but then later, to abandon it, and just stare at these maps for a while. This is a great way to catch misspellings or to find collateral kin you'd not known were in the area.

Each Land Patent Map represents one Congressional Township containing approximately 36-square miles. Each of these square miles is labeled by an accompanying Section Number (1 through 36, in most cases). Keep in mind, that this book concerns itself solely with Jones County's patents. Townships which creep into one or more other counties will not be shown in their entirety in any one book. You will need to consult other books, as they become available, in order to view other countys' patents, cities, cemeteries, etc.

But getting back to Jones County: each Land Patent Map contains a Statistical Chart that looks like the following:

Township Statistics

Parcels Mapped	:	173
Number of Patents	:	163
Number of Individuals	:	152
Patentees Identified	:	151
Number of Surnames	:	137
Multi-Patentee Parcels	:	4
Oldest Patent Date	:	11/27/1820
Most Recent Patent	:	9/28/1917
Block/Lot Parcels	:	0
Parcels Re-Issued	:	3
Parcels that Overlap	:	8
Cities and Towns	:	6
Cemeteries	:	6

This information may be of more use to a social statistician or historian than a genealogist, but I think all three will find it interesting.

Most of the statistics are self-explanatory, and what is not, was described in the above discussion of the Index's Legend, but I do want to mention a few of them that may affect your understanding of the Land Patent Maps.

First of all, Patents often contain more than one Parcel of land, so it is common for there to be more Parcels than Patents. Also, the Number of Individuals will more often than not, not match the number of Patentees. A Patentee is literally the person or PERSONS named in a patent. So, a Patent may have a multi-person Patentee or a single-person patentee. Nonetheless, we account for all these individuals in our indexes.

On the lower-righthand side of the Patent Map is a Legend which describes various features in the map, including Section Boundaries, Patent (land) Boundaries, Lots (numbered), and Multi-Patentee Group Numbers. You'll also find a "Helpful Hints" Box that will assist you.

One important note: though the vast majority of Patents mapped in this series will prove to be reasonably accurate representations of their actual locations, we cannot claim this for patents lying along state and county lines, or waterways, or that have been platted (lots).

Shifting boundaries and sparse legal descriptions in the GLO data make this a reality that we have nonetheless tried to overcome by estimating these patents' locations the best that we can.

Road Map

On the two-page spread following each Patent Map you will find a Road Map covering the exact same area (the same Congressional Township).

For me, fully exploring the past means that every once in a while I must leave the library and travel to the actual locations where my ancestors once walked and worked the land. Our Township Road Maps are a great place to begin such a quest.

Keep in mind that the scaling and proportion of these maps was chosen in order to squeeze hundreds of people-names, road-names, and place-names into tinier spaces than you would traditionally see. These are not professional road-maps, and like any secondary genealogical source, should be looked upon as an entry-way to original sources—in this case, original patents and applications, professionally produced maps and surveys, etc.

Both our Road Maps and Historical Maps contain cemeteries and city-centers, along with a listing of these on the left-hand side of the map. I should note that I am showing you city center-points, rather than city-limit boundaries, because in many instances, this will represent a place where settlement began. This may be a good time to mention that many cemeteries are located on private property, Always check with a local historical or genealogical society to see if a particular cemetery is publicly accessible (if it is not obviously so). As a final point, look for your surnames among the road-names. You will often be surprised by what you find.

Historical Map

The third and final map in each Map Group is our attempt to display what each Township might have looked like before the advent of modern roads. In frontier times, people were usually more determined to settle near rivers and creeks than they were near roads, which were often few and

far between. As was the case with the Road Map, we've included the same cemeteries and city-centers. We've also included railroads, many of which came along before most roads.

While some may claim "Historical Map" to be a bit of a misnomer for this tool, we settled for this label simply because it was almost as accurate as saying "Railroads, Lakes, Rivers, Cities, and Cemeteries," and it is much easier to remember.

In Closing . . .

By way of example, here is *A Really Good Way to Use a Township Map Group.* First, find the person you are researching in the Township's Index to Land Patents, which will direct you to the proper Section and parcel on the Patent Map. But before leaving the Index, scan all the patents within it, looking for other names of interest. Now, turn to the Patent Map and locate your parcels of land. Pay special attention to the names of patent-holders who own land surrounding your person of interest. Next, turn the page and look at the same Section(s) on the Road Map. Note which roads are closest to your parcels and also the names of nearby towns and cemeteries. Using other resources, you may be able to learn of kin who have been buried here, plus, you may choose to visit these cemeteries the next time you are in the area.

Finally, turn to the Historical Map. Look once more at the same Sections where you found your research subject's land. Note the nearby streams, creeks, and other geographical features. You may be surprised to find family names were used to name them, or you may see a name you haven't heard mentioned in years and years—and a new research possibility is born.

Many more techniques for using these *Family Maps* volumes will no doubt be discovered. If from time to time, you will navigate to Jones County's web-page at www.arphax.com (use the "Research" link), you can learn new tricks as they become known (or you can share ones you have employed). But for now, you are ready to get started. So, go, and good luck.

– Part I –

The Big Picture

Map A - Where Jones County, Mississippi Lies Within the State

---- Legend ----

State Boundary

County Boundaries

Jones County, Mississippi

---- Helpful Hints ----

1 We start with Map "A" which simply shows us where within the State this county lies.

2 Map "B" zooms in further to help us more easily identify surrounding Counties.

3 Map "C" zooms in even further to reveal the Congressional Townships that either lie within or intersect Jones County.

Map B - Jones County, Mississippi and Surrounding Counties

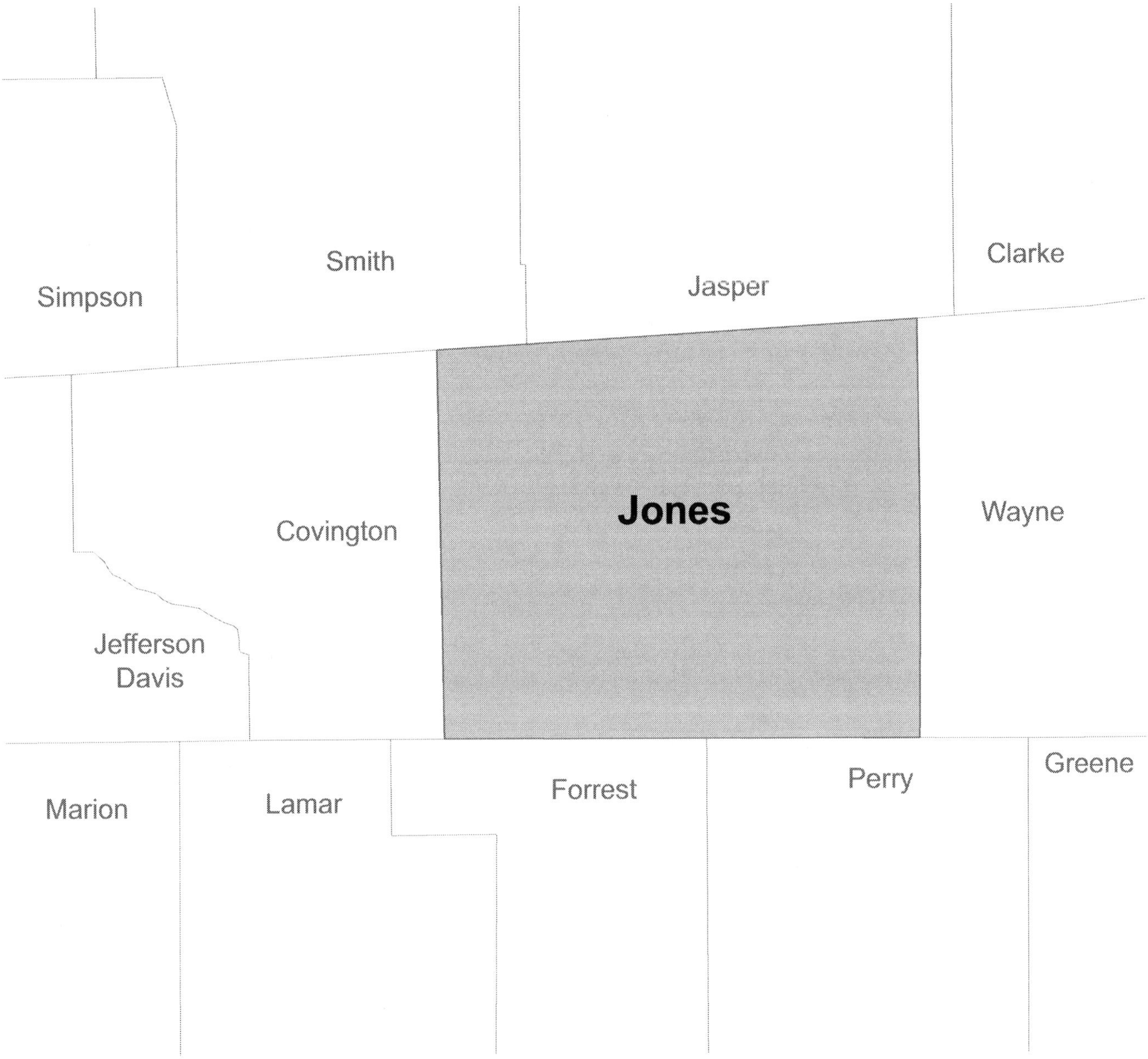

Simpson

Smith

Jasper

Clarke

Covington

Jones

Wayne

Jefferson
Davis

Greene

Marion

Lamar

Forrest

Perry

Legend

State Boundaries (when applicable)

County Boundary

Helpful Hints
---

1 Many Patent-holders and their families settled across county lines. It is always a good idea to check nearby counties for your families.

2 Refer to Map "A" to see a broader view of where this County lies within the State, and Map "C" to see which Congressional Townships lie within Jones County.

Map C - Congressional Townships of Jones County, Mississippi

Map Group 1 Township 10-N Range 14-W	Map Group 2 Township 10-N Range 13-W	Map Group 3 Township 10-N Range 12-W	Map Group 4 Township 10-N Range 11-W	Map Group 5 Township 10-N Range 10-W
Map Group 6 Township 9-N Range 14-W	Map Group 7 Township 9-N Range 13-W	Map Group 8 Township 9-N Range 12-W	Map Group 9 Township 9-N Range 11-W	Map Group 10 Township 9-N Range 10-W
Map Group 11 Township 8-N Range 14-W	Map Group 12 Township 8-N Range 13-W	Map Group 13 Township 8-N Range 12-W	Map Group 14 Township 8-N Range 11-W	Map Group 15 Township 8-N Range 10-W
Map Group 16 Township 7-N Range 14-W	Map Group 17 Township 7-N Range 13-W	Map Group 18 Township 7-N Range 12-W	Map Group 19 Township 7-N Range 11-W	Map Group 20 Township 7-N Range 10-W
Map Group 21 Township 6-N Range 14-W	Map Group 22 Township 6-N Range 13-W	Map Group 23 Township 6-N Range 12-W	Map Group 24 Township 6-N Range 11-W	Map Group 25 Township 6-N Range 10-W

--- Legend ---

Jones County, Mississippi

Congressional Townships

--- Helpful Hints ---

1   Many Patent-holders and their families settled across county lines. It is always a good idea to check nearby counties for your families (See Map "B").

2   Refer to Map "A" to see a broader view of where this county lies within the State, and Map "B" for a view of the counties surrounding Jones County.

Map D Index: Cities & Towns of Jones County, Mississippi

The following represents the Cities and Towns of Jones County, along with the corresponding Map Group in which each is found. Cities and Towns are displayed in both the Road and Historical maps in the Group.

City/Town	Map Group No.
Albeison	22
Amy	7
Antioch	14
Benson	18
Blodgett	25
Bonner	4
Calhoun	13
Cleo	10
Crotts	19
Currie	13
Eastview	9
Ellisville	18
Errata	9
Flynt	8
Gitano	7
Glade	14
Glaston	14
Haney	5
Hawkes	9
Hebron	6
Hoy	9
Jenkins	18
Johnson	19
Lanham	19
Laurel	14
Matthews	3
Mill Creek	15
Monarch	24
Moselle	22
Mount Olive	9
Mount Zion	13
Myrick	15
Oak Bowery	11
Oak Grove	18
Ovett	25
Pecan Grove	19
Pendorff	13
Pleasant Ridge	13
Powers	9
Queensburg	14
Rainey	21
Sand Hill	12
Sandersville	5
Service	8
Shady Grove	8
Sharon	4
Shelton	21
Soso	7
Springhill	8
Tallahomo	19
Tawanta	17
Tuckers Crossing	14
Union	23
Walters	13
Whitfield	24

Map D - Cities & Towns of Jones County, Mississippi

Map Group 1 Township 10-N Range 14-W	Map Group 2 Township 10-N Range 13-W	Matthews ● Map Group 3 Township 10-N Range 12-W	Bonner ● Map Group 4 Township 10-N Range 11-W ● Sharon	● Haney Map Group 5 Township 10-N Range 10-W ● Sandersville

Map Group 6
Township 9-N
Range 14-W
 	
Hebron ●
	Gitano ● Amy ●
	Soso ●
	Map Group 7
	Township 9-N Range 13-W
		Shady Grove ●
		● Springhill
		● Service
		Map Group 8
		Township 9-N Range 12-W
			● Hoy
			          Errata ●
			Hawkes ●
			        Mount Olive ●
			Map Group 9
			Township 9-N Range 11-W
				Map Group 10
				Township 9-N Range 10-W

Map Group 11 Township 8-N Range 14-W ● Oak Bowery	Map Group 12 Township 8-N Range 13-W Sand Hill ●	Calhoun ● ● Flynt ● Pleasant Ridge Pendorff ● ● Mount Zion ● Walters Map Group 13 Township 8-N Range 12-W Currie ●	Powers ● Eastview Laurel ● Queensburg Glade ● ● Glaston Map Group 14 Township 8-N Range 11-W Antioch ● ● Tuckers Crossing	● Cleo Mill Creek ● ● Myrick Map Group 15 Township 8-N Range 10-W
Map Group 16 Township 7-N Range 14-W Rainey ●	Map Group 17 Township 7-N Range 13-W Tawanta ●	Ellisville ● Jenkins ● Map Group 18 Township 7-N Range 12-W ● Benson ● Oak Grove	● Pecan Grove Lanham ● Map Group 19 Township 7-N Range 11-W ● Crotts ● Johnson ● Tallahomo	Map Group 20 Township 7-N Range 10-W
Shelton ● Map Group 21 Township 6-N Range 14-W	Moselle ● ● Albeison Map Group 22 Township 6-N Range 13-W	Map Group 23 Township 6-N Range 12-W Union ●	● Monarch Map Group 24 Township 6-N Range 11-W Whitfield ●	● Ovett Map Group 25 Township 6-N Range 10-W ● Blodgett

Legend

Jones County, Mississippi

Congressional Townships

Helpful Hints

1 Cities and towns are marked only at their center-points as published by the USGS and/or NationalAtlas.gov. This often enables us to more closely approximate where these might have existed when first settled.

2 To see more specifically where these Cities & Towns are located within the county, refer to both the Road and Historical maps in the Map-Group referred to above. See also, the Map "D" Index on the opposite page.

Map E Index: Cemeteries of Jones County, Mississippi

The following represents many of the Cemeteries of Jones County, along with the corresponding Township Map Group in which each is found. Cemeteries are displayed in both the Road and Historical maps in the Map Groups referred to below.

Cemetery	Map Group No.	Cemetery	Map Group No.
Anderson-Minter Cem.	18	Mount Moriah Cem.	19
Antioch Cem.	7	Mount Olive Cem.	6
Antioch Cem.	14	Mount Olive Cem.	9
Beech Cem.	24	Mount Oral Cem.	14
Benson Cem.	17	Mount Vernon Cem.	14
Bethel Cem.	5	Mount Zion Cem.	12
Big Creek Cem.	12	Murphy Cem.	23
Blackledge Cem.	10	Myrick Cem.	15
Brown Cem.	18	New Bethany Cem.	12
Brown Cem.	25	Nora Davis Memorial Cem.	9
Bynum Cem.	18	Odom Cem.	24
Calhoun Cem.	8	Old Sharon Cem.	4
Callahan Cem.	22	Our Home Universalist Cem.	12
Center Ridge Cem.	6	Ovett Cem.	25
Centreville Cem.	12	Palestine Cem.	9
Choctaw Cem.	5	Pickering Cem.	11
Clark Cem.	15	Pilgrim Cem.	18
Coats Cem.	7	Pilgrims Rest Cem.	13
Coltins Cem.	23	Pine Grove Cem.	17
County Line Cem.	11	Pleasant Ridge Cem.	13
County Line Cem.	24	Sandersville Cem.	5
Crosby Cem.	17	Shady Grove Cem.	8
Crossroads Cem.	16	Shady Grove Cem.	22
Currie Cem.	13	Sharon Cem.	4
Dennis Blackledge Cem.	15	Shelton Cem.	21
Eastabuchie Cem.	22	Shows Cem.	8
Edmonson Cem.	22	Shows Cem.	13
Ellisville Cem.	18	Shows Cem.	23
Erratta Cem.	9	Spring Hill Cem.	8
Fairchild Cem.	22	Taylor Cem.	13
Fairfield Cem.	16	Tucker Cem.	19
Fall Cem.	10	Tularosa Cem.	18
Florence Cem.	5	Union Cem.	23
Gandy Cem.	17	Union Line Cem.	2
Harper Cem.	7	Walters Cem.	16
Hatton Cem.	6	Walters Cem.	18
Hebron Cem.	6	Walters Cem.	23
Hebron Lodge Cem.	6	Welborn Cem.	3
Hill Cem.	7	Welch Cem.	12
Hinton Cem.	1	Windham Cem.	14
Hinton Cem.	17	Woodlawn Cem.	13
Hopewell Cem.	22		
Indian Springs Cem.	13		
Jack Knight Cem.	6		
Johnson Cem.	18		
Jordan Cem.	17		
Jordan Cem.	18		
Jordan Cem.	23		
Kirland Cem.	23		
Knight Cem.	22		
Knights Mill Cem.	7		
Lancaster Cem.	24		
Laurel Cem.	9		
Lebanon Cem.	8		
Matthews Cem.	3		
May Cem.	10		
McGill Cem.	5		
Memorial Park Cem.	9		
Mill Creek Cem.	15		

Map E - Cemeteries of Jones County, Mississippi

	Map Group 1 Township 10-N Range 14-W Hinton ⚲	Map Group 2 Township 10-N Range 13-W Union Line ⚲ Knights Mill ⚲ Coats⚲ ⚲Antioch ⚲Harper	Matthews ⚲ Map Group 3 Township 10-N Range 12-W Welborn ⚲	McGill ⚲ Map Group 5 Township 10-N Sandersville ⚲ Choctaw⚲ Range 10-W Florence⚲ Bethel⚲
	Center Ridge ⚲ **Map Group 6** Township 9-N Range 14-W ⚲Hatton ⚲Mount Olive ⚲ Jack Knight ⚲Hebron Lodge Hebron⚲	**Map Group 7** Township 9-N Range 13-W Hill ⚲	**Map Group 8** Township 9-N Range 12-W Shady Grove ⚲ ⚲Spring Hill ⚲Shows ⚲Lebanon Calhoun⚲	**Map Group 4** Township 10-N Range 11-W ⚲Old Sharon Sharon ⚲ **Map Group 9** Township 9-N Range 11-W Erratta ⚲ Mount Olive ⚲ ⚲Palestine Nora Davis ⚲ Memorial ⚲Laurel Memorial Park ⚲	⚲May Blackledge ⚲ **Map Group 10** Township 9-N Range 10-W ⚲Fall
	⚲Pickering **Map Group 11** Township 8-N Range 14-W ⚲County Line	Big Creek⚲ ⚲Centreville Welch ⚲ Mount Zion⚲ **Map Group 12** Township 8-N Range 13-W ⚲New Bethany	Taylor⚲ ⚲ Shows ⚲Our Home ⚲Indian Springs Universalist ⚲Pilgrims Rest ⚲Pleasant Ridge ⚲Woodlawn **Map Group 13** Township 8-N Range 12-W Currie ⚲	Mount Oral ⚲ ⚲Windham ⚲Mount Vernon Antioch ⚲ **Map Group 14** Township 8-N Range 11-W	Mill Creek ⚲ Dennis Blackledge ⚲ ⚲Clark Myrick ⚲ **Map Group 15** Township 8-N Range 10-W
	Map Group 16 Township 7-N Range 14-W ⚲ Walters Crossroads ⚲ Fairfield ⚲	Hinton ⚲ **Map Group 17** Township 7-N Range 13-W Pine Grove⚲ Gandy ⚲ Jordan⚲ ⚲Crosby Benson⚲	Anderson-Minter ⚲ Bynum ⚲ Ellisville ⚲ Walters ⚲ Tularosa ⚲ ⚲Jordan **Map Group 18** Township 7-N Range 12-W Brown ⚲ Pilgrim⚲ Johnson ⚲	⚲Tucker **Map Group 19** Township 7-N Range 11-W Mount Moriah ⚲	**Map Group 20** Township 7-N Range 10-W
	Shelton⚲ **Map Group 21** Township 6-N Range 14-W	**Map Group 22** Township 6-N Range 13-W ⚲Callahan ⚲Hopewell ⚲ Fairchild ⚲Edmonson ⚲Knight Shady Grove ⚲ ⚲Eastabuchie	**Map Group 23** Township 6-N Range 12-W Shows⚲ Murphy ⚲ ⚲ Coltins ⚲ Union Kirland ⚲ Jordan Walters⚲	⚲Odom ⚲Beech Lancaster⚲ **Map Group 24** Township 6-N Range 11-W County Line ⚲	Ovett⚲ **Map Group 25** Township 6-N Range 10-W ⚲ Brown

—— Legend ——

Jones County, Mississippi

Congressional Townships

—— Helpful Hints ——

1 Cemeteries are marked at locations as published by the USGS and/or NationalAtlas.gov.

2 To see more specifically where these Cemeteries are located, refer to the Road & Historical maps in the Map-Group referred to above. See also, the Map "E" Index on the opposite page to make sure you don't miss any of the Cemeteries located within this Congressional township.

Surnames in Jones County, Mississippi Patents

The following list represents the surnames that we have located in Jones County, Mississippi Patents and the number of parcels that we have mapped for each one. Here is a quick way to determine the existence (or not) of Patents to be found in the subsequent indexes and maps of this volume.

Surname	# of Land Parcels	Surname	# of Land Parcels	Surname	# of Land Parcels	Surname	# of Land Parcels
ABNY	2	BRYAN	1	DEASON	6	GLIDEWELL	1
ACKENHAUSEN	7	BRYANT	25	DEAVENPORT	1	GLOVER	1
ADAMS	2	BUCHANAN	2	DELANCY	3	GORE	2
ADCOX	3	BUCKOLEW	3	DELK	9	GRAFTON	1
AGEE	1	BULLARD	2	DEMENT	3	GRAHAM	18
AGNEW	1	BUNKLEY	3	DENT	2	GRANBERRY	9
AINSWORTH	1	BURK	1	DEVALL	1	GRANISON	1
ALLEN	6	BURKHALTER	1	DEVINPORT	5	GRANTHAM	17
ALWAY	6	BUSBY	5	DICKENSON	2	GRAVES	29
ANDERSON	42	BUSH	29	DILLARD	3	GRAY	1
ANDREWS	5	BUTLER	1	DONALD	8	GRAYSON	8
APLIN	1	BYNUM	36	DOSSETT	12	GREEN	3
ARCHEY	1	BYRD	10	DOSSETTE	3	GRISSETT	2
ARRINGTON	3	CALLAHAM	8	DOWNING	2	GRISSOM	16
ATWOOD	1	CALLAHAN	1	DRAUGHN	2	GUI	3
BAILEY	5	CAMPBELL	3	DRENNAN	2	GUNTER	27
BALFOUR	28	CARAWAY	2	DREW	3	GUYE	3
BALY	2	CARLISLE	5	DRYDEN	3	HADDOX	1
BARKLEY	6	CARLTON	3	DUCKWORTH	19	HAFTER	2
BARKLY	1	CARPENTER	24	DYE	2	HAIGLER	2
BARLOW	6	CARTER	26	DYESS	1	HALES	3
BARNES	13	CHAMBLESS	1	DYKES	12	HALL	3
BARNETT	3	CHAPMAN	2	EASLEY	3	HAMILTON	6
BARTNE	3	CHARLESCRAFT	1	EASTERLING	33	HANSON	5
BATES	1	CHATHAM	1	EATON	1	HARDY	9
BAYLIS	16	CHISHOLM	1	EDWARDS	2	HARE	1
BEARD	1	CLARK	23	ELLZEY	8	HARGROVE	2
BEAVERS	1	COATES	9	ELLZY	2	HARPER	14
BEDWELL	1	COATNEY	4	ELZEY	1	HARREL	1
BEECH	13	COATS	17	EVANS	3	HARRELL	4
BEESLEY	1	COBB	2	EVERETT	2	HARRING	1
BELL	2	COLE	3	EWING	1	HARRIS	1
BENSON	1	COLEMAN	1	EZELL	3	HARVEY	1
BEWICK	6	COLLEY	14	FAIRCHILD	3	HATTON	5
BIRKETT	32	COLLINS	33	FAIRCHILDS	16	HAWKINS	5
BLACK	10	COMPANY	15	FALER	2	HAYS	5
BLACKLEDGE	6	COOLEY	6	FERGUSON	47	HENNIS	3
BLACKLIDGE	22	COOPER	13	FERRILL	3	HENSARLING	2
BLACKWELL	5	COPELAND	6	FEWOX	1	HERINGTON	2
BLODGETT	29	CORLEY	7	FLYNT	14	HERRING	1
BLUE	1	COTTON	1	FOKES	1	HERRINGTON	40
BONNER	10	COX	1	FOLKS	5	HICKS	3
BOOTH	1	CRABTREE	5	FREEMAN	3	HILBURN	3
BOROUGH	1	CRAFT	11	FURR	2	HILL	16
BOUTWELL	10	CRAKER	1	GAINEY	1	HINTON	20
BOWDEN	3	CRANFORD	2	GAMBRELL	8	HOBGOOD	2
BOWEN	3	CRAVEN	16	GANDY	5	HODGES	5
BOYCE	5	CRAWFORD	6	GARNER	3	HOGAN	1
BOYKIN	2	CREEL	20	GARRICK	5	HOLDER	12
BOYLES	4	CRENSHAW	5	GASKIN	2	HOLIFIELD	53
BRADLEY	4	CROMWELL	3	GATLIN	13	HOLLEY	8
BRADSHAW	3	CROSBY	9	GATTIS	1	HOLLIFIELD	1
BRAKENRIDGE	15	CRUMBY	7	GAVIN	3	HOLLIMAN	6
BRASHIER	2	CRUMITY	2	GEDDIE	7	HOLLIMON	8
BRASWELL	2	CULPEPPER	3	GEIGER	5	HOLT	3
BREAZEALE	3	CURTIS	1	GEIGGER	2	HOLYFIELD	15
BRELAND	4	DARRAH	1	GIEGER	3	HOOD	14
BRIDGES	5	DAVIDSON	3	GILENDER	4	HOPKINS	17
BROOMFIELD	2	DAVIS	37	GILLANDER	2	HOSKINS	4
BROWN	18	DEAN	4	GILLENDER	1	HOSSEY	2
BRUCE	2	DEARMAN	4	GILLEY	2	HOUGH	2
BRUMFIELD	2	DEASE	1	GILLINDER	1	HOWARD	7

Surname	# of Land Parcels	Surname	# of Land Parcels	Surname	# of Land Parcels	Surname	# of Land Parcels
HOWSE	5	MCBRIDE	3	NORDMAN	7	RUSHTON	18
HUFF	5	MCCALLUM	7	NORWOOD	3	RUSSELL	1
HULSEY	1	MCCRANEY	2	NOWELL	6	RUSTIN	1
HURST	1	MCCRAW	1	OBER	1	SAGE	12
HUTTO	7	MCCULLUM	2	ODOM	18	SANDERS	2
INGRAIM	3	MCDANIEL	9	OVERSTREET	6	SANDERSON	2
INGRAM	2	MCDONALD	20	OWEN	18	SANFORD	2
JACKSON	18	MCDUGALD	3	OWENS	2	SANTSON	2
JEFCOAT	16	MCGAHEY	3	PAGE	9	SAUL	2
JENKINS	10	MCGEE	5	PARISH	6	SAUNDERS	3
JIMISON	2	MCGILBERRY	12	PARKER	16	SCANLAN	3
JOHNSON	66	MCGILL	33	PARROT	1	SCARBROUGH	2
JOHNSTON	17	MCGILVERRY	1	PATERSON	2	SCHONE	2
JONES	27	MCGILVRAY	9	PATES	1	SCOTT	4
JORDAN	9	MCINNIS	3	PATRICK	8	SCRIVENER	1
JOSEY	4	MCKAY	3	PATTERSON	8	SCRIVNER	1
KAMPER	215	MCKEOWN	85	PATTON	2	SCRUGGS	1
KEETON	6	MCKINLEY	1	PEARCEY	1	SEAMAN	1
KELLEY	7	MCLAMORE	1	PEARSON	8	SELLERS	17
KELLY	12	MCLAURIN	2	PEOPLES	4	SHARP	2
KENNEDY	4	MCLEAIN	1	PERRY	1	SHELBY	3
KENT	8	MCLEMORE	2	PHILLIPS	3	SHERLY	1
KERVIN	1	MCLENDON	2	PICKERING	6	SHOEMAKE	10
KILGORE	10	MCMANUS	4	PINNELL	1	SHOLAR	2
KING	3	MCMILLAN	2	PITMAN	5	SHOWE	1
KIRKLAND	9	MCMULLEN	3	PITTMAN	6	SHOWES	1
KITCHENS	9	MCNAT	3	PITTS	11	SHOWS	86
KNIGHT	83	MCNIECE	2	PLOCK	42	SIMPSON	5
LAMPORT	3	MCPHERSON	49	PONDER	3	SIMS	6
LANDRUM	27	MCVEY	1	POOL	14	SINGELTARY	2
LANE	2	MEADOR	5	POWELL	35	SINGLETON	1
LANGLEY	1	MEDEARIS	3	PRESCOTT	3	SKELLY	3
LARD	3	MELVIN	10	PRESSCOAT	5	SMITH	104
LARRE	1	MERCHANT	2	PRICE	3	SPEARS	5
LAWSON	2	MERRITT	1	PRIDGEN	3	SPEED	1
LEE	8	MILEY	4	PRINCE	2	STAFFORD	3
LEWIS	21	MILLER	5	PRINE	3	STEELMON	2
LIGHTSEY	1	MILLSAP	10	PRYOR	6	STENNETT	1
LINDER	1	MILLSAPS	1	PURVIS	1	STEPHENS	4
LINDSEY	1	MISSISSIPPI	2	QUANCE	11	STEVENS	2
LITTLE	4	MITCHEL	2	QUICK	3	STEVENSON	3
LOCKHART	1	MITCHELL	9	RABUN	2	STEVISON	3
LOFTIN	1	MIXON	1	RAINEY	16	STEWART	7
LOFTON	1	MOFFETT	7	RAMSEY	3	STINSON	2
LONG	3	MONTGOMERY	3	RAYNER	1	STOCKTON	1
LOPER	1	MOORES	59	READ	1	STRANGE	3
LOTT	13	MORGAN	22	REAVES	2	STRICKLAND	10
LOURY	1	MORRELL	2	REDDECK	1	STRINGER	4
LOVE	2	MORRIS	2	REDDOCH	1	STULMAN	2
LOVETT	1	MORSE	4	REDDOCK	4	STUTMAN	1
LOVITT	1	MOSS	9	REESE	1	SUGGS	5
LOWE	9	MOTT	3	REEVES	3	SUMMERS	1
LOWERY	2	MOULDS	6	RIALS	6	SUMRALL	45
LOWRY	2	MURFEY	2	RICHARDSON	8	SYMES	9
LUMSEY	3	MURPHY	3	RIDGWAY	4	TAYLOR	4
LYNES	4	MURRAH	2	RIELS	4	TEMPLES	6
LYON	62	MURRAY	16	RIVERS	11	THACH	1
MAGEE	1	MURRY	3	ROBERTS	14	THATCH	3
MARTIN	2	MUSGROVE	26	ROBERTSON	8	THIGPEN	1
MASKEW	2	MYERS	3	ROBINSON	3	THOMAS	5
MASON	2	MYRICK	8	ROBISON	6	THOMPSON	7
MATHEWS	5	NALL	1	RODGERS	6	THOMSON	6
MATTHEWS	4	NELSON	12	ROGERS	11	THORNTON	3
MATTREN	1	NESOM	2	ROSE	5	THRASH	3
MAULDIN	3	NETTLES	2	ROUNSAVILL	3	TINNON	2
MAXCEY	2	NEWELL	1	ROWELL	1	TIPPIN	22
MAXEY	4	NEWSOM	4	ROYALS	9	TISDALE	40
MAXWELL	1	NICHOLES	1	RUMPH	3	TISDALL	1
MCADAMS	1	NIX	7	RUNNELLS	3	TODD	7
MCARTHUR	2	NOBLES	10	RUSH	8	TOUCHSTONE	5

Surname	# of Land Parcels
TRAVIS	1
TREST	24
TRIGGS	5
TUCKER	29
TURNER	9
ULMER	7
UNDERWOOD	8
UPSHAW	3
VALENTINE	36
VAN	2
VARNER	1
VAUGHAN	34
VAUGHN	2
VICK	1
VOLENTINE	2
VOLKING	2
VOLLENTINE	2
WADDELL	67
WADE	21
WAITES	3
WALL	1
WALLACE	3
WALLEY	2
WALTERS	117
WALTMAN	6
WARD	7
WARE	28
WARNER	14
WARREN	4
WATKINS	3
WATSON	180
WATTERS	8
WATTS	1
WEAVER	3
WEEKS	1
WELBORN	57
WELBORNE	6
WELCH	40
WELDY	1
WELLS	4
WEST	3
WHEELER	5
WHITE	2
WHITEHEAD	2
WHITTLE	3
WILBORN	11
WILLIAMS	16
WILLIS	3
WILSON	5
WINDHAM	16
WISE	1
WOODARD	6
WOODDARD	2
WOULARD	2
YATES	4
YAWN	4
YOUNG	1

Surname/Township Index

This Index allows you to determine which *Township Map Group(s)* contain individuals with the following surnames. Each *Map Group* has a corresponding full-name index of all individuals who obtained patents for land within its Congressional township's borders. After each index you will find the Patent Map to which it refers, and just thereafter, you can view the township's Road Map and Historical Map, with the latter map displaying streams, railroads, and more.

So, once you find your Surname here, proceed to the Index at the beginning of the **Map Group** indicated below.

Surname	Map Group	Parcels of Land	Meridian/Township/Range
ABNY	**4**	2	St Stephens 10-N 11-W
ACKENHAUSEN	**13**	7	St Stephens 8-N 12-W
ADAMS	**19**	2	St Stephens 7-N 11-W
ADCOX	**16**	3	St Stephens 7-N 14-W
AGEE	**8**	1	St Stephens 9-N 12-W
AGNEW	**24**	1	St Stephens 6-N 11-W
AINSWORTH	**13**	1	St Stephens 8-N 12-W
ALLEN	**7**	5	St Stephens 9-N 13-W
" "	**22**	1	St Stephens 6-N 13-W
ALWAY	**15**	5	St Stephens 8-N 10-W
" "	**7**	1	St Stephens 9-N 13-W
ANDERSON	**4**	15	St Stephens 10-N 11-W
" "	**13**	11	St Stephens 8-N 12-W
" "	**18**	6	St Stephens 7-N 12-W
" "	**17**	4	St Stephens 7-N 13-W
" "	**23**	3	St Stephens 6-N 12-W
" "	**1**	1	St Stephens 10-N 14-W
" "	**22**	1	St Stephens 6-N 13-W
" "	**6**	1	St Stephens 9-N 14-W
ANDREWS	**10**	3	St Stephens 9-N 10-W
" "	**9**	2	St Stephens 9-N 11-W
APLIN	**18**	1	St Stephens 7-N 12-W
ARCHEY	**22**	1	St Stephens 6-N 13-W
ARRINGTON	**5**	1	St Stephens 10-N 10-W
" "	**14**	1	St Stephens 8-N 11-W
" "	**10**	1	St Stephens 9-N 10-W
ATWOOD	**22**	1	St Stephens 6-N 13-W
BAILEY	**12**	4	St Stephens 8-N 13-W
" "	**13**	1	St Stephens 8-N 12-W
BALFOUR	**17**	24	St Stephens 7-N 13-W
" "	**22**	4	St Stephens 6-N 13-W
BALY	**12**	2	St Stephens 8-N 13-W
BARKLEY	**10**	4	St Stephens 9-N 10-W
" "	**5**	2	St Stephens 10-N 10-W
BARKLY	**10**	1	St Stephens 9-N 10-W
BARLOW	**23**	4	St Stephens 6-N 12-W
" "	**11**	2	St Stephens 8-N 14-W
BARNES	**5**	6	St Stephens 10-N 10-W
" "	**6**	4	St Stephens 9-N 14-W
" "	**2**	3	St Stephens 10-N 13-W
BARNETT	**13**	3	St Stephens 8-N 12-W
BARTNE	**13**	3	St Stephens 8-N 12-W
BATES	**18**	1	St Stephens 7-N 12-W
BAYLIS	**22**	6	St Stephens 6-N 13-W

Surname	Map Group	Parcels of Land	Meridian/Township/Range
BAYLIS (Cont'd)	17	4	St Stephens 7-N 13-W
" "	11	4	St Stephens 8-N 14-W
" "	25	1	St Stephens 6-N 10-W
" "	12	1	St Stephens 8-N 13-W
BEARD	23	1	St Stephens 6-N 12-W
BEAVERS	6	1	St Stephens 9-N 14-W
BEDWELL	15	1	St Stephens 8-N 10-W
BEECH	18	6	St Stephens 7-N 12-W
" "	24	3	St Stephens 6-N 11-W
" "	19	2	St Stephens 7-N 11-W
" "	14	2	St Stephens 8-N 11-W
BEESLEY	22	1	St Stephens 6-N 13-W
BELL	9	2	St Stephens 9-N 11-W
BENSON	17	1	St Stephens 7-N 13-W
BEWICK	19	6	St Stephens 7-N 11-W
BIRKETT	19	18	St Stephens 7-N 11-W
" "	24	9	St Stephens 6-N 11-W
" "	23	5	St Stephens 6-N 12-W
BLACK	12	5	St Stephens 8-N 13-W
" "	6	5	St Stephens 9-N 14-W
BLACKLEDGE	10	4	St Stephens 9-N 10-W
" "	15	2	St Stephens 8-N 10-W
BLACKLIDGE	15	9	St Stephens 8-N 10-W
" "	10	8	St Stephens 9-N 10-W
" "	8	3	St Stephens 9-N 12-W
" "	5	1	St Stephens 10-N 10-W
" "	17	1	St Stephens 7-N 13-W
BLACKWELL	3	2	St Stephens 10-N 12-W
" "	12	2	St Stephens 8-N 13-W
" "	1	1	St Stephens 10-N 14-W
BLODGETT	25	29	St Stephens 6-N 10-W
BLUE	10	1	St Stephens 9-N 10-W
BONNER	9	7	St Stephens 9-N 11-W
" "	4	2	St Stephens 10-N 11-W
" "	5	1	St Stephens 10-N 10-W
BOOTH	6	1	St Stephens 9-N 14-W
BOROUGH	12	1	St Stephens 8-N 13-W
BOUTWELL	23	4	St Stephens 6-N 12-W
" "	18	3	St Stephens 7-N 12-W
" "	20	1	St Stephens 7-N 10-W
" "	19	1	St Stephens 7-N 11-W
" "	15	1	St Stephens 8-N 10-W
BOWDEN	8	3	St Stephens 9-N 12-W
BOWEN	18	2	St Stephens 7-N 12-W
" "	21	1	St Stephens 6-N 14-W
BOYCE	4	2	St Stephens 10-N 11-W
" "	10	2	St Stephens 9-N 10-W
" "	21	1	St Stephens 6-N 14-W
BOYKIN	11	2	St Stephens 8-N 14-W
BOYLES	5	4	St Stephens 10-N 10-W
BRADLEY	23	2	St Stephens 6-N 12-W
" "	22	1	St Stephens 6-N 13-W
" "	18	1	St Stephens 7-N 12-W
BRADSHAW	18	2	St Stephens 7-N 12-W
" "	19	1	St Stephens 7-N 11-W
BRAKENRIDGE	20	9	St Stephens 7-N 10-W
" "	19	6	St Stephens 7-N 11-W
BRASHIER	9	2	St Stephens 9-N 11-W
BRASWELL	2	2	St Stephens 10-N 13-W
BREAZEALE	16	2	St Stephens 7-N 14-W

Surname	Map Group	Parcels of Land	Meridian/Township/Range		
BREAZEALE (Cont'd)	**17**	1	St Stephens	7-N	13-W
BRELAND	**15**	4	St Stephens	8-N	10-W
BRIDGES	**9**	5	St Stephens	9-N	11-W
BROOMFIELD	**7**	2	St Stephens	9-N	13-W
BROWN	**24**	9	St Stephens	6-N	11-W
" "	**25**	5	St Stephens	6-N	10-W
" "	**21**	2	St Stephens	6-N	14-W
" "	**1**	1	St Stephens	10-N	14-W
" "	**14**	1	St Stephens	8-N	11-W
BRUCE	**7**	2	St Stephens	9-N	13-W
BRUMFIELD	**6**	2	St Stephens	9-N	14-W
BRYAN	**15**	1	St Stephens	8-N	10-W
BRYANT	**21**	16	St Stephens	6-N	14-W
" "	**16**	3	St Stephens	7-N	14-W
" "	**9**	3	St Stephens	9-N	11-W
" "	**8**	2	St Stephens	9-N	12-W
" "	**4**	1	St Stephens	10-N	11-W
BUCHANAN	**5**	2	St Stephens	10-N	10-W
BUCKOLEW	**4**	3	St Stephens	10-N	11-W
BULLARD	**21**	2	St Stephens	6-N	14-W
BUNKLEY	**7**	3	St Stephens	9-N	13-W
BURK	**13**	1	St Stephens	8-N	12-W
BURKHALTER	**6**	1	St Stephens	9-N	14-W
BUSBY	**18**	5	St Stephens	7-N	12-W
BUSH	**13**	11	St Stephens	8-N	12-W
" "	**8**	7	St Stephens	9-N	12-W
" "	**9**	6	St Stephens	9-N	11-W
" "	**14**	2	St Stephens	8-N	11-W
" "	**12**	2	St Stephens	8-N	13-W
" "	**17**	1	St Stephens	7-N	13-W
BUTLER	**11**	1	St Stephens	8-N	14-W
BYNUM	**8**	13	St Stephens	9-N	12-W
" "	**13**	8	St Stephens	8-N	12-W
" "	**21**	3	St Stephens	6-N	14-W
" "	**17**	3	St Stephens	7-N	13-W
" "	**16**	3	St Stephens	7-N	14-W
" "	**11**	3	St Stephens	8-N	14-W
" "	**7**	2	St Stephens	9-N	13-W
" "	**18**	1	St Stephens	7-N	12-W
BYRD	**5**	7	St Stephens	10-N	10-W
" "	**18**	2	St Stephens	7-N	12-W
" "	**4**	1	St Stephens	10-N	11-W
CALLAHAM	**22**	8	St Stephens	6-N	13-W
CALLAHAN	**22**	1	St Stephens	6-N	13-W
CAMPBELL	**24**	2	St Stephens	6-N	11-W
" "	**22**	1	St Stephens	6-N	13-W
CARAWAY	**5**	2	St Stephens	10-N	10-W
CARLISLE	**25**	3	St Stephens	6-N	10-W
" "	**4**	2	St Stephens	10-N	11-W
CARLTON	**24**	3	St Stephens	6-N	11-W
CARPENTER	**20**	24	St Stephens	7-N	10-W
CARTER	**16**	21	St Stephens	7-N	14-W
" "	**23**	3	St Stephens	6-N	12-W
" "	**21**	2	St Stephens	6-N	14-W
CHAMBLESS	**25**	1	St Stephens	6-N	10-W
CHAPMAN	**24**	2	St Stephens	6-N	11-W
CHARLESCRAFT	**17**	1	St Stephens	7-N	13-W
CHATHAM	**17**	1	St Stephens	7-N	13-W
CHISHOLM	**7**	1	St Stephens	9-N	13-W
CLARK	**15**	14	St Stephens	8-N	10-W

Surname	Map Group	Parcels of Land	Meridian/Township/Range
CLARK (Cont'd)	**8**	8	St Stephens 9-N 12-W
" "	**23**	1	St Stephens 6-N 12-W
COATES	**7**	8	St Stephens 9-N 13-W
" "	**6**	1	St Stephens 9-N 14-W
COATNEY	**14**	4	St Stephens 8-N 11-W
COATS	**7**	15	St Stephens 9-N 13-W
" "	**2**	1	St Stephens 10-N 13-W
" "	**6**	1	St Stephens 9-N 14-W
COBB	**25**	2	St Stephens 6-N 10-W
COLE	**16**	3	St Stephens 7-N 14-W
COLEMAN	**11**	1	St Stephens 8-N 14-W
COLLEY	**14**	9	St Stephens 8-N 11-W
" "	**13**	5	St Stephens 8-N 12-W
COLLINS	**8**	17	St Stephens 9-N 12-W
" "	**23**	6	St Stephens 6-N 12-W
" "	**13**	4	St Stephens 8-N 12-W
" "	**2**	3	St Stephens 10-N 13-W
" "	**7**	3	St Stephens 9-N 13-W
COMPANY	**18**	6	St Stephens 7-N 12-W
" "	**14**	6	St Stephens 8-N 11-W
" "	**9**	3	St Stephens 9-N 11-W
COOLEY	**24**	5	St Stephens 6-N 11-W
" "	**12**	1	St Stephens 8-N 13-W
COOPER	**4**	8	St Stephens 10-N 11-W
" "	**13**	3	St Stephens 8-N 12-W
" "	**9**	2	St Stephens 9-N 11-W
COPELAND	**9**	2	St Stephens 9-N 11-W
" "	**7**	2	St Stephens 9-N 13-W
" "	**22**	1	St Stephens 6-N 13-W
" "	**12**	1	St Stephens 8-N 13-W
CORLEY	**9**	5	St Stephens 9-N 11-W
" "	**7**	2	St Stephens 9-N 13-W
COTTON	**4**	1	St Stephens 10-N 11-W
COX	**13**	1	St Stephens 8-N 12-W
CRABTREE	**5**	5	St Stephens 10-N 10-W
CRAFT	**8**	5	St Stephens 9-N 12-W
" "	**18**	4	St Stephens 7-N 12-W
" "	**22**	1	St Stephens 6-N 13-W
" "	**19**	1	St Stephens 7-N 11-W
CRAKER	**17**	1	St Stephens 7-N 13-W
CRANFORD	**16**	2	St Stephens 7-N 14-W
CRAVEN	**15**	12	St Stephens 8-N 10-W
" "	**10**	4	St Stephens 9-N 10-W
CRAWFORD	**12**	2	St Stephens 8-N 13-W
" "	**11**	2	St Stephens 8-N 14-W
" "	**6**	2	St Stephens 9-N 14-W
CREEL	**14**	9	St Stephens 8-N 11-W
" "	**22**	3	St Stephens 6-N 13-W
" "	**6**	3	St Stephens 9-N 14-W
" "	**23**	2	St Stephens 6-N 12-W
" "	**17**	2	St Stephens 7-N 13-W
" "	**9**	1	St Stephens 9-N 11-W
CRENSHAW	**25**	3	St Stephens 6-N 10-W
" "	**16**	2	St Stephens 7-N 14-W
CROMWELL	**23**	3	St Stephens 6-N 12-W
CROSBY	**17**	5	St Stephens 7-N 13-W
" "	**1**	2	St Stephens 10-N 14-W
" "	**9**	2	St Stephens 9-N 11-W
CRUMBY	**9**	7	St Stephens 9-N 11-W
CRUMITY	**21**	2	St Stephens 6-N 14-W

Surname	Map Group	Parcels of Land	Meridian/Township/Range		
CULPEPPER	**22**	2	St Stephens	6-N	13-W
" "	**21**	1	St Stephens	6-N	14-W
CURTIS	**24**	1	St Stephens	6-N	11-W
DARRAH	**20**	1	St Stephens	7-N	10-W
DAVIDSON	**11**	3	St Stephens	8-N	14-W
DAVIS	**13**	7	St Stephens	8-N	12-W
" "	**8**	7	St Stephens	9-N	12-W
" "	**15**	5	St Stephens	8-N	10-W
" "	**1**	4	St Stephens	10-N	14-W
" "	**10**	4	St Stephens	9-N	10-W
" "	**5**	3	St Stephens	10-N	10-W
" "	**4**	3	St Stephens	10-N	11-W
" "	**2**	2	St Stephens	10-N	13-W
" "	**16**	2	St Stephens	7-N	14-W
DEAN	**7**	3	St Stephens	9-N	13-W
" "	**8**	1	St Stephens	9-N	12-W
DEARMAN	**9**	3	St Stephens	9-N	11-W
" "	**2**	1	St Stephens	10-N	13-W
DEASE	**12**	1	St Stephens	8-N	13-W
DEASON	**17**	6	St Stephens	7-N	13-W
DEAVENPORT	**5**	1	St Stephens	10-N	10-W
DELANCY	**7**	3	St Stephens	9-N	13-W
DELK	**21**	9	St Stephens	6-N	14-W
DEMENT	**25**	3	St Stephens	6-N	10-W
DENT	**21**	2	St Stephens	6-N	14-W
DEVALL	**17**	1	St Stephens	7-N	13-W
DEVINPORT	**10**	5	St Stephens	9-N	10-W
DICKENSON	**22**	2	St Stephens	6-N	13-W
DILLARD	**10**	3	St Stephens	9-N	10-W
DONALD	**4**	6	St Stephens	10-N	11-W
" "	**24**	1	St Stephens	6-N	11-W
" "	**18**	1	St Stephens	7-N	12-W
DOSSETT	**22**	5	St Stephens	6-N	13-W
" "	**16**	4	St Stephens	7-N	14-W
" "	**21**	3	St Stephens	6-N	14-W
DOSSETTE	**21**	3	St Stephens	6-N	14-W
DOWNING	**17**	2	St Stephens	7-N	13-W
DRAUGHN	**25**	1	St Stephens	6-N	10-W
" "	**23**	1	St Stephens	6-N	12-W
DRENNAN	**8**	2	St Stephens	9-N	12-W
DREW	**18**	3	St Stephens	7-N	12-W
DRYDEN	**18**	3	St Stephens	7-N	12-W
DUCKWORTH	**6**	19	St Stephens	9-N	14-W
DYE	**21**	2	St Stephens	6-N	14-W
DYESS	**13**	1	St Stephens	8-N	12-W
DYKES	**2**	8	St Stephens	10-N	13-W
" "	**12**	4	St Stephens	8-N	13-W
EASLEY	**9**	2	St Stephens	9-N	11-W
" "	**8**	1	St Stephens	9-N	12-W
EASTERLING	**6**	6	St Stephens	9-N	14-W
" "	**25**	5	St Stephens	6-N	10-W
" "	**19**	4	St Stephens	7-N	11-W
" "	**24**	3	St Stephens	6-N	11-W
" "	**21**	3	St Stephens	6-N	14-W
" "	**20**	3	St Stephens	7-N	10-W
" "	**18**	3	St Stephens	7-N	12-W
" "	**23**	2	St Stephens	6-N	12-W
" "	**22**	2	St Stephens	6-N	13-W
" "	**17**	2	St Stephens	7-N	13-W
EATON	**22**	1	St Stephens	6-N	13-W

Surname	Map Group	Parcels of Land	Meridian/Township/Range		
EDWARDS	17	2	St Stephens	7-N	13-W
ELLZEY	12	4	St Stephens	8-N	13-W
" "	11	2	St Stephens	8-N	14-W
" "	7	2	St Stephens	9-N	13-W
ELLZY	12	2	St Stephens	8-N	13-W
ELZEY	12	1	St Stephens	8-N	13-W
EVANS	12	2	St Stephens	8-N	13-W
" "	22	1	St Stephens	6-N	13-W
EVERETT	19	1	St Stephens	7-N	11-W
" "	18	1	St Stephens	7-N	12-W
EWING	17	1	St Stephens	7-N	13-W
EZELL	18	3	St Stephens	7-N	12-W
FAIRCHILD	16	3	St Stephens	7-N	14-W
FAIRCHILDS	17	10	St Stephens	7-N	13-W
" "	16	6	St Stephens	7-N	14-W
FALER	9	2	St Stephens	9-N	11-W
FERGUSON	10	29	St Stephens	9-N	10-W
" "	23	8	St Stephens	6-N	12-W
" "	9	7	St Stephens	9-N	11-W
" "	5	3	St Stephens	10-N	10-W
FERRILL	9	3	St Stephens	9-N	11-W
FEWOX	14	1	St Stephens	8-N	11-W
FLYNT	12	7	St Stephens	8-N	13-W
" "	7	5	St Stephens	9-N	13-W
" "	8	2	St Stephens	9-N	12-W
FOKES	14	1	St Stephens	8-N	11-W
FOLKS	17	3	St Stephens	7-N	13-W
" "	22	2	St Stephens	6-N	13-W
FREEMAN	18	2	St Stephens	7-N	12-W
" "	23	1	St Stephens	6-N	12-W
FURR	23	2	St Stephens	6-N	12-W
GAINEY	22	1	St Stephens	6-N	13-W
GAMBRELL	1	5	St Stephens	10-N	14-W
" "	6	3	St Stephens	9-N	14-W
GANDY	17	5	St Stephens	7-N	13-W
GARNER	7	2	St Stephens	9-N	13-W
" "	18	1	St Stephens	7-N	12-W
GARRICK	16	3	St Stephens	7-N	14-W
" "	7	2	St Stephens	9-N	13-W
GASKIN	5	2	St Stephens	10-N	10-W
GATLIN	5	13	St Stephens	10-N	10-W
GATTIS	20	1	St Stephens	7-N	10-W
GAVIN	3	3	St Stephens	10-N	12-W
GEDDIE	19	3	St Stephens	7-N	11-W
" "	14	3	St Stephens	8-N	11-W
" "	18	1	St Stephens	7-N	12-W
GEIGER	6	3	St Stephens	9-N	14-W
" "	9	2	St Stephens	9-N	11-W
GEIGGER	3	2	St Stephens	10-N	12-W
GIEGER	3	3	St Stephens	10-N	12-W
GILENDER	22	4	St Stephens	6-N	13-W
GILLANDER	22	1	St Stephens	6-N	13-W
" "	12	1	St Stephens	8-N	13-W
GILLENDER	22	1	St Stephens	6-N	13-W
GILLEY	25	2	St Stephens	6-N	10-W
GILLINDER	22	1	St Stephens	6-N	13-W
GLIDEWELL	21	1	St Stephens	6-N	14-W
GLOVER	21	1	St Stephens	6-N	14-W
GORE	9	2	St Stephens	9-N	11-W
GRAFTON	8	1	St Stephens	9-N	12-W

Surname	Map Group	Parcels of Land	Meridian/Township/Range		
GRAHAM	**17**	7	St Stephens	7-N	13-W
" "	**25**	6	St Stephens	6-N	10-W
" "	**16**	4	St Stephens	7-N	14-W
" "	**13**	1	St Stephens	8-N	12-W
GRANBERRY	**21**	9	St Stephens	6-N	14-W
GRANISON	**24**	1	St Stephens	6-N	11-W
GRANTHAM	**23**	17	St Stephens	6-N	12-W
GRAVES	**11**	13	St Stephens	8-N	14-W
" "	**7**	13	St Stephens	9-N	13-W
" "	**6**	2	St Stephens	9-N	14-W
" "	**2**	1	St Stephens	10-N	13-W
GRAY	**9**	1	St Stephens	9-N	11-W
GRAYSON	**16**	3	St Stephens	7-N	14-W
" "	**22**	2	St Stephens	6-N	13-W
" "	**21**	2	St Stephens	6-N	14-W
" "	**17**	1	St Stephens	7-N	13-W
GREEN	**12**	3	St Stephens	8-N	13-W
GRISSETT	**6**	2	St Stephens	9-N	14-W
GRISSOM	**1**	13	St Stephens	10-N	14-W
" "	**2**	3	St Stephens	10-N	13-W
GUI	**16**	3	St Stephens	7-N	14-W
GUNTER	**7**	9	St Stephens	9-N	13-W
" "	**2**	8	St Stephens	10-N	13-W
" "	**23**	2	St Stephens	6-N	12-W
" "	**18**	2	St Stephens	7-N	12-W
" "	**11**	2	St Stephens	8-N	14-W
" "	**6**	2	St Stephens	9-N	14-W
" "	**3**	1	St Stephens	10-N	12-W
" "	**8**	1	St Stephens	9-N	12-W
GUYE	**16**	3	St Stephens	7-N	14-W
HADDOX	**21**	1	St Stephens	6-N	14-W
HAFTER	**9**	2	St Stephens	9-N	11-W
HAIGLER	**21**	2	St Stephens	6-N	14-W
HALES	**5**	3	St Stephens	10-N	10-W
HALL	**18**	2	St Stephens	7-N	12-W
" "	**23**	1	St Stephens	6-N	12-W
HAMILTON	**8**	4	St Stephens	9-N	12-W
" "	**21**	2	St Stephens	6-N	14-W
HANSON	**5**	5	St Stephens	10-N	10-W
HARDY	**18**	8	St Stephens	7-N	12-W
" "	**4**	1	St Stephens	10-N	11-W
HARE	**23**	1	St Stephens	6-N	12-W
HARGROVE	**4**	1	St Stephens	10-N	11-W
" "	**10**	1	St Stephens	9-N	10-W
HARPER	**7**	8	St Stephens	9-N	13-W
" "	**12**	2	St Stephens	8-N	13-W
" "	**8**	2	St Stephens	9-N	12-W
" "	**6**	2	St Stephens	9-N	14-W
HARREL	**21**	1	St Stephens	6-N	14-W
HARRELL	**21**	4	St Stephens	6-N	14-W
HARRING	**6**	1	St Stephens	9-N	14-W
HARRIS	**19**	1	St Stephens	7-N	11-W
HARVEY	**6**	1	St Stephens	9-N	14-W
HATTON	**6**	5	St Stephens	9-N	14-W
HAWKINS	**10**	5	St Stephens	9-N	10-W
HAYS	**9**	3	St Stephens	9-N	11-W
" "	**14**	2	St Stephens	8-N	11-W
HENNIS	**18**	3	St Stephens	7-N	12-W
HENSARLING	**23**	2	St Stephens	6-N	12-W
HERINGTON	**8**	2	St Stephens	9-N	12-W

Surname	Map Group	Parcels of Land	Meridian/Township/Range		
HERRING	**23**	1	St Stephens	6-N	12-W
HERRINGTON	**23**	8	St Stephens	6-N	12-W
" "	**5**	7	St Stephens	10-N	10-W
" "	**16**	6	St Stephens	7-N	14-W
" "	**4**	5	St Stephens	10-N	11-W
" "	**12**	5	St Stephens	8-N	13-W
" "	**18**	3	St Stephens	7-N	12-W
" "	**24**	2	St Stephens	6-N	11-W
" "	**13**	2	St Stephens	8-N	12-W
" "	**8**	2	St Stephens	9-N	12-W
HICKS	**6**	3	St Stephens	9-N	14-W
HILBURN	**12**	3	St Stephens	8-N	13-W
HILL	**7**	11	St Stephens	9-N	13-W
" "	**12**	5	St Stephens	8-N	13-W
HINTON	**7**	11	St Stephens	9-N	13-W
" "	**1**	3	St Stephens	10-N	14-W
" "	**24**	3	St Stephens	6-N	11-W
" "	**9**	2	St Stephens	9-N	11-W
" "	**17**	1	St Stephens	7-N	13-W
HOBGOOD	**10**	2	St Stephens	9-N	10-W
HODGES	**5**	4	St Stephens	10-N	10-W
" "	**15**	1	St Stephens	8-N	10-W
HOGAN	**3**	1	St Stephens	10-N	12-W
HOLDER	**3**	9	St Stephens	10-N	12-W
" "	**16**	2	St Stephens	7-N	14-W
" "	**10**	1	St Stephens	9-N	10-W
HOLIFIELD	**8**	19	St Stephens	9-N	12-W
" "	**9**	10	St Stephens	9-N	11-W
" "	**14**	8	St Stephens	8-N	11-W
" "	**15**	7	St Stephens	8-N	10-W
" "	**13**	5	St Stephens	8-N	12-W
" "	**23**	3	St Stephens	6-N	12-W
" "	**7**	1	St Stephens	9-N	13-W
HOLLEY	**10**	8	St Stephens	9-N	10-W
HOLLIFIELD	**4**	1	St Stephens	10-N	11-W
HOLLIMAN	**25**	3	St Stephens	6-N	10-W
" "	**22**	3	St Stephens	6-N	13-W
HOLLIMON	**14**	4	St Stephens	8-N	11-W
" "	**25**	2	St Stephens	6-N	10-W
" "	**24**	2	St Stephens	6-N	11-W
HOLT	**18**	3	St Stephens	7-N	12-W
HOLYFIELD	**8**	8	St Stephens	9-N	12-W
" "	**9**	4	St Stephens	9-N	11-W
" "	**4**	2	St Stephens	10-N	11-W
" "	**13**	1	St Stephens	8-N	12-W
HOOD	**22**	7	St Stephens	6-N	13-W
" "	**21**	2	St Stephens	6-N	14-W
" "	**17**	2	St Stephens	7-N	13-W
" "	**12**	2	St Stephens	8-N	13-W
" "	**16**	1	St Stephens	7-N	14-W
HOPKINS	**7**	6	St Stephens	9-N	13-W
" "	**12**	3	St Stephens	8-N	13-W
" "	**11**	3	St Stephens	8-N	14-W
" "	**3**	2	St Stephens	10-N	12-W
" "	**8**	2	St Stephens	9-N	12-W
" "	**6**	1	St Stephens	9-N	14-W
HOSKINS	**16**	3	St Stephens	7-N	14-W
" "	**17**	1	St Stephens	7-N	13-W
HOSSEY	**4**	2	St Stephens	10-N	11-W
HOUGH	**10**	2	St Stephens	9-N	10-W

Surname	Map Group	Parcels of Land	Meridian/Township/Range		
HOWARD	9	4	St Stephens	9-N	11-W
" "	5	2	St Stephens	10-N	10-W
" "	4	1	St Stephens	10-N	11-W
HOWSE	14	3	St Stephens	8-N	11-W
" "	15	2	St Stephens	8-N	10-W
HUFF	6	5	St Stephens	9-N	14-W
HULSEY	12	1	St Stephens	8-N	13-W
HURST	22	1	St Stephens	6-N	13-W
HUTTO	25	5	St Stephens	6-N	10-W
" "	4	2	St Stephens	10-N	11-W
INGRAIM	9	2	St Stephens	9-N	11-W
" "	8	1	St Stephens	9-N	12-W
INGRAM	8	2	St Stephens	9-N	12-W
JACKSON	8	12	St Stephens	9-N	12-W
" "	22	3	St Stephens	6-N	13-W
" "	2	2	St Stephens	10-N	13-W
" "	21	1	St Stephens	6-N	14-W
JEFCOAT	7	8	St Stephens	9-N	13-W
" "	23	4	St Stephens	6-N	12-W
" "	6	4	St Stephens	9-N	14-W
JENKINS	20	5	St Stephens	7-N	10-W
" "	15	5	St Stephens	8-N	10-W
JIMISON	17	2	St Stephens	7-N	13-W
JOHNSON	24	34	St Stephens	6-N	11-W
" "	19	6	St Stephens	7-N	11-W
" "	18	6	St Stephens	7-N	12-W
" "	9	4	St Stephens	9-N	11-W
" "	8	4	St Stephens	9-N	12-W
" "	22	3	St Stephens	6-N	13-W
" "	3	2	St Stephens	10-N	12-W
" "	12	2	St Stephens	8-N	13-W
" "	6	2	St Stephens	9-N	14-W
" "	2	1	St Stephens	10-N	13-W
" "	25	1	St Stephens	6-N	10-W
" "	23	1	St Stephens	6-N	12-W
JOHNSTON	17	7	St Stephens	7-N	13-W
" "	7	4	St Stephens	9-N	13-W
" "	2	3	St Stephens	10-N	13-W
" "	12	1	St Stephens	8-N	13-W
" "	9	1	St Stephens	9-N	11-W
" "	6	1	St Stephens	9-N	14-W
JONES	12	5	St Stephens	8-N	13-W
" "	2	4	St Stephens	10-N	13-W
" "	23	4	St Stephens	6-N	12-W
" "	22	4	St Stephens	6-N	13-W
" "	19	3	St Stephens	7-N	11-W
" "	13	3	St Stephens	8-N	12-W
" "	9	2	St Stephens	9-N	11-W
" "	5	1	St Stephens	10-N	10-W
" "	15	1	St Stephens	8-N	10-W
JORDAN	17	6	St Stephens	7-N	13-W
" "	23	3	St Stephens	6-N	12-W
JOSEY	14	2	St Stephens	8-N	11-W
" "	20	1	St Stephens	7-N	10-W
" "	19	1	St Stephens	7-N	11-W
KAMPER	8	73	St Stephens	9-N	12-W
" "	9	43	St Stephens	9-N	11-W
" "	7	43	St Stephens	9-N	13-W
" "	14	25	St Stephens	8-N	11-W
" "	13	17	St Stephens	8-N	12-W

Surname	Map Group	Parcels of Land	Meridian/Township/Range
KAMPER (Cont'd)	**4**	8	St Stephens 10-N 11-W
" "	**12**	4	St Stephens 8-N 13-W
" "	**3**	2	St Stephens 10-N 12-W
KEETON	**9**	4	St Stephens 9-N 11-W
" "	**17**	2	St Stephens 7-N 13-W
KELLEY	**16**	3	St Stephens 7-N 14-W
" "	**22**	2	St Stephens 6-N 13-W
" "	**21**	1	St Stephens 6-N 14-W
" "	**10**	1	St Stephens 9-N 10-W
KELLY	**22**	6	St Stephens 6-N 13-W
" "	**16**	3	St Stephens 7-N 14-W
" "	**6**	2	St Stephens 9-N 14-W
" "	**21**	1	St Stephens 6-N 14-W
KENNEDY	**13**	3	St Stephens 8-N 12-W
" "	**1**	1	St Stephens 10-N 14-W
KENT	**6**	7	St Stephens 9-N 14-W
" "	**7**	1	St Stephens 9-N 13-W
KERVIN	**7**	1	St Stephens 9-N 13-W
KILGORE	**13**	8	St Stephens 8-N 12-W
" "	**22**	2	St Stephens 6-N 13-W
KING	**8**	3	St Stephens 9-N 12-W
KIRKLAND	**23**	7	St Stephens 6-N 12-W
" "	**18**	2	St Stephens 7-N 12-W
KITCHENS	**25**	7	St Stephens 6-N 10-W
" "	**20**	2	St Stephens 7-N 10-W
KNIGHT	**11**	21	St Stephens 8-N 14-W
" "	**2**	18	St Stephens 10-N 13-W
" "	**12**	17	St Stephens 8-N 13-W
" "	**7**	12	St Stephens 9-N 13-W
" "	**6**	6	St Stephens 9-N 14-W
" "	**16**	3	St Stephens 7-N 14-W
" "	**23**	2	St Stephens 6-N 12-W
" "	**22**	2	St Stephens 6-N 13-W
" "	**9**	2	St Stephens 9-N 11-W
LAMPORT	**22**	3	St Stephens 6-N 13-W
LANDRUM	**19**	17	St Stephens 7-N 11-W
" "	**25**	3	St Stephens 6-N 10-W
" "	**15**	3	St Stephens 8-N 10-W
" "	**23**	2	St Stephens 6-N 12-W
" "	**24**	1	St Stephens 6-N 11-W
" "	**20**	1	St Stephens 7-N 10-W
LANE	**13**	1	St Stephens 8-N 12-W
" "	**7**	1	St Stephens 9-N 13-W
LANGLEY	**15**	1	St Stephens 8-N 10-W
LARD	**8**	3	St Stephens 9-N 12-W
LARRE	**19**	1	St Stephens 7-N 11-W
LAWSON	**24**	2	St Stephens 6-N 11-W
LEE	**21**	4	St Stephens 6-N 14-W
" "	**10**	2	St Stephens 9-N 10-W
" "	**22**	1	St Stephens 6-N 13-W
" "	**14**	1	St Stephens 8-N 11-W
LEWIS	**14**	10	St Stephens 8-N 11-W
" "	**7**	7	St Stephens 9-N 13-W
" "	**19**	3	St Stephens 7-N 11-W
" "	**11**	1	St Stephens 8-N 14-W
LIGHTSEY	**10**	1	St Stephens 9-N 10-W
LINDER	**5**	1	St Stephens 10-N 10-W
LINDSEY	**4**	1	St Stephens 10-N 11-W
LITTLE	**12**	2	St Stephens 8-N 13-W
" "	**7**	2	St Stephens 9-N 13-W

Surname	Map Group	Parcels of Land	Meridian/Township/Range		
LOCKHART	**22**	1	St Stephens	6-N	13-W
LOFTIN	**24**	1	St Stephens	6-N	11-W
LOFTON	**22**	1	St Stephens	6-N	13-W
LONG	**4**	3	St Stephens	10-N	11-W
LOPER	**25**	1	St Stephens	6-N	10-W
LOTT	**16**	8	St Stephens	7-N	14-W
" "	**20**	2	St Stephens	7-N	10-W
" "	**15**	2	St Stephens	8-N	10-W
" "	**21**	1	St Stephens	6-N	14-W
LOURY	**17**	1	St Stephens	7-N	13-W
LOVE	**8**	2	St Stephens	9-N	12-W
LOVETT	**11**	1	St Stephens	8-N	14-W
LOVITT	**17**	1	St Stephens	7-N	13-W
LOWE	**8**	4	St Stephens	9-N	12-W
" "	**14**	3	St Stephens	8-N	11-W
" "	**4**	2	St Stephens	10-N	11-W
LOWERY	**17**	2	St Stephens	7-N	13-W
LOWRY	**18**	2	St Stephens	7-N	12-W
LUMSEY	**21**	3	St Stephens	6-N	14-W
LYNES	**19**	4	St Stephens	7-N	11-W
LYON	**12**	28	St Stephens	8-N	13-W
" "	**17**	13	St Stephens	7-N	13-W
" "	**13**	8	St Stephens	8-N	12-W
" "	**18**	7	St Stephens	7-N	12-W
" "	**8**	6	St Stephens	9-N	12-W
MAGEE	**8**	1	St Stephens	9-N	12-W
MARTIN	**17**	2	St Stephens	7-N	13-W
MASKEW	**21**	2	St Stephens	6-N	14-W
MASON	**4**	2	St Stephens	10-N	11-W
MATHEWS	**3**	4	St Stephens	10-N	12-W
" "	**8**	1	St Stephens	9-N	12-W
MATTHEWS	**3**	2	St Stephens	10-N	12-W
" "	**8**	2	St Stephens	9-N	12-W
MATTREN	**19**	1	St Stephens	7-N	11-W
MAULDIN	**2**	3	St Stephens	10-N	13-W
MAXCEY	**7**	2	St Stephens	9-N	13-W
MAXEY	**13**	2	St Stephens	8-N	12-W
" "	**12**	2	St Stephens	8-N	13-W
MAXWELL	**1**	1	St Stephens	10-N	14-W
MCADAMS	**24**	1	St Stephens	6-N	11-W
MCARTHUR	**9**	2	St Stephens	9-N	11-W
MCBRIDE	**14**	3	St Stephens	8-N	11-W
MCCALLUM	**4**	5	St Stephens	10-N	11-W
" "	**17**	2	St Stephens	7-N	13-W
MCCRANEY	**21**	2	St Stephens	6-N	14-W
MCCRAW	**9**	1	St Stephens	9-N	11-W
MCCULLUM	**6**	2	St Stephens	9-N	14-W
MCDANIEL	**6**	5	St Stephens	9-N	14-W
" "	**10**	4	St Stephens	9-N	10-W
MCDONALD	**5**	13	St Stephens	10-N	10-W
" "	**22**	3	St Stephens	6-N	13-W
" "	**24**	1	St Stephens	6-N	11-W
" "	**23**	1	St Stephens	6-N	12-W
" "	**17**	1	St Stephens	7-N	13-W
" "	**10**	1	St Stephens	9-N	10-W
MCDUGALD	**18**	3	St Stephens	7-N	12-W
MCGAHEY	**18**	3	St Stephens	7-N	12-W
MCGEE	**9**	3	St Stephens	9-N	11-W
" "	**13**	1	St Stephens	8-N	12-W
" "	**8**	1	St Stephens	9-N	12-W

Surname	Map Group	Parcels of Land	Meridian/Township/Range		
MCGILBERRY	**10**	5	St Stephens	9-N	10-W
" "	**25**	4	St Stephens	6-N	10-W
" "	**24**	3	St Stephens	6-N	11-W
MCGILL	**5**	15	St Stephens	10-N	10-W
" "	**10**	14	St Stephens	9-N	10-W
" "	**18**	3	St Stephens	7-N	12-W
" "	**23**	1	St Stephens	6-N	12-W
MCGILVERRY	**24**	1	St Stephens	6-N	11-W
MCGILVRAY	**24**	9	St Stephens	6-N	11-W
MCINNIS	**21**	3	St Stephens	6-N	14-W
MCKAY	**24**	3	St Stephens	6-N	11-W
MCKEOWN	**20**	51	St Stephens	7-N	10-W
" "	**15**	30	St Stephens	8-N	10-W
" "	**19**	4	St Stephens	7-N	11-W
MCKINLEY	**23**	1	St Stephens	6-N	12-W
MCLAMORE	**11**	1	St Stephens	8-N	14-W
MCLAURIN	**10**	1	St Stephens	9-N	10-W
" "	**9**	1	St Stephens	9-N	11-W
MCLEAIN	**15**	1	St Stephens	8-N	10-W
MCLEMORE	**21**	1	St Stephens	6-N	14-W
" "	**11**	1	St Stephens	8-N	14-W
MCLENDON	**15**	2	St Stephens	8-N	10-W
MCMANUS	**13**	3	St Stephens	8-N	12-W
" "	**24**	1	St Stephens	6-N	11-W
MCMILLAN	**4**	2	St Stephens	10-N	11-W
MCMULLEN	**18**	3	St Stephens	7-N	12-W
MCNAT	**3**	3	St Stephens	10-N	12-W
MCNIECE	**17**	2	St Stephens	7-N	13-W
MCPHERSON	**24**	24	St Stephens	6-N	11-W
" "	**19**	20	St Stephens	7-N	11-W
" "	**23**	5	St Stephens	6-N	12-W
MCVEY	**4**	1	St Stephens	10-N	11-W
MEADOR	**6**	3	St Stephens	9-N	14-W
" "	**7**	2	St Stephens	9-N	13-W
MEDEARIS	**16**	3	St Stephens	7-N	14-W
MELVIN	**23**	9	St Stephens	6-N	12-W
" "	**18**	1	St Stephens	7-N	12-W
MERCHANT	**13**	2	St Stephens	8-N	12-W
MERRITT	**23**	1	St Stephens	6-N	12-W
MILEY	**4**	4	St Stephens	10-N	11-W
MILLER	**15**	4	St Stephens	8-N	10-W
" "	**13**	1	St Stephens	8-N	12-W
MILLSAP	**10**	6	St Stephens	9-N	10-W
" "	**5**	3	St Stephens	10-N	10-W
" "	**9**	1	St Stephens	9-N	11-W
MILLSAPS	**10**	1	St Stephens	9-N	10-W
MISSISSIPPI	**25**	1	St Stephens	6-N	10-W
" "	**22**	1	St Stephens	6-N	13-W
MITCHEL	**15**	2	St Stephens	8-N	10-W
MITCHELL	**10**	5	St Stephens	9-N	10-W
" "	**21**	2	St Stephens	6-N	14-W
" "	**17**	2	St Stephens	7-N	13-W
MIXON	**21**	1	St Stephens	6-N	14-W
MOFFETT	**22**	3	St Stephens	6-N	13-W
" "	**17**	3	St Stephens	7-N	13-W
" "	**18**	1	St Stephens	7-N	12-W
MONTGOMERY	**12**	2	St Stephens	8-N	13-W
" "	**7**	1	St Stephens	9-N	13-W
MOORES	**19**	34	St Stephens	7-N	11-W
" "	**14**	22	St Stephens	8-N	11-W

Surname	Map Group	Parcels of Land	Meridian/Township/Range		
MOORES (Cont'd)	**18**	3	St Stephens	7-N	12-W
MORGAN	**21**	9	St Stephens	6-N	14-W
" "	**16**	9	St Stephens	7-N	14-W
" "	**15**	2	St Stephens	8-N	10-W
" "	**24**	1	St Stephens	6-N	11-W
" "	**18**	1	St Stephens	7-N	12-W
MORRELL	**8**	2	St Stephens	9-N	12-W
MORRIS	**25**	1	St Stephens	6-N	10-W
" "	**16**	1	St Stephens	7-N	14-W
MORSE	**4**	4	St Stephens	10-N	11-W
MOSS	**3**	3	St Stephens	10-N	12-W
" "	**4**	2	St Stephens	10-N	11-W
" "	**8**	2	St Stephens	9-N	12-W
" "	**7**	2	St Stephens	9-N	13-W
MOTT	**18**	2	St Stephens	7-N	12-W
" "	**15**	1	St Stephens	8-N	10-W
MOULDS	**22**	3	St Stephens	6-N	13-W
" "	**21**	3	St Stephens	6-N	14-W
MURFEY	**23**	2	St Stephens	6-N	12-W
MURPHY	**23**	2	St Stephens	6-N	12-W
" "	**3**	1	St Stephens	10-N	12-W
MURRAH	**16**	2	St Stephens	7-N	14-W
MURRAY	**6**	16	St Stephens	9-N	14-W
MURRY	**6**	3	St Stephens	9-N	14-W
MUSGROVE	**7**	11	St Stephens	9-N	13-W
" "	**4**	7	St Stephens	10-N	11-W
" "	**8**	4	St Stephens	9-N	12-W
" "	**6**	4	St Stephens	9-N	14-W
MYERS	**25**	1	St Stephens	6-N	10-W
" "	**23**	1	St Stephens	6-N	12-W
" "	**17**	1	St Stephens	7-N	13-W
MYRICK	**4**	6	St Stephens	10-N	11-W
" "	**21**	1	St Stephens	6-N	14-W
" "	**15**	1	St Stephens	8-N	10-W
NALL	**23**	1	St Stephens	6-N	12-W
NELSON	**9**	7	St Stephens	9-N	11-W
" "	**4**	3	St Stephens	10-N	11-W
" "	**14**	2	St Stephens	8-N	11-W
NESOM	**4**	2	St Stephens	10-N	11-W
NETTLES	**4**	1	St Stephens	10-N	11-W
" "	**14**	1	St Stephens	8-N	11-W
NEWELL	**9**	1	St Stephens	9-N	11-W
NEWSOM	**9**	4	St Stephens	9-N	11-W
NICHOLES	**25**	1	St Stephens	6-N	10-W
NIX	**16**	4	St Stephens	7-N	14-W
" "	**4**	3	St Stephens	10-N	11-W
NOBLES	**24**	10	St Stephens	6-N	11-W
NORDMAN	**13**	7	St Stephens	8-N	12-W
NORWOOD	**12**	1	St Stephens	8-N	13-W
" "	**11**	1	St Stephens	8-N	14-W
" "	**6**	1	St Stephens	9-N	14-W
NOWELL	**15**	6	St Stephens	8-N	10-W
OBER	**4**	1	St Stephens	10-N	11-W
ODOM	**24**	6	St Stephens	6-N	11-W
" "	**22**	5	St Stephens	6-N	13-W
" "	**23**	3	St Stephens	6-N	12-W
" "	**16**	3	St Stephens	7-N	14-W
" "	**17**	1	St Stephens	7-N	13-W
OVERSTREET	**25**	4	St Stephens	6-N	10-W
" "	**24**	2	St Stephens	6-N	11-W

Surname	Map Group	Parcels of Land	Meridian/Township/Range
OWEN	**13**	6	St Stephens 8-N 12-W
" "	**5**	5	St Stephens 10-N 10-W
" "	**18**	4	St Stephens 7-N 12-W
" "	**10**	3	St Stephens 9-N 10-W
OWENS	**8**	2	St Stephens 9-N 12-W
PAGE	**17**	3	St Stephens 7-N 13-W
" "	**21**	2	St Stephens 6-N 14-W
" "	**18**	2	St Stephens 7-N 12-W
" "	**23**	1	St Stephens 6-N 12-W
" "	**9**	1	St Stephens 9-N 11-W
PARISH	**13**	3	St Stephens 8-N 12-W
" "	**8**	2	St Stephens 9-N 12-W
" "	**7**	1	St Stephens 9-N 13-W
PARKER	**18**	6	St Stephens 7-N 12-W
" "	**24**	4	St Stephens 6-N 11-W
" "	**23**	2	St Stephens 6-N 12-W
" "	**19**	2	St Stephens 7-N 11-W
" "	**25**	1	St Stephens 6-N 10-W
" "	**22**	1	St Stephens 6-N 13-W
PARROT	**9**	1	St Stephens 9-N 11-W
PATERSON	**10**	2	St Stephens 9-N 10-W
PATES	**13**	1	St Stephens 8-N 12-W
PATRICK	**15**	7	St Stephens 8-N 10-W
" "	**13**	1	St Stephens 8-N 12-W
PATTERSON	**4**	2	St Stephens 10-N 11-W
" "	**10**	2	St Stephens 9-N 10-W
" "	**9**	2	St Stephens 9-N 11-W
" "	**22**	1	St Stephens 6-N 13-W
" "	**21**	1	St Stephens 6-N 14-W
PATTON	**11**	2	St Stephens 8-N 14-W
PEARCEY	**10**	1	St Stephens 9-N 10-W
PEARSON	**14**	8	St Stephens 8-N 11-W
PEOPLES	**1**	3	St Stephens 10-N 14-W
" "	**2**	1	St Stephens 10-N 13-W
PERRY	**21**	1	St Stephens 6-N 14-W
PHILLIPS	**17**	3	St Stephens 7-N 13-W
PICKERING	**6**	4	St Stephens 9-N 14-W
" "	**21**	2	St Stephens 6-N 14-W
PINNELL	**12**	1	St Stephens 8-N 13-W
PITMAN	**18**	2	St Stephens 7-N 12-W
" "	**12**	2	St Stephens 8-N 13-W
" "	**19**	1	St Stephens 7-N 11-W
PITTMAN	**17**	6	St Stephens 7-N 13-W
PITTS	**13**	6	St Stephens 8-N 12-W
" "	**19**	4	St Stephens 7-N 11-W
" "	**25**	1	St Stephens 6-N 10-W
PLOCK	**18**	20	St Stephens 7-N 12-W
" "	**5**	10	St Stephens 10-N 10-W
" "	**13**	7	St Stephens 8-N 12-W
" "	**22**	4	St Stephens 6-N 13-W
" "	**23**	1	St Stephens 6-N 12-W
PONDER	**18**	2	St Stephens 7-N 12-W
" "	**14**	1	St Stephens 8-N 11-W
POOL	**18**	11	St Stephens 7-N 12-W
" "	**14**	2	St Stephens 8-N 11-W
" "	**11**	1	St Stephens 8-N 14-W
POWELL	**7**	13	St Stephens 9-N 13-W
" "	**13**	8	St Stephens 8-N 12-W
" "	**6**	6	St Stephens 9-N 14-W
" "	**12**	4	St Stephens 8-N 13-W

Surname	Map Group	Parcels of Land	Meridian/Township/Range
POWELL (Cont'd)	2	2	St Stephens 10-N 13-W
" "	17	2	St Stephens 7-N 13-W
PRESCOTT	24	2	St Stephens 6-N 11-W
" "	9	1	St Stephens 9-N 11-W
PRESSCOAT	18	5	St Stephens 7-N 12-W
PRICE	12	2	St Stephens 8-N 13-W
" "	11	1	St Stephens 8-N 14-W
PRIDGEN	6	3	St Stephens 9-N 14-W
PRINCE	19	2	St Stephens 7-N 11-W
PRINE	19	2	St Stephens 7-N 11-W
" "	14	1	St Stephens 8-N 11-W
PRYOR	15	5	St Stephens 8-N 10-W
" "	3	1	St Stephens 10-N 12-W
PURVIS	5	1	St Stephens 10-N 10-W
QUANCE	19	7	St Stephens 7-N 11-W
" "	20	4	St Stephens 7-N 10-W
QUICK	17	3	St Stephens 7-N 13-W
RABUN	12	2	St Stephens 8-N 13-W
RAINEY	16	6	St Stephens 7-N 14-W
" "	21	5	St Stephens 6-N 14-W
" "	17	5	St Stephens 7-N 13-W
RAMSEY	24	3	St Stephens 6-N 11-W
RAYNER	23	1	St Stephens 6-N 12-W
READ	18	1	St Stephens 7-N 12-W
REAVES	24	1	St Stephens 6-N 11-W
" "	9	1	St Stephens 9-N 11-W
REDDECK	6	1	St Stephens 9-N 14-W
REDDOCH	6	1	St Stephens 9-N 14-W
REDDOCK	6	4	St Stephens 9-N 14-W
REESE	10	1	St Stephens 9-N 10-W
REEVES	13	3	St Stephens 8-N 12-W
RIALS	21	6	St Stephens 6-N 14-W
RICHARDSON	18	6	St Stephens 7-N 12-W
" "	22	1	St Stephens 6-N 13-W
" "	11	1	St Stephens 8-N 14-W
RIDGWAY	17	3	St Stephens 7-N 13-W
" "	22	1	St Stephens 6-N 13-W
RIELS	21	3	St Stephens 6-N 14-W
" "	16	1	St Stephens 7-N 14-W
RIVERS	9	6	St Stephens 9-N 11-W
" "	8	3	St Stephens 9-N 12-W
" "	4	2	St Stephens 10-N 11-W
ROBERTS	11	13	St Stephens 8-N 14-W
" "	21	1	St Stephens 6-N 14-W
ROBERTSON	11	5	St Stephens 8-N 14-W
" "	16	3	St Stephens 7-N 14-W
ROBINSON	19	2	St Stephens 7-N 11-W
" "	17	1	St Stephens 7-N 13-W
ROBISON	18	6	St Stephens 7-N 12-W
RODGERS	5	2	St Stephens 10-N 10-W
" "	21	2	St Stephens 6-N 14-W
" "	15	2	St Stephens 8-N 10-W
ROGERS	5	3	St Stephens 10-N 10-W
" "	16	3	St Stephens 7-N 14-W
" "	10	3	St Stephens 9-N 10-W
" "	19	2	St Stephens 7-N 11-W
ROSE	4	2	St Stephens 10-N 11-W
" "	19	2	St Stephens 7-N 11-W
" "	5	1	St Stephens 10-N 10-W
ROUNSAVILL	24	3	St Stephens 6-N 11-W

Surname	Map Group	Parcels of Land	Meridian/Township/Range		
ROWELL	11	1	St Stephens	8-N	14-W
ROYALS	7	6	St Stephens	9-N	13-W
" "	6	3	St Stephens	9-N	14-W
RUMPH	6	3	St Stephens	9-N	14-W
RUNNELLS	9	3	St Stephens	9-N	11-W
RUSH	21	5	St Stephens	6-N	14-W
" "	22	3	St Stephens	6-N	13-W
RUSHTON	10	12	St Stephens	9-N	10-W
" "	9	6	St Stephens	9-N	11-W
RUSSELL	11	1	St Stephens	8-N	14-W
RUSTIN	10	1	St Stephens	9-N	10-W
SAGE	3	12	St Stephens	10-N	12-W
SANDERS	18	2	St Stephens	7-N	12-W
SANDERSON	17	2	St Stephens	7-N	13-W
SANFORD	16	2	St Stephens	7-N	14-W
SANTSON	15	2	St Stephens	8-N	10-W
SAUL	9	2	St Stephens	9-N	11-W
SAUNDERS	5	2	St Stephens	10-N	10-W
" "	3	1	St Stephens	10-N	12-W
SCANLAN	19	2	St Stephens	7-N	11-W
" "	24	1	St Stephens	6-N	11-W
SCARBROUGH	7	2	St Stephens	9-N	13-W
SCHONE	19	2	St Stephens	7-N	11-W
SCOTT	8	4	St Stephens	9-N	12-W
SCRIVENER	18	1	St Stephens	7-N	12-W
SCRIVNER	23	1	St Stephens	6-N	12-W
SCRUGGS	5	1	St Stephens	10-N	10-W
SEAMAN	13	1	St Stephens	8-N	12-W
SELLERS	22	11	St Stephens	6-N	13-W
" "	2	2	St Stephens	10-N	13-W
" "	21	2	St Stephens	6-N	14-W
" "	11	2	St Stephens	8-N	14-W
SHARP	22	2	St Stephens	6-N	13-W
SHELBY	8	3	St Stephens	9-N	12-W
SHERLY	5	1	St Stephens	10-N	10-W
SHOEMAKE	24	5	St Stephens	6-N	11-W
" "	19	4	St Stephens	7-N	11-W
" "	4	1	St Stephens	10-N	11-W
SHOLAR	23	2	St Stephens	6-N	12-W
SHOWE	18	1	St Stephens	7-N	12-W
SHOWES	18	1	St Stephens	7-N	12-W
SHOWS	23	34	St Stephens	6-N	12-W
" "	18	19	St Stephens	7-N	12-W
" "	13	9	St Stephens	8-N	12-W
" "	24	4	St Stephens	6-N	11-W
" "	21	3	St Stephens	6-N	14-W
" "	19	3	St Stephens	7-N	11-W
" "	12	3	St Stephens	8-N	13-W
" "	8	3	St Stephens	9-N	12-W
" "	7	3	St Stephens	9-N	13-W
" "	25	2	St Stephens	6-N	10-W
" "	17	2	St Stephens	7-N	13-W
" "	22	1	St Stephens	6-N	13-W
SIMPSON	1	3	St Stephens	10-N	14-W
" "	2	2	St Stephens	10-N	13-W
SIMS	4	3	St Stephens	10-N	11-W
" "	7	3	St Stephens	9-N	13-W
SINGELTARY	9	2	St Stephens	9-N	11-W
SINGLETON	14	1	St Stephens	8-N	11-W
SKELLY	19	2	St Stephens	7-N	11-W

Surname	Map Group	Parcels of Land	Meridian/Township/Range		
SKELLY (Cont'd)	**18**	1	St Stephens	7-N	12-W
SMITH	**9**	47	St Stephens	9-N	11-W
" "	**25**	18	St Stephens	6-N	10-W
" "	**7**	12	St Stephens	9-N	13-W
" "	**4**	4	St Stephens	10-N	11-W
" "	**22**	4	St Stephens	6-N	13-W
" "	**21**	4	St Stephens	6-N	14-W
" "	**19**	3	St Stephens	7-N	11-W
" "	**17**	3	St Stephens	7-N	13-W
" "	**11**	3	St Stephens	8-N	14-W
" "	**14**	2	St Stephens	8-N	11-W
" "	**1**	1	St Stephens	10-N	14-W
" "	**24**	1	St Stephens	6-N	11-W
" "	**16**	1	St Stephens	7-N	14-W
" "	**15**	1	St Stephens	8-N	10-W
SPEARS	**13**	5	St Stephens	8-N	12-W
SPEED	**8**	1	St Stephens	9-N	12-W
STAFFORD	**17**	3	St Stephens	7-N	13-W
STEELMON	**10**	2	St Stephens	9-N	10-W
STENNETT	**18**	1	St Stephens	7-N	12-W
STEPHENS	**24**	3	St Stephens	6-N	11-W
" "	**14**	1	St Stephens	8-N	11-W
STEVENS	**25**	1	St Stephens	6-N	10-W
" "	**23**	1	St Stephens	6-N	12-W
STEVENSON	**23**	3	St Stephens	6-N	12-W
STEVISON	**23**	2	St Stephens	6-N	12-W
" "	**19**	1	St Stephens	7-N	11-W
STEWART	**5**	4	St Stephens	10-N	10-W
" "	**12**	2	St Stephens	8-N	13-W
" "	**10**	1	St Stephens	9-N	10-W
STINSON	**25**	2	St Stephens	6-N	10-W
STOCKTON	**17**	1	St Stephens	7-N	13-W
STRANGE	**6**	3	St Stephens	9-N	14-W
STRICKLAND	**23**	4	St Stephens	6-N	12-W
" "	**18**	3	St Stephens	7-N	12-W
" "	**15**	2	St Stephens	8-N	10-W
" "	**13**	1	St Stephens	8-N	12-W
STRINGER	**16**	3	St Stephens	7-N	14-W
" "	**23**	1	St Stephens	6-N	12-W
STULMAN	**10**	2	St Stephens	9-N	10-W
STUTMAN	**10**	1	St Stephens	9-N	10-W
SUGGS	**2**	5	St Stephens	10-N	13-W
SUMMERS	**17**	1	St Stephens	7-N	13-W
SUMRALL	**23**	7	St Stephens	6-N	12-W
" "	**15**	6	St Stephens	8-N	10-W
" "	**7**	6	St Stephens	9-N	13-W
" "	**9**	5	St Stephens	9-N	11-W
" "	**20**	4	St Stephens	7-N	10-W
" "	**19**	4	St Stephens	7-N	11-W
" "	**8**	4	St Stephens	9-N	12-W
" "	**4**	2	St Stephens	10-N	11-W
" "	**25**	2	St Stephens	6-N	10-W
" "	**24**	2	St Stephens	6-N	11-W
" "	**14**	2	St Stephens	8-N	11-W
" "	**2**	1	St Stephens	10-N	13-W
SYMES	**13**	7	St Stephens	8-N	12-W
" "	**12**	2	St Stephens	8-N	13-W
TAYLOR	**5**	3	St Stephens	10-N	10-W
" "	**13**	1	St Stephens	8-N	12-W
TEMPLES	**9**	6	St Stephens	9-N	11-W

Surname	Map Group	Parcels of Land	Meridian/Township/Range		
THACH	**5**	1	St Stephens	10-N	10-W
THATCH	**5**	3	St Stephens	10-N	10-W
THIGPEN	**7**	1	St Stephens	9-N	13-W
THOMAS	**7**	4	St Stephens	9-N	13-W
" "	**6**	1	St Stephens	9-N	14-W
THOMPSON	**17**	2	St Stephens	7-N	13-W
" "	**16**	2	St Stephens	7-N	14-W
" "	**21**	1	St Stephens	6-N	14-W
" "	**13**	1	St Stephens	8-N	12-W
" "	**9**	1	St Stephens	9-N	11-W
THOMSON	**25**	3	St Stephens	6-N	10-W
" "	**24**	3	St Stephens	6-N	11-W
THORNTON	**4**	1	St Stephens	10-N	11-W
" "	**22**	1	St Stephens	6-N	13-W
" "	**10**	1	St Stephens	9-N	10-W
THRASH	**16**	3	St Stephens	7-N	14-W
TINNON	**6**	2	St Stephens	9-N	14-W
TIPPIN	**23**	18	St Stephens	6-N	12-W
" "	**24**	4	St Stephens	6-N	11-W
TISDALE	**17**	19	St Stephens	7-N	13-W
" "	**16**	7	St Stephens	7-N	14-W
" "	**12**	6	St Stephens	8-N	13-W
" "	**11**	5	St Stephens	8-N	14-W
" "	**22**	3	St Stephens	6-N	13-W
TISDALL	**18**	1	St Stephens	7-N	12-W
TODD	**12**	4	St Stephens	8-N	13-W
" "	**7**	3	St Stephens	9-N	13-W
TOUCHSTONE	**14**	2	St Stephens	8-N	11-W
" "	**15**	1	St Stephens	8-N	10-W
" "	**10**	1	St Stephens	9-N	10-W
" "	**9**	1	St Stephens	9-N	11-W
TRAVIS	**22**	1	St Stephens	6-N	13-W
TREST	**10**	22	St Stephens	9-N	10-W
" "	**15**	1	St Stephens	8-N	10-W
" "	**14**	1	St Stephens	8-N	11-W
TRIGGS	**16**	5	St Stephens	7-N	14-W
TUCKER	**24**	15	St Stephens	6-N	11-W
" "	**14**	9	St Stephens	8-N	11-W
" "	**16**	3	St Stephens	7-N	14-W
" "	**25**	2	St Stephens	6-N	10-W
TURNER	**12**	5	St Stephens	8-N	13-W
" "	**6**	4	St Stephens	9-N	14-W
ULMER	**4**	4	St Stephens	10-N	11-W
" "	**3**	3	St Stephens	10-N	12-W
UNDERWOOD	**5**	5	St Stephens	10-N	10-W
" "	**10**	3	St Stephens	9-N	10-W
UPSHAW	**19**	2	St Stephens	7-N	11-W
" "	**24**	1	St Stephens	6-N	11-W
VALENTINE	**2**	21	St Stephens	10-N	13-W
" "	**15**	5	St Stephens	8-N	10-W
" "	**7**	4	St Stephens	9-N	13-W
" "	**6**	3	St Stephens	9-N	14-W
" "	**3**	2	St Stephens	10-N	12-W
" "	**8**	1	St Stephens	9-N	12-W
VAN	**24**	2	St Stephens	6-N	11-W
VARNER	**10**	1	St Stephens	9-N	10-W
VAUGHAN	**24**	34	St Stephens	6-N	11-W
VAUGHN	**7**	2	St Stephens	9-N	13-W
VICK	**22**	1	St Stephens	6-N	13-W
VOLENTINE	**7**	2	St Stephens	9-N	13-W

Surname	Map Group	Parcels of Land	Meridian/Township/Range
VOLKING	**9**	2	St Stephens 9-N 11-W
VOLLENTINE	**2**	1	St Stephens 10-N 13-W
ʺ　　ʺ	**1**	1	St Stephens 10-N 14-W
WADDELL	**10**	40	St Stephens 9-N 10-W
ʺ　ʺ	**15**	27	St Stephens 8-N 10-W
WADE	**12**	14	St Stephens 8-N 13-W
ʺ　ʺ	**2**	4	St Stephens 10-N 13-W
ʺ　ʺ	**11**	2	St Stephens 8-N 14-W
ʺ　ʺ	**6**	1	St Stephens 9-N 14-W
WAITES	**21**	3	St Stephens 6-N 14-W
WALL	**23**	1	St Stephens 6-N 12-W
WALLACE	**16**	2	St Stephens 7-N 14-W
ʺ　ʺ	**9**	1	St Stephens 9-N 11-W
WALLEY	**24**	2	St Stephens 6-N 11-W
WALTERS	**15**	22	St Stephens 8-N 10-W
ʺ　ʺ	**19**	20	St Stephens 7-N 11-W
ʺ　ʺ	**14**	17	St Stephens 8-N 11-W
ʺ　ʺ	**12**	11	St Stephens 8-N 13-W
ʺ　ʺ	**9**	10	St Stephens 9-N 11-W
ʺ　ʺ	**10**	9	St Stephens 9-N 10-W
ʺ　ʺ	**13**	7	St Stephens 8-N 12-W
ʺ　ʺ	**24**	5	St Stephens 6-N 11-W
ʺ　ʺ	**16**	5	St Stephens 7-N 14-W
ʺ　ʺ	**18**	4	St Stephens 7-N 12-W
ʺ　ʺ	**23**	2	St Stephens 6-N 12-W
ʺ　ʺ	**17**	2	St Stephens 7-N 13-W
ʺ　ʺ	**8**	2	St Stephens 9-N 12-W
ʺ　ʺ	**20**	1	St Stephens 7-N 10-W
WALTMAN	**13**	3	St Stephens 8-N 12-W
ʺ　ʺ	**6**	3	St Stephens 9-N 14-W
WARD	**23**	3	St Stephens 6-N 12-W
ʺ　ʺ	**7**	3	St Stephens 9-N 13-W
ʺ　ʺ	**4**	1	St Stephens 10-N 11-W
WARE	**25**	15	St Stephens 6-N 10-W
ʺ　ʺ	**20**	13	St Stephens 7-N 10-W
WARNER	**14**	9	St Stephens 8-N 11-W
ʺ　ʺ	**13**	5	St Stephens 8-N 12-W
WARREN	**12**	2	St Stephens 8-N 13-W
ʺ　ʺ	**11**	2	St Stephens 8-N 14-W
WATKINS	**17**	2	St Stephens 7-N 13-W
ʺ　ʺ	**16**	1	St Stephens 7-N 14-W
WATSON	**25**	63	St Stephens 6-N 10-W
ʺ　ʺ	**24**	40	St Stephens 6-N 11-W
ʺ　ʺ	**23**	35	St Stephens 6-N 12-W
ʺ　ʺ	**20**	24	St Stephens 7-N 10-W
ʺ　ʺ	**22**	10	St Stephens 6-N 13-W
ʺ　ʺ	**13**	5	St Stephens 8-N 12-W
ʺ　ʺ	**16**	3	St Stephens 7-N 14-W
WATTERS	**15**	2	St Stephens 8-N 10-W
ʺ　ʺ	**14**	2	St Stephens 8-N 11-W
ʺ　ʺ	**13**	2	St Stephens 8-N 12-W
ʺ　ʺ	**10**	1	St Stephens 9-N 10-W
ʺ　ʺ	**9**	1	St Stephens 9-N 11-W
WATTS	**22**	1	St Stephens 6-N 13-W
WEAVER	**16**	3	St Stephens 7-N 14-W
WEEKS	**23**	1	St Stephens 6-N 12-W
WELBORN	**2**	14	St Stephens 10-N 13-W
ʺ　ʺ	**3**	13	St Stephens 10-N 12-W
ʺ　ʺ	**18**	7	St Stephens 7-N 12-W
ʺ　ʺ	**8**	7	St Stephens 9-N 12-W

Surname	Map Group	Parcels of Land	Meridian/Township/Range
WELBORN (Cont'd)	4	4	St Stephens 10-N 11-W
" "	15	3	St Stephens 8-N 10-W
" "	13	3	St Stephens 8-N 12-W
" "	10	3	St Stephens 9-N 10-W
" "	7	2	St Stephens 9-N 13-W
" "	1	1	St Stephens 10-N 14-W
WELBORNE	15	3	St Stephens 8-N 10-W
" "	7	3	St Stephens 9-N 13-W
WELCH	3	8	St Stephens 10-N 12-W
" "	2	7	St Stephens 10-N 13-W
" "	12	7	St Stephens 8-N 13-W
" "	11	7	St Stephens 8-N 14-W
" "	7	7	St Stephens 9-N 13-W
" "	14	2	St Stephens 8-N 11-W
" "	9	1	St Stephens 9-N 11-W
" "	8	1	St Stephens 9-N 12-W
WELDY	16	1	St Stephens 7-N 14-W
WELLS	4	2	St Stephens 10-N 11-W
" "	13	2	St Stephens 8-N 12-W
WEST	14	2	St Stephens 8-N 11-W
" "	9	1	St Stephens 9-N 11-W
WHEELER	21	4	St Stephens 6-N 14-W
" "	6	1	St Stephens 9-N 14-W
WHITE	5	2	St Stephens 10-N 10-W
WHITEHEAD	21	2	St Stephens 6-N 14-W
WHITTLE	4	3	St Stephens 10-N 11-W
WILBORN	2	4	St Stephens 10-N 13-W
" "	8	4	St Stephens 9-N 12-W
" "	3	2	St Stephens 10-N 12-W
" "	7	1	St Stephens 9-N 13-W
WILLIAMS	2	4	St Stephens 10-N 13-W
" "	13	4	St Stephens 8-N 12-W
" "	22	3	St Stephens 6-N 13-W
" "	20	3	St Stephens 7-N 10-W
" "	1	1	St Stephens 10-N 14-W
" "	24	1	St Stephens 6-N 11-W
WILLIS	1	2	St Stephens 10-N 14-W
" "	9	1	St Stephens 9-N 11-W
WILSON	11	4	St Stephens 8-N 14-W
" "	22	1	St Stephens 6-N 13-W
WINDHAM	17	8	St Stephens 7-N 13-W
" "	22	3	St Stephens 6-N 13-W
" "	14	2	St Stephens 8-N 11-W
" "	11	2	St Stephens 8-N 14-W
" "	3	1	St Stephens 10-N 12-W
WISE	23	1	St Stephens 6-N 12-W
WOODARD	25	3	St Stephens 6-N 10-W
" "	23	3	St Stephens 6-N 12-W
WOODDARD	25	2	St Stephens 6-N 10-W
WOULARD	17	2	St Stephens 7-N 13-W
YATES	11	3	St Stephens 8-N 14-W
" "	12	1	St Stephens 8-N 13-W
YAWN	23	4	St Stephens 6-N 12-W
YOUNG	16	1	St Stephens 7-N 14-W

– Part II –

Township Map Groups

Map Group 1: Index to Land Patents

Township 10-North Range 14-West (St Stephens)

After you locate an individual in this Index, take note of the Section and Section Part then proceed to the Land Patent map on the pages immediately following. You should have no difficulty locating the corresponding parcel of land.

The "For More Info" Column will lead you to more information about the underlying Patents. See the *Legend* at right, and the "How to Use this Book" chapter, for more information.

```
┌─────────────────────────────────────────────────────┐
│                    LEGEND                            │
│          "For More Info . . . " column               │
│ ─────────────────────────────────────────────────── │
│ A = Authority (Legislative Act, See Appendix "A")    │
│ B = Block or Lot (location in Section unknown)       │
│ C = Cancelled Patent                                 │
│ F = Fractional Section                               │
│ G = Group (Multi-Patentee Patent, see Appendix "C")  │
│ V = Overlaps another Parcel                          │
│ R = Re-Issued (Parcel patented more than once)       │
│                                                      │
│ (A & G items require you to look in the Appendixes   │
│ referred to above. All other Letter-designations     │
│ followed by a number require you to locate line-items │
│ in this index that possess the ID number found after │
│ the letter).                                         │
└─────────────────────────────────────────────────────┘
```

ID	Individual in Patent	Sec.	Sec. Part	Date Issued	Other Counties	For More Info . . .
21	ANDERSON, Latson D	34	3	1892-03-23	Smith	A3
40	BLACKWELL, Warren	25	NWNW	1882-03-04	Smith	A3 V41
16	BROWN, John R	36	S½SW	1859-11-10		A2
13	CROSBY, John	35	S½SE	1901-11-08	Smith	A3
14	" "	35	SESW	1901-11-08	Smith	A3
33	DAVIS, Thomas S	25	12	1898-01-19	Smith	A3
34	" "	25	5	1898-01-19	Smith	A3
35	" "	25	6	1898-01-19	Smith	A3
36	" "	25	7	1898-01-19	Smith	A3
6	GAMBRELL, C B	35	N½N½	1960-05-25	Smith	A1 F
7	GAMBRELL, Emmette W	34	1	1902-03-07	Smith	A3
8	" "	34	E½1	1902-03-07	Smith	A3
17	GAMBRELL, John S	34	E½2	1911-06-26	Smith	A2 R25
25	GAMBRELL, Mary M	34	E½2	1899-04-01	Smith	A3 R17
26	" "	34	W½1	1899-04-01	Smith	A3
10	GRISSOM, James	35	N½SE	1860-07-02	Smith	A2
11	" "	35	NESW	1860-07-02	Smith	A2
12	" "	35	S½NE	1860-07-02	Smith	A2
29	GRISSOM, Reubin W	25	10	1898-01-19	Smith	A3
30	" "	25	15	1898-01-19	Smith	A3
31	" "	25	16	1898-01-19	Smith	A3
37	GRISSOM, Wade M	35	N½1	1892-04-29	Smith	A3
38	" "	36	NWSW	1892-04-29		A3
39	" "	36	W½NW	1892-04-29		A3
44	GRISSOM, William	25	E½SW	1861-05-01	Smith	A2 V41
43	" "	25	13	1889-10-15	Smith	A3
41	GRISSOM, William G	25		1902-02-07	Smith	A2
42	" "	36	NENW	1902-02-07		A2
20	HINTON, Joshua H	35	W½SW	1859-05-02	Smith	A2
18	" "	35	3	1859-11-10	Smith	A2
19	" "	35	4	1859-11-10	Smith	A2
5	KENNEDY, Benjamin F	25	3	1874-11-05	Smith	A2
9	MAXWELL, George F	36	N½NE	1906-05-01		A2
1	PEOPLES, Andrew D	25	1	1896-09-29	Smith	A3
2	" "	25	8	1896-09-29	Smith	A3
3	" "	25	9	1896-09-29	Smith	A3
22	SIMPSON, Mary E	36	NESW	1859-05-02		A2
23	" "	36	S½NE	1859-05-02		A2
24	" "	36	SENW	1859-05-02		A2
45	SMITH, William H	35	N½2	1899-05-31	Smith	A3
15	VOLLENTINE, John J	36	SE	1859-05-02		A2
4	WELBORN, Ann	25	2	1905-02-13	Smith	A3
32	WILLIAMS, Thomas D	34	W½2	1897-04-14	Smith	A2
27	WILLIS, Mary	34	5	1901-03-23	Smith	A2
28	" "	34	6	1901-03-23	Smith	A2

3	2	1
10	11	12
15	14	13
22	23	24
27	26	25

Smith

Jones

Patent Map

T10-N R14-W
St Stephens Meridian

Map Group 1

Township Statistics

Parcels Mapped	:	45
Number of Patents	:	26
Number of Individuals	:	24
Patentees Identified	:	24
Number of Surnames	:	17
Multi-Patentee Parcels	:	0
Oldest Patent Date	:	5/2/1859
Most Recent Patent	:	5/25/1960
Block/Lot Parcels	:	26
Parcels Re - Issued	:	1
Parcels that Overlap	:	2
Cities and Towns	:	0
Cemeteries	:	1

Note: the area contained in this map amounts to far less than a full Township. Therefore, its contents are completely on this single page (instead of a "normal" 2-page spread).

Section 25

BLACKWELL
Warren
1882

GRISSOM
William G
1902

GRISSOM
William
1861

GRISSOM
William G
1902

MAXWELL
George F
1906

GRISSOM
Wade M
1892

SIMPSON
Mary E
1859

SIMPSON
Mary E
1859

GRISSOM
Wade M
1892

SIMPSON
Mary E
1859

BROWN
John R
1859

VOLLENTINE
John J
1859

Section 36

Lots-Sec. 34

1	GAMBRELL, Emmette W	1902
3	ANDERSON, Latson D	1892
5	WILLIS, Mary	1901
6	WILLIAMS, Thomas D	1897
6	GAMBRELL, Mary M	1899
6	GAMBRELL, John S	1911
6	GAMBRELL, Mary M	1899
6	GAMBRELL, Emmette W	1902
6	WILLIS, Mary	1901

Lots-Sec. 25

1	PEOPLES, Andrew D	1896
2	WELBORN, Ann	1905
3	KENNEDY, Benjamin F	1874
5	DAVIS, Thomas S	1898
6	DAVIS, Thomas S	1898
7	DAVIS, Thomas S	1898
8	PEOPLES, Andrew D	1896
9	PEOPLES, Andrew D	1896
10	GRISSOM, Reubin W	1898
12	DAVIS, Thomas S	1898
13	GRISSOM, William	1889
15	GRISSOM, Reubin W	1898
16	GRISSOM, Reubin W	1898

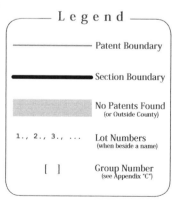

Legend

———— Patent Boundary

━━━━ Section Boundary

▨ No Patents Found
(or Outside County)

1., 2., 3., ... Lot Numbers
(when beside a name)

[ ] Group Number
(see Appendix "C")

Scale: Section = 1 mile X 1 mile
(generally, with some exceptions)

43

Road Map

T10-N R14-W
St Stephens Meridian

Map Group 1

Note: the area contained in this map amounts to far less than a full Township. Therefore, its contents are completely on this single page (instead of a "normal" 2-page spread).

Cities & Towns
None

Cemeteries
Hinton Cemetery

Legend

────────	Section Lines
════════	Interstates
────────	Highways
────────	Other Roads
●	Cities/Towns
✝	Cemeteries

Scale: Section = 1 mile X 1 mile
(generally, with some exceptions)

3	2	1
10	11	12
15	14	13
22	23	24
27	26	25

Smith

Jones

S H 28

| 34 | 25 | |
| | Gambrell ✝ *Hinton Cem.* | 36 |

Carter Dees

Summerland

3

2

1

Note: the area contained in this map amounts to far less than a full Township. Therefore, its contents are completely on this single page (instead of a "normal" 2-page spread).

10

11

12

Cities & Towns
None

15

14

13

Cemeteries
Hinton Cemetery

22

23

24

26

25

27

Smith

Jones

26

25

34

⚱ *Hinton Cem.*

36

Little Creek

L e g e n d

———— Section Lines

+++++ Railroads

▭ Large Rivers & Bodies of Water

- - - - - Streams/Creeks & Small Rivers

● Cities/Towns

⚱ Cemeteries

Scale: Section = 1 mile X 1 mile
(there are some exceptions)

Map Group 2: Index to Land Patents

Township 10-North Range 13-West (St Stephens)

After you locate an individual in this Index, take note of the Section and Section Part then proceed to the Land Patent map on the pages immediately following. You should have no difficulty locating the corresponding parcel of land.

The "For More Info" Column will lead you to more information about the underlying Patents. See the *Legend* at right, and the "How to Use this Book" chapter, for more information.

```
LEGEND
        "For More Info . . . " column
A = Authority (Legislative Act, See Appendix "A")
B = Block or Lot (location in Section unknown)
C = Cancelled Patent
F = Fractional Section
G = Group  (Multi-Patentee Patent, see Appendix "C")
V = Overlaps another Parcel
R = Re-Issued (Parcel patented more than once)

(A & G items require you to look in the Appendixes referred
to above. All other Letter-designations followed by a number
require you to locate line-items in this index that possess
the ID number found after the letter).
```

ID	Individual in Patent	Sec.	Sec. Part	Date Issued	Other Counties	For More Info . . .
148	BARNES, Richard	30	10	1895-05-11	Smith	A3
149	" "	30	11	1895-05-11	Smith	A3
150	" "	30	13	1895-05-11	Smith	A3
99	BRASWELL, Henry	29	1	1897-04-10	Smith	A3
100	" "	32	NWNE	1897-04-10		A3
80	COATS, Daniel	36	NWNW	1841-01-05		A2
155	COLLINS, Riley J	36	E½SE	1859-05-02		A2
157	" "	36	W½SE	1859-05-02		A2
156	" "	36	SWNE	1859-11-10		A2
142	DAVIS, Orange	31	NESW	1841-01-05		A2
143	" "	31	SWNW	1841-01-05		A2
160	DEARMAN, William	29	N½NE	1906-05-01	Smith	A3
67	DYKES, Benjamin F	25	8	1884-12-30	Jasper	A3
68	" "	26	5	1884-12-30	Jasper	A3
65	" "	25	6	1889-11-23	Jasper	A3
66	" "	25	7	1889-11-23	Jasper	A3
96	DYKES, George W	25	10	1861-05-01	Jasper	A2
97	" "	25	4	1861-05-01	Jasper	A2
98	" "	25	9	1861-05-01	Jasper	A2
129	DYKES, Luther C	26	12	1906-06-26	Jasper	A3
79	GRAVES, Claborn	35	SESW	1906-05-01		A2
123	GRISSOM, Joseph C	29	3	1899-04-28	Smith	A3
124	" "	29	4	1899-04-28	Smith	A3
125	" "	29	9	1899-04-28	Smith	A3
48	GUNTER, Albert L	28	NWNW	1901-12-12	Jasper	A2
50	GUNTER, Allen	25	3	1859-05-02	Jasper	A2
52	" "	36	NENW	1859-05-02		A2
51	" "	35	NENE	1859-06-01		A2
53	" "	36	SENW	1860-04-02		A2
122	GUNTER, John H	28	1	1898-12-12	Jasper	A3
126	GUNTER, Joseph M	30	S½	1859-05-02	Smith	A2 F
127	" "	31	E½NE	1859-05-02		A2
171	JACKSON, Wyly W	34	NENE	1906-06-30		A3
172	" "	35	NWNW	1906-06-30		A3
131	JOHNSON, Marvin	35	SWNE	1908-07-01		A2
162	JOHNSTON, William T	26	2	1893-10-13	Jasper	A3
163	" "	26	3	1893-10-13	Jasper	A3
164	" "	35	NENW	1893-10-13		A3
117	JONES, John D	28	13	1881-05-10	Jasper	A3
118	" "	28	14	1881-05-10	Jasper	A3
119	" "	28	2	1881-05-10	Jasper	A3
120	" "	28	3	1881-05-10	Jasper	A3
73	KNIGHT, Benjamin	31	NWSW	1859-05-02		A2
74	" "	31	SE	1859-05-02		A2
75	" "	31	SESW	1859-05-02		A2
76	" "	31	SWNE	1859-05-02		A2

ID	Individual in Patent	Sec.	Sec. Part	Date Issued	Other Counties	For More Info . . .
77	KNIGHT, Benjamin (Cont'd)	32	NWSW	1859-05-02		A2
78	" "	32	SWSW	1859-05-02		A2
103	KNIGHT, Jack	30	12	1896-10-10	Smith	A3
104	" "	30	5	1896-10-10	Smith	A3
105	" "	30	6	1896-10-10	Smith	A3
106	" "	30	7	1896-10-10	Smith	A3
107	KNIGHT, James	32	SWSE	1859-11-10		A2
111	KNIGHT, Jeff Early	27	12	1911-02-09	Jasper	A3
121	KNIGHT, John F	26	4	1901-08-12	Jasper	A3
137	KNIGHT, Newton	26	8	1881-05-10	Jasper	A3
158	KNIGHT, Seaborn A	31	SWSW	1906-06-21		A3
168	KNIGHT, Wyatt D	31	N½NW	1895-01-17		A3
169	" "	31	NWNE	1895-01-17		A3
170	" "	31	SENW	1895-01-17		A3
69	MAULDIN, Benjamin F	26	10	1894-12-17	Jasper	A3
70	" "	26	14	1894-12-17	Jasper	A3
71	" "	26	9	1894-12-17	Jasper	A3
64	PEOPLES, Andrew D	30	4	1896-09-29	Smith	A3
101	POWELL, Hiram W	34	SESW	1859-11-10		A2
102	" "	34	SWSE	1859-11-10		A2
115	SELLERS, John C	25	S½1	1841-01-05	Jasper	A2 F
116	" "	25	S½2	1841-01-05	Jasper	A2 F
49	SIMPSON, Alfred M	30	9	1859-06-01	Smith	A2
128	SIMPSON, Josiah	29	6	1859-05-02	Smith	A2
63	SUGGS, Amy J	30	3	1896-12-18	Smith	A3
108	SUGGS, James S	29	7	1891-06-30	Smith	A3
109	" "	30	1	1891-06-30	Smith	A3
110	" "	30	8	1891-06-30	Smith	A3
141	SUGGS, Oliver C	30	2	1906-06-30	Smith	A3
72	SUMRALL, Benjamin F	27	8	1885-05-25	Jasper	A3
54	VALENTINE, Allen	34	SENE	1859-11-10		A2
55	" "	34	W½NE	1859-11-10		A2
56	" "	35	NESW	1859-11-10		A2
57	" "	35	SENW	1859-11-10		A2
58	" "	35	SWNW	1859-11-10		A2
92	VALENTINE, George A	34	W½NW	1889-01-12		A3
93	" "	34	W½SW	1889-01-12		A3
87	" "	28	10	1889-04-23	Jasper	A2
88	" "	28	11	1890-03-28	Jasper	A3
89	" "	28	12	1890-03-28	Jasper	A3
90	" "	28	15	1896-11-04	Jasper	A3
91	" "	28	7	1896-11-04	Jasper	A3
130	VALENTINE, Martin E	27	13	1904-10-27	Jasper	A3
134	VALENTINE, Millard F	32	E½NE	1894-12-17		A3
135	" "	33	NWSW	1894-12-17		A3
136	" "	33	SWNW	1894-12-17		A3
151	VALENTINE, Richard H	34	E½SE	1882-03-30		A3
152	" "	35	W½SW	1882-03-30		A3
165	VALENTINE, William W	28	4	1893-04-12	Jasper	A3
166	" "	33	N½NW	1893-04-12		A3
167	" "	33	NWNE	1893-04-12		A3
59	VOLLENTINE, Allen	27	1	1859-11-10	Jasper	A2
144	WADE, Pinkney D	28	16	1897-02-15	Jasper	A3
145	" "	28	9	1897-02-15	Jasper	A3
146	" "	29	10	1897-02-15	Smith	A3
147	" "	29	11	1897-02-15	Smith	A3
46	WELBORN, Aaron	33	E½NE	1859-05-02		A2
47	" "	33	SE	1859-05-02		A2
86	WELBORN, Franklin M	33	SWSW	1859-05-02		A2
85	" "	32	SWNE	1859-11-10		A2
83	" "	32	N½SE	1925-04-02		A2
84	" "	32	SESE	1925-04-02		A2
95	WELBORN, George Buckhanan	25	N½1	1914-07-29	Jasper	A3
112	WELBORN, Joel H	26	1	1897-02-15	Jasper	A3
113	" "	35	NWNE	1897-02-15		A3
114	" "	35	SENE	1897-02-15		A3
138	WELBORN, Norris M	25	11	1893-04-12	Jasper	A3
139	" "	25	12	1893-04-12	Jasper	A3
140	" "	25	5	1893-04-12	Jasper	A3
161	WELBORN, William S	36	SWNW	1901-03-23		A3
60	WELCH, Alson M	33	E½SW	1894-12-17		A3
61	" "	33	SENW	1894-12-17		A3
62	" "	33	SWNE	1894-12-17		A3

ID	Individual in Patent	Sec.	Sec. Part	Date Issued	Other Counties	For More Info . . .
94	WELCH, George B	36	SW	1886-03-20		A3
153	WELCH, Richard J	36	E½NE	1859-05-02		A2
154	" "	36	NWNE	1859-05-02		A2
159	WELCH, Timothy	35	SE	1859-05-02		A2
173	WILBORN, Younger	26	11	1861-05-01	Jasper	A2
174	" "	26	13	1861-05-01	Jasper	A2
175	" "	26	6	1861-05-01	Jasper	A2
176	" "	26	7	1861-05-01	Jasper	A2
81	WILLIAMS, Eli E	28	5	1892-06-15	Jasper	A3
82	" "	28	6	1892-06-15	Jasper	A3
132	WILLIAMS, Matthew H	29	12	1899-04-01	Smith	A2
133	" "	29	14	1899-04-01	Smith	A2

Patent Map

T10-N R13-W
St Stephens Meridian

Map Group 2

Township Statistics

Parcels Mapped	:	131
Number of Patents	:	72
Number of Individuals	:	58
Patentees Identified	:	58
Number of Surnames	:	29
Multi-Patentee Parcels	:	0
Oldest Patent Date	:	1/5/1841
Most Recent Patent	:	4/2/1925
Block/Lot Parcels	:	69
Parcels Re - Issued	:	0
Parcels that Overlap	:	0
Cities and Towns	:	0
Cemeteries	:	1

Note: the area contained in this map amounts to far less than a full Township. Therefore, its contents are completely on this single page (instead of a "normal" 2-page spread).

Legend

Patent Boundary

Section Boundary

No Patents Found (or Outside County)

1., 2., 3., ...   Lot Numbers (when beside a name)

[ ]   Group Number (see Appendix "C")

Scale: Section = 1 mile X 1 mile (generally, with some exceptions)

N

49

Map Sections

Section 30 (Lots-Sec. 30):
1 SUGGS, James S 1891
2 SUGGS, Oliver C 1906
3 SUGGS, Amy J 1896
4 PEOPLES, Andrew D 1896
5 KNIGHT, Jack 1896
6 KNIGHT, Jack 1896
7 KNIGHT, Jack 1896
8 KNIGHT, Jack 1896
9 SIMPSON, Alfred M 1891
10 SUGGS, James S 1891
11 BARNES, Richard 1895
12 BARNES, Richard 1895
12 KNIGHT, Jack 1896
13 BARNES, Richard

30 GUNTER, Joseph M 1859

Left edge:
KNIGHT Seaborn A 1906
KNIGHT Benjamin 1859
KNIGHT Wyatt D 1895
DAVIS Orange 1841
KNIGHT Benjamin 1859
KNIGHT Wyatt D 1895
DAVIS Orange 1841
KNIGHT Wyatt D 1895
KNIGHT Joseph M 1859
GUNTER Joseph M 1859

31 KNIGHT Benjamin 1859

Section 29 (Lots-Sec. 29):
1 BRASWELL, Henry 1897
2 GRISSOM, Joseph C 1899
3 GRISSOM, Joseph C 1899
4 GRISSOM, Joseph C 1899
5 SIMPSON, Josiah 1859
6 GRISSOM, James S 1891
7 SUGGS, James S 1891
8 GRISSOM, Joseph C 1899
9 WADE, Pinkney D 1897
10 WADE, Pinkney D 1897
11 WADE, Pinkney D 1897
12 WILLIAMS, Matthew H 1899
14 WILLIAMS, Matthew H 1899

29 DEARMAN William 1906

20 Smith

Section 32:
KNIGHT Benjamin 1859
KNIGHT Benjamin 1859
WELBORN Franklin M 1859
BRASWELL Henry 1897
VALENTINE William F 1894
KNIGHT James 1859
WELBORN Franklin M 1925
WELBORN Franklin M 1859

32

Section 28 (Lots-Sec. 28):
GUNTER, Albert L 1901
1 GUNTER, John H 1898
2 JONES, John D 1881
3 JONES, John D 1881
4 VALENTINE, William W 1893
5 WILLIAMS, Eli E 1892
6 VALENTINE, William F 1892
7 WILLIAMS, Eli E 1892
8 VALENTINE, George A 1896
9 WADE, Pinkney D 1897
10 VALENTINE, George A 1889
11 VALENTINE, George A 1890
13 JONES, John D 1881
14 JONES, John D 1881
15 VALENTINE, George A 1896
16 WADE, Pinkney D 1897

28

21

Section 33:
WELBORN Franklin M 1894
VALENTINE William W 1893
VALENTINE Millard F 1894
VALENTINE Millard F 1894
WELCH Alson M 1894
WELCH Alson M 1894
WELCH Alson M 1894
WELBORN Aaron 1859

33

Section 27 (Lots-Sec. 27):
1 VOLLENTINE, Allen 1859
8 SUMRALL, Benjamin F 1885
12 KNIGHT, Jeff Early 1911
13 VALENTINE, Martin E 1904

VALENTINE George A 1889
VALENTINE George A 1889

27 Jasper

Jones

22

Section 34:
VALENTINE George A 1889
POWELL Hiram W 1859
POWELL Hiram W 1859
VALENTINE Allen 1859
VALENTINE Allen 1859
VALENTINE Richard H 1882

34

Section 26 (Lots-Sec. 26):
1 WELBORN, Joel H 1897
2 JOHNSTON, William T 1893
3 JOHNSTON, William T 1893
4 KNIGHT, John F 1901
5 DYKES, Benjamin F 1884
6 WELBORN, Younger 1861
7 WELBORN, Younger 1861
8 KNIGHT, Newton 1859
9 KNIGHT, Benjamin F 1894
10 MAULDIN, Benjamin F 1894
11 WELBORN, Younger 1861
12 DYKES, Luther C 1906
13 WILBORN, Younger 1861
14 MAULDIN, Benjamin F 1894

26

Section 35:
JACKSON Wyly W 1906
JACKSON Wyly W 1906
JOHNSTON William T 1893
WELBORN Joel H 1897
JOHNSON Marvin 1908
VALENTINE Allen 1859/1859
VALENTINE Allen 1859
VALENTINE Richard H 1882
WELCH Timothy 1859
WELCH Joel H 1897
GUNTER Allen 1859
GRAVES Claborn 1906

35

23

Section 25 (Lots-Sec. 25):
3 GUNTER, Allen 1859
4 DYKES, George W 1861
5 WELBORN, Norris M 1893
6 DYKES, Benjamin F 1889
7 DYKES, Benjamin F 1889
8 DYKES, Benjamin F 1884
9 SELLERS, John C 1841
10 WELBORN, George Buck 1914
11 DYKES, George W 1861
12 WELBORN, Norris M 1893
13 DYKES, George W 1861
14 WELBORN, Norris M 1893

Section 36:
WELBORN William S 1901
COATS Daniel 1841
GUNTER Richard J 1859
WELCH Richard J
WELBORN William S 1901
GUNTER Allen 1860
GUNTER Allen 1859
COLLINS Riley J 1859
WELCH George B 1886
COLLINS Riley J 1859
COLLINS Riley J 1859

36

24

25

Road Map

T10-N R13-W
St Stephens Meridian

Map Group 2

Note: the area contained in this map amounts to far less than a full Township. Therefore, its contents are completely on this single page (instead of a "normal" 2-page spread).

Cities & Towns
None

Cemeteries
Union Line Cemetery

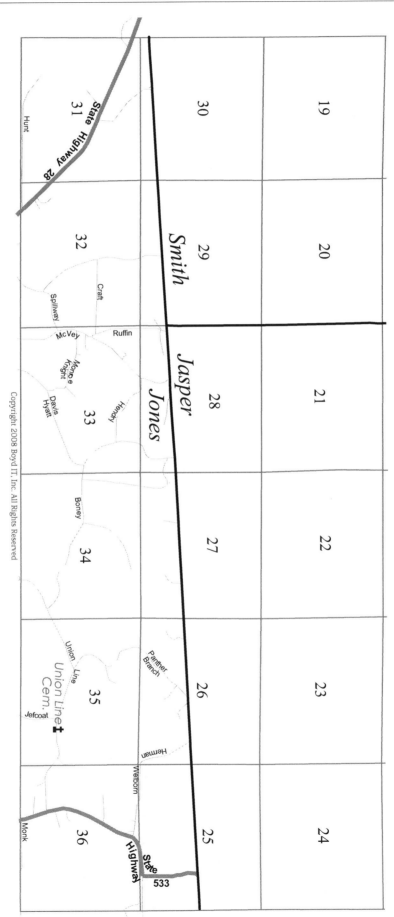

Legend

—— Section Lines

══ Interstates

══ Highways

—— Other Roads

● Cities/Towns

✝ Cemeteries

Scale: Section = 1 mile X 1 mile
(generally, with some exceptions)

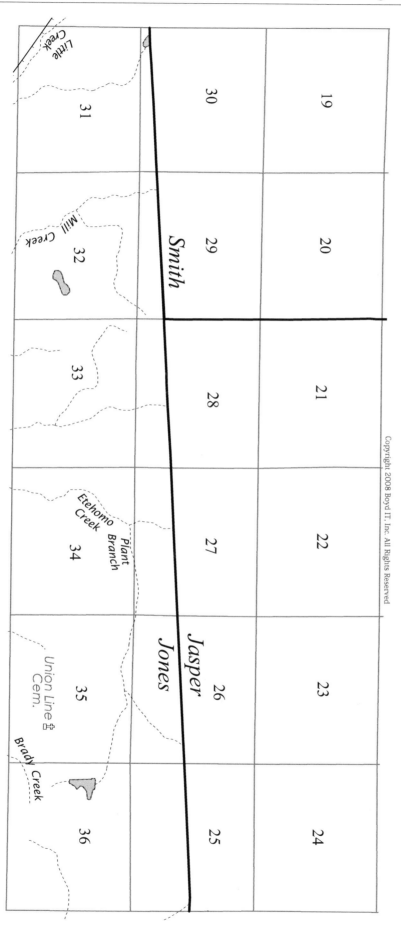

Historical Map

T10-N R13-W
St Stephens Meridian

Map Group 2

Note: the area contained in this map amounts to far less than a full Township. Therefore, its contents are completely on this single page (instead of a "normal" 2-page spread).

Cities & Towns

None

Cemeteries

Union Line Cemetery

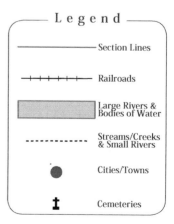

Legend

- Section Lines
- Railroads
- Large Rivers & Bodies of Water
- Streams/Creeks & Small Rivers
- Cities/Towns
- Cemeteries

Scale: Section = 1 mile X 1 mile
(there are some exceptions)

Map Group 3: Index to Land Patents

Township 10-North Range 12-West (St Stephens)

After you locate an individual in this Index, take note of the Section and Section Part then proceed to the Land Patent map on the pages immediately following. You should have no difficulty locating the corresponding parcel of land.

The "For More Info" Column will lead you to more information about the underlying Patents. See the *Legend* at right, and the "How to Use this Book" chapter, for more information.

ID	Individual in Patent	Sec.	Sec. Part	Date Issued	Other Counties	For More Info . . .
182	BLACKWELL, Alonzo	33	NESW	1897-09-09		A3
183	"	33	S½NW	1897-09-09		A3
233	GAVIN, Joseph	35	SESE	1892-07-25		A3
234	"	36	NESW	1892-07-25		A3
235	"	36	S½SW	1892-07-25		A3
246	GEIGGER, Samuel	36	SESE	1888-04-05		A3
247	"	36	W½SE	1888-04-05		A3
178	GIEGER, Abram M	25	6	1859-05-02	Jasper	A2
179	"	25	7	1859-05-02	Jasper	A2
180	"	25	8	1859-05-02	Jasper	A2
181	GUNTER, Allen	30	S½4	1860-04-02	Jasper	A2
190	HOGAN, George H	33	SESE	1900-02-02		A3
207	HOLDER, James	27	S½5	1859-05-02	Jasper	A2
208	"	27	S½6	1859-05-02	Jasper	A2
209	"	34	NESW	1859-05-02		A2
210	"	34	NW	1859-05-02		A2
211	"	34	W½SW	1859-05-02		A2
219	HOLDER, James R	26	3	1859-05-02	Jasper	A2
220	"	26	4	1859-05-02	Jasper	A2
221	"	26	5	1859-05-02	Jasper	A2
222	"	27	1	1859-05-02	Jasper	A2
243	HOPKINS, Robert J	33	SESW	1892-07-25		A3
244	"	33	SWSE	1892-07-25		A3
252	JOHNSON, William H	33	NWSE	1893-08-23		A3
253	"	33	SWNE	1893-08-23		A3
231	KAMPER, John	36	NESE	1890-07-03		A2
232	"	36	SENE	1890-07-03		A2
229	MATHEWS, John H	32	E½NW	1897-09-09		A3
230	"	32	N½NE	1897-09-09		A3
237	MATHEWS, Lazarus	32	N½SE	1892-03-07		A3
238	"	32	S½NE	1892-03-07		A3
212	MATTHEWS, James L	32	SESE	1898-11-11		A3
254	MATTHEWS, William L	33	W½SW	1894-03-12		A3
256	MCNAT, William	31	NESW	1859-05-02		A2
257	"	31	NWSE	1859-05-02		A2
258	"	31	SENW	1859-05-02		A2
184	MOSS, Benjamin F	26	10	1881-09-17	Jasper	A3
224	MOSS, Jefferson D	28	8	1895-02-21	Jasper	A3
225	"	28	9	1895-02-21	Jasper	A3
203	MURPHY, Irydell M	27	9	1895-02-15	Jasper	A3
255	PRYOR, William L	33	NENE	1904-08-30		A3
191	SAGE, Henry W	29	2	1890-04-25	Jasper	A2
192	"	29	3	1890-04-25	Jasper	A2
193	"	29	4	1890-04-25	Jasper	A2
194	"	29	7	1890-04-25	Jasper	A2
195	"	29	8	1890-04-25	Jasper	A2

ID	Individual in Patent	Sec.	Sec. Part	Date Issued	Other Counties	For More Info . . .
196	SAGE, Henry W (Cont'd)	30	1	1890-04-25	Jasper	A2
197	" "	30	2	1890-04-25	Jasper	A2
198	" "	30	5	1890-04-25	Jasper	A2
199	" "	30	6	1890-04-25	Jasper	A2
200	" "	30	7	1890-04-25	Jasper	A2
201	" "	30	8	1890-04-25	Jasper	A2
202	" "	30	N½4	1890-04-25	Jasper	A2
259	SAUNDERS, William	26	9	1854-03-15	Jasper	A2
205	ULMER, Jacob F	28	5	1888-02-25	Jasper	A3
206	" "	28	6	1888-02-25	Jasper	A3
204	" "	28	1	1889-04-23	Jasper	A2
248	VALENTINE, Susannah	31	N½NE	1897-08-09		A2
249	" "	32	W½NW	1897-08-09		A2
177	WELBORN, Aaron S	25	1	1859-11-10	Jasper	A2
213	WELBORN, James L	35	NENE	1859-05-02		A2
214	" "	36	NENW	1859-05-02		A2
217	" "	36	SWNW	1859-05-02		A2
215	" "	36	SENW	1859-11-10		A2
216	" "	36	SWNE	1859-11-10		A2
226	WELBORN, Jefferson G	35	N½SE	1860-07-02		A2
227	" "	35	SESW	1860-07-02		A2
228	" "	35	SWSE	1860-07-02		A2
236	WELBORN, Lazarus E	33	N½NW	1894-04-10		A3
239	WELBORN, Millard F	36	N½NE	1892-04-29		A3
245	WELBORN, Robert T	30	3	1904-10-17	Jasper	A3
250	WELBORN, Thomas N	29	6	1893-04-12	Jasper	A3
185	WELCH, Catherine	32	SWSE	1859-11-10		A2
186	WELCH, Cathorine	31	E½SE	1859-05-02		A2
187	" "	31	S½NE	1859-05-02		A2
188	" "	31	SESW	1859-05-02		A2
189	" "	31	SWSE	1859-05-02		A2
240	WELCH, Richard J	31	NENW	1859-05-02		A2
241	" "	31	W½NW	1859-05-02		A2
242	" "	31	W½SW	1859-05-02		A2
218	WILBORN, James L	36	NWNW	1859-05-02		A2
251	WILBORN, Thomas N	29	1	1861-05-01	Jasper	A2
223	WINDHAM, Jared C	27	N½5	1898-12-01	Jasper	A3

Patent Map

T10-N R12-W
St Stephens Meridian

Map Group 3

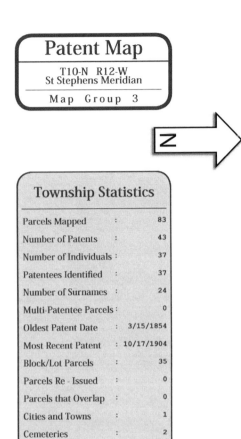

N

Township Statistics

Parcels Mapped	:	83
Number of Patents	:	43
Number of Individuals	:	37
Patentees Identified	:	37
Number of Surnames	:	24
Multi-Patentee Parcels	:	0
Oldest Patent Date	:	3/15/1854
Most Recent Patent	:	10/17/1904
Block/Lot Parcels	:	35
Parcels Re-Issued	:	0
Parcels that Overlap	:	0
Cities and Towns	:	1
Cemeteries	:	2

Note: the area contained in this map amounts to far less than a full Township. Therefore, its contents are completely on this single page (instead of a "normal" 2-page spread).

Legend

— Patent Boundary

▬ Section Boundary

▒ No Patents Found (or Outside County)

1., 2., 3., ... Lot Numbers (when beside a name)

[ ] Group Number (see Appendix "C")

Scale: Section = 1 mile X 1 mile (generally, with some exceptions)

Map (Patent Map, T10-N R12-W, Map Group 3)

Sections with No Patents Found (or Outside County): 19, 20, 21, 22, 23, 24

Lots-Sec. 30
1 SAGE, Henry W 1890
2 SAGE, Henry W 1890
3 WELBORN, Robert T 1904
5 SAGE, Henry W 1890
6 SAGE, Henry W 1890
7 SAGE, Henry W 1890
8 GUNTER, Allen 1860
8 SAGE, Henry W 1890
8 SAGE, Henry W 1890

Section 30 / 31 area
WELCH, Richard J 1859
MCNAT, William 1859
WELCH, Richard J 1859
MCNAT, William 1859
WELCH, Cathorine 1859
WELCH, Cathorine 1859
WELCH, William 1859
MCNAT, Cathorine 1859 (31)
VALENTINE, Susannah 1897
WELCH, Cathorine 1859

Lots-Sec. 29
1 WILBORN, Thomas N 1861
2 SAGE, Henry W 1890
3 SAGE, Henry W 1890
4 SAGE, Henry W 1890
6 WELBORN, Thomas N 1893
7 SAGE, Henry W 1890
8 SAGE, Henry W 1890

Section 32
VALENTINE, Susannah 1897
MATHEWS, John H 1897
MATHEWS, John H 1897 (32)
MATHEWS, Lazarus 1892
MATHEWS, Lazarus 1892
WELCH, Catherine 1859
MATTHEWS, James L 1888

Lots-Sec. 28
1 ULMER, Jacob F 1889
2 ULMER, Jacob F 1888
6 ULMER, Jacob F 1888
8 MOSS, Jefferson D 1895
9 MOSS, Jefferson D 1895

Section 33 / 28 area
WELBORN, Lazarus E 1894
MATTHEWS, William L 1894
BLACKWELL, Alonzo 1897 (33)
BLACKWELL, Alonzo 1897
HOPKINS, Robert J 1892
JOHNSON, William H 1893
JOHNSON, William H 1893
HOPKINS, Robert J 1892 / HOGAN, George H 1900
PRYOR, William L 1904

Lots-Sec. 27
1 HOLDER, James R 1859
3 HOLDER, James 1859
6 HOLDER, James 1859
9 WINDHAM, Jared C 1898
9 MURPHY, Irydell M 1895

Section 34
HOLDER, James 1859
HOLDER, James 1859
HOLDER, James 1859 (34)

Lots-Sec. 26
3 HOLDER, James R 1859
4 HOLDER, James R 1859
9 HOLDER, James R 1859
9 SAUNDERS, William 1854
10 MOSS, Benjamin F 1881

Section 35
WELBORN, Jefferson G 1860
WELBORN, Jefferson G 1860
WELBORN, Jefferson G 1860 (35)
GAVIN, Joseph 1892
WELBORN, James L 1859

Lots-Sec. 25
1 WELBORN, Aaron S 1859
6 GEIGER, Abram M 1859
7 GEIGER, Abram M 1859
8 GEIGER, Abram M 1859

Section 25 area
WELBORN, James L 1859
WELBORN, James L 1859
WELBORN, Millard F 1892
WELBORN, John 1890

Section 36
WELBORN, James L 1859
WELBORN, James L 1859 (36)
GAVIN, Joseph 1892
KAMPER, John 1890
GEIGER, Samuel 1888
GEIGER, Samuel 1888
KAMPER, John 1890

County labels: Jones / Jasper

Sections (numbered on map): 19, 20, 21, 22, 23, 24, 29, 28, 27, 26, 25, 30, 31, 32, 33, 34, 35, 36

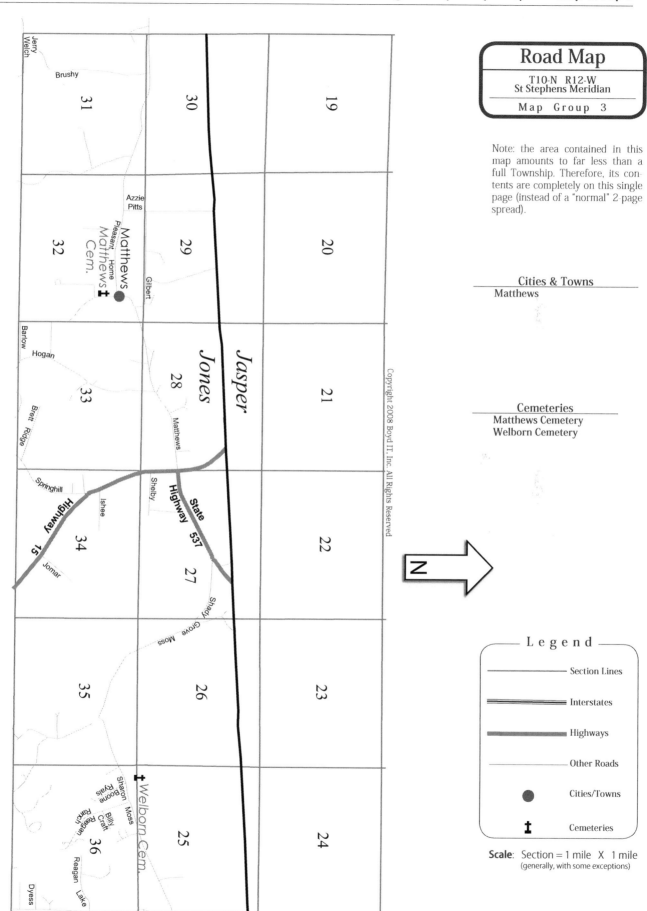

Road Map
T10-N R12-W
St Stephens Meridian

Map Group 3

Note: the area contained in this map amounts to far less than a full Township. Therefore, its contents are completely on this single page (instead of a "normal" 2-page spread).

Cities & Towns
Matthews

Cemeteries
Matthews Cemetery
Welborn Cemetery

Legend
——— Section Lines
═══ Interstates
▬▬▬ Highways
——— Other Roads
● Cities/Towns
✝ Cemeteries

Scale: Section = 1 mile X 1 mile
(generally, with some exceptions)

Historical Map

T10-N R12-W
St Stephens Meridian

Map Group 3

Note: the area contained in this map amounts to far less than a full Township. Therefore, its contents are completely on this single page (instead of a "normal" 2-page spread).

Cities & Towns
Matthews

Cemeteries
Matthews Cemetery
Welborn Cemetery

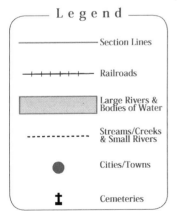

Legend

———————	Section Lines
+++++++	Railroads
▭	Large Rivers & Bodies of Water
- - - - -	Streams/Creeks & Small Rivers
●	Cities/Towns
♰	Cemeteries

Scale: Section = 1 mile X 1 mile
(there are some exceptions)

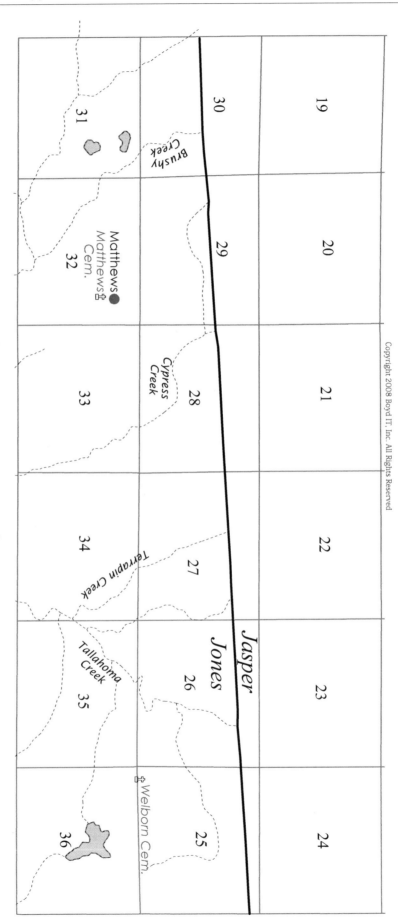

Map Group 4: Index to Land Patents

Township 10-North Range 11-West (St Stephens)

After you locate an individual in this Index, take note of the Section and Section Part then proceed to the Land Patent map on the pages immediately following. You should have no difficulty locating the corresponding parcel of land.

The "For More Info" Column will lead you to more information about the underlying Patents. See the *Legend* at right, and the "How to Use this Book" chapter, for more information.

```
                            LEGEND
                  "For More Info . . . " column

A = Authority (Legislative Act, See Appendix "A")
B = Block or Lot (location in Section unknown)
C = Cancelled Patent
F = Fractional Section
G = Group  (Multi-Patentee Patent, see Appendix "C")
V = Overlaps another Parcel
R = Re-Issued (Parcel patented more than once)

(A & G items require you to look in the Appendixes referred
to above. All other Letter-designations followed by a number
require you to locate line-items in this index that possess
the ID number found after the letter).
```

ID	Individual in Patent	Sec.	Sec. Part	Date Issued	Other Counties	For More Info . . .
388	ABNY, Theodore F	24	14	1873-09-20	Jasper	A3
389	" "	24	3	1873-09-20	Jasper	A3
280	ANDERSON, Daiton A	20	11	1892-06-15	Jasper	A3
281	" "	20	12	1892-06-15	Jasper	A3
282	" "	20	13	1892-06-15	Jasper	A3
283	" "	20	14	1892-06-15	Jasper	A3
302	ANDERSON, Eli S	33	NENW	1859-05-02		A2
308	ANDERSON, George H	36	W½SW	1859-05-02		A2
320	ANDERSON, Isaac	21	9	1859-05-02	Jasper	A2
321	" "	22	13	1859-11-10	Jasper	A2
322	" "	22	14	1859-11-10	Jasper	A2
323	" "	22	15	1859-11-10	Jasper	A2
325	ANDERSON, James A	22	2	1859-05-02	Jasper	A2
326	" "	27	N½NW	1859-05-02		A2
324	" "	22	1	1859-06-01	Jasper	A2
327	" "	28	NENE	1859-06-01		A2
386	ANDERSON, Stacy W	29	NE	1861-05-01	Jasper	A2
391	BONNER, Thomas F	24	15	1897-06-07	Jasper	A2
392	" "	24	4	1897-06-07	Jasper	A2
378	BOYCE, Robert P	34	SESW	1859-11-10		A2
379	" "	34	SWSE	1859-11-10		A2
390	BRYANT, Thomas C	34	SESE	1953-07-27		A2
369	BUCKOLEW, Oneismus	21	11	1892-08-08	Jasper	A3
370	" "	21	12	1892-08-08	Jasper	A3
371	" "	21	13	1892-08-08	Jasper	A3
387	BYRD, Sylvester B	25	E½NE	1895-02-21		A3
312	CARLISLE, Henry J	20	3	1899-05-12	Jasper	A2
313	" "	20	4	1899-05-12	Jasper	A2
363	COOPER, Moses D	24	2	1859-05-02	Jasper	A2
364	" "	25	W½NE	1859-06-01		A2
365	COOPER, Nathan	33	E½NE	1861-05-01		A2
366	" "	34	NWNW	1861-05-01		A2
374	COOPER, Robert	34	N½SW	1859-05-02		A2
375	" "	34	SENW	1859-05-02		A2
376	" "	34	SWNW	1859-05-02		A2
377	" "	34	SWSW	1859-05-02		A2
269	COTTON, Andrew B	24	8	1888-04-05	Jasper	A3
383	DAVIS, Sidney A	36	SENW	1861-05-01		A2
384	" "	36	SWNE	1861-05-01		A2
385	" "	36	W½SE	1861-05-01		A2
267	DONALD, Alexander	20	5	1860-05-02	Jasper	A2
268	" "	20	6	1860-05-02	Jasper	A2
303	DONALD, Eli S	30	S½6	1890-08-16	Jasper	A3
304	" "	31	E½NW	1890-08-16		A3
305	" "	31	SWNW	1890-08-16		A3
336	DONALD, John	28	E½NW	1859-05-02		A2

ID	Individual in Patent	Sec.	Sec. Part	Date Issued	Other Counties	For More Info . . .
352	HARDY, Lawrence H	20	1	1895-10-09	Jasper	A3
328	HARGROVE, James A	24	1	1848-09-01	Jasper	A2 F
397	HERRINGTON, William	25	SWSE	1859-05-02		A2
400	"	36	NWNE	1859-05-02		A2
398	"	36	E½NE	1859-11-10		A2
399	"	36	NESE	1859-11-10		A2
396	HERRINGTON, William C	25	E½SE	1859-05-02		A2
331	HOLLIFIELD, James	32	S½NE	1861-05-01		A2
332	HOLYFIELD, James	32	E½SE	1859-11-10		A2
333	"	32	NWSE	1859-11-10		A2
265	HOSSEY, Abner	21	1	1841-01-05	Jasper	A2 F
266	"	21	8	1841-01-05	Jasper	A2 F
372	HOWARD, Prince E	25	N½SW	1859-05-02		A2
314	HUTTO, Henry L	29		1911-06-26	Jasper	A2 F
315	"	30		1911-06-26	Jasper	A2 F
337	KAMPER, John	29	3	1890-07-03	Jasper	A2
338	"	29	7	1890-07-03	Jasper	A2
339	"	29	N½4	1890-07-03	Jasper	A2
340	"	29	S½5	1890-07-03	Jasper	A2
341	"	30	N½3	1890-07-03	Jasper	A2
342	"	31	NWNE	1890-07-03		A2
343	"	31	W½SW	1890-07-03		A2
344	"	32	SWSE	1890-07-03		A2
335	LINDSEY, James M	36	NENW	1884-12-30		A2
274	LONG, Benjamin A	30	1	1892-08-08	Jasper	A3
275	"	30	2	1892-08-08	Jasper	A3
334	LONG, James	29	8	1881-09-17	Jasper	A3
286	LOWE, Daniel W	31	E½SE	1884-12-30		A3
287	"	31	S½NE	1884-12-30		A3
407	MASON, Zebedee	27	E½SW	1881-09-17		A3
408	"	27	SENW	1881-09-17		A3
260	MCCALLUM, Aaron	24	11	1889-12-19	Jasper	A3
261	"	24	12	1889-12-19	Jasper	A3
262	"	24	5	1889-12-19	Jasper	A3
263	"	24	6	1889-12-19	Jasper	A3
401	MCCALLUM, William	24	13	1895-11-11	Jasper	A3
350	MCMILLAN, King G	34	NWSE	1901-03-23		A3
351	"	34	W½NE	1901-03-23		A3
301	MCVEY, Eli	32	N½NE	1862-04-10		A2
290	MILEY, David	30	3	-12:00:00 AM	Jasper	A3
291	"	30	N½6	-12:00:00 AM	Jasper	A3
288	MILEY, David M	31	E½SW	1891-05-20		A3
289	"	31	W½SE	1891-05-20		A3
270	MORSE, Andrew J	21	10	1861-05-01	Jasper	A2
271	"	21	14	1861-05-01	Jasper	A2
272	"	21	2	1861-05-01	Jasper	A2
273	"	21	7	1861-05-01	Jasper	A2
381	MOSS, Samuel	27	NWSE	1859-05-02		A2
382	"	27	W½NE	1859-05-02		A2
309	MUSGROVE, George	33	NWSE	1890-06-25		A3
310	"	33	SENW	1890-06-25		A3
311	"	33	W½NE	1890-06-25		A3
345	MUSGROVE, John R	32	E½NW	1862-04-10		A2
346	"	32	NWSW	1862-04-10		A2
347	"	32	SWNW	1862-04-10		A2
406	MUSGROVE, Willis S	30	8	1862-04-10	Jasper	A2
316	MYRICK, Henry	25	SESW	1859-05-02		A2
317	"	25	SWSW	1859-05-02		A2
318	"	36	NWNW	1859-05-02		A2
319	"	36	SWNW	1859-06-01		A2
360	MYRICK, Miley	25	N½NW	1859-06-01		A2
402	MYRICK, William	25	S½NW	1861-05-01		A2
393	NELSON, Washington	27	NESE	1859-06-01		A2
395	"	27	SWSE	1859-06-01		A2
394	"	27	SESE	1899-01-30		A2
329	NESOM, James F	27	SWSW	1886-02-10		A2
330	"	28	SE	1890-02-21		A3
373	NETTLES, Rebecca A	36	E½SW	1884-12-30		A3
298	NIX, Edward	29	N½SW	1859-05-02	Jasper	A2
299	"	29	SESW	1859-05-02	Jasper	A2
300	"	29	SWNW	1859-05-02	Jasper	A2
278	OBER, Charles A	33	SWSE	1859-05-02		A2
367	PATTERSON, Niell	22	7	1841-01-05	Jasper	A2 F

ID	Individual in Patent	Sec.	Sec. Part	Date Issued	Other Counties	For More Info . . .
368	PATTERSON, Niell (Cont'd)	22	8	1841-01-05	Jasper	A2 F
353	RIVERS, Mark	32	SESW	1859-11-10		A2
354	RIVERS, Mark S	32	SWSW	1854-03-15		A2
403	ROSE, William	23	10	1860-07-02	Jasper	A2
404	" "	23	3	1860-07-02	Jasper	A2
380	SHOEMAKE, Sampson	20	15	1901-08-12	Jasper	A3
358	SIMS, Miles	28	SENE	1886-07-20		A2
359	" "	28	W½NE	1886-07-20		A2
405	SIMS, William	33	E½SW	1897-08-09		A2
276	SMITH, Benjamin F	28	E½SW	1895-02-21		A3
277	SMITH, Berry	34	NENW	1859-05-02		A2
284	SMITH, Daniel C	35	SESE	1854-03-15		A2
285	" "	35	SWSE	1859-05-02		A2
296	SUMRALL, Drury	22	3	1859-05-02	Jasper	A2
297	" "	22	4	1859-05-02	Jasper	A2
307	THORNTON, George A	25	NWSE	1884-12-30		A2
292	ULMER, Demarius	21	3	1890-06-25	Jasper	A3
293	" "	21	4	1890-06-25	Jasper	A3
294	" "	21	5	1890-06-25	Jasper	A3
295	" "	21	6	1890-06-25	Jasper	A3
279	WARD, Charles L	20	17	1964-08-19	Jasper	A1
264	WELBORN, Aaron S	30	4	1859-11-10	Jasper	A2
306	WELBORN, Elisha Y	21		1902-01-25		A2
361	WELBORN, Millard F	30	S½5	1892-04-29	Jasper	A3
362	" "	31	NWNW	1892-04-29		A3
348	WELLS, Joseph M	27	NWSW	1859-05-02		A2
349	" "	27	SWNW	1859-05-02		A2
355	WHITTLE, Michael C	24	10	1861-05-01	Jasper	A2
356	" "	24	7	1861-05-01	Jasper	A2
357	" "	24	9	1861-05-01	Jasper	A2

Patent Map

T10-N R11-W
St Stephens Meridian

Map Group 4

Township Statistics

Parcels Mapped	:	149
Number of Patents	:	86
Number of Individuals	:	74
Patentees Identified	:	74
Number of Surnames	:	51
Multi-Patentee Parcels	:	0
Oldest Patent Date	:	1/5/1841
Most Recent Patent	:	8/19/1964
Block/Lot Parcels	:	65
Parcels Re - Issued	:	0
Parcels that Overlap	:	0
Cities and Towns	:	2
Cemeteries	:	2

Note: the area contained in this map amounts to far less than a full Township. Therefore, its contents are completely on this single page (instead of a "normal" 2-page spread).

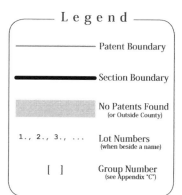

Legend

— Patent Boundary

━ Section Boundary

▨ No Patents Found (or Outside County)

1., 2., 3., ... Lot Numbers (when beside a name)

[ ] Group Number (see Appendix "C")

Scale: Section = 1 mile X 1 mile (generally, with some exceptions)

N

Section 19

19

Section 30 (Lots-Sec. 30)

1 LONG, Benjamin A 1892
2 LONG, Benjamin A 1892
3 MILEY, David -12.
4 WELBORN, David 1892
8 DONALD, Aaron S 1859
8 WELBORN, Ellis 1890
8 WELBORN, Millard F 1892
8 MILEY, David -12.
8 KAMPER, John 1890
8 MUSGROVE, Willis S 1862

WELBORN, Millard F 1892

DONALD, Elli S 1890

31

KAMPER, John 1890

MILEY, David M 1891

MILEY, David M 1891

DONALD, Elli S 1890

KAMPER, John 1890

LOWE, Daniel W 1884

LOWE, Daniel W 1884

KAMPER, John 1890

Section 20 (Lots-Sec. 20)

1 HARDY, Lawrence H 1895
3 CARLISLE, Henry J 1899
4 CARLISLE, Henry J 1899
5 DONALD, Alexander 1860
6 DONALD, Alexander 1860
11 ANDERSON, Dalton A 1892
12 ANDERSON, Dalton A 1892
13 ANDERSON, Dalton A 1892
14 ANDERSON, Dalton A 1892
15 SHOEMAKE, Sampson 1901
17 WARD, Charles L 1964

Section 32

RIVERS, Mark S 1854

MUSGROVE, John R 1862

MUSGROVE, John R 1862

RIVERS, Mark 1859

32

MUSGROVE, John R 1862

KAMPER, John 1890

HUTTO, Henry L 1911

NIX, Edward 1859

NIX, Edward 1859

NIX, Edward 1859

Section 29 (Lots-Sec. 29)

3 KAMPER, John 1890
7 KAMPER, John 1890
8 KAMPER, John 1890
8 KAMPER, John 1890
8 LONG, James 1881

HUTTO, Henry L 1911

ANDERSON, Stacy W 1861

20

Section 30

30

HUTTO, Henry L 1911

29

Section 21 (Lots-Sec. 21)

1 HOSSEY, Abner 1861
2 MORSE, Andrew J 1890
3 ULMER, Demarius 1890
4 ULMER, Demarius 1890
5 ULMER, Demarius 1890
6 ULMER, Demarius 1890
7 MORSE, Andrew J 1890
8 HOSSEY, Abner 1841
9 ANDERSON, Isaac 1859
10 MORSE, Andrew J 1861
11 BUCKOLEW, Oneismus 1892
12 BUCKOLEW, Oneismus 1892
13 BUCKOLEW, Oneismus 1892
14 MORSE, Andrew J 1861

Section 33

MOVEY, Eli 1862

HOLYFIELD, James 1861

HOLLIFIELD, James 1861

HOLYFIELD, James 1859

SIMS, William 1897

MUSGROVE, George 1890

MUSGROVE, George 1890

ANDERSON, Elli S 1859

33

MUSGROVE, George 1890

OBER, Charles A 1859

SMITH, Benjamin F 1895

MUSGROVE, George 1890

NESOM, James F 1890

DONALD, John 1859

SIMS, Miles 1886

SIMS, Miles 1886

COOPER, Nathan 1861

28

Section 22 (Lots-Sec. 22)

1 ANDERSON, James A 1859
2 ANDERSON, James A 1859
3 SUMRALL, Drury 1859
4 SUMRALL, Drury 1859
5 PATTERSON, Niell 1841
6 PATTERSON, Niell 1841
7 PATTERSON, Niell 1841
13 ANDERSON, Isaac 1859
14 ANDERSON, Isaac 1859
15 ANDERSON, Isaac 1859

WELBORN, Elisha Y 1902

ANDERSON, James A 1859

21

22

Section 34

COOPER, Robert 1859

COOPER, Robert 1859

COOPER, Robert 1859

COOPER, Nathan Berry 1861

WELLS, Joseph M 1859

WELLS, Joseph M 1859

COOPER, Nathan Berry 1861

34

COOPER, Robert 1859

COOPER, Robert King G 1901

NESOM, James F 1886

NESOM, Joseph M 1859

SMITH, Berry 1859

MASON, Zebedee 1881

ANDERSON, James A 1859

27

MASON, Zebedee 1881

MOSS, Samuel 1859

MOSS, Samuel 1859

BOYCE, Robert P 1859

BOYCE, Robert P 1859

BOYCE BRYANT, Robert P Thomas C 1859 1953

MCMILLAN, King G 1901

MCMILLAN, King G 1901

NELSON, Washington 1859

NELSON, Washington 1859

NELSON, Washington 1899

Section 23 (Lots-Sec. 23)

3 ROSE, William 1860
10 ROSE, William 1860

23

Section 35

35

SMITH, Daniel C 1859

SMITH, Daniel C 1854

Section 26

26

Jones / Jasper

Jones

Jasper

Section 36

ANDERSON, George H 1859

MYRICK, Henry 1859

MYRICK, Henry 1859

DAVIS, Sidney A 1861

DAVIS, Sidney A 1861

36

NETTLES, Rebecca A 1884

DAVIS, Sidney A 1861

Section 25

MYRICK, Henry 1859

LINDSEY, James M 1859

HERRINGTON, William 1859

MYRICK, Henry 1859

MYRICK, William 1861

MYRICK, Henry 1859

MYRICK, Henry HERRINGTON 1859 William 1859

HOWARD, Prince E 1861

THORNTON, George A 1884

HERRINGTON, William C 1859

25

COOPER, Moses D 1897

BYRD, Sylvester B 1895

HERRINGTON, William C 1859

Section 24 (Lots-Sec. 24)

1 HARGROVE, James A 1848
2 COOPER, Moses D 1859
3 ABNY, Theodore F 1873
4 BONNER, Thomas F 1897
5 MCCALLUM, Aaron 1889
6 MCCALLUM, Aaron 1889
7 COTTON, Andrew B 1888
8 WHITTLE, Michael C 1861
9 WHITTLE, Michael C 1861
10 MCGHLOW, Michael C 1861
12 MCCALLUM, Aaron 1889
13 MCCALLUM, William 1895
14 ABNY, Theodore F 1873
15 BONNER, Thomas F 1897

MYRICK, Miley 1859

COOPER, Moses D 1897

24

Road Map

T10-N R11-W
St Stephens Meridian

Map Group 4

Note: the area contained in this map amounts to far less than a full Township. Therefore, its contents are completely on this single page (instead of a "normal" 2-page spread).

Cities & Towns

Bonner
Sharon

Cemeteries

Old Sharon Cemetery
Sharon Cemetery

Legend

Section Lines	
Interstates	
Highways	
Other Roads	
●	Cities/Towns
✝	Cemeteries

Scale: Section = 1 mile X 1 mile
(generally, with some exceptions)

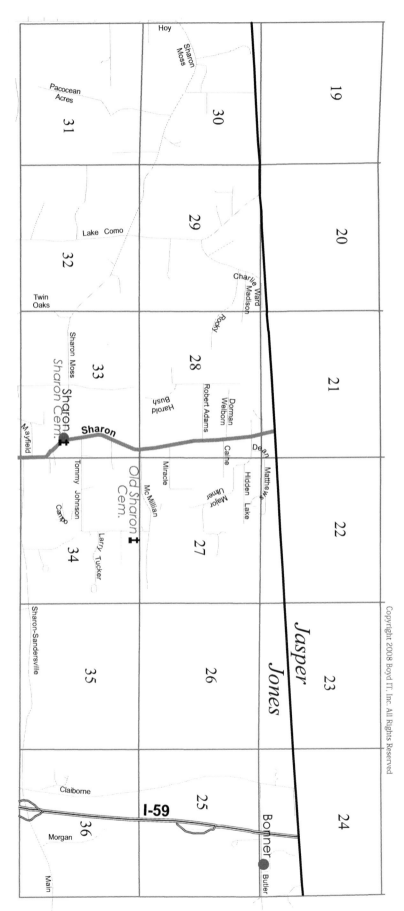

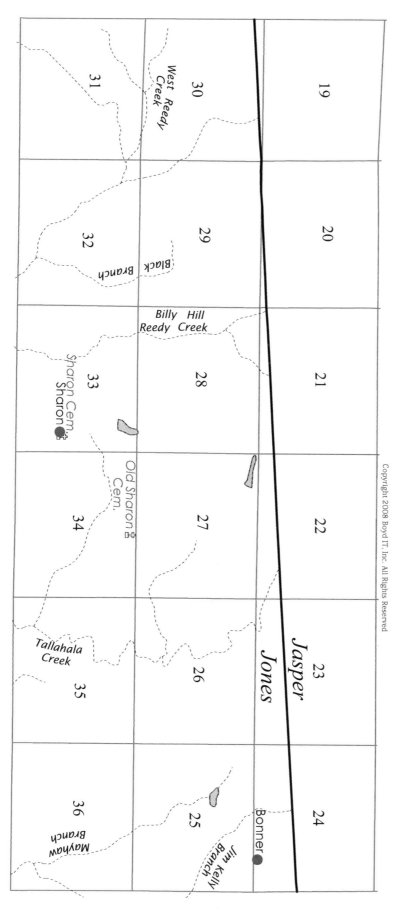

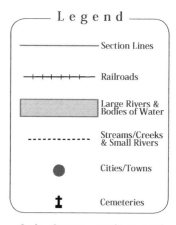

Historical Map

T10-N R11-W
St Stephens Meridian

Map Group 4

Note: the area contained in this map amounts to far less than a full Township. Therefore, its contents are completely on this single page (instead of a "normal" 2-page spread).

Cities & Towns
Bonner
Sharon

Cemeteries
Old Sharon Cemetery
Sharon Cemetery

Legend

——————— Section Lines

+—+—+—+—+ Railroads

▭ Large Rivers & Bodies of Water

- - - - - - Streams/Creeks & Small Rivers

● Cities/Towns

✝ Cemeteries

Scale: Section = 1 mile X 1 mile
(there are some exceptions)

Map Group 5: Index to Land Patents

Township 10-North Range 10-West (St Stephens)

After you locate an individual in this Index, take note of the Section and Section Part then proceed to the Land Patent map on the pages immediately following. You should have no difficulty locating the corresponding parcel of land.

The "For More Info" Column will lead you to more information about the underlying Patents. See the *Legend* at right, and the "How to Use this Book" chapter, for more information.

```
LEGEND
"For More Info . . . " column

A = Authority (Legislative Act, See Appendix "A")
B = Block or Lot (location in Section unknown)
C = Cancelled Patent
F = Fractional Section
G = Group  (Multi-Patentee Patent, see Appendix "C")
V = Overlaps another Parcel
R = Re-Issued (Parcel patented more than once)

(A & G items require you to look in the Appendixes referred
to above. All other Letter-designations followed by a number
require you to locate line-items in this index that possess
the ID number found after the letter).
```

ID	Individual in Patent	Sec.	Sec. Part	Date Issued	Other Counties	For More Info . . .
419	ARRINGTON, Cicero	22	8	1893-04-12	Jasper	A3
480	BARKLEY, John L	27	SWSE	1895-08-30		A3
481	" "	34	N½NE	1895-08-30		A3
447	BARNES, Jacob	30	NESE	1897-08-09		A2
448	" "	30	S½NE	1897-08-09		A2
543	BARNES, Thomas J	19	11	1861-02-01	Jasper	A2
545	" "	19	14	1861-02-01	Jasper	A2
542	" "	19	1	1861-07-01	Jasper	A2
544	" "	19	13	1927-07-22	Jasper	A2
560	BLACKLIDGE, Zachariah	24	6	1896-05-29	Jasper	A2
489	BONNER, John T	30	NWSE	1921-10-15		A3
452	BOYLES, James H	34	NW	1861-02-01		A2
449	" "	20	10	1881-08-20	Jasper	A3
450	" "	20	8	1881-08-20	Jasper	A3
451	" "	20	9	1881-08-20	Jasper	A3
446	BUCHANAN, Hugh	22	10	1859-05-02	Jasper	A2
467	BUCHANAN, John A	22	9	1859-05-02	Jasper	A2
493	BYRD, Joseph	19	12	1860-04-02	Jasper	A2
491	BYRD, Joseph B	19	5	1891-06-30	Jasper	A3
492	" "	19	6	1891-06-30	Jasper	A3
507	BYRD, Obadiah	19	7	1859-11-10	Jasper	A2
508	BYRD, Obediah	19	10	1860-04-02	Jasper	A2
509	" "	19	9	1860-04-02	Jasper	A2
548	BYRD, William	31	NWSW	1859-05-02		A2
427	CARAWAY, Ellis	27	NWSE	1861-02-01		A2
428	" "	27	SWNE	1861-02-01		A2
441	CRABTREE, Haynes	31	E½NE	1859-05-02		A2
442	" "	32	NENW	1859-05-02		A2
444	" "	32	W½NW	1859-05-02		A2
440	" "	30	S½SE	1861-07-01		A2
443	" "	32	SENW	1861-07-01		A2 R540
526	DAVIS, Robert H	31	E½SE	1860-04-10		A2
527	" "	32	W½SW	1860-04-10		A2
549	DAVIS, William E	27	S½SW	1890-06-25		A3
494	DEAVENPORT, Calvin A	26	NENE	1911-08-24		A3 G9
494	DEAVENPORT, Laura L	26	NENE	1911-08-24		A3 G9
410	FERGUSON, Angus G	33	SESE	1890-02-21		A3
473	FERGUSON, John	33	SWSW	1854-03-15		A2
472	" "	33	SWSE	1884-08-20		A2
528	GASKIN, Samuel P	23	7	1885-05-25	Jasper	A3
529	" "	23	8	1885-05-25	Jasper	A3
431	GATLIN, Francis M	26	NESW	1859-05-02		A2
432	" "	26	NW	1859-05-02		A2
429	" "	23	S½4	1892-05-26	Jasper	A3
430	" "	23	S½5	1892-05-26	Jasper	A3
433	" "	26	W½NE	1892-05-26		A3

ID	Individual in Patent	Sec.	Sec. Part	Date Issued	Other Counties	For More Info . . .
495	GATLIN, Mitchel	26	SWSE	1860-04-02		A2
498	GATLIN, Mitchell	26	W½SW	1859-05-02		A2
500	" "	27	SESE	1859-05-02		A2
496	" "	26	N½SE	1860-04-02		A2
497	" "	26	SENE	1860-04-02		A2
499	" "	27	NESE	1860-04-02		A2
530	GATLIN, Sarah J	36	E½NE	1899-06-28		A3
531	" "	36	E½SE	1899-06-28		A3
424	HALES, Elias	23	2	1892-05-26	Jasper	A3 R522
425	" "	23	N½4	1892-05-26	Jasper	A3
426	" "	23	N½5	1892-05-26	Jasper	A3
453	HANSON, James	24	2	1860-10-01	Jasper	A2
454	" "	24	3	1860-10-01	Jasper	A2
455	" "	24	4	1860-10-01	Jasper	A2
456	" "	24	5	1860-10-01	Jasper	A2
457	" "	25	N½NW	1860-10-01		A2
483	HERRINGTON, John M	31	NENW	1859-06-01		A2
485	" "	31	NWNE	1859-06-01		A2
482	" "	30	SESW	1860-07-02		A2
484	" "	31	NESW	1860-07-02		A2
486	" "	31	S½NW	1860-07-02		A2
487	" "	31	SWNE	1860-07-02		A2
488	" "	31	SWSW	1860-07-02		A2
474	HODGES, John	25	SWNW	1859-05-02		A2
475	" "	25	W½SW	1859-05-02		A2
476	" "	27	SENW	1859-05-02		A2
477	" "	36	NENW	1859-05-02		A2
409	HOWARD, Alfred J	22	N½5	1892-03-23	Jasper	A3
541	HOWARD, Thomas Alford	22	1	1914-08-27	Jasper	A3
520	JONES, Polly	19	8	1906-06-16	Jasper	A3
546	LINDER, Thomas W	19	4	1846-09-01	Jasper	A2 F
417	MCDONALD, Benjamin F	34	SWSW	1898-02-24		A3
420	MCDONALD, Daniel	22	11	1860-10-01	Jasper	A2
422	" "	22	N½	1860-10-01	Jasper	A2
421	" "	22	12	1861-02-01	Jasper	A2
434	MCDONALD, Francis M	33	E½NE	1859-06-01		A2
436	" "	33	NWSE	1859-06-01		A2
437	" "	33	SWNE	1859-06-01		A2
435	" "	33	NESE	1861-05-01		A2
445	MCDONALD, Hugh A	22	N½4	1859-06-01	Jasper	A2
468	MCDONALD, John A	21	1	1859-05-02	Jasper	A2
469	" "	21	2	1859-05-02	Jasper	A2
470	" "	21	7	1859-05-02	Jasper	A2
471	" "	21	8	1859-05-02	Jasper	A2
411	MCGILL, Archibald	20	7	1841-01-05	Jasper	A2 F
413	" "	21	3	1841-01-05	Jasper	A2 F R414
416	" "	21	6	1841-01-05	Jasper	A2 F
412	" "	20	N½1	1859-05-02	Jasper	A2
414	" "	21	3	1859-05-02	Jasper	A2 R413
415	" "	21	4	1859-05-02	Jasper	A2
458	MCGILL, James	20	12	1859-11-10	Jasper	A2
459	" "	20	5	1859-11-10	Jasper	A2
461	" "	28	NWNW	1860-10-01		A2
460	" "	21	5	1900-02-14	Jasper	A2
501	MCGILL, Neil	29	E½NE	1860-07-02		A2
502	" "	29	NWSE	1860-07-02		A2
503	" "	29	SESW	1860-07-02		A2
504	" "	29	SWNE	1860-07-02		A2
505	" "	32	NWNE	1860-07-02		A2
506	MCGILL, Neill	29	SWSE	1859-05-02		A2
521	MILLSAP, Richard	23	1	1893-09-08	Jasper	A3
522	" "	23	2	1893-09-08	Jasper	A3 R424
523	" "	23	6	1893-09-08	Jasper	A3
550	OWEN, William L	34	E½SW	1860-04-02		A2
551	" "	34	NWSE	1860-04-02		A2
552	" "	34	NWSW	1860-04-02		A2
553	" "	34	SENE	1860-04-02		A2
554	" "	34	SWNE	1860-04-02		A2
510	PLOCK, Otto	20	11	1882-04-20	Jasper	A2
511	" "	20	2	1882-04-20	Jasper	A2
512	" "	20	3	1882-04-20	Jasper	A2
513	" "	20	4	1882-04-20	Jasper	A2
514	" "	20	6	1882-04-20	Jasper	A2

ID	Individual in Patent	Sec.	Sec. Part	Date Issued	Other Counties	For More Info . . .
515	PLOCK, Otto (Cont'd)	20	S½1	1882-04-20	Jasper	A2
516	" "	29	NESW	1882-04-20		A2
517	" "	29	NW	1882-04-20		A2
518	" "	29	NWNE	1882-04-20		A2
519	" "	29	W½SW	1882-04-20		A2
418	PURVIS, Benjamin F	36	NWNE	1901-03-23		A3
465	RODGERS, Jefferson	22	SESW	1859-05-02	Jasper	A2
466	" "	22	SWSE	1859-05-02	Jasper	A2
532	ROGERS, Silas J	27	NENW	1860-07-02		A2
533	" "	27	NWNE	1860-07-02		A2
555	ROGERS, William P	27	E½NE	1889-01-05		A3
556	ROSE, William	19	3	1859-11-10	Jasper	A2
524	SAUNDERS, Robert B	31	SESW	1860-04-02		A2
525	" "	31	W½SE	1860-04-02		A2
547	SCRUGGS, Washington J	30	NENE	1892-08-01		A2
490	SHERLY, John W	35	SESE	1884-12-30		A2
537	STEWART, Thomas A	30	SESE	1860-07-02		A2 C
538	" "	30	SWNE	1860-07-02		A2 C
539	" "	30	W½SE	1860-07-02		A2 C
540	" "	32	SENW	1860-07-02		A2 C R443
557	TAYLOR, William	22	7	1890-02-21	Jasper	A3
558	" "	23	10	1890-02-21	Jasper	A3
559	" "	23	9	1890-02-21	Jasper	A3
423	THACH, David	24	7	1859-06-01	Jasper	A2
534	THATCH, Simeon D	24	10	1897-09-09	Jasper	A3
535	" "	24	8	1897-09-09	Jasper	A3
536	" "	24	9	1897-09-09	Jasper	A3
462	UNDERWOOD, James	36	N½SW	1884-12-30		A3
463	" "	36	SENW	1884-12-30		A3
464	" "	36	SWNE	1884-12-30		A3
478	UNDERWOOD, John J	36	S½SW	1884-12-30		A3
479	" "	36	W½SE	1884-12-30		A3
438	WHITE, Greenberry	30	NENW	1859-11-10		A2
439	" "	30	W½NW	1859-11-10		A2

Patent Map

T10-N R10-W
St Stephens Meridian

Map Group 5

Township Statistics

Parcels Mapped	:	152
Number of Patents	:	78
Number of Individuals	:	62
Patentees Identified	:	61
Number of Surnames	:	40
Multi-Patentee Parcels	:	1
Oldest Patent Date	:	1/5/1841
Most Recent Patent	:	7/22/1927
Block/Lot Parcels	:	65
Parcels Re - Issued	:	3
Parcels that Overlap	:	0
Cities and Towns	:	2
Cemeteries	:	5

Note: the area contained in this map amounts to far less than a full Township. Therefore, its contents are completely on this single page (instead of a "normal" 2-page spread).

Legend

— Patent Boundary

— Section Boundary

No Patents Found (or Outside County)

1., 2., 3., ... Lot Numbers (when beside a name)

[ ] Group Number (see Appendix "C")

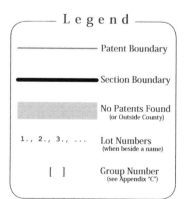

Scale: Section = 1 mile X 1 mile (generally, with some exceptions)

Section 19

Lots-Sec. 19
1. BARNES, Thomas J 1861
3. ROSE, William 1859
4. LINDER, Thomas W 1846
5. BYRD, Joseph B 1891
6. BYRD, Joseph B 1891
7. BYRD, Obadiah 1859
8. JONES, Polly 1906
9. BYRD, Obadiah 1860

WHITE, Greenberry 1859

10. BYRD, Obadiah 1860
11. BARNES, Thomas A 1861
12. BYRD, Joseph B 1860
13. BARNES, Thomas J 1927
14. BARNES, Thomas J 1861

Section 30

HERRINGTON John M 1859
HERRINGTON John M 1859
BYRD William 1860
SAUNDERS Robert B 1860

HERRINGTON Thomas A 1860
STEWART Thomas A 1860
WHITE Greenberry 1859
SCRUGGS Washington J 1892

BONNER John T 1921
BARNES Jacob 1897
STEWART Thomas A 1860
BARNES Jacob 1897
CRABTREE Haynes 1861
STEWART Thomas A 1860

Section 31

HERRINGTON John M 1860
HERRINGTON John M 1859
HERRINGTON John M
SAUNDERS Robert B 1860
DAVIS Robert H 1860

Section 20

Lots-Sec. 20
1. PLOCK Otto 1882
2. PLOCK Otto 1882
3. PLOCK Otto 1882
4. MCGILL James 1859
5. PLOCK Otto 1882
6. PLOCK Otto 1882
7. MCGILL Archibald 1841
8. BOYLES James H 1881

9. PLOCK Otto 1882
9. MCGILL, Archibald 1859
9. BOYLES, Archibald 1859
9. BOYLES, James H 1881
11. PLOCK Otto 1882
12. MCGILL, James 1859

PLOCK Otto 1882

Section 29

PLOCK Otto 1882
MCGILL Neill 1860
MCGILL Neil 1859

Section 32

DAVIS Robert H 1860
CRABTREE Haynes 1859
CRABTREE Thomas A 1860
CRABTREE Haynes 1861
MCGILL Neil 1860

PLOCK Otto 1882
MCGILL Neil 1860

Section 21

Lots-Sec. 21
1. MCDONALD, John A 1859
2. MCDONALD, John A 1859
3. MCGILL, Archibald 1841
4. MCGILL, Archibald 1859
5. MCGILL, James 1900
6. MCGILL, Archibald 1841
7. MCDONALD, John A 1859
8. MCDONALD, John A 1859

MCGILL James 1860

Section 33

FERGUSON John 1854
FERGUSON John 1884
FERGUSON Angus G 1890

MCDONALD Francis M 1859
MCDONALD Francis M 1859
MCDONALD Francis M 1869

Section 28

Section 22

Lots-Sec. 22
1. MCDONALD Daniel 1860
2. HALES, Elias 1892
3. HOWARD, Thomas A 1914
7. TAYLOR, William 1890
8. ARRINGTON, Cicero 1893

8. MCDONALD Hugh A 1859
9. BUCHANAN, John A 1859
9. HOWARD, Alfred J 1892
10. HOWARD, Hugh 1859
10. MCDONALD, Daniel 1860
11. BUCHANAN, Hugh 1859
12. MCDONALD, Daniel 1860
RODGERS, Daniel 1861
Jefferson 1859

RODGERS Jefferson 1859

ROGERS Silas J 1859
ROGERS Silas J 1860
ROGERS William P 1889

Section 34

MCDONALD Benjamin F 1898
OWEN William L 1860
OWEN William L 1860
OWEN William L 1860

BOYLES James H 1861
DAVIS William E 1890
OWEN William L 1860
OWEN William L 1860

Section 27

HODGES John 1859
CARAWAY Ellis 1861
CARAWAY Ellis 1861

BARKLEY John L 1895
GATLIN Mitchell 1860
BARKLEY John L 1895

Section 23

Lots-Sec. 23
1. MILLSAP, Richard 1893
2. HALES, Elias 1892
3. MILLSAP, Richard 1893
4. MILLSAP, Richard 1893

2. GASKIN, Samuel P 1885
3. GASKIN, Samuel P 1885
4. GATLIN, Francis M 1892
5. GATLIN, Francis M 1892
6. HALES, Elias 1892
7. HALES, Elias 1892
8. TAYLOR, William 1890
9. TAYLOR, William 1890
10. TAYLOR, William 1890

Section 26

GATLIN Mitchell 1859
GATLIN Francis M 1859
GATLIN Francis M 1859
GATLIN Francis M 1892
GATLIN Mitchell 1860
GATLIN Mitchell 1860

DEAVENPORT [9] Laura L 1911

Section 35

GATLIN Mitchell 1859

Section 25

HODGES John 1859
HODGES John 1859
HODGES John 1859

UNDERWOOD James 1884

Section 24

Lots-Sec. 24
2. HANSON, James 1860
3. HANSON, James 1860
4. HANSON, James 1860
5. BLACKLIDGE, Zachariah 1896
6. THACH, David 1859
7. THACH, Zachariah 1896
8. THATCH, Simeon D 1897
9. THATCH, Simeon D 1897
10. THATCH, Simeon D 1897

HANSON James 1860

PURVIS Benjamin F 1901
GATLIN Sarah J 1899

Section 36

SHERLY John W 1884
UNDERWOOD John J 1884
UNDERWOOD James 1884
UNDERWOOD John J 1884
UNDERWOOD James 1884
UNDERWOOD James 1884
GATLIN Sarah J 1899

Jasper
Jones

Road Map

T10-N R10-W
St Stephens Meridian

Map Group 5

Note: the area contained in this map amounts to far less than a full Township. Therefore, its contents are completely on this single page (instead of a "normal" 2-page spread).

Cities & Towns

Haney
Sandersville

Cemeteries

Bethel Cemetery
Choctaw Cemetery
Florence Cemetery
McGill Cemetery
Sandersville Cemetery

Legend

———————	Section Lines
═══════════	Interstates
━━━━━━━	Highways
───────────	Other Roads
●	Cities/Towns
✝	Cemeteries

Scale: Section = 1 mile X 1 mile
(generally, with some exceptions)

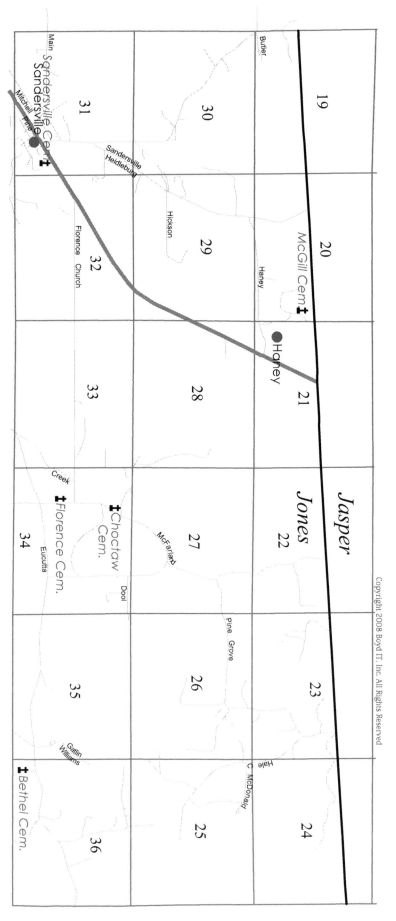

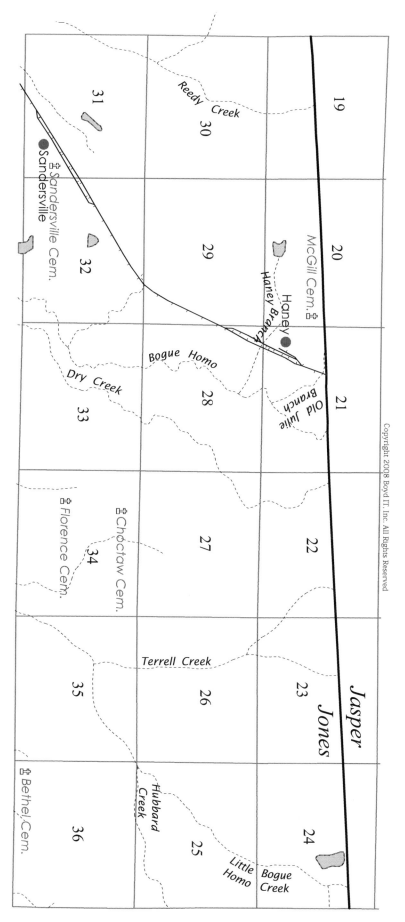

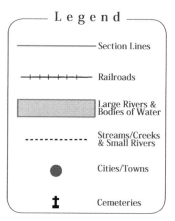

Historical Map

T10-N R10-W
St Stephens Meridian

Map Group 5

Note: the area contained in this map amounts to far less than a full Township. Therefore, its contents are completely on this single page (instead of a "normal" 2-page spread).

Cities & Towns
Haney
Sandersville

Cemeteries
Bethel Cemetery
Choctaw Cemetery
Florence Cemetery
McGill Cemetery
Sandersville Cemetery

N

Legend
Section Lines
Railroads
Large Rivers & Bodies of Water
Streams/Creeks & Small Rivers
Cities/Towns
Cemeteries

Scale: Section = 1 mile X 1 mile
(there are some exceptions)

Map Group 6: Index to Land Patents

Township 9-North Range 14-West (St Stephens)

After you locate an individual in this Index, take note of the Section and Section Part then proceed to the Land Patent map on the pages immediately following. You should have no difficulty locating the corresponding parcel of land.

The "For More Info" Column will lead you to more information about the underlying Patents. See the *Legend* at right, and the "How to Use this Book" chapter, for more information.

```
                         LEGEND
              "For More Info . . . " column
A = Authority (Legislative Act, See Appendix "A")
B = Block or Lot (location in Section unknown)
C = Cancelled Patent
F = Fractional Section
G = Group   (Multi-Patentee Patent, see Appendix "C")
V = Overlaps another Parcel
R = Re-Issued (Parcel patented more than once)

(A & G items require you to look in the Appendixes referred
to above. All other Letter-designations followed by a number
require you to locate line-items in this index that possess
the ID number found after the letter).
```

ID	Individual in Patent	Sec.	Sec. Part	Date Issued	Other Counties	For More Info . . .
688	ANDERSON, Latson D	3	N½NW	1892-03-23		A3
616	BARNES, Gus	10	NENE	1898-09-28		A3
617	" "	11	N½NW	1898-09-28		A3
618	" "	11	SENW	1898-09-28		A3
687	BARNES, Joseph T	15	SWNE	1901-03-23		A3
675	BEAVERS, Martin	14	SE	1846-09-01		A2 G40
663	BLACK, John L	10	NESE	1897-02-15		A3
664	" "	11	SWNW	1897-02-15		A3
665	" "	11	W½SW	1897-02-15		A3
720	BLACK, W J	10	SESW	1895-12-14		A3
721	" "	15	NENW	1895-12-14		A3
699	BOOTH, Matilda	13	NESW	1906-06-04		A3 G4
610	BRUMFIELD, George M	10	S½SE	1896-01-25		A3
611	" "	15	N½NE	1896-01-25		A3
600	BURKHALTER, Garson	15	SESW	1901-08-12		A3
725	COATES, William	1	E½NE	1860-07-02		A2
632	COATS, Ive	1	W½NE	1899-06-13		A3
659	CRAWFORD, John H	27	W½NE	1894-03-12		A3
660	" "	27	W½SE	1894-03-12		A3
580	CREEL, Burt	10	SENE	1897-02-15		A3
581	" "	10	W½NE	1897-02-15		A3
582	" "	3	SWSE	1897-02-15		A3
561	DUCKWORTH, A W	24	N½NW	1902-12-30		A3
562	" "	24	W½NE	1902-12-30		A3
577	DUCKWORTH, Benjamin C	23	SWSE	1841-01-05		A2
579	" "	26	NWNE	1841-01-05		A2
572	" "	14	SENE	1859-05-02		A2
573	" "	14	W½NE	1859-05-02		A2
574	" "	23	NESW	1859-05-02		A2
575	" "	23	NWSE	1859-05-02		A2
576	" "	23	SENW	1859-05-02		A2
578	" "	23	SWSW	1889-01-05		A3
592	DUCKWORTH, Fannie F	14	NWSW	1901-08-12		A3 G13
593	" "	14	S½SW	1901-08-12		A3 G13
628	DUCKWORTH, Hulon P	14	NESW	1881-05-10		A3
629	" "	14	S½NW	1881-05-10		A3
630	" "	15	SENE	1881-05-10		A3
633	DUCKWORTH, Jacob H	35	SENE	1891-05-20		A3
634	" "	35	W½NE	1891-05-20		A3
702	DUCKWORTH, Patrick C	23	W½NE	1841-01-05		A2
701	" "	10	W½NW	1859-11-10		A2
592	DUCKWORTH, William B	14	NWSW	1901-08-12		A3 G13
593	" "	14	S½SW	1901-08-12		A3 G13
656	EASTERLING, John C	3	NESW	1895-02-21		A3
657	" "	3	NWSE	1895-02-21		A3
658	" "	3	W½SW	1895-02-21		A3

ID	Individual in Patent	Sec.	Sec. Part	Date Issued	Other Counties	For More Info . . .
722	EASTERLING, William A	15	NESW	1895-01-17		A3
723	" "	15	SENW	1895-01-17		A3
724	" "	15	W½SW	1895-01-17		A3
676	GAMBRELL, John W	26	E½SW	1895-06-28		A3
677	" "	26	SWSE	1895-06-28		A3
678	" "	26	SWSW	1895-06-28		A3
619	GEIGER, Harriet	23	NWSW	1892-05-26		A3
620	" "	23	SWNW	1892-05-26		A3
621	" "	24	E½NE	1906-06-04		A3
612	GRAVES, George T	13	NENE	1905-02-13		A3
704	GRAVES, Robert	36	NWSW	1884-08-20		A2
726	GRISSETT, William	34	E½SW	1841-01-05		A2
727	" "	34	NWSE	1841-01-05		A2
592	GUNTER, Fannie F	14	NWSW	1901-08-12		A3 G13
593	" "	14	S½SW	1901-08-12		A3 G13
705	HARPER, Robert O	2	5	1899-06-13		A3
706	" "	3	E½SE	1899-06-13		A3
699	HARRING, Matilda	13	NESW	1906-06-04		A3 G4
679	HARVEY, John W	10	SWSW	1859-11-10		A2
571	HATTON, Author	23	N½NW	1906-06-26		A3
685	HATTON, Joseph	22	S½NE	1896-08-26		A3
686	" "	22	S½NW	1896-08-26		A3
689	HATTON, Lev	2	3	1900-10-04		A3
690	" "	2	6	1900-10-04		A3
691	HICKS, Lonzo	2	SESE	1897-05-07		A3
692	" "	2	SWNE	1897-05-07		A3
693	" "	2	W½SE	1897-05-07		A3
732	HOPKINS, William W	36	NE	1896-10-10		A3
703	HUFF, Philip	23	SESW	1859-11-10		A2
714	HUFF, Thomas J	26	NWSW	1859-05-02		A2
716	" "	27	SENE	1859-05-02		A2
713	" "	26	NWNW	1895-06-19		A3
715	" "	27	NENE	1895-06-19		A3
585	JEFCOAT, Daniel W	25	SENE	1906-06-21		A3
613	JEFCOAT, George W	13	NENW	1898-12-01		A3
614	" "	13	NWNE	1898-12-01		A3
615	" "	13	S½NE	1898-12-01		A3
601	JOHNSON, George	11	NENE	1899-04-01		A3
602	" "	12	NWNW	1899-04-01		A3
591	JOHNSTON, Emery A	36	NW	1896-12-26		A2
680	KELLY, John W	22	N½NE	1892-07-20		A3
681	" "	22	N½NW	1892-07-20		A3
603	KENT, George	13	SE	1889-04-20		A2
604	" "	13	SESW	1889-04-20		A2
605	" "	25	E½SE	1889-04-20		A2
606	" "	25	N½NE	1889-04-20		A2
607	" "	25	NW	1889-04-20		A2
608	" "	25	SWNE	1889-04-20		A2
609	" "	25	W½SW	1889-04-20		A2
565	KNIGHT, Albert	35	NW	1859-11-10		A2
566	" "	35	SE	1859-11-10		A2
645	KNIGHT, James	27	E½SE	1841-01-05		A2
661	KNIGHT, John	22	S½SW	1859-05-02		A2
662	" "	27	N½NW	1859-05-02		A2
729	KNIGHT, William	34	E½NE	1841-01-05		A2
647	MCCULLUM, James	3	S½NW	1913-02-10		A3
648	" "	3	W½NE	1913-02-10		A3
594	MCDANIEL, Ferdinand	1	NWSW	1891-06-30		A3
595	" "	1	SWNW	1891-06-30		A3
596	" "	2	NESE	1891-06-30		A3
597	" "	2	SENE	1891-06-30		A3
730	MCDANIEL, William	15	SE	1895-11-11		A3
643	MEADOR, James K	23	E½NE	1905-03-30		A3
644	" "	23	NESE	1905-03-30		A3
646	MEADOR, James M	36	SWSE	1899-08-03		A3
589	MURRAY, Delpha M	13	S½NW	1883-04-30		A3 G28
590	" "	13	W½SW	1883-04-30		A3 G28
667	MURRAY, John R	11	SESE	1860-07-02		A2
669	" "	14	NENE	1860-07-02		A2
666	" "	11	NESW	1889-01-05		A3
668	" "	11	W½SE	1889-01-05		A3
673	MURRAY, John S	1	S½SW	1897-04-02		A3
674	" "	12	NENW	1897-04-02		A3

ID	Individual in Patent	Sec.	Sec. Part	Date Issued	Other Counties	For More Info . . .
694	MURRAY, Martha A	12	N½NE	1897-06-07		A3
695	" "	12	SENW	1897-06-07		A3
696	" "	12	SWNE	1897-06-07		A3
711	MURRAY, Sarah A	12	E½SW	1897-06-07		A3
712	" "	12	W½SE	1897-06-07		A3
717	MURRAY, Thomas J	11	SENE	1889-01-05		A3
718	" "	11	W½NE	1889-01-05		A3
719	" "	12	SWNW	1889-01-05		A3
589	MURRAY, W W	13	S½NW	1883-04-30		A3 G28
590	" "	13	W½SW	1883-04-30		A3 G28
670	MURRY, John R	11	NESE	1878-01-15		A2
671	" "	12	W½SW	1878-01-15		A2
672	" "	13	NWNW	1878-01-15		A2
598	MUSGROVE, Frank	2	W½NW	1901-03-23		A3
599	" "	3	E½NE	1901-03-23		A3
650	MUSGROVE, Jefferson	12	E½SE	1898-12-01		A3
651	" "	12	SENE	1898-12-01		A3
728	NORWOOD, William K	36	E½SE	1896-02-13		A3
653	PICKERING, John B	26	E½NE	1898-08-27		A3
654	" "	26	SENW	1898-08-27		A3
655	" "	26	SWNE	1898-08-27		A3
707	PICKERING, Robert W	35	SW	1893-12-18		A3
682	POWELL, John W	1	N½SE	1895-02-21		A3
683	" "	1	NESW	1895-02-21		A3
684	" "	1	SENW	1895-02-21		A3
708	POWELL, Samuel R	10	N½SW	1892-03-23		A3
709	" "	10	NWSE	1892-03-23		A3
710	" "	10	SENW	1892-03-23		A3
622	PRIDGEN, Henry C	26	E½SE	1896-10-10		A3
623	" "	26	NWSE	1896-10-10		A3
624	" "	35	NENE	1896-10-10		A3
649	REDDECK, James	27	W½SW	1841-01-05		A2
731	REDDOCH, William	34	NESE	1859-11-10		A2
638	REDDOCK, James C	34	SENW	1851-10-01		A2
637	" "	27	S½NW	1859-05-02		A2
636	" "	27	E½SW	1896-06-06		A2
639	" "	34	W½NW	1896-06-06		A2
640	ROYALS, James E	23	SESE	1895-10-09		A3
641	" "	24	SWNW	1895-10-09		A3
642	" "	24	W½SW	1895-10-09		A3
625	RUMPH, Henry L	36	E½SW	1894-04-10		A3
626	" "	36	NWSE	1894-04-10		A3
627	" "	36	SWSW	1894-04-10		A3
586	STRANGE, David	24	N½SE	1901-08-12		A3
587	" "	24	NESW	1901-08-12		A3
588	" "	24	SENW	1901-08-12		A3
675	THOMAS, John	14	SE	1846-09-01		A2 G40
563	TINNON, Absalom A	11	SESW	1906-06-21		A3
564	" "	14	N½NW	1906-06-21		A3
567	TURNER, Allen G	10	NENW	1878-06-24		A3
568	" "	3	SESW	1878-06-24		A3
569	TURNER, Alvin H	25	E½SW	1893-12-21		A3
570	" "	25	W½SE	1893-12-21		A3
583	VALENTINE, Daniel N	1	N½NW	1897-02-15		A3
584	" "	2	N½NE	1897-02-15		A3
635	VALENTINE, James A	1	S½SE	1899-05-12		A2
631	WADE, Isaac	22	N½SW	1895-11-11		A3
697	WALTMAN, Mary E	24	S½SE	1898-11-11		A3
698	" "	24	SESW	1898-11-11		A3
700	WALTMAN, Moses O	22	SE	1889-01-12		A3
652	WHEELER, John A	34	SWSE	1841-01-05		A2

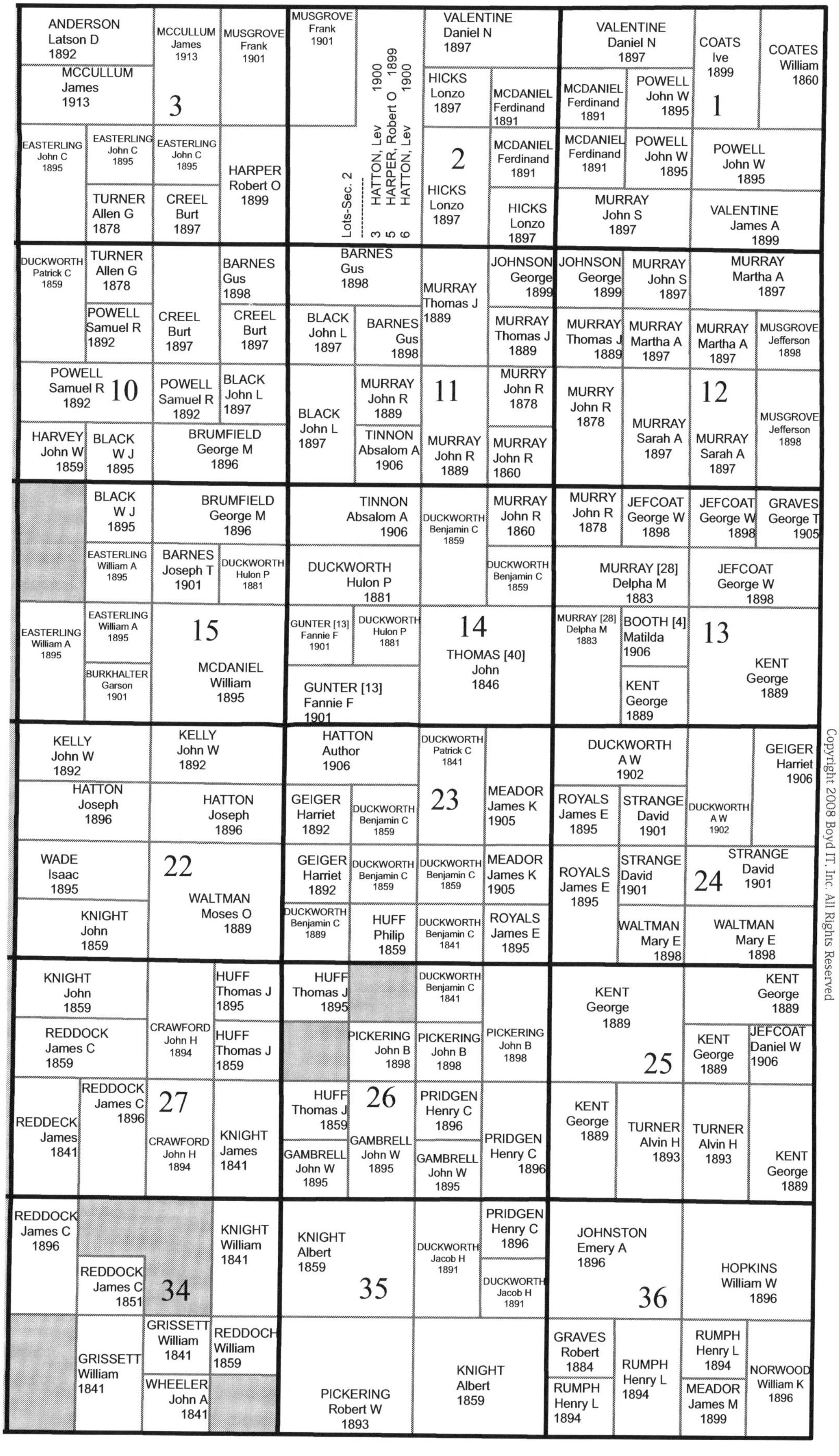

Map Grid (Sections)

Section 3 area:
ANDERSON Latson D 1892 | MCCULLUM James 1913 | MUSGROVE Frank 1901
MCCULLUM James 1913 | **3**
EASTERLING John C 1895 | EASTERLING John C 1895 | EASTERLING John C 1895 | HARPER Robert O 1899
TURNER Allen G 1878 | CREEL Burt 1897

MUSGROVE Frank 1901

HATTON, Lev 1900 | HARPER, Robert O 1899 | HATTON, Lev 1900 (Lots-Sec. 2, 3 5 6)

Section 2 area:
VALENTINE Daniel N 1897
HICKS Lonzo 1897 | MCDANIEL Ferdinand 1891
MCDANIEL Ferdinand 1891 | **2**
HICKS Lonzo 1897

Section 1 area:
VALENTINE Daniel N 1897 | COATS Ive 1899 | COATES William 1860
MCDANIEL Ferdinand 1891 | POWELL John W 1895 | **1**
MCDANIEL Ferdinand 1891 | POWELL John W 1895 | POWELL John W 1895
MURRAY John S 1897 | VALENTINE James A 1899

Section 10 area:
DUCKWORTH Patrick C 1859 | TURNER Allen G 1878 | BARNES Gus 1898
POWELL Samuel R 1892 | CREEL Burt 1897 | CREEL Burt 1897
POWELL Samuel R 1892 **10** | POWELL Samuel R 1892 | BLACK John L 1897
HARVEY John W 1859 | BLACK W J 1895 | BRUMFIELD George M 1896

Section 11 area:
BARNES Gus 1898 | JOHNSON George 1899
MURRAY Thomas J 1889 | BLACK John L 1897 | BARNES Gus 1898 | MURRAY Thomas J 1889
MURRAY John R 1889 **11** | MURRY John R 1878
BLACK John L 1897 | TINNON Absalom A 1906 | MURRAY John R 1889 | MURRAY John R 1860

Section 12 area:
JOHNSON George 1899 | MURRAY John S 1897 | MURRAY Martha A 1897
MURRAY Thomas J 1889 | MURRAY Martha A 1897 | MURRAY Martha A 1897 | MUSGROVE Jefferson 1898
MURRY John R 1878 **12** | MUSGROVE Jefferson 1898
MURRAY Sarah A 1897 | MURRAY Sarah A 1897

Section 15 area:
BLACK W J 1895 | BRUMFIELD George M 1896
EASTERLING William A 1895 | BARNES Joseph T 1901 | DUCKWORTH Hulon P 1881
EASTERLING William A 1895 | EASTERLING William A 1895 **15**
BURKHALTER Garson 1901 | MCDANIEL William 1895

Section 14 area:
TINNON Absalom A 1906 | DUCKWORTH Benjamin C 1859 | MURRAY John R 1860
DUCKWORTH Hulon P 1881 | DUCKWORTH Benjamin C 1859
GUNTER [13] Fannie F 1901 | DUCKWORTH Hulon P 1881 | **14** | MURRAY [28] Delpha M 1883
THOMAS [40] John 1846
GUNTER [13] Fannie F 1901

Section 13 area:
MURRAY John R 1878 | JEFCOAT George W 1898 | JEFCOAT George W 1898 | GRAVES George T 1905
MURRAY [28] Delpha M 1883 | JEFCOAT George W 1898
MURRAY [28] Delpha M 1883 | BOOTH [4] Matilda 1906 **13**
KENT George 1889
KENT George 1889

Section 22 area:
KELLY John W 1892 | KELLY John W 1892
HATTON Joseph 1896 | HATTON Joseph 1896
WADE Isaac 1895 **22** | WALTMAN Moses O 1889
KNIGHT John 1859

Section 23 area:
HATTON Author 1906 | DUCKWORTH Patrick C 1841
GEIGER Harriet 1892 | DUCKWORTH Benjamin C 1859 | **23** | MEADOR James K 1905
GEIGER Harriet 1892 | DUCKWORTH Benjamin C 1859 | DUCKWORTH Benjamin C 1859 | MEADOR James K 1905
DUCKWORTH Benjamin C 1889 | HUFF Philip 1859 | DUCKWORTH Benjamin C 1841 | ROYALS James E 1895

Section 24 area:
DUCKWORTH A W 1902 | GEIGER Harriet 1906
ROYALS James E 1895 | STRANGE David 1901 | DUCKWORTH A W 1902
ROYALS James E 1895 | STRANGE David 1901 | STRANGE David 1901 **24**
WALTMAN Mary E 1898 | WALTMAN Mary E 1898

Section 27 area:
KNIGHT John 1859 | HUFF Thomas J 1895
REDDOCK James C 1859 | CRAWFORD John H 1894 | HUFF Thomas J 1859
REDDOCK James C 1896 **27**
REDDECK James 1841 | CRAWFORD John H 1894 | KNIGHT James 1841

Section 26 area:
HUFF Thomas J 1895 | DUCKWORTH Benjamin C 1841
PICKERING John B 1898 | PICKERING John B 1898 | PICKERING John B 1898
HUFF Thomas J 1859 **26** | PRIDGEN Henry C 1896
GAMBRELL John W 1895 | GAMBRELL John W 1895 | PRIDGEN Henry C 1896

Section 25 area:
KENT George 1889 | KENT George 1889
KENT George 1889 | JEFCOAT Daniel W 1906
25
KENT George 1889 | TURNER Alvin H 1893 | TURNER Alvin H 1893 | KENT George 1889

Section 34 area:
REDDOCK James C 1896 | KNIGHT William 1841
REDDOCK James C 1851 **34**
GRISSETT William 1841 | GRISSETT William 1841 | REDDOCH William 1859
WHEELER John A 1841

Section 35 area:
KNIGHT Albert 1859 | DUCKWORTH Jacob H 1891
35 | DUCKWORTH Jacob H 1891
KNIGHT Albert 1859
PICKERING Robert W 1893

Section 36 area:
PRIDGEN Henry C 1896 | JOHNSTON Emery A 1896 | HOPKINS William W 1896
36
GRAVES Robert 1884 | RUMPH Henry L 1894 | RUMPH Henry L 1894 | NORWOOD William K 1896
RUMPH Henry L 1894 | MEADOR James M 1899

Patent Map

T9-N R14-W
St Stephens Meridian

Map Group 6

Township Statistics

Parcels Mapped	:	172
Number of Patents	:	91
Number of Individuals	:	85
Patentees Identified	:	80
Number of Surnames	:	54
Multi-Patentee Parcels	:	6
Oldest Patent Date	:	1/5/1841
Most Recent Patent	:	2/10/1913
Block/Lot Parcels	:	3
Parcels Re-Issued	:	0
Parcels that Overlap	:	0
Cities and Towns	:	1
Cemeteries	:	6

Note: the area contained in this map amounts to far less than a full Township. Therefore, its contents are completely on this single page (instead of a "normal" 2-page spread).

Legend

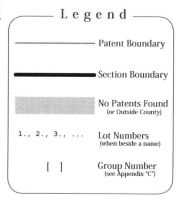

———— Patent Boundary

━━━━ Section Boundary

▓▓▓▓ No Patents Found (or Outside County)

1., 2., 3., ... Lot Numbers (when beside a name)

[ ] Group Number (see Appendix "C")

Scale: Section = 1 mile X 1 mile (generally, with some exceptions)

Road Map

T9-N R14-W
St Stephens Meridian

Map Group 6

Note: the area contained in this map amounts to far less than a full Township. Therefore, its contents are completely on this single page (instead of a "normal" 2-page spread).

Cities & Towns
Hebron

Cemeteries
Center Ridge Cemetery
Hatton Cemetery
Hebron Cemetery
Hebron Lodge Cemetery
Jack Knight Cemetery
Mount Olive Cemetery

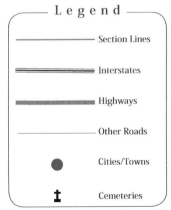

Legend

Section Lines	
Interstates	
Highways	
Other Roads	
Cities/Towns	
Cemeteries	

Scale: Section = 1 mile X 1 mile
(generally, with some exceptions)

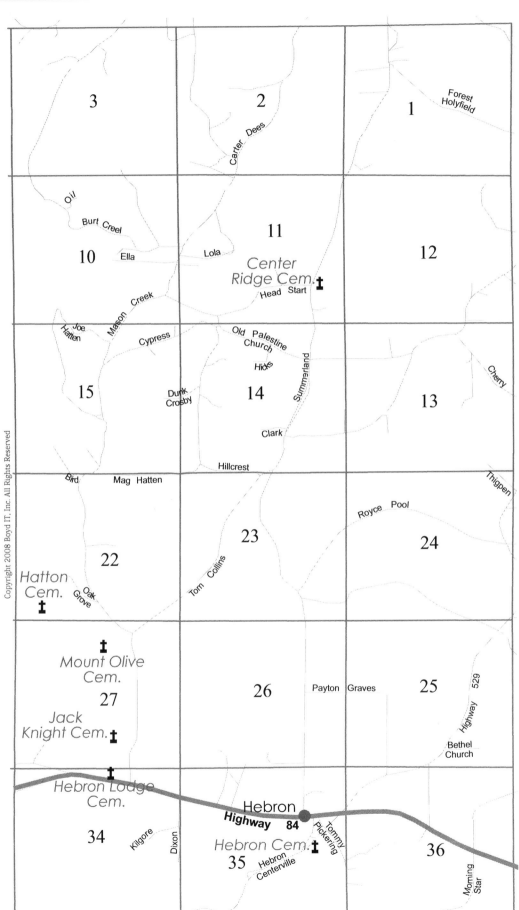

3

2

1

Forest Holyfield

Oil

Burt Creel

10

Ella

Lola

11

Center Ridge Cem.

Head Start

12

Mason Creek

Joe Hatten

Cypress

Old Palestine Church

Hites

Summerland

Cherry

15

Dunk Crosby

14

Clark

13

Hillcrest

Bird

Mag Hatten

Thigpen

Royce Pool

22

23

24

Hatton Cem.

Oak Grove

Tom Collins

Mount Olive Cem.

27

Jack Knight Cem.

26

Payton Graves

25

Highway 529

Bethel Church

Hebron Lodge Cem.

34

Kilgore

Dixon

Hebron

Highway 84

Hebron Cem.

35

Hebron Centerville

Tommy Pickering

36

Morning Star

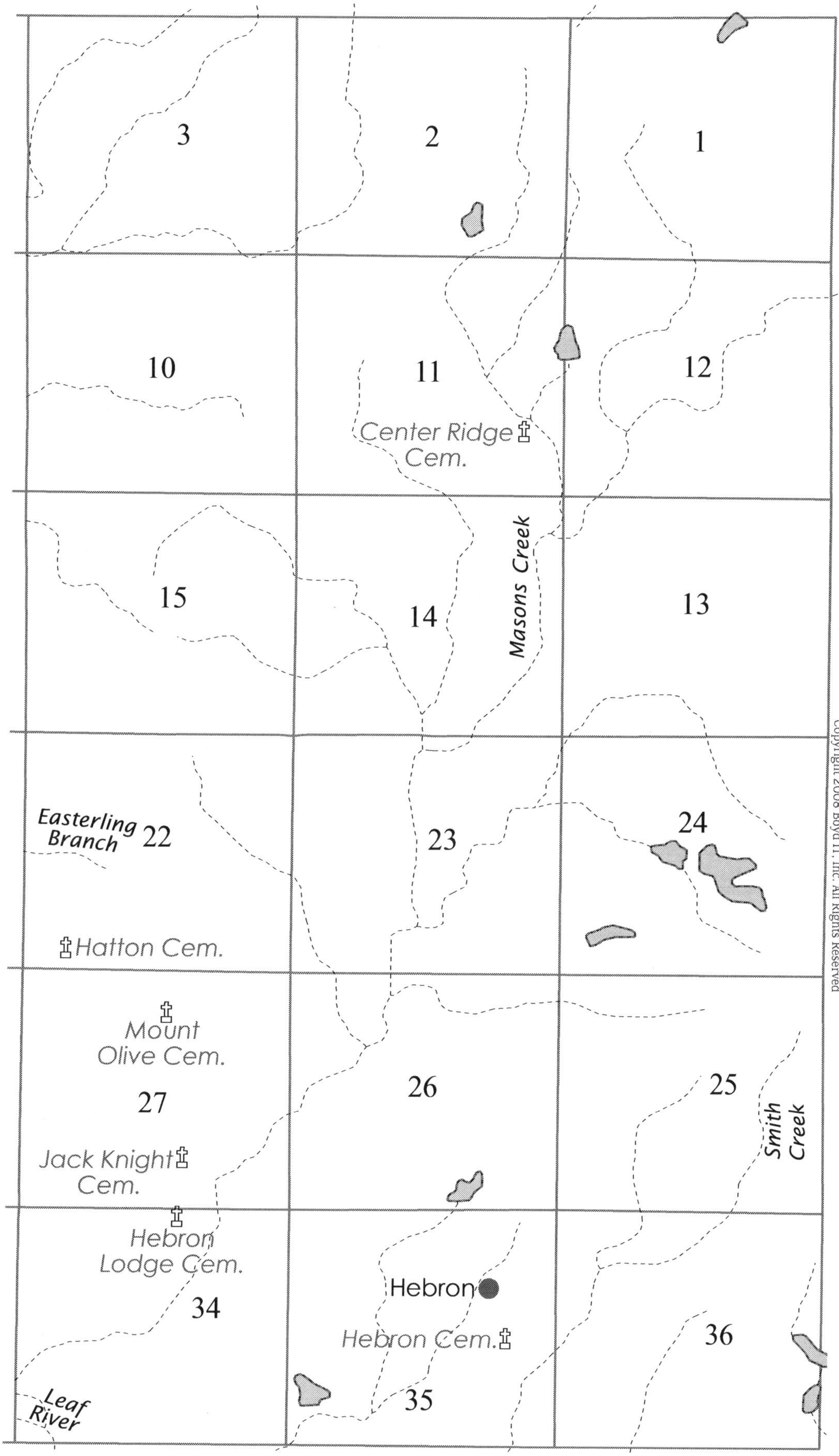

3
2
1
10
11
12
Center Ridge Cem.
Masons Creek
15
14
13
Easterling Branch
22
23
24
Hatton Cem.
Mount Olive Cem.
27
26
25
Jack Knight Cem.
Smith Creek
Hebron Lodge Cem.
34
Hebron
Hebron Cem.
35
36
Leaf River

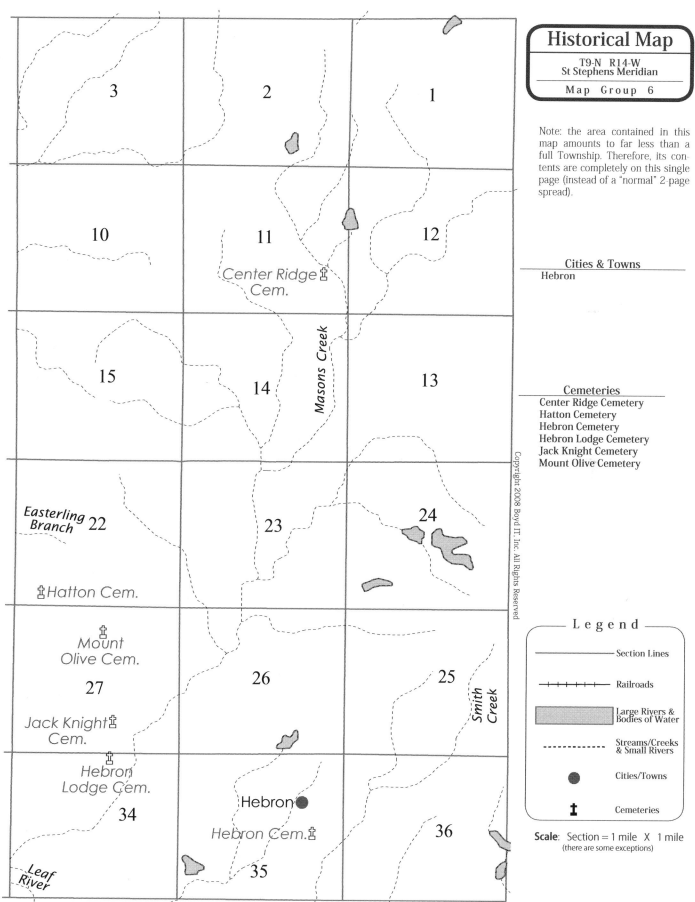

Historical Map

T9-N R14-W
St Stephens Meridian

Map Group 6

Note: the area contained in this map amounts to far less than a full Township. Therefore, its contents are completely on this single page (instead of a "normal" 2-page spread).

Cities & Towns

Hebron

Cemeteries

Center Ridge Cemetery
Hatton Cemetery
Hebron Cemetery
Hebron Lodge Cemetery
Jack Knight Cemetery
Mount Olive Cemetery

Legend

- Section Lines
- Railroads
- Large Rivers & Bodies of Water
- Streams/Creeks & Small Rivers
- Cities/Towns
- Cemeteries

Scale: Section = 1 mile X 1 mile
(there are some exceptions)

Map Group 7: Index to Land Patents

Township 9-North Range 13-West (St Stephens)

After you locate an individual in this Index, take note of the Section and Section Part then proceed to the Land Patent map on the pages immediately following. You should have no difficulty locating the corresponding parcel of land.

The "For More Info" Column will lead you to more information about the underlying Patents. See the *Legend* at right, and the "How to Use this Book" chapter, for more information.

ID	Individual in Patent	Sec.	Sec. Part	Date Issued	Other Counties	For More Info . . .
979	ALLEN, Robert B	29	N½SW	1889-04-20		A2
980	" "	29	SENW	1889-04-20		A2
981	" "	29	SWNE	1889-04-20		A2
982	" "	29	W½NW	1889-04-20		A2
983	" "	29	W½SE	1889-04-20		A2
794	ALWAY, Frederick	31		1889-04-20		A2
935	BROOMFIELD, Joseph	3	E½SE	1892-07-20		A3
936	" "	3	SENE	1892-07-20		A3
995	BRUCE, Simpson	33	SENE	1882-06-01		A2
996	" "	34	NWNW	1882-06-01		A2
864	BUNKLEY, John J	27	E½NW	1878-06-24		A3
865	" "	27	W½NE	1878-06-24		A3
951	BUNKLEY, Lewis L	34	NESE	1896-08-26		A2
750	BYNUM, Benjamin	33	NW	1841-01-05		A2 G7
807	BYNUM, Hiram	25	E½NE	1859-05-02		A2
750	BYNUM, William	33	NW	1841-01-05		A2 G7
814	CHISHOLM, Hugh	32	SENW	1901-10-09		A2
767	COATES, Daniel	5	SWNE	1851-10-01		A2
768	" "	5	W½SE	1851-10-01		A2
769	" "	8	NENW	1859-06-01		A2
770	" "	8	NWSE	1859-06-01		A2
771	" "	8	SWNE	1859-06-01		A2
1010	COATES, William	6	NWSW	1860-07-02		A2
1008	" "	6	NESW	1860-10-01		A2
1009	" "	6	NW	1860-10-01		A2
738	COATS, Adam L	7	E½SE	1898-12-01		A3
739	" "	7	NWSE	1898-12-01		A3
740	" "	8	SWSW	1898-12-01		A3
772	COATS, Daniel	5	E½SE	1860-07-02		A2
773	" "	5	E½SW	1860-07-02		A2
774	" "	8	NWNE	1860-07-02		A2
787	COATS, Elizabeth	21	NWNE	1890-02-21		A3
788	" "	21	S½NE	1890-02-21		A3
789	" "	21	SENW	1890-02-21		A3
831	COATS, James B	20	N½NW	1897-02-15		A3
832	" "	20	NWNE	1897-02-15		A3
833	" "	20	SWNW	1897-02-15		A3
853	COATS, Jefferson D	21	N½SE	1899-06-13		A3
965	COATS, Morgan M	9	SESE	1897-02-15		A3
966	" "	9	W½SE	1897-02-15		A3
858	COLLINS, John C	10	W½SW	1906-05-01		A2
977	COLLINS, Riley J	1	NENE	1859-05-02		A2
978	" "	1	SENE	1859-06-01		A2
850	COPELAND, James W	22	SWNW	1901-03-23		A2
997	COPELAND, Stephen J	23	S½NW	1898-10-04		A3
1015	CORLEY, William G	10	E½SW	1897-02-23		A3

ID	Individual in Patent	Sec.	Sec. Part	Date Issued	Other Counties	For More Info . . .
1016	CORLEY, William G (Cont'd)	15	N½NW	1897-02-23		A3
733	DEAN, Abel	12	NESE	1890-02-21		A3
734	"	12	S½NE	1890-02-21		A3
1011	DEAN, William	11	SE	1896-04-28		A3
777	DELANCY, David S	15	SWNW	1859-05-02		A2
989	DELANCY, Sarah	12	SESW	1859-05-02		A2
990	"	12	SWSE	1859-05-02		A2
751	ELLZEY, Bennett M	33	E½SW	1854-03-15		A2
752	"	33	SWNE	1859-05-02		A2
792	FLYNT, Franklin M	34	SESW	1861-05-01		A2
793	"	34	W½SW	1861-05-01		A2
920	FLYNT, John Q	29	SWSW	1896-02-13		A3
921	"	30	E½SE	1896-02-13		A3
922	"	30	SENE	1896-02-13		A3
986	GARNER, Samuel J	22	NENE	1895-02-21		A3
987	"	23	NWNW	1895-02-21		A3
866	GARRICK, John J	21	S½SE	1884-11-20		A3
867	"	28	N½NE	1884-11-20		A3
785	GRAVES, Elijah	33	NWSW	1859-05-02		A2
803	GRAVES, Green M	32	N½SE	1896-08-26		A3
804	"	32	NESW	1896-08-26		A3
805	"	32	SWNE	1896-08-26		A3
820	GRAVES, Jack	2	SWNE	1892-06-15		A3
821	"	2	W½SE	1892-06-15		A3
948	GRAVES, Lewis	2	N½NW	1895-06-19		A3
949	"	2	NWNE	1895-06-19		A3
950	"	2	SENW	1895-06-19		A3
970	GRAVES, Phillip	18	N½NE	1888-02-25		A3
972	"	18	NWSE	1888-02-25		A3
973	"	18	SWNE	1888-02-25		A3
971	"	18	NW	1898-10-04		A3
992	GUNTER, Allen	13	NWSW	1895-11-11		A3 G15
993	"	13	W½NW	1895-11-11		A3 G15
994	"	14	NESE	1895-11-11		A3 G15
741	GUNTER, Americus	4	SWSE	1859-11-10		A2
742	"	9	NWNE	1859-11-10		A2
837	GUNTER, James	13	NESE	1859-06-01		A2
838	"	13	SENW	1859-06-01		A2
839	"	13	SESW	1859-06-01		A2
840	"	13	SWNE	1859-06-01		A2
992	GUNTER, Sarah R	13	NWSW	1895-11-11		A3 G15
993	"	13	W½NW	1895-11-11		A3 G15
994	"	14	NESE	1895-11-11		A3 G15
795	HARPER, George	5	NENW	1841-01-05		A2
797	HARPER, George W	13	E½NE	1895-11-11		A3
798	"	13	NENW	1895-11-11		A3
799	"	13	NWNE	1895-11-11		A3
915	HARPER, John L	21	NENW	1899-05-05		A3
937	HARPER, Josiah	17	NWSE	1859-05-02		A2
938	"	17	SWNE	1859-05-02		A2
939	"	17	SWSE	1859-11-10		A2
753	HILL, Caleb A	27	SWSW	1884-11-20		A3
754	"	28	E½SE	1884-11-20		A3
755	"	33	NENE	1884-11-20		A3
756	HILL, Caleb L	35	NE	1890-06-25		A3
822	HILL, James A	35	NESE	1902-01-17		A3
823	"	36	N½SW	1902-01-17		A3
824	"	36	SWNW	1902-01-17		A3
998	HILL, Thomas F	34	SESE	1891-03-16		A3
999	"	34	W½SE	1891-03-16		A3
1000	"	35	SWSW	1891-03-16		A3
1019	HILL, William M	32	S½SE	1896-01-25		A3
735	HINTON, Abner A	15	NESW	1892-03-07		A3
736	"	15	NWSE	1892-03-07		A3
737	"	15	S½SE	1892-03-07		A3
825	HINTON, James A	12	NESW	1885-05-25		A3
826	"	12	SWNW	1885-05-25		A3
827	"	12	W½SW	1885-05-25		A3
931	HINTON, John W	5	SWSW	1895-02-21		A3
932	"	6	E½SE	1895-02-21		A3
974	HINTON, Richard H	6	SESW	1888-02-25		A3
975	"	6	W½SE	1888-02-25		A3
976	"	7	NWNE	1888-02-25		A3

ID	Individual in Patent	Sec.	Sec. Part	Date Issued	Other Counties	For More Info . . .
991	HOLIFIELD, Sarah F	24	NWSW	1901-03-23		A2
943	HOPKINS, Lemuel W	18	E½SE	1896-01-30		A2
944	" "	18	SENE	1896-01-30		A2
945	" "	18	SWSE	1896-01-30		A2
958	HOPKINS, Martha V	29	SESW	1896-10-31		A3
959	" "	32	N½NW	1896-10-31		A3
960	" "	32	NWNE	1896-10-31		A3
775	JEFCOAT, David	29	E½SE	1884-12-30		A3
776	" "	32	E½NE	1884-12-30		A3
778	JEFCOAT, Dempsy D	34	NENW	1893-12-21		A3
779	" "	34	NESW	1893-12-21		A3
780	" "	34	S½NW	1893-12-21		A3
815	JEFCOAT, Hughie D	20	W½SW	1906-06-21		A3
929	JEFCOAT, John V	26	N½SW	1890-06-25		A3
930	" "	26	S½NW	1890-06-25		A3
746	JOHNSTON, Beadson S	20	SESW	1874-11-05		A2
747	" "	20	SWSE	1874-11-05		A2
748	" "	29	NENW	1874-11-05		A2
749	" "	29	NWNE	1874-11-05		A2
888	KAMPER, John	22	SESE	1889-11-29		A2
889	" "	22	W½NE	1889-11-29		A2
890	" "	22	W½SE	1889-11-29		A2
891	" "	23	E½SE	1889-11-29		A2
892	" "	23	NENW	1889-11-29		A2
893	" "	23	NESW	1889-11-29		A2
894	" "	23	NWSE	1889-11-29		A2
895	" "	23	SENE	1889-11-29		A2
896	" "	25	S½	1889-11-29		A2
897	" "	25	SENW	1889-11-29		A2
898	" "	25	W½NE	1889-11-29		A2
899	" "	26	E½NE	1889-11-29		A2
900	" "	26	N½NW	1889-11-29		A2
901	" "	26	S½SW	1889-11-29		A2
902	" "	26	SWNE	1889-11-29		A2
903	" "	27	E½NE	1889-11-29		A2
904	" "	27	E½SW	1889-11-29		A2
905	" "	27	NWSW	1889-11-29		A2
906	" "	27	SE	1889-11-29		A2
907	" "	27	W½NW	1889-11-29		A2
908	" "	35	E½SW	1889-11-29		A2
909	" "	35	NW	1889-11-29		A2
910	" "	35	NWSW	1889-11-29		A2
911	" "	35	W½SE	1889-11-29		A2
912	" "	36	E½	1889-11-29		A2
913	" "	36	E½NW	1889-11-29		A2
914	" "	36	NWNW	1889-11-29		A2
872	" "	11	E½NE	1890-07-03		A2
873	" "	11	NESW	1890-07-03		A2
874	" "	11	SENW	1890-07-03		A2
875	" "	11	SWNE	1890-07-03		A2
876	" "	12	NWNW	1890-07-03		A2
877	" "	12	SESE	1890-07-03		A2
878	" "	14	E½NE	1890-07-03		A2
879	" "	14	NWNE	1890-07-03		A2
880	" "	14	S½NW	1890-07-03		A2
881	" "	14	SESE	1890-07-03		A2
882	" "	14	SESW	1890-07-03		A2
883	" "	14	W½SW	1890-07-03		A2
884	" "	15	E½NE	1890-07-03		A2
885	" "	15	NESE	1890-07-03		A2
886	" "	15	SESW	1890-07-03		A2
887	" "	15	W½SW	1890-07-03		A2
796	KENT, George	19		1889-04-20		A2
988	KERVIN, Samuel W	1	SE	1892-07-20		A3
743	KNIGHT, Andy	11	N½NW	1892-06-15		A3
744	" "	11	NWNE	1892-06-15		A3
745	" "	2	SESW	1892-06-15		A3
806	KNIGHT, Henry T	22	SW	1896-01-10		A3
841	KNIGHT, James	5	NWSW	1859-05-02		A2
842	" "	5	SENW	1859-05-02		A2
843	" "	5	W½NW	1859-05-02		A2
844	" "	6	NE	1859-05-02		A2
868	KNIGHT, John J	17	N½NE	1882-03-30		A3

ID	Individual in Patent	Sec.	Sec. Part	Date Issued	Other Counties	For More Info . . .
916	KNIGHT, John M	3	NENE	1906-05-01		A3
917	" "	3	W½NE	1906-05-01		A3
984	KNIGHT, Sam	2	SESE	1897-09-09		A3
816	LANE, Ida E	17	W½	1890-07-03		A2
781	LEWIS, Ela	13	NESW	1859-05-02		A2
782	" "	13	NWSE	1859-05-02		A2
810	LEWIS, Howell	10	E½NW	1859-05-02		A2
811	" "	10	NWNE	1859-05-02		A2
809	" "	10	E½NE	1861-02-01		A2
812	" "	10	SWNE	1861-02-01		A2
813	" "	11	SWNW	1861-02-01		A2
1006	LITTLE, William C	35	SESE	1892-03-23		A3
1007	" "	36	SWSW	1892-03-23		A3
786	MAXCEY, Elizabeth A	1	SW	1890-02-18		A3
790	MAXCEY, Elizabeth F	1	NWNW	1884-12-30		A2
1017	MEADOR, William L	30	N½SW	1898-02-24		A3
1018	" "	30	S½NW	1898-02-24		A3
1022	MONTGOMERY, William N	36	SESW	1892-07-25		A3
956	MOSS, Madison	1	E½NW	1890-02-18		A3
957	" "	1	W½NE	1890-02-18		A3
791	MUSGROVE, Flavilla	24	S½NE	1895-06-28		A3
854	MUSGROVE, Jefferson	7	SWNW	1898-12-01		A3
918	MUSGROVE, John M	13	S½SE	1889-01-12		A3
919	" "	24	N½NE	1889-01-12		A3
933	MUSGROVE, Johnson J	24	S½SE	1892-03-23		A3
934	" "	24	SESW	1892-03-23		A3
964	MUSGROVE, Mary H	7	SW	1901-08-12		A3
1026	MUSGROVE, Willis S	24	SWSW	1895-01-17		A3
1027	" "	25	NENW	1895-01-17		A3
1028	" "	25	W½NW	1895-01-17		A3
1029	MUSGROVE, Willis W	26	SE	1896-04-28		A3
985	PARISH, Samuel C	34	NE	1895-02-21		A3
760	POWELL, Cathrine	6	SWSW	1897-06-07		A3
761	" "	7	N½NW	1897-06-07		A3
762	" "	7	SENW	1897-06-07		A3
801	POWELL, George W	3	S½SW	1892-07-20		A3
802	" "	3	SWSE	1892-07-20		A3
800	" "	3	NWSW	1893-08-23		A3
808	POWELL, Hiram W	3	N½NW	1859-11-10		A2
845	POWELL, James M	4	E½SE	1897-02-15		A3
851	POWELL, James W	28	SWSE	1859-05-02		A2
852	" "	33	NWNE	1859-05-02		A2
961	POWELL, Mary C	3	NESW	1886-03-20		A3
962	" "	3	NWSE	1886-03-20		A3
963	" "	3	S½NW	1886-03-20		A3
763	ROYALS, Clarissa A	20	NESW	1895-10-09		A3
764	" "	20	NWSE	1895-10-09		A3
765	" "	20	SENW	1895-10-09		A3
766	" "	20	SWNE	1895-10-09		A3
923	ROYALS, John S	8	SESW	1896-01-30		A2
924	" "	8	SWSE	1896-01-30		A2
859	SCARBROUGH, John E	30	S½SW	1897-02-15		A3
860	" "	30	W½SE	1897-02-15		A3
834	SHOWS, James D	23	S½SW	1898-10-04		A3
835	" "	23	SWSE	1898-10-04		A3
836	" "	26	NWNE	1898-10-04		A3
925	SIMS, John T	24	N½SE	1889-01-12		A3
926	" "	24	NESW	1889-01-12		A3
927	" "	24	SENW	1889-01-12		A3
940	SMITH, Abram	14	NESW	1895-12-14		A3 G37
941	" "	14	SWNE	1895-12-14		A3 G37
942	" "	14	W½SE	1895-12-14		A3 G37
783	SMITH, Eli L	7	SWNE	1901-08-08		A2
784	" "	7	SWSE	1901-08-08		A2
828	SMITH, James A	22	NESE	1859-05-02		A2
829	" "	22	SENE	1859-05-02		A2
830	" "	23	NWSW	1859-05-02		A2
940	SMITH, Laura	14	NESW	1895-12-14		A3 G37
941	" "	14	SWNE	1895-12-14		A3 G37
942	" "	14	W½SE	1895-12-14		A3 G37
952	SMITH, Lewis	13	SWSW	1859-06-01		A2
953	" "	23	NENE	1859-06-01		A2
954	" "	24	NENW	1859-06-01		A2

ID	Individual in Patent	Sec.	Sec. Part	Date Issued	Other Counties	For More Info . . .
955	SMITH, Lewis (Cont'd)	24	W½NW	1859-06-01		A2
757	SUMRALL, Carney S	21	NENE	1899-04-28		A3
758	" "	22	N½NW	1899-04-28		A3
759	" "	22	SENW	1899-04-28		A3
861	SUMRALL, John H	28	NWSE	1890-06-25		A3
863	" "	28	SWNE	1890-06-25		A3
862	" "	28	SENE	1895-02-21		A3
928	THIGPEN, John	18	SW	1898-10-04		A3
848	THOMAS, James	9	NESE	1859-05-02		A2
849	" "	9	SWNE	1859-05-02		A2
846	" "	10	W½NW	1859-06-01		A2
847	" "	9	E½NE	1859-06-01		A2
1012	TODD, William F	32	NWSW	1895-06-22		A2
1013	" "	32	S½SW	1895-06-22		A2
1014	" "	32	SWNW	1895-06-22		A2
857	VALENTINE, John A	23	W½NE	1898-02-24		A3
869	VALENTINE, John J	2	NESW	1874-11-05		A2
870	" "	2	SWNW	1874-11-05		A2
871	" "	2	W½SW	1874-11-05		A2
1004	VAUGHN, Tobe R	30	N½NE	1896-08-26		A2
1005	" "	30	N½NW	1896-08-26		A2
946	VOLENTINE, Levi	15	SENW	1861-07-01		A2
947	" "	15	W½NE	1861-07-01		A2
819	WARD, Isaac	12	NWSE	1884-12-30		A2
817	" "	12	E½NW	1890-02-21		A3
818	" "	12	N½NE	1890-02-21		A3
1023	WELBORN, William	11	S½SW	1861-07-01		A2
1024	" "	14	N½NW	1861-07-01		A2
967	WELBORNE, Needham	10	NESE	1861-02-01		A2
968	" "	10	W½SE	1861-02-01		A2
969	" "	11	NWSW	1861-02-01		A2
855	WELCH, Joel W	8	N½SW	1897-02-15		A3
856	" "	8	SENW	1897-02-15		A3
1001	WELCH, Timothy	1	SWNW	1861-07-01		A2
1002	" "	2	E½NE	1861-07-01		A2
1003	" "	2	NESE	1861-07-01		A2
1020	WELCH, William M	7	E½NE	1861-05-01		A2
1021	" "	8	W½NW	1861-05-01		A2
1025	WILBORN, William	10	SESE	1859-05-02		A2

Patent Map

T9-N R13-W
St Stephens Meridian

Map Group 7

Township Statistics

Parcels Mapped	:	297
Number of Patents	:	141
Number of Individuals	:	120
Patentees Identified	:	117
Number of Surnames	:	58
Multi-Patentee Parcels	:	7
Oldest Patent Date	:	1/5/1841
Most Recent Patent	:	6/21/1906
Block/Lot Parcels	:	0
Parcels Re - Issued	:	0
Parcels that Overlap	:	0
Cities and Towns	:	3
Cemeteries	:	5

Section 6
COATES William 1860
KNIGHT James 1859
COATES William 1860
COATES William 1860
HINTON Richard H 1888
HINTON John W 1895
POWELL Cathrine 1897
HINTON Richard H 1888

Section 5
HARPER George 1841
KNIGHT James 1859
KNIGHT James 1859
COATES Daniel 1851
KNIGHT James 1859
COATS Daniel 1860
COATES Daniel 1851
HINTON John W 1895
COATS Daniel 1860

Section 4
COATS Daniel 1860
GUNTER Americus 1859
POWELL James M 1897

Section 7
POWELL Cathrine 1897
HINTON Richard H 1888
MUSGROVE Jefferson 1898
POWELL Cathrine 1897
SMITH Eli L 1901
MUSGROVE Mary H 1901
COATS Adam L 1898
SMITH Eli L 1901
COATS Adam L 1898

Section 8
WELCH William M 1861
COATES Daniel 1859
COATS Daniel 1860
WELCH William M 1861
WELCH Joel W 1897
COATES Daniel 1859
WELCH Joel W 1897
COATES Daniel 1859
COATS Adam L 1898
ROYALS John S 1896
ROYALS John S 1896

Section 9
GUNTER Americus 1859
THOMAS James 1859
THOMAS James 1859
COATS Morgan M 1897
THOMAS James 1859
COATS Morgan M 1897

Section 18
GRAVES Phillip 1898
GRAVES Phillip 1888
GRAVES Phillip 1888
HOPKINS Lemuel W 1896
GRAVES Phillip 1888
HOPKINS Lemuel W 1896
THIGPEN John 1898
HOPKINS Lemuel W 1896

Section 17
LANE Ida E 1890
KNIGHT John J 1882
HARPER Josiah 1859
HARPER Josiah 1859
HARPER Josiah 1859

Section 16

Section 19
KENT George 1889

Section 20
COATS James B 1897
COATS James B 1897
COATS James B 1897
ROYALS Clarissa A 1895
ROYALS Clarissa A 1895
JEFCOAT Hughie D 1906
ROYALS Clarissa A 1895
ROYALS Clarissa A 1895
JOHNSTON Beadson S 1874
JOHNSTON Beadson S 1874

Section 21
HARPER John L 1899
COATS Elizabeth 1890
SUMRALL Carney S 1899
COATS Elizabeth 1890
COATS Elizabeth 1890
COATS Jefferson D 1899
GARRICK John J 1884

Section 30
VAUGHN Tobe R 1896
VAUGHN Tobe R 1896
MEADOR William L 1898
FLYNT John Q 1896
MEADOR William L 1898
SCARBROUGH John E 1897
FLYNT John Q 1896
SCARBROUGH John E 1897

Section 29
ALLEN Robert B 1889
JOHNSTON Beadson S 1874
JOHNSTON Beadson S 1874
ALLEN Robert B 1889
ALLEN Robert B 1889
ALLEN Robert B 1889
ALLEN Robert B 1889
FLYNT John Q 1896
HOPKINS Martha V 1896
JEFCOAT David 1884

Section 28
GARRICK John J 1884
SUMRALL John H 1890
SUMRALL John H 1895
SUMRALL John H 1890
HILL Caleb A 1884
POWELL James W 1859

Section 31
ALWAY Frederick 1889

Section 32
HOPKINS Martha V 1896
HOPKINS Martha V 1896
JEFCOAT David 1884
TODD William F 1895
CHISHOLM Hugh 1901
GRAVES Green M 1896
TODD William F 1895
GRAVES Green M 1896
GRAVES Green M 1896
TODD William F 1895
HILL William M 1896

Section 33
BYNUM [7] Benjamin 1841
GRAVES Elijah 1859
POWELL James W 1859
HILL Caleb A 1884
ELLZEY Bennett M 1859
BRUCE Simpson 1882
ELLZEY Bennett M 1854

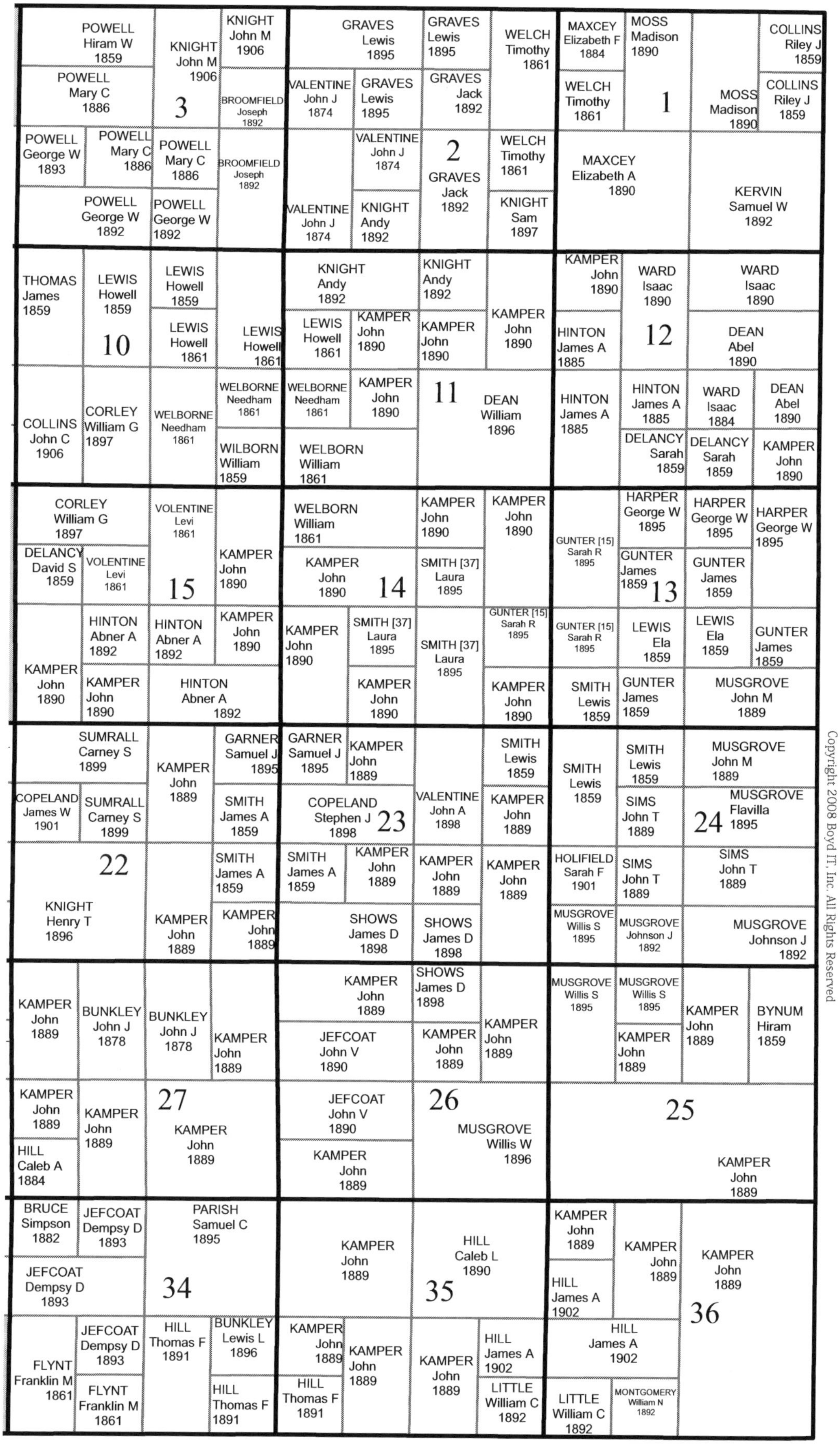

Section 3 / 1 area (top row)

POWELL Hiram W 1859
POWELL Mary C 1886
KNIGHT John M 1906
3
KNIGHT John M 1906
BROOMFIELD Joseph 1892
GRAVES Lewis 1895
VALENTINE John J 1874
GRAVES Lewis 1895
GRAVES Lewis 1895
GRAVES Jack 1892
WELCH Timothy 1861
MAXCEY Elizabeth F 1884
WELCH Timothy 1861
1
MOSS Madison 1890
MOSS Madison 1890
COLLINS Riley J 1859
COLLINS Riley J 1859

POWELL George W 1893
POWELL Mary C 1886
POWELL Mary C 1886
POWELL George W 1892
BROOMFIELD Joseph 1892
POWELL George W 1892
VALENTINE John J 1874
VALENTINE John J 1874
KNIGHT Andy 1892
2
GRAVES Jack 1892
GRAVES Jack 1892
WELCH Timothy 1861
KNIGHT Sam 1897
MAXCEY Elizabeth A 1890
KERVIN Samuel W 1892

Sections 10 / 11 / 12

THOMAS James 1859
LEWIS Howell 1859
LEWIS Howell 1859
LEWIS Howell 1861
LEWIS Howell 1861
10
LEWIS Howell 1861
KNIGHT Andy 1892
LEWIS Howell 1861
KAMPER John 1890
KNIGHT Andy 1892
KAMPER John 1890
KAMPER John 1890
KAMPER John 1890
WARD Isaac 1890
12
WARD Isaac 1890
HINTON James A 1885
DEAN Abel 1890

COLLINS John C 1906
CORLEY William G 1897
WELBORNE Needham 1861
WELBORNE Needham 1861
WILBORN William 1859
WELBORNE Needham 1861
WELBORN William 1861
KAMPER John 1890
11
DEAN William 1896
HINTON James A 1885
HINTON James A 1885
WARD Isaac 1884
DELANCY Sarah 1859
DEAN Abel 1890
DELANCY Sarah 1859
KAMPER John 1890

Sections 15 / 14 / 13

CORLEY William G 1897
VOLENTINE Levi 1861
DELANCY David S 1859
VOLENTINE Levi 1861
KAMPER John 1890
15
WELBORN William 1861
KAMPER John 1890
KAMPER John 1890
KAMPER John 1890
SMITH [37] Laura 1895
HARPER George W 1895
GUNTER [15] Sarah R 1895
HARPER George W 1895
GUNTER James 1859
13
HARPER George W 1895
GUNTER James 1859

HINTON Abner A 1892
HINTON Abner A 1892
KAMPER John 1890
KAMPER John 1890
KAMPER John 1890
SMITH [37] Laura 1895
SMITH [37] Laura 1895
GUNTER [15] Sarah R 1895
GUNTER [15] Sarah R 1895
LEWIS Ela 1859
LEWIS Ela 1859
GUNTER James 1859

KAMPER John 1890
KAMPER John 1890
HINTON Abner A 1892
KAMPER John 1890
KAMPER John 1890
SMITH Lewis 1859
GUNTER James 1859
MUSGROVE John M 1889

Sections 22 / 23 / 24

SUMRALL Carney S 1899
KAMPER John 1889
GARNER Samuel J 1895
GARNER Samuel J 1895
KAMPER John 1889
SMITH Lewis 1859
SMITH Lewis 1859
SMITH Lewis 1859
MUSGROVE John M 1889

COPELAND James W 1901
SUMRALL Carney S 1899
SMITH James A 1859
COPELAND Stephen J 1898
23
VALENTINE John A 1898
KAMPER John 1889
SMITH Lewis 1859
SIMS John T 1889
MUSGROVE Flavilla 1895
24

22
SMITH James A 1859
KAMPER John 1889
SMITH James A 1859
KAMPER John 1889
KAMPER John 1889
KAMPER John 1889
HOLIFIELD Sarah F 1901
SIMS John T 1889
SIMS John T 1889

KNIGHT Henry T 1896
KAMPER John 1889
KAMPER John 1889
SHOWS James D 1898
SHOWS James D 1898
MUSGROVE Willis S 1895
MUSGROVE Johnson J 1892
MUSGROVE Johnson J 1892

Sections 27 / 26 / 25

KAMPER John 1889
BUNKLEY John J 1878
BUNKLEY John J 1878
KAMPER John 1889
KAMPER John 1889
SHOWS James D 1898
KAMPER John 1889
MUSGROVE Willis S 1895
MUSGROVE Willis S 1895
KAMPER John 1889
BYNUM Hiram 1859

JEFCOAT John V 1890
KAMPER John 1889
KAMPER John 1889

KAMPER John 1889
KAMPER John 1889
27
KAMPER John 1889
JEFCOAT John V 1890
26
MUSGROVE Willis W 1896
25

HILL Caleb A 1884
KAMPER John 1889
KAMPER John 1889
KAMPER John 1889

Sections 34 / 35 / 36

BRUCE Simpson 1882
JEFCOAT Dempsy D 1893
PARISH Samuel C 1895
KAMPER John 1889
KAMPER John 1889
HILL Caleb L 1890
KAMPER John 1889
KAMPER John 1889
KAMPER John 1889

JEFCOAT Dempsy D 1893
34
35
HILL James A 1902
36

FLYNT Franklin M 1861
JEFCOAT Dempsy D 1893
HILL Thomas F 1891
BUNKLEY Lewis L 1896
KAMPER John 1889
KAMPER John 1889
KAMPER John 1889
HILL James A 1902
HILL James A 1902

FLYNT Franklin M 1861
FLYNT Franklin M 1861
HILL Thomas F 1891
HILL Thomas F 1891
HILL James A 1902
LITTLE William C 1892
LITTLE William C 1892
MONTGOMERY William N 1892

Helpful Hints

1. This Map's INDEX can be found on the preceding pages.

2. Refer to Map "C" to see where this Township lies within Jones County, Mississippi.

3. Numbers within square brackets [ ] denote a multi-patentee land parcel (multi-owner). Refer to Appendix "C" for a full list of members in this group.

4. Areas that look to be crowded with Patentees usually indicate multiple sales of the same parcel (Re-issues) or Overlapping parcels. See this Township's Index for an explanation of these and other circumstances that might explain "odd" groupings of Patentees on this map.

Legend

— Patent Boundary
— Section Boundary
No Patents Found (or Outside County)
1., 2., 3., ... Lot Numbers (when beside a name)
[ ] Group Number (see Appendix "C")

Scale: Section = 1 mile X 1 mile (generally, with some exceptions)

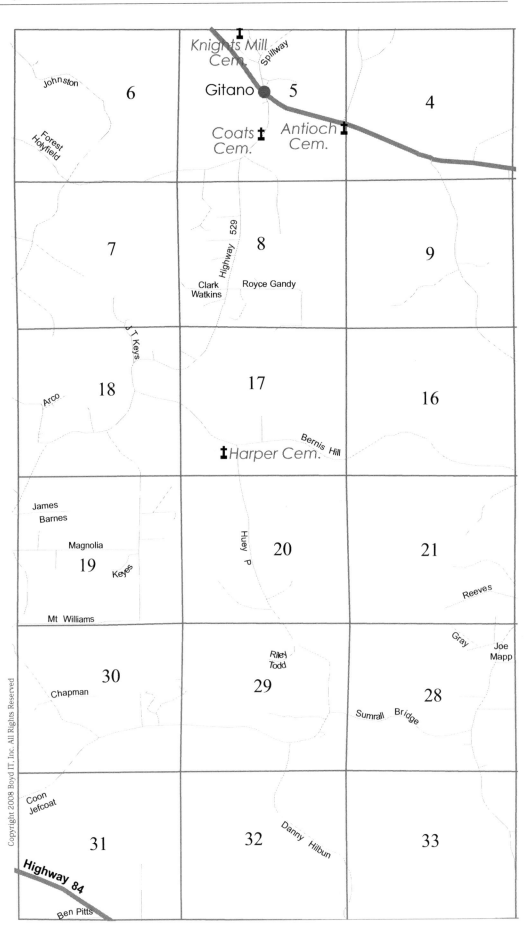

Road Map

T9-N R13-W
St Stephens Meridian

Map Group 7

Cities & Towns
Amy
Gitano
Soso

Cemeteries
Antioch Cemetery
Coats Cemetery
Harper Cemetery
Hill Cemetery
Knights Mill Cemetery

Knights Mill Cem.

Spillway

Johnston

6

Gitano

5

4

Coats Cem.

Antioch Cem.

Forest Holyfield

7

Highway 529

8

9

Clark Watkins

Royce Gandy

J T Keys

18

17

16

Arco

Bernis Hill

Harper Cem.

James Barnes

Magnolia

Huey P

20

21

19

Keyes

Reeves

Mt Williams

Gray

Joe Mapp

Riley Todd

30

29

28

Chapman

Sumrall Bridge

Coon Jefcoat

31

32

Danny Hilbun

33

Highway 84

Ben Pitts

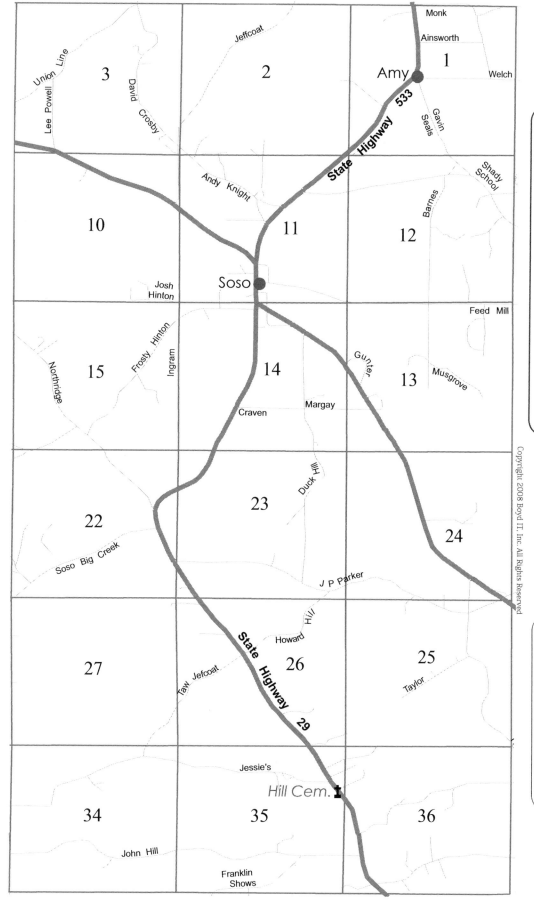

3

Union Line

Lee Powell

David Crosby

Jeffcoat

2

Monk

Ainsworth

Amy

1

Welch

State Highway 533

Gavin

Seals

Shady School

10

Andy Knight

11

Barnes

12

Soso

Josh Hinton

Feed Mill

15

Northridge

Frosty Hinton

Ingram

14

Gunter

Musgrove

13

Craven

Margay

22

Soso Big Creek

23

Duck Hill

24

J P Parker

27

Taw Jefcoat

State Highway 29

Howard

Hill

26

Taylor

25

34

John Hill

Jessie's

Hill Cem.

35

Franklin Shows

36

Helpful Hints

1. This road map has a number of uses, but primarily it is to help you: a) find the present location of land owned by your ancestors (at least the general area), b) find cemeteries and city-centers, and c) estimate the route/roads used by Census-takers & tax-assessors.

2. If you plan to travel to Jones County to locate cemeteries or land parcels, please pick up a modern travel map for the area before you do. Mapping old land parcels on modern maps is not as exact a science as you might think. Just the slightest variations in public land survey coordinates, estimates of parcel boundaries, or road-map deviations can greatly alter a map's representation of how a road either does or doesn't cross a particular parcel of land.

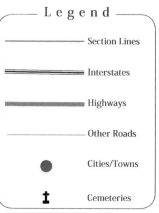

Legend

———————— Section Lines

═══════════ Interstates

━━━━━━━━━ Highways

———————— Other Roads

● Cities/Towns

✝ Cemeteries

Scale: Section = 1 mile X 1 mile
(generally, with some exceptions)

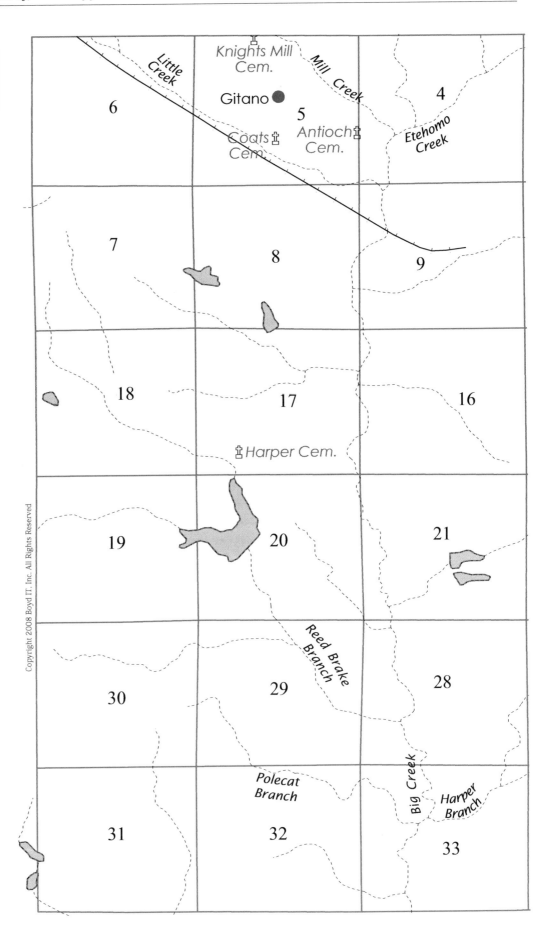

Historical Map

T9-N R13-W
St Stephens Meridian

Map Group 7

Cities & Towns

Amy
Gitano
Soso

Cemeteries

Antioch Cemetery
Coats Cemetery
Harper Cemetery
Hill Cemetery
Knights Mill Cemetery

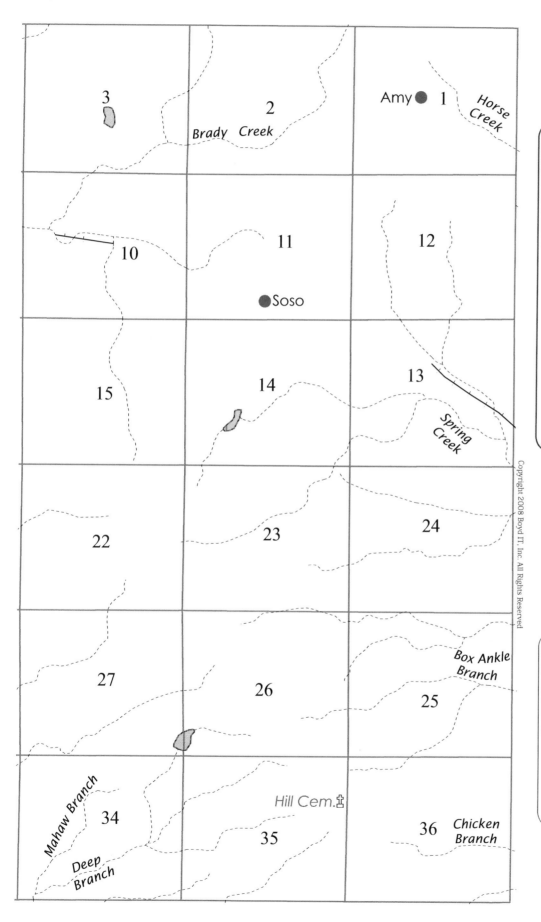

3

2

Brady Creek

Amy ● 1

Horse Creek

10

11

12

● Soso

15

14

13

Spring Creek

22

23

24

27

26

Box Ankle Branch

25

Mahaw Branch

34

Hill Cem. ✝

35

36

Chicken Branch

Deep Branch

Helpful Hints

1. This Map takes a different look at the same Congressional Township displayed in the preceding two maps. It presents features that can help you better envision the historical development of the area: a) Water-bodies (lakes & ponds), b) Water-courses (rivers, streams, etc.), c) Railroads, d) City/town center-points (where they were oftentimes located when first settled), and e) Cemeteries.

2. Using this "Historical" map in tandem with this Township's Patent Map and Road Map, may lead you to some interesting discoveries. You will often find roads, towns, cemeteries, and waterways are named after nearby landowners: sometimes those names will be the ones you are researching. See how many of these research gems you can find here in Jones County.

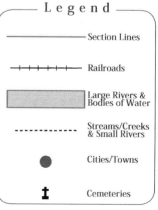

L e g e n d

————————	Section Lines
+++++++	Railroads
▨	Large Rivers & Bodies of Water
- - - - - -	Streams/Creeks & Small Rivers
●	Cities/Towns
✝	Cemeteries

Scale: Section = 1 mile X 1 mile
(there are some exceptions)

Map Group 8: Index to Land Patents

Township 9-North Range 12-West (St Stephens)

After you locate an individual in this Index, take note of the Section and Section Part then proceed to the Land Patent map on the pages immediately following. You should have no difficulty locating the corresponding parcel of land.

The "For More Info" Column will lead you to more information about the underlying Patents. See the *Legend* at right, and the "How to Use this Book" chapter, for more information.

```
                    LEGEND
            "For More Info . . . " column

A = Authority (Legislative Act, See Appendix "A")
B = Block or Lot (location in Section unknown)
C = Cancelled Patent
F = Fractional Section
G = Group  (Multi-Patentee Patent, see Appendix "C")
V = Overlaps another Parcel
R = Re-Issued (Parcel patented more than once)

(A & G items require you to look in the Appendixes referred
to above. All other Letter-designations followed by a number
require you to locate line-items in this index that possess
the ID number found after the letter).
```

ID	Individual in Patent	Sec.	Sec. Part	Date Issued	Other Counties	For More Info . . .
1074	AGEE, Henry	28	NESE	1899-05-12		A2
1075	BLACKLIDGE, Henry H	13	N½SE	1892-04-16		A2
1076	" "	13	SWNE	1892-04-16		A2
1077	" "	13	SWSE	1892-04-16		A2
1102	BOWDEN, Jesse M	26	E½NW	1859-05-02		A2
1103	" "	26	NESW	1859-05-02		A2
1104	" "	26	SWNW	1859-05-02		A2
1267	BRYANT, William C	25	NENW	1902-07-03		A3
1268	" "	25	W½NW	1902-07-03		A3
1085	BUSH, James H	13	E½NE	1889-01-05		A3
1092	BUSH, James M	13	SWSW	1895-11-11		A3
1093	" "	14	E½SE	1895-11-11		A3
1094	" "	14	NWSE	1895-11-11		A3
1209	BUSH, Leacy	25	E½NE	1889-01-12		A3 G46
1222	BUSH, Mason	25	SENW	1859-05-02		A2
1240	BUSH, Rosier	20	SESW	1901-03-23		A3
1048	BYNUM, Benjamin	33	N½SW	1859-05-02		A2
1049	" "	33	NWSE	1859-05-02		A2
1050	" "	33	S½NW	1859-05-02		A2
1051	" "	33	SESW	1859-05-02		A2
1052	" "	33	SWNE	1859-05-02		A2
1071	BYNUM, Gustavus A	33	SWSW	1891-05-20		A3
1078	BYNUM, Hiram	30	N½NW	1859-05-02		A2
1079	BYNUM, Hiram G	15	E½SW	1861-05-01		A2
1080	" "	15	NWSW	1861-05-01		A2
1081	" "	15	SWSE	1861-05-01		A2
1218	BYNUM, Mark	4	E½SE	1859-05-02		A2
1219	" "	4	SENE	1859-05-02		A2
1245	BYNUM, Tapley	33	E½SE	1859-05-02		A2
1082	CLARK, James	23	NESE	1859-06-01		A2
1083	" "	24	E½SW	1859-06-01		A2
1223	CLARK, Matilda	6	E½NW	1895-11-11		A3
1224	" "	6	NWNE	1895-11-11		A3
1225	" "	6	SWNW	1895-11-11		A3
1235	CLARK, Ransom	17	NESE	1895-10-09		A3
1236	" "	17	S½NE	1895-10-09		A3
1241	CLARK, Samuel J	24	NWSW	1859-05-02		A2
1056	COLLINS, Clay C	31	E½NE	1884-12-30		A3
1057	" "	32	W½NW	1884-12-30		A3
1100	COLLINS, Jasper J	23	SESW	1859-05-02		A2
1096	" "	22	NESE	1859-11-10		A2
1097	" "	22	SENE	1859-11-10		A2
1098	" "	23	N½SW	1859-11-10		A2
1099	" "	23	S½NW	1859-11-10		A2
1229	COLLINS, Newton W	33	SWSE	1885-05-25		A3
1237	COLLINS, Riley J	6	NWNW	1859-05-02		A2

ID	Individual in Patent	Sec.	Sec. Part	Date Issued	Other Counties	For More Info . . .
1244	COLLINS, Stacy	29	NWNE	1841-01-05		A2
1254	COLLINS, Vincent A	30	E½SE	1859-05-02		A2
1255	" "	30	NWSE	1859-05-02		A2
1256	" "	30	SENE	1859-05-02		A2
1257	" "	30	SWSE	1859-05-02		A2
1258	" "	31	NENW	1859-05-02		A2
1259	" "	31	NWNE	1859-05-02		A2
1260	" "	31	NWNW	1859-05-02		A2
1206	CRAFT, Julia A	11	E½NE	1891-08-19		A3
1207	" "	11	NESE	1891-08-19		A3
1208	" "	12	SWNW	1891-08-19		A3
1230	CRAFT, Noah R	12	E½NW	1892-06-15		A3
1231	" "	12	N½SW	1892-06-15		A3
1032	DAVIS, Abel	30	NENE	1859-05-02		A2
1033	" "	30	NESW	1859-05-02		A2
1030	" "	20	N½SW	1860-07-02		A2
1031	" "	20	SWSW	1860-07-02		A2
1035	DAVIS, Abel M	19	NWSE	1860-07-02		A2
1036	" "	19	S½SE	1860-07-02		A2
1042	DAVIS, Alfred	19	E½SW	1859-05-02		A2
1034	DEAN, Abel	7	NWSW	1890-02-21		A3
1107	DRENNAN, John B	21	S½NW	1890-08-16		A3
1108	" "	21	W½NE	1890-08-16		A3
1210	EASLEY, Loranza F	13	SESE	1892-04-29		A3
1059	FLYNT, David J	26	W½SW	1891-06-30		A3
1060	" "	35	W½NW	1891-06-30		A3
1061	GRAFTON, David W	35	NWSW	1917-04-19		A2 R1215
1043	GUNTER, Allen	30	NWSW	1859-06-01		A2
1105	HAMILTON, Jesse M	1	NWSE	1892-07-25		A3
1106	" "	1	W½NE	1892-07-25		A3
1115	HAMILTON, John J	1	NW	1884-12-30		A3
1114	" "	1	NESE	1886-07-20		A2
1284	HARPER, William T	29	NESW	1892-06-30		A3
1285	" "	29	W½SW	1892-06-30		A3
1214	HERINGTON, Madison	34	NWSE	1860-07-02		A2
1215	" "	35	NWSW	1860-07-02		A2 R1061
1101	HERRINGTON, Jefferson T	23	NENE	1884-12-30		A2
1216	HERRINGTON, Madison	34	E½SE	1859-05-02		A2
1040	HOLIFIELD, Albert E	5	E½SW	1900-11-28		A3
1041	" "	5	SWSE	1900-11-28		A3
1044	HOLIFIELD, Andrew A	5	NENW	1901-04-09		A2
1045	" "	5	SWNW	1901-04-09		A2
1064	HOLIFIELD, Frederick	36	NESW	1859-11-10		A2
1065	" "	36	SENW	1859-11-10		A2
1066	" "	36	SWSW	1859-11-10		A2
1095	HOLIFIELD, James M	11	N½NW	1889-01-12		A3
1118	HOLIFIELD, John J	9	SESW	1890-06-25		A3
1119	" "	9	SWSE	1890-06-25		A3
1116	" "	9	NESW	1892-08-20		A3
1117	" "	9	SENW	1892-08-20		A3
1195	HOLIFIELD, John M	15	SWSW	1902-02-12		A3
1200	HOLIFIELD, Jonathan	12	SESE	1892-05-26		A3
1201	" "	12	SESW	1892-05-26		A3
1202	" "	12	W½SE	1892-05-26		A3
1228	HOLIFIELD, Moses	2	S½SW	1889-01-05		A3
1263	HOLIFIELD, Warren W	9	SWNW	1898-03-15		A3
1264	" "	9	W½SW	1898-03-15		A3
1067	HOLYFIELD, Frederick	36	NWSW	1860-07-02		A2
1068	" "	36	SWNW	1860-07-02		A2
1112	HOLYFIELD, John	10	NENE	1860-07-02		A2
1113	" "	3	SESE	1860-07-02		A2
1273	HOLYFIELD, William	10	NESE	1897-08-09		A2
1274	" "	10	SENE	1897-08-09		A2
1275	" "	11	NWSW	1897-08-09		A2
1276	" "	11	SWNW	1897-08-09		A2
1238	HOPKINS, Robert J	4	NENW	1892-07-25		A3
1239	" "	4	NWNE	1892-07-25		A3
1277	INGRAIM, William	24	SENE	1890-04-22		A2
1261	INGRAM, Warren	24	E½NW	1890-09-26		A3
1262	" "	24	W½NE	1890-09-26		A3
1084	JACKSON, James F	6	SW	1885-05-25		A3
1086	JACKSON, James L	6	E½NE	1892-07-20		A3
1087	" "	6	NWSE	1892-07-20		A3

ID	Individual in Patent	Sec.	Sec. Part	Date Issued	Other Counties	For More Info . . .
1088	JACKSON, James L (Cont'd)	6	SWNE	1892-07-20		A3
1251	JACKSON, Thomas M	18	NENE	1894-02-28		A3
1252	" "	7	N½SE	1894-02-28		A3
1253	" "	7	SESE	1894-02-28		A3
1279	JACKSON, William M	7	NENW	1885-05-25		A3
1280	" "	7	S½NW	1885-05-25		A3
1281	" "	7	SWNE	1885-05-25		A3
1282	JACKSON, William R	5	W½SW	1890-03-28		A3
1283	" "	6	E½SE	1890-03-28		A3
1198	JOHNSON, John T	12	NWNW	1908-02-13		A2
1286	JOHNSON, William T	11	S½SE	1890-08-16		A3
1287	" "	12	SWSW	1890-08-16		A3
1288	" "	14	NENE	1890-08-16		A3
1161	KAMPER, John	25	E½SW	1887-05-27		A2
1162	" "	25	SE	1887-05-27		A2
1189	" "	36	NENW	1887-05-27		A2 G21
1190	" "	36	NWNE	1887-05-27		A2 G21
1191	" "	36	SENE	1887-05-27		A2 G21
1192	" "	36	SESE	1887-05-27		A2 G21
1122	" "	12	NESE	1889-04-09		A2
1123	" "	12	S½NE	1889-04-09		A2
1124	" "	13	N½NW	1889-04-09		A2
1125	" "	13	NWNE	1889-04-09		A2
1126	" "	13	SENW	1889-04-09		A2
1127	" "	13	SESW	1889-04-09		A2
1157	" "	24	N½SE	1889-04-09		A2
1158	" "	24	NENE	1889-04-09		A2
1159	" "	24	SWSE	1889-04-09		A2
1160	" "	24	W½NW	1889-04-09		A2
1135	" "	18	E½NW	1889-04-10		A2
1137	" "	18	SENE	1889-04-10		A2
1138	" "	18	W½NE	1889-04-10		A2
1128	" "	14	NENW	1889-05-06		A2
1129	" "	14	NWNE	1889-05-06		A2
1132	" "	17	SW	1889-05-06		A2
1136	" "	18	E½SE	1889-05-06		A2
1139	" "	20	NENW	1889-05-06		A2
1140	" "	20	W½NE	1889-05-06		A2
1155	" "	23	SENE	1889-05-06		A2
1164	" "	27		1889-05-06		A2
1166	" "	28	NENW	1889-05-06		A2
1179	" "	34	SENE	1889-05-06		A2
1130	" "	17	NENW	1889-11-21		A2
1131	" "	17	NWNE	1889-11-21		A2
1133	" "	17	SWSE	1889-11-21		A2
1134	" "	17	W½NW	1889-11-21		A2
1142	" "	21	N½NW	1889-11-21		A2
1143	" "	21	NENE	1889-11-21		A2
1146	" "	22	NENW	1889-11-21		A2
1147	" "	22	NESW	1889-11-21		A2
1149	" "	22	SESE	1889-11-21		A2
1156	" "	23	SWSW	1889-11-21		A2
1163	" "	26	NWNW	1889-11-21		A2
1165	" "	28	E½NE	1889-11-21		A2
1167	" "	28	SWSW	1889-11-21		A2
1168	" "	29	SESW	1889-11-21		A2
1170	" "	31	NESE	1889-11-21		A2
1172	" "	31	SW	1889-11-21		A2
1174	" "	31	W½SE	1889-11-21		A2
1175	" "	32	E½NW	1889-11-21		A2
1176	" "	32	S½SE	1889-11-21		A2
1177	" "	32	SWSW	1889-11-21		A2
1178	" "	33	NWNW	1889-11-21		A2
1120	" "	1	E½NE	1889-11-29		A2
1121	" "	11	SENW	1889-11-29		A2
1145	" "	21	SE	1889-11-29		A2
1148	" "	22	SENW	1889-11-29		A2
1150	" "	22	SESW	1889-11-29		A2
1151	" "	22	W½NE	1889-11-29		A2
1152	" "	22	W½NW	1889-11-29		A2
1153	" "	22	W½SE	1889-11-29		A2
1154	" "	22	W½SW	1889-11-29		A2
1169	" "	30	S½SW	1889-11-29		A2

ID	Individual in Patent	Sec.	Sec. Part	Date Issued	Other Counties	For More Info . . .
1180	KAMPER, John (Cont'd)	7	E½NE	1889-11-29		A2
1181	" "	7	NESW	1889-11-29		A2
1182	" "	7	S½SW	1889-11-29		A2
1183	" "	7	SWSE	1889-11-29		A2
1184	" "	8	NENE	1889-11-29		A2
1185	" "	8	W½	1889-11-29		A2
1186	" "	8	W½NE	1889-11-29		A2
1187	" "	8	W½SE	1889-11-29		A2
1188	" "	9	NWNW	1889-11-29		A2
1141	" "	21	E½SW	1890-07-03		A2
1144	" "	21	NWSW	1890-07-03		A2
1171	" "	31	S½NW	1890-07-03		A2
1173	" "	31	SWNE	1890-07-03		A2
1203	KING, Joseph S	36	N½SE	1897-05-12		A2
1204	" "	36	SESW	1897-05-12		A2
1205	" "	36	SWSE	1897-05-12		A2
1037	LARD, Abraham	18	E½SW	1897-08-09		A2
1038	" "	18	NWSW	1897-08-09		A2
1039	" "	18	SWNW	1897-08-09		A2
1193	LOVE, John	11	NWNE	1885-12-19		A3
1194	" "	2	SWSE	1885-12-19		A3
1070	LOWE, George W	1	SW	1889-01-12		A3
1246	LOWE, Thomas J	11	E½SW	1890-03-28		A3
1247	" "	11	NWSE	1890-03-28		A3
1248	" "	11	SWNE	1890-03-28		A3
1054	LYON, Cisero E	2	E½NW	1889-01-12		A3
1055	" "	2	W½NE	1889-01-12		A3
1226	LYON, Matilda	2	NESW	1890-06-25		A3
1227	" "	2	NWSE	1890-06-25		A3
1265	LYON, William A	2	NWSW	1859-05-02		A2
1266	" "	2	W½NW	1859-05-02		A2
1220	MAGEE, Mary	26	SESW	1859-11-10		A2
1278	MATHEWS, William L	5	SWNE	1907-05-13		A3
1046	MATTHEWS, Benajah	4	W½NW	1897-08-09		A2
1047	" "	5	E½NE	1897-08-09		A2
1221	MCGEE, Mary	35	E½NW	1859-05-02		A2
1296	MORRELL, Wilson B	1	S½SE	1906-06-16		A3
1297	" "	12	N½NE	1906-06-16		A3
1196	MOSS, John	14	SENW	1859-05-02		A2
1197	" "	14	SWNE	1859-05-02		A2
1199	MUSGROVE, Johnson J	19	SWSW	1892-03-23		A3
1211	MUSGROVE, Luke J	17	NENE	1895-06-28		A3
1212	" "	8	E½SE	1895-06-28		A3
1213	" "	8	SENE	1895-06-28		A3
1242	OWENS, Seaborn P	32	E½SW	1859-05-02		A2
1243	" "	32	NWSW	1859-05-02		A2
1289	PARISH, William T	29	S½SE	1894-03-15		A2
1290	" "	32	N½NE	1894-03-15		A2
1109	RIVERS, John C	13	N½SW	1892-04-29		A3
1110	" "	13	SWNW	1892-04-29		A3
1111	" "	14	SENE	1892-04-29		A3
1189	SCOTT, Edward	36	NENW	1887-05-27		A2 G21
1190	" "	36	NWNE	1887-05-27		A2 G21
1191	" "	36	SENE	1887-05-27		A2 G21
1192	" "	36	SESE	1887-05-27		A2 G21
1062	SHELBY, Ellis	6	SWSE	1911-01-05		A3
1063	" "	7	NWNE	1911-01-05		A3
1234	SHELBY, Polly	7	NWNW	1910-09-01		A3
1089	SHOWS, James L	34	NENE	1889-01-12		A3
1090	" "	34	NENW	1889-01-12		A3
1091	" "	34	W½NE	1889-01-12		A3
1069	SPEED, George	18	NWNW	1904-12-31		A3
1072	SUMRALL, Harmon L	19	NESE	1860-07-02		A2
1073	" "	19	NWSW	1860-07-02		A2
1294	SUMRALL, William W	32	N½SE	1892-07-20		A3
1295	" "	32	S½NE	1892-07-20		A3
1058	VALENTINE, Columbus M	28	W½NE	1897-06-07		A3
1209	WALTERS, Leacy	25	E½NE	1889-01-12		A3 G46
1217	WALTERS, Marion	24	SESE	1894-12-17		A3
1232	WELBORN, Norvell P	2	E½NE	1896-07-11		A3
1233	" "	2	E½SE	1896-07-11		A3
1249	WELBORN, Thomas J	29	SENW	1860-04-02		A2
1250	" "	29	SWNE	1860-04-02		A2

ID	Individual in Patent	Sec.	Sec. Part	Date Issued	Other Counties	For More Info . . .
1291	WELBORN, William T	10	SESE	1859-05-02		A2
1292	" "	11	SWSW	1859-05-02		A2
1293	" "	14	NWNW	1859-05-02		A2
1053	WELCH, Catherine	5	NWNE	1859-11-10		A2
1269	WILBORN, William E	4	NESW	1861-04-01		A2
1270	" "	4	NWSE	1861-04-01		A2
1271	" "	4	SENW	1861-04-01		A2
1272	" "	4	SWNE	1861-04-01		A2

Patent Map

T9-N R12-W
St Stephens Meridian

Map Group 8

Township Statistics

Parcels Mapped	:	268
Number of Patents	:	123
Number of Individuals	:	99
Patentees Identified	:	98
Number of Surnames	:	53
Multi-Patentee Parcels	:	5
Oldest Patent Date	:	1/5/1841
Most Recent Patent	:	4/19/1917
Block/Lot Parcels	:	0
Parcels Re - Issued	:	1
Parcels that Overlap	:	0
Cities and Towns	:	4
Cemeteries	:	5

Section 6
COLLINS Riley J 1859
CLARK Matilda 1895
CLARK Matilda 1895
CLARK Matilda 1895
JACKSON James L 1892
JACKSON James L 1892
JACKSON James L 1892
JACKSON James F 1885
SHELBY Ellis 1911
JACKSON William R 1890

Section 5
HOLIFIELD Andrew A 1901
HOLIFIELD Andrew A 1901
WELCH Catherine 1859
MATHEWS William L 1907
MATTHEWS Benajah 1897
JACKSON William R 1890
JACKSON William R 1890
HOLIFIELD Albert E 1900
HOLIFIELD Albert E 1900

Section 4
MATTHEWS Benajah 1897
HOPKINS Robert J 1892
HOPKINS Robert J 1892
WILBORN William E 1861
WILBORN William E 1861
BYNUM Mark 1859
WILBORN William E 1861
WILBORN William E 1861
BYNUM Mark 1859

Section 7
SHELBY Polly 1910
JACKSON William M 1885
SHELBY Ellis 1911
JACKSON William M 1885
JACKSON William M 1885
KAMPER John 1889
DEAN Abel 1890
KAMPER John 1889
JACKSON Thomas M 1894
KAMPER John 1889
KAMPER John 1889
JACKSON Thomas M 1894

Section 8
KAMPER John 1889
KAMPER John 1889
KAMPER John 1889
MUSGROVE Luke J 1895
KAMPER John 1889
KAMPER John 1889
MUSGROVE Luke J 1895

Section 9
HOLIFIELD Warren W 1898
HOLIFIELD John J 1892
HOLIFIELD Warren W 1898
HOLIFIELD John J 1892
HOLIFIELD John J 1890
HOLIFIELD John J 1890

Section 18
SPEED George 1904
LARD Abraham 1897
KAMPER John 1889
KAMPER John 1889
JACKSON Thomas M 1894
KAMPER John 1889
LARD Abraham 1897
LARD Abraham 1897
KAMPER John 1889

Section 17
KAMPER John 1889
KAMPER John 1889
KAMPER John 1889
CLARK Ransom 1895
CLARK Ransom 1895
KAMPER John 1889
MUSGROVE Luke J 1895

Section 16

Section 19
SUMRALL Harmon L 1860
DAVIS Abel M 1860
SUMRALL Harmon L 1860
DAVIS Alfred 1859
MUSGROVE Johnson J 1892
DAVIS Abel M 1860

Section 20
KAMPER John 1889
KAMPER John 1889
DAVIS Abel 1860
DAVIS Abel 1860
BUSH Rosier 1901

Section 21
KAMPER John 1889
DRENNAN John B 1890
KAMPER John 1889
DRENNAN John B 1890
KAMPER John 1890
KAMPER John 1890
KAMPER John 1889

Section 30
BYNUM Hiram 1859
DAVIS Abel 1859
COLLINS Vincent A 1859
GUNTER Allen 1859
DAVIS Abel 1859
COLLINS Vincent A 1859
KAMPER John 1889
COLLINS Vincent A 1859

Section 29
COLLINS Stacy 1841
WELBORN Thomas J 1860
WELBORN Thomas J 1860
HARPER William T 1892
HARPER William T 1892
KAMPER John 1889
PARISH William T 1894
PARISH William T 1894

Section 28
KAMPER John 1889
VALENTINE Columbus M 1897
KAMPER John 1889
AGEE Henry 1899
KAMPER John 1889

Section 31
COLLINS Vincent A 1859
COLLINS Vincent A 1859
COLLINS Vincent A 1859
KAMPER John 1890
KAMPER John 1890
COLLINS Clay C 1884
KAMPER John 1889
KAMPER John 1889

Section 32
COLLINS Clay C 1884
KAMPER John 1889
OWENS Seaborn P 1859
OWENS Seaborn P 1859
KAMPER John 1889

Section 33
PARISH William T 1894
SUMRALL William W 1892
SUMRALL William W 1892
BYNUM Benjamin 1859
BYNUM Benjamin 1859
BYNUM Benjamin 1859
BYNUM Benjamin 1859
KAMPER John 1889
BYNUM Gustavus A 1891
BYNUM Benjamin 1859
COLLINS Newton W 1885
BYNUM Tapley 1859

Section 3

3

Section 2

LYON William A 1859

2

LYON Cisero E 1889

LYON Cisero E 1889

WELBORN Norvell P 1896

LYON William A 1859

LYON Matilda 1890

LYON Matilda 1890

WELBORN Norvell P 1896

HOLYFIELD John 1860

HOLIFIELD Moses 1889

LOVE John 1885

Section 1

HAMILTON John J 1884

1

HAMILTON Jesse M 1892

KAMPER John 1889

HAMILTON Jesse M 1892

HAMILTON John J 1886

LOWE George W 1889

MORRELL Wilson B 1906

Section 10

HOLYFIELD John 1860

HOLYFIELD William 1897

HOLIFIELD William 1897

HOLIFIELD William 1897

10

WELBORN William T 1859

Section 11

HOLIFIELD James M 1889

HOLYFIELD William 1897

KAMPER John 1889

LOWE Thomas J 1890

11

LOWE Thomas J 1890

WELBORN William T 1859

LOVE John 1885

CRAFT Julia A 1891

LOWE Thomas J 1890

CRAFT Julia A 1891

JOHNSON William T 1890

Section 12

JOHNSON John T 1908

CRAFT Julia A 1891

CRAFT Noah R 1892

CRAFT Noah R 1892

JOHNSON William T 1890

MORRELL Wilson B 1906

12

HOLIFIELD Jonathan 1892

HOLIFIELD Jonathan 1892

KAMPER John 1889

KAMPER John 1889

HOLIFIELD Jonathan 1892

Section 15

15

BYNUM Hiram G 1861

HOLIFIELD John M 1902

BYNUM Hiram G 1861

BYNUM Hiram G 1861

Section 14

WELBORN William T 1859

KAMPER John 1889

KAMPER John 1889

JOHNSON William T 1890

MOSS John 1859

MOSS John 1859

RIVERS John C 1892

14

BUSH James M 1895

BUSH James M 1895

Section 13

KAMPER John 1889

RIVERS John C 1892

KAMPER John 1889

BUSH James H 1889

KAMPER John 1889

BLACKLIDGE Henry H 1892

RIVERS John C 1892

BLACKLIDGE Henry H 1892

13

BUSH James M 1895

KAMPER John 1889

BLACKLIDGE Henry H 1892

EASLEY Loranza F 1892

Section 22

KAMPER John 1889

KAMPER John 1889

KAMPER John 1889

KAMPER John 1889

22

KAMPER John 1889

KAMPER John 1889

KAMPER John 1889

KAMPER John 1889

KAMPER John 1889

COLLINS Jasper J 1859

COLLINS Jasper J 1859

COLLINS Jasper J 1859

KAMPER John 1889

Section 23

COLLINS Jasper J 1859

23

COLLINS Jasper J 1859

KAMPER John 1889

COLLINS Jasper J 1859

HERRINGTON Jefferson T 1884

KAMPER John 1889

KAMPER John 1889

CLARK James 1859

Section 24

KAMPER John 1889

INGRAM Warren 1890

INGRAM Warren 1890

KAMPER John 1889

INGRAIM William 1890

CLARK Samuel J 1859

CLARK James 1859

24

KAMPER John 1889

KAMPER John 1889

WALTERS Marion 1894

Section 27

KAMPER John 1889

27

Section 26

KAMPER John 1889

BOWDEN Jesse M 1859

BOWDEN Jesse M 1859

26

BOWDEN Jesse M 1859

FLYNT David J 1891

MAGEE Mary 1859

Section 25

BRYANT William C 1902

BRYANT William C 1902

WALTERS [46] Leacy 1889

BUSH Mason 1859

25

KAMPER John 1887

KAMPER John 1887

Section 34

SHOWS James L 1889

SHOWS James L 1889

SHOWS James L 1889

34

KAMPER John 1889

HERINGTON Madison 1860

Section 35

FLYNT David J 1891

MCGEE Mary 1859

GRAFTON David W 1917

HERINGTON Madison 1860

HERRINGTON Madison 1859

35

Section 36

KAMPER [21] John 1887

KAMPER [21] John 1887

HOLYFIELD Frederick 1860

HOLIFIELD Frederick 1859

KAMPER [21] John 1887

HOLYFIELD Frederick 1860

HOLIFIELD Frederick 1859

KING Joseph S 1897

36

HOLIFIELD Frederick 1859

KING Joseph S 1897

KING Joseph S 1897

KAMPER [21] John 1887

Helpful Hints

1. This Map's INDEX can be found on the preceding pages.

2. Refer to Map "C" to see where this Township lies within Jones County, Mississippi.

3. Numbers within square brackets [ ] denote a multi-patentee land parcel (multi-owner). Refer to Appendix "C" for a full list of members in this group.

4. Areas that look to be crowded with Patentees usually indicate multiple sales of the same parcel (Re-issues) or Overlapping parcels. See this Township's Index for an explanation of these and other circumstances that might explain "odd" groupings of Patentees on this map.

Legend

———————— Patent Boundary

———————— Section Boundary

No Patents Found (or Outside County)

1., 2., 3., ... Lot Numbers (when beside a name)

[ ] Group Number (see Appendix "C")

Scale: Section = 1 mile X 1 mile (generally, with some exceptions)

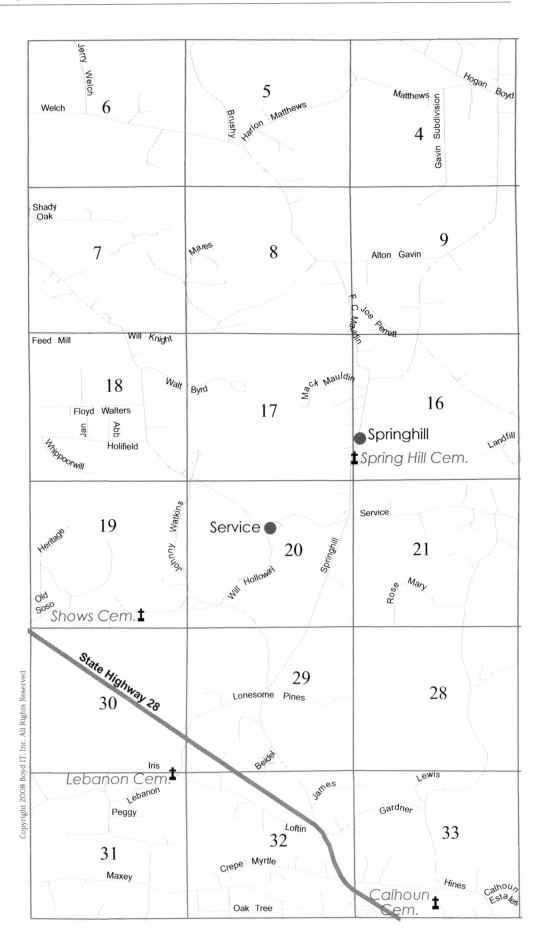

Road Map

T9-N R12-W
St Stephens Meridian

Map Group 8

Cities & Towns

Flynt
Service
Shady Grove
Springhill

Cemeteries

Calhoun Cemetery
Lebanon Cemetery
Shady Grove Cemetery
Shows Cemetery
Spring Hill Cemetery

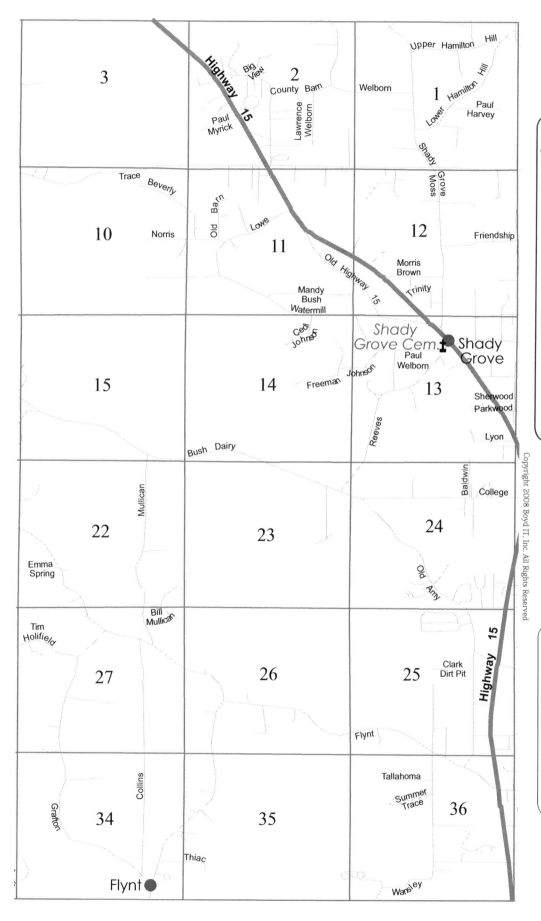

3

Highway 15

Big View

2

County Barn

Paul Myrick

Lawrence Welborn

Welborn

Upper Hamilton Hill

Lower Hamilton Hill

1

Paul Harvey

Shady Grove

Trace

Beverly

Old Barn

Lowe

Norris

10

11

12

Moss

Friendship

Old Highway 15

Mandy Bush Watermill

Morris Brown

Trinity

Ceal Johnson

Shady Grove Cem.

Paul Welborn

Shady Grove

15

Johnson

14

Freeman

13

Sherwood

Parkwood

Reeves

Lyon

Bush   Dairy

Mullican

Baldwin

College

22

23

24

Emma Spring

Old Amy

Bill Mullican

Tim Holifield

27

26

25

Clark Dirt Pit

Highway 15

Flynt

Collins

Tallahoma

34

35

Summer Trace

36

Grafton

Thiac

Flynt

Wareley

Helpful Hints

1. This road map has a number of uses, but primarily it is to help you: a) find the present location of land owned by your ancestors (at least the general area), b) find cemeteries and city-centers, and c) estimate the route/roads used by Census-takers & tax-assessors.

2. If you plan to travel to Jones County to locate cemeteries or land parcels, please pick up a modern travel map for the area before you do. Mapping old land parcels on modern maps is not as exact a science as you might think. Just the slightest variations in public land survey coordinates, estimates of parcel boundaries, or road-map deviations can greatly alter a map's representation of how a road either does or doesn't cross a particular parcel of land.

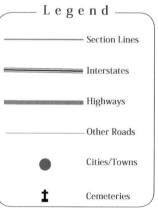

Legend

———	Section Lines
═══	Interstates
▬▬▬	Highways
———	Other Roads
●	Cities/Towns
✝	Cemeteries

Scale: Section = 1 mile X 1 mile
(generally, with some exceptions)

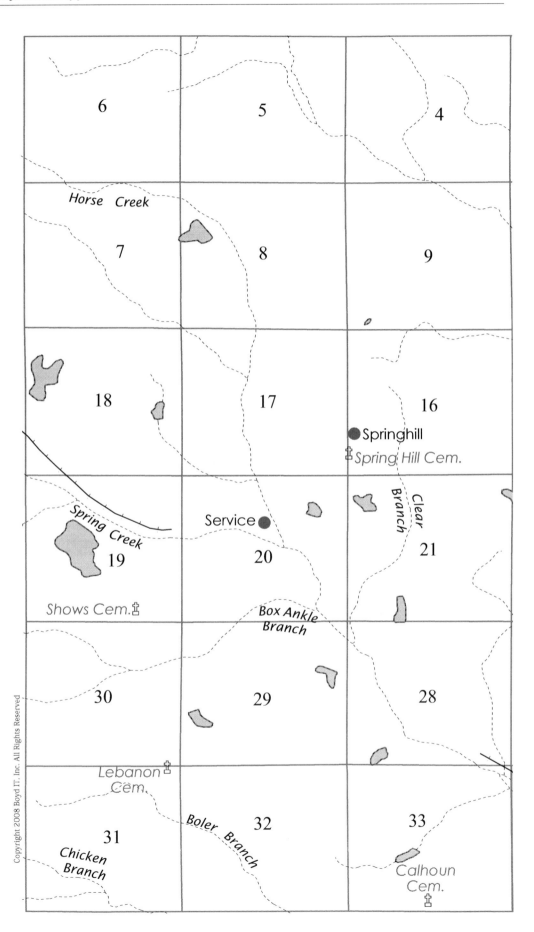

Historical Map

T9-N R12-W
St Stephens Meridian

Map Group 8

Cities & Towns
Flynt
Service
Shady Grove
Springhill

Cemeteries
Calhoun Cemetery
Lebanon Cemetery
Shady Grove Cemetery
Shows Cemetery
Spring Hill Cemetery

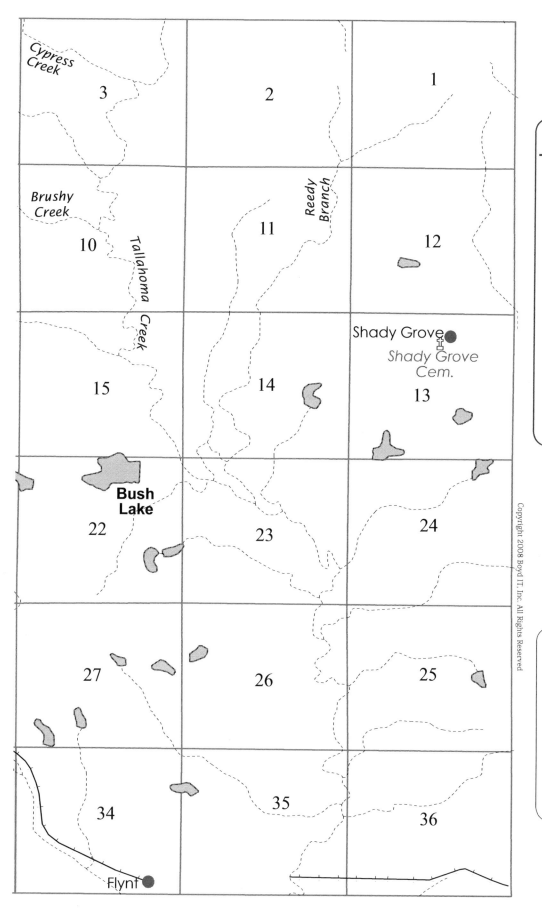

3 Cypress Creek

2

1

Brushy Creek

10

Tallahoma Creek

11

Reedy Branch

12

15

14

Shady Grove

Shady Grove Cem.

13

Bush Lake

22

23

24

27

26

25

34

35

36

Flynt

Helpful Hints

1. This Map takes a different look at the same Congressional Township displayed in the preceding two maps. It presents features that can help you better envision the historical development of the area: a) Water-bodies (lakes & ponds), b) Water-courses (rivers, streams, etc.), c) Railroads, d) City/town center-points (where they were oftentimes located when first settled), and e) Cemeteries.

2. Using this "Historical" map in tandem with this Township's Patent Map and Road Map, may lead you to some interesting discoveries. You will often find roads, towns, cemeteries, and waterways are named after nearby landowners: sometimes those names will be the ones you are researching. See how many of these research gems you can find here in Jones County.

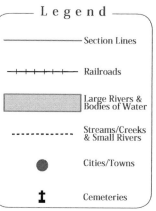

Legend

———————— Section Lines

+—+—+—+—+ Railroads

� Large Rivers & Bodies of Water

- - - - - - Streams/Creeks & Small Rivers

● Cities/Towns

♱ Cemeteries

Scale: Section = 1 mile X 1 mile
(there are some exceptions)

Map Group 9: Index to Land Patents

Township 9-North Range 11-West (St Stephens)

After you locate an individual in this Index, take note of the Section and Section Part then proceed to the Land Patent map on the pages immediately following. You should have no difficulty locating the corresponding parcel of land.

The "For More Info" Column will lead you to more information about the underlying Patents. See the *Legend* at right, and the "How to Use this Book" chapter, for more information.

LEGEND
"For More Info . . . " column

A – Authority (Legislative Act, See Appendix "A")
B = Block or Lot (location in Section unknown)
C = Cancelled Patent
F = Fractional Section
G = Group (Multi-Patentee Patent, see Appendix "C")
V = Overlaps another Parcel
R = Re-Issued (Parcel patented more than once)

(A & G items require you to look in the Appendixes referred to above. All other Letter-designations followed by a number require you to locate line-items in this index that possess the ID number found after the letter).

ID	Individual in Patent	Sec.	Sec. Part	Date Issued	Other Counties	For More Info . . .
1556	ANDREWS, William	12	SESE	1859-05-02		A2
1557	" "	13	NENE	1859-05-02		A2
1359	BELL, Frank	25	S½SW	1896-04-28		A3
1360	" "	36	N½NW	1896-04-28		A3
1369	BONNER, George W	34	N½SW	1892-08-01		A2
1370	" "	34	SESW	1892-08-01		A2
1371	" "	34	SWSE	1892-08-01		A2
1398	BONNER, James J	29	NWSW	1888-12-29		A2
1399	" "	29	SWNW	1888-12-29		A2
1400	" "	30	NESE	1888-12-29		A2
1401	" "	30	SENE	1888-12-29		A2
1472	BRASHIER, John W	21	SESW	1884-08-20		A2
1473	" "	21	SWSE	1884-08-20		A2
1389	BRIDGES, Isaac	13	S½SE	1888-04-05		A3
1390	" "	24	E½NE	1888-04-05		A3
1477	BRIDGES, Joseph	24	E½SW	1892-06-15		A3
1478	" "	24	NWSE	1892-06-15		A3
1479	" "	24	SWNE	1892-06-15		A3
1547	BRYANT, Thomas C	9	NESW	1861-05-01		A2
1548	" "	9	NWSE	1861-05-01		A2
1549	" "	9	SWNE	1861-05-01		A2
1397	BUSH, James H	18	W½NW	1889-01-05		A3
1408	BUSH, Jefferson J	30	NWSE	1890-08-16		A3
1409	" "	30	SWNE	1890-08-16		A3
1410	BUSH, Jesse M	19	S½SE	1890-02-21		A3
1411	" "	30	N½NE	1890-02-21		A3
1489	BUSH, Leacy	30	W½NW	1889-01-12		A3 G46
1560	COMPANY, William F Evans And	31		1882-05-10		A2
1561	" "	32	N½SW	1882-05-10		A2
1562	" "	32	NW	1882-05-10		A2
1319	COOPER, Benjamin R	8	E½SW	1893-08-14		A3
1320	" "	8	NWSE	1893-08-14		A3
1419	COPELAND, John	25	N½SW	1892-06-15		A3
1420	" "	25	S½NW	1892-06-15		A3
1316	CORLEY, Balaam	3	NESW	1859-11-10		A2
1317	" "	3	W½SE	1859-11-10		A2
1361	CORLEY, Franklin P	10	NWNW	1861-05-01		A2
1362	" "	3	SESW	1861-05-01		A2
1363	" "	3	W½SW	1861-05-01		A2
1528	CREEL, Reuben	32	S½SW	1859-05-02		A2
1364	CROSBY, George	22	SENW	1897-05-07		A3
1365	" "	22	SWNE	1897-05-07		A3
1340	CRUMBY, Daniel C	24	SWNW	1885-05-09		A2
1337	" "	13	SESW	1888-04-05		A3
1338	" "	24	E½NW	1888-04-05		A3
1339	" "	24	NWNE	1888-04-05		A3

ID	Individual in Patent	Sec.	Sec. Part	Date Issued	Other Counties	For More Info . . .
1519	CRUMBY, Peter M	23	N½SE	1892-03-23		A3
1520	" "	23	SWSE	1892-03-23		A3
1521	" "	26	NWNE	1892-03-23		A3
1391	DEARMAN, Isaac W	18	NENE	1894-04-14		A3
1392	" "	7	NWSE	1894-04-14		A3
1393	" "	7	S½SE	1894-04-14		A3
1490	EASLEY, Loranza F	18	W½SW	1892-04-29		A3
1491	" "	19	NWNW	1892-04-29		A3
1328	FALER, Charley	24	S½SE	1892-06-15		A3
1329	" "	25	N½NE	1892-06-15		A3
1385	FERGUSON, Henry	13	N½SW	1888-02-25		A3
1386	" "	13	S½NW	1888-02-25		A3
1525	FERGUSON, Prince	13	SWSW	1892-06-30		A3
1526	" "	23	N½NE	1892-06-30		A3
1527	" "	24	NWNW	1892-06-30		A3
1563	FERGUSON, William	13	NWSE	1895-06-27		A3
1564	" "	13	W½NE	1895-06-27		A3
1531	FERRILL, Richard S	32	NWSE	1906-06-30		A2
1533	FERRILL, Samuel E	26	E½NE	1892-06-15		A3
1534	" "	26	E½SE	1892-06-15		A3
1554	GEIGER, Wesly W	9	SESW	1894-07-24		A3
1555	" "	9	SWSE	1894-07-24		A3
1366	GORE, George	24	W½SW	1892-03-23		A3
1367	" "	25	N½NW	1892-03-23		A3
1407	GRAY, James W	29	NWNE	1897-02-15		A3
1394	HAFTER, Jacob	1	NWSW	1862-04-10		A2
1395	" "	2	NESE	1862-04-10		A2
1485	HAYS, June	18	E½SE	1894-02-10		A2
1486	" "	18	SESW	1894-02-10		A2
1487	" "	18	SWSE	1894-02-10		A2
1558	HINTON, William C	13	NESE	1895-06-28		A3
1559	" "	13	SENE	1895-06-28		A3
1423	HOLIFIELD, John	9	W½SW	1859-05-02		A2
1421	" "	8	SENE	1859-11-10		A2
1422	" "	8	SWSE	1859-11-10		A2
1483	HOLIFIELD, Joshua	19	E½NE	1888-04-05		A3
1484	" "	20	W½NW	1888-04-05		A3
1507	HOLIFIELD, Moses	20	NWSE	1854-05-01		A2
1508	" "	20	SWNE	1854-05-01		A2
1509	" "	8	NW	1861-05-01		A2
1572	HOLIFIELD, William R	17	E½NW	1894-12-17		A3
1573	" "	17	NESW	1894-12-17		A3
1476	HOLYFIELD, Jonathan	9	E½NW	1859-05-02		A2 V1466
1510	HOLYFIELD, Moses	17	NESE	1859-05-02		A2
1511	" "	17	SENE	1859-05-02		A2
1512	" "	17	W½NE	1859-05-02		A2
1372	HOWARD, George W	34	NESE	1894-09-18		A2
1373	" "	34	SENE	1894-09-18		A2
1374	" "	35	NWSW	1894-09-18		A2
1375	" "	35	SWNW	1894-09-18		A2
1569	INGRAIM, William	19	NWSW	1890-04-22		A2
1570	" "	19	S½NW	1890-04-22		A2
1298	JOHNSON, Abner	10	N½SW	1861-05-01		A2
1305	JOHNSON, Alfred	10	SWNW	1861-05-01		A2
1306	" "	9	E½NE	1861-05-01		A2
1396	JOHNSON, Jacob	15	NW	1859-11-10		A2
1299	JOHNSTON, Abner	9	E½SE	1859-05-02		A2 V1465
1517	JONES, Peter	23	S½SW	1901-08-12		A3
1518	" "	26	NWNW	1901-08-12		A3
1442	KAMPER, John	30	E½NW	1887-05-27		A2
1443	" "	30	NWSW	1887-05-27		A2
1424	" "	18	NENW	1889-04-10		A2
1425	" "	18	NWNE	1889-04-10		A2
1426	" "	18	SENE	1889-04-10		A2
1427	" "	19	NENW	1889-04-10		A2
1428	" "	19	NWSE	1889-04-10		A2
1456	" "	36	SWSW	1889-04-10		A2
1462	" "	7	W½	1889-04-10		A2
1458	" "	6	N½NE	1889-04-20		A2
1459	" "	6	NENW	1889-04-20		A2
1460	" "	6	S½	1889-04-20		A2
1461	" "	6	W½NW	1889-04-20		A2
1437	" "	27	E½NW	1889-04-23		A2

ID	Individual in Patent	Sec.	Sec. Part	Date Issued	Other Counties	For More Info . . .
1438	KAMPER, John (Cont'd)	27	E½SW	1889-04-23		A2
1439	" "	27	SWNE	1889-04-23		A2
1440	" "	28	E½NE	1889-04-23		A2
1441	" "	28	E½SE	1889-04-23		A2
1444	" "	33	E½NE	1889-04-23		A2
1445	" "	33	NWNE	1889-04-23		A2
1446	" "	33	SESE	1889-04-23		A2
1447	" "	34	NWSE	1889-04-23		A2
1448	" "	34	SESE	1889-04-23		A2
1449	" "	34	W½NE	1889-04-23		A2
1450	" "	35	NESW	1889-04-23		A2
1451	" "	35	SENW	1889-04-23		A2
1452	" "	35	SESE	1889-04-23		A2
1453	" "	35	SWSW	1889-04-23		A2
1429	" "	22	E½SE	1889-11-29		A2
1430	" "	22	E½SW	1889-11-29		A2
1431	" "	22	SWNW	1889-11-29		A2
1432	" "	23	S½NE	1889-11-29		A2
1433	" "	23	SESE	1889-11-29		A2
1434	" "	25	W½SE	1889-11-29		A2
1435	" "	26	N½SW	1889-11-29		A2
1436	" "	26	NWSE	1889-11-29		A2
1454	" "	36	N½SE	1889-11-29		A2
1455	" "	36	NE	1889-11-29		A2
1457	" "	5	NESW	1889-11-29		A2
1463	" "	8	NWSW	1889-11-29		A2
1464	" "	8	SWNE	1889-11-29		A2
1465	" "	9	NESE	1889-11-29		A2 V1299
1466	" "	9	SENW	1889-11-29		A2 V1476
1404	KEETON, James	22	N½NE	1859-05-02		A2
1402	" "	15	NESW	1859-06-01		A2
1403	" "	15	W½SW	1859-06-01		A2
1550	KEETON, Thomas J	15	SESE	1859-11-10		A2
1303	KNIGHT, Albert	4	E½SW	1861-05-01		A2
1304	" "	4	N½SE	1861-05-01		A2
1343	MCARTHUR, Daniel	22	W½SE	1862-04-10		A2
1344	" "	27	N½NE	1862-04-10		A2
1357	MCCRAW, Edwin H	7	NE	1861-07-01		A2
1537	MCGEE, Seaborn	5	NWSE	1859-11-10		A2
1538	MCGEE, Seborn	4	E½NW	1861-05-01		A2
1539	" "	4	W½NE	1861-05-01		A2
1388	MCLAURIN, Hugh N	14	SE	1897-09-09		A3
1513	MILLSAP, Moses	24	NESE	1897-09-09		A3
1376	NELSON, George W	35	NESE	1894-02-10		A2
1377	" "	35	SWNE	1894-02-10		A2
1378	" "	35	W½SE	1894-02-10		A2
1467	NELSON, John	36	N½SW	1892-06-15		A3
1468	" "	36	S½NW	1892-06-15		A3
1565	NELSON, William H	36	SESW	1892-06-15		A3
1566	" "	36	SWSE	1892-06-15		A3
1551	NEWELL, Thomas	27	N½SE	1895-07-18		A2
1542	NEWSOM, Solomon	26	SWSW	1861-05-01		A2 C R1535
1543	" "	35	E½NE	1861-05-01		A2 C R1544
1545	" "	35	NWNE	1861-05-01		A2 C R1546
1541	" "	26	SWSE	1894-11-15		A2
1544	" "	35	E½NE	1894-11-15		A2 R1543
1546	" "	35	NWNE	1894-11-15		A2 R1545
1318	PAGE, Ben	26	NENW	1898-08-27		A3
1368	PARROT, George	12	SWSE	1890-02-21		A3
1326	PATTERSON, Charles	23	N½SW	1898-05-16		A3
1327	" "	23	SENW	1898-05-16		A3
1552	PRESCOTT, Thomas	4	E½NE	1896-12-14		A3
1406	REAVES, James	30	E½SW	1859-11-10		A2
1492	RIVERS, Luke	6	S½NE	1862-04-10		A2
1493	" "	6	SENW	1862-04-10		A2
1503	RIVERS, Mark	5	NWNW	1859-11-10		A2
1504	RIVERS, Mary S	5	SESE	1892-04-29		A3
1505	" "	5	SWNW	1892-04-29		A3
1506	" "	5	W½SW	1892-04-29		A3
1480	RUNNELLS, Joseph	20	SESE	1890-08-16		A3
1481	" "	21	W½SW	1890-08-16		A3
1482	" "	28	NWNW	1890-08-16		A3
1307	RUSHTON, Andrew	26	S½NW	1891-06-30		A3

ID	Individual in Patent	Sec.	Sec. Part	Date Issued	Other Counties	For More Info . . .
1308	RUSHTON, Andrew (Cont'd)	26	SWNE	1891-06-30		A3
1309	" "	27	SENE	1891-06-30		A3
1516	RUSHTON, Obulus E	25	SWNE	1889-04-23		A2
1514	" "	25	NESE	1897-05-07		A3
1515	" "	25	SENE	1897-05-07		A3
1529	SAUL, Richard M	12	E½NE	1861-07-01		A2
1530	" "	12	N½SE	1861-07-01		A2
1567	SINGELTARY, William H	12	E½NW	1862-04-10		A2
1568	" "	12	W½NE	1862-04-10		A2
1300	SMITH, Albert B	26	SESW	1891-03-16		A3
1301	" "	34	NENE	1891-03-16		A3
1302	" "	35	N½NW	1891-03-16		A3
1310	SMITH, Andy	14	NWNE	1898-11-11		A3
1311	SMITH, Angus E	13	N½NW	1895-05-11		A3
1312	" "	14	E½NE	1895-05-11		A3
1313	SMITH, Annie M	1	SESW	1882-08-03		A2
1321	SMITH, Berry	18	NESW	1889-01-12		A3
1322	" "	18	NWSE	1889-01-12		A3
1323	" "	18	SENW	1889-01-12		A3
1324	" "	18	SWNE	1889-01-12		A3
1330	SMITH, Chester B	11	SESE	1890-04-22		A2
1331	" "	12	E½SW	1890-04-22		A2
1332	" "	12	SWSW	1890-04-22		A2
1335	SMITH, D P	21	E½SE	1879-05-06		A3
1336	" "	22	W½SW	1879-05-06		A3
1348	SMITH, Daniel	2	E½NE	1841-01-05		A2
1345	" "	1	NESW	1874-11-05		A2
1346	" "	1	SWNE	1874-11-05		A2
1347	" "	1	W½SE	1874-11-05		A2
1341	SMITH, Daniel C	1	W½NW	1859-05-02		A2
1342	SMITH, Daniel F	15	E½NE	1874-04-10		A3
1354	SMITH, Edward H	14	N½SW	1861-05-01		A2
1355	" "	14	SENW	1861-05-01		A2
1356	" "	14	SWNE	1861-05-01		A2
1379	SMITH, H C	11	SENE	1879-05-06		A3
1380	" "	12	NWSW	1879-05-06		A3
1381	" "	12	W½NW	1879-05-06		A3
1470	SMITH, John	11	NESE	1841-01-05		A2
1471	" "	11	W½SE	1841-01-05		A2
1413	SMITH, John C	10	NWSE	1854-03-15		A2
1414	" "	10	SESE	1854-03-15		A2
1415	" "	15	SESW	1854-03-15		A2
1412	" "	10	E½NW	1859-05-02		A2
1416	" "	22	SENE	1897-09-09		A3
1417	" "	23	NENW	1897-09-09		A3
1418	" "	23	W½NW	1897-09-09		A3
1488	SMITH, Laurence	27	S½SE	1895-06-22		A2
1494	SMITH, Malcolm	5	S½SE	1897-08-09		A2
1495	" "	8	N½NE	1897-08-09		A2
1496	SMITH, Malcom C	1	E½NW	1878-06-24		A3
1497	" "	1	NWNE	1896-07-11		A3
1498	SMITH, Malcom F	1	SWSW	1859-05-02		A2
1499	" "	2	SESE	1859-05-02		A2
1500	SMITH, Malcom H	14	S½SW	1901-03-23		A3
1535	SMITH, Sarah	26	SWSW	1906-05-01		A3 R1542
1571	SMITH, William J	5	NENW	1902-04-08		A3
1349	SUMRALL, Drury	21	N½NE	1859-05-02		A2
1350	" "	21	N½NW	1859-05-02		A2
1351	" "	21	NESW	1859-05-02		A2
1352	" "	21	SENW	1859-05-02		A2
1353	" "	21	SWNE	1859-05-02		A2
1314	TEMPLES, Asa R	4	S½SE	1892-06-15		A3
1315	" "	9	NWNE	1892-06-15		A3
1522	TEMPLES, Pinckney M	19	NESE	1892-03-07		A3
1523	" "	20	W½SW	1892-03-07		A3
1524	" "	29	NWNW	1892-03-07		A3
1574	TEMPLES, William	3	NW	1859-11-10		A2
1536	THOMPSON, Sarah	19	W½NE	1895-06-22		A2
1469	TOUCHSTONE, John P	36	SESE	1895-12-14		A3
1474	VOLKING, John W	27	W½NW	1892-06-06		A2
1475	" "	27	W½SW	1892-06-06		A2
1405	WALLACE, James N	1	E½SE	1873-09-20		A3
1325	WALTERS, Charles C	34	NW	1895-09-05		A2

ID	Individual in Patent	Sec.	Sec. Part	Date Issued	Other Counties	For More Info . . .
1333	WALTERS, Collins W	29	SWSW	1888-04-05		A3
1334	" "	30	S½SE	1888-04-05		A3
1382	WALTERS, Henry B	20	E½SW	1859-05-02		A2
1383	" "	33	N½SE	1859-05-02		A2
1384	" "	33	SWNE	1859-05-02		A2
1489	WALTERS, Leacy	30	W½NW	1889-01-12		A3 G46
1501	WALTERS, Marion	19	NESW	1894-12-17		A3
1502	" "	19	S½SW	1894-12-17		A3
1532	WALTERS, Robert	32	NENE	1859-11-10		A2
1358	WATTERS, Elisha	32	S½SE	1860-04-10		A2
1553	WELCH, Timothy L	33	SWSE	1885-05-25		A3
1540	WEST, Shannon R	34	SWSW	1892-08-01		A2
1387	WILLIS, Henry	29	SWNE	1898-02-24		A3

Patent Map

T9-N R11-W
St Stephens Meridian

Map Group 9

Township Statistics

Parcels Mapped	:	277
Number of Patents	:	140
Number of Individuals	:	115
Patentees Identified	:	114
Number of Surnames	:	65
Multi-Patentee Parcels	:	1
Oldest Patent Date	:	1/5/1841
Most Recent Patent	:	6/30/1906
Block/Lot Parcels	:	0
Parcels Re - Issued	:	3
Parcels that Overlap	:	4
Cities and Towns	:	6
Cemeteries	:	6

Section 6
- KAMPER John 1889
- KAMPER John 1889
- KAMPER John 1889
- RIVERS Luke 1862
- RIVERS Luke 1862
- KAMPER John 1889

Section 5
- RIVERS Mark 1859
- SMITH William J 1902
- RIVERS Mary S 1892
- RIVERS Mary S 1892
- KAMPER John 1889
- MCGEE Seaborn 1859
- RIVERS Mary S 1892
- SMITH Malcolm 1897

Section 4
- MCGEE Seborn 1861
- MCGEE Seborn 1861
- PRESCOTT Thomas 1896
- KNIGHT Albert 1861
- KNIGHT Albert 1861
- TEMPLES Asa R 1892

Section 7
- MCCRAW Edwin H 1861
- DEARMAN Isaac W 1894
- DEARMAN Isaac W 1894
- KAMPER John 1889

Section 8
- HOLIFIELD Moses 1861
- SMITH Malcolm 1897
- KAMPER John 1889
- HOLIFIELD John 1859
- KAMPER John 1889
- COOPER Benjamin R 1893
- COOPER Benjamin R 1893
- HOLIFIELD John 1859

Section 9
- HOLYFIELD Jonathan 1859
- TEMPLES Asa R 1892
- KAMPER John 1889
- BRYANT Thomas C 1861
- JOHNSON Alfred 1861
- HOLIFIELD John 1859
- BRYANT Thomas C 1861
- BRYANT Thomas C 1861
- KAMPER John 1889
- GEIGER Wesly W 1894
- GEIGER Wesly W 1894
- JOHNSTON Abner 1859

Section 18
- BUSH James H 1889
- KAMPER John 1889
- KAMPER John 1889
- DEARMAN Isaac W 1894
- SMITH Berry 1889
- SMITH Berry 1889
- KAMPER John 1889
- EASLEY Loranza F 1892
- SMITH Berry 1889
- SMITH Berry 1889
- HAYS June 1894
- HAYS June 1894
- HAYS June 1894

Section 17
- HOLIFIELD William R 1894
- HOLYFIELD Moses 1859
- HOLYFIELD Moses 1859
- HOLIFIELD William R 1894
- HOLYFIELD Moses 1859

Section 16
- (blank)

Section 19
- EASLEY Loranza F 1892
- KAMPER John 1889
- THOMPSON Sarah 1895
- HOLIFIELD Joshua 1888
- INGRAIM William 1890
- INGRAIM William 1890
- WALTERS Marion 1894
- KAMPER John 1889
- TEMPLES Pinckney M 1892
- WALTERS Marion 1894
- BUSH Jesse M 1890

Section 20
- HOLIFIELD Joshua 1888
- HOLIFIELD Moses 1854
- TEMPLES Pinckney M 1892
- HOLIFIELD Moses 1854
- WALTERS Henry B 1859
- RUNNELLS Joseph 1890

Section 21
- SUMRALL Drury 1859
- SUMRALL Drury 1859
- SUMRALL Drury 1859
- SUMRALL Drury 1859
- SUMRALL Drury 1859
- RUNNELLS Joseph 1890
- BRASHIER John W 1884
- BRASHIER John W 1884
- SMITH D P 1879

Section 30
- WALTERS [46] Leacy 1889
- KAMPER John 1887
- BUSH Jesse M 1890
- BUSH Jefferson J 1890
- BONNER James J 1888
- KAMPER John 1887
- BUSH Jefferson J 1890
- BONNER James J 1888
- REAVES James 1859
- WALTERS Collins W 1888

Section 29
- TEMPLES Pinckney M 1892
- BONNER James J 1888
- GRAY James W 1897
- WILLIS Henry 1898
- WALTERS Collins W 1888

Section 28
- RUNNELLS Joseph 1890
- KAMPER John 1889
- KAMPER John 1889

Section 31
- COMPANY William F Evans And 1882

Section 32
- COMPANY William F Evans And 1882
- WALTERS Robert 1859
- COMPANY William F Evans And 1882
- FERRILL Richard S 1906
- CREEL Reuben 1859
- WATTERS Elisha 1860

Section 33
- KAMPER John 1889
- WALTERS Henry B 1859
- KAMPER John 1889
- WALTERS Henry B 1859
- WELCH Timothy L 1885
- KAMPER John 1889

Section 3
TEMPLES William 1859
3
CORLEY Franklin P 1861
CORLEY Balaam 1859
CORLEY Franklin P 1861
CORLEY Balaam 1859

Section 2
2
SMITH Daniel 1841
HAFTER Jacob 1862
HAFTER Jacob 1862
SMITH Malcom F 1859
SMITH Malcom F 1859

Section 1
SMITH Malcom C 1878
SMITH Malcom C 1896
SMITH Daniel C 1859
1
SMITH Daniel 1874
SMITH Daniel 1874
SMITH Daniel 1874
SMITH Annie M 1882
WALLACE James N 1873

Section 10
CORLEY Franklin P 1861
SMITH John C 1859
JOHNSON Alfred 1861
10
JOHNSON Abner 1861
SMITH John C 1854
SMITH John C 1854

Section 11
11
SMITH H C 1879
SMITH H C 1879
SMITH John 1841
SMITH Chester B 1890

Section 12
SINGELTARY William H 1862
SINGELTARY William H 1862
SAUL Richard M 1861
12
SMITH H C 1879
SAUL Richard M 1861
SMITH Chester B 1890
SMITH Chester B 1890
PARROT George 1890
ANDREWS William 1859

Section 15
JOHNSON Jacob 1859
15
SMITH Daniel F 1874
KEETON James 1859
KEETON James 1859
SMITH John C 1854
KEETON Thomas J 1859

Section 14
SMITH Andy 1898
SMITH Edward H 1861
SMITH Edward H 1861
14
SMITH Edward H 1861
SMITH Malcom H 1901
MCLAURIN Hugh N 1897
SMITH Angus E 1895

Section 13
SMITH Angus E 1895
FERGUSON William 1895
ANDREWS William 1859
FERGUSON Henry 1888
13
HINTON William C 1895
FERGUSON Henry 1888
FERGUSON William 1895
HINTON William C 1895
FERGUSON Prince 1892
CRUMBY Daniel C 1888
BRIDGES Isaac 1888

Section 22
KEETON James 1859
KAMPER John 1889
CROSBY George 1897
CROSBY George 1897
SMITH John C 1897
22
SMITH D P 1879
KAMPER John 1889
MCARTHUR Daniel 1862
KAMPER John 1889

Section 23
SMITH John C 1897
SMITH John C 1897
PATTERSON Charles 1898
23
PATTERSON Charles 1898
JONES Peter 1901
FERGUSON Prince 1892
KAMPER John 1889
CRUMBY Peter M 1892
CRUMBY Peter M 1892

Section 24
FERGUSON Prince 1892
CRUMBY Daniel C 1888
CRUMBY Daniel C 1888
CRUMBY Daniel C 1885
24
GORE George 1892
BRIDGES Joseph 1892
BRIDGES Joseph 1892
BRIDGES Joseph 1892
BRIDGES Isaac 1888
MILLSAP Moses 1897
FALER Charley 1892

Section 27
VOLKING John W 1892
KAMPER John 1889
27
VOLKING John W 1892
KAMPER John 1889
MCARTHUR Daniel 1862
KAMPER John 1889
RUSHTON Andrew 1891
NEWELL Thomas 1895
SMITH Laurence 1895

Section 26
JONES Peter 1901
PAGE Ben 1898
CRUMBY Peter M 1892
RUSHTON Andrew 1891
26
RUSHTON Andrew 1891
FERRILL Samuel E 1892
KAMPER John 1889
KAMPER John 1889
NEWSOM Solomon 1861
SMITH Sarah 1906
SMITH Albert B 1891
NEWSOM Solomon 1894

Section 25
GORE George 1892
GORE George 1892
COPELAND John 1892
25
COPELAND John 1892
FERRILL Samuel E 1892
FALER Charley 1892
RUSHTON Obulus E 1889
RUSHTON Obulus E 1897
RUSHTON Obulus E 1897
KAMPER John 1889
BELL Frank 1896

Section 34
WALTERS Charles C 1895
KAMPER John 1889
SMITH Albert B 1891
34
HOWARD George W 1894
BONNER George W 1892
KAMPER John 1889
HOWARD George W 1894
WEST Shannon R 1892
BONNER George W 1892
BONNER George W 1892
KAMPER John 1889

Section 35
SMITH Albert B 1891
HOWARD George W 1894
KAMPER John 1889
HOWARD George W 1894
KAMPER John 1889
35
KAMPER John 1889
KAMPER John 1889
SMITH Albert B 1891
NELSON George W 1894
NELSON George W 1894
NELSON George W 1894

Section 36
NEWSOM Solomon 1861
NEWSOM Solomon 1894
BELL Frank 1896
NEWSOM Solomon 1861
NEWSOM Solomon 1894
BELL Frank 1896
KAMPER John 1889
NELSON John 1892
36
NELSON John 1892
KAMPER John 1889
KAMPER John 1889
KAMPER John 1889
NELSON William H 1892
NELSON William H 1892
TOUCHSTONE John P 1895

Helpful Hints

1. This Map's INDEX can be found on the preceding pages.

2. Refer to Map "C" to see where this Township lies within Jones County, Mississippi.

3. Numbers within square brackets [ ] denote a multi-patentee land parcel (multi-owner). Refer to Appendix "C" for a full list of members in this group.

4. Areas that look to be crowded with Patentees usually indicate multiple sales of the same parcel (Re-issues) or Overlapping parcels. See this Township's Index for an explanation of these and other circumstances that might explain "odd" groupings of Patentees on this map.

Legend

— Patent Boundary

— Section Boundary

No Patents Found (or Outside County)

1., 2., 3., ... Lot Numbers (when beside a name)

[ ] Group Number (see Appendix "C")

Scale: Section = 1 mile X 1 mile (generally, with some exceptions)

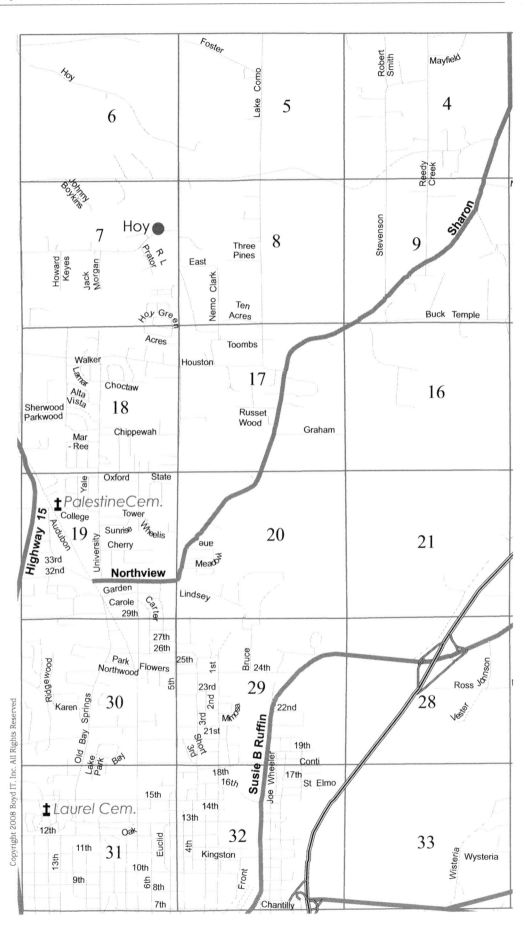

Road Map

T9-N R11-W
St Stephens Meridian

Map Group 9

Cities & Towns

Eastview
Errata
Hawkes
Hoy
Mount Olive
Powers

Cemeteries

Erratta Cemetery
Laurel Cemetery
Memorial Park Cemetery
Mount Olive Cemetery
Nora Davis Memorial Cemetery
Palestine Cemetery

Copyright 2008 Boyd IT, Inc. All Rights Reserved

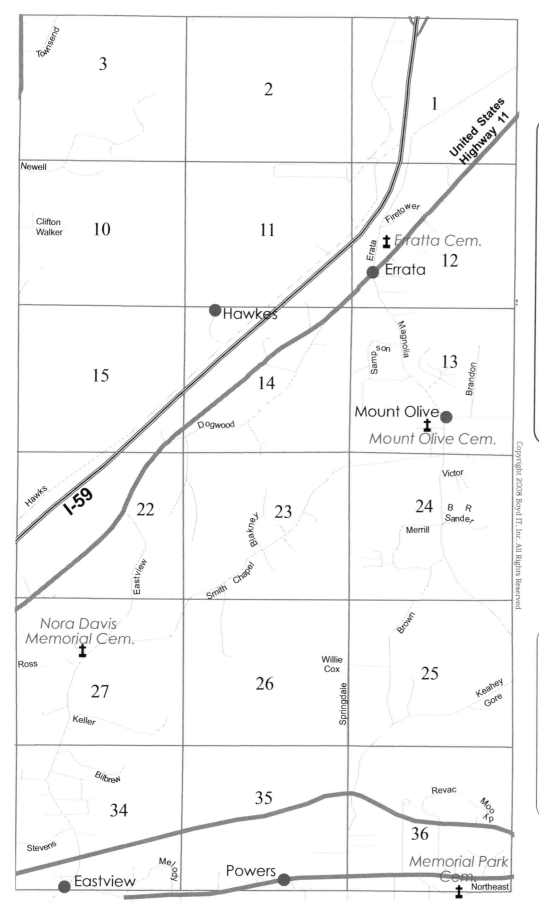

Helpful Hints

1. This road map has a number of uses, but primarily it is to help you: a) find the present location of land owned by your ancestors (at least the general area), b) find cemeteries and city-centers, and c) estimate the route/roads used by Census-takers & tax-assessors.

2. If you plan to travel to Jones County to locate cemeteries or land parcels, please pick up a modern travel map for the area before you do. Mapping old land parcels on modern maps is not as exact a science as you might think. Just the slightest variations in public land survey coordinates, estimates of parcel boundaries, or road-map deviations can greatly alter a map's representation of how a road either does or doesn't cross a particular parcel of land.

Legend

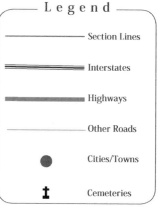

————	Section Lines
══════	Interstates
━━━━━	Highways
‥‥‥‥	Other Roads
●	Cities/Towns
⚰	Cemeteries

Scale: Section = 1 mile X 1 mile
(generally, with some exceptions)

109

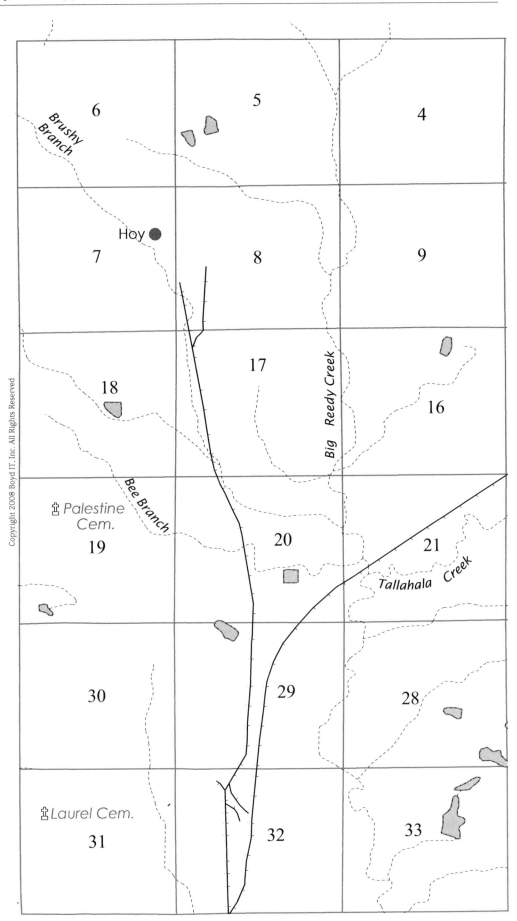

Historical Map

T9-N R11-W
St Stephens Meridian

Map Group 9

Cities & Towns

Eastview
Errata
Hawkes
Hoy
Mount Olive
Powers

Cemeteries

Erratta Cemetery
Laurel Cemetery
Memorial Park Cemetery
Mount Olive Cemetery
Nora Davis Memorial Cemetery
Palestine Cemetery

Copyright 2008 Boyd IT, Inc. All Rights Reserved

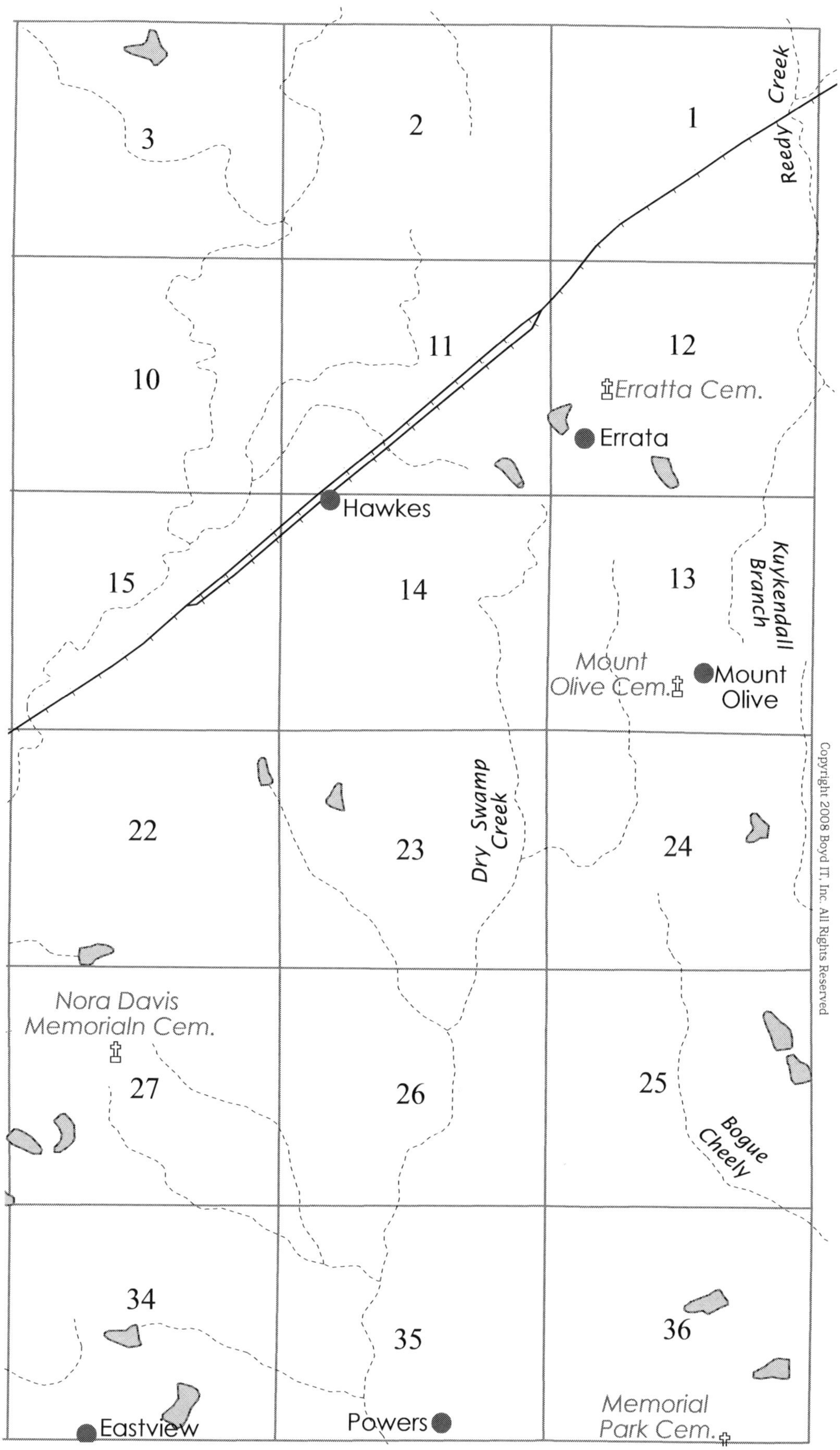
3
2
1
Reedy Creek
10
11
12
Erratta Cem.
Errata
15
Hawkes
14
13
Kuykendall Branch
Mount Olive Cem.
Mount Olive
22
23
Dry Swamp Creek
24
Nora Davis Memorialn Cem.
27
26
25
Bogue Cheely
34
35
36
Eastview
Powers
Memorial Park Cem.

Helpful Hints

1. This Map takes a different look at the same Congressional Township displayed in the preceding two maps. It presents features that can help you better envision the historical development of the area: a) Water-bodies (lakes & ponds), b) Water-courses (rivers, streams, etc.), c) Railroads, d) City/town center-points (where they were oftentimes located when first settled), and e) Cemeteries.
2. Using this "Historical" map in tandem with this Township's Patent Map and Road Map, may lead you to some interesting discoveries. You will often find roads, towns, cemeteries, and waterways are named after nearby landowners: sometimes those names will be the ones you are researching. See how many of these research gems you can find here in Jones County.

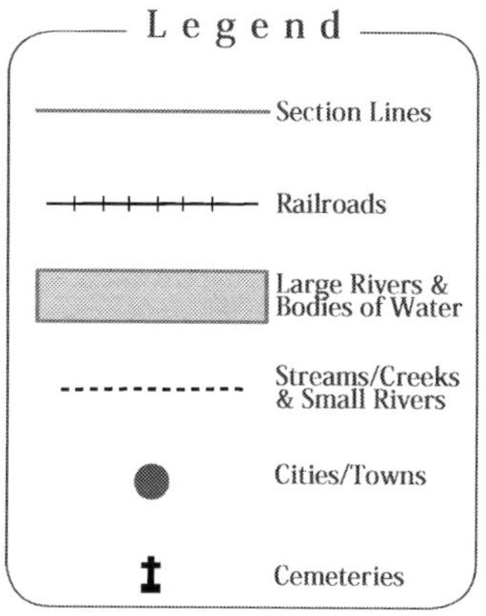
Legend
Section Lines
Railroads
Large Rivers & Bodies of Water
Streams/Creeks & Small Rivers
Cities/Towns
Cemeteries

Scale: Section = 1 mile X 1 mile
(there are some exceptions)

Map Group 10: Index to Land Patents

Township 9-North Range 10-West (St Stephens)

After you locate an individual in this Index, take note of the Section and Section Part then proceed to the Land Patent map on the pages immediately following. You should have no difficulty locating the corresponding parcel of land.

The "For More Info" Column will lead you to more information about the underlying Patents. See the *Legend* at right, and the "How to Use this Book" chapter, for more information.

```
┌─────────────────────────────────────────────────────────┐
│                        LEGEND                            │
│           "For More Info . . . " column                  │
│ ──────────────────────────────────────────────────────  │
│ A = Authority (Legislative Act, See Appendix "A")        │
│ B = Block or Lot (location in Section unknown)           │
│ C = Cancelled Patent                                     │
│ F = Fractional Section                                   │
│ G = Group  (Multi-Patentee Patent, see Appendix "C")     │
│ V = Overlaps another Parcel                              │
│ R = Re-Issued (Parcel patented more than once)           │
│                                                          │
│ (A & G items require you to look in the Appendixes       │
│ referred to above. All other Letter-designations         │
│ followed by a number require you to locate line-items    │
│ in this index that possess the ID number found after     │
│ the letter).                                             │
└─────────────────────────────────────────────────────────┘
```

ID	Individual in Patent	Sec.	Sec. Part	Date Issued	Other Counties	For More Info . . .
1789	ANDREWS, William	18	W½NW	1859-05-02		A2
1788	" "	18	E½SW	1859-11-10		A2
1790	"	7	SWSW	1859-11-10		A2
1600	ARRINGTON, Arther	17	E½SE	1846-09-01		A2
1715	BARKLEY, Moses H	29	E½SE	1859-11-10		A2
1716	" "	29	NE	1859-11-10		A2
1717	" "	29	NWSE	1859-11-10		A2
1718	" "	3	SENE	1859-11-10		A2
1735	BARKLY, Samuel M	1	NWNW	1901-03-23		A3
1665	BLACKLEDGE, James R	14	SESW	1901-12-04		A3
1700	BLACKLEDGE, Joseph J	1	NENW	1860-04-02		A2
1701	" "	1	NWNE	1860-04-02		A2
1794	BLACKLEDGE, William	11	NESW	1859-05-02		A2
1660	BLACKLIDGE, James G	13	SWNW	1888-07-24		A3
1661	" "	14	SENE	1888-07-24		A3
1667	BLACKLIDGE, Jesse C	27	NWNE	1897-06-07		A3
1668	" "	27	S½NE	1897-06-07		A3
1674	BLACKLIDGE, John	14	NWNE	1889-11-29		A2
1711	BLACKLIDGE, Mary	11	NWSE	1884-12-30		A3
1712	" "	11	SWNE	1884-12-30		A3 R1742
1782	BLACKLIDGE, Thomas B	26	SENW	1906-09-14		A3
1626	BLUE, David	3	NENW	1894-12-17		A3
1730	BOYCE, Robert P	6	E½NW	1861-07-01		A2
1731	" "	6	NESW	1861-07-01		A2
1611	CRAVEN, Columbus C	34	S½SE	1888-02-25		A3
1666	CRAVEN, Jenkins R	32	SESE	1859-05-02		A2
1669	CRAVEN, Jinkins R	33	E½SW	1859-11-10		A2
1670	" "	33	SWSW	1859-11-10		A2
1646	DAVIS, George W	6	W½NW	1859-11-10		A2
1647	" "	9	SWSE	1891-05-20		A3
1702	DAVIS, Josiah J	29	NWNW	1860-04-10		A2
1703	" "	30	NENE	1860-04-10		A2
1801	DEVINPORT, William	10	N½NW	1861-02-01		A2
1802	" "	3	NWSW	1861-02-01		A2
1803	" "	3	SWSW	1861-02-01		A2
1804	" "	4	NESE	1861-02-01		A2
1805	" "	4	W½SE	1861-02-01		A2
1671	DILLARD, John A	19	E½SE	1859-06-01		A2
1672	" "	19	S½NE	1859-06-01		A2
1673	" "	20	W½SW	1859-06-01		A2
1593	FERGUSON, Angus	8	W½NW	1854-03-15		A2
1590	" "	7	E½NE	1859-05-02		A2
1591	" "	7	E½SE	1859-05-02		A2
1589	" "	6	SESW	1859-11-10		A2
1592	" "	7	NENW	1859-11-10		A2
1588	" "	6	S½SE	1860-07-02		A2

ID	Individual in Patent	Sec.	Sec. Part	Date Issued	Other Counties	For More Info . . .
1594	FERGUSON, Angus G	3	NWNW	1890-02-21		A3
1595	" "	4	E½NE	1890-02-21		A3
1616	FERGUSON, Daniel	9	NWNW	1860-10-01		A2
1614	" "	6	NWSE	1861-07-01		A2
1615	" "	6	SWNE	1861-07-01		A2
1638	FERGUSON, Flora	5	SWNW	1860-07-02		A2
1639	" "	6	NESE	1860-07-02		A2
1650	FERGUSON, Hamp	30	NENW	1897-06-07		A3
1683	FERGUSON, John	5	E½NE	1854-03-15		A2
1681	" "	4	SWNW	1859-05-02		A2
1684	" "	5	NWNW	1859-11-10		A2
1685	" "	6	NENE	1859-11-10		A2
1686	" "	6	NWNE	1861-07-01		A2
1687	" "	6	SENE	1861-07-01		A2
1682	" "	4	W½NE	1884-08-20		A2
1651	" "	8	E½NW	1917-11-14		A2 G17
1704	FERGUSON, Malcolm	5	E½SE	1841-01-05		A2
1706	FERGUSON, Malcom	4	W½SW	1859-05-02		A2
1705	" "	4	SESW	1859-11-10		A2
1707	" "	9	NENW	1859-11-10		A2
1708	FERGUSON, Malcomb	4	E½NW	1958-11-10		A1
1709	" "	4	NESW	1958-11-10		A1
1710	" "	4	NWNW	1958-11-10		A1
1651	HARGROVE, Hardy	8	E½NW	1917-11-14		A2 G17
1633	HAWKINS, Ellis W	30	SWSW	1859-11-10		A2
1634	" "	31	E½SW	1859-11-10		A2
1635	" "	31	NWSW	1859-11-10		A2
1636	" "	31	W½NW	1859-11-10		A2
1637	" "	31	W½SE	1859-11-10		A2
1813	HOBGOOD, William P	19	NENW	1859-11-10		A2
1814	" "	19	NWNE	1859-11-10		A2
1806	HOLDER, William F	3	SWNW	1898-09-28		A3
1648	HOLLEY, Godfrey D	33	NE	1861-05-01		A2
1649	" "	33	NWSE	1861-05-01		A2
1795	HOLLEY, William D	21	E½NE	1860-04-02		A2
1796	" "	21	NESE	1860-04-02		A2
1797	" "	21	NWNE	1860-04-02		A2
1798	" "	21	SESE	1860-10-01		A2
1799	" "	28	NENE	1860-10-01		A2
1800	" "	28	SESE	1860-10-01		A2
1640	HOUGH, Francis	30	SESE	1859-11-10		A2
1641	" "	30	SWSE	1859-11-10		A2
1693	KELLEY, John O	24	NESE	1904-09-28		A3
1792	LEE, William B	7	W½NE	1859-05-02		A2
1791	" "	14	NWSW	1859-11-10		A2
1787	LIGHTSEY, William A	25	NENE	1889-11-29		A2
1612	MCDANIEL, Cyrus	23	N½SE	1897-06-07		A3
1613	" "	23	S½NE	1897-06-07		A3
1675	MCDANIEL, John C	23	E½NW	1901-03-23		A3
1676	" "	23	N½NE	1901-03-23		A3
1617	MCDONALD, Daniel	9	E½SE	1846-09-01		A2
1688	MCGILBERRY, John	10	SESW	1859-05-02		A2
1689	" "	11	S½SW	1859-05-02		A2
1690	" "	11	SWSE	1859-05-02		A2
1691	" "	14	N½NW	1859-05-02		A2
1692	" "	14	SENW	1859-11-10		A2
1579	MCGILL, Allen P	3	E½SE	1859-05-02		A2
1581	" "	3	NWSE	1859-05-02		A2
1583	" "	3	SWSE	1859-05-02		A2
1584	" "	3	W½NE	1859-05-02		A2
1580	" "	3	NENE	1860-07-02		A2
1582	" "	3	SESW	1860-07-02		A2
1618	MCGILL, Daniel	10	NESW	1859-05-02		A2
1619	" "	10	S½NW	1859-05-02		A2
1655	MCGILL, James A	22	SESE	1897-05-07		A3
1656	" "	23	SWSW	1897-05-07		A3
1657	" "	26	NWNW	1897-05-07		A3
1658	" "	27	NENE	1897-05-07		A3
1811	MCGILL, William	3	NESW	1885-12-19		A3
1812	" "	3	SENW	1885-12-19		A3
1807	MCLAURIN, William F	9	NWNE	1924-10-03		A3
1576	MILLSAP, Alexander	23	NWSW	1891-05-20		A3
1577	" "	23	SWNW	1891-05-20		A3

ID	Individual in Patent	Sec.	Sec. Part	Date Issued	Other Counties	For More Info . . .
1609	MILLSAP, Charley A	22	N½SE	1894-02-17		A3
1610	" "	22	S½NE	1894-02-17		A3
1732	MILLSAP, Sam	22	NESW	1897-06-07		A3
1733	" "	22	SENW	1897-06-07		A3
1578	MILLSAPS, Alexander	22	N½NE	1889-05-23		A3
1714	MITCHELL, Morgan	21	SWNE	1859-11-10		A2
1736	MITCHELL, Samuel	21	W½SE	1860-07-02		A2
1737	" "	28	NWNE	1860-07-02		A2
1738	" "	36	E½NW	1891-05-20		A3
1739	" "	36	E½SW	1891-05-20		A3
1662	OWEN, James L	1	SWNW	1859-11-10		A2
1663	" "	2	E½SW	1859-11-10		A2
1664	" "	2	SWNE	1859-11-10		A2
1596	PATERSON, Archabald	31	SWNE	1908-10-29		A2
1597	" "	32	NWNW	1908-10-29		A2
1598	PATTERSON, Archabald	31	E½NW	1859-11-10		A2
1599	" "	31	NWNE	1859-11-10		A2
1713	PEARCEY, Miles W	8	NESE	1895-06-27		A3
1575	REESE, Alex	23	E½SW	1904-10-17		A3
1653	ROGERS, Jacob	10	SWSW	1859-11-10		A2
1652	" "	10	NWSW	1860-07-02		A2
1654	" "	9	NWSE	1860-07-02		A2
1601	RUSHTON, Bennett J	30	E½SW	1859-11-10		A2
1602	" "	30	NWSE	1859-11-10		A2
1603	" "	30	SENW	1859-11-10		A2
1604	" "	30	W½NE	1859-11-10		A2
1605	" "	30	W½NW	1859-11-10		A2
1721	RUSHTON, Obulus E	19	E½SW	1859-11-10		A2
1722	" "	19	NWSW	1859-11-10		A2
1723	" "	19	SENW	1859-11-10		A2
1725	" "	19	W½NW	1859-11-10		A2
1726	" "	19	W½SE	1859-11-10		A2
1724	" "	19	SWSW	1886-10-22		A2
1727	" "	30	NWSW	1897-05-07		A3
1622	RUSTIN, Daniel W	23	NWNW	1898-09-28		A3
1719	STEELMON, Nancy C	12	S½SE	1892-03-23		A3
1720	" "	12	S½SW	1892-03-23		A3
1781	STEWART, Thomas A	7	W½SE	1859-11-10		A2
1606	STULMAN, Charles C	2	SENW	1859-11-10		A2
1607	" "	2	SWNW	1859-11-10		A2
1608	STUTMAN, Charles C	2	NENW	1859-05-02		A2
1680	THORNTON, John E	29	SWSW	1882-06-01		A2
1694	TOUCHSTONE, John P	31	SWSW	1895-12-14		A3
1585	TREST, Angus B	22	NWSW	1891-08-19		A3
1586	" "	22	S½SW	1891-08-19		A3
1587	" "	22	SWNW	1891-08-19		A3
1632	TREST, Elizabeth	8	SWSE	1859-11-10		A2
1630	" "	17	NENE	1860-08-01		A2
1631	" "	8	SESE	1860-08-01		A2
1695	TREST, John	17	NWSE	1841-01-05		A2
1698	" "	8	NE	1841-01-05		A2
1699	" "	8	NWSE	1841-01-05		A2
1696	" "	21	W½NW	1846-09-01		A2
1697	" "	8	E½SW	1846-09-01		A2
1677	TREST, John D	30	NESE	1859-11-10		A2
1678	" "	30	SENE	1859-11-10		A2
1679	" "	32	SWSE	1859-11-10		A2
1728	TREST, Richard C	9	S½NW	1859-11-10		A2
1729	" "	9	SW	1859-11-10		A2
1734	TREST, Samuel C	22	SWSE	1889-11-29		A2
1740	TREST, Sap L	17	SENE	1905-05-02		A3
1793	TREST, William B	20	SWNW	1859-05-02		A2
1808	TREST, William J	4	SESE	1891-06-30		A3
1809	" "	9	E½NE	1891-06-30		A3
1810	" "	9	SWNE	1891-06-30		A3
1783	UNDERWOOD, Thomas H	1	E½NE	1895-01-17		A3
1784	" "	1	SENW	1895-01-17		A3
1785	" "	1	SWNE	1895-01-17		A3
1642	VARNER, Franklin W	24	SESE	1889-11-29		A2
1741	WADDELL, Seid	11	E½SE	1890-04-25		A2
1742	" "	11	SWNE	1890-04-25		A2 R1712
1743	" "	12	N½SE	1890-04-25		A2
1744	" "	12	N½SW	1890-04-25		A2

ID	Individual in Patent	Sec.	Sec. Part	Date Issued	Other Counties	For More Info . . .
1745	WADDELL, Seid (Cont'd)	12	S½NE	1890-04-25		A2
1746	" "	12	S½NW	1890-04-25		A2
1747	" "	13	E½NW	1890-04-25		A2
1748	" "	13	N½SW	1890-04-25		A2
1749	" "	13	NE	1890-04-25		A2
1750	" "	13	NWNW	1890-04-25		A2
1751	" "	14	NENE	1890-04-25		A2
1752	" "	14	NESW	1890-04-25		A2
1753	" "	14	SE	1890-04-25		A2
1754	" "	14	SWNE	1890-04-25		A2
1755	" "	14	SWNW	1890-04-25		A2
1756	" "	24	E½SW	1890-04-25		A2
1757	" "	24	NE	1890-04-25		A2
1758	" "	24	W½SE	1890-04-25		A2
1759	" "	25	NW	1890-04-25		A2
1760	" "	25	S½	1890-04-25		A2
1761	" "	25	SENE	1890-04-25		A2
1762	" "	25	W½NE	1890-04-25		A2
1763	" "	26	E½SW	1890-04-25		A2
1764	" "	26	S½SE	1890-04-25		A2
1765	" "	26	SWSW	1890-04-25		A2
1766	" "	27	S½SE	1890-04-25		A2
1767	" "	27	S½SW	1890-04-25		A2
1768	" "	34	E½SW	1890-04-25		A2
1769	" "	34	N½	1890-04-25		A2
1770	" "	34	N½SE	1890-04-25		A2
1771	" "	34	NWSW	1890-04-25		A2
1772	" "	35	E½SW	1890-04-25		A2
1773	" "	35	NENE	1890-04-25		A2
1774	" "	35	W½NE	1890-04-25		A2
1775	" "	35	W½SE	1890-04-25		A2
1776	" "	36	NENE	1890-04-25		A2
1777	" "	36	NWSE	1890-04-25		A2
1778	" "	36	SWSW	1890-04-25		A2
1779	" "	36	W½NE	1890-04-25		A2
1780	" "	36	W½NW	1890-04-25		A2
1620	WALTERS, Daniel T	26	N½SE	1888-04-05		A3
1621	" "	26	W½NE	1888-04-05		A3
1624	WALTERS, Darcus	14	SWSW	1860-10-01		A2
1625	" "	15	SESE	1860-10-01		A2
1643	WALTERS, Gabriel B	35	E½SE	1892-06-15		A3
1644	" "	35	SENE	1892-06-15		A3
1645	" "	36	NWSW	1892-06-15		A3
1659	WALTERS, James E	35	W½SW	1891-03-16		A3
1786	WALTERS, Thomas N	36	SWSE	1861-05-01		A2
1623	WATTERS, Darcas	15	SWSE	1859-11-10		A2
1627	WELBORN, E C	33	E½SE	1878-06-24		A3
1628	" "	33	SWSE	1878-06-24		A3
1629	" "	34	SWSW	1878-06-24		A3

Patent Map

T9-N R10-W
St Stephens Meridian

Map Group 10

Township Statistics

Parcels Mapped	:	240
Number of Patents	:	131
Number of Individuals	:	89
Patentees Identified	:	89
Number of Surnames	:	51
Multi-Patentee Parcels	:	1
Oldest Patent Date	:	1/5/1841
Most Recent Patent	:	11/10/1958
Block/Lot Parcels	:	0
Parcels Re - Issued	:	1
Parcels that Overlap	:	0
Cities and Towns	:	1
Cemeteries	:	3

Copyright 2008 Boyd IT. Inc. All Rights Reserved

FERGUSON Angus G 1890	BLUE David 1894	MCGILL Allen P 1859	MCGILL Allen P 1860		STUTMAN Charles C 1859		BARKLY Samuel M 1901	BLACKLEDGE Joseph J 1860

Section 3 area:
- FERGUSON Angus G 1890
- BLUE David 1894
- MCGILL Allen P 1859
- MCGILL Allen P 1860
- HOLDER William F 1898
- MCGILL William 1885
- **3**
- BARKLEY Moses H 1859
- DEVINPORT William 1861
- MCGILL William 1885
- MCGILL Allen P 1859
- MCGILL Allen P 1859
- DEVINPORT William 1861
- MCGILL Allen P 1860
- MCGILL Allen P 1859

Section 2 area:
- STUTMAN Charles C 1859
- STULMAN Charles C 1859
- STULMAN Charles C 1859
- OWEN James L 1859
- **2**
- OWEN James L 1859

Section 1 area:
- BARKLY Samuel M 1901
- BLACKLEDGE Joseph J 1860
- BLACKLEDGE Joseph J 1860
- UNDERWOOD Thomas H 1895
- OWEN James L 1859
- UNDERWOOD Thomas H 1895
- UNDERWOOD Thomas H 1895
- **1**

Section 10 area:
- DEVINPORT William 1861
- MCGILL Daniel 1859
- **10**
- ROGERS Jacob 1860
- MCGILL Daniel 1859
- ROGERS Jacob 1859
- MCGILBERRY John 1859

Section 11 area:
- **11**
- BLACKLIDGE Mary 1884
- WADDELL Seid 1890
- BLACKLEDGE William 1859
- BLACKLIDGE Mary 1884
- MCGILBERRY John 1859
- MCGILBERRY John 1859

Section 12 area:
- WADDELL Seid 1890
- **12**
- WADDELL Seid 1890
- WADDELL Seid 1890
- WADDELL Seid 1890
- WADDELL Seid 1890
- STEELMON Nancy C 1892
- STEELMON Nancy C 1892

Section 15 area:
- **15**
- WATTERS Darcas 1859
- WALTERS Darcus 1860

Section 14 area:
- MCGILBERRY John 1859
- BLACKLIDGE John 1889
- WADDELL Seid 1890
- WADDELL Seid 1890
- WADDELL Seid 1890
- MCGILBERRY John 1859
- WADDELL Seid 1890
- BLACKLIDGE James G 1888
- BLACKLIDGE James G 1888
- WADDELL Seid 1890
- LEE William B 1859
- WADDELL Seid 1890
- **14**
- WADDELL Seid 1890
- WALTERS Darcus 1860
- BLACKLEDGE James R 1901
- WADDELL Seid 1890

Section 13 area:
- WADDELL Seid 1890
- WADDELL Seid 1890
- **13**

Section 22 area:
- MILLSAPS Alexander 1889
- TREST Angus B 1891
- MILLSAP Sam 1897
- **22**
- MILLSAP Charley A 1894
- TREST Angus B 1891
- MILLSAP Sam 1897
- MILLSAP Charley A 1894
- TREST Angus B 1891
- TREST Samuel C 1889
- MCGILL James A 1897

Section 23 area:
- RUSTIN Daniel W 1898
- MCDANIEL John C 1901
- MCDANIEL John C 1901
- MILLSAP Alexander 1891
- MCDANIEL Cyrus 1897
- MILLSAP Alexander 1891
- REESE Alex 1904
- **23**
- MCDANIEL Cyrus 1897
- MCGILL James A 1897

Section 24 area:
- WADDELL Seid 1890
- **24**
- WADDELL Seid 1890
- WADDELL Seid 1890
- KELLEY John O 1904
- VARNER Franklin W 1889

Section 27 area:
- BLACKLIDGE Jesse C 1897
- MCGILL James A 1897
- MCGILL James A 1897
- BLACKLIDGE Jesse C 1897
- **27**
- WADDELL Seid 1890
- WADDELL Seid 1890

Section 26 area:
- WALTERS Daniel T 1888
- BLACKLIDGE Thomas B 1906
- WALTERS Daniel T 1888
- **26**
- WADDELL Seid 1890
- WADDELL Seid 1890

Section 25 area:
- LIGHTSEY William A 1889
- WADDELL Seid 1890
- WADDELL Seid 1890
- WADDELL Seid 1890
- **25**
- WADDELL Seid 1890

Section 34 area:
- WADDELL Seid 1890
- **34**
- WADDELL Seid 1890
- WELBORN E C 1878
- WADDELL Seid 1890
- CRAVEN Columbus C 1888

Section 35 area:
- **35**
- WADDELL Seid 1890
- WADDELL Seid 1890
- WADDELL Seid 1890
- WALTERS Gabriel B 1892
- WALTERS James E 1891
- WADDELL Seid 1890
- WADDELL Seid 1890
- WALTERS Gabriel B 1892

Section 36 area:
- WADDELL Seid 1890
- MITCHELL Samuel 1891
- WADDELL Seid 1890
- WADDELL Seid 1890
- WALTERS Gabriel B 1892
- **36**
- WADDELL Seid 1890
- WADDELL Seid 1890
- MITCHELL Samuel 1891
- WALTERS Thomas N 1861

Helpful Hints

1. This Map's INDEX can be found on the preceding pages.

2. Refer to Map "C" to see where this Township lies within Jones County, Mississippi.

3. Numbers within square brackets [ ] denote a multi-patentee land parcel (multi-owner). Refer to Appendix "C" for a full list of members in this group.

4. Areas that look to be crowded with Patentees usually indicate multiple sales of the same parcel (Re-issues) or Overlapping parcels. See this Township's Index for an explanation of these and other circumstances that might explain "odd" groupings of Patentees on this map.

Legend

——— Patent Boundary

▬▬▬ Section Boundary

▨ No Patents Found (or Outside County)

1., 2., 3., ... Lot Numbers (when beside a name)

[ ] Group Number (see Appendix "C")

Scale: Section = 1 mile X 1 mile (generally, with some exceptions)

Road Map

T9-N R10-W
St Stephens Meridian

Map Group 10

Cities & Towns
Cleo

Cemeteries
Blackledge Cemetery
Fall Cemetery
May Cemetery

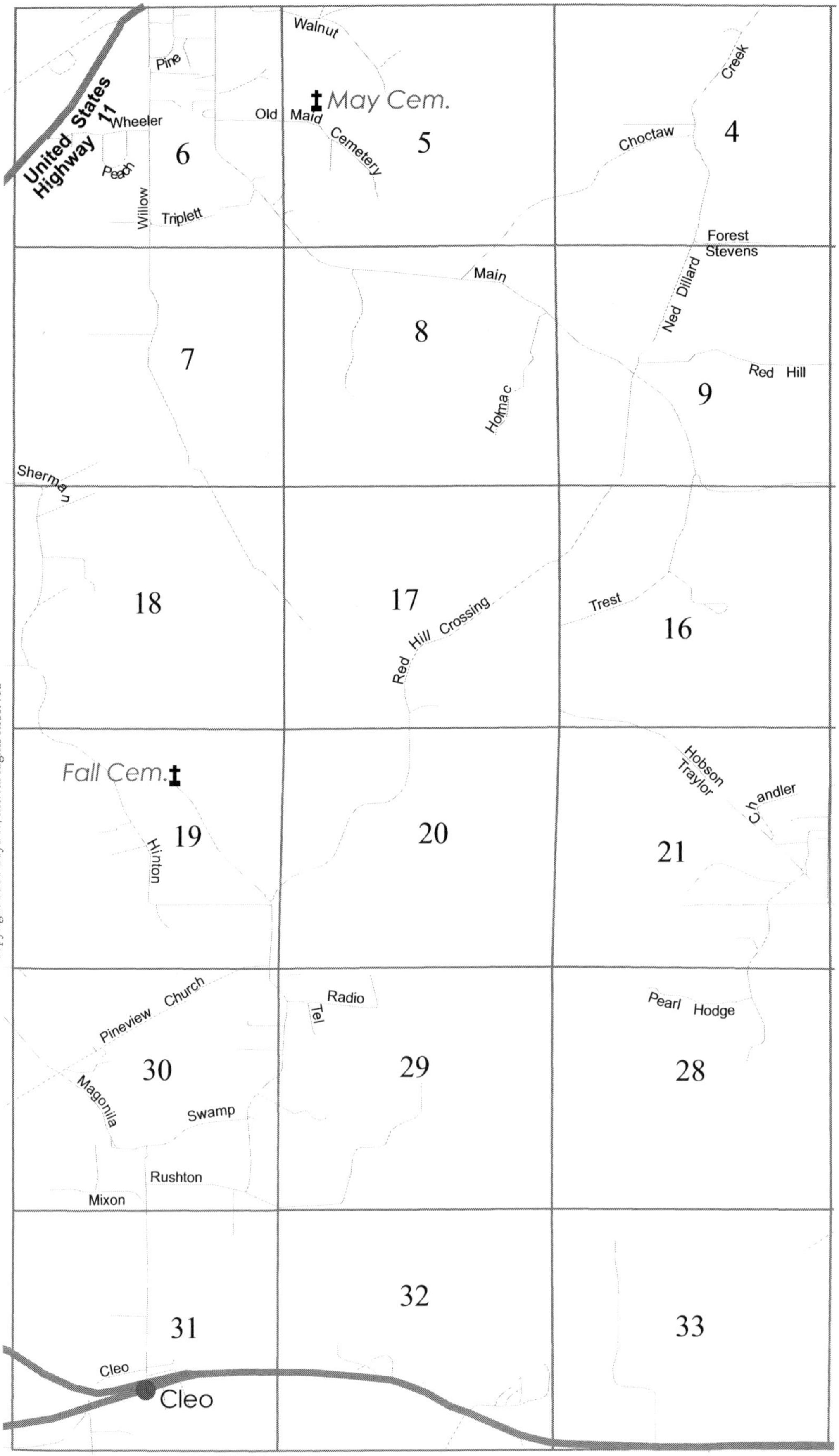

United States Highway 11

Walnut

Pine

Wheeler

May Cem.

Old Maid Cemetery

Creek

Choctaw

Peach

6

Willow

Triplett

5

4

Main

Forest
Stevens

Ned Dillard

Red Hill

7

8

Homa c

9

Sherman

18

17

Red Hill Crossing

Trest

16

Fall Cem.

Hinton

19

20

Hobson
Traylor

Chandler

21

Pineview Church

Radio

Tel

Pearl Hodge

Magonila

30

Swamp

29

28

Rushton

Mixon

31

32

33

Cleo

Cleo

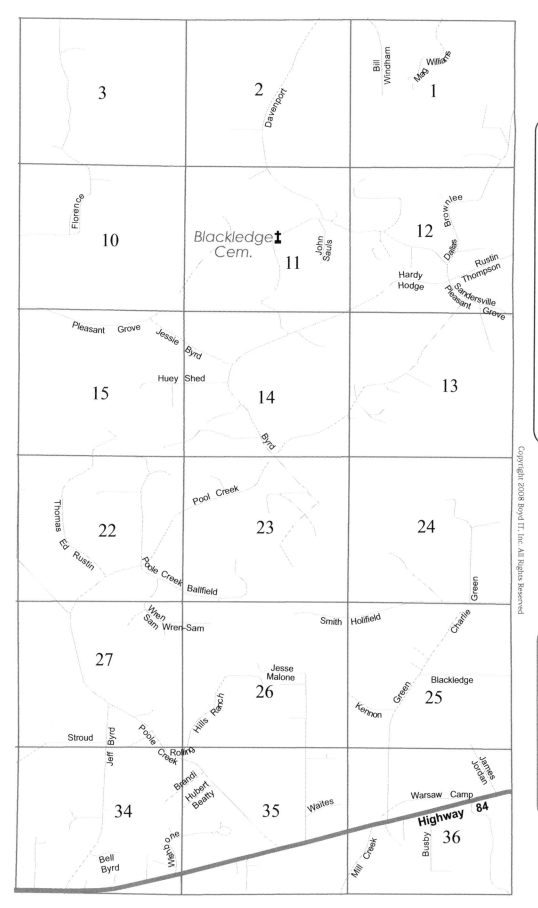

3

2

Davenport

Bill
Windham

Mag Williams

1

Florence

10

Blackledge †
Cem.

11

John
Sauls

Brownlee

12

Dallas

Rustin
Thompson

Hardy
Hodge

Sandersville

Pleasant

Grove

Pleasant Grove Jessie Byrd

Huey Shed

15

14

Byrd

13

Thomas
Ed Rustin

22

Pool Creek

23

24

Poole Creek

Ballfield

Green

Wren
Sam Wren-Sam

Smith Holifield

Charlie

27

Jesse
Malone

26

Hills Ranch

Green

Blackledge

Kennon

25

Stroud

Jeff Byrd

Poole
Creek

Rolling

Brandi
Hubert
Beatty

34

Wisho

35

Waites

James
Jordan

Warsaw Camp

Highway 84

Bell
Byrd

Mill Creek

Busby

36

Helpful Hints

1. This road map has a number of uses, but primarily it is to help you: a) find the present location of land owned by your ancestors (at least the general area), b) find cemeteries and city-centers, and c) estimate the route/roads used by Census-takers & tax-assessors.

2. If you plan to travel to Jones County to locate cemeteries or land parcels, please pick up a modern travel map for the area before you do. Mapping old land parcels on modern maps is not as exact a science as you might think. Just the slightest variations in public land survey coordinates, estimates of parcel boundaries, or road-map deviations can greatly alter a map's representation of how a road either does or doesn't cross a particular parcel of land.

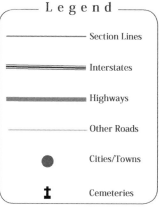

L e g e n d

———————— Section Lines

════════════ Interstates

━━━━━━━━ Highways

———————— Other Roads

● Cities/Towns

† Cemeteries

Scale: Section = 1 mile X 1 mile
(generally, with some exceptions)

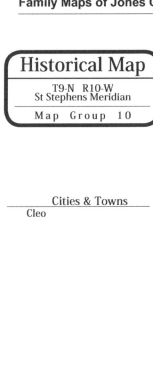

Historical Map

T9-N R10-W
St Stephens Meridian

Map Group 10

Cities & Towns

Cleo

Cemeteries

Blackledge Cemetery
Fall Cemetery
May Cemetery

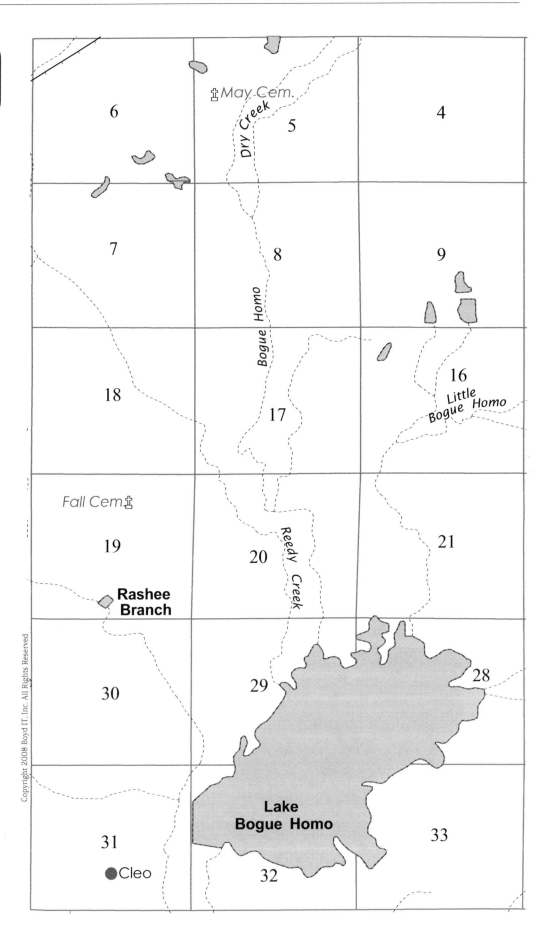

‡ May Cem.

6

5

4

Dry Creek

7

8

9

Bogue Homo

18

17

16

Little
Bogue Homo

Fall Cem ‡

19

20

21

Reedy Creek

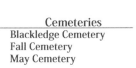

**Rashee
Branch**

30

29

28

**Lake
Bogue Homo**

31

● Cleo

32

33

Copyright 2008 Boyd IT. Inc. All Rights Reserved

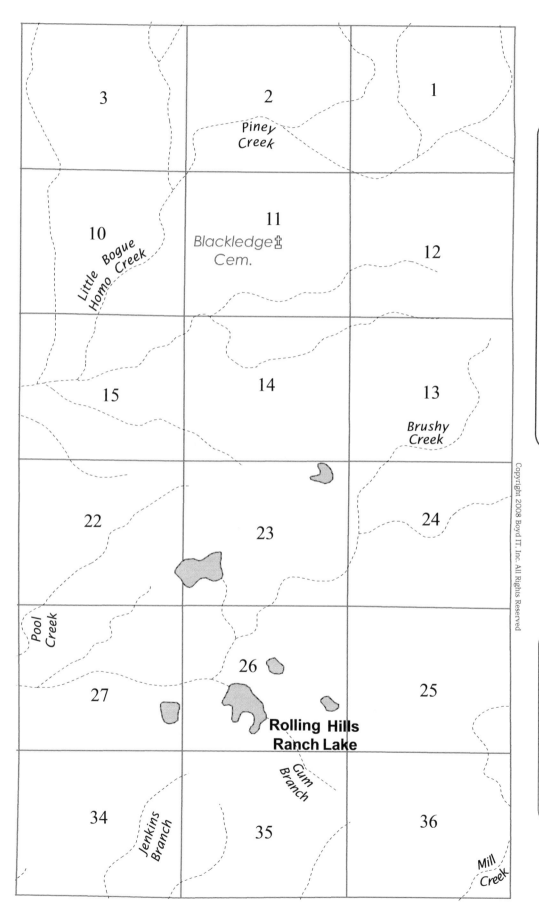

3

2

1

Piney
Creek

10

11

Blackledge⚓
Cem.

12

Little Bogue Homo Creek

15

14

13

Brushy
Creek

22

23

24

Pool Creek

26

27

**Rolling Hills
Ranch Lake**

25

34

Gum Branch

Jenkins Branch

35

36

Mill
Creek

Helpful Hints

1. This Map takes a different look at the same Congressional Township displayed in the preceding two maps. It presents features that can help you better envision the historical development of the area: a) Water-bodies (lakes & ponds), b) Water-courses (rivers, streams, etc.), c) Railroads, d) City/town center-points (where they were oftentimes located when first settled), and e) Cemeteries.

2. Using this "Historical" map in tandem with this Township's Patent Map and Road Map, may lead you to some interesting discoveries. You will often find roads, towns, cemeteries, and waterways are named after nearby landowners: sometimes those names will be the ones you are researching. See how many of these research gems you can find here in Jones County.

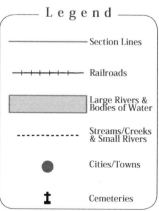

Legend

———————— Section Lines

+–+–+–+–+ Railroads

Large Rivers &
Bodies of Water

- - - - - - - Streams/Creeks
& Small Rivers

● Cities/Towns

✝ Cemeteries

Scale: Section = 1 mile X 1 mile
(there are some exceptions)

Map Group 11: Index to Land Patents

Township 8-North Range 14-West (St Stephens)

After you locate an individual in this Index, take note of the Section and Section Part then proceed to the Land Patent map on the pages immediately following. You should have no difficulty locating the corresponding parcel of land.

The "For More Info" Column will lead you to more information about the underlying Patents. See the *Legend* at right, and the "How to Use this Book" chapter, for more information.

```
                    LEGEND
          "For More Info . . . " column
A = Authority (Legislative Act, See Appendix "A")
B = Block or Lot (location in Section unknown)
C = Cancelled Patent
F = Fractional Section
G = Group  (Multi-Patentee Patent, see Appendix "C")
V = Overlaps another Parcel
R = Re-Issued (Parcel patented more than once)

(A & G items require you to look in the Appendixes referred
to above. All other Letter-designations followed by a number
require you to locate line-items in this index that possess
the ID number found after the letter).
```

ID	Individual in Patent	Sec.	Sec. Part	Date Issued	Other Counties	For More Info . . .
1852	BARLOW, Henry H	12	W½NE	1896-10-10		A3
1851	"	12	NENE	1912-06-27		A2
1836	BAYLIS, George	24	NENW	1841-01-05		A2
1837	"	24	NWSE	1841-01-05		A2
1838	"	24	SENW	1841-01-05		A2
1835	"	24	E½SE	1846-09-01		A2
1905	BOYKIN, Robert L	22	E½SW	1898-03-15		A3
1906	"	22	N½SE	1898-03-15		A3
1816	BUTLER, Amos O	11	SESE	1912-10-18		A2
1817	BYNUM, Benjamin	13	NWSW	1841-01-05		A2
1828	BYNUM, Drury	13	SWSW	1841-01-05		A2
1829	"	14	SENE	1841-01-05		A2
1910	COLEMAN, Thomas J	14	NESE	1846-09-01		A2
1914	CRAWFORD, Thomas P	34	NWSW	1886-03-20		A3
1915	"	34	S½NW	1886-03-20		A3
1839	DAVIDSON, George W	1	NESW	1861-05-01		A2
1840	"	1	NWSE	1861-05-01		A2
1841	"	1	S½SW	1861-05-01		A2
1920	ELLZEY, William	22	S½SE	1892-07-11		A3
1921	"	23	S½SW	1892-07-11		A3
1818	GRAVES, Benjamin D	1	S½SE	1896-12-14		A3
1831	GRAVES, Franklin L	1	N½NW	1892-07-20		A3
1832	"	1	NWNE	1892-07-20		A3
1833	"	1	SENW	1892-07-20		A3
1882	GRAVES, Joseph	3	NESE	1854-03-15		A2
1896	GRAVES, Robert	10	NENE	1854-03-15		A2
1900	"	2	SWNW	1854-03-15		A2
1898	"	2	E½NW	1859-05-02		A2
1899	"	2	SWNE	1859-05-02		A2
1901	"	3	SENE	1859-05-02		A2
1894	"	1	NWSW	1884-08-20		A2
1895	"	1	SWNW	1884-08-20		A2
1897	"	2	E½NE	1884-08-20		A2
1885	GUNTER, Joseph M	11	E½NE	1861-05-01		A2
1886	"	12	S½NW	1861-05-01		A2
1902	HOPKINS, Robert J	13	NESE	1884-12-30		A3
1903	"	13	S½SE	1884-12-30		A3
1904	"	24	NWNE	1884-12-30		A3
1819	KNIGHT, Benjamin F	12	E½SE	1874-11-05		A2
1820	"	12	SENE	1874-11-05		A2
1823	KNIGHT, Casander	13	NWSE	1896-10-31		A3
1824	"	13	SWNE	1896-10-31		A3
1834	KNIGHT, George B	13	SENE	1892-03-07		A3
1862	KNIGHT, Jesse D	11	SWSE	1854-03-15		A2
1859	"	11	NESE	1859-05-02		A2
1861	"	11	SWNE	1859-05-02		A2

ID	Individual in Patent	Sec.	Sec. Part	Date Issued	Other Counties	For More Info . . .
1863	KNIGHT, Jesse D (Cont'd)	13	SESW	1859-05-02		A2 R1923
1864	" "	24	SENE	1859-05-02		A2 V1850
1860	" "	11	NWSE	1898-08-15		A2
1871	KNIGHT, John	3	W½NE	1841-01-05		A2
1908	KNIGHT, Sarah A	13	NENW	1896-12-14		A3
1909	" "	13	NWNE	1896-12-14		A3
1919	KNIGHT, Warren W	27	SWSW	1897-05-07		A3
1925	KNIGHT, William H	14	NENE	1854-03-15		A2
1923	" "	13	SESW	1859-05-02		A2 R1863
1924	" "	13	SWNW	1859-05-02		A2
1926	" "	14	NWNE	1859-05-02		A2
1922	" "	13	NENE	1891-05-20		A3
1929	KNIGHT, William M	12	S½SW	1892-09-09		A3
1930	" "	12	W½SE	1892-09-09		A3
1830	LEWIS, Elbert	22	W½SW	1861-05-01		A2
1854	LOVETT, Isaac	26	W½NW	1859-11-10		A2
1872	MCLAMORE, John	10	NWSW	1841-01-05		A2
1934	MCLEMORE, Willis D	1	SWNE	1898-12-01		A3
1928	NORWOOD, William K	1	NENE	1896-02-13		A3
1842	PATTON, George W	27	N½NE	1859-05-02		A2
1843	" "	27	NENW	1859-06-01		A2
1827	POOL, Daniel R	22	NW	1890-03-28		A3
1887	PRICE, Joseph W	2	NWNE	1896-10-31		A3
1891	RICHARDSON, Moses	26	E½NW	1861-05-01		A2
1865	ROBERTS, Jesse N	10	NWSE	1846-09-01		A2
1866	" "	10	SWSE	1848-09-01		A2
1867	" "	15	NENW	1848-09-01		A2
1868	" "	15	NWNW	1859-11-10		A2
1869	" "	15	SENW	1859-11-10		A2
1870	" "	15	SWNE	1859-11-10		A2
1875	ROBERTS, John W	10	NESW	1854-03-15		A2
1876	" "	15	NWNE	1854-03-15		A2
1877	" "	25	N½SW	1861-05-01		A2
1878	" "	26	NESE	1861-05-01		A2
1879	" "	26	SENE	1861-05-01		A2
1889	ROBERTS, Marshall O	15	NESW	1898-08-15		A3
1890	" "	15	SWNW	1898-08-15		A3
1825	ROBERTSON, Cornelius R	27	NWNW	1901-06-25		A3
1826	" "	27	SWNE	1901-06-25		A3
1855	ROBERTSON, James N	35	N½SE	1896-12-14		A3
1856	" "	35	NESW	1896-12-14		A3
1857	" "	35	SENW	1896-12-14		A3
1858	ROWELL, James	25	SWNE	1899-04-17		A3
1844	RUSSELL, George W	25	SENE	1894-03-08		A2
1873	SELLERS, John	10	SWSW	1841-01-05		A2
1874	" "	10	W½NW	1841-01-05		A2
1931	SMITH, William	2	W½SW	1841-01-05		A2
1932	" "	3	NWSE	1841-01-05		A2
1933	" "	3	SESE	1841-01-05		A2
1815	TISDALE, Albert G	25	NW	1898-10-04		A3
1845	TISDALE, George W	11	NWNE	1897-11-01		A3
1846	" "	2	S½SE	1897-11-01		A3
1892	TISDALE, Oliver C	2	N½SE	1896-01-25		A3
1893	" "	2	NESW	1896-01-25		A3
1853	WADE, Hiram B	12	N½NW	1905-03-30		A3
1927	WADE, William J	12	N½SW	1897-01-21		A3
1883	WARREN, Joseph L	1	NESE	1860-04-10		A2
1884	" "	1	SENE	1860-04-10		A2
1821	WELCH, Caleb	27	NWSW	1859-11-10		A2
1822	" "	27	SWNW	1859-11-10		A2
1850	WELCH, Harrison T	24	E½NE	1885-05-25		A3 V1864
1907	WELCH, Samuel	10	SESE	1854-03-15		A2
1917	WELCH, Timothy	23	N½SW	1859-05-02		A2
1918	" "	23	NW	1859-05-02		A2
1916	WELCH, Timothy A	15	SE	1897-09-09		A3
1847	WILSON, George W	34	SESW	1892-07-25		A3
1848	" "	34	SWNE	1892-07-25		A3
1849	" "	34	W½SE	1892-07-25		A3
1888	WILSON, Joseph W	23	SE	1881-09-17		A3
1880	WINDHAM, Joseph A	15	SESW	1895-10-09		A3
1881	" "	15	W½SW	1895-10-09		A3
1911	YATES, Thomas J	27	SESW	1891-03-16		A3
1912	" "	34	N½NW	1891-03-16		A3

ID	Individual in Patent	Sec.	Sec. Part	Date Issued	Other Counties	For More Info . . .
1913	YATES, Thomas J (Cont'd)	34	NWNE	1891-03-16		A3

Map Grid

Section 3
KNIGHT John 1841
GRAVES Robert 1859
SMITH William 1841
GRAVES Joseph 1854
SMITH William 1841

Section 2
GRAVES Robert 1854
GRAVES Robert 1859
PRICE Joseph W 1896
GRAVES Robert 1859
SMITH William 1841
TISDALE Oliver C 1896
GRAVES Robert 1884
TISDALE Oliver C 1896
TISDALE George W 1897

Section 1
GRAVES Franklin L 1892
GRAVES Franklin L 1892
NORWOOD William K 1896
GRAVES Robert 1884
GRAVES Franklin L 1892
MCLEMORE Willis D 1898
WARREN Joseph L 1860
GRAVES Robert 1884
DAVIDSON George W 1861
DAVIDSON George W 1861
WARREN Joseph L 1860
DAVIDSON George W 1861
GRAVES Benjamin D 1896

Section 10
SELLERS John 1841
GRAVES Robert 1854
MCLAMORE John 1841
ROBERTS John W 1854
ROBERTS Jesse N 1846
SELLERS John 1841
WELCH Samuel 1854
ROBERTS Jesse N 1848

Section 11
TISDALE George W 1897
GUNTER Joseph M 1861
KNIGHT Jesse D 1859
KNIGHT Jesse D 1898
KNIGHT Jesse D 1859
KNIGHT Jesse D 1854
BUTLER Amos O 1912

Section 12
WADE Hiram B 1905
BARLOW Henry H 1896
BARLOW Henry H 1912
GUNTER Joseph M 1861
KNIGHT Benjamin F 1874
WADE William J 1897
KNIGHT William M 1892
KNIGHT Benjamin F 1874
KNIGHT William M 1892

Section 15
ROBERTS Jesse N 1859
ROBERTS Jesse N 1848
ROBERTS John W 1854
ROBERTS Marshall O 1898
ROBERTS Jesse N 1859
ROBERTS Jesse N 1859
WINDHAM Joseph A 1895
ROBERTS Marshall O 1898
WELCH Timothy A 1897
WINDHAM Joseph A 1895

Section 14
KNIGHT William H 1859
KNIGHT William H 1854
BYNUM Drury 1841
COLEMAN Thomas J 1846

Section 13
KNIGHT Sarah A 1896
KNIGHT Sarah A 1896
KNIGHT William H 1891
KNIGHT William H 1859
KNIGHT Casander 1896
KNIGHT George B 1892
BYNUM Benjamin 1841
KNIGHT Casander 1896
HOPKINS Robert J 1884
BYNUM Drury 1841
KNIGHT William H 1859
KNIGHT Jesse D 1859
HOPKINS Robert J 1884

Section 22
POOL Daniel R 1890
LEWIS Elbert 1861
BOYKIN Robert L 1898
BOYKIN Robert L 1898
ELLZEY William 1892

Section 23
WELCH Timothy 1859
WELCH Timothy 1859
ELLZEY William 1892
WILSON Joseph W 1881

Section 24
BAYLIS George 1841
HOPKINS Robert J 1884
WELCH Harrison T 1885
BAYLIS George 1841
KNIGHT Jesse D 1859
BAYLIS George 1841
BAYLIS George 1846

Section 27
ROBERTSON Comelius R 1901
PATTON George W 1859
PATTON George W 1859
WELCH Caleb 1859
ROBERTSON Comelius R 1901
WELCH Caleb 1859
KNIGHT Warren W 1897
YATES Thomas J 1891

Section 26
LOVETT Isaac 1859
RICHARDSON Moses 1861
ROBERTS John W 1861
ROBERTS John W 1861

Section 25
TISDALE Albert G 1898
ROWELL James 1899
RUSSELL George W 1894
ROBERTS John W 1861

Section 34
YATES Thomas J 1891
YATES Thomas J 1891
CRAWFORD Thomas P 1886
WILSON George W 1892
CRAWFORD Thomas P 1886
WILSON George W 1892
WILSON George W 1892

Section 35
ROBERTSON James N 1896
ROBERTSON James N 1896
ROBERTSON James N 1896

Section 36

Patent Map

T8-N R14-W
St Stephens Meridian

Map Group 11

Township Statistics

Parcels Mapped	:	120
Number of Patents	:	76
Number of Individuals	:	58
Patentees Identified	:	58
Number of Surnames	:	35
Multi-Patentee Parcels	:	0
Oldest Patent Date	:	1/5/1841
Most Recent Patent	:	10/18/1912
Block/Lot Parcels	:	0
Parcels Re - Issued	:	1
Parcels that Overlap	:	2
Cities and Towns	:	1
Cemeteries	:	2

Note: the area contained in this map amounts to far less than a full Township. Therefore, its contents are completely on this single page (instead of a "normal" 2-page spread).

Legend

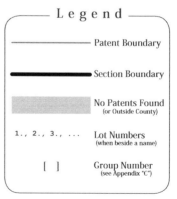

—— Patent Boundary

━━ Section Boundary

No Patents Found (or Outside County)

1., 2., 3., ... Lot Numbers (when beside a name)

[ ] Group Number (see Appendix "C")

Scale: Section = 1 mile X 1 mile (generally, with some exceptions)

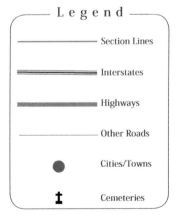

Road Map

T8-N R14-W
St Stephens Meridian

Map Group 11

Note: the area contained in this map amounts to far less than a full Township. Therefore, its contents are completely on this single page (instead of a "normal" 2-page spread).

Cities & Towns
Oak Bowery

Cemeteries
County Line Cemetery
Pickering Cemetery

Legend

———— Section Lines

════ Interstates

━━━━ Highways

———— Other Roads

● Cities/Towns

✝ Cemeteries

Scale: Section = 1 mile X 1 mile
(generally, with some exceptions)

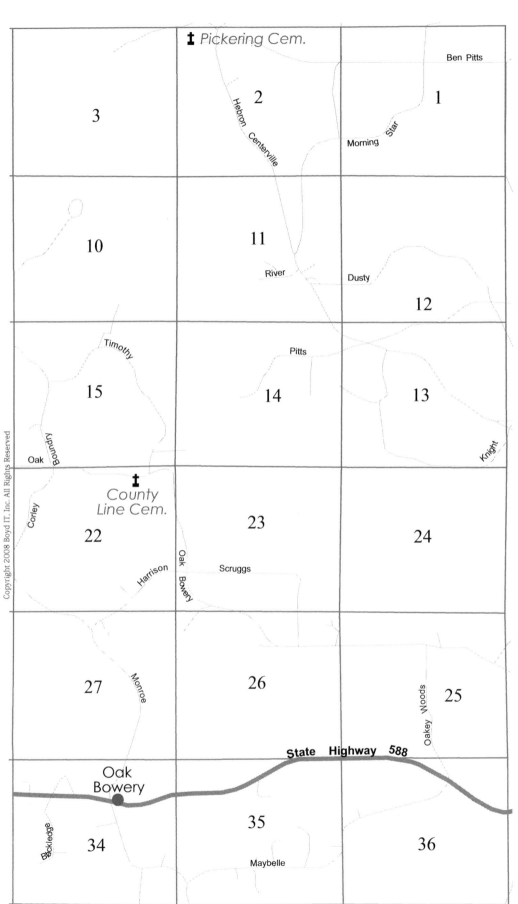

✝ *Pickering Cem.*

Ben Pitts

3

2

1

Hebron Centerville

Morning Star

10

11

River

Dusty

12

Timothy

Pitts

15

14

13

Oak Bounny

Knight

Corley

✝

County Line Cem.

22

23

24

Harrison

Oak Bowery

Scruggs

Monroe

27

26

Oakey Woods

25

State Highway 588

Oak Bowery ●

Blackledge

34

35

Maybelle

36

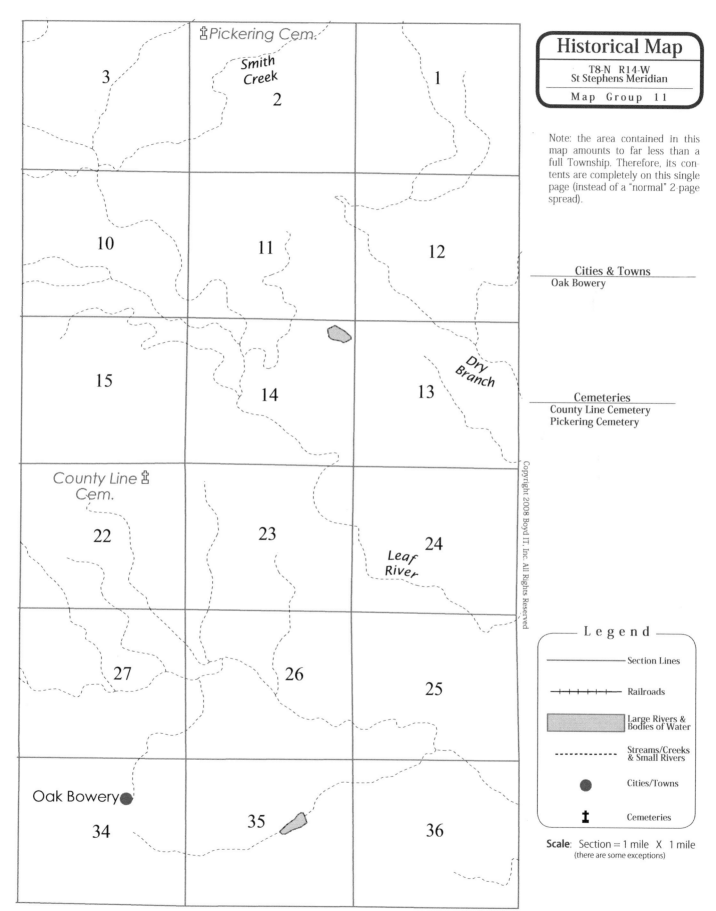

Historical Map

T8-N R14-W
St Stephens Meridian

Map Group 11

Note: the area contained in this map amounts to far less than a full Township. Therefore, its contents are completely on this single page (instead of a "normal" 2-page spread).

Cities & Towns
Oak Bowery

Cemeteries
County Line Cemetery
Pickering Cemetery

Legend
Section Lines
Railroads
Large Rivers & Bodies of Water
Streams/Creeks & Small Rivers
Cities/Towns
Cemeteries

Scale: Section = 1 mile X 1 mile
(there are some exceptions)

Map Group 12: Index to Land Patents

Township 8-North Range 13-West (St Stephens)

After you locate an individual in this Index, take note of the Section and Section Part then proceed to the Land Patent map on the pages immediately following. You should have no difficulty locating the corresponding parcel of land.

The "For More Info" Column will lead you to more information about the underlying Patents. See the *Legend* at right, and the "How to Use this Book" chapter, for more information.

ID	Individual in Patent	Sec.	Sec. Part	Date Issued	Other Counties	For More Info . . .
2047	BAILEY, John	17	NENE	1859-05-02		A2
2048	" "	17	SESE	1859-05-02		A2
2049	" "	17	SWNE	1859-05-02		A2
2050	" "	8	SESE	1859-05-02		A2
2051	BALY, John	17	SENE	1854-03-15		A2
2052	" "	8	NESE	1859-05-02		A2
1979	BAYLIS, George	19	SENW	1848-09-01		A2
2076	BLACK, Lewis C	33	NENE	1884-12-30		A2
2077	" "	33	S½NE	1884-12-30		A2
2078	" "	33	SE	1884-12-30		A2
2079	" "	33	SENW	1884-12-30		A2
2080	" "	34		1884-12-30		A2
2092	BLACKWELL, Richerd M	30	N½SE	1896-03-04		A3
2093	" "	30	N½SW	1896-03-04		A3
2106	BOROUGH, Thomas	31	SWSE	1853-11-01		A2
1959	BUSH, Elder W	7	E½NE	1895-06-27		A3
1960	" "	8	W½NW	1895-06-27		A3
1953	COOLEY, Curt C	31	NENW	1906-10-15		A3
2094	COPELAND, Ripley	28	NWNW	1841-01-05		A2
2125	CRAWFORD, William M	31	NWSE	1891-05-20		A3
2126	" "	31	W½NE	1891-05-20		A3
1958	DEASE, Edward	32	SE	1917-07-06		A2
1986	DYKES, Henry	3	E½SE	1895-06-27		A3
1987	" "	3	SWSE	1895-06-27		A3
2025	DYKES, James L	2	N½SW	1897-05-07		A3
2026	" "	2	SENW	1897-05-07		A3
1971	ELLZEY, Evan	33	N½SW	1884-12-30		A3
1972	" "	33	W½NW	1884-12-30		A3
1980	ELLZEY, George	21	E½NW	1859-06-01		A2
1988	ELLZEY, Henry	21	NE	1890-08-16		A3
1973	ELLZY, Evan	20	NESE	1841-01-05		A2
2114	ELLZY, Vandon	33	SWSW	1906-10-09		A2
1974	ELZEY, Evan	29	E½NE	1841-01-05		A2
2068	EVANS, Joseph	3	NESW	1861-05-01		A2
2069	" "	3	NWSE	1861-05-01		A2
1975	FLYNT, Franklin M	3	NENW	1861-05-01		A2
1976	" "	5	E½NE	1896-08-26		A3
2108	FLYNT, Thomas	9	W½SW	1861-05-01		A2
2107	" "	8	N½NE	1891-05-20		A3
2111	FLYNT, Thomas R	5	SESW	1896-04-11		A2
2112	" "	5	SWSE	1896-04-11		A2
2113	" "	8	NENW	1896-04-11		A2
1989	GILLANDER, Hugh	32	NE	1917-07-06		A2
1939	GREEN, Andrew J	36	E½SW	1890-12-20		A2
1940	" "	36	SWSE	1890-12-20		A2
1941	" "	36	SWSW	1890-12-20		A2

ID	Individual in Patent	Sec.	Sec. Part	Date Issued	Other Counties	For More Info . . .
2053	HARPER, John H	8	NWSE	1860-07-02		A2
2054	" "	8	SWNE	1860-07-02		A2
2033	HERRINGTON, Jasper	1	S½SE	1885-05-25		A3
2034	" "	12	E½NE	1885-05-25		A3
2085	HERRINGTON, Orange S	12	E½SE	1898-12-27		A3
2086	" "	12	NESW	1898-12-27		A3
2087	" "	12	NWSE	1898-12-27		A3
2066	HILBURN, John W	6	NE	1879-12-15		A3
2105	HILBURN, Stephen F	9	SESE	1896-02-13		A3
2129	HILBURN, William P	6	E½SE	1896-08-26		A2
2067	HILL, John W	3	W½NE	1897-11-01		A3
2081	HILL, Martin D	2	W½NW	1892-05-04		A3
2082	" "	3	E½NE	1892-05-04		A3
2109	HILL, Thomas	4	NENW	1854-03-15		A2
2110	" "	4	SWNW	1854-03-15		A2
1947	HOOD, Benjamin	31	SESE	1854-03-15		A2
1948	" "	31	SESW	1859-05-02		A2
2098	HOPKINS, Robert J	10	NENW	1859-05-02		A2
2099	" "	10	NWNE	1859-05-02		A2
2100	" "	3	SESW	1859-05-02		A2
1942	HULSEY, Avery M	24	NENE	1897-05-12		A2
1969	JOHNSON, Emerd A	4	N½SE	1860-10-01		A2
2101	JOHNSON, Samuel J	13	SESW	1890-08-13		A2
1970	JOHNSTON, Emriah A	4	E½SW	1859-05-02		A2
1951	JONES, Chesley E	13	E½NE	1890-02-21		A3
1952	" "	13	SWNE	1890-02-21		A3
1966	JONES, Elizabeth E	35	E½SE	1890-12-20		A2
1967	" "	35	SENE	1890-12-20		A2
1968	" "	36	NWSW	1890-12-20		A2
2060	KAMPER, John	1	E½NE	1889-11-29		A2
2061	" "	1	NESE	1889-11-29		A2
2062	" "	1	SWNW	1889-11-29		A2
2063	" "	1	SWSW	1889-11-29		A2
1935	KNIGHT, Alpheus	28	S½SE	1883-07-10		A3
1936	"	33	NENW	1883-07-10		A3
1937	"	33	NWNE	1883-07-10		A3
1938	"	33	SESW	1883-09-15		A2
1943	KNIGHT, Benjamin F	7	SWSW	1874-11-05		A2
1977	KNIGHT, George B	18	NWSW	1892-03-07		A3 V1978
1978	"	18	W½SW	1892-03-07		A3 V1984, 1977
2035	KNIGHT, Jesse D	19	E½SW	1859-05-02		A2
2036	" "	19	NENW	1859-05-02		A2
2037	" "	19	SWNW	1859-05-02		A2
2038	" "	19	W½NE	1859-05-02		A2
2039	" "	7	NWSW	1891-05-20		A3
2040	" "	7	W½NW	1891-05-20		A3
2041	KNIGHT, Jesse M	35	N½NW	1891-03-16		A3
2042	" "	35	W½NE	1891-03-16		A3
2132	KNIGHT, William W	17	NESE	1854-03-15		A2
2133	KNIGHT, Zachariah T	22	SWSW	1901-08-12		A3
2115	LITTLE, William C	1	NWNW	1892-03-23		A3
2116	" "	2	NENE	1892-03-23		A3
1995	LYON, Isaac L	10	E½SW	1884-12-30		A2
1996	" "	10	SE	1884-12-30		A2
1997	" "	11	S½	1884-12-30		A2
1998	" "	11	S½NE	1884-12-30		A2
1999	" "	11	S½NW	1884-12-30		A2
2000	" "	12	SWNW	1884-12-30		A2
2001	" "	12	W½SW	1884-12-30		A2
2002	" "	13	SENW	1884-12-30		A2
2003	" "	13	W½NW	1884-12-30		A2
2004	" "	14	N½NE	1884-12-30		A2
2005	" "	14	N½NW	1884-12-30		A2
2006	" "	14	W½SW	1884-12-30		A2
2007	" "	15	E½	1884-12-30		A2
2008	" "	15	E½NW	1884-12-30		A2
2009	" "	15	E½SW	1884-12-30		A2
2010	" "	22	E½SE	1884-12-30		A2
2011	" "	22	N½	1884-12-30		A2
2012	" "	23	NWNW	1884-12-30		A2
2013	" "	23	SW	1884-12-30		A2
2014	" "	23	SWSE	1884-12-30		A2
2015	" "	26	W½	1884-12-30		A2

ID	Individual in Patent	Sec.	Sec. Part	Date Issued	Other Counties	For More Info . . .
2016	LYON, Isaac L (Cont'd)	26	W½NE	1884-12-30		A2
2017	" "	26	W½SE	1884-12-30		A2
2018	" "	27	E½	1884-12-30		A2
2019	" "	27	E½SW	1884-12-30		A2
2020	" "	35	S½NW	1884-12-30		A2
2021	" "	35	SW	1884-12-30		A2
2022	" "	35	W½SE	1884-12-30		A2
1949	MAXEY, Charles F	2	NENW	1896-04-11		A2
1950	" "	2	W½NE	1896-04-11		A2
2127	MONTGOMERY, William N	1	NENW	1892-07-25		A3
2128	" "	1	W½NE	1892-07-25		A3
2124	NORWOOD, William K	6	NWNW	1896-02-13		A3
2090	PINNELL, Richard	8	SENE	1860-04-02		A2
2088	PITMAN, Reuben J	30	N½NW	1888-04-05		A3
2089	" "	30	NWNE	1888-04-05		A3
2119	POWELL, William H	28	SWNW	1889-01-12		A3
2117	" "	28	NESE	1895-10-09		A3
2118	" "	28	SENE	1895-10-09		A3
2131	POWELL, William T	18	W½SE	1888-02-25		A3
2083	PRICE, O W	2	E½SE	1897-01-08		A2
2084	" "	2	SENE	1897-01-08		A2
2027	RABUN, James	20	SESE	1841-01-05		A2
2028	" "	21	W½NW	1841-01-05		A2
1992	SHOWS, Isaac B	8	N½SW	1859-05-02		A2
1994	" "	8	SESW	1859-05-02		A2
1993	" "	8	SENW	1859-06-01		A2
2058	STEWART, John J	29	W½NW	1860-07-02		A2
2059	" "	30	NENE	1860-07-02		A2
2023	SYMES, Frank J	24	SE	1884-12-30		A2 G39
2024	" "	25	E½NE	1884-12-30		A2 G39
2023	SYMES, George B	24	SE	1884-12-30		A2 G39
2024	" "	25	E½NE	1884-12-30		A2 G39
2023	SYMES, James E	24	SE	1884-12-30		A2 G39
2024	" "	25	E½NE	1884-12-30		A2 G39
1957	TISDALE, Edward C	31	NESE	1897-09-09		A3
1961	TISDALE, Elijah W	30	S½NE	1890-06-25		A3
1962	" "	30	S½NW	1890-06-25		A3
2095	TISDALE, Robert E	30	S½SW	1897-02-15		A3
2096	" "	30	SWSE	1897-02-15		A3
2097	" "	31	NWNW	1897-02-15		A3
2030	TODD, James	3	S½NW	1859-05-02		A2
2029	" "	3	NWNW	1860-04-02		A2
2031	" "	4	NWSW	1861-05-01		A2
2032	" "	5	E½SE	1861-05-01		A2
2055	TURNER, John H	1	SENW	1859-05-02		A2
2121	TURNER, William H	9	NESE	1861-05-01		A2
2122	" "	9	SENE	1861-05-01		A2
2123	" "	9	W½SE	1861-05-01		A2
2120	" "	10	NENE	1879-05-06		A3
1955	WADE, Daniel W	18	E½SW	1859-05-02		A2
1954	" "	10	W½NW	1861-05-01		A2
1956	" "	3	W½SW	1861-05-01		A2
1963	WADE, Elisha	4	E½SW	1841-01-05		A2
1964	" "	9	E½SW	1841-01-05		A2
1965	" "	9	W½NE	1841-01-05		A2
1990	WADE, Irvin	4	SWSW	1841-01-05		A2
1991	" "	9	W½NW	1841-01-05		A2
2064	WADE, John Q	17	NWNE	1890-06-25		A3
2065	" "	8	SWSE	1890-06-25		A3
2102	WADE, Seaborn	4	SWNE	1841-01-05		A2
2103	WADE, Seborn	4	S½SE	1854-03-15		A2
2104	" "	9	NENE	1854-03-15		A2
2130	WADE, William S	17	W½SE	1890-02-21		A3
1981	WALTERS, George M	1	N½SW	1891-05-20		A3
1982	" "	1	NWSE	1891-05-20		A3
1983	" "	1	SESW	1891-05-20		A3
2046	WALTERS, Jesse	32	S½NW	1854-03-15		A2
2043	" "	29	W½SW	1859-05-02		A2
2044	" "	30	SESE	1859-05-02		A2
2045	" "	31	E½NE	1859-05-02		A2
2072	WALTERS, Justice W	12	SESW	1879-05-06		A3
2073	" "	12	SWSE	1879-05-06		A3
2074	" "	13	NENW	1879-05-06		A3

ID	Individual in Patent	Sec.	Sec. Part	Date Issued	Other Counties	For More Info . . .
2075	WALTERS, Justice W (Cont'd)	13	NWNE	1879-05-06		A3
2070	WARREN, Joseph L	6	S½NW	1859-05-02		A2
2071	" "	6	W½SW	1860-04-10		A2
1944	WELCH, Benjamin F	21	N½SE	1891-05-20		A3
1945	" "	21	NESW	1891-05-20		A3
1946	" "	22	NWSW	1891-05-20		A3
1984	WELCH, Harrison T	18	SWSW	1885-05-25		A3 V1978
1985	" "	19	NWNW	1885-05-25		A3
2056	WELCH, John I	21	S½SE	1895-11-11		A3
2057	" "	28	N½NE	1895-11-11		A3
2091	YATES, Richard W	6	NENW	1901-03-23		A3

Patent Map

T8-N R13-W
St Stephens Meridian

Map Group 12

Township Statistics

Parcels Mapped	:	199
Number of Patents	:	108
Number of Individuals	:	87
Patentees Identified	:	85
Number of Surnames	:	52
Multi-Patentee Parcels	:	2
Oldest Patent Date	:	1/5/1841
Most Recent Patent	:	7/6/1917
Block/Lot Parcels	:	0
Parcels Re-Issued	:	0
Parcels that Overlap	:	3
Cities and Towns	:	1
Cemeteries	:	6

TODD James 1860	FLYNT Franklin M 1861		HILL Martin D 1892	HILL Martin D 1892	MAXEY Charles F 1896	MAXEY Charles F 1896	LITTLE William C 1892	LITTLE William C 1892	MONTGOMERY William N 1892	MONTGOMERY William N 1892	
TODD James 1859	**3**	HILL John W 1897		DYKES James L 1897		**2**	PRICE O W 1897	KAMPER John 1889	TURNER John H 1859	**1**	KAMPER John 1889
WADE Daniel W 1861	EVANS Joseph 1861	EVANS Joseph 1861	DYKES Henry 1895	DYKES James L 1897			PRICE O W 1897	WALTERS George M 1891		WALTERS George M 1891	KAMPER John 1889
	HOPKINS Robert J 1859	DYKES Henry 1895						KAMPER John 1889	WALTERS George M 1891	HERRINGTON Jasper 1885	

WADE Daniel W 1861	HOPKINS Robert J 1859	HOPKINS Robert J 1859	TURNER William H 1879							HERRINGTON Jasper 1885	
	10			LYON Isaac L 1884	**11**	LYON Isaac L 1884	LYON Isaac L 1884	**12**			
LYON Isaac L 1884	LYON Isaac L 1884			LYON Isaac L 1884				HERRINGTON Orange S 1898	HERRINGTON Orange S 1898	HERRINGTON Orange S 1898	
							LYON Isaac L 1884	WALTERS Justice W 1879	WALTERS Justice W 1879		

LYON Isaac L 1884	LYON Isaac L 1884		LYON Isaac L 1884	LYON Isaac L 1884		WALTERS Justice W 1879	WALTERS Justice W 1879	JONES Chesley E 1890
LYON Isaac L 1884	**15**		**14**		LYON Isaac L 1884	LYON Isaac L 1884	JONES Chesley E 1890	
		LYON Isaac L 1884				**13**		
					JOHNSON Samuel J 1890			

LYON Isaac L 1884		LYON Isaac L 1884			HULSEY Avery M 1897
		23		**24**	
WELCH Benjamin F 1891	**22**	LYON Isaac L 1884	LYON Isaac L 1884	LYON Isaac L 1884	SYMES [39] James E 1884
KNIGHT Zachariah T 1901					

27	LYON Isaac L 1884		**26**	LYON Isaac L 1884		SYMES [39] James E 1884
LYON Isaac L 1884	LYON Isaac L 1884	LYON Isaac L 1884	LYON Isaac L 1884	LYON Isaac L 1884	**25**	

34	KNIGHT Jesse M 1891		KNIGHT Jesse M 1891		
	LYON Isaac L 1884		JONES Elizabeth E 1890		**36**
BLACK Lewis C 1884	LYON Isaac L 1884	**35**	JONES Elizabeth E 1890	JONES Elizabeth E 1890	
	LYON Isaac L 1884		GREEN Andrew J 1890	GREEN Andrew J 1890	GREEN Andrew J 1890

Helpful Hints

1. This Map's INDEX can be found on the preceding pages.

2. Refer to Map "C" to see where this Township lies within Jones County, Mississippi.

3. Numbers within square brackets [ ] denote a multi-patentee land parcel (multi-owner). Refer to Appendix "C" for a full list of members in this group.

4. Areas that look to be crowded with Patentees usually indicate multiple sales of the same parcel (Re-issues) or Overlapping parcels. See this Township's Index for an explanation of these and other circumstances that might explain "odd" groupings of Patentees on this map.

Legend

— Patent Boundary

━ Section Boundary

▨ No Patents Found (or Outside County)

1., 2., 3., ... Lot Numbers (when beside a name)

[ ] Group Number (see Appendix "C")

Scale: Section = 1 mile X 1 mile (generally, with some exceptions)

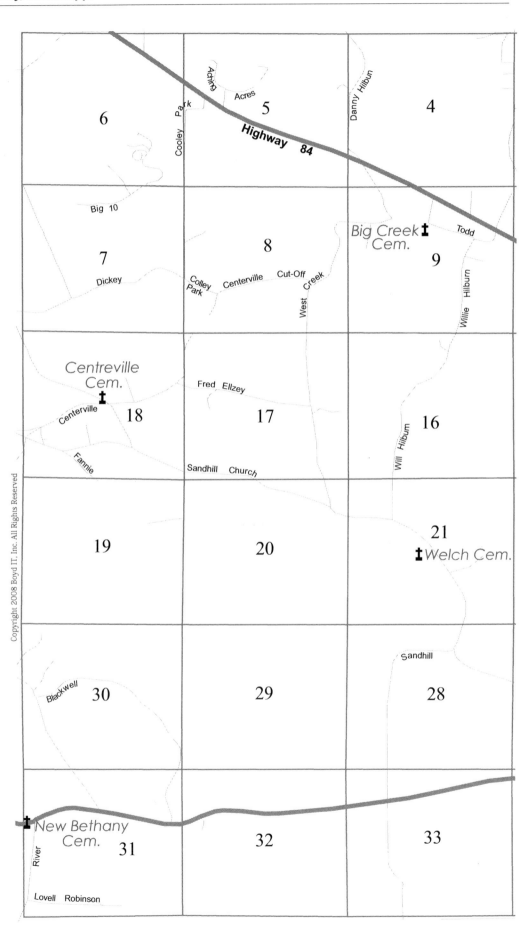

Road Map

T8-N R13-W
St Stephens Meridian

Map Group 12

Cities & Towns
Sand Hill

Cemeteries
Big Creek Cemetery
Centreville Cemetery
Mount Zion Cemetery
New Bethany Cemetery
Our Home Universalist
 Cemetery
Welch Cemetery

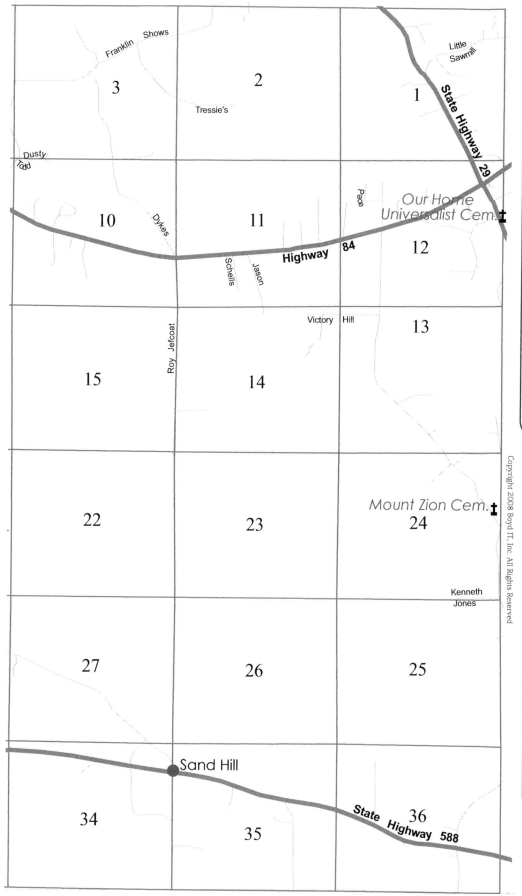

3

Franklin   Shows

2

Little
Sawmill

1

State Highway 29

Tressie's

Dusty
Todd

10

Dykes

11

Pace

Our Home
Universalist Cem.

Highway 84

Schells

Jason

12

Victory   Hill

13

Roy   Jefcoat

15

14

22

23

Mount Zion Cem.

24

Kenneth
Jones

27

26

25

Sand Hill

State Highway 588

34

35

36

Helpful Hints

1. This road map has a number of uses, but primarily it is to help you: a) find the present location of land owned by your ancestors (at least the general area), b) find cemeteries and city-centers, and c) estimate the route/roads used by Census-takers & tax-assessors.

2. If you plan to travel to Jones County to locate cemeteries or land parcels, please pick up a modern travel map for the area before you do. Mapping old land parcels on modern maps is not as exact a science as you might think. Just the slightest variations in public land survey coordinates, estimates of parcel boundaries, or road-map deviations can greatly alter a map's representation of how a road either does or doesn't cross a particular parcel of land.

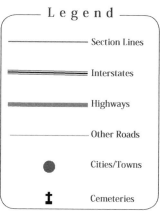

L e g e n d

———————— Section Lines

════════════ Interstates

━━━━━━━━ Highways

———————— Other Roads

● Cities/Towns

✝ Cemeteries

Scale: Section = 1 mile X 1 mile
(generally, with some exceptions)

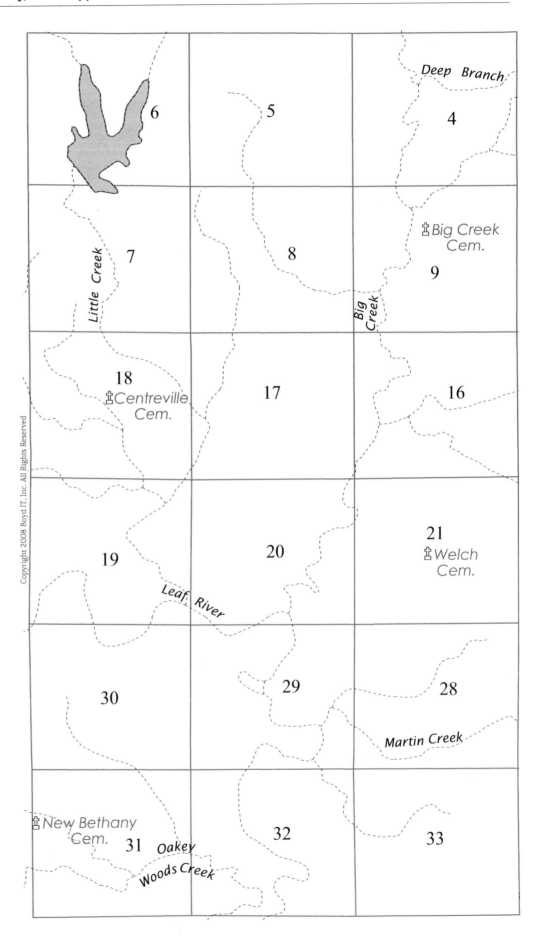

Historical Map

T8-N R13-W
St Stephens Meridian

Map Group 12

Cities & Towns

Sand Hill

Cemeteries

Big Creek Cemetery
Centreville Cemetery
Mount Zion Cemetery
New Bethany Cemetery
Our Home Universalist
 Cemetery
Welch Cemetery

6

5

Deep Branch

4

Little Creek

7

8

⚓Big Creek
Cem.

9

Big Creek

18

⚓Centreville
Cem.

17

16

19

20

21
⚓Welch
Cem.

Leaf River

30

29

28

Martin Creek

⚓New Bethany
Cem.

31

Oakey

Woods Creek

32

33

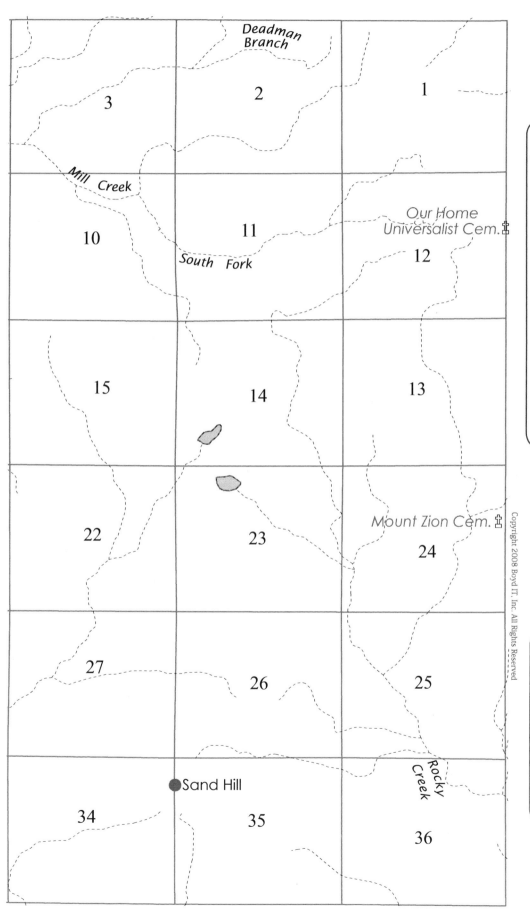

3

2

1

Deadman
Branch

Mill Creek

10

11

South Fork

Our Home
Universalist Cem.

12

15

14

13

22

23

Mount Zion Cem.

24

27

26

25

34

Sand Hill

35

Rocky Creek

36

Helpful Hints

1. This Map takes a different look at the same Congressional Township displayed in the preceding two maps. It presents features that can help you better envision the historical development of the area: a) Water-bodies (lakes & ponds), b) Water-courses (rivers, streams, etc.), c) Railroads, d) City/town center-points (where they were oftentimes located when first settled), and e) Cemeteries.

2. Using this "Historical" map in tandem with this Township's Patent Map and Road Map, may lead you to some interesting discoveries. You will often find roads, towns, cemeteries, and waterways are named after nearby landowners: sometimes those names will be the ones you are researching. See how many of these research gems you can find here in Jones County.

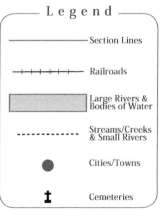

L e g e n d

————	Section Lines
+++++	Railroads
�	Large Rivers & Bodies of Water
- - - -	Streams/Creeks & Small Rivers
●	Cities/Towns
☩	Cemeteries

Scale: Section = 1 mile X 1 mile
(there are some exceptions)

Map Group 13: Index to Land Patents

Township 8-North Range 12-West (St Stephens)

After you locate an individual in this Index, take note of the Section and Section Part then proceed to the Land Patent map on the pages immediately following. You should have no difficulty locating the corresponding parcel of land.

The "For More Info" Column will lead you to more information about the underlying Patents. See the *Legend* at right, and the "How to Use this Book" chapter, for more information.

```
                        LEGEND
               "For More Info . . . " column
A = Authority (Legislative Act, See Appendix "A")
B = Block or Lot (location in Section unknown)
C = Cancelled Patent
F = Fractional Section
G = Group (Multi-Patentee Patent, see Appendix "C")
V = Overlaps another Parcel
R = Re-Issued (Parcel patented more than once)

(A & G items require you to look in the Appendixes referred
to above. All other Letter-designations followed by a number
require you to locate line-items in this index that possess
the ID number found after the letter).
```

ID	Individual in Patent	Sec.	Sec. Part	Date Issued	Other Counties	For More Info . . .
2329	ACKENHAUSEN, William	28	SENW	1884-12-30		A2 G1
2330	" "	28	SWNE	1884-12-30		A2 G1
2331	" "	28	W½SE	1884-12-30		A2 G1
2332	" "	29	N½SE	1884-12-30		A2 G1
2333	" "	29	S½NE	1884-12-30		A2 G1
2334	" "	29	S½SE	1884-12-30		A2 G1
2335	" "	29	SESW	1884-12-30		A2 G1
2259	AINSWORTH, John T	30	NENE	1894-11-22		A3
2137	ANDERSON, Amos	18	NESW	1898-02-24		A3
2138	" "	18	SENW	1898-02-24		A3
2139	" "	18	W½SW	1898-02-24		A3
2140	ANDERSON, Amos D	20	NENW	1908-07-23		A2
2174	ANDERSON, Hyrom	34	SWSE	1846-09-01		A2
2176	ANDERSON, Isaac	35	E½SE	1841-01-05		A2
2177	" "	35	NESW	1841-01-05		A2
2178	" "	35	NWSE	1841-01-05		A2
2179	" "	35	W½NE	1841-01-05		A2
2180	" "	35	W½SW	1841-01-05		A2
2175	" "	2	SENE	1854-03-15		A2 C R2337
2267	BAILEY, Martha O	20	NWSE	1904-10-28		A2
2171	BARNETT, Henry F	20	N½SW	1892-07-25		A3
2172	" "	20	SENW	1892-07-25		A3
2173	" "	20	SWNE	1892-07-25		A3
2274	BARTNE, Maston C	29	NWSW	1896-06-06		A2
2275	" "	30	E½SE	1896-06-06		A2
2276	" "	30	SENE	1896-06-06		A2
2195	BURK, James F	22	SESE	1886-10-22		A2
2199	BUSH, James M	17	S½NE	1892-07-25		A3
2200	" "	17	S½SE	1892-07-25		A3 R2279
2210	BUSH, James R	26	NWSW	1888-04-05		A3
2251	BUSH, John P	17	NENW	1890-06-25		A3
2252	" "	17	NWNE	1890-06-25		A3
2253	" "	8	SESW	1890-06-25		A3
2254	" "	8	SWSE	1890-06-25		A3
2273	BUSH, Mason	12	E½NE	1890-08-16		A3
2336	BUSH, William H	2	NESE	1861-05-01		A2
2337	" "	2	SENE	1861-05-01		A2 R2175
2338	" "	2	W½SE	1861-05-01		A2
2149	BYNUM, Annie	31	SWSE	1886-10-22		A2
2151	BYNUM, Benjamin	4	NWSE	1859-05-02		A2
2168	BYNUM, Gustavus A	4	E½NW	1891-05-20		A3
2169	" "	4	NWNW	1891-05-20		A3
2283	BYNUM, Nancy A	31	S½SW	1883-09-15		A2
2281	" "	22	NESE	1884-12-30		A2
2282	" "	31	NWSW	1884-12-30		A2
2284	" "	31	SESE	1884-12-30		A2

ID	Individual in Patent	Sec.	Sec. Part	Date Issued	Other Counties	For More Info . . .
2318	COLLEY, Thomas S	25	E½	1882-05-20		A2 G8
2319	" "	25	SW	1882-05-20		A2 G8
2320	" "	36	E½SW	1882-05-20		A2 G8
2321	" "	36	N½	1882-05-20		A2 G8
2322	" "	36	SE	1882-05-20		A2 G8
2285	COLLINS, Newton W	4	NENE	1885-05-25		A3
2286	" "	4	W½NE	1885-05-25		A3
2308	COLLINS, Stacy	26	E½NE	1978-09-01		A2 G38
2324	COLLINS, Vincent A	12	SESE	1859-05-02		A2
2187	COOPER, James	36	W½SW	1859-05-02		A2
2197	COOPER, James I	18	NENE	1896-02-13		A3
2198	" "	18	S½NE	1896-02-13		A3
2150	COX, Augustus B	20	S½SW	1897-08-05		A3
2136	DAVIS, Alfred J	29	SWSW	1901-03-23		A3
2227	DAVIS, John	15	NWNE	1851-10-01		A2
2226	" "	15	NENE	1859-05-02		A2
2224	" "	11	SWSW	1859-06-01		A2
2225	" "	14	NWNW	1859-06-01		A2
2302	DAVIS, Rosier	7	N½SE	1861-05-01		A2
2303	" "	7	S½NE	1861-05-01		A2
2323	DYESS, Thomas S	15	W½SE	1859-05-02		A2
2186	GRAHAM, Isaac N	21	NESE	1859-05-02		A2
2279	HERRINGTON, Morgan H	17	S½SE	1891-05-20		A3 R2200
2280	" "	20	N½NE	1891-05-20		A3
2233	HOLIFIELD, John	7	W½NW	1884-12-30		A2
2263	HOLIFIELD, Joshua	11	NWNE	1859-11-10		A2
2264	" "	2	SESW	1859-11-10		A2
2287	HOLIFIELD, Norval N	7	NESW	1894-02-01		A3
2288	" "	7	W½SW	1894-02-01		A3
2265	HOLYFIELD, Joshua	11	E½SW	1859-05-02		A2
2157	JONES, Chesley E	18	SWNW	1890-02-21		A3
2339	JONES, William	5	SESW	1859-05-02		A2
2340	" "	8	NENW	1859-05-02		A2
2241	KAMPER, John	4	E½SW	1889-11-21		A2
2242	" "	5	NENE	1889-11-21		A2
2243	" "	5	NENW	1889-11-21		A2
2244	" "	5	SWSW	1889-11-21		A2
2245	" "	5	W½NE	1889-11-21		A2
2246	" "	6	SE	1889-11-21		A2
2247	" "	6	W½	1889-11-21		A2
2248	" "	6	W½NE	1889-11-21		A2
2234	" "	17	E½SW	1889-11-29		A2
2235	" "	17	NENE	1889-11-29		A2
2236	" "	17	NWSW	1889-11-29		A2
2237	" "	17	S½NW	1889-11-29		A2
2249	" "	8	NWSE	1889-11-29		A2
2250	" "	8	W½NW	1889-11-29		A2
2238	" "	19	E½SE	1890-07-03		A2
2239	" "	29	NESW	1890-07-03		A2
2240	" "	29	S½NW	1890-07-03		A2
2211	KENNEDY, James W	20	SWSW	1892-06-15		A3
2212	" "	29	N½NW	1892-06-15		A3
2213	" "	29	NWNE	1892-06-15		A3
2277	KILGORE, Matthew T	10	NWSW	1859-05-02		A2
2278	" "	10	SWNW	1859-05-02		A2
2297	KILGORE, Peter	4	NESE	1859-05-02		A2
2298	" "	4	SENE	1859-05-02		A2
2307	KILGORE, Samuel	3	S½SW	1859-05-02		A2
2304	" "	10	N½NW	1859-06-01		A2
2305	" "	3	NESW	1859-06-01		A2
2306	" "	3	NWSE	1859-06-01		A2
2196	LANE, James H	21	SW	1890-12-20		A2
2181	LYON, Isaac L	31	N½SE	1884-12-30		A2
2182	" "	31	NESW	1884-12-30		A2
2183	" "	31	NW	1884-12-30		A2
2184	" "	31	W½NE	1884-12-30		A2
2185	" "	32	E½NW	1884-12-30		A2
2315	LYON, Thomas J	5	NWSW	1861-05-01		A2
2316	" "	5	SWNW	1861-05-01		A2
2317	" "	6	E½NE	1861-05-01		A2
2255	MAXEY, John P	7	E½NW	1892-09-09		A3
2256	" "	7	N½NE	1892-09-09		A3
2165	MCGEE, George B	18	SWSE	1898-02-24		A3

ID	Individual in Patent	Sec.	Sec. Part	Date Issued	Other Counties	For More Info . . .
2309	MCMANUS, Sylvanus V	28	N½NW	1896-12-14		A3
2310	" "	28	NWNE	1896-12-14		A3
2311	" "	28	SWNW	1896-12-14		A3
2158	MERCHANT, David	31	E½NE	1891-05-20		A3
2159	" "	32	W½NW	1891-05-20		A3
2156	MILLER, Charles J	21	NWNW	1898-03-15		A3
2329	NORDMAN, John	28	SENW	1884-12-30		A2 G1
2330	" "	28	SWNE	1884-12-30		A2 G1
2331	" "	28	W½SE	1884-12-30		A2 G1
2332	" "	29	N½SE	1884-12-30		A2 G1
2333	" "	29	S½NE	1884-12-30		A2 G1
2334	" "	29	S½SE	1884-12-30		A2 G1
2335	" "	29	SESW	1884-12-30		A2 G1
2152	OWEN, Beuage C	4	NWSW	1874-11-05		A2
2153	" "	4	SWNW	1874-11-05		A2
2154	" "	5	NESE	1874-11-05		A2
2155	" "	5	SENE	1874-11-05		A2
2341	OWEN, William L	9	SENW	1860-07-02		A2
2342	" "	9	SWNE	1860-07-02		A2
2162	PARISH, Edward	9	NENW	-12:00:00 AM-		A3
2214	PARISH, Jasper J	8	E½SE	1891-05-20		A3
2215	" "	9	W½SW	1891-05-20		A3
2289	PATES, Otto	28	SW	1895-12-14		A3
2216	PATRICK, Jeremiah	27	SESE	1859-05-02		A2
2201	PITTS, James M	21	SESE	1859-06-01		A2
2202	" "	28	E½NE	1859-06-01		A2
2229	PITTS, John G	27	NWSE	1854-03-15		A2
2231	" "	27	SWNE	1854-03-15		A2
2228	" "	27	NESE	1859-05-02		A2
2230	" "	27	SENE	1859-05-02		A2
2293	PLOCK, Otto	32	E½	1882-04-20		A2
2294	" "	33	N½	1882-04-20		A2
2295	" "	33	SW	1882-04-20		A2
2296	" "	33	W½SE	1882-04-20		A2
2290	" "	1		1882-05-20		A2
2291	" "	12	NW	1882-05-20		A2
2292	" "	12	W½NE	1882-05-20		A2
2203	POWELL, James M	10	NESW	1859-05-02		A2
2204	" "	10	SENW	1859-05-02		A2
2205	" "	9	E½SE	1859-05-02		A2
2206	" "	9	NENE	1859-05-02		A2
2207	" "	9	NESW	1859-05-02		A2
2208	" "	9	SENE	1859-05-02		A2
2209	" "	9	SESW	1859-05-02		A2
2232	POWELL, John H	9	SWSE	1848-09-01		A2
2312	REEVES, Thomas F	11	E½NE	1885-05-25		A3
2313	" "	11	SWNE	1885-05-25		A3
2314	" "	2	SESE	1885-05-25		A3
2170	SEAMAN, Henry E	8	NE	1874-11-05		A2
2257	SHOWS, John	24	E½NE	1841-01-05		A2
2258	" "	24	SWNE	1841-01-05		A2
2268	SHOWS, Martin L	17	NWNW	1894-04-10		A3
2269	" "	8	NESW	1894-04-10		A3
2270	" "	8	W½SW	1894-04-10		A3
2325	SHOWS, Warren M	2	NENW	1854-03-15		A2
2326	SHOWS, Warren W	3	SENW	1859-05-02		A2
2327	" "	3	SWNE	1859-05-02		A2
2328	" "	3	W½NW	1859-05-02		A2
2143	SPEARS, Amos J	28	E½SE	1859-05-02		A2
2141	" "	27	NENE	1860-07-02		A2
2142	" "	27	NWNW	1860-07-02		A2
2144	" "	34	NWNW	1860-07-02		A2
2145	" "	34	SWNW	1900-02-14		A2
2308	STRICKLAND, Simeon	26	E½NE	1978-09-01		A2 G38
2188	SYMES, Frank J	18	SESW	1884-12-30		A2 G39
2189	" "	19	W½	1884-12-30		A2 G39
2190	" "	19	W½NE	1884-12-30		A2 G39
2191	" "	19	W½SE	1884-12-30		A2 G39
2192	" "	30	W½	1884-12-30		A2 G39
2193	" "	30	W½NE	1884-12-30		A2 G39
2194	" "	30	W½SE	1884-12-30		A2 G39
2188	SYMES, George B	18	SESW	1884-12-30		A2 G39
2189	" "	19	W½	1884-12-30		A2 G39

ID	Individual in Patent	Sec.	Sec. Part	Date Issued	Other Counties	For More Info . . .
2190	SYMES, George B (Cont'd)	19	W½NE	1884-12-30		A2 G39
2191	" "	19	W½SE	1884-12-30		A2 G39
2192	" "	30	W½	1884-12-30		A2 G39
2193	" "	30	W½NE	1884-12-30		A2 G39
2194	" "	30	W½SE	1884-12-30		A2 G39
2188	SYMES, James E	18	SESW	1884-12-30		A2 G39
2189	" "	19	W½	1884-12-30		A2 G39
2190	" "	19	W½NE	1884-12-30		A2 G39
2191	" "	19	W½SE	1884-12-30		A2 G39
2192	" "	30	W½	1884-12-30		A2 G39
2193	" "	30	W½NE	1884-12-30		A2 G39
2194	" "	30	W½SE	1884-12-30		A2 G39
2163	TAYLOR, Elisha J	32	SW	1890-08-16		A3
2164	THOMPSON, Elizabeth	4	SWSW	1860-07-02		A2
2222	WALTERS, Jesse	35	SESW	1841-01-05		A2
2219	WALTERS, Jesse M	18	NENW	1888-02-25		A3
2220	" "	7	S½SE	1888-02-25		A3
2221	" "	7	SESW	1888-02-25		A3
2260	WALTERS, John W	23	SESW	1859-05-02		A2
2261	" "	23	SWSE	1859-05-02		A2
2262	" "	26	NENW	1859-05-02		A2
2146	WALTMAN, Andrew	17	SWSW	1861-05-01		A2
2147	" "	18	E½SE	1861-05-01		A2
2148	" "	18	NWSE	1861-05-01		A2
2318	WARNER, Leslie	25	E½	1882-05-20		A2 G8
2319	" "	25	SW	1882-05-20		A2 G8
2320	" "	36	E½SW	1882-05-20		A2 G8
2321	" "	36	N½	1882-05-20		A2 G8
2322	" "	36	SE	1882-05-20		A2 G8
2134	WATSON, Albert	20	E½SE	1901-11-08		A3
2135	" "	20	SENE	1901-11-08		A3
2166	WATSON, George W	19	E½NE	1897-09-09		A3
2167	" "	20	W½NW	1897-09-09		A3
2266	WATSON, Lemuel	21	W½SE	1879-05-06		A3
2271	WATTERS, Mary	27	NWSW	1860-07-02		A2
2272	" "	27	SWNW	1860-07-02		A2
2160	WELBORN, Dewit C	33	E½SE	1859-05-02		A2
2161	" "	34	W½SW	1859-05-02		A2
2223	WELBORN, Joel E	34	E½SW	1860-07-02		A2
2217	WELLS, Jesse C	4	S½SE	1874-11-05		A2
2218	" "	9	NWNE	1874-11-05		A2
2299	WILLIAMS, Richard	21	E½NW	1892-03-17		A3
2300	" "	21	SWNE	1892-03-17		A3
2301	" "	21	SWNW	1892-03-17		A3
2343	WILLIAMS, Willie H	29	NENE	1909-12-01		A2

Patent Map

T8-N R12-W
St Stephens Meridian

Map Group 13

Township Statistics

Parcels Mapped	:	210
Number of Patents	:	109
Number of Individuals	:	90
Patentees Identified	:	85
Number of Surnames	:	54
Multi-Patentee Parcels	:	20
Oldest Patent Date	:	1/5/1841
Most Recent Patent	:	9/1/1978
Block/Lot Parcels	:	0
Parcels Re - Issued	:	2
Parcels that Overlap	:	0
Cities and Towns	:	6
Cemeteries	:	7

SHOWS Warren W 1859	SHOWS Warren W 1859	SHOWS Warren W 1859 **3**
	KILGORE Samuel 1859	KILGORE Samuel 1859
KILGORE Samuel 1859		

2

SHOWS
Warren M
1854

ANDERSON
Isaac 1854
BUSH
William H
1861

BUSH
William H
1861

HOLIFIELD
Joshua
1859

BUSH
William H
1861

BUSH
William H
1861

REEVES
Thomas F
1885

1

PLOCK
Otto
1882

KILGORE
Samuel
1859

KILGORE
Matthew T
1859

POWELL
James M
1859

KILGORE
Matthew T
1859

POWELL
James M
1859

10

11

HOLIFIELD
Joshua
1859

REEVES
Thomas F
1885

REEVES
Thomas F
1885

HOLYFIELD
Joshua
1859

DAVIS
John
1859

PLOCK
Otto
1882

PLOCK
Otto
1882

BUSH
Mason
1890

12

COLLINS
Vincent A
1859

DAVIS
John
1851

DAVIS
John
1859

DAVIS
John
1859

15

DYESS
Thomas S
1859

14

13

22

BYNUM
Nancy A
1884

BURK
James F
1886

23

WALTERS
John W
1859

WALTERS
John W
1859

24

SHOWS
John
1841

SHOWS
John
1841

SPEARS
Amos J
1860

WATTERS
Mary
1860

WATTERS
Mary
1860

27

PITTS
John G
1854

PITTS
John G
1854

SPEARS
Amos J
1860

PITTS
John G
1859

PITTS
John G
1859

PATRICK
Jeremiah
1859

WALTERS
John W
1859

BUSH
James R
1888

26

STRICKLAND [38]
Simeon
1978

25

COLLEY [8]
Thomas S
1882

COLLEY [8]
Thomas S
1882

SPEARS
Amos J
1860

SPEARS
Amos J
1900

34

WELBORN
Dewit C
1859

WELBORN
Joel E
1860

ANDERSON
Hyrom
1846

35

ANDERSON
Isaac
1841

ANDERSON
Isaac
1841

ANDERSON
Isaac
1841

ANDERSON
Isaac
1841

WALTERS
Jesse
1841

ANDERSON
Isaac
1841

COOPER
James
1859

COLLEY [8]
Thomas S
1882 **36**

COLLEY [8]
Thomas S
1882

COLLEY [8]
Thomas S
1882

Helpful Hints

1. This Map's INDEX can be found on the preceding pages.

2. Refer to Map "C" to see where this Township lies within Jones County, Mississippi.

3. Numbers within square brackets [ ] denote a multi-patentee land parcel (multi-owner). Refer to Appendix "C" for a full list of members in this group.

4. Areas that look to be crowded with Patentees usually indicate multiple sales of the same parcel (Re-issues) or Overlapping parcels. See this Township's Index for an explanation of these and other circumstances that might explain "odd" groupings of Patentees on this map.

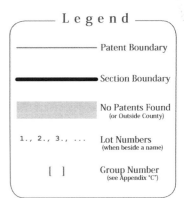

Legend

— Patent Boundary

━ Section Boundary

No Patents Found
(or Outside County)

1., 2., 3., ... Lot Numbers
(when beside a name)

[ ] Group Number
(see Appendix "C")

Scale: Section = 1 mile X 1 mile
(generally, with some exceptions)

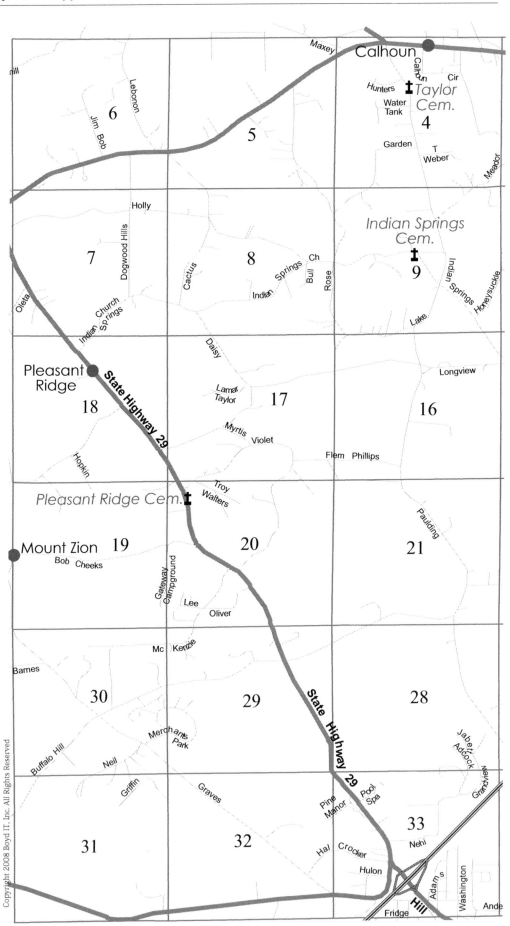

Road Map

T8-N R12-W
St Stephens Meridian

Map Group 13

Cities & Towns
Calhoun
Currie
Mount Zion
Pendorff
Pleasant Ridge
Walters

Cemeteries
Currie Cemetery
Indian Springs Cemetery
Pilgrims Rest Cemetery
Pleasant Ridge Cemetery
Shows Cemetery
Taylor Cemetery
Woodlawn Cemetery

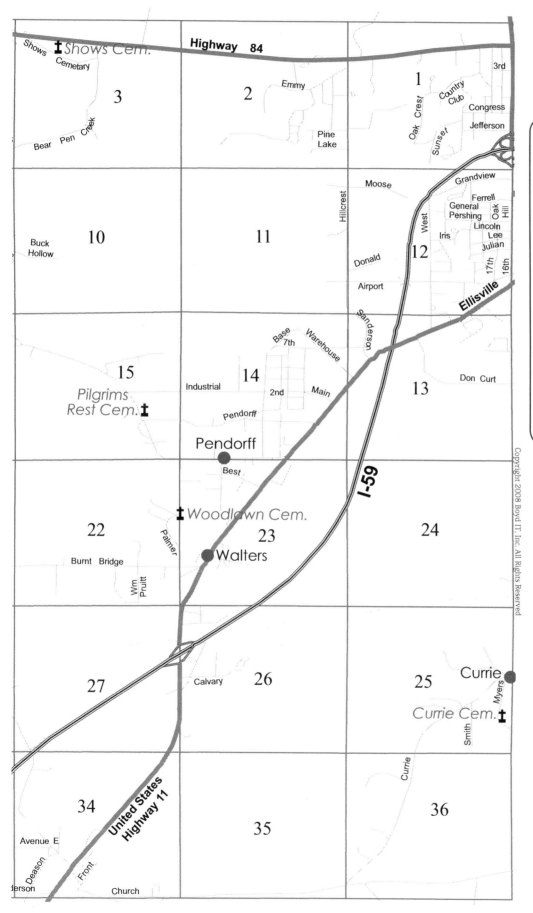

Highway 84

Shows Cemetery
✝ Shows Cem.

3

2

Emmy

1

3rd

Oak Crest

Country Club

Congress

Sunset

Jefferson

Bear Pen Creek

Pine Lake

Moose

Grandview

Hillcrest

Ferrell

General Pershing

Oak Hill

10

11

West

Iris

Lincoln

Lee

Julian

Buck Hollow

12

17th

16th

Donald

Airport

Sanderson

Ellisville

Base

Warehouse

7th

15

14

Industrial

2nd

Main

13

Don Curt

Pilgrims Rest Cem. ✝

Pendorff

Pendorff ●

Best

✝ Woodlawn Cem.

22

Palmer

23

24

Burnt Bridge

● **Walters**

Wm Pruitt

27

Calvary

26

25

Currie ●

Myers

Currie Cem. ✝

Smith

34

United States Highway 11

35

Currie

36

Avenue E

Deason

Front

Church

derson

I-59

Helpful Hints

1. This road map has a number of uses, but primarily it is to help you: a) find the present location of land owned by your ancestors (at least the general area), b) find cemeteries and city-centers, and c) estimate the route/roads used by Census-takers & tax-assessors.

2. If you plan to travel to Jones County to locate cemeteries or land parcels, please pick up a modern travel map for the area before you do. Mapping old land parcels on modern maps is not as exact a science as you might think. Just the slightest variations in public land survey coordinates, estimates of parcel boundaries, or road-map deviations can greatly alter a map's representation of how a road either does or doesn't cross a particular parcel of land.

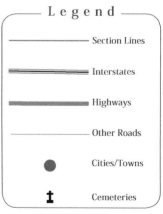

― L e g e n d ―

――――― Section Lines

══════ Interstates

━━━━━ Highways

――――― Other Roads

● Cities/Towns

✝ Cemeteries

Scale: Section = 1 mile X 1 mile
(generally, with some exceptions)

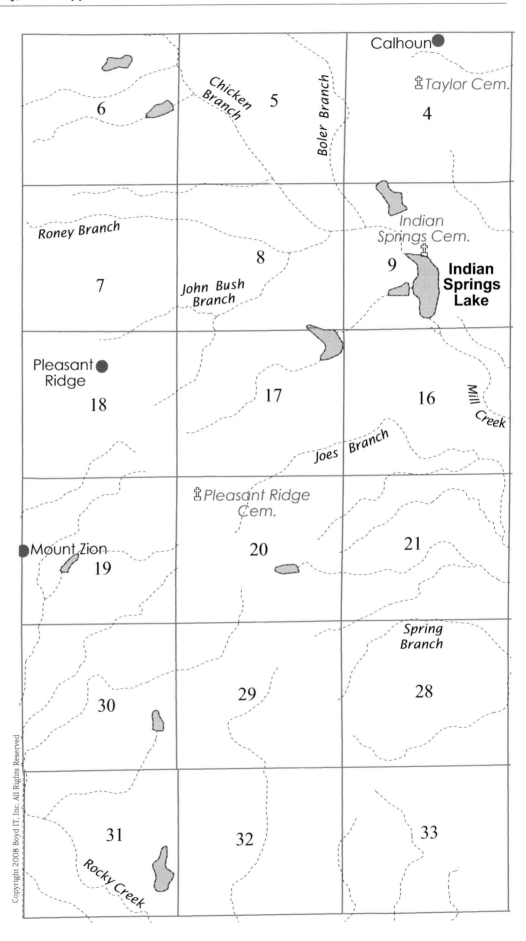

Historical Map

T8-N R12-W
St Stephens Meridian

Map Group 13

Cities & Towns
Calhoun
Currie
Mount Zion
Pendorff
Pleasant Ridge
Walters

Cemeteries
Currie Cemetery
Indian Springs Cemetery
Pilgrims Rest Cemetery
Pleasant Ridge Cemetery
Shows Cemetery
Taylor Cemetery
Woodlawn Cemetery

Calhoun

⚰ Taylor Cem.

Chicken Branch

Boler Branch

6

5

4

Indian Springs Cem.

Roney Branch

8

9

Indian Springs Lake

John Bush Branch

7

Pleasant Ridge

18

17

16

Mill Creek

Joes Branch

⚰ Pleasant Ridge Cem.

Mount Zion

19

20

21

Spring Branch

30

29

28

31

32

33

Rocky Creek

Copyright 2008 Boyd IT, Inc. All Rights Reserved

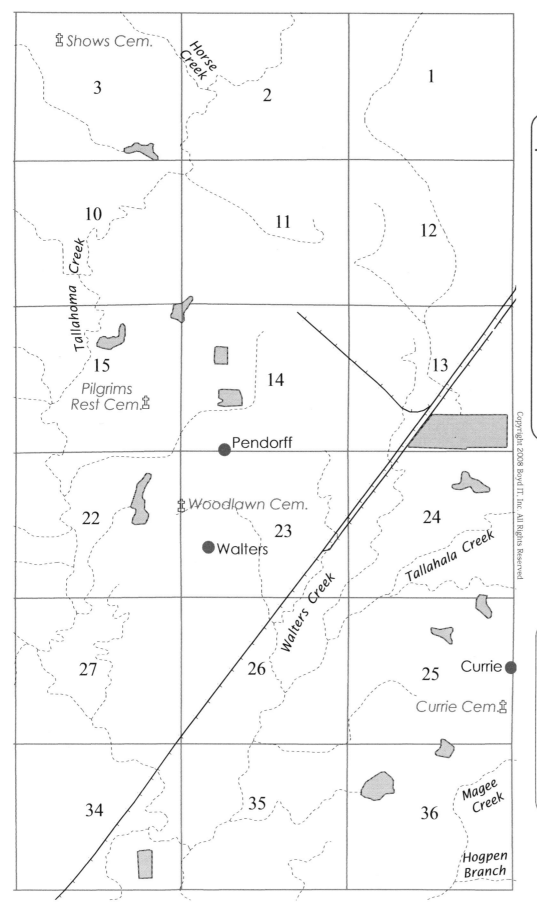

‡ *Shows Cem.*

Horse Creek

3

2

1

10

11

12

Tallahoma Creek

15

Pilgrims Rest Cem. ‡

14

13

● Pendorff

‡ *Woodlawn Cem.*

22

23

24

● Walters

Tallahala Creek

27

26

Walters Creek

25 Currie ●

Currie Cem. ‡

34

35

36

Magee Creek

Hogpen Branch

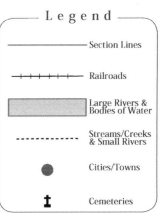

L e g e n d

———— Section Lines

+++++ Railroads

▨ Large Rivers & Bodies of Water

----- Streams/Creeks & Small Rivers

● Cities/Towns

‡ Cemeteries

Scale: Section = 1 mile X 1 mile
(there are some exceptions)

Map Group 14: Index to Land Patents

Township 8-North Range 11-West (St Stephens)

After you locate an individual in this Index, take note of the Section and Section Part then proceed to the Land Patent map on the pages immediately following. You should have no difficulty locating the corresponding parcel of land.

The "For More Info" Column will lead you to more information about the underlying Patents. See the *Legend* at right, and the "How to Use this Book" chapter, for more information.

```
                        LEGEND
              "For More Info . . . " column

A = Authority (Legislative Act, See Appendix "A")
B = Block or Lot (location in Section unknown)
C = Cancelled Patent
F = Fractional Section
G = Group  (Multi-Patentee Patent, see Appendix "C")
V = Overlaps another Parcel
R = Re-Issued (Parcel patented more than once)

(A & G items require you to look in the Appendixes referred
to above. All other Letter-designations followed by a number
require you to locate line-items in this index that possess
the ID number found after the letter).
```

ID	Individual in Patent	Sec.	Sec. Part	Date Issued	Other Counties	For More Info . . .
2421	ARRINGTON, James T	12	NESW	1897-09-09		A3
2387	BEECH, Henry	34	S½NW	1884-12-30		A3
2388	" "	34	W½SW	1884-12-30		A3
2347	BROWN, Albert	11	SW	1892-07-25		A3
2385	BUSH, Green A	18	NWNW	1901-06-08		A3
2462	BUSH, Mason	7	W½NW	1890-08-16		A3
2358	COATNEY, Alzana	3	W½NE	1897-05-07		A3
2359	" "	3	W½SE	1897-05-07		A3
2425	COATNEY, John D	2	W½NW	1892-04-16		A2
2426	" "	3	E½NE	1892-04-16		A2
2492	COLLEY, Thomas S	19	NENE	1882-05-20		A2 G8
2493	" "	19	S½	1882-05-20		A2 G8
2494	" "	19	S½NE	1882-05-20		A2 G8
2495	" "	19	SENW	1882-05-20		A2 G8
2496	" "	20		1882-05-20		A2 G8
2497	" "	29		1882-05-20		A2 G8
2498	" "	30		1882-05-20		A2 G8
2499	" "	31		1882-05-20		A2 G8
2500	" "	32		1882-05-20		A2 G8
2508	COMPANY, William F Evans And	6		1882-05-10		A2
2509	" "	7	NENE	1882-05-10		A2
2510	" "	7	NWSW	1882-05-10		A2
2511	" "	7	SESW	1882-05-10		A2
2512	" "	7	W½NE	1882-05-10		A2
2513	" "	7	W½SE	1882-05-10		A2
2390	CREEL, Isiah	15	E½SW	1890-08-16		A3
2391	" "	15	W½SE	1890-08-16		A3
2414	CREEL, J R	25	N½NE	1879-12-15		A3
2415	" "	25	NESE	1879-12-15		A3
2416	" "	25	SENE	1879-12-15		A3
2473	CREEL, Reuben	4	SWNW	1854-03-15		A2
2477	CREEL, Reubin	5	E½NW	1859-05-02		A2
2481	CREEL, Ruben	5	W½NW	1859-11-10		A2
2485	CREEL, Syreen S	8	NWNW	1860-07-02		A2
2427	FEWOX, John E	1	E½NE	1861-05-01		A2
2417	FOKES, James A	10	NW	1892-04-16		A2
2478	GEDDIE, Robert	27	N½NW	1892-03-23		A3
2479	" "	27	NESW	1892-03-23		A3
2480	" "	27	SENW	1892-03-23		A3
2474	HAYS, Reuben	17	E½SE	1891-06-30		A3
2475	" "	17	SENE	1891-06-30		A3
2349	HOLIFIELD, Albert	21	SESW	1892-04-29		A3
2350	" "	21	SWSE	1892-04-29		A3
2351	" "	21	W½SW	1892-04-29		A3
2355	HOLIFIELD, Alvin	28	N½NE	1893-08-23		A3
2356	" "	28	SENW	1893-08-23		A3

ID	Individual in Patent	Sec.	Sec. Part	Date Issued	Other Counties	For More Info . . .
2357	HOLIFIELD, Alvin (Cont'd)	28	SWNE	1893-08-23		A3
2379	HOLIFIELD, Elijah	21	NW	1892-04-29		A3
2461	HOLIFIELD, Mark	22	SW	1892-04-29		A3 G20
2461	HOLIFIELD, Mary T	22	SW	1892-04-29		A3 G20
2380	HOLLIMON, Elizabeth B	13	NESW	1892-02-12		A3
2381	" "	13	NWSE	1892-02-12		A3
2382	" "	13	SENW	1892-02-12		A3
2383	" "	13	SWNE	1892-02-12		A3
2363	HOWSE, Benjamin B	12	NENE	1895-06-27		A3
2367	HOWSE, Buckner O	1	S½SE	1892-06-15		A3
2368	" "	12	NWNE	1892-06-15		A3
2455	JOSEY, Madison A	21	E½NE	1890-06-25		A3
2456	" "	22	W½NW	1890-06-25		A3
2430	KAMPER, John	1	SENW	1889-04-10		A2
2431	" "	1	SESW	1889-04-10		A2
2432	" "	1	SWNE	1889-04-10		A2
2433	" "	1	W½NW	1889-04-10		A2
2435	" "	12	NENW	1889-04-10		A2
2436	" "	12	NWSW	1889-04-10		A2
2437	" "	12	SWNW	1889-04-10		A2
2434	" "	11	SENE	1889-04-23		A2
2438	" "	14	W½NW	1889-04-23		A2
2439	" "	15	W½SW	1889-04-23		A2
2440	" "	17	NWNE	1889-04-23		A2
2441	" "	2	E½NW	1889-04-23		A2
2442	" "	2	N½SW	1889-04-23		A2
2443	" "	2	NE	1889-04-23		A2
2444	" "	2	W½SE	1889-04-23		A2
2451	" "	3	E½NW	1889-04-23		A2
2452	" "	3	E½SE	1889-04-23		A2
2453	" "	4	NESE	1889-04-23		A2
2454	" "	4	SENE	1889-04-23		A2
2445	" "	22	W½SE	1889-11-29		A2
2448	" "	26	NWSW	1889-11-29		A2
2450	" "	27	W½NE	1889-11-29		A2
2446	" "	23	SENW	1890-07-03		A2
2447	" "	24	N½SW	1890-07-03		A2
2449	" "	27	SESW	1890-07-03		A2
2516	LEE, William T	15	NW	1894-11-22		A3
2348	LEWIS, Albert G	14	SE	1891-05-20		A3
2389	LEWIS, Henry E	14	NE	1892-05-26		A3
2428	LEWIS, John H	23	N½NW	1892-07-25		A3
2429	" "	23	W½NE	1892-07-25		A3
2470	LEWIS, Reece D	23	N½SE	1892-09-15		A3
2471	" "	23	NESW	1892-09-15		A3
2472	" "	23	SENE	1892-09-15		A3
2505	LEWIS, Wallace F	14	SW	1891-12-26		A2
2519	LEWIS, Willis	12	S½SW	1892-05-16		A3
2520	" "	13	N½NW	1892-05-16		A3
2344	LOWE, Alafair	10	NWSW	1892-07-11		A3 G44
2345	" "	10	S½SW	1892-07-11		A3 G44
2346	" "	9	SESE	1892-07-11		A3 G44
2422	MCBRIDE, Jasper N	21	NESW	1891-05-20		A3
2423	" "	21	NWSE	1891-05-20		A3
2424	" "	21	W½NE	1891-05-20		A3 R2404
2392	MOORES, J H	10	E½	1889-04-23		A2
2393	" "	10	NESW	1889-04-23		A2
2394	" "	11	S½NW	1889-04-23		A2
2395	" "	11	W½NE	1889-04-23		A2
2396	" "	13	NWSW	1889-04-23		A2
2397	" "	13	S½SW	1889-04-23		A2
2398	" "	13	SWNW	1889-04-23		A2
2399	" "	13	SWSE	1889-04-23		A2
2400	" "	14	E½NW	1889-04-23		A2
2401	" "	17	SWSW	1889-04-23		A2
2402	" "	2	S½SW	1889-04-23		A2
2403	" "	21	E½SE	1889-04-23		A2
2404	" "	21	W½NE	1889-04-23		A2 R2424
2405	" "	22	E½NW	1889-04-23		A2
2407	" "	24	N½NW	1889-04-23		A2
2408	" "	28	NWNW	1889-04-23		A2
2409	" "	28	NWSW	1889-04-23		A2
2410	" "	9	NESE	1889-04-23		A2

ID	Individual in Patent	Sec.	Sec. Part	Date Issued	Other Counties	For More Info . . .
2411	MOORES, J H (Cont'd)	9	NWSW	1889-04-23		A2
2412	" "	9	SESW	1889-04-23		A2
2413	" "	9	SWSE	1889-04-23		A2
2406	" "	23	NENE	1890-04-25		A2
2514	NELSON, William H	1	NENW	1892-06-15		A3
2515	" "	1	NWNE	1892-06-15		A3
2482	NETTLES, Samuel E	24	E½SE	1859-05-02		A2
2466	PEARSON, Nathan L	28	SESW	1883-05-25		A3
2467	" "	33	N½NE	1883-05-25		A3
2468	" "	33	NENW	1883-05-25		A3
2469	" "	33	S½NE	1886-07-20		A2
2465	" "	28	NENW	1889-04-23		A2
2488	PEARSON, Thomas A	28	SWSW	1892-09-15		A2
2489	" "	33	SENW	1892-09-15		A2
2490	" "	33	W½NW	1892-09-15		A2
2476	PONDER, Reuben	33	S½	1886-07-20		A2
2506	POOL, Warren S	24	S½NW	1892-05-26		A3
2507	" "	24	W½NE	1892-05-26		A3
2386	PRINE, Harriett	27	W½SE	1859-05-02		A2
2352	SINGLETON, Albert	11	SE	1891-09-18		A2
2354	SMITH, Allen	8	SWNW	1859-05-02		A2
2353	" "	7	SENE	1859-06-01		A2
2491	STEPHENS, Thomas J	3	NESW	1896-12-21		A2
2486	SUMRALL, Theodore T	12	NESE	1894-11-22		A3
2487	" "	12	S½NE	1894-11-22		A3
2419	TOUCHSTONE, James L	1	N½SE	1892-06-15		A3
2420	" "	1	NESW	1892-06-15		A3
2378	TREST, Edmond	17	SWNE	1859-05-02		A2
2360	TUCKER, Angus M	23	SESW	1894-04-10		A3
2361	" "	23	SWNW	1894-04-10		A3
2362	" "	23	W½SW	1894-04-10		A3
2457	TUCKER, Martin V	27	NWSW	1884-12-30		A3
2458	" "	27	SWNW	1884-12-30		A3
2459	" "	28	NESE	1884-12-30		A3
2460	" "	28	SENE	1884-12-30		A3
2463	TUCKER, Mathew	35	NWNE	1854-03-15		A2
2464	" "	36	N½NW	1859-05-02		A2
2344	WALTERS, Alafair	10	NWSW	1892-07-11		A3 G44
2345	" "	10	S½SW	1892-07-11		A3 G44
2346	" "	9	SESE	1892-07-11		A3 G44
2364	WALTERS, Benjamin W	3	SESW	1892-04-16		A2
2365	" "	3	SWNW	1892-04-16		A2
2366	" "	3	W½SW	1892-04-16		A2
2369	WALTERS, Calvin R	15	NE	1894-04-14		A3
2370	WALTERS, Dan F	9	NESW	1885-04-04		A3
2371	" "	9	NWSE	1885-04-04		A3
2372	" "	9	S½NE	1885-04-04		A3
2374	WALTERS, Daniel	9	E½NW	1859-05-02		A2
2376	" "	9	NWNE	1859-05-02		A2
2377	" "	9	SWNW	1859-05-02		A2
2373	" "	4	S½SE	1896-04-28		A3
2375	" "	9	NENE	1896-04-28		A3
2384	WALTERS, George	18	W½SW	1846-09-01		A2
2418	WALTERS, James A	25	SENW	1896-12-14		A3
2492	WARNER, Leslie	19	NENE	1882-05-20		A2 G8
2493	" "	19	S½	1882-05-20		A2 G8
2494	" "	19	S½NE	1882-05-20		A2 G8
2495	" "	19	SENW	1882-05-20		A2 G8
2496	" "	20		1882-05-20		A2 G8
2497	" "	29		1882-05-20		A2 G8
2498	" "	30		1882-05-20		A2 G8
2499	" "	31		1882-05-20		A2 G8
2500	" "	32		1882-05-20		A2 G8
2517	WATTERS, William	5	NESW	1859-05-02		A2
2518	" "	5	W½SW	1859-05-02		A2
2503	WELCH, Timothy L	4	NWSE	1885-05-25		A3
2504	" "	4	W½NE	1885-05-25		A3
2483	WEST, Shannon R	3	NWNW	1892-08-01		A2
2484	" "	4	NENE	1892-08-01		A2
2501	WINDHAM, Thomas W	17	E½SW	1884-12-30		A3
2502	" "	17	W½SE	1884-12-30		A3

Patent Map

T8-N R11-W
St Stephens Meridian

Map Group 14

Township Statistics

Parcels Mapped	:	177
Number of Patents	:	81
Number of Individuals	:	67
Patentees Identified	:	64
Number of Surnames	:	41
Multi-Patentee Parcels	:	13
Oldest Patent Date	:	9/1/1846
Most Recent Patent	:	6/8/1901
Block/Lot Parcels	:	0
Parcels Re - Issued	:	1
Parcels that Overlap	:	0
Cities and Towns	:	6
Cemeteries	:	4

Section 6
COMPANY
William F Evans And
1882

Section 5
CREEL Ruben 1859
CREEL Reubin 1859
WATTERS William 1859
WATTERS William 1859

Section 4
CREEL Reuben 1854
WELCH Timothy L 1885
WELCH Timothy L 1885
WEST Shannon R 1892
KAMPER John 1889
KAMPER John 1889
WALTERS Daniel 1896

Section 7
BUSH Mason 1890
COMPANY William F Evans And 1882
COMPANY William F Evans And 1882
COMPANY William F Evans And 1882
COMPANY William F Evans And 1882

Section 8
CREEL Syreen S 1860
SMITH Allen 1859
SMITH Allen 1859

Section 9
WALTERS Daniel 1859
WALTERS Daniel 1859
WALTERS Daniel 1859
WALTERS Dan F 1885
WALTERS Daniel 1896
MOORES J H 1889
WALTERS Dan F 1885
WALTERS Dan F 1885
MOORES J H 1889
MOORES J H 1889
MOORES J H 1889
WALTERS [44] Alafair 1892

Section 18
BUSH Green A 1901
WALTERS George 1846

Section 17
KAMPER John 1889
TREST Edmond 1859
HAYS Reuben 1891
WINDHAM Thomas W 1884
WINDHAM Thomas W 1884
HAYS Reuben 1891
MOORES J H 1889

Section 16

Section 19
COLLEY [8] Thomas S 1882
COLLEY [8] Thomas S 1882
COLLEY [8] Thomas S 1882
COLLEY [8] Thomas S 1882

Section 20
COLLEY [8] Thomas S 1882

Section 21
HOLIFIELD Elijah 1892
MOORES J H 1889
MCBRIDE Jasper N 1891
JOSEY Madison A 1890
HOLIFIELD Albert 1892
MCBRIDE Jasper N 1891
MCBRIDE Jasper N 1891
MOORES J H 1889
HOLIFIELD Albert 1892
HOLIFIELD Albert 1892

Section 30
COLLEY [8] Thomas S 1882

Section 29
COLLEY [8] Thomas S 1882

Section 28
MOORES J H 1889
PEARSON Nathan L 1889
HOLIFIELD Alvin 1893
HOLIFIELD Alvin 1893
HOLIFIELD Alvin 1893
TUCKER Martin V 1884
MOORES J H 1889
TUCKER Martin V 1884
PEARSON Thomas A 1892
PEARSON Nathan L 1883

Section 31
COLLEY [8] Thomas S 1882

Section 32
COLLEY [8] Thomas S 1882

Section 33
PEARSON Thomas A 1892
PEARSON Nathan L 1883
PEARSON Nathan L 1883
PEARSON Thomas A 1892
PEARSON Nathan L 1886
PONDER Reuben 1886

152

		COATNEY John D 1892					KAMPER John 1889	NELSON William H 1892	NELSON William H 1892	
WEST Shannon R 1892	KAMPER John 1889	COATNEY Alzana 1897	COATNEY John D 1892	KAMPER John 1889	KAMPER John 1889			KAMPER John 1889	KAMPER John 1889	FEWOX John E 1861
WALTERS Benjamin W 1892	**3**				**2**					

3 / **2** / **1**

WEST Shannon R 1892 / KAMPER John 1889 / WALTERS Benjamin W 1892 — Section 3

STEPHENS Thomas J 1896 / WALTERS Benjamin W 1892 / COATNEY Alzana 1897 / KAMPER John 1889 / KAMPER John 1889 / MOORES J H 1889 / KAMPER John 1889

TOUCHSTONE James L 1892 / TOUCHSTONE James L 1892 / KAMPER John 1889 / HOWSE Buckner O 1892 — Section 1

10 — FOKES James A 1892 / MOORES J H 1889 / WALTERS [44] Alafair 1892 / MOORES J H 1889 / WALTERS [44] Alafair 1892

11 — MOORES J H 1889 / MOORES J H 1889 / KAMPER John 1889 / SINGLETON Albert 1891 / BROWN Albert 1892

12 — KAMPER John 1889 / SUMRALL Theodore T 1894 / KAMPER John 1889 / ARRINGTON James T 1897 / SUMRALL Theodore T 1894 / LEWIS Willis 1892 / HOWSE Buckner O 1892 / HOWSE Benjamin B 1895

15 — LEE William T 1894 / WALTERS Calvin R 1894 / KAMPER John 1889 / CREEL Isiah 1890 / CREEL Isiah 1890

14 — KAMPER John 1889 / MOORES J H 1889 / LEWIS Henry E 1892 / LEWIS Wallace F 1891 / LEWIS Albert G 1891

13 — LEWIS Willis 1892 / MOORES J H 1889 / HOLLIMON Elizabeth B 1892 / HOLLIMON Elizabeth B 1892 / MOORES J H 1889 / HOLLIMON Elizabeth B 1892 / HOLLIMON Elizabeth B 1892 / MOORES J H 1889 / MOORES J H 1889

22 — JOSEY Madison A 1890 / MOORES J H 1889 / HOLIFIELD [20] Mary T 1892 / KAMPER John 1889

23 — LEWIS John H 1892 / LEWIS John H 1892 / TUCKER Angus M 1894 / KAMPER John 1890 / MOORES J H 1890 / LEWIS Reece D 1892 / LEWIS Reece D 1892 / LEWIS Reece D 1892 / TUCKER Angus M 1894 / TUCKER Angus M 1894

24 — MOORES J H 1889 / POOL Warren S 1892 / POOL Warren S 1892 / KAMPER John 1890 / NETTLES Samuel E 1859

27 — GEDDIE Robert 1892 / TUCKER Martin V 1884 / GEDDIE Robert 1892 / KAMPER John 1889 / TUCKER Martin V 1884 / GEDDIE Robert 1892 / PRINE Harriett 1859 / KAMPER John 1890

26 — KAMPER John 1889

25 — CREEL J R 1879 / WALTERS James A 1896 / CREEL J R 1879 / CREEL J R 1879

34 — BEECH Henry 1884 / BEECH Henry 1884

35 — TUCKER Mathew 1854

36 — TUCKER Mathew 1859

Helpful Hints

1. This Map's INDEX can be found on the preceding pages.

2. Refer to Map "C" to see where this Township lies within Jones County, Mississippi.

3. Numbers within square brackets [ ] denote a multi-patentee land parcel (multi-owner). Refer to Appendix "C" for a full list of members in this group.

4. Areas that look to be crowded with Patentees usually indicate multiple sales of the same parcel (Re-issues) or Overlapping parcels. See this Township's Index for an explanation of these and other circumstances that might explain "odd" groupings of Patentees on this map.

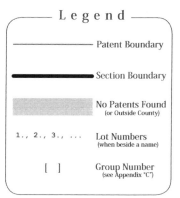

Legend

—————— Patent Boundary

━━━━━━ Section Boundary

▓▓▓▓▓▓ No Patents Found
(or Outside County)

1., 2., 3., ... Lot Numbers
(when beside a name)

[ ] Group Number
(see Appendix "C")

Scale: Section = 1 mile X 1 mile
(generally, with some exceptions)

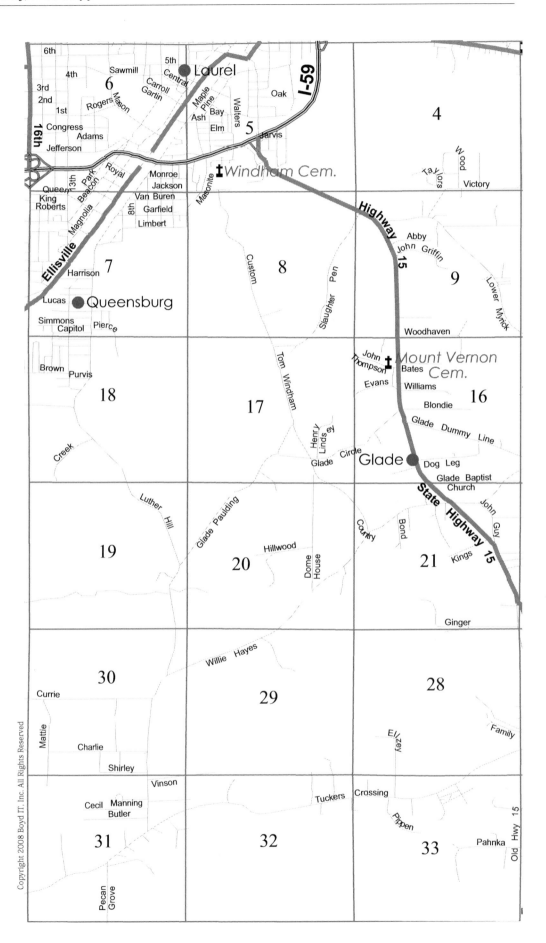

Road Map

T8-N R11-W
St Stephens Meridian

Map Group 14

Cities & Towns

Antioch
Glade
Glaston
Laurel
Queensburg
Tuckers Crossing

Cemeteries

Antioch Cemetery
Mount Oral Cemetery
Mount Vernon Cemetery
Windham Cemetery

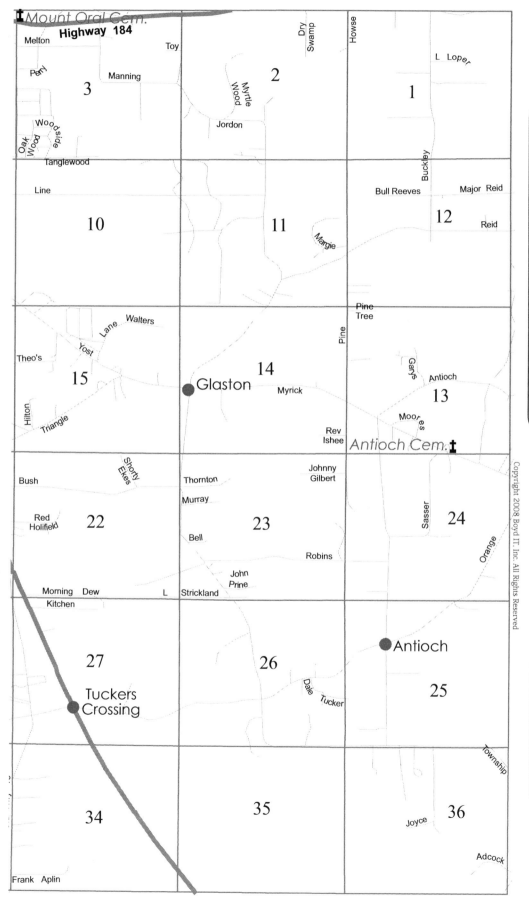

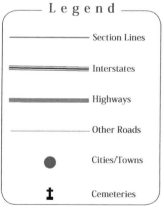

Helpful Hints

1. This road map has a number of uses, but primarily it is to help you: a) find the present location of land owned by your ancestors (at least the general area), b) find cemeteries and city-centers, and c) estimate the route/roads used by Census-takers & tax-assessors.

2. If you plan to travel to Jones County to locate cemeteries or land parcels, please pick up a modern travel map for the area before you do. Mapping old land parcels on modern maps is not as exact a science as you might think. Just the slightest variations in public land survey coordinates, estimates of parcel boundaries, or road-map deviations can greatly alter a map's representation of how a road either does or doesn't cross a particular parcel of land.

— Legend —

———	Section Lines
═══	Interstates
▬▬▬	Highways
———	Other Roads
●	Cities/Towns
✝	Cemeteries

Scale: Section = 1 mile X 1 mile
(generally, with some exceptions)

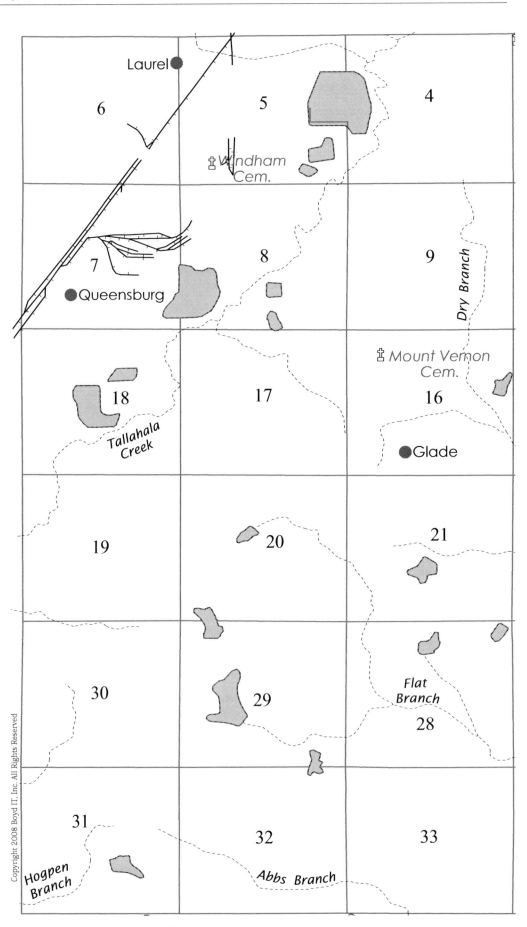

Historical Map

T8-N R11-W
St Stephens Meridian

Map Group 14

Laurel ●

6

5

4

✞ Windham
Cem.

Cities & Towns
Antioch
Glade
Glaston
Laurel
Queensburg
Tuckers Crossing

7

8

9

Dry Branch

● Queensburg

✞ Mount Vernon
Cem.

18

17

16

Tallahala
Creek

● Glade

Cemeteries
Antioch Cemetery
Mount Oral Cemetery
Mount Vernon Cemetery
Windham Cemetery

19

20

21

30

29

Flat
Branch

28

31

32

33

Hogpen
Branch

Abbs Branch

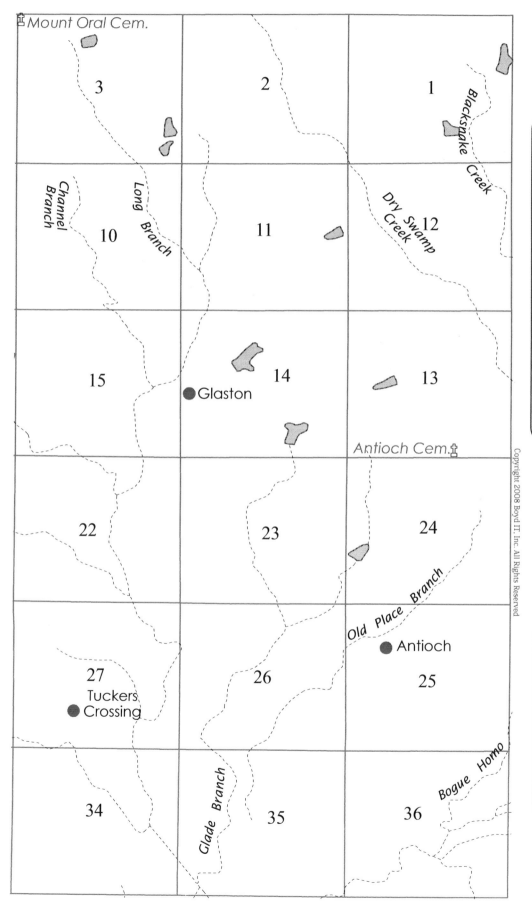

‡Mount Oral Cem.

3

2

1

Blacksnake Creek

Channel Branch

Long Branch

Dry Swamp Creek

10

11

12

15

●Glaston

14

13

Antioch Cem.‡

22

23

24

Old Place Branch

27

Tuckers
●Crossing

26

●Antioch

25

Glade Branch

34

35

36

Bogue Homo

Helpful Hints

1. This Map takes a different look at the same Congressional Township displayed in the preceding two maps. It presents features that can help you better envision the historical development of the area: a) Water-bodies (lakes & ponds), b) Water-courses (rivers, streams, etc.), c) Railroads, d) City/town center-points (where they were oftentimes located when first settled), and e) Cemeteries.

2. Using this "Historical" map in tandem with this Township's Patent Map and Road Map, may lead you to some interesting discoveries. You will often find roads, towns, cemeteries, and waterways are named after nearby landowners: sometimes those names will be the ones you are researching. See how many of these research gems you can find here in Jones County.

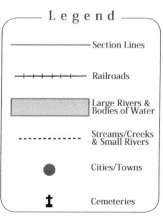

Legend

————————	Section Lines
+++++++	Railroads
�▬	Large Rivers & Bodies of Water
- - - - - - -	Streams/Creeks & Small Rivers
●	Cities/Towns
‡	Cemeteries

Scale: Section = 1 mile X 1 mile
(there are some exceptions)

Map Group 15: Index to Land Patents

Township 8-North Range 10-West (St Stephens)

After you locate an individual in this Index, take note of the Section and Section Part then proceed to the Land Patent map on the pages immediately following. You should have no difficulty locating the corresponding parcel of land.

The "For More Info" Column will lead you to more information about the underlying Patents. See the *Legend* at right, and the "How to Use this Book" chapter, for more information.

```
LEGEND
          "For More Info . . . " column
A = Authority (Legislative Act, See Appendix "A")
B = Block or Lot (location in Section unknown)
C = Cancelled Patent
F = Fractional Section
G = Group  (Multi-Patentee Patent, see Appendix "C")
V = Overlaps another Parcel
R = Re-Issued (Parcel patented more than once)

(A & G items require you to look in the Appendixes referred
to above. All other Letter-designations followed by a number
require you to locate line-items in this index that possess
the ID number found after the letter).
```

ID	Individual in Patent	Sec.	Sec. Part	Date Issued	Other Counties	For More Info . . .
2564	ALWAY, Fredrick	31	E½SE	1889-04-10		A2
2565	" "	31	S½SW	1889-04-10		A2
2566	" "	31	SWSE	1889-04-10		A2
2567	" "	32	SESW	1889-04-10		A2
2568	" "	32	W½SW	1889-04-10		A2
2521	BEDWELL, Albert	15	W½SE	1893-08-14		A3
2544	BLACKLEDGE, Daniel	1	NWSW	1859-05-02		A2
2545	" "	1	SWNW	1860-04-02		A2
2549	BLACKLIDGE, Dennis C	2	N½SW	1891-05-20		A3
2550	" "	2	W½SE	1891-05-20		A3
2584	BLACKLIDGE, James E	1	NWNW	1896-02-13		A3
2585	" "	2	N½NE	1896-02-13		A3
2600	BLACKLIDGE, John	11	NENW	1882-04-20		A2
2601	" "	11	NWNW	1886-02-10		A2
2610	BLACKLIDGE, John L	10	N½NW	1888-02-25		A3
2611	" "	10	SWNW	1888-02-25		A3
2612	" "	3	SESW	1888-02-25		A3
2571	BOUTWELL, George B	31	N½SW	1905-08-26		A3
2645	BRELAND, John W	12	SWSW	1890-08-16		A3
2646	" "	13	NWSW	1890-08-16		A3
2647	" "	13	W½NW	1890-08-16		A3
2730	BRELAND, William T	13	NWSE	1887-05-27		A2
2552	BRYAN, Edward	10	NENE	1860-10-01		A2
2553	CLARK, Edward	8	NESW	1859-05-02		A2
2554	" "	8	NWSE	1859-05-02		A2
2555	" "	8	SENW	1859-05-02		A2
2557	" "	8	SWNE	1859-05-02		A2
2556	" "	8	SESW	1859-11-10		A2
2558	" "	8	SWSE	1859-11-10		A2
2572	CLARK, George E	9	E½SW	1892-06-15		A3
2573	" "	9	SENW	1892-06-15		A3
2574	" "	9	SWNE	1892-06-15		A3
2603	CLARK, John	17	SWSW	1859-05-02		A2
2606	" "	18	SESE	1859-05-02		A2
2602	" "	17	NWSW	1860-07-02		A2 R2718
2604	" "	18	NESE	1860-07-02		A2
2605	" "	18	SENE	1860-07-02		A2
2543	CRAVEN, Columbus C	3	E½NE	1888-02-25		A3
2597	CRAVEN, Jinkins R	4	NWNW	1859-11-10		A2
2598	" "	5	NENE	1859-11-10		A2
2666	CRAVEN, Malden M	6	NWNE	1859-11-10		A2
2668	" "	6	W½NW	1860-04-02		A2
2667	" "	6	NWSW	1860-07-02		A2
2669	CRAVEN, Maldon M	6	NESW	1859-11-10		A2
2670	" "	6	SENW	1859-11-10		A2
2682	CRAVEN, Ritchmon Z	9	NENW	1897-04-02		A3

ID	Individual in Patent	Sec.	Sec. Part	Date Issued	Other Counties	For More Info . . .
2683	CRAVEN, Ritchmon Z (Cont'd)	9	NWNE	1897-04-02		A3
2723	CRAVEN, William E	24	SENW	1899-06-13		A3
2724	" "	24	W½NE	1899-06-13		A3
2608	DAVIS, John J	36	E½SE	1898-12-27		A3
2609	" "	36	NENE	1898-12-27		A3
2654	DAVIS, Josiah J	13	NENW	1860-04-02		A2
2655	" "	13	NESW	1860-04-02		A2
2656	" "	13	SWNE	1860-04-02		A2
2678	HODGES, Powhattan E	4	NENW	1861-02-01		A2
2595	HOLIFIELD, Jesse J	4	W½NE	1895-02-21		A3
2596	" "	4	W½SE	1895-02-21		A3
2714	HOLIFIELD, Swinton	3	SWNW	1892-09-02		A3
2715	" "	4	E½NE	1892-09-02		A3
2716	" "	4	NESE	1892-09-02		A3
2727	HOLIFIELD, William M	8	E½NE	1894-11-22		A3
2728	" "	8	E½SE	1894-11-22		A3
2537	HOWSE, Benjamin B	7	W½NW	1895-06-27		A3
2538	HOWSE, Buckner O	6	SWSW	1892-06-15		A3
2559	JENKINS, Elijah J	22	NESE	1884-12-30		A3
2560	" "	22	S½SE	1884-12-30		A3
2561	" "	22	SENE	1884-12-30		A3
2731	JENKINS, William T	22	NWSE	1905-02-13		A3
2732	" "	22	NWSW	1905-02-13		A3
2542	JONES, Christopher C	17	NE	1894-12-17		A3
2719	LANDRUM, Wiley H	13	SENW	1859-05-02		A2
2725	LANDRUM, William H	3	E½NW	1894-04-10		A3
2726	" "	3	NESW	1894-04-10		A3
2657	LANGLEY, Josiah	24	NESE	1902-07-22		A2
2672	LOTT, Mary E	35	SESW	1898-07-18		A3
2673	" "	35	SWSE	1898-07-18		A3
2614	MCKEOWN, John	23	E½SW	1884-12-30		A2
2615	" "	23	S½SE	1884-12-30		A2
2616	" "	24	S½SE	1884-12-30		A2
2617	" "	24	S½SW	1884-12-30		A2
2618	" "	25	E½SE	1884-12-30		A2
2619	" "	25	NWNE	1884-12-30		A2
2620	" "	25	SWSE	1884-12-30		A2
2621	" "	25	W½	1884-12-30		A2
2622	" "	26	E½	1884-12-30		A2
2623	" "	26	E½NW	1884-12-30		A2
2624	" "	26	SW	1884-12-30		A2
2625	" "	26	SWNW	1884-12-30		A2
2626	" "	27	E½SW	1884-12-30		A2
2627	" "	27	SE	1884-12-30		A2
2628	" "	33	E½SE	1884-12-30		A2
2629	" "	33	SESW	1884-12-30		A2
2630	" "	33	SWSE	1884-12-30		A2
2631	" "	34	E½	1884-12-30		A2
2632	" "	34	E½NW	1884-12-30		A2
2633	" "	34	SW	1884-12-30		A2
2634	" "	35	E½NW	1884-12-30		A2
2635	" "	35	N½SE	1884-12-30		A2
2636	" "	35	NE	1884-12-30		A2
2637	" "	35	NESW	1884-12-30		A2
2638	" "	35	NWNW	1884-12-30		A2
2639	" "	35	SESE	1884-12-30		A2
2640	" "	35	SWSW	1884-12-30		A2
2641	" "	36	W½	1884-12-30		A2
2642	" "	36	W½NE	1884-12-30		A2
2643	" "	36	W½SE	1884-12-30		A2
2576	MCLEAIN, Harvey M	23	SENE	1906-09-14		A3
2562	MCLENDON, Frank	21	S½SE	1895-06-27		A3
2563	" "	22	S½SW	1895-06-27		A3
2658	MILLER, Laura	9	SENE	1906-06-16		A3 G45
2663	MILLER, Lewis W	29	SESW	1899-05-31		A3
2664	" "	29	SWSE	1899-05-31		A3
2665	MILLER, Louis N	33	SWSW	1907-05-09		A3
2578	MITCHEL, Henry	29	SWSW	1859-11-10		A2
2579	" "	32	NWNW	1859-11-10		A2
2569	MORGAN, Gaines G	21	E½NW	1898-11-11		A3
2570	" "	21	N½NE	1898-11-11		A3
2575	MOTT, George M	17	SE	1892-03-17		A3
2674	MYRICK, Mary E	15	SW	1892-06-30		A3

ID	Individual in Patent	Sec.	Sec. Part	Date Issued	Other Counties	For More Info . . .
2588	NOWELL, James	13	E½SE	1898-12-27		A3
2589	" "	13	SWSE	1898-12-27		A3
2590	" "	24	NENE	1898-12-27		A3
2651	NOWELL, Joshua	25	E½NE	1890-03-28		A3
2652	" "	25	NWSE	1890-03-28		A3
2653	" "	25	SWNE	1890-03-28		A3
2539	PATRICK, Cathrine	3	W½SW	1897-05-07		A3
2540	" "	4	SESE	1897-05-07		A3
2541	" "	9	NENE	1897-05-07		A3
2659	PATRICK, Lewis D	20	E½SE	1895-07-11		A2
2660	" "	20	SWSE	1895-07-11		A2
2661	" "	21	NWSW	1895-07-11		A2
2662	" "	21	SWNW	1895-07-11		A2
2534	PRYOR, Barnett	4	SESW	1888-04-05		A3
2535	" "	4	W½SW	1888-04-05		A3
2536	" "	9	NWNW	1888-04-05		A3
2591	PRYOR, James	5	E½SE	1888-03-15		A3
2592	" "	5	NWSE	1888-03-15		A3
2644	RODGERS, John	7	W½SW	1859-11-10		A2
2607	RODGERS, John D	18	W½NW	1860-08-01		A2
2675	SANTSON, Oliver	9	SWNW	1897-09-09		A3
2676	" "	9	W½SW	1897-09-09		A3
2729	SMITH, William N	2	S½NW	1908-02-06		A3
2720	STRICKLAND, William A	35	NWSW	1893-12-19		A3
2721	" "	35	SWNW	1893-12-19		A3
2593	SUMRALL, James	17	E½NW	1893-09-08		A3
2580	SUMRALL, James A	28	NWSW	1895-02-21		A3
2581	" "	28	SWNW	1895-02-21		A3
2582	" "	29	NESE	1895-02-21		A3
2583	" "	29	SENE	1895-02-21		A3
2594	SUMRALL, Jefferson	17	SWNW	1893-09-08		A3
2733	TOUCHSTONE, Wilson Wesley	4	NESW	1921-01-24		A3
2677	TREST, Peter N	6	NENW	1859-05-02		A2
2551	VALENTINE, Drayton V	20	SESW	1910-05-19		A3
2671	VALENTINE, Martin B	27	NW	1898-01-19		A3
2711	VALENTINE, Susan A	26	NWNW	1900-11-28		A3
2712	" "	27	N½NE	1900-11-28		A3
2713	" "	27	SENE	1900-11-28		A3
2684	WADDELL, Seid	10	SESE	1889-11-29		A2
2685	" "	11	S½SW	1889-11-29		A2
2686	" "	11	SE	1889-11-29		A2
2687	" "	12	E½SW	1889-11-29		A2
2688	" "	12	NWSW	1889-11-29		A2
2689	" "	12	S½NE	1889-11-29		A2
2690	" "	12	S½NW	1889-11-29		A2
2691	" "	12	SE	1889-11-29		A2
2692	" "	13	E½NE	1889-11-29		A2
2693	" "	13	NWNE	1889-11-29		A2
2694	" "	14		1889-11-29		A2
2695	" "	15	E½SE	1889-11-29		A2
2696	" "	15	N½	1889-11-29		A2
2697	" "	23	W½SW	1889-11-29		A2
2698	" "	27	SWNE	1889-11-29		A2
2699	" "	27	W½SW	1889-11-29		A2
2704	" "	32	E½	1889-11-29		A2
2705	" "	32	E½NW	1889-11-29		A2
2706	" "	32	NESW	1889-11-29		A2
2707	" "	33	N½	1889-11-29		A2
2708	" "	33	N½SW	1889-11-29		A2
2709	" "	33	NWSE	1889-11-29		A2
2710	" "	34	W½NW	1889-11-29		A2
2700	" "	28	E½	1890-08-13		A2
2701	" "	28	E½NW	1890-08-13		A2
2702	" "	28	E½SW	1890-08-13		A2
2703	" "	28	NWNW	1890-08-13		A2
2528	WALTERS, Albert	10	SESW	1911-10-19		A3
2529	" "	10	SWSE	1911-10-19		A3
2531	WALTERS, Archibald M	29	E½NW	1859-11-10		A2
2532	" "	29	NWNW	1859-11-10		A2
2533	WALTERS, Archibald W	29	N½NE	1859-05-02		A2
2547	WALTERS, Daniel E	2	NESE	1859-11-10		A2
2548	" "	2	S½NE	1859-11-10		A2
2546	" "	1	SWSW	1898-10-04		A3

ID	Individual in Patent	Sec.	Sec. Part	Date Issued	Other Counties	For More Info . . .
2577	WALTERS, Henry E	2	S½SW	1901-03-23		A3
2586	WALTERS, James E	2	NWNW	1891-03-16		A3
2599	WALTERS, Joel W	3	NWNW	1859-05-02		A2
2613	WALTERS, John M	11	NWNE	1906-06-16		A3
2648	WALTERS, John W	31	NWSE	1895-06-28		A3
2649	"	31	S½NE	1895-06-28		A3
2650	"	32	SWNW	1895-06-28		A3
2658	WALTERS, Laura	9	SENE	1906-06-16		A3 G45
2679	WALTERS, Richard M	13	SESW	1897-07-03		A3
2680	"	24	N½NW	1897-07-03		A3
2681	"	24	SWNW	1897-07-03		A3
2717	WALTERS, Tabitha J	17	E½SW	1889-01-12		A3
2718	"	17	NWSW	1889-01-12		A3 R2602
2722	WALTERS, William C	2	SESE	1911-01-05		A3
2530	WATTERS, Archabald	20	W½SW	1859-11-10		A2
2587	WATTERS, James E	2	NENW	1859-05-02		A2
2522	WELBORN, Albert G	5	SWSE	1859-11-10		A2
2523	"	8	NENW	1859-11-10		A2
2524	"	8	NWNE	1859-11-10		A2
2525	WELBORNE, Albert G	17	NWNW	1860-10-01		A2
2526	"	18	NENE	1860-10-01		A2
2527	"	8	SWSW	1860-10-01		A2

Patent Map

T8-N R10-W
St Stephens Meridian

Map Group 15

Township Statistics

Parcels Mapped	:	213
Number of Patents	:	102
Number of Individuals	:	82
Patentees Identified	:	81
Number of Surnames	:	42
Multi-Patentee Parcels	:	1
Oldest Patent Date	:	5/2/1859
Most Recent Patent	:	1/24/1921
Block/Lot Parcels	:	0
Parcels Re-Issued	:	1
Parcels that Overlap	:	0
Cities and Towns	:	2
Cemeteries	:	4

Copyright 2008 Boyd IT, Inc. All Rights Reserved

Section 6
- CRAVEN Malden M 1860
- TREST Peter N 1859
- CRAVEN Malden M 1859
- CRAVEN Maldon M 1859
- CRAVEN Malden M 1860
- CRAVEN Maldon M 1859
- HOWSE Buckner O 1892

Section 5

- CRAVEN Jinkins R 1859
- PRYOR James 1888
- WELBORN Albert G 1859
- PRYOR James 1888

Section 4
- CRAVEN Jinkins R 1859
- HODGES Powhattan E 1861
- HOLIFIELD Jesse J 1895
- HOLIFIELD Swinton 1892
- PRYOR Barnett 1888
- TOUCHSTONE Wilson Wesley 1921
- HOLIFIELD Swinton 1892
- HOLIFIELD Jesse J 1895
- PRYOR Barnett 1888
- PATRICK Cathrine 1897

Section 7
- HOWSE Benjamin B 1895
- RODGERS John 1859

Section 8
- WELBORN Albert G 1859
- WELBORN Albert G 1859
- HOLIFIELD William M 1894
- CLARK Edward 1859
- CLARK Edward 1859
- CLARK Edward 1859
- CLARK Edward 1859
- WELBORNE Albert G 1860
- CLARK Edward 1859
- CLARK Edward 1859
- HOLIFIELD William M 1894

Section 9
- PRYOR Barnett 1888
- CRAVEN Ritchmon Z 1897
- CRAVEN Ritchmon Z 1897
- PATRICK Cathrine 1897
- SANTSON Oliver 1897
- CLARK George E 1892
- CLARK George E 1892
- WALTERS [45] Laura 1906
- CLARK George E 1892
- SANTSON Oliver 1897

Section 18
- RODGERS John D 1860
- WELBORNE Albert G 1860
- CLARK John 1860
- CLARK John 1860
- CLARK John 1859

Section 17
- WELBORNE Albert G 1860
- SUMRALL James 1893
- SUMRALL Jefferson 1893
- WALTERS Tabitha J / CLARK 1889 John 1860
- CLARK John 1859
- WALTERS Tabitha J 1889
- JONES Christopher C 1894
- MOTT George M 1892

Section 16

Section 19

Section 20
- WATTERS Archabald 1859
- VALENTINE Drayton V 1910
- PATRICK Lewis D 1895
- PATRICK Lewis D 1895

Section 21
- PATRICK Lewis D 1895
- MORGAN Gaines G 1898
- MORGAN Gaines G 1898
- PATRICK Lewis D 1895
- MCLENDON Frank 1895

Section 30

Section 29
- WALTERS Archibald M 1859
- WALTERS Archibald M 1859
- WALTERS Archibald W 1859
- SUMRALL James A 1895
- SUMRALL James A 1895

Section 28
- WADDELL Seid 1890
- WADDELL Seid 1890
- SUMRALL James A 1895
- WADDELL Seid 1890
- WADDELL Seid 1890

Section 31
- WALTERS John W 1895
- BOUTWELL George B 1905
- WALTERS John W 1895
- ALWAY Fredrick 1889
- ALWAY Fredrick 1889
- ALWAY Fredrick 1889

Section 32
- MITCHEL Henry 1859
- MILLER Lewis W 1899
- MILLER Lewis W 1899
- MITCHEL Henry 1859
- WADDELL Seid 1889
- WALTERS John W 1895
- ALWAY Fredrick 1889
- WADDELL Seid 1889
- WADDELL Seid 1889
- ALWAY Fredrick 1889

Section 33
- WADDELL Seid 1889
- WADDELL Seid 1889
- WADDELL Seid 1889
- WADDELL Seid 1889
- MCKEOWN John 1884
- MILLER Louis N 1907
- MCKEOWN John 1884
- MCKEOWN John 1884

WALTERS Joel W 1859	LANDRUM William H 1894		CRAVEN Columbus C 1888	WALTERS James E 1891	WATTERS James E 1859

3

2

1

WALTERS
Joel W
1859

HOLIFIELD
Swinton
1892

LANDRUM
William H
1894

LANDRUM
William H
1894

PATRICK
Cathrine
1897

BLACKLIDGE
John L
1888

CRAVEN
Columbus C
1888

WALTERS
James E
1891

WATTERS
James E
1859

BLACKLIDGE
James E
1896

SMITH
William N
1908

WALTERS
Daniel E
1859

BLACKLIDGE
Dennis C
1891

WALTERS
Daniel E
1859

BLACKLIDGE
Dennis C
1891

WALTERS
Henry E
1901

WALTERS
William C
1911

BLACKLIDGE
James E
1896

BLACKLEDGE
Daniel
1860

BLACKLEDGE
Daniel
1859

WALTERS
Daniel E
1898

10

BLACKLIDGE
John L
1888

BLACKLIDGE
John L
1888

BRYAN
Edward
1860

BLACKLIDGE
John
1886

BLACKLIDGE
John
1882

WALTERS
John M
1906

WALTERS
Albert
1911

WALTERS
Albert
1911

WADDELL
Seid
1889

11

WADDELL
Seid
1889

WADDELL
Seid
1889

WADDELL
Seid
1889

12

WADDELL
Seid
1889

WADDELL
Seid
1889

BRELAND
John W
1890

WADDELL
Seid
1889

WADDELL
Seid
1889

15

WADDELL
Seid
1889

MYRICK
Mary E
1892

BEDWELL
Albert
1893

WADDELL
Seid
1889

14

WADDELL
Seid
1889

WADDELL
Seid
1889

BRELAND
John W
1890

DAVIS
Josiah J
1860

LANDRUM
Wiley H
1859

WADDELL
Seid
1889

DAVIS
Josiah J
1860

WADDELL
Seid
1889

13

BRELAND
John W
1890

DAVIS
Josiah J
1860

BRELAND
William T
1887

NOWELL
James
1898

WALTERS
Richard M
1897

NOWELL
James
1898

22

JENKINS
Elijah J
1884

23

WALTERS
Richard M
1897

NOWELL
James
1898

CRAVEN
William E
1899

JENKINS
William T
1905

JENKINS
William T
1905

JENKINS
Elijah J
1884

MCLEAIN
Harvey M
1906

WALTERS
Richard M
1897

CRAVEN
William E
1899

24

MCLENDON
Frank
1895

JENKINS
Elijah J
1884

WADDELL
Seid
1889

MCKEOWN
John
1884

MCKEOWN
John
1884

MCKEOWN
John
1884

MCKEOWN
John
1884

LANGLEY
Josiah
1902

VALENTINE
Martin B
1898

VALENTINE
Susan A
1900

WADDELL
Seid
1889

VALENTINE
Susan A
1900

VALENTINE
Susan A
1900

MCKEOWN
John
1884

MCKEOWN
John
1884

MCKEOWN
John
1884

NOWELL
Joshua
1890

WADDELL
Seid
1889

MCKEOWN
John
1884

27

MCKEOWN
John
1884

26

MCKEOWN
John
1884

MCKEOWN
John
1884

25

MCKEOWN
John
1884

NOWELL
Joshua
1890

NOWELL
Joshua
1890

MCKEOWN
John
1884

MCKEOWN
John
1884

WADDELL
Seid
1889

MCKEOWN
John
1884

34

MCKEOWN
John
1884

MCKEOWN
John
1884

STRICKLAND
William A
1893

MCKEOWN
John
1884

35

MCKEOWN
John
1884

36

MCKEOWN
John
1884

DAVIS
John J
1898

MCKEOWN
John
1884

STRICKLAND
William A
1893

MCKEOWN
John
1884

MCKEOWN
John
1884

MCKEOWN
John
1884

MCKEOWN
John
1884

LOTT
Mary E
1898

LOTT
Mary E
1898

MCKEOWN
John
1884

DAVIS
John J
1898

Helpful Hints

1. This Map's INDEX can be found on the preceding pages.

2. Refer to Map "C" to see where this Township lies within Jones County, Mississippi.

3. Numbers within square brackets [ ] denote a multi-patentee land parcel (multi-owner). Refer to Appendix "C" for a full list of members in this group.

4. Areas that look to be crowded with Patentees usually indicate multiple sales of the same parcel (Re-issues) or Overlapping parcels. See this Township's Index for an explanation of these and other circumstances that might explain "odd" groupings of Patentees on this map.

Legend

———————	Patent Boundary
━━━━━━━	Section Boundary
░░░░░░	No Patents Found (or Outside County)
1., 2., 3., . . .	Lot Numbers (when beside a name)
[ ]	Group Number (see Appendix "C")

Scale: Section = 1 mile X 1 mile
(generally, with some exceptions)

Road Map

T8-N R10-W
St Stephens Meridian

Map Group 15

Cities & Towns
Mill Creek
Myrick

Cemeteries
Clark Cemetery
Dennis Blackledge Cemetery
Mill Creek Cemetery
Myrick Cemetery

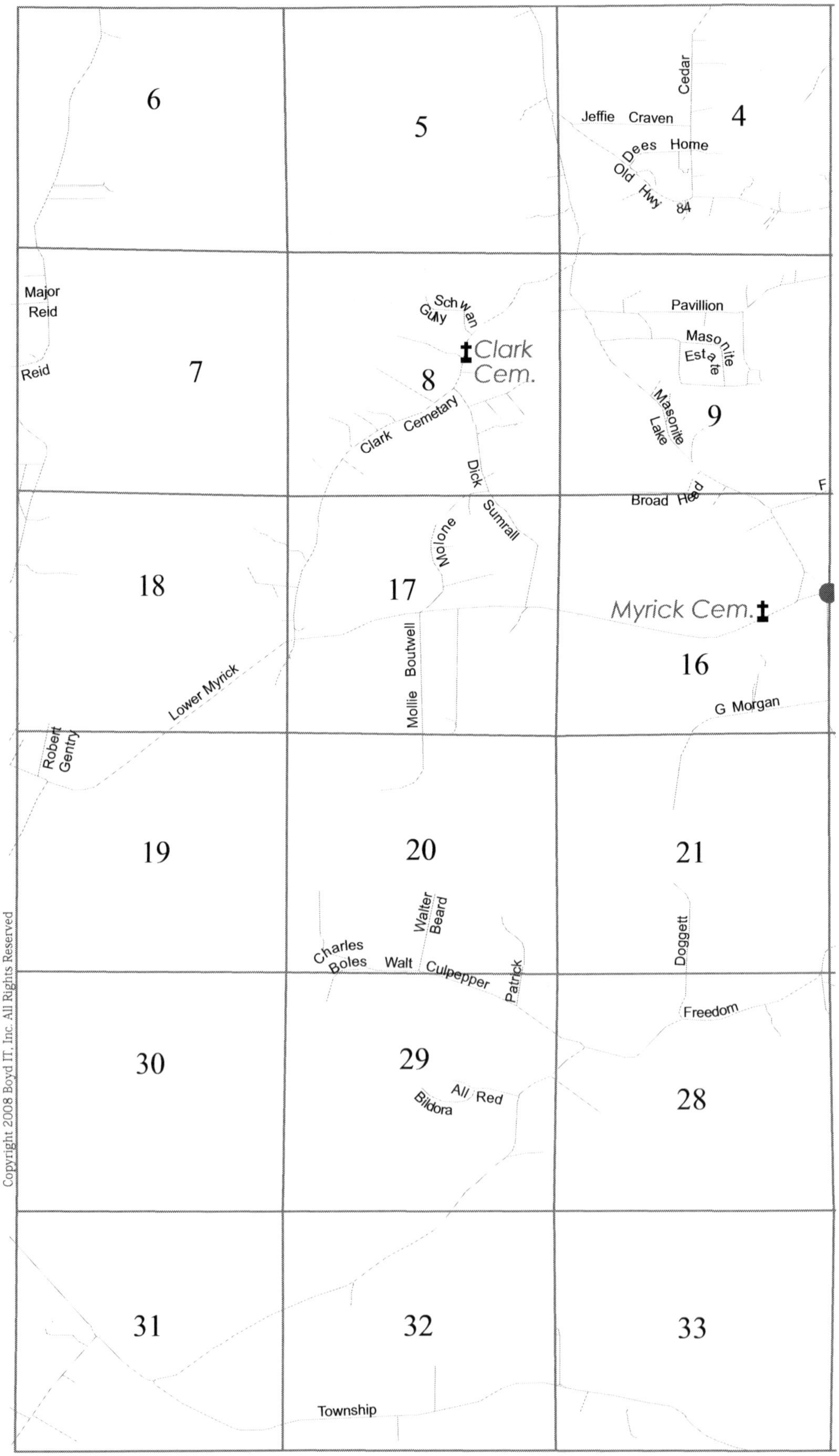

6

5

Cedar

Jeffie Craven   4

Dees Home

Old Hwy 84

Major
Reid

Schwan

Reid   7

Guy

8   Clark
Cem.

Pavillion

Masonite
Estate

Clark Cemetary

Masonite
Lake   9

Dick
Sumrall

Broad Head   F

18   Molone   17

Myrick Cem.

16

Mollie Boutwell

Lower Myrick

G Morgan

Robert
Gentry

19   20   21

Walter
Beard

Doggett

Charles
Boles   Walt Culpepper

Patrick

Freedom

30   29   28

All Red

Bildora

31   32   33

Township

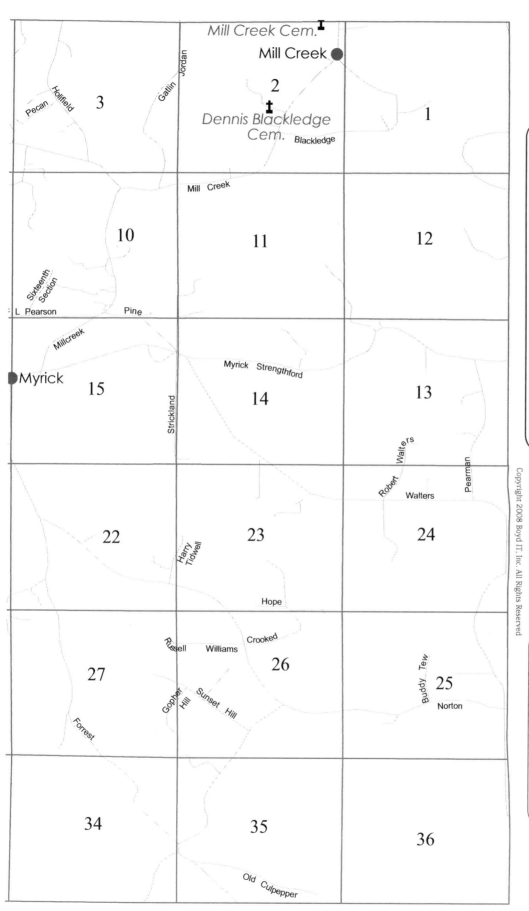

3

Pecan

Holifield

Gatlin

Jordan

Mill Creek Cem.

Mill Creek

2

Dennis Blackledge
Cem.

Blackledge

1

Mill   Creek

10

11

12

Sixteenth
Section

L. Pearson

Pine

Millcreek

Myrick   Strengthford

Myrick

15

Strickland

14

13

Robert Walters

Pearman

Robert

Walters

22

Harry
Tidwell

23

24

Hope

Crooked

Russell   Williams

26

Buddy Tew

25

27

Gopher
Hill   Sunset Hill

Norton

Forrest

34

35

36

Old   Culpepper

Helpful Hints

1. This road map has a number of uses, but primarily it is to help you: a) find the present location of land owned by your ancestors (at least the general area), b) find cemeteries and city-centers, and c) estimate the route/roads used by Census-takers & tax-assessors.

2. If you plan to travel to Jones County to locate cemeteries or land parcels, please pick up a modern travel map for the area before you do. Mapping old land parcels on modern maps is not as exact a science as you might think. Just the slightest variations in public land survey coordinates, estimates of parcel boundaries, or road-map deviations can greatly alter a map's representation of how a road either does or doesn't cross a particular parcel of land.

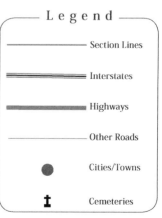

Legend

————————	Section Lines
════════════	Interstates
▬▬▬▬▬▬▬▬	Highways
————————	Other Roads
●	Cities/Towns
✝	Cemeteries

Scale: Section = 1 mile X 1 mile
(generally, with some exceptions)

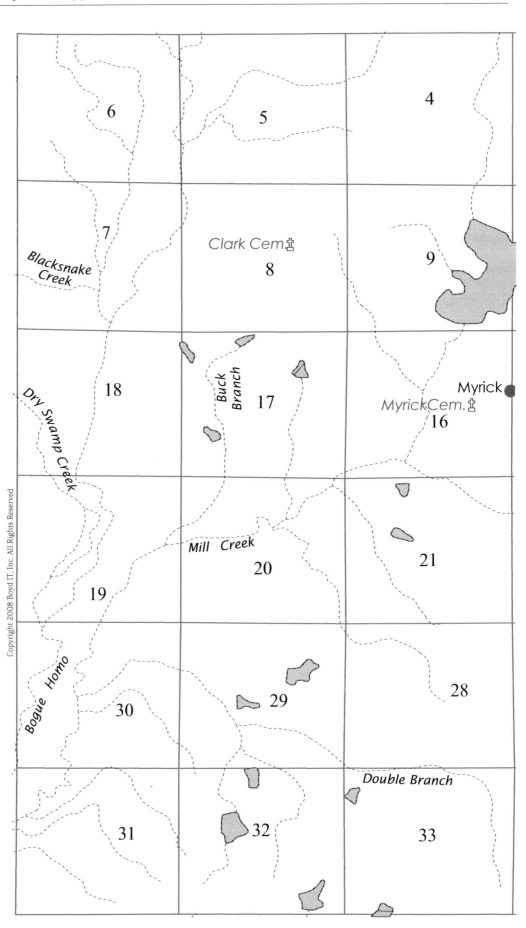

Historical Map

T8-N R10-W
St Stephens Meridian

Map Group 15

Cities & Towns
Mill Creek
Myrick

Cemeteries
Clark Cemetery
Dennis Blackledge Cemetery
Mill Creek Cemetery
Myrick Cemetery

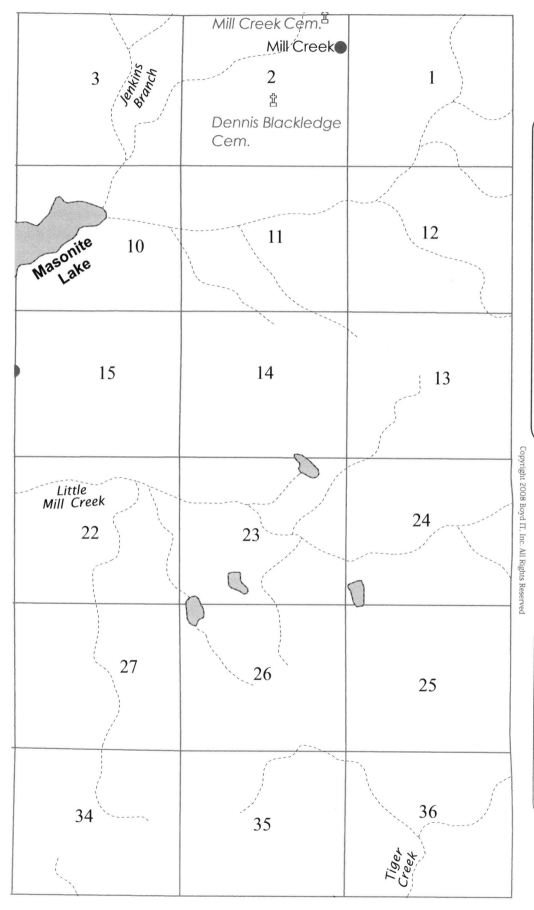

3

Mill Creek Cem. ✝

Mill Creek ●

2

✝

Dennis Blackledge
Cem.

1

Jenkins Branch

10

Masonite Lake

11

12

15

14

13

Little Mill Creek

22

23

24

27

26

25

34

35

36

Tiger Creek

Helpful Hints

1. This Map takes a different look at the same Congressional Township displayed in the preceding two maps. It presents features that can help you better envision the historical development of the area: a) Water-bodies (lakes & ponds), b) Water-courses (rivers, streams, etc.), c) Railroads, d) City/town center-points (where they were oftentimes located when first settled), and e) Cemeteries.

2. Using this "Historical" map in tandem with this Township's Patent Map and Road Map, may lead you to some interesting discoveries. You will often find roads, towns, cemeteries, and waterways are named after nearby landowners: sometimes those names will be the ones you are researching. See how many of these research gems you can find here in Jones County.

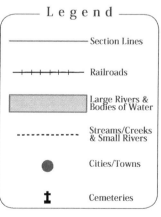

Legend

———————— Section Lines

+++++++ Railroads

Large Rivers &
Bodies of Water

------------- Streams/Creeks
& Small Rivers

● Cities/Towns

✝ Cemeteries

Scale: Section = 1 mile X 1 mile
(there are some exceptions)

Map Group 16: Index to Land Patents

Township 7-North Range 14-West (St Stephens)

After you locate an individual in this Index, take note of the Section and Section Part then proceed to the Land Patent map on the pages immediately following. You should have no difficulty locating the corresponding parcel of land.

The "For More Info" Column will lead you to more information about the underlying Patents. See the *Legend* at right, and the "How to Use this Book" chapter, for more information.

```
                        LEGEND
            "For More Info . . . " column
A = Authority (Legislative Act, See Appendix "A")
B = Block or Lot (location in Section unknown)
C = Cancelled Patent
F = Fractional Section
G = Group  (Multi-Patentee Patent, see Appendix "C")
V = Overlaps another Parcel
R = Re-Issued (Parcel patented more than once)

(A & G items require you to look in the Appendixes referred
to above. All other Letter-designations followed by a number
require you to locate line-items in this index that possess
the ID number found after the letter).
```

ID	Individual in Patent	Sec.	Sec. Part	Date Issued	Other Counties	For More Info . . .
2866	ADCOX, Sarah	3	SESW	1906-05-01		A3 G47
2867	" "	3	SWNE	1906-05-01		A3 G47
2868	" "	3	W½SE	1906-05-01		A3 G47
2737	BREAZEALE, Alfred A	11	S½NE	1901-03-23		A3
2738	" "	12	SWNW	1901-03-23		A3
2848	BRYANT, Richmon E	36	N½NW	1897-02-23		A3
2849	" "	36	NWNE	1897-02-23		A3
2850	" "	36	SWNW	1897-02-23		A3
2882	BYNUM, William A	24	NWSE	1883-04-30		A3
2883	" "	24	SENE	1883-04-30		A3
2884	" "	24	W½NE	1883-04-30		A3
2746	CARTER, Asa	12	NESW	1884-12-30		A3
2747	" "	12	NWSE	1895-02-21		A3
2748	" "	12	SENW	1895-02-21		A3
2749	" "	12	SESW	1895-02-21		A3
2743	CARTER, Asa B	12	W½SW	1892-04-29		A3
2744	" "	13	W½NW	1892-04-29		A3
2783	CARTER, George W	34	E½NW	1895-10-09		A3
2784	" "	34	NESW	1895-10-09		A3
2785	" "	34	SWNE	1895-10-09		A3
2815	CARTER, John W	26	SENW	1891-05-20		A3
2816	" "	26	SWNE	1891-05-20		A3
2817	" "	26	W½NW	1891-05-20		A3
2818	" "	34	S½SW	1900-11-28		A3
2819	" "	34	W½SE	1900-11-28		A3
2834	CARTER, Mary A	26	SW	1896-12-14		A3
2874	CARTER, Thomas A	13	NWSW	1896-08-26		A3
2875	" "	13	S½SW	1896-08-26		A3
2876	" "	14	NESE	1896-08-26		A3
2891	CARTER, William M	11	E½NW	1891-03-16		A3
2892	" "	11	NESW	1891-03-16		A3
2893	" "	11	NWSE	1891-03-16		A3
2779	COLE, Frank C	1	N½SW	1897-09-09		A3
2780	" "	1	SESW	1897-09-09		A3
2781	" "	12	NENW	1897-09-09		A3
2763	CRANFORD, Della	3	N½NW	1897-05-20		A3 G43
2764	" "	3	NWNE	1897-05-20		A3 G43
2763	CRANFORD, John W	3	N½NW	1897-05-20		A3 G43
2764	" "	3	NWNE	1897-05-20		A3 G43
2869	CRENSHAW, Sylvester C	25	W½NW	1885-05-25		A3
2870	" "	26	E½NE	1885-05-25		A3
2840	DAVIS, Nathaniel N	13	SENW	1899-04-28		A3
2841	" "	13	SWNE	1899-04-28		A3
2797	DOSSETT, Hansford D	15	SE	1859-05-02		A2
2798	" "	15	SENE	1859-05-02		A2
2799	" "	22	N½NE	1859-05-02		A2

ID	Individual in Patent	Sec.	Sec. Part	Date Issued	Other Counties	For More Info . . .
2800	DOSSETT, Hansford D (Cont'd)	22	SWNE	1859-05-02		A2
2829	FAIRCHILD, Littleton A	35	N½NE	1859-05-02		A2
2865	FAIRCHILD, Robert J	22	S½SW	1894-12-17		A3 G12
2865	FAIRCHILD, Sarah E	22	S½SW	1894-12-17		A3 G12
2825	FAIRCHILD, William A	1	SWNE	1889-11-29		A2 G19
2830	FAIRCHILDS, Littleton A	35	NESE	1859-05-02		A2
2831	" "	35	SENE	1859-05-02		A2
2857	FAIRCHILDS, Robert	14	NESW	1859-06-01		A2
2858	" "	14	S½NW	1859-06-01		A2
2859	" "	14	W½SW	1859-06-01		A2
2860	" "	23	NWNW	1859-06-01		A2
2802	GARRICK, Jacob V	10	E½SW	1892-04-29		A3
2803	" "	10	SWSW	1892-04-29		A3
2804	" "	15	NWNW	1892-04-29		A3
2772	GRAHAM, Francis M	24	E½SE	1897-02-15		A3
2773	" "	24	SESW	1897-02-15		A3
2774	" "	24	SWSE	1897-02-15		A3
2890	GRAHAM, William H	1	SENE	1854-03-15		A2
2735	GRAYSON, Alexander E	35	E½SW	1894-07-24		A2
2736	" "	35	W½SE	1894-07-24		A2
2856	GRAYSON, Robert C	27	SE	1894-03-15		A2
2758	GUI, Charles H	10	NESE	1861-05-01		A2
2759	" "	10	SENE	1861-05-01		A2
2760	" "	10	W½NE	1861-05-01		A2
2756	GUYE, Charles	3	NWSW	1876-02-15		A3
2757	" "	3	S½NW	1876-02-15		A3
2755	" "	3	NESW	1893-07-31		A3
2822	HERRINGTON, Jordan A	11	N½NE	1884-12-30		A3
2823	" "	12	NWNW	1884-12-30		A3
2824	" "	2	SESE	1884-12-30		A3
2825	" "	1	SWNE	1889-11-29		A2 G19
2832	HERRINGTON, Martin B	14	W½SE	1894-12-17		A3
2833	" "	23	N½NE	1894-12-17		A3
2786	HOLDER, George W	2	S½SW	1897-05-07		A3
2787	" "	2	W½SE	1897-05-07		A3
2814	HOOD, John Q	36	SE	1899-06-13		A3
2794	HOSKINS, Green	11	E½SE	1859-06-01		A2
2795	" "	11	SWSE	1859-06-01		A2
2796	" "	14	NENE	1859-06-01		A2
2791	KELLEY, Green A	15	NESW	1892-08-08		A3
2792	" "	15	S½SW	1892-08-08		A3
2793	" "	22	NENW	1892-08-08		A3
2879	KELLY, Warren	15	E½NW	1899-09-30		A3
2880	" "	15	NWSW	1899-09-30		A3
2881	" "	15	SWNW	1899-09-30		A3
2826	KNIGHT, Joseph E	36	NENE	1896-12-14		A3
2827	" "	36	S½NE	1896-12-14		A3
2828	" "	36	SENW	1896-12-14		A3
2739	LOTT, Allen J	23	NWSE	1891-03-16		A3
2740	" "	23	S½NE	1891-03-16		A3
2768	LOTT, Erastus W	23	NESW	1911-05-03		A2
2770	LOTT, Eugene J	12	E½SE	1906-06-16		A3
2771	" "	12	S½NE	1906-06-16		A3
2808	LOTT, James M	23	NESE	1895-11-11		A3
2809	" "	24	N½SW	1895-11-11		A3
2810	" "	24	SWSW	1895-11-11		A3
2842	MEDEARIS, Phillip N	13	N½SE	1889-01-05		A3
2843	" "	13	NESW	1889-01-05		A3
2844	" "	13	SWSE	1889-01-05		A3
2745	MORGAN, Asa B	27	S½NE	1898-09-28		A3
2775	MORGAN, Francis M	22	S½SE	1890-02-21		A3
2777	" "	27	NWNE	1890-02-21		A3
2776	" "	27	NENE	1895-11-11		A3
2885	MORGAN, William C	27	S½SW	1897-06-07		A3
2894	MORGAN, William N	26	NENW	1889-01-05		A3
2895	" "	26	NWNE	1889-01-05		A3
2899	MORGAN, William V	27	NWSW	1901-03-23		A3
2900	" "	27	SWNW	1901-03-23		A3
2886	MORRIS, William E	25	NE	1895-12-14		A3
2741	MURRAH, Andrew J	34	E½NE	1894-03-27		A2
2742	" "	34	E½SE	1894-03-27		A2
2765	NIX, Edward	34	NWNE	1900-02-02		A3
2788	NIX, George W	14	NENW	1895-02-21		A3

ID	Individual in Patent	Sec.	Sec. Part	Date Issued	Other Counties	For More Info . . .
2789	NIX, George W (Cont'd)	14	SENE	1895-02-21		A3
2790	" "	14	W½NE	1895-02-21		A3
2754	ODOM, Catharine	24	NW	1898-01-19		A3
2836	ODOM, Mathew T	25	NENW	1914-03-25		A3
2901	ODOM, Willie C	13	SENE	1906-06-26		A3
2862	RAINEY, Appleton	25	NESW	1888-02-25		A3 G36
2863	" "	25	SENW	1888-02-25		A3 G36
2864	" "	25	W½SW	1888-02-25		A3 G36
2782	RAINEY, Franklin T	26	SE	1889-01-05		A3
2811	RAINEY, Jefferson D	10	NW	1895-12-14		A3
2862	RAINEY, Sarah A	25	NESW	1888-02-25		A3 G36
2863	" "	25	SENW	1888-02-25		A3 G36
2864	" "	25	W½SW	1888-02-25		A3 G36
2898	RAINEY, William T	36	W½SW	1891-05-20		A3
2778	RIELS, Francis M	22	W½NW	1893-04-12		A3
2845	ROBERTSON, Richard	22	SENE	1860-07-02		A2
2846	" "	23	E½NW	1860-07-02		A2
2847	" "	23	SWNW	1860-07-02		A2
2871	ROGERS, Terrel R	27	N½NW	1893-04-12		A3
2872	" "	27	NESW	1893-04-12		A3
2873	" "	27	SENW	1893-04-12		A3
2855	SANFORD, Robert A	11	W½NW	1904-12-31		A3
2902	SANFORD, Willis H	3	SWSW	1901-04-22		A3
2801	SMITH, Hays	35	SESE	1859-05-02		A2
2750	STRINGER, Benjamin W	14	SESE	1898-01-19		A3
2761	STRINGER, Charles W	10	NWSW	1902-07-03		A3
2769	STRINGER, Ervin H	14	SESE	1907-07-15		A2
2820	THOMPSON, John W	34	NWSW	1901-04-22		A3
2821	" "	34	W½NW	1901-04-22		A3
2837	THRASH, Nathaniel J	12	SWSE	1899-04-17		A3
2838	" "	13	N½NE	1899-04-17		A3
2839	" "	13	NENW	1899-04-17		A3
2734	TISDALE, Albert B	13	SESE	1884-12-30		A3
2812	TISDALE, John H	1	NWSE	1894-12-17		A3
2813	" "	1	S½SE	1894-12-17		A3
2861	TISDALE, Robert W	24	NENE	1906-06-21		A3
2896	TISDALE, William P	11	SWSW	1859-05-02		A2
2897	" "	14	NWNW	1859-05-02		A2
2903	TISDALE, Wyatt W	15	W½NE	1897-05-07		A3
2751	TRIGGS, Bruce	35	E½NW	1896-03-09		A3
2752	" "	35	NWNW	1896-03-09		A3
2753	" "	35	SWNE	1896-03-09		A3
2766	TRIGGS, Edward	35	SWNW	1894-07-24		A2
2767	" "	35	W½SW	1894-07-24		A2
2887	TUCKER, William G	2	N½NW	1905-12-13		A3
2888	" "	2	NWNE	1905-12-13		A3
2889	" "	3	NENE	1905-12-13		A3
2763	WALLACE, Della	3	N½NW	1897-05-20		A3 G43
2764	" "	3	NWNE	1897-05-20		A3 G43
2851	WALTERS, Richmon	10	SESE	1889-01-05		A3
2852	" "	10	W½SE	1889-01-05		A3
2854	" "	15	NENE	1889-01-05		A3
2853	" "	11	NWSW	1889-11-29		A2
2877	WALTERS, Thomas J	11	SESW	1899-06-13		A3
2762	WATKINS, Dayton O	25	NESE	1895-11-11		A3
2866	WATSON, Sarah	3	SESE	1906-05-01		A3 G47
2867	" "	3	SWNE	1906-05-01		A3 G47
2868	" "	3	W½SE	1906-05-01		A3 G47
2805	WEAVER, James G	25	SESE	1896-08-26		A3
2806	" "	25	SESW	1896-08-26		A3
2807	" "	25	W½SE	1896-08-26		A3
2878	WELDY, Thomas	1	NENW	1854-03-15		A2
2835	YOUNG, Mary A	36	E½SW	1897-11-01		A3

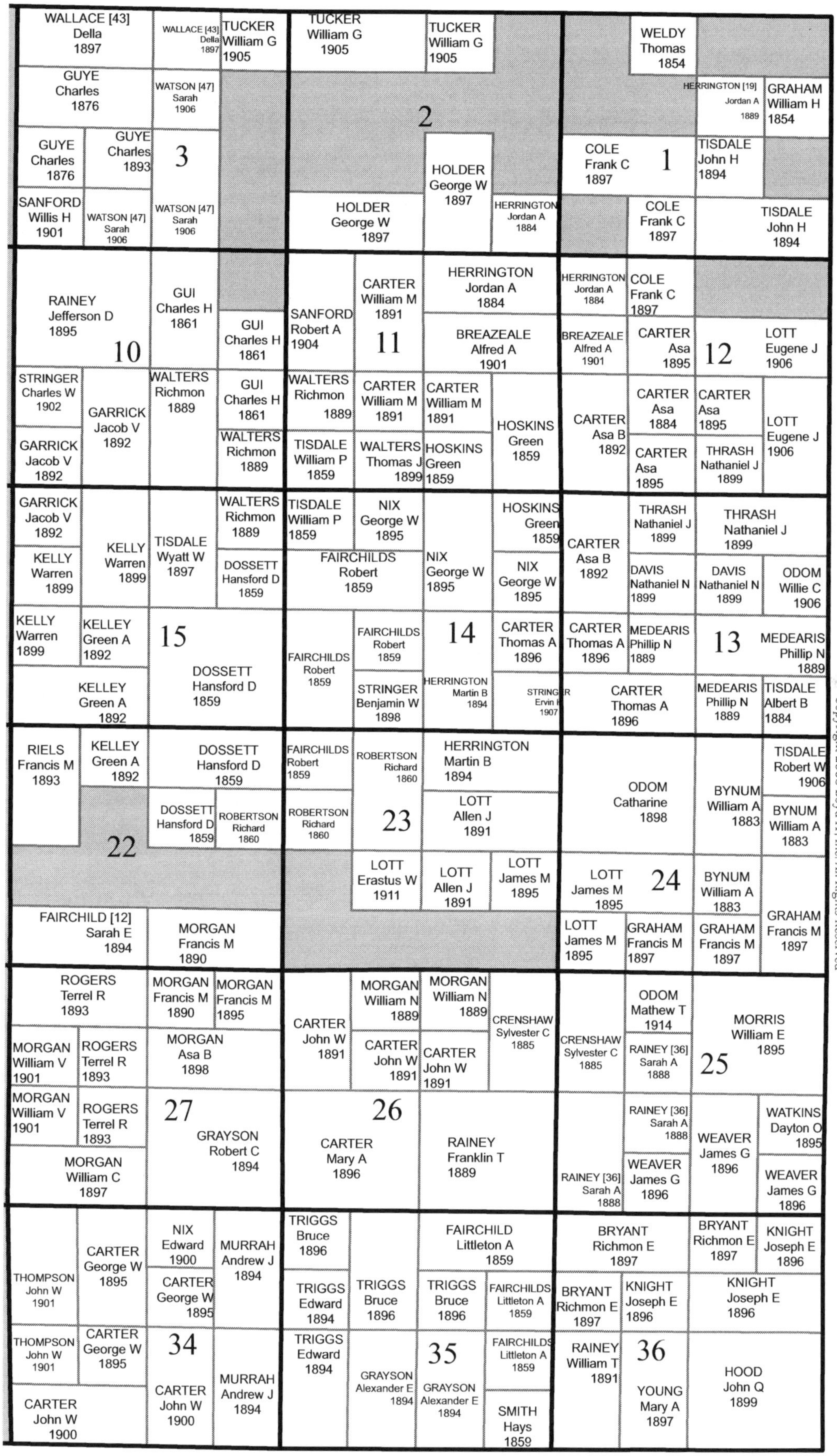
WALLACE [43] Della 1897
WALLACE [43] Della 1897
TUCKER William G 1905
TUCKER William G 1905
TUCKER William G 1905
WELDY Thomas 1854
GUYE Charles 1876
WATSON [47] Sarah 1906
2
HERRINGTON [19] Jordan A 1889
GRAHAM William H 1854
GUYE Charles 1876
GUYE Charles 1893
3
HOLDER George W 1897
COLE Frank C 1897
1
TISDALE John H 1894
SANFORD Willis H 1901
WATSON [47] Sarah 1906
WATSON [47] Sarah 1906
HOLDER George W 1897
HERRINGTON Jordan A 1884
COLE Frank C 1897
TISDALE John H 1894
RAINEY Jefferson D 1895
10
GUI Charles H 1861
GUI Charles H 1861
SANFORD Robert A 1904
CARTER William M 1891
11
HERRINGTON Jordan A 1884
BREAZEALE Alfred A 1901
HERRINGTON Jordan A 1884
COLE Frank C 1897
BREAZEALE Alfred A 1901
CARTER Asa 1895
12
LOTT Eugene J 1906
STRINGER Charles W 1902
GARRICK Jacob V 1892
WALTERS Richmon 1889
GUI Charles H 1861
WALTERS Richmon 1889
CARTER William M 1891
CARTER William M 1891
CARTER Asa B 1892
CARTER Asa 1884
CARTER Asa 1895
LOTT Eugene J 1906
GARRICK Jacob V 1892
WALTERS Richmon 1889
TISDALE William P 1859
WALTERS Thomas J 1899
HOSKINS Green 1859
HOSKINS Green 1859
CARTER Asa 1895
THRASH Nathaniel J 1899
GARRICK Jacob V 1892
KELLY Warren 1899
TISDALE Wyatt W 1897
WALTERS Richmon 1889
TISDALE William P 1859
NIX George W 1895
HOSKINS Green 1859
CARTER Asa B 1892
THRASH Nathaniel J 1899
THRASH Nathaniel J 1899
KELLY Warren 1899
DOSSETT Hansford D 1859
FAIRCHILDS Robert 1859
NIX George W 1895
NIX George W 1895
DAVIS Nathaniel N 1899
DAVIS Nathaniel N 1899
ODOM Willie C 1906
KELLY Warren 1899
KELLEY Green A 1892
15
DOSSETT Hansford D 1859
FAIRCHILDS Robert 1859
FAIRCHILDS Robert 1859
14
CARTER Thomas A 1896
CARTER Thomas A 1896
MEDEARIS Phillip N 1889
13
MEDEARIS Phillip N 1889
KELLEY Green A 1892
HERRINGTON Martin B 1894
STRINGER Benjamin W 1898
STRINGER Ervin 1907
CARTER Thomas A 1896
MEDEARIS Phillip N 1889
TISDALE Albert B 1884
RIELS Francis M 1893
KELLEY Green A 1892
DOSSETT Hansford D 1859
FAIRCHILDS Robert 1859
ROBERTSON Richard 1860
HERRINGTON Martin B 1894
ODOM Catharine 1898
BYNUM William A 1883
TISDALE Robert W 1906
22
DOSSETT Hansford D 1859
ROBERTSON Richard 1860
ROBERTSON Richard 1860
23
LOTT Allen J 1891
BYNUM William A 1883
LOTT Erastus W 1911
LOTT Allen J 1891
LOTT James M 1895
LOTT James M 1895
24
BYNUM William A 1883
FAIRCHILD [12] Sarah E 1894
MORGAN Francis M 1890
LOTT James M 1895
GRAHAM Francis M 1897
GRAHAM Francis M 1897
GRAHAM Francis M 1897
ROGERS Terrel R 1893
MORGAN Francis M 1890
MORGAN Francis M 1895
MORGAN William N 1889
MORGAN William N 1889
CARTER John W 1891
CRENSHAW Sylvester C 1885
ODOM Mathew T 1914
MORRIS William E 1895
MORGAN William V 1901
ROGERS Terrel R 1893
MORGAN Asa B 1898
CARTER John W 1891
CARTER John W 1891
CRENSHAW Sylvester C 1885
RAINEY [36] Sarah A 1888
25
MORGAN William V 1901
ROGERS Terrel R 1893
27
26
GRAYSON Robert C 1894
CARTER Mary A 1896
RAINEY Franklin T 1889
RAINEY [36] Sarah A 1888
WATKINS Dayton O 1895
WEAVER James G 1896
MORGAN William C 1897
WEAVER James G 1896
RAINEY [36] Sarah A 1888
WEAVER James G 1896
NIX Edward 1900
TRIGGS Bruce 1896
FAIRCHILD Littleton A 1859
BRYANT Richmon E 1897
BRYANT Richmon E 1897
KNIGHT Joseph E 1896
CARTER George W 1895
MURRAH Andrew J 1894
THOMPSON John W 1901
CARTER George W 1895
TRIGGS Edward 1894
TRIGGS Bruce 1896
TRIGGS Bruce 1896
FAIRCHILDS Littleton A 1859
BRYANT Richmon E 1897
KNIGHT Joseph E 1896
KNIGHT Joseph E 1896
THOMPSON John W 1901
CARTER George W 1895
34
TRIGGS Edward 1894
35
FAIRCHILDS Littleton A 1859
RAINEY William T 1891
36
GRAYSON Alexander E 1894
GRAYSON Alexander E 1894
HOOD John Q 1899
CARTER John W 1900
CARTER John W 1900
MURRAH Andrew J 1894
SMITH Hays 1859
YOUNG Mary A 1897

Patent Map

T7-N R14-W
St Stephens Meridian

Map Group 16

Township Statistics

Parcels Mapped	:	170
Number of Patents	:	87
Number of Individuals	:	87
Patentees Identified	:	82
Number of Surnames	:	50
Multi-Patentee Parcels	:	10
Oldest Patent Date	:	3/15/1854
Most Recent Patent	:	3/25/1914
Block/Lot Parcels	:	0
Parcels Re - Issued	:	0
Parcels that Overlap	:	0
Cities and Towns	:	0
Cemeteries	:	3

Note: the area contained in this map amounts to far less than a full Township. Therefore, its contents are completely on this single page (instead of a "normal" 2-page spread).

Legend

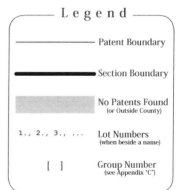

(thin line)	Patent Boundary
(thick line)	Section Boundary
(shaded)	No Patents Found (or Outside County)
1., 2., 3., ...	Lot Numbers (when beside a name)
[ ]	Group Number (see Appendix "C")

Scale: Section = 1 mile X 1 mile
(generally, with some exceptions)

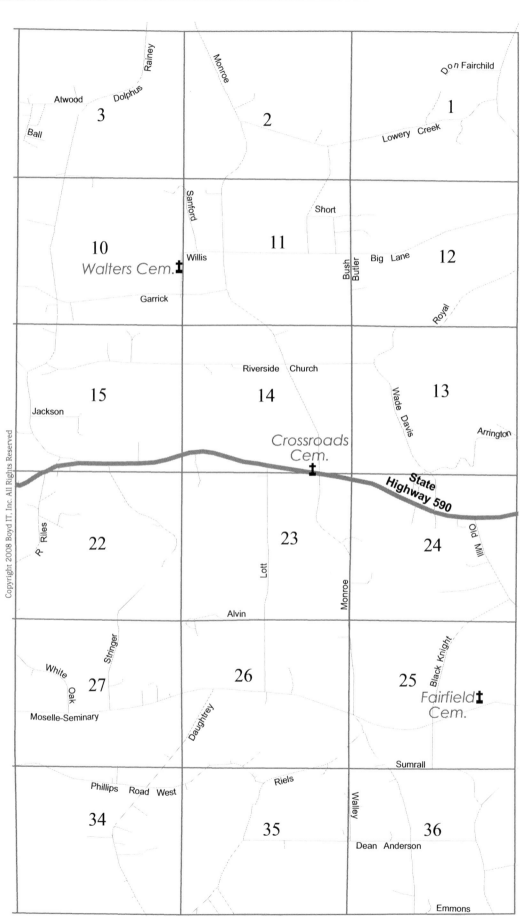

Road Map

T7-N R14-W
St Stephens Meridian

Map Group 16

Note: the area contained in this map amounts to far less than a full Township. Therefore, its contents are completely on this single page (instead of a "normal" 2-page spread).

Cities & Towns
None

Cemeteries
Crossroads Cemetery
Fairfield Cemetery
Walters Cemetery

Legend

———	Section Lines
═══	Interstates
▬▬▬	Highways
——	Other Roads
●	Cities/Towns
✝	Cemeteries

Scale: Section = 1 mile X 1 mile
(generally, with some exceptions)

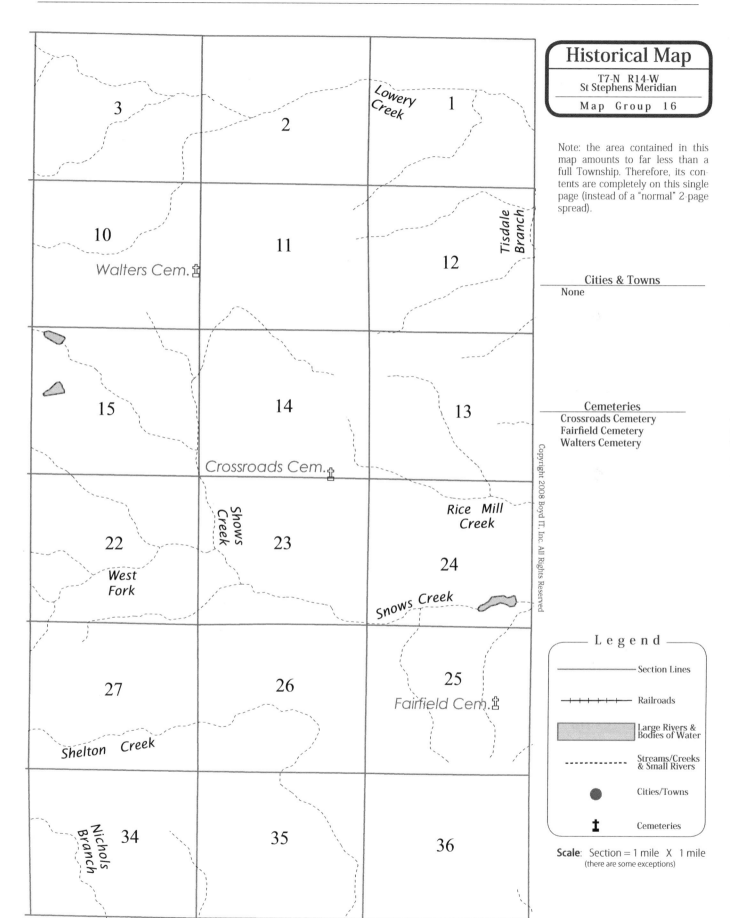

Historical Map

T7-N R14-W
St Stephens Meridian

M a p   G r o u p   1 6

Note: the area contained in this map amounts to far less than a full Township. Therefore, its contents are completely on this single page (instead of a "normal" 2-page spread).

Cities & Towns
None

Cemeteries
Crossroads Cemetery
Fairfield Cemetery
Walters Cemetery

L e g e n d

——————— Section Lines

+—+—+—+—+ Railroads

▭ Large Rivers & Bodies of Water

- - - - - - - Streams/Creeks & Small Rivers

● Cities/Towns

✝ Cemeteries

Scale: Section = 1 mile X 1 mile
(there are some exceptions)

Map Group 17: Index to Land Patents

Township 7-North Range 13-West (St Stephens)

After you locate an individual in this Index, take note of the Section and Section Part then proceed to the Land Patent map on the pages immediately following. You should have no difficulty locating the corresponding parcel of land.

The "For More Info" Column will lead you to more information about the underlying Patents. See the *Legend* at right, and the "How to Use this Book" chapter, for more information.

```
LEGEND
"For More Info . . . " column
A = Authority (Legislative Act, See Appendix "A")
B = Block or Lot (location in Section unknown)
C = Cancelled Patent
F = Fractional Section
G = Group  (Multi-Patentee Patent, see Appendix "C")
V = Overlaps another Parcel
R = Re-Issued (Parcel patented more than once)

(A & G items require you to look in the Appendixes referred
to above. All other Letter-designations followed by a number
require you to locate line-items in this index that possess
the ID number found after the letter).
```

ID	Individual in Patent	Sec.	Sec. Part	Date Issued	Other Counties	For More Info . . .
2957	ANDERSON, Isaac	1	NENE	1889-11-29		A2
3080	ANDERSON, Susanah	13	E½NE	1884-12-30		A3
3081	" "	13	NESE	1884-12-30		A3
3082	" "	13	SWNE	1884-12-30		A3
2977	BALFOUR, James	22	E½NE	1882-12-30		A2
2978	" "	22	E½SE	1882-12-30		A2
2979	" "	23	E½	1882-12-30		A2
2980	" "	23	NW	1882-12-30		A2
2981	" "	24	SW	1882-12-30		A2
2982	" "	24	W½NW	1882-12-30		A2
2983	" "	24	W½SE	1882-12-30		A2
2984	" "	25	NW	1882-12-30		A2
2985	" "	25	W½NE	1882-12-30		A2
2986	" "	26	E½SW	1882-12-30		A2
2987	" "	26	NENE	1882-12-30		A2
2988	" "	26	SE	1882-12-30		A2
2989	" "	26	SWSW	1882-12-30		A2
2990	" "	27	E½NW	1882-12-30		A2
2991	" "	27	N½NE	1882-12-30		A2
2992	" "	27	NESW	1882-12-30		A2
2993	" "	27	SESE	1882-12-30		A2
2994	" "	27	SWSW	1882-12-30		A2
2995	" "	27	W½SE	1882-12-30		A2
2998	" "	35	E½NE	1882-12-30		A2
2999	" "	35	N½NW	1882-12-30		A2
3000	" "	36	NW	1882-12-30		A2
2996	" "	28	5	1883-09-15		A2
2997	" "	28	6	1883-09-15		A2
2943	BAYLIS, George	19	SENE	1859-11-10		A2
2944	" "	20	S½SW	1859-11-10		A2
2945	" "	29	NWNW	1859-11-10		A2
2946	" "	30	NENE	1859-11-10		A2
2971	BENSON, Isom	25	W½SW	1893-04-12		A3
3086	BLACKLIDGE, William	20	6	1881-08-20		A3
3092	BREAZEALE, William H	13	NESW	1902-07-22		A2
3066	BUSH, Priscilla	21	N½NE	1892-04-29		A3
3043	BYNUM, Leon S	18	N½SW	1905-03-30		A3
3044	" "	18	SESW	1905-03-30		A3
3045	" "	18	SWSE	1905-03-30		A3
2920	CHARLESCRAFT, Anson	5	2	1853-11-01		A2 F
3056	CHATHAM, Mary	32	NENE	1859-05-02		A2
3029	CRAKER, John W	10	NWSW	1901-12-17		A3
3010	CREEL, James R	34	NWSE	1859-05-02		A2
3011	" "	34	SWNE	1859-05-02		A2
3047	CROSBY, Mack C	19	E½SW	1899-06-13		A3
3048	" "	19	S½SE	1899-06-13		A3

ID	Individual in Patent	Sec.	Sec. Part	Date Issued	Other Counties	For More Info . . .
3067	CROSBY, Ransom	20	S½7	1891-03-16		A3
3068	" "	29	N½NE	1891-03-16		A3
3069	" "	29	NENW	1891-03-16		A3
2911	DEASON, Amos	14	SENE	1854-03-15		A2
2912	" "	14	SWNE	1854-03-15		A2
2907	" "	11	SESE	1859-05-02		A2
2908	" "	13	SWNW	1859-05-02		A2
2909	" "	14	N½NE	1859-05-02		A2
2910	" "	14	NENW	1859-05-02		A2
3046	DEVALL, Luther E	24	E½NW	1894-11-17		A2
3027	DOWNING, John R	31	SENE	1894-07-24		A2
3028	"	31	W½NE	1894-07-24		A2
2975	EASTERLING, James A	25	E½NE	1895-02-07		A2
2976	" "	25	N½SE	1895-02-07		A2
2916	EDWARDS, Andrew	30	E½NW	1884-12-30		A3
2917	" "	30	W½NE	1884-12-30		A3
2904	EWING, Albert B	36	NE	1895-06-22		A2
2923	FAIRCHILDS, Charity	17	SE	1846-09-01		A2 F
2954	FAIRCHILDS, Hiram	22	NWSW	1859-05-02		A2
2956	" "	22	SWNW	1859-05-02		A2
2953	" "	22	NESW	1859-06-01		A2
2955	" "	22	SENW	1859-06-01		A2
3087	FAIRCHILDS, William	15	SESW	1859-05-02		A2
3088	" "	15	SWNE	1859-05-02		A2
3089	" "	15	W½SE	1859-05-02		A2
3090	" "	22	N½NW	1859-05-02		A2
3091	" "	22	NWNE	1859-05-02		A2
3015	FOLKS, John	23	NESW	1859-06-01		A2
3016	" "	23	SESW	1859-06-01		A2
3017	" "	23	W½SW	1859-06-01		A2
3021	GANDY, John	15	NESW	1859-05-02		A2
3022	" "	15	W½SW	1859-05-02		A2
3023	" "	17	NE	1859-05-02		A2 F
3013	GANDY, John B	4	SWSW	1897-05-07		A3
3024	GANDY, John H	10	E½NW	1898-05-10		A3
3094	GRAHAM, William H	6	NESW	1859-05-02		A2
3097	" "	6	SENW	1859-05-02		A2
3095	" "	6	NWSE	1859-11-10		A2
3096	" "	6	S½SE	1859-11-10		A2
3098	" "	6	SESW	1859-11-10		A2
3099	" "	6	SWNE	1859-11-10		A2
3093	" "	6	NESE	1860-07-02		A2
3041	GRAYSON, Joseph W	31	SW	1897-04-02		A3
3079	HINTON, Samuel	12	N½NW	1897-11-01		A3
2922	HOOD, Benjamin	6	SENE	1854-03-15		A2
2921	" "	6	NENE	1859-05-02		A2
2948	HOSKINS, Henry	5	4	1853-11-01		A2 F
3030	JIMISON, John W	34	E½NE	1896-10-31		A3
3031	" "	34	E½SE	1896-10-31		A3
3001	JOHNSTON, James	4	E½SW	1884-12-30		A2
3002	" "	4	NW	1884-12-30		A2
3003	" "	4	NWSW	1884-12-30		A2
3004	" "	4	W½NE	1884-12-30		A2
3005	" "	9	NWNW	1884-12-30		A2
3006	" "	9	S½SW	1884-12-30		A2
3007	" "	9	SE	1884-12-30		A2
3032	JORDAN, John W	11	SESW	1894-09-28		A3
3033	" "	11	SWSE	1894-09-28		A3
3052	JORDAN, Mark C	14	E½SE	1896-12-14		A3
3059	JORDAN, Matthew P	14	S½SW	1890-03-28		A3
3060	" "	14	SWSE	1890-03-28		A3
3061	" "	15	SESE	1890-03-28		A3
3062	KEETON, Nancy	15	E½NW	1891-06-30		A3
3063	" "	15	N½NE	1891-06-30		A3
2924	LOURY, Chim N	6	SWNW	1854-03-15		A2
3078	LOVITT, Samuel Archie	33	8	1912-07-05		A3
3065	LOWERY, Peter	6	NWSW	1841-01-05		A2
3114	LOWERY, Willis Otis	32	NWNW	1922-05-16		A3
2958	LYON, Isaac L	10	NESE	1884-12-30		A2
2959	" "	11	N½SW	1884-12-30		A2
2960	" "	11	NW	1884-12-30		A2
2961	" "	11	NWSE	1884-12-30		A2
2962	" "	11	W½NE	1884-12-30		A2

ID	Individual in Patent	Sec.	Sec. Part	Date Issued	Other Counties	For More Info . . .
2963	LYON, Isaac L (Cont'd)	12	N½SW	1884-12-30		A2
2964	" "	12	S½NW	1884-12-30		A2
2965	" "	2	E½SW	1884-12-30		A2
2966	" "	2	W½NE	1884-12-30		A2
2967	" "	2	W½SE	1884-12-30		A2
2968	" "	3	E½NW	1884-12-30		A2
2969	" "	3	N½NE	1884-12-30		A2
2970	" "	3	SWNW	1884-12-30		A2
2930	MARTIN, Daniel W	19	S½NW	1890-07-03		A2
2931	" "	29	S½6	1890-07-03		A2
3057	MCCALLUM, March	35	S½NW	1885-12-19		A3 G24
3058	" "	35	W½NE	1885-12-19		A3 G24
3057	MCCALLUM, Matilda	35	S½NW	1885-12-19		A3 G24
3058	" "	35	W½NE	1885-12-19		A3 G24
3064	MCDONALD, Norman	36	SE	1894-07-24		A2
3008	MCNIECE, James	34	NESW	1859-05-02		A2
3009	" "	34	W½NW	1859-05-02		A2
3105	MITCHELL, William W	24	E½SE	1892-09-15		A2
3106	" "	24	S½NE	1892-09-15		A2
2925	MOFFETT, Daniel T	26	SENE	1885-12-19		A3
2926	" "	26	SENW	1885-12-19		A3
2927	" "	26	W½NE	1885-12-19		A3
3025	MYERS, John H	13	NWSE	1854-03-15		A2
3113	ODOM, Willie C	18	W½NW	1906-06-26		A3
2951	PAGE, Hezekiah W	26	NENW	1859-05-02		A2
2952	" "	26	W½NW	1859-05-02		A2
3014	PAGE, John C	27	SESW	1859-05-02		A2
2936	PHILLIPS, Eli E	22	SESW	1890-08-16		A3
2937	" "	22	SWNE	1890-08-16		A3
2938	" "	22	W½SE	1890-08-16		A3
3018	PITTMAN, John G	14	N½SW	1893-07-31		A3
3019	" "	14	NWSE	1893-07-31		A3
3020	" "	14	SENW	1893-07-31		A3
3107	PITTMAN, William W	14	W½NW	1895-12-14		A3
3108	" "	15	NESE	1895-12-14		A3
3109	" "	15	SENE	1895-12-14		A3
2941	POWELL, Francis M	5	E½NE	1892-03-23		A3
2942	" "	5	E½SE	1892-03-23		A3
3034	QUICK, John W	13	E½NW	1896-12-21		A2
3035	" "	13	NWNE	1896-12-21		A2
3036	" "	13	NWNW	1896-12-21		A2
3037	RAINEY, John W	32	S½NE	1890-02-21		A3
3038	" "	33	5	1890-02-21		A3
3049	RAINEY, Marion M	29	N½SE	1888-02-25		A3
3050	" "	29	NESW	1888-02-25		A3
3051	" "	29	SENW	1888-02-25		A3
3110	RIDGWAY, William W	29	S½7	1896-10-31		A3
3111	" "	29	S½8	1896-10-31		A3
3112	" "	32	NWNE	1896-10-31		A3
2947	ROBINSON, Govan	5	3	1954-07-23		A3
3026	SANDERSON, John H	31	NW	1891-03-16		A3
3042	SANDERSON, Joseph W	15	W½NW	1895-06-28		A3
2928	SHOWS, Daniel T	34	SESW	1892-03-07		A3
2929	" "	34	SWSE	1892-03-07		A3
3100	SMITH, William J	33	E½NE	1888-02-25		A3
3101	" "	33	NESE	1888-02-25		A3
3102	" "	34	NWSW	1888-02-25		A3
2972	STAFFORD, Jacob	26	NWSW	1861-05-01		A2
2973	" "	27	NESE	1861-05-01		A2
2974	" "	27	S½NE	1861-05-01		A2
2935	STOCKTON, Edward	12	SWSW	1901-03-23		A3
3077	SUMMERS, Russell A	33	7	1954-07-26		A1
2918	THOMPSON, Andrew J	29	S½1	1897-06-07		A3
2919	" "	29	S½2	1897-06-07		A3
2905	TISDALE, Albert B	18	SWSW	1884-12-30		A3
2906	" "	19	N½NW	1884-12-30		A3
2913	TISDALE, Amos W	30	E½SW	1894-12-17		A3
2914	" "	30	SWSE	1894-12-17		A3
2915	" "	30	SWSW	1894-12-17		A3
2934	TISDALE, Edward C	6	NWNE	1897-09-09		A3
2949	TISDALE, Henry T	19	N½SE	1896-08-26		A3
2950	" "	19	SWNE	1896-08-26		A3
3012	TISDALE, John A	6	SWSW	1854-03-15		A2

ID	Individual in Patent	Sec.	Sec. Part	Date Issued	Other Counties	For More Info . . .
3053	TISDALE, Martha	29	SWNW	1890-02-21		A3
3054	" "	30	N½SE	1890-02-21		A3
3055	" "	30	SENE	1890-02-21		A3
3083	TISDALE, Washington S	18	SESE	1859-06-01		A2
3084	" "	19	N½NE	1859-06-01		A2
3104	TISDALE, William	20	N½5	1841-01-05		A2 F
3103	TISDALE, William J	33	S½10	1897-06-07		A3
3115	TISDALE, Zacariah T	29	W½SW	1884-12-30		A3
3116	" "	30	SESE	1884-12-30		A3
3117	" "	31	NENE	1884-12-30		A3
3039	WALTERS, Joseph M	10	SESE	1890-06-25		A3
3040	" "	11	SWSW	1890-06-25		A3
2932	WATKINS, Dayton O	30	NWSW	1895-11-11		A3
2933	" "	30	W½NW	1895-11-11		A3
3072	WINDHAM, Robert C	32	SESE	1848-09-01		A2
3073	" "	32	SESW	1859-05-02		A2
3075	" "	32	SWSE	1859-05-02		A2
3076	" "	32	W½SW	1859-06-01		A2
3070	" "	32	E½NW	1881-09-17		A3
3071	" "	32	NESW	1881-09-17		A3
3074	" "	32	SWNW	1881-09-17		A3
3085	WINDHAM, William A	31	SE	1890-08-16		A3
2939	WOULARD, Erasmus A	25	E½SW	1894-09-28		A3
2940	" "	25	S½SE	1894-09-28		A3

Patent Map

T7-N R13-W
St Stephens Meridian

Map Group 17

Township Statistics

Parcels Mapped	:	214
Number of Patents	:	106
Number of Individuals	:	87
Patentees Identified	:	86
Number of Surnames	:	63
Multi-Patentee Parcels	:	2
Oldest Patent Date	:	1/5/1841
Most Recent Patent	:	7/26/1954
Block/Lot Parcels	:	17
Parcels Re - Issued	:	0
Parcels that Overlap	:	0
Cities and Towns	:	1
Cemeteries	:	6

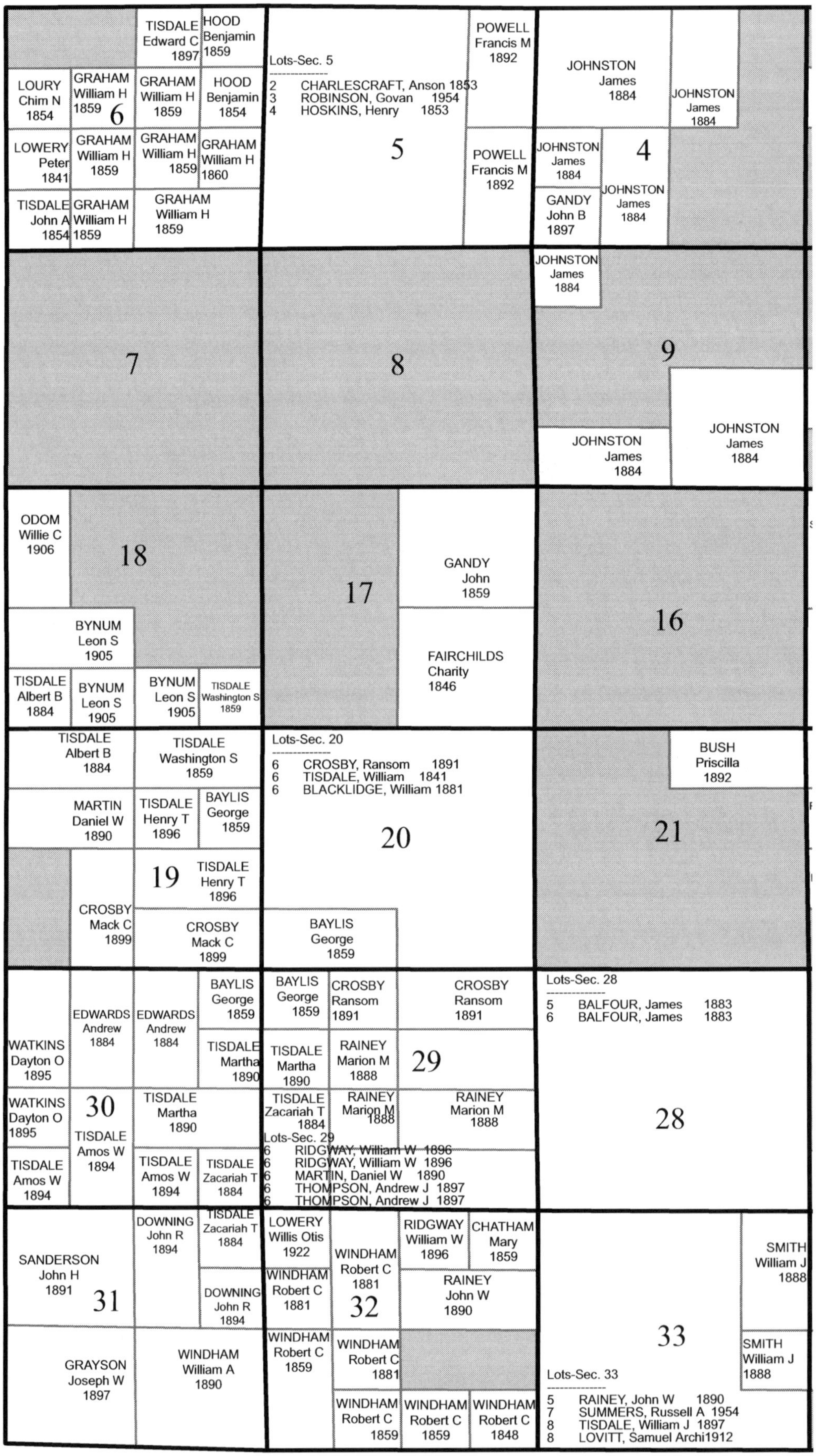

Map content (parcel owners by section):

Section 6: LOURY Chim N 1854; GRAHAM William H 1859; GRAHAM William H 1859; TISDALE Edward C 1897; HOOD Benjamin 1859; HOOD Benjamin 1854; LOWERY Peter 1841; GRAHAM William H 1859; GRAHAM William H 1859; GRAHAM William H 1860; GRAHAM William H 1859; TISDALE John A 1854; GRAHAM William H 1859; GRAHAM William H 1859

Section 5: Lots-Sec. 5
2 CHARLESCRAFT, Anson 1853
3 ROBINSON, Govan 1954
4 HOSKINS, Henry 1853
POWELL Francis M 1892; POWELL Francis M 1892

Section 4: JOHNSTON James 1884; JOHNSTON James 1884; JOHNSTON James 1884; GANDY John B 1897; JOHNSTON James 1884

Section 7

Section 8

Section 9: JOHNSTON James 1884; JOHNSTON James 1884; JOHNSTON James 1884

Section 18: ODOM Willie C 1906; BYNUM Leon S 1905; TISDALE Albert B 1884; BYNUM Leon S 1905; BYNUM Leon S 1905; TISDALE Washington S 1859

Section 17: GANDY John 1859; FAIRCHILDS Charity 1846

Section 16

Section 19: TISDALE Albert B 1884; TISDALE Washington S 1859; MARTIN Daniel W 1890; TISDALE Henry T 1896; BAYLIS George 1859; TISDALE Henry T 1896; CROSBY Mack C 1899; CROSBY Mack C 1899

Section 20: Lots-Sec. 20
6 CROSBY, Ransom 1891
6 TISDALE, William 1841
6 BLACKLIDGE, William 1881
BAYLIS George 1859

Section 21: BUSH Priscilla 1892

Section 30: WATKINS Dayton O 1895; EDWARDS Andrew 1884; EDWARDS Andrew 1884; WATKINS Dayton O 1895; TISDALE Amos W 1894; TISDALE Amos W 1894; TISDALE Martha 1890; TISDALE Amos W 1894

Section 29: BAYLIS George 1859; CROSBY Ransom 1891; CROSBY Ransom 1891; TISDALE Martha 1890; RAINEY Marion M 1888; RAINEY Marion M 1888; RAINEY Marion M 1888; TISDALE Zacariah T 1884; TISDALE Martha 1890; TISDALE Zacariah T 1884
Lots-Sec. 29
6 RIDGWAY, William W 1896
6 RIDGWAY, William W 1896
6 MARTIN, Daniel W 1890
6 THOMPSON, Andrew J 1897
6 THOMPSON, Andrew J 1897

Section 28: Lots-Sec. 28
5 BALFOUR, James 1883
6 BALFOUR, James 1883

Section 31: SANDERSON John H 1891; GRAYSON Joseph W 1897; WINDHAM William A 1890

Section 32: DOWNING John R 1894; TISDALE Zacariah T 1884; DOWNING John R 1894; LOWERY Willis Otis 1922; WINDHAM Robert C 1881; WINDHAM Robert C 1859; RIDGWAY William W 1896; WINDHAM Robert C 1881; RAINEY John W 1890; CHATHAM Mary 1859; WINDHAM Robert C 1881; WINDHAM Robert C 1859; WINDHAM Robert C 1859; WINDHAM Robert C 1848

Section 33: SMITH William J 1888; SMITH William J 1888
Lots-Sec. 33
5 RAINEY, John W 1890
7 SUMMERS, Russell A 1954
8 TISDALE, William J 1897
8 LOVITT, Samuel Archi 1912

Map grid

Section 3
LYON Isaac L 1884
LYON Isaac L 1884
LYON Isaac L 1884
3

Section 2
LYON Isaac L 1884
2
LYON Isaac L 1884
LYON Isaac L 1884

Section 1
ANDERSON Isaac 1889
1

Section 10
GANDY John H 1898
CRAKER John W 1901
10

Section 11
LYON Isaac L 1884
LYON Isaac L 1884
11
LYON Isaac L 1884
LYON Isaac L 1884
LYON Isaac L 1884
WALTERS Joseph M 1890

Section 12
HINTON Samuel 1897
LYON Isaac L 1884
12
LYON Isaac L 1884

WALTERS Joseph M 1890 | JORDAN John W 1894 | JORDAN John W 1894 | DEASON Amos 1859 | STOCKTON Edward 1901

Section 15
SANDERSON Joseph W 1895
KEETON Nancy 1891
KEETON Nancy 1891
FAIRCHILDS William 1859
PITTMAN William W 1895
GANDY John 1859
GANDY John 1859
15
PITTMAN William W 1895
FAIRCHILDS William 1859

Section 14
PITTMAN William W 1895
DEASON Amos 1859
DEASON Amos 1859
PITTMAN John G 1893
DEASON Amos 1854
DEASON Amos 1854
PITTMAN John G 1893
14
PITTMAN John G 1893
JORDAN Mark C 1896
JORDAN Matthew P 1890
JORDAN Matthew P 1890
JORDAN Matthew P 1890

Section 13
QUICK John W 1896
QUICK John W 1896
QUICK John W 1896
ANDERSON Susanah 1884
DEASON Amos 1859
ANDERSON Susanah 1884
13
BREAZEALE William H 1902
MYERS John H 1854
ANDERSON Susanah 1884

Section 22
FAIRCHILDS William 1859
FAIRCHILDS William 1859
FAIRCHILDS Hiram 1859
FAIRCHILDS Hiram 1859
PHILLIPS Eli E 1890
FAIRCHILDS Hiram 1859
FAIRCHILDS Hiram 1859
22
PHILLIPS Eli E 1890
PHILLIPS Eli E 1890

Section 23
BALFOUR James 1882
BALFOUR James 1882
23
BALFOUR James 1882
FOLKS John 1859
BALFOUR James 1882
FOLKS John 1859
FOLKS John 1859

Section 24
BALFOUR James 1882
DEVALL Luther E 1894
MITCHELL William W 1892
24
BALFOUR James 1882
BALFOUR James 1882
MITCHELL William W 1892

Section 27
BALFOUR James 1882
STAFFORD Jacob 1861
BALFOUR James 1882
27
BALFOUR James 1882
BALFOUR James 1882
STAFFORD Jacob 1861
BALFOUR James 1882
PAGE John C 1859
BALFOUR James 1882

Section 26
PAGE Hezekiah W 1859
PAGE Hezekiah W 1859
MOFFETT Daniel T 1885
STAFFORD Jacob 1861
MOFFETT Daniel T 1885
26
BALFOUR James 1882
BALFOUR James 1882
BALFOUR James 1882

Section 25
BALFOUR James 1882
MOFFETT Daniel T 1885
BALFOUR James 1882
25
BALFOUR James 1882
EASTERLING James A 1895
BENSON Isom 1893
WOULARD Erasmus A 1894
EASTERLING James A 1895
WOULARD Erasmus A 1894

Section 34
MCNIECE James 1859
34
JIMISON John W 1896
CREEL James R 1859
SMITH William J 1888
MCNIECE James 1859
CREEL James R 1859
JIMISON John W 1896
SHOWS Daniel T 1892
SHOWS Daniel T 1892

Section 35
BALFOUR James 1882
MCCALLUM [24] Matilda 1885
MCCALLUM [24] Matilda 1885
BALFOUR James 1882
35

Section 36
BALFOUR James 1882
36
EWING Albert B 1895
MCDONALD Norman 1894

Helpful Hints

1. This Map's INDEX can be found on the preceding pages.

2. Refer to Map "C" to see where this Township lies within Jones County, Mississippi.

3. Numbers within square brackets [ ] denote a multi-patentee land parcel (multi-owner). Refer to Appendix "C" for a full list of members in this group.

4. Areas that look to be crowded with Patentees usually indicate multiple sales of the same parcel (Re-issues) or Overlapping parcels. See this Township's Index for an explanation of these and other circumstances that might explain "odd" groupings of Patentees on this map.

Legend

——— Patent Boundary

━━━ Section Boundary

No Patents Found (or Outside County)

1., 2., 3., ... Lot Numbers (when beside a name)

[ ] Group Number (see Appendix "C")

Scale: Section = 1 mile X 1 mile (generally, with some exceptions)

Road Map

T7-N R13-W
St Stephens Meridian

Map Group 17

Cities & Towns
Tawanta

Cemeteries
Benson Cemetery
Crosby Cemetery
Gandy Cemetery
Hinton Cemetery
Jordan Cemetery
Pine Grove Cemetery

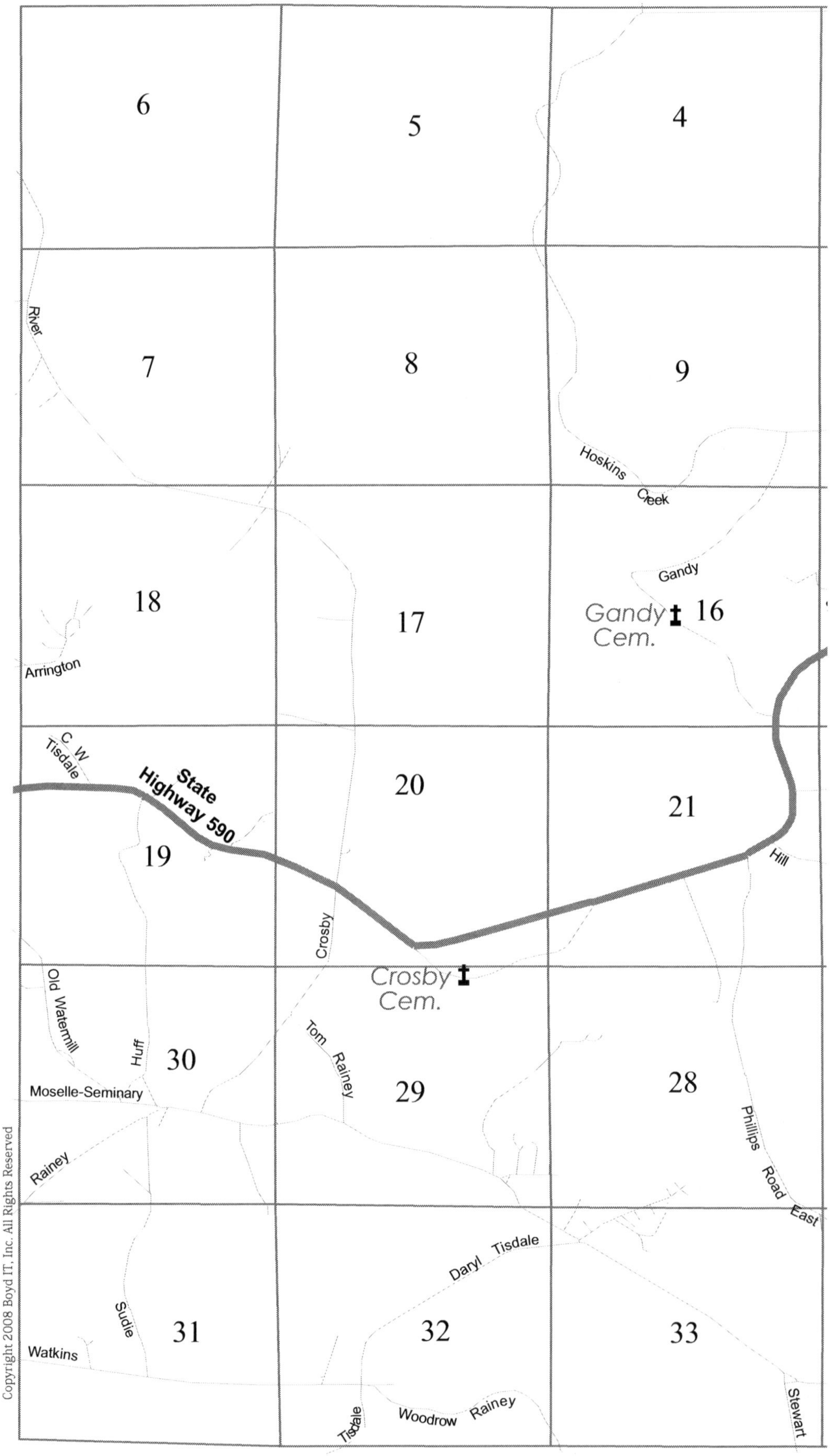

6	5	4
7	8	9
18	17	Gandy ✝ 16 Cem.
19	20	21
30	29	28
31	32	33

River

Hoskins Creek

Gandy

Arrington

C W Tisdale

State Highway 590

Crosby ✝ Cem.

Hill

Old Watermill

Huff

Moselle-Seminary

Rainey

Tom Rainey

Phillips Road East

Sudie

Watkins

Daryl Tisdale

Tisdale

Woodrow Rainey

Stewart

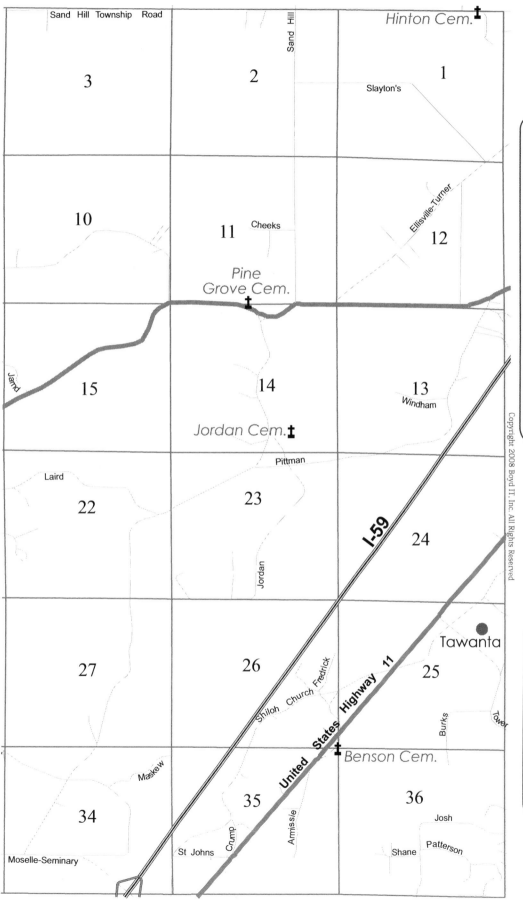

Sand Hill Township Road

Sand Hill

Hinton Cem.

3

2

1

Slayton's

Ellisville-Turner

10

11

Cheeks

12

Pine Grove Cem.

Jarrd

15

14

13

Windham

Jordan Cem.

Pittman

Laird

22

23

24

Jordan

I-59

27

26

25

Tawanta

Shiloh Church Fredrick

United States Highway 11

Burks

Tower

Benson Cem.

Maskew

35

36

34

Crump

Armissie

Josh

St Johns

Shane

Patterson

Moselle-Seminary

Helpful Hints

1. This road map has a number of uses, but primarily it is to help you: a) find the present location of land owned by your ancestors (at least the general area), b) find cemeteries and city-centers, and c) estimate the route/roads used by Census-takers & tax-assessors.

2. If you plan to travel to Jones County to locate cemeteries or land parcels, please pick up a modern travel map for the area before you do. Mapping old land parcels on modern maps is not as exact a science as you might think. Just the slightest variations in public land survey coordinates, estimates of parcel boundaries, or road-map deviations can greatly alter a map's representation of how a road either does or doesn't cross a particular parcel of land.

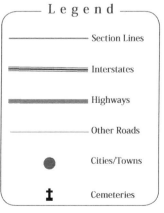

Legend

——————	Section Lines
═══════	Interstates
——————	Highways
··············	Other Roads
●	Cities/Towns
✝	Cemeteries

Scale: Section = 1 mile X 1 mile
(generally, with some exceptions)

181

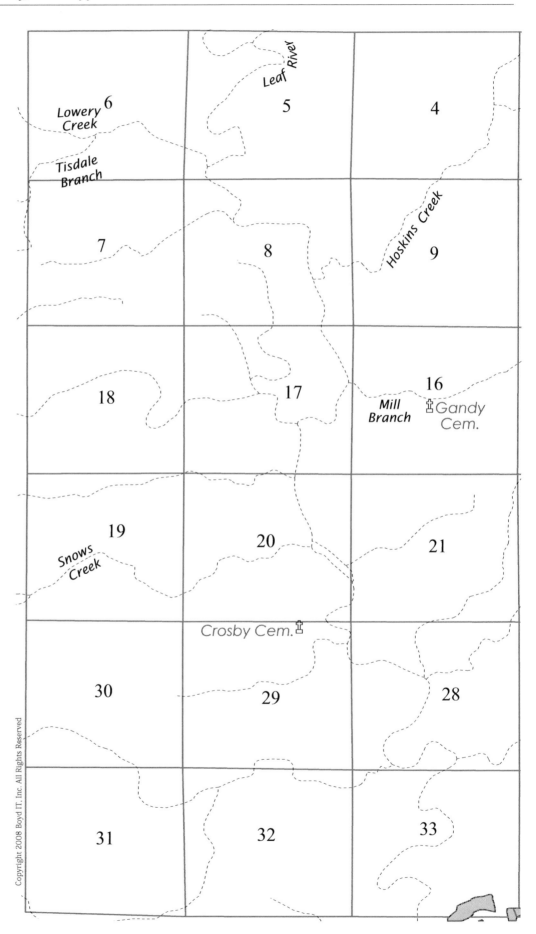

Historical Map

T7-N R13-W
St Stephens Meridian

Map Group 17

Cities & Towns
Tawanta

Cemeteries
Benson Cemetery
Crosby Cemetery
Gandy Cemetery
Hinton Cemetery
Jordan Cemetery
Pine Grove Cemetery

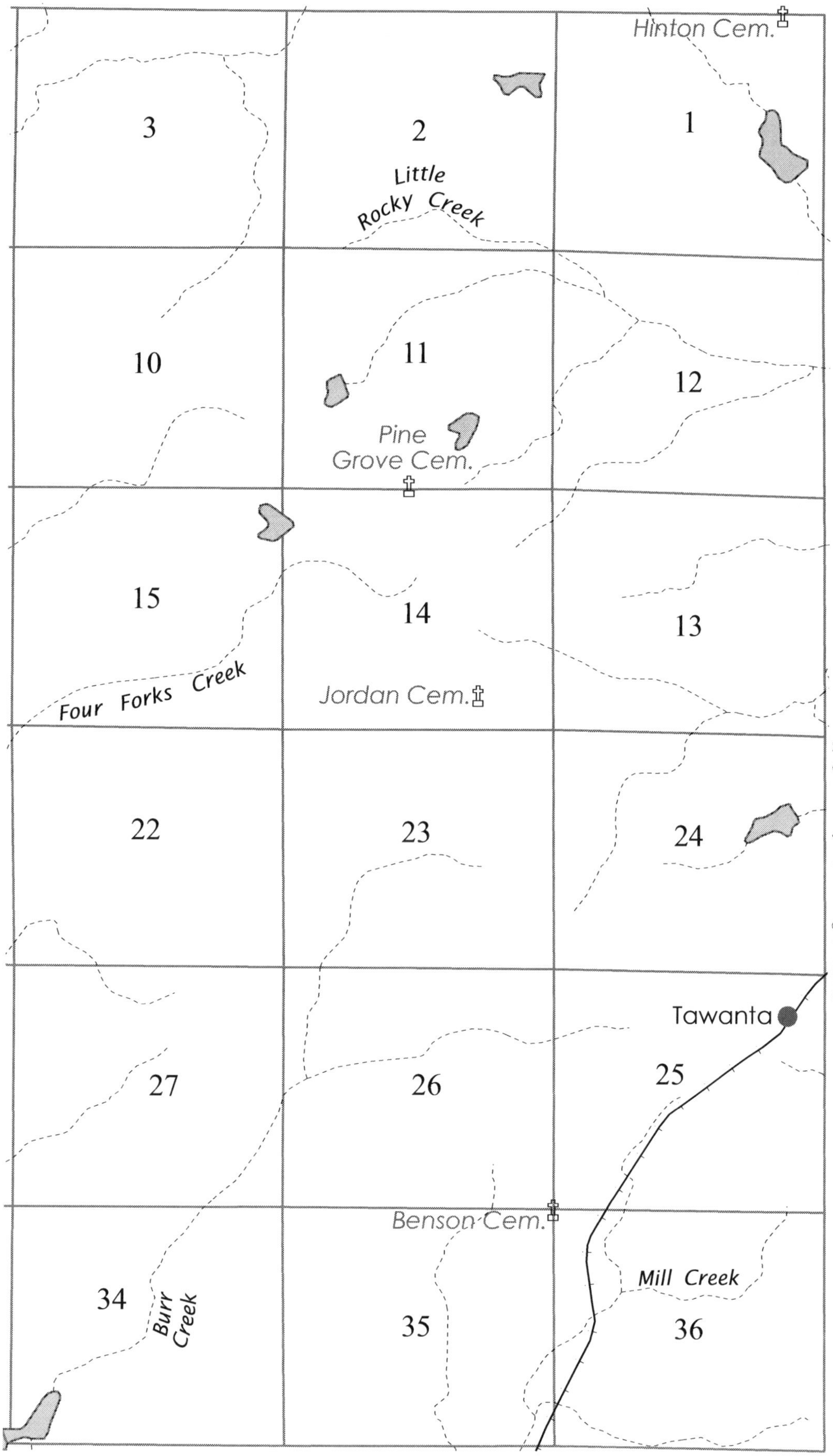

Helpful Hints

1. This Map takes a different look at the same Congressional Township displayed in the preceding two maps. It presents features that can help you better envision the historical development of the area: a) Water-bodies (lakes & ponds), b) Water-courses (rivers, streams, etc.), c) Railroads, d) City/town center-points (where they were oftentimes located when first settled), and e) Cemeteries.
2. Using this "Historical" map in tandem with this Township's Patent Map and Road Map, may lead you to some interesting discoveries. You will often find roads, towns, cemeteries, and waterways are named after nearby landowners: sometimes those names will be the ones you are researching. See how many of these research gems you can find here in Jones County.

Legend

- Section Lines
- Railroads
- Large Rivers & Bodies of Water
- Streams/Creeks & Small Rivers
- Cities/Towns
- Cemeteries

Scale: Section = 1 mile X 1 mile
(there are some exceptions)

Map Group 18: Index to Land Patents

Township 7-North Range 12-West (St Stephens)

After you locate an individual in this Index, take note of the Section and Section Part then proceed to the Land Patent map on the pages immediately following. You should have no difficulty locating the corresponding parcel of land.

The "For More Info" Column will lead you to more information about the underlying Patents. See the *Legend* at right, and the "How to Use this Book" chapter, for more information.

```
                        LEGEND
              "For More Info . . . " column
A = Authority (Legislative Act, See Appendix "A")
B = Block or Lot (location in Section unknown)
C = Cancelled Patent
F = Fractional Section
G = Group  (Multi-Patentee Patent, see Appendix "C")
V = Overlaps another Parcel
R = Re-Issued (Parcel patented more than once)

(A & G items require you to look in the Appendixes referred
to above. All other Letter-designations followed by a number
require you to locate line-items in this index that possess
the ID number found after the letter).
```

ID	Individual in Patent	Sec.	Sec. Part	Date Issued	Other Counties	For More Info . . .
3133	ANDERSON, Allen	22	NESE	1841-01-05		A2
3134	" "	3	NWNE	1841-01-05		A2
3132	" "	1	W½SW	1859-05-02		A2
3176	ANDERSON, Hiram	2	SESE	1848-09-01		A2
3178	ANDERSON, Isaac	22	SENE	1837-02-02		A2
3177	" "	2	SENE	1857-06-19		A2
3151	APLIN, David W	36	SE	1895-06-27		A3
3216	BATES, John M	10	SESW	1859-05-02		A2
3207	BEECH, John	24	E½NW	1898-07-18		A3
3208	" "	24	NWSW	1898-07-18		A3
3209	" "	24	SWNW	1898-07-18		A3
3234	BEECH, Josiah S	27	NWSW	1892-07-25		A3
3235	" "	28	E½NE	1892-07-25		A3
3236	" "	28	NESE	1892-07-25		A3
3201	BOUTWELL, Jeremiah	26	SESW	1886-03-20		A3
3199	" "	25	NWSW	1895-11-11		A3
3200	" "	26	E½SE	1895-11-11		A3
3301	BOWEN, Thomas H	15	SESW	1860-04-10		A2
3302	" "	22	NENW	1860-04-10		A2
3188	BRADLEY, James M	36	S½SW	1897-04-02		A3
3295	BRADSHAW, Sanford F	13	SESE	1886-07-20		A2
3296	" "	24	NWNE	1886-07-20		A2
3243	BUSBY, Lovick A	12	NE	1889-01-12		A3
3255	BUSBY, Matt C	1	S½SE	1891-06-30		A3
3256	" "	1	SESW	1891-06-30		A3
3289	BUSBY, Sampson	12	N½NW	1895-10-09		A3
3290	" "	12	SENW	1895-10-09		A3
3259	BYNUM, Nancy A	21	NESE	1884-12-30		A2
3257	BYRD, Moses	21	SESE	1859-05-02		A2
3258	" "	22	SWSW	1859-05-02		A2
3308	COMPANY, William F Evans And	17	NESW	1882-04-20		A2
3309	" "	17	SENW	1882-04-20		A2
3310	" "	7	NWSE	1882-04-20		A2
3311	" "	7	SWNE	1882-04-20		A2
3312	" "	8	NENW	1882-04-20		A2
3313	" "	8	NWNE	1882-04-20		A2
3166	CRAFT, George W	28	NESW	1896-10-31		A3
3167	" "	28	NWSE	1896-10-31		A3
3168	" "	28	SENW	1896-10-31		A3
3169	" "	28	SWNE	1896-10-31		A3
3118	DONALD, Alexander	14	NENW	1841-01-05		A2
3304	DREW, Thomas P	28	SESE	1894-03-15		A2
3305	" "	33	NWNE	1894-03-15		A2
3306	" "	33	SENE	1894-03-15		A2
3213	DRYDEN, John L	28	NWSW	1892-08-01		A2
3214	" "	28	S½SW	1892-08-01		A2

ID	Individual in Patent	Sec.	Sec. Part	Date Issued	Other Counties	For More Info . . .
3215	DRYDEN, John L (Cont'd)	28	SWSE	1892-08-01		A2
3140	EASTERLING, Asa B	26	SWNE	1882-04-20		A2
3138	" "	26	NWNE	1882-06-01		A2
3139	" "	26	SENE	1882-06-01		A2
3210	EVERETT, John E	25	S½NW	1906-06-26		A3
3261	EZELL, Hugh F	5	NWNE	1884-12-30		A2 G26
3262	" "	5	S½SW	1884-12-30		A2 G26
3263	" "	6	W½SW	1884-12-30		A2 G26
3211	FREEMAN, John	34	S½SW	1895-02-21		A3
3212	" "	34	SWSE	1895-02-21		A3
3330	GARNER, Willie C	13	W½SW	1912-06-20		A2
3119	GEDDIE, Alexander	1	NENE	1882-04-20		A2
3250	GUNTER, Mary S	33	SESE	1898-08-27		A3 G14
3251	" "	33	W½SE	1898-08-27		A3 G14
3145	HALL, Cleveland	34	NENW	1914-08-27		A3
3225	HALL, Jonathan T	27	SWSW	1911-01-05		A3
3314	HARDY, William H	10	NWNE	1882-05-10		A2
3315	" "	10	W½NW	1882-05-10		A2
3316	" "	10	W½SW	1882-05-10		A2
3317	" "	4	E½NW	1882-05-10		A2
3318	" "	4	SWNE	1882-05-10		A2
3319	" "	4	W½SE	1882-05-10		A2
3320	" "	9	N½NE	1882-05-10		A2
3321	" "	9	SENE	1882-05-10		A2
3298	HENNIS, Susan	35	NESE	1890-08-16		A3
3299	" "	36	N½SW	1890-08-16		A3
3300	" "	36	SENW	1890-08-16		A3
3135	HERRINGTON, Andrew J	32	NESW	1897-05-07		A3
3136	" "	32	NWSE	1897-05-07		A3
3137	" "	32	S½SE	1897-05-07		A3
3261	HOLT, Thomas B	5	NWNE	1884-12-30		A2 G26
3262	" "	5	S½SW	1884-12-30		A2 G26
3263	" "	6	W½SW	1884-12-30		A2 G26
3143	JOHNSON, Charles B	25	SWSW	1897-11-01		A3
3144	" "	36	W½NW	1897-11-01		A3
3293	JOHNSON, Samuel J	25	NESW	1886-07-20		A2
3294	" "	25	NWSE	1886-07-20		A2
3292	" "	23	SENE	1889-11-21		A2
3291	" "	23	NESE	1889-11-29		A2
3141	KIRKLAND, Caleb R	12	E½SW	1889-01-12		A3
3142	" "	12	W½SE	1889-01-12		A3
3284	LOWRY, Peter	3	W½SW	1861-02-01		A2
3285	" "	4	E½SE	1861-02-01		A2
3158	LYON, Elijah	26	NWSE	1841-01-05		A2
3159	LYON, Elisha	11	SWSE	1841-01-05		A2
3160	" "	13	E½SW	1841-01-05		A2
3161	" "	13	W½SE	1841-01-05		A2
3162	" "	14	SENW	1841-01-05		A2
3163	" "	14	W½SW	1841-01-05		A2
3260	LYON, Nicholas	11	W½SW	1928-02-18		A2
3146	MCDUGALD, Daniel	32	NESE	1895-06-28		A3
3147	" "	33	N½SW	1895-06-28		A3
3148	" "	33	SESW	1895-06-28		A3
3261	MCGAHEY, Otto	5	NWNE	1884-12-30		A2 G26
3262	" "	5	S½SW	1884-12-30		A2 G26
3263	" "	6	W½SW	1884-12-30		A2 G26
3250	MCGILL, Mary S	33	SESE	1898-08-27		A3 G14
3251	" "	33	W½SE	1898-08-27		A3 G14
3297	MCGILL, Sarah A	32	S½NW	1893-04-12		A3
3155	MCMULLEN, Eli S	36	NENW	1895-06-28		A3
3156	" "	36	NWNE	1895-06-28		A3
3157	" "	36	S½NE	1895-06-28		A3
3170	MELVIN, George W	35	SESE	1889-12-19		A3
3217	MOFFETT, John	2	NESE	1841-01-05		A2
3179	MOORES, J H	12	NESE	1889-04-23		A2
3180	" "	13	NESE	1889-04-23		A2
3181	" "	13	S½NE	1889-04-23		A2
3218	MORGAN, John	28	W½NW	1896-02-13		A3
3223	MOTT, John W	14	NESE	1846-09-01		A2
3224	" "	14	NWSE	1846-09-01		A2
3185	OWEN, Jacob L	11	SENW	1851-10-01		A2
3183	" "	10	E½SE	1859-11-10		A2
3184	" "	10	SENE	1859-11-10		A2

ID	Individual in Patent	Sec.	Sec. Part	Date Issued	Other Counties	For More Info . . .
3186	OWEN, Jacob L (Cont'd)	11	SWNW	1859-11-10		A2
3164	PAGE, Franklin D	23	SESE	1889-11-29		A2
3165	" "	33	NENE	1889-11-29		A2
3171	PARKER, Hardy	11	SESE	1841-01-05		A2
3172	" "	14	W½NE	1841-01-05		A2
3189	PARKER, James	14	E½SW	1841-01-05		A2
3190	" "	23	NWNW	1841-01-05		A2
3219	PARKER, John	35	W½SE	1918-08-12		A2 G33
3242	PARKER, Littleberry A	24	E½SW	1875-07-01		A3
3197	PITMAN, James W	25	E½NE	1895-06-28		A3
3198	" "	25	SWNE	1895-06-28		A3
3264	PLOCK, Otto	18	S½SE	1882-04-20		A2
3265	" "	18	SW	1882-04-20		A2
3268	" "	19	S½SW	1882-04-20		A2
3270	" "	20	S½SE	1882-04-20		A2
3271	" "	20	S½SW	1882-04-20		A2
3272	" "	21	W½NW	1882-04-20		A2
3273	" "	21	W½SW	1882-04-20		A2
3274	" "	29	E½	1882-04-20		A2
3275	" "	29	E½SW	1882-04-20		A2
3276	" "	29	NW	1882-04-20		A2
3277	" "	29	NWSW	1882-04-20		A2
3278	" "	30	N½	1882-04-20		A2
3279	" "	30	N½SE	1882-04-20		A2
3280	" "	30	SW	1882-04-20		A2
3281	" "	31	S½NE	1882-04-20		A2
3282	" "	31	SE	1882-04-20		A2
3283	" "	31	W½	1882-04-20		A2
3266	" "	19	N½SW	1882-05-20		A2
3267	" "	19	NW	1882-05-20		A2
3269	" "	20	NE	1882-05-20		A2
3286	PONDER, Reuben	1	NWNE	1885-06-12		A2
3287	" "	1	SENE	1885-06-12		A2
3123	POOL, Alfred G	10	NENE	1859-05-02		A2
3124	" "	11	NWNW	1859-05-02		A2
3125	" "	2	W½SW	1859-05-02		A2
3126	" "	3	E½SE	1859-05-02		A2
3127	" "	3	SWSE	1859-05-02		A2 R3205
3226	POOL, Joseph	10	SWSE	1859-05-02		A2
3227	" "	12	SWSW	1859-05-02		A2
3228	" "	13	W½NW	1859-05-02		A2
3229	" "	15	NWSE	1859-05-02		A2
3230	" "	15	SENE	1859-05-02		A2
3231	" "	15	W½NE	1859-05-02		A2
3237	PRESSCOAT, Lewis B	10	E½NW	1859-11-10		A2
3238	" "	10	NESW	1859-11-10		A2
3239	" "	10	NWSE	1859-11-10		A2
3240	" "	10	SWNE	1859-11-10		A2
3241	" "	3	SESW	1859-11-10		A2
3206	READ, John B	9	SWSE	1854-03-15		A2
3322	RICHARDSON, William P	17	S½NE	1882-05-10		A2
3323	" "	17	S½SW	1882-05-10		A2
3324	" "	17	SE	1882-05-10		A2
3325	" "	19	N½SE	1882-05-10		A2
3326	" "	19	NE	1882-05-10		A2
3327	" "	20	NW	1882-05-10		A2
3128	ROBISON, Alfred T	21	SESW	1892-07-25		A3
3129	" "	21	SWSE	1892-07-25		A3
3130	" "	28	NENW	1892-07-25		A3
3131	" "	28	NWNE	1892-07-25		A3
3154	ROBISON, Doctor C	24	SE	1893-04-12		A3
3249	ROBISON, Mary Edna	30	SWSE	1931-01-27		A3
3232	SANDERS, Joseph	32	SESE	1897-07-03		A3
3233	" "	32	W½SW	1897-07-03		A3
3219	SCRIVENER, Jesse	35	W½SE	1918-08-12		A2 G33
3187	SHOWE, James J	34	NWSE	1882-04-20		A2
3182	SHOWES, Jackson	1	NESE	1890-06-25		A3
3149	SHOWS, Daniel	27	S½NE	1841-01-05		A2
3173	SHOWS, Henry	12	SESE	1892-04-29		A3
3174	" "	13	N½NE	1892-04-29		A3
3175	" "	13	NENW	1892-04-29		A3
3193	SHOWS, James	35	NENW	1841-01-05		A2
3194	" "	35	NWNE	1854-03-15		A2

ID	Individual in Patent	Sec.	Sec. Part	Date Issued	Other Counties	For More Info . . .
3192	SHOWS, James (Cont'd)	35	E½NE	1859-05-02		A2
3195	" "	35	SENW	1859-05-02		A2
3196	" "	35	SWNE	1859-05-02		A2
3220	SHOWS, John R	24	SWSW	1901-02-27		A3
3221	" "	25	N½NW	1901-02-27		A3
3222	" "	26	NENE	1901-02-27		A3
3244	SHOWS, Lucinda	26	SWSE	1859-05-02		A2
3246	SHOWS, Martha	25	SESE	1884-12-30		A3
3247	" "	36	NENE	1884-12-30		A3
3252	SHOWS, Mary	25	NESE	1892-06-15		A3
3253	" "	25	SESW	1892-06-15		A3
3254	" "	25	SWSE	1892-06-15		A3
3307	SHOWS, Warren W	11	NENW	1848-09-01		A2
3248	SKELLY, Martha	24	S½NE	1885-06-20		A3
3245	STENNETT, Mark	34	SWNE	1910-07-05		A3
3191	STRICKLAND, James S	24	NENE	1896-12-14		A3
3288	STRICKLAND, Richard Franklin	25	NWNE	1938-04-05		A3
3328	STRICKLAND, William P	35	E½SW	1917-11-14		A3
3329	TISDALL, William	11	NESW	1848-09-01		A2
3120	WALTERS, Alfred B	1	NESW	1891-05-20		A3
3121	" "	1	NWSE	1891-05-20		A3
3122	" "	1	SWNE	1891-05-20		A3
3150	WALTERS, Daniel Webster	33	SWSW	1925-04-20		A3
3152	WELBORN, Dewit C	4	E½NE	1859-05-02		A2
3153	" "	4	NWNE	1859-05-02		A2
3205	WELBORN, Joel E	3	SWSE	1859-05-02		A2 R3127
3202	" "	3	NESW	1860-07-02		A2
3203	" "	3	NW	1860-07-02		A2
3204	" "	3	SWNE	1860-07-02		A2
3303	WELBORN, Thomas J	23	W½SE	1860-04-02		A2

Patent Map

T7-N R12-W
St Stephens Meridian

Map Group 18

Township Statistics

Parcels Mapped	:	213
Number of Patents	:	116
Number of Individuals	:	91
Patentees Identified	:	87
Number of Surnames	:	63
Multi-Patentee Parcels	:	6
Oldest Patent Date	:	2/2/1837
Most Recent Patent	:	4/5/1938
Block/Lot Parcels	:	0
Parcels Re - Issued	:	1
Parcels that Overlap	:	0
Cities and Towns	:	4
Cemeteries	:	9

WELBORN Joel E 1860	ANDERSON Allen 1841			PONDER Reuben 1885	GEDDIE Alexander 1882
	WELBORN Joel E 1860		ANDERSON Isaac 1857	WALTERS Alfred B 1891	PONDER Reuben 1885
3		2	MOFFETT John 1841	WALTERS Alfred B 1891	WALTERS Alfred B 1891	SHOWES Jackson 1890
LOWRY Peter 1861	WELBORN Joel E 1860	POOL Alfred G 1859		ANDERSON Allen 1859	BUSBY Matt C 1891	BUSBY Matt C 1891
	PRESSCOAT Lewis B 1859	WELBORN Joel E 1859 / POOL Alfred G 1859	POOL Alfred G 1859	ANDERSON Hiram 1848		

Helpful Hints

1. This Map's INDEX can be found on the preceding pages.

2. Refer to Map "C" to see where this Township lies within Jones County, Mississippi.

3. Numbers within square brackets [ ] denote a multi-patentee land parcel (multi-owner). Refer to Appendix "C" for a full list of members in this group.

4. Areas that look to be crowded with Patentees usually indicate multiple sales of the same parcel (Re-issues) or Overlapping parcels. See this Township's Index for an explanation of these and other circumstances that might explain "odd" groupings of Patentees on this map.

HARDY William H 1882	PRESSCOAT Lewis B 1859	HARDY William H 1882	POOL Alfred G 1859	POOL Alfred G 1859	SHOWS Warren W 1848	BUSBY Sampson 1895	
10		PRESSCOAT Lewis B 1859	OWEN Jacob L 1859	OWEN Jacob L 1859	OWEN Jacob L 1851	BUSBY Sampson 1895	BUSBY Lovick A 1889
	PRESSCOAT Lewis B 1859	PRESSCOAT Lewis B 1859	OWEN Jacob L 1859	TISDALL William 1848	11	12	MOORES J H 1889
HARDY William H 1882	BATES John M 1859	POOL Joseph 1859	LYON Nicholas 1928	LYON Elisha 1841	PARKER Hardy 1841	POOL Joseph 1859	KIRKLAND Caleb R 1889	KIRKLAND Caleb R 1889	SHOWS Henry 1892

	POOL Joseph 1859		DONALD Alexander 1841	PARKER Hardy 1841	POOL Joseph 1859	SHOWS Henry 1892	SHOWS Henry 1892
15	POOL Joseph 1859		LYON Elisha 1841	14	13	MOORES J H 1889
	POOL Joseph 1859	LYON Elisha 1841	PARKER James 1841	MOTT John W 1846	MOTT John W 1846	GARNER Willie C 1912	LYON Elisha 1841	LYON Elisha 1841	MOORES J H 1889
BOWEN Thomas H 1860						BRADSHAW Sanford F 1886

BOWEN Thomas H 1860		PARKER James 1841			BRADSHAW Sanford F 1886	STRICKLAND James S 1896
22	ANDERSON Isaac 1837	23	JOHNSON Samuel J 1889	BEECH John 1898	BEECH John 1898	SKELLY Martha 1885
	ANDERSON Allen 1841	WELBORN Thomas J 1860	JOHNSON Samuel J 1889	BEECH John 1898	PARKER Littleberry A 1875	24
BYRD Moses 1859			PAGE Franklin D 1889	SHOWS John R 1901	ROBISON Doctor C 1893	

27	SHOWS Daniel 1841		EASTERLING Asa B 1882	SHOWS John R 1901	SHOWS John R 1901	STRICKLAND Richard Franklin 1938	PITMAN James W 1895
			EASTERLING Asa B 1882	EASTERLING Asa B 1882	EVERETT John E 1906	25	PITMAN James W 1895
BEECH Josiah S 1892		26	LYON Elijah 1841	BOUTWELL Jeremiah 1895	BOUTWELL Jeremiah 1895	JOHNSON Samuel J 1886	JOHNSON Samuel J 1886	SHOWS Mary 1892
HALL Jonathan T 1911		BOUTWELL Jeremiah 1886	SHOWS Lucinda 1859	JOHNSON Charles B 1897	SHOWS Mary 1892	SHOWS Mary 1892	SHOWS Martha 1884

	HALL Cleveland 1914	SHOWS James 1841	SHOWS James 1854	JOHNSON Charles B 1897	MCMULLEN Eli S 1895	MCMULLEN Eli S 1895	SHOWS Martha 1884
34	STENNETT Mark 1910	SHOWS James 1859	SHOWS James 1859	SHOWS James 1859	HENNIS Susan 1890	MCMULLEN Eli S 1895
	SHOWE James J 1882	35	PARKER [33] John 1918	HENNIS Susan 1890	HENNIS Susan 1890	36	APLIN David W 1895
FREEMAN John 1895	FREEMAN John 1895	STRICKLAND William P 1917	MELVIN George W 1889	BRADLEY James M 1897		

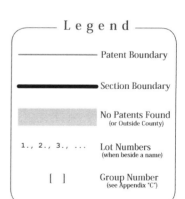

L e g e n d

———— Patent Boundary

▬▬▬▬ Section Boundary

▓▓▓▓ No Patents Found (or Outside County)

1., 2., 3., ... Lot Numbers (when beside a name)

[ ] Group Number (see Appendix "C")

Scale: Section = 1 mile X 1 mile (generally, with some exceptions)

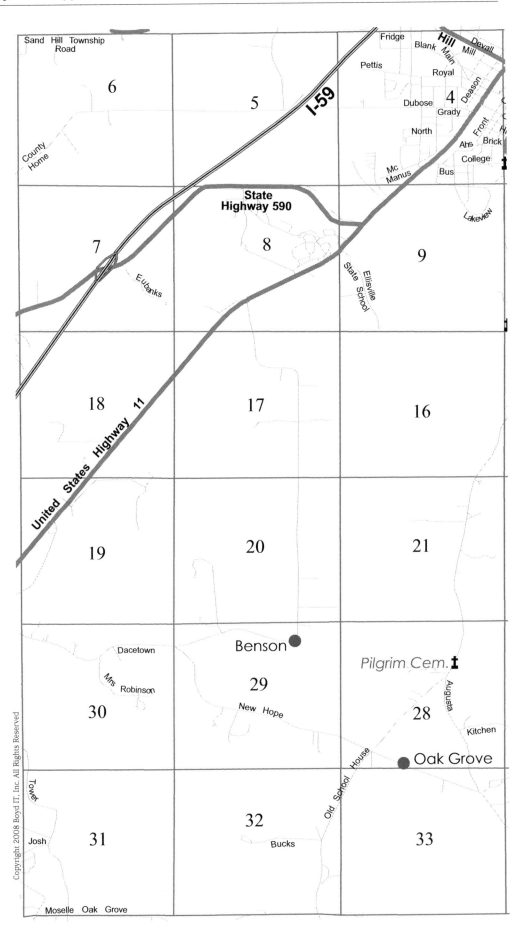

Road Map

T7-N R12-W
St Stephens Meridian

Map Group 18

Cities & Towns

Benson
Ellisville
Jenkins
Oak Grove

Cemeteries

Anderson-Minter Cemetery
Brown Cemetery
Bynum Cemetery
Ellisville Cemetery
Johnson Cemetery
Jordan Cemetery
Pilgrim Cemetery
Tularosa Cemetery
Walters Cemetery

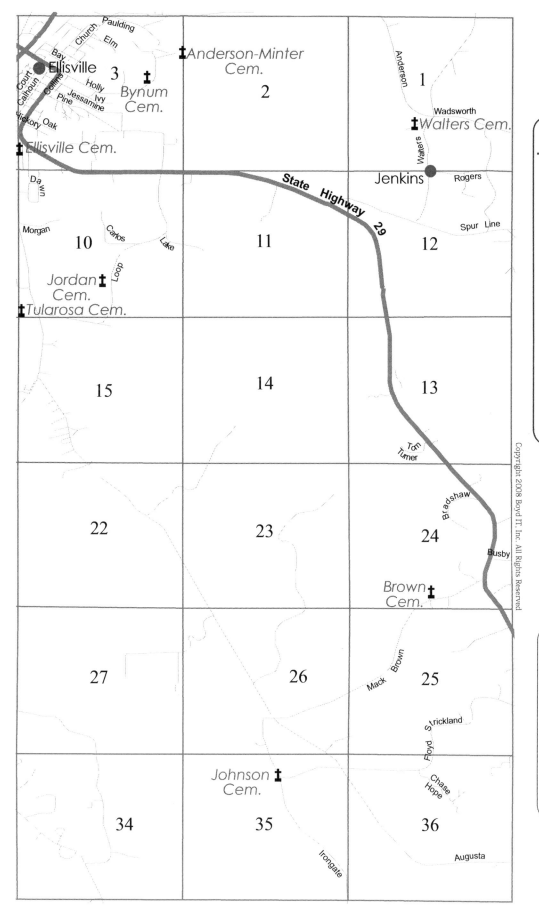

Ellisville

Paulding
Church
Elm
Bay
Collins
Holly
Ivy
Jessamine
Pine
Hickory
Oak
Court
Calhoun

3

Bynum
Cem.

† Anderson-Minter
Cem.

2

Anderson

1

Wadsworth
† Walters Cem.

Walters

† Ellisville Cem.

Dawn

Jenkins

Rogers

Spur   Line

State   Highway   29

Morgan

Carlos

Lake

10

Loop

Jordan †
Cem.
† Tularosa Cem.

11

12

15

14

13

Tom
Turner

22

23

Bradshaw

24

Busby

Brown †
Cem.

27

Mack   Brown

26

25

Strickland

Floyd

Johnson †
Cem.

Chase
Hope

34

35

36

Irongate

Augusta

Copyright 2008 Boyd IT, Inc. All Rights Reserved

Helpful Hints

1. This road map has a number of uses, but primarily it is to help you: a) find the present location of land owned by your ancestors (at least the general area), b) find cemeteries and city-centers, and c) estimate the route/roads used by Census-takers & tax-assessors.

2. If you plan to travel to Jones County to locate cemeteries or land parcels, please pick up a modern travel map for the area before you do. Mapping old land parcels on modern maps is not as exact a science as you might think. Just the slightest variations in public land survey coordinates, estimates of parcel boundaries, or road-map deviations can greatly alter a map's representation of how a road either does or doesn't cross a particular parcel of land.

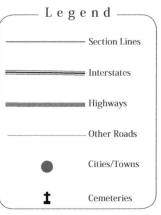

L e g e n d

——————— Section Lines

══════════ Interstates

━━━━━━━━ Highways

——————— Other Roads

● Cities/Towns

† Cemeteries

Scale: Section = 1 mile X 1 mile
(generally, with some exceptions)

191

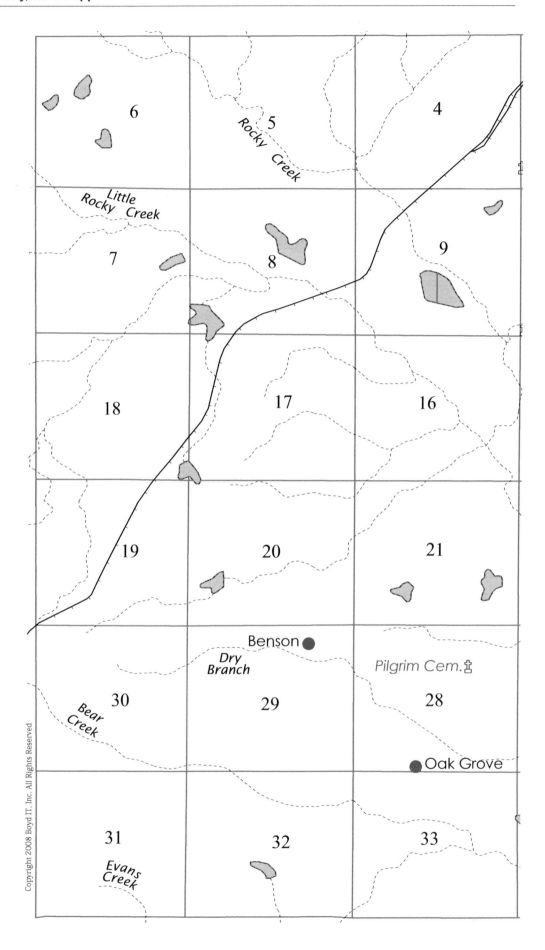

Historical Map

T7-N R12-W
St Stephens Meridian

Map Group 18

Cities & Towns
Benson
Ellisville
Jenkins
Oak Grove

Cemeteries
Anderson-Minter Cemetery
Brown Cemetery
Bynum Cemetery
Ellisville Cemetery
Johnson Cemetery
Jordan Cemetery
Pilgrim Cemetery
Tularosa Cemetery
Walters Cemetery

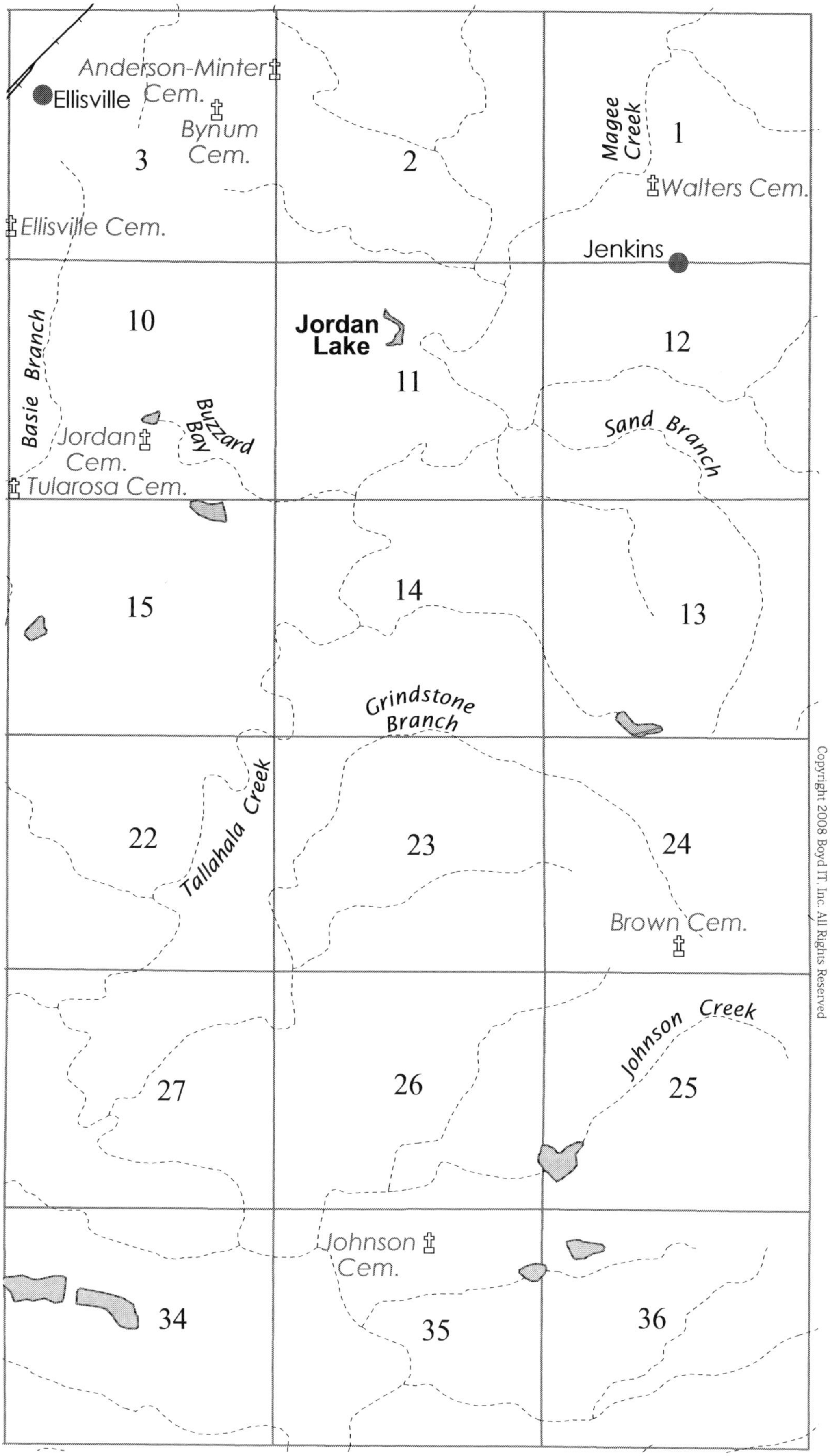
Anderson-Minter Cem.
Ellisville
Bynum Cem.
3
2
Magee Creek
1
Walters Cem.
Ellisville Cem.
Jenkins
10
Basie Branch
Jordan Lake
11
12
Buzzard Bay
Jordan Cem.
Tularosa Cem.
Sand Branch
15
14
13
Grindstone Branch
22
Tallahala Creek
23
24
Brown Cem.
Johnson Creek
27
26
25
Johnson Cem.
34
35
36

Helpful Hints

1. This Map takes a different look at the same Congressional Township displayed in the preceding two maps. It presents features that can help you better envision the historical development of the area: a) Water-bodies (lakes & ponds), b) Water-courses (rivers, streams, etc.), c) Railroads, d) City/town center-points (where they were oftentimes located when first settled), and e) Cemeteries.

2. Using this "Historical" map in tandem with this Township's Patent Map and Road Map, may lead you to some interesting discoveries. You will often find roads, towns, cemeteries, and waterways are named after nearby landowners: sometimes those names will be the ones you are researching. See how many of these research gems you can find here in Jones County.

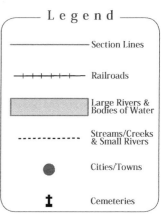

Legend

- Section Lines
- Railroads
- Large Rivers & Bodies of Water
- Streams/Creeks & Small Rivers
- Cities/Towns
- Cemeteries

Scale: Section = 1 mile X 1 mile
(there are some exceptions)

Map Group 19: Index to Land Patents

Township 7-North Range 11-West (St Stephens)

After you locate an individual in this Index, take note of the Section and Section Part then proceed to the Land Patent map on the pages immediately following. You should have no difficulty locating the corresponding parcel of land.

The "For More Info" Column will lead you to more information about the underlying Patents. See the *Legend* at right, and the "How to Use this Book" chapter, for more information.

```
┌─────────────────────────────────────────────────┐
│                     LEGEND                        │
│          "For More Info . . . " column            │
│  A = Authority (Legislative Act, See Appendix "A")│
│  B = Block or Lot (location in Section unknown)   │
│  C = Cancelled Patent                             │
│  F = Fractional Section                           │
│  G = Group  (Multi-Patentee Patent, see Appendix "C")│
│  V = Overlaps another Parcel                      │
│  R = Re-Issued (Parcel patented more than once)   │
│                                                   │
│  (A & G items require you to look in the Appendixes referred│
│  to above. All other Letter-designations followed by a number│
│  require you to locate line-items in this index that possess│
│  the ID number found after the letter).           │
└─────────────────────────────────────────────────┘
```

ID	Individual in Patent	Sec.	Sec. Part	Date Issued	Other Counties	For More Info . . .
3447	ADAMS, Lewin	11	NESE	1859-05-02		A2
3448	" "	11	S½NE	1859-05-02		A2
3434	BEECH, John	19	NESW	1886-07-20		A2
3435	" "	19	SENW	1886-07-20		A2
3343	BEWICK, Charles	4	N½	1882-10-10		A2
3344	" "	4	NWSW	1882-10-10		A2
3345	" "	5		1882-10-10		A2
3346	" "	6		1882-10-10		A2
3347	" "	7		1882-10-10		A2
3348	" "	8		1882-10-10		A2
3486	BIRKETT, Thomas	27	SESW	1884-12-30		A2 G3
3487	" "	27	W½SW	1884-12-30		A2 G3
3488	" "	28	N½SE	1884-12-30		A2 G3
3489	" "	28	NESW	1884-12-30		A2 G3
3490	" "	28	NWSW	1884-12-30		A2 G3
3491	" "	29	E½SE	1884-12-30		A2 G3
3492	" "	29	S½SW	1884-12-30		A2 G3
3493	" "	29	W½SE	1884-12-30		A2 G3
3494	" "	32	N½NE	1884-12-30		A2 G3
3495	" "	32	NENW	1884-12-30		A2 G3
3496	" "	32	NWNW	1884-12-30		A2 G3
3497	" "	32	SENW	1884-12-30		A2 G3
3498	" "	33	N½NW	1884-12-30		A2 G3
3499	" "	33	NENE	1884-12-30		A2 G3
3500	" "	33	SENW	1884-12-30		A2 G3
3501	" "	33	SWNW	1884-12-30		A2 G3
3502	" "	33	W½NE	1884-12-30		A2 G3
3503	" "	34	NENW	1884-12-30		A2 G3
3418	BOUTWELL, James A	35	SENW	1859-05-02		A2
3371	BRADSHAW, Featherston	18	NWNW	1894-07-24		A2
3358	BRAKENRIDGE, Edward A	12	E½NW	1884-12-30		A2
3359	" "	12	N½SE	1884-12-30		A2
3360	" "	12	NE	1884-12-30		A2
3361	" "	13	E½	1884-12-30		A2
3362	" "	13	E½SW	1884-12-30		A2
3363	" "	24	E½	1884-12-30		A2
3469	CRAFT, Rankin C	15	NWSW	1901-03-23		A3
3372	EASTERLING, Giles B	25	NESW	1889-01-12		A3
3373	" "	25	NWSE	1889-01-12		A3
3374	" "	25	SENW	1889-01-12		A3
3375	" "	25	SWNE	1889-01-12		A3
3504	EVERETT, Thomas	32	SWNW	1905-03-30		A3
3430	GEDDIE, Joel J	18	NESW	1895-06-27		A3
3431	" "	18	NWSE	1895-06-27		A3
3432	" "	18	S½SW	1895-06-27		A3
3458	HARRIS, Mary E	11	S½SE	1859-05-02		A2

ID	Individual in Patent	Sec.	Sec. Part	Date Issued	Other Counties	For More Info . . .
3428	JOHNSON, James	15	NW	1885-04-04		A3
3480	JOHNSON, Samuel J	30	NWSW	1886-07-20		A2
3481	" "	30	SENW	1886-07-20		A2
3477	" "	17	NWNW	1889-04-23		A2
3478	" "	19	N½NW	1889-04-23		A2
3479	" "	20	SWNW	1889-04-23		A2
3370	JONES, Enoch R	19	SWNE	1886-07-20		A2
3368	" "	18	S½SE	1890-02-21		A3
3369	" "	19	NWNE	1890-02-21		A3
3367	JOSEY, Elizabeth	12	SESE	1894-07-24		A2
3351	LANDRUM, Daniel M	13	SWSW	1911-01-05		A3
3379	LANDRUM, Henry M	24	S½SW	1885-04-04		A3
3380	" "	25	NENW	1885-04-04		A3
3381	" "	25	NWNE	1885-04-04		A3
3420	LANDRUM, James C	12	S½SW	1898-03-15		A3
3421	" "	12	SWSE	1898-03-15		A3
3422	" "	13	NENW	1898-03-15		A3
3425	LANDRUM, James J	13	SWNW	1859-11-10		A2
3426	" "	14	E½NE	1859-11-10		A2
3427	" "	14	NESE	1859-11-10		A2
3424	" "	13	NWSW	1860-07-02		A2
3449	LANDRUM, Lewis L	35	NENW	1898-12-01		A3
3450	LANDRUM, Linson B	24	W½NW	1859-11-10		A2
3465	LANDRUM, Palm	34	NENE	1892-06-15		A3
3466	" "	35	NWSW	1892-06-15		A3
3467	" "	35	W½NW	1892-06-15		A3
3468	LANDRUM, Pinkney H	34	S½SE	1896-09-16		A3
3464	LARRE, Oscar Dugas	2	SWSW	1931-02-17		A2 G22
3505	LEWIS, Walden	4	SWSE	1881-05-10		A3
3506	" "	9	N½NE	1881-05-10		A3
3507	" "	9	NENW	1881-05-10		A3
3482	LYNES, Albert G	35	W½NE	1895-06-28		A3 G23
3483	" "	35	W½SE	1895-06-28		A3 G23
3462	LYNES, Obidiah	9	N½SE	1881-08-20		A3
3463	" "	9	S½NE	1881-08-20		A3
3482	LYNES, Sarah	35	W½NE	1895-06-28		A3 G23
3483	" "	35	W½SE	1895-06-28		A3 G23
3464	MATTREN, Joel	2	SWSW	1931-02-17		A2 G22
3436	MCKEOWN, John	1	E½SE	1884-12-30		A2
3437	" "	1	SWSE	1884-12-30		A2
3438	" "	12	NESW	1884-12-30		A2
3439	" "	13	SENW	1884-12-30		A2
3486	MCPHERSON, Alexander	27	SESW	1884-12-30		A2 G3
3487	" "	27	W½SW	1884-12-30		A2 G3
3488	" "	28	N½SE	1884-12-30		A2 G3
3489	" "	28	NESW	1884-12-30		A2 G3
3490	" "	28	NWSW	1884-12-30		A2 G3
3491	" "	29	E½SE	1884-12-30		A2 G3
3492	" "	29	S½SW	1884-12-30		A2 G3
3493	" "	29	W½SE	1884-12-30		A2 G3
3494	" "	32	N½NE	1884-12-30		A2 G3
3495	" "	32	NENW	1884-12-30		A2 G3
3496	" "	32	NWNW	1884-12-30		A2 G3
3497	" "	32	SENW	1884-12-30		A2 G3
3498	" "	33	N½NW	1884-12-30		A2 G3
3499	" "	33	NENE	1884-12-30		A2 G3
3500	" "	33	SENW	1884-12-30		A2 G3
3501	" "	33	SWNW	1884-12-30		A2 G3
3502	" "	33	W½NE	1884-12-30		A2 G3
3503	" "	34	NENW	1884-12-30		A2 G3
3515	" "	30	SENE	1889-04-10		A2 G27
3516	" "	34	SENW	1889-04-10		A2 G27
3486	MCPHERSON, Edward	27	SESW	1884-12-30		A2 G3
3487	" "	27	W½SW	1884-12-30		A2 G3
3488	" "	28	N½SE	1884-12-30		A2 G3
3489	" "	28	NESW	1884-12-30		A2 G3
3490	" "	28	NWSW	1884-12-30		A2 G3
3491	" "	29	E½SE	1884-12-30		A2 G3
3492	" "	29	S½SW	1884-12-30		A2 G3
3493	" "	29	W½SE	1884-12-30		A2 G3
3494	" "	32	N½NE	1884-12-30		A2 G3
3495	" "	32	NENW	1884-12-30		A2 G3
3496	" "	32	NWNW	1884-12-30		A2 G3

ID	Individual in Patent	Sec.	Sec. Part	Date Issued	Other Counties	For More Info . . .
3497	MCPHERSON, Edward (Cont'd)	32	SENW	1884-12-30		A2 G3
3498	" "	33	N½NW	1884-12-30		A2 G3
3499	" "	33	NENE	1884-12-30		A2 G3
3500	" "	33	SENW	1884-12-30		A2 G3
3501	" "	33	SWNW	1884-12-30		A2 G3
3502	" "	33	W½NE	1884-12-30		A2 G3
3503	" "	34	NENW	1884-12-30		A2 G3
3515	MCPHERSON, Edward G	30	SENE	1889-04-10		A2 G27
3516	" "	34	SENW	1889-04-10		A2 G27
3486	MCPHERSON, Martin	27	SESW	1884-12-30		A2 G3
3487	" "	27	W½SW	1884-12-30		A2 G3
3488	" "	28	N½SE	1884-12-30		A2 G3
3489	" "	28	NESW	1884-12-30		A2 G3
3490	" "	28	NWSW	1884-12-30		A2 G3
3491	" "	29	E½SE	1884-12-30		A2 G3
3492	" "	29	S½SW	1884-12-30		A2 G3
3493	" "	29	W½SE	1884-12-30		A2 G3
3494	" "	32	N½NE	1884-12-30		A2 G3
3495	" "	32	NENW	1884-12-30		A2 G3
3496	" "	32	NWNW	1884-12-30		A2 G3
3497	" "	32	SENW	1884-12-30		A2 G3
3498	" "	33	N½NW	1884-12-30		A2 G3
3499	" "	33	NENE	1884-12-30		A2 G3
3500	" "	33	SENW	1884-12-30		A2 G3
3501	" "	33	SWNW	1884-12-30		A2 G3
3502	" "	33	W½NE	1884-12-30		A2 G3
3503	" "	34	NENW	1884-12-30		A2 G3
3515	MCPHERSON, Martin J	30	SENE	1889-04-10		A2 G27
3516	" "	34	SENW	1889-04-10		A2 G27
3486	MCPHERSON, William	27	SESW	1884-12-30		A2 G3
3487	" "	27	W½SW	1884-12-30		A2 G3
3488	" "	28	N½SE	1884-12-30		A2 G3
3489	" "	28	NESW	1884-12-30		A2 G3
3490	" "	28	NWSW	1884-12-30		A2 G3
3491	" "	29	E½SE	1884-12-30		A2 G3
3492	" "	29	S½SW	1884-12-30		A2 G3
3493	" "	29	W½SE	1884-12-30		A2 G3
3494	" "	32	N½NE	1884-12-30		A2 G3
3495	" "	32	NENW	1884-12-30		A2 G3
3496	" "	32	NWNW	1884-12-30		A2 G3
3497	" "	32	SENW	1884-12-30		A2 G3
3498	" "	33	N½NW	1884-12-30		A2 G3
3499	" "	33	NENE	1884-12-30		A2 G3
3500	" "	33	SENW	1884-12-30		A2 G3
3501	" "	33	SWNW	1884-12-30		A2 G3
3502	" "	33	W½NE	1884-12-30		A2 G3
3503	" "	34	NENW	1884-12-30		A2 G3
3515	" "	30	SENE	1889-04-10		A2 G27
3516	" "	34	SENW	1889-04-10		A2 G27
3384	MOORES, J H	15	SWSW	1889-04-23		A2
3385	" "	17	N½NE	1889-04-23		A2
3386	" "	18	NWSW	1889-04-23		A2
3387	" "	18	SWNW	1889-04-23		A2
3388	" "	19	E½SE	1889-04-23		A2
3389	" "	20	S½	1889-04-23		A2
3390	" "	21	E½NE	1889-04-23		A2
3391	" "	21	SWSW	1889-04-23		A2
3392	" "	27	E½NW	1889-04-23		A2
3393	" "	27	NESW	1889-04-23		A2
3394	" "	27	NWSE	1889-04-23		A2
3395	" "	27	SWNW	1889-04-23		A2
3397	" "	28	S½SE	1889-04-23		A2
3398	" "	28	S½SW	1889-04-23		A2
3401	" "	30	NENE	1889-04-23		A2
3402	" "	30	W½NE	1889-04-23		A2
3403	" "	31	E½NE	1889-04-23		A2
3404	" "	31	NESE	1889-04-23		A2
3405	" "	32	S½SE	1889-04-23		A2
3406	" "	32	SW	1889-04-23		A2
3407	" "	33	SENE	1889-04-23		A2
3408	" "	34	N½SE	1889-04-23		A2
3409	" "	34	N½SW	1889-04-23		A2
3411	" "	34	W½NW	1889-04-23		A2

ID	Individual in Patent	Sec.	Sec. Part	Date Issued	Other Counties	For More Info . . .
3412	MOORES, J H (Cont'd)	35	SWSW	1889-04-23	A2	
3414	" "	9	SENW	1889-04-23	A2	
3415	" "	9	SW	1889-04-23	A2	
3416	" "	9	SWSE	1889-04-23	A2	
3417	" "	9	W½NW	1889-04-23	A2	
3399	" "	29	N½NW	1889-11-29	A2	
3396	" "	27	SWSE	1890-04-25	A2	
3400	" "	3	NWNW	1890-04-25	A2	
3410	" "	34	NWNE	1890-04-25	A2	
3413	" "	4	NWSE	1890-04-25	A2	
3451	PARKER, Little B	18	E½NW	1892-06-15	A3	
3452	" "	18	W½NE	1892-06-15	A3	
3429	PITMAN, James W	30	SWNW	1895-06-28	A3	
3352	PITTS, Daniel	22	N½NE	1859-05-02	A2	
3353	" "	22	SENE	1859-05-02	A2	
3354	" "	22	SWNE	1859-05-02	A2	
3433	PITTS, John A	22	SE	1895-11-11	A3	
3446	PRINCE, Levi	17	NENW	1901-06-08	A3	
3510	PRINCE, Wiley W	19	W½SE	1913-05-21	A3	
3423	PRINE, James H	4	SESE	1906-08-16	A2	
3517	PRINE, William Wesley	11	NENW	1915-05-18	A3	
3470	QUANCE, Richard	1	E½NE	1889-04-10	A2 G35	
3471	" "	1	NWSE	1889-04-10	A2 G35	
3472	" "	1	S½NW	1889-04-10	A2 G35	
3473	" "	1	SW	1889-04-10	A2 G35	
3474	" "	1	SWNE	1889-04-10	A2 G35	
3475	" "	12	NWSW	1889-04-10	A2 G35	
3476	" "	12	W½NW	1889-04-10	A2 G35	
3470	QUANCE, Samuel H	1	E½NE	1889-04-10	A2 G35	
3471	" "	1	NWSE	1889-04-10	A2 G35	
3472	" "	1	S½NW	1889-04-10	A2 G35	
3473	" "	1	SW	1889-04-10	A2 G35	
3474	" "	1	SWNE	1889-04-10	A2 G35	
3475	" "	12	NWSW	1889-04-10	A2 G35	
3476	" "	12	W½NW	1889-04-10	A2 G35	
3511	ROBINSON, William B	31	E½NW	1894-02-28	A3	
3512	" "	31	W½NE	1894-02-28	A3	
3341	ROGERS, Britain L	24	E½NW	1892-04-29	A3	
3342	" "	24	N½SW	1892-04-29	A3	
3382	ROSE, Henry	21	E½NW	1888-02-25	A3	
3383	" "	21	W½NE	1888-02-25	A3	
3513	SCANLAN, William J	31	SWNW	1905-03-30	A3	
3514	" "	31	W½SW	1905-03-30	A3	
3349	SCHONE, Charles H	30	E½SW	1892-07-25	A3	
3350	" "	30	S½SE	1892-07-25	A3	
3444	SHOEMAKE, Julius H	20	E½NE	1890-02-21	A3	
3445	" "	21	W½NW	1890-02-21	A3	
3484	SHOEMAKE, Stephen G	20	E½NW	1891-05-20	A3	
3485	" "	20	W½NE	1891-05-20	A3	
3454	SHOWS, Martha	31	E½SW	1874-11-05	A2	
3453	" "	30	SWSW	1884-12-30	A3	
3455	" "	31	NWNW	1884-12-30	A3	
3456	SKELLY, Martha	19	NWSW	1885-06-20	A3	
3457	" "	19	SWNW	1885-06-20	A3	
3364	SMITH, Eliza	17	S½NW	1895-05-11	A3	
3365	" "	18	NESE	1895-05-11	A3	
3366	" "	18	SENE	1895-05-11	A3	
3459	STEVISON, Mary J	18	NENE	1894-07-24	A2	
3340	SUMRALL, Benjamin H	36	E½NE	1898-12-01	A3	
3355	SUMRALL, David M	19	SENE	1901-06-08	A3	
3419	SUMRALL, James A	36	E½SE	1890-02-21	A3	
3518	SUMRALL, Willie Cranford	2	SENE	1957-07-11	A1	
3356	UPSHAW, Drury	31	SESE	1891-05-20	A3	
3357	" "	31	W½SE	1891-05-20	A3	
3331	WALTERS, Albert	3	NWSW	1859-05-02	A2	
3332	" "	3	SWNW	1859-05-02	A2	
3333	" "	4	NESE	1859-05-02	A2	
3334	WALTERS, Amon E	11	NENE	1896-08-26	A3	
3335	" "	2	SESE	1896-08-26	A3	
3336	WALTERS, Asa	10	NWNW	1859-05-02	A2	
3337	" "	27	SENE	1894-03-12	A3	
3338	" "	27	W½NE	1894-03-12	A3	
3339	WALTERS, Benjamin D	1	N½NW	1859-05-02	A2	

ID	Individual in Patent	Sec.	Sec. Part	Date Issued	Other Counties	For More Info . . .
3376	WALTERS, Hansford A	10	NWSW	1882-04-20		A2
3377	WALTERS, Hanson A	10	SWSW	1897-09-09		A3
3378	" "	9	SESE	1897-09-09		A3
3441	WALTERS, John	2	NWSE	1859-05-02		A2
3442	" "	2	SESW	1859-05-02		A2
3443	" "	2	SWSE	1859-05-02		A2
3440	" "	11	NWNE	1860-07-02		A2
3460	WALTERS, Nellie	4	E½SW	1896-01-25		A3
3461	" "	4	SWSW	1896-01-25		A3
3508	WALTERS, Warren W	21	N½SE	1892-07-11		A3
3509	" "	21	N½SW	1892-07-11		A3

Patent Map

T7-N R11-W
St Stephens Meridian

Map Group 19

Township Statistics

Parcels Mapped	:	188
Number of Patents	:	86
Number of Individuals	:	73
Patentees Identified	:	65
Number of Surnames	:	42
Multi-Patentee Parcels	:	30
Oldest Patent Date	:	5/2/1859
Most Recent Patent	:	7/11/1957
Block/Lot Parcels	:	0
Parcels Re-Issued	:	0
Parcels that Overlap	:	0
Cities and Towns	:	5
Cemeteries	:	2

Map grid

Section 6 — BEWICK Charles 1882

Section 5 — BEWICK Charles 1882

Section 4 — BEWICK Charles 1882; BEWICK Charles 1882; WALTERS Nellie 1896; MOORES J H 1890; WALTERS Albert 1859; WALTERS Nellie 1896; LEWIS Walden 1881; PRINE James H 1906

Section 7 — BEWICK Charles 1882

Section 8 — BEWICK Charles 1882

Section 9 — MOORES J H 1889; LEWIS Walden 1881; LEWIS Walden 1881; MOORES J H 1889; LYNES Obidiah 1881; LYNES Obidiah 1881; MOORES J H 1889; MOORES J H 1889; WALTERS Hanson A 1897

Section 18 — BRADSHAW Featherston 1894; PARKER Little B 1892; STEVISON Mary J 1894; MOORES J H 1889; PARKER Little B 1892; SMITH Eliza 1895; MOORES J H 1889; GEDDIE Joel J 1895; GEDDIE Joel J 1895; SMITH Eliza 1895; GEDDIE Joel J 1895; JONES Enoch R 1890

Section 17 — JOHNSON Samuel J 1889; PRINCE Levi 1901; MOORES J H 1889; SMITH Eliza 1895

Section 16

Section 19 — JOHNSON Samuel J 1889; JONES Enoch R 1890; SKELLY Martha 1885; BEECH John 1886; JONES Enoch R 1886; SUMRALL David M 1901; SKELLY Martha 1885; BEECH John 1886; MOORES J H 1889; PRINCE Wiley W 1913

Section 20 — JOHNSON Samuel J 1889; SHOEMAKE Stephen G 1891; SHOEMAKE Stephen G 1891; SHOEMAKE Julius H 1890; MOORES J H 1889

Section 21 — SHOEMAKE Julius H 1890; ROSE Henry 1888; ROSE Henry 1888; MOORES J H 1889; WALTERS Warren W 1892; WALTERS Warren W 1892; MOORES J H 1889

Section 30 — PITMAN James W 1895; JOHNSON Samuel J 1886; MOORES J H 1889; MOORES J H 1889; MOORES J H 1889; MCPHERSON [27] William 1889; JOHNSON Samuel J 1886; SCHONE Charles H 1892; SHOWS Martha 1884; SCHONE Charles H 1892

Section 29 — BIRKETT [3] Thomas 1884; BIRKETT [3] Thomas 1884; BIRKETT [3] Thomas 1884

Section 28 — BIRKETT [3] Thomas 1884; BIRKETT [3] Thomas 1884; BIRKETT [3] Thomas 1884; MOORES J H 1889; MOORES J H 1889

Section 31 — SHOWS Martha 1884; ROBINSON William B 1894; BIRKETT [3] Thomas 1884; BIRKETT [3] Thomas 1884; ROBINSON William B 1894; MOORES J H 1889; SCANLAN William J 1905; SCANLAN William J 1905; SHOWS Martha 1874; UPSHAW Drury 1891; MOORES J H 1889; UPSHAW Drury 1891

Section 32 — EVERETT Thomas 1905; BIRKETT [3] Thomas 1884; BIRKETT [3] Thomas 1884; MOORES J H 1889; MOORES J H 1889

Section 33 — BIRKETT [3] Thomas 1884; BIRKETT [3] Thomas 1884; BIRKETT [3] Thomas 1884; BIRKETT [3] Thomas 1884; BIRKETT [3] Thomas 1884; BIRKETT [3] Thomas 1884; MOORES J H 1889

MOORES
J H
1890

WALTERS
Albert
1859

WALTERS
Albert
1859

3

2

SUMRALL
Willie Cranford
1957

WALTERS
John
1859

LARRE [22]
Oscar Dugas
1931

WALTERS
John
1859

WALTERS
John
1859

WALTERS
Amon E
1896

WALTERS
Benjamin D
1859

QUANCE [35]
Richard
1889

1

QUANCE [35]
Richard
1889

QUANCE [35]
Richard
1889

QUANCE [35]
Richard
1889

MCKEOWN
John
1884

QUANCE [35]
Richard
1889

MCKEOWN
John
1884

WALTERS
Asa
1859

10

WALTERS
Hansford A
1882

WALTERS
Hanson A
1897

PRINE
William Wesley
1915

WALTERS
John
1860

11

WALTERS
Amon E
1896

ADAMS
Lewin
1859

ADAMS
Lewin
1859

HARRIS
Mary E
1859

QUANCE [35]
Richard
1889

BRAKENRIDGE
Edward A
1884

12

QUANCE [35]
Richard
1889

MCKEOWN
John
1884

LANDRUM
James C
1898

BRAKENRIDGE
Edward A
1884

BRAKENRIDGE
Edward A
1884

LANDRUM
James C
1898

JOSEY
Elizabeth
1894

JOHNSON
James
1885

15

CRAFT
Rankin C
1901

MOORES
J H
1889

LANDRUM
James J
1859

14

LANDRUM
James J
1859

LANDRUM
James C
1898

LANDRUM
James J
1859

MCKEOWN
John
1884

LANDRUM
James J
1860

LANDRUM
Daniel M
1911

BRAKENRIDGE
Edward A
1884

BRAKENRIDGE
Edward A
1884

13

PITTS
Daniel
1859

PITTS
Daniel
1859

PITTS
Daniel
1859

PITTS
John A
1895

22

23

LANDRUM
Linson B
1859

ROGERS
Britain L
1892

ROGERS
Britain L
1892

LANDRUM
Henry M
1885

24

BRAKENRIDGE
Edward A
1884

MOORES
J H
1889

MOORES
J H
1889

WALTERS
Asa
1894

WALTERS
Asa
1894

MOORES
J H
1889

MOORES
J H
1889

BIRKETT [3]
Thomas
1884

BIRKETT [3]
Thomas
1884

MOORES
J H
1890

27

26

LANDRUM
Henry M
1885

LANDRUM
Henry M
1885

EASTERLING
Giles B
1889

EASTERLING
Giles B
1889

EASTERLING
Giles B
1889

EASTERLING
Giles B
1889

25

MOORES
J H
1889

BIRKETT [3]
Thomas
1884

MCPHERSON [27]
William
1889

MOORES
J H
1890

LANDRUM
Palm
1892

34

MOORES
J H
1889

MOORES
J H
1889

LANDRUM
Pinkney H
1896

LANDRUM
Palm
1892

LANDRUM
Lewis L
1898

BOUTWELL
James A
1859

LYNES [23]
Sarah
1895

LANDRUM
Palm
1892

MOORES
J H
1889

35

LYNES [23]
Sarah
1895

36

SUMRALL
Benjamin H
1898

SUMRALL
James A
1890

Helpful Hints

1. This Map's INDEX can be found on the preceding pages.

2. Refer to Map "C" to see where this Township lies within Jones County, Mississippi.

3. Numbers within square brackets [ ] denote a multi-patentee land parcel (multi-owner). Refer to Appendix "C" for a full list of members in this group.

4. Areas that look to be crowded with Patentees usually indicate multiple sales of the same parcel (Re-issues) or Overlapping parcels. See this Township's Index for an explanation of these and other circumstances that might explain "odd" groupings of Patentees on this map.

Legend

Patent Boundary

Section Boundary

No Patents Found
(or Outside County)

1., 2., 3., ... Lot Numbers
(when beside a name)

[ ] Group Number
(see Appendix "C")

Scale: Section = 1 mile X 1 mile
(generally, with some exceptions)

Road Map

T7-N R11-W
St Stephens Meridian

Map Group 19

Cities & Towns
Crotts
Johnson
Lanham
Pecan Grove
Tallahomo

Cemeteries
Mount Moriah Cemetery
Tucker Cemetery

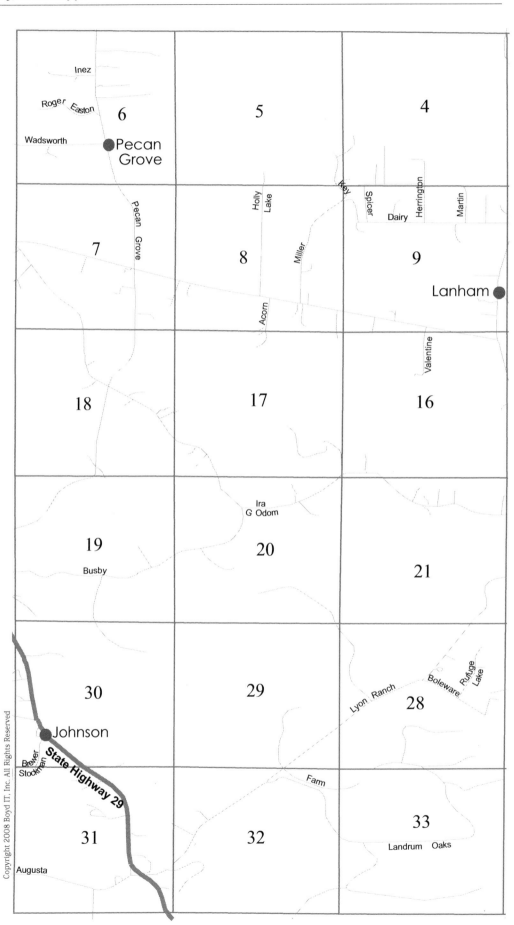

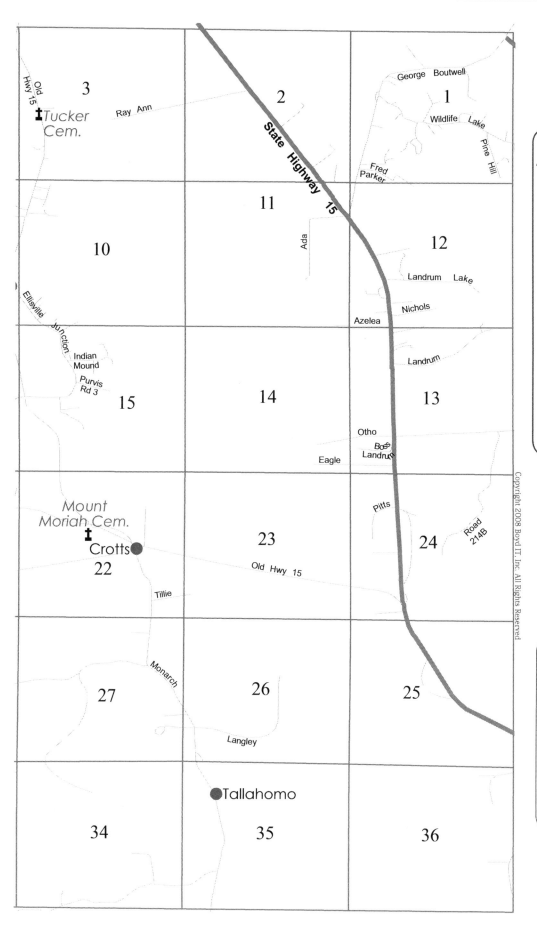

3

Old Hwy 15

✝ *Tucker Cem.*

Ray Ann

2

1

George Boutwell

Wildlife Lake

Pine Hill

Fred Parker

11

Ada

10

State Highway 15

12

Landrum Lake

Nichols

Azelea

Ellisville Junction

Indian Mound

Purvis Rd 3

15

14

13

Landrum

Otho

Bo Landrum

Eagle

Mount Moriah Cem.

✝

Crotts ●

22

23

Old Hwy 15

Pitts

24

Road 214B

Tillie

27

Monarch

26

Langley

25

● Tallahomo

34

35

36

Helpful Hints

1. This road map has a number of uses, but primarily it is to help you: a) find the present location of land owned by your ancestors (at least the general area), b) find cemeteries and city-centers, and c) estimate the route/roads used by Census-takers & tax-assessors.

2. If you plan to travel to Jones County to locate cemeteries or land parcels, please pick up a modern travel map for the area before you do. Mapping old land parcels on modern maps is not as exact a science as you might think. Just the slightest variations in public land survey coordinates, estimates of parcel boundaries, or road-map deviations can greatly alter a map's representation of how a road either does or doesn't cross a particular parcel of land.

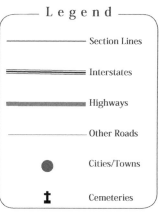

L e g e n d

———————	Section Lines
═══════════	Interstates
▬▬▬▬▬▬	Highways
———————	Other Roads
●	Cities/Towns
✝	Cemeteries

Scale: Section = 1 mile X 1 mile
(generally, with some exceptions)

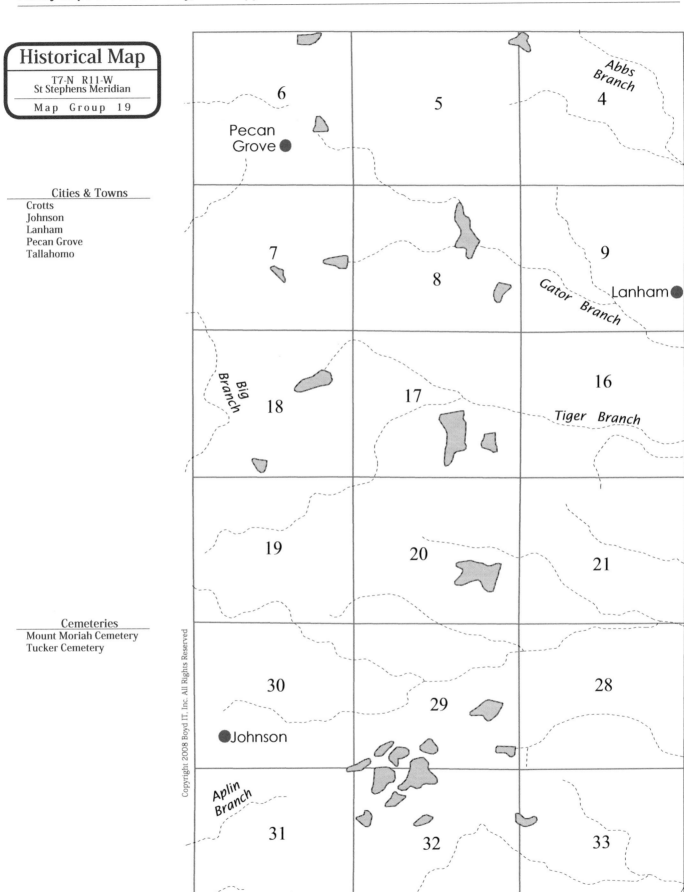

Historical Map

T7-N R11-W
St Stephens Meridian

Map Group 19

Cities & Towns
Crotts
Johnson
Lanham
Pecan Grove
Tallahomo

Cemeteries
Mount Moriah Cemetery
Tucker Cemetery

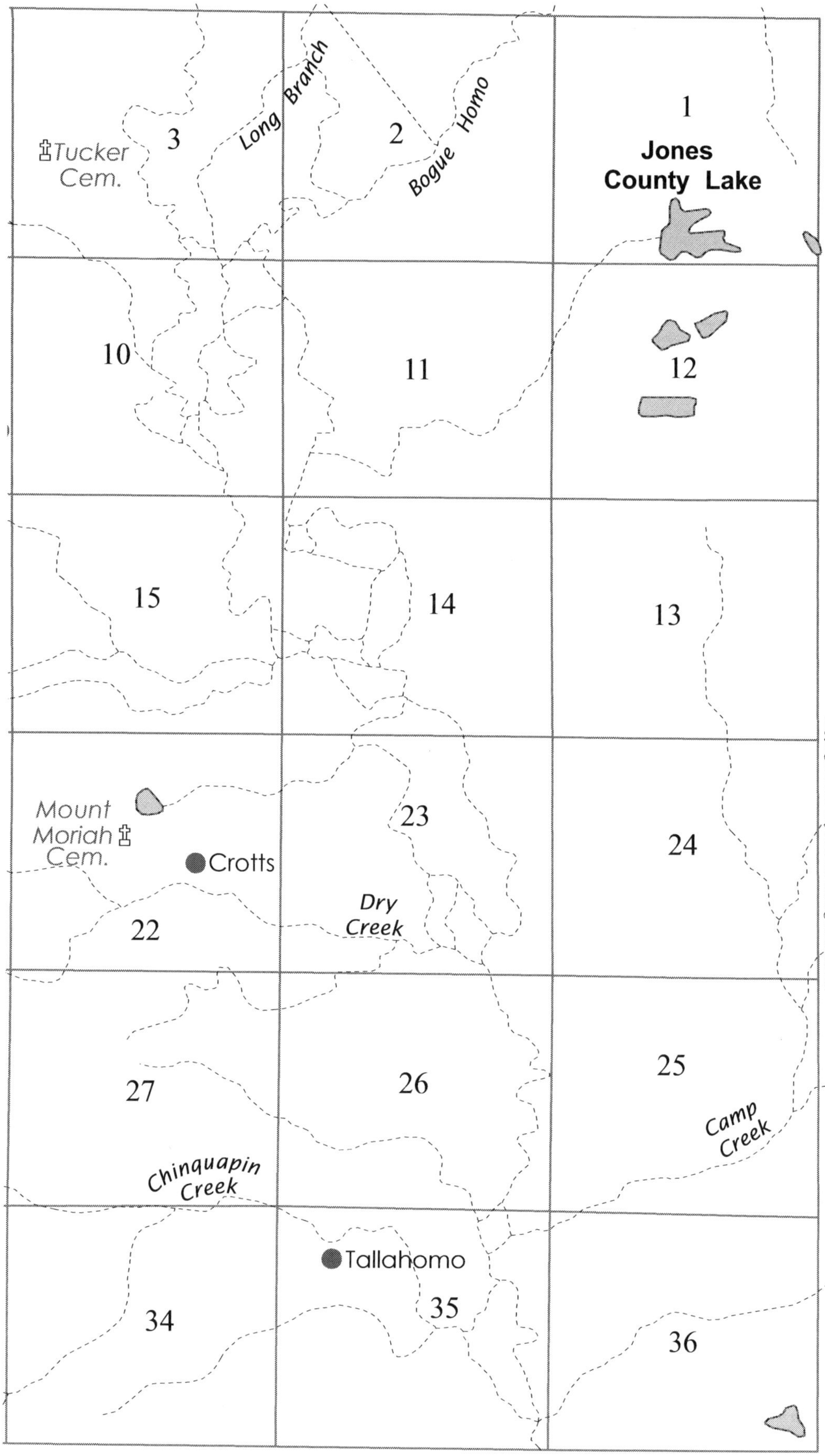
3
Tucker Cem.
Long Branch
2
Bogue Homo
1
Jones County Lake
10
11
12
15
14
13
Mount Moriah Cem.
Crotts
23
24
22
Dry Creek
27
26
25
Camp Creek
Chinquapin Creek
Tallahomo
34
35
36

Helpful Hints

1. This Map takes a different look at the same Congressional Township displayed in the preceding two maps. It presents features that can help you better envision the historical development of the area: a) Water-bodies (lakes & ponds), b) Water-courses (rivers, streams, etc.), c) Railroads, d) City/town center-points (where they were oftentimes located when first settled), and e) Cemeteries.
2. Using this "Historical" map in tandem with this Township's Patent Map and Road Map, may lead you to some interesting discoveries. You will often find roads, towns, cemeteries, and waterways are named after nearby landowners: sometimes those names will be the ones you are researching. See how many of these research gems you can find here in Jones County.

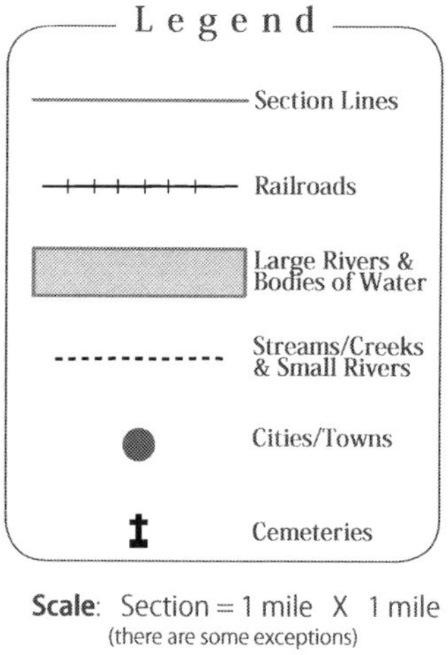
Legend
Section Lines
Railroads
Large Rivers & Bodies of Water
Streams/Creeks & Small Rivers
Cities/Towns
Cemeteries

Scale: Section = 1 mile X 1 mile
(there are some exceptions)

Map Group 20: Index to Land Patents

Township 7-North Range 10-West (St Stephens)

After you locate an individual in this Index, take note of the Section and Section Part then proceed to the Land Patent map on the pages immediately following. You should have no difficulty locating the corresponding parcel of land.

The "For More Info" Column will lead you to more information about the underlying Patents. See the *Legend* at right, and the "How to Use this Book" chapter, for more information.

```
┌─────────────────────────────────────────────────────┐
│                      LEGEND                           │
│          "For More Info . . . " column                │
│ ───────────────────────────────────────────────      │
│ A = Authority (Legislative Act, See Appendix "A")     │
│ B = Block or Lot (location in Section unknown)        │
│ C = Cancelled Patent                                  │
│ F = Fractional Section                                │
│ G = Group  (Multi-Patentee Patent, see Appendix "C")  │
│ V = Overlaps another Parcel                           │
│ R = Re-Issued (Parcel patented more than once)        │
│                                                       │
│ (A & G items require you to look in the Appendixes     │
│ referred to above. All other Letter-designations      │
│ followed by a number require you to locate line-items  │
│ in this index that possess the ID number found after  │
│ the letter).                                          │
└─────────────────────────────────────────────────────┘
```

ID	Individual in Patent		Sec.	Sec. Part	Date Issued	Other Counties	For More Info . . .
3544	BOUTWELL, Daniel B		3	N½NW	1904-10-27		A3
3545	BRAKENRIDGE, Edward A		18	NE	1884-12-30		A2
3546	"	"	18	W½	1884-12-30		A2
3547	"	"	19	E½	1884-12-30		A2
3548	"	"	19	E½SW	1884-12-30		A2
3549	"	"	20		1884-12-30		A2
3550	"	"	6	SW	1884-12-30		A2
3551	"	"	7	E½	1884-12-30		A2
3552	"	"	7	N½SW	1884-12-30		A2
3553	"	"	7	NW	1884-12-30		A2
3569	CARPENTER, George W		12	E½SW	1890-07-03		A2
3570	"	"	13	E½NW	1890-07-03		A2
3571	"	"	14	E½SE	1890-07-03		A2
3572	"	"	14	N½NW	1890-07-03		A2
3573	"	"	15	NENE	1890-07-03		A2
3574	"	"	19	W½SW	1890-07-03		A2
3575	"	"	24	N½	1890-07-03		A2
3576	"	"	24	SW	1890-07-03		A2
3577	"	"	25	E½NW	1890-07-03		A2
3578	"	"	25	NWNW	1890-07-03		A2
3579	"	"	25	W½NE	1890-07-03		A2
3580	"	"	27	SESE	1890-07-03		A2
3581	"	"	27	SESW	1890-07-03		A2
3582	"	"	30	NESW	1890-07-03		A2
3583	"	"	30	NW	1890-07-03		A2
3584	"	"	30	NWSE	1890-07-03		A2
3585	"	"	30	SESE	1890-07-03		A2
3586	"	"	30	SWNE	1890-07-03		A2
3587	"	"	31	E½NE	1890-07-03		A2 V3543
3588	"	"	31	SWNE	1890-07-03		A2 V3543
3589	"	"	31	W½SE	1890-07-03		A2
3590	"	"	32	SWNW	1890-07-03		A2
3591	"	"	34	E½SE	1890-07-03		A2
3592	"	"	34	NWSW	1890-07-03		A2
3554	DARRAH, Edward H		15	S½	1886-02-10		A2
3598	EASTERLING, Jefferson D		12	E½SE	1897-09-09		A3
3599	"	"	12	SENE	1897-09-09		A3
3600	"	"	12	SWSE	1897-09-09		A3
3597	GATTIS, James		34	NWNW	1915-03-22		A3
3662	JENKINS, Roderick		13	E½SW	1891-05-20		A3
3663	"	"	13	W½SE	1891-05-20		A3
3664	JENKINS, Rodrick F		11	SESE	1893-04-12		A3
3665	"	"	14	N½NE	1893-04-12		A3
3666	"	"	14	SENE	1893-04-12		A3
3555	JOSEY, Elizabeth		7	S½SW	1894-07-24		A2
3655	KITCHENS, Marion Franklin		25	SWSW	1914-03-31		A3

ID	Individual in Patent	Sec.	Sec. Part	Date Issued	Other Counties	For More Info . . .
3667	KITCHENS, Sarah E	26	NWNE	1911-01-05		A3
3668	LANDRUM, Turner H	31	S½SW	1901-12-17		A3
3656	LOTT, Mary E	2	NENW	1898-07-18		A3
3657	" "	2	NWNE	1898-07-18		A3
3602	MCKEOWN, John	1	NW	1884-12-30		A2
3604	" "	1	SENE	1884-12-30		A2
3605	" "	1	W½NE	1884-12-30		A2
3606	" "	10		1884-12-30		A2
3609	" "	11	W½	1884-12-30		A2
3610	" "	11	W½NE	1884-12-30		A2
3611	" "	11	W½SE	1884-12-30		A2
3616	" "	13	E½SE	1884-12-30		A2
3617	" "	13	NE	1884-12-30		A2
3618	" "	14	S½NW	1884-12-30		A2
3619	" "	14	SW	1884-12-30		A2
3620	" "	14	SWNE	1884-12-30		A2
3621	" "	14	W½SE	1884-12-30		A2
3622	" "	15	NW	1884-12-30		A2
3623	" "	15	SENE	1884-12-30		A2
3624	" "	15	W½NE	1884-12-30		A2
3625	" "	17	NE	1884-12-30		A2
3626	" "	17	S½	1884-12-30		A2
3627	" "	2	E½NE	1884-12-30		A2
3629	" "	2	SENW	1884-12-30		A2
3630	" "	2	SW	1884-12-30		A2
3631	" "	2	SWNE	1884-12-30		A2
3632	" "	2	W½NW	1884-12-30		A2
3633	" "	2	W½SE	1884-12-30		A2
3634	" "	21		1884-12-30		A2
3635	" "	22		1884-12-30		A2
3636	" "	23	W½	1884-12-30		A2
3637	" "	23	W½NE	1884-12-30		A2
3638	" "	23	W½SE	1884-12-30		A2
3639	" "	24	SE	1884-12-30		A2
3640	" "	25	NENE	1884-12-30		A2
3641	" "	3	E½	1884-12-30		A2
3642	" "	3	SW	1884-12-30		A2
3643	" "	30	N½NE	1884-12-30		A2
3644	" "	4		1884-12-30		A2
3645	" "	4	S½NW	1884-12-30		A2 V3644
3646	" "	5	S½	1884-12-30		A2
3647	" "	5	S½NE	1884-12-30		A2
3648	" "	5	S½NW	1884-12-30		A2
3649	" "	6	S½NE	1884-12-30		A2
3650	" "	6	SE	1884-12-30		A2
3651	" "	8		1884-12-30		A2
3652	" "	9		1884-12-30		A2
3603	" "	1	S½	1886-02-10		A2
3607	" "	11	E½NE	1886-02-10		A2
3608	" "	11	NESE	1886-02-10		A2
3612	" "	12	E½NW	1886-02-10		A2
3613	" "	12	NENE	1886-02-10		A2
3614	" "	12	NWSE	1886-02-10		A2
3615	" "	12	W½NE	1886-02-10		A2
3628	" "	2	E½SE	1886-02-10		A2
3658	QUANCE, Richard	5	N½NE	1889-04-10		A2 G35
3659	" "	5	N½NW	1889-04-10		A2 G35
3660	" "	6	N½NE	1889-04-10		A2 G35
3661	" "	6	NW	1889-04-10		A2 G35
3658	QUANCE, Samuel H	5	N½NE	1889-04-10		A2 G35
3659	" "	5	N½NW	1889-04-10		A2 G35
3660	" "	6	N½NE	1889-04-10		A2 G35
3661	" "	6	NW	1889-04-10		A2 G35
3593	SUMRALL, Henry	30	S½SW	1892-04-29		A3
3594	" "	30	SWSE	1892-04-29		A3
3595	" "	31	NWNE	1892-04-29		A3 V3543
3596	SUMRALL, James A	31	N½SW	1890-02-21		A3
3601	WALTERS, Joel W	1	NENE	1901-12-17		A3
3556	WARE, Emmor	28	W½	1882-12-30		A2
3557	" "	29	E½	1882-12-30		A2
3558	" "	29	E½NW	1882-12-30		A2
3559	" "	29	E½SW	1882-12-30		A2
3560	" "	29	SWNW	1882-12-30		A2

ID	Individual in Patent	Sec.	Sec. Part	Date Issued	Other Counties	For More Info . . .
3561	WARE, Emmor (Cont'd)	29	SWSW	1882-12-30		A2
3562	" "	32	E½	1882-12-30		A2
3563	" "	32	E½NW	1882-12-30		A2
3564	" "	32	E½SW	1882-12-30		A2
3565	" "	32	NWNW	1882-12-30		A2
3566	" "	33	N½	1882-12-30		A2
3567	" "	33	SESE	1882-12-30		A2
3568	" "	33	SW	1882-12-30		A2
3519	WATSON, Amasa B	25	E½SW	1884-12-30		A2
3520	" "	25	SE	1884-12-30		A2
3521	" "	25	SENE	1884-12-30		A2
3522	" "	26	SWNE	1884-12-30		A2
3523	" "	26	W½	1884-12-30		A2
3524	" "	26	W½SE	1884-12-30		A2
3525	" "	27	N½	1884-12-30		A2
3526	" "	27	NESE	1884-12-30		A2
3527	" "	27	NESW	1884-12-30		A2
3528	" "	27	W½SE	1884-12-30		A2
3529	" "	27	W½SW	1884-12-30		A2
3530	" "	28	E½	1884-12-30		A2
3531	" "	34	E½NW	1884-12-30		A2
3532	" "	34	E½SW	1884-12-30		A2
3533	" "	34	NE	1884-12-30		A2
3534	" "	34	SWNW	1884-12-30		A2
3535	" "	34	SWSW	1884-12-30		A2
3536	" "	34	W½SE	1884-12-30		A2
3537	" "	35	W½	1884-12-30		A2
3538	" "	35	W½NE	1884-12-30		A2
3539	" "	35	W½SE	1884-12-30		A2
3540	" "	36	E½SE	1884-12-30		A2
3541	" "	36	W½	1884-12-30		A2
3542	" "	36	W½NE	1884-12-30		A2
3543	WILLIAMS, Charles	31	NE	1859-05-02		A2 V3587, 3588, 3595
3653	WILLIAMS, John	31	E½SE	1891-06-30		A3
3654	" "	32	W½SW	1891-06-30		A3

Patent Map

T7-N R10-W
St Stephens Meridian

Map Group 20

Township Statistics

Parcels Mapped	:	150
Number of Patents	:	49
Number of Individuals	:	23
Patentees Identified	:	22
Number of Surnames	:	18
Multi-Patentee Parcels	:	4
Oldest Patent Date	:	5/2/1859
Most Recent Patent	:	3/22/1915
Block/Lot Parcels	:	0
Parcels Re-Issued	:	0
Parcels that Overlap	:	5
Cities and Towns	:	0
Cemeteries	:	0

Section 6
QUANCE [35] Richard 1889
QUANCE [35] Richard 1889
MCKEOWN John 1884
BRAKENRIDGE Edward A 1884
MCKEOWN John 1884

Section 5
QUANCE [35] Richard 1889
MCKEOWN John 1884
QUANCE [35] Richard 1889
MCKEOWN John 1884
MCKEOWN John 1884

Section 4
MCKEOWN John 1884
MCKEOWN John 1884

Section 7
BRAKENRIDGE Edward A 1884
BRAKENRIDGE Edward A 1884
JOSEY Elizabeth 1894
BRAKENRIDGE Edward A 1884

Section 8
MCKEOWN John 1884

Section 9
MCKEOWN John 1884

Section 18
BRAKENRIDGE Edward A 1884
BRAKENRIDGE Edward A 1884

Section 17
BRAKENRIDGE Edward A 1884
MCKEOWN John 1884
MCKEOWN John 1884

Section 16

Section 19
CARPENTER George W 1890
BRAKENRIDGE Edward A 1884

Section 20
BRAKENRIDGE Edward A 1884
BRAKENRIDGE Edward A 1884

Section 21
MCKEOWN John 1884

Section 30
CARPENTER George W 1890
MCKEOWN John 1884
CARPENTER George W 1890
CARPENTER George W 1890
CARPENTER George W 1890
SUMRALL Henry 1892
SUMRALL Henry 1892

Section 29
WARE Emmor 1882
WARE Emmor 1882
WARE Emmor 1882
WARE Emmor 1882
CARPENTER George W 1890
WARE Emmor 1882

Section 28
WARE Emmor 1882
WATSON Amasa B 1884

Section 31
SUMRALL Henry 1892
CARPENTER George W 1890
WILLIAMS Charles 1859
SUMRALL James A 1890
LANDRUM Turner H 1901
CARPENTER George W 1890
WILLIAMS John 1891

Section 32
WARE Emmor 1882
CARPENTER George W 1890
WARE Emmor 1882
WILLIAMS John 1891
WARE Emmor 1882
WARE Emmor 1882

Section 33
WARE Emmor 1882
WARE Emmor 1882
WARE Emmor 1882

		LOTT Mary E 1898	LOTT Mary E 1898					WALTERS Joel W 1901

BOUTWELL
Daniel B
1904

3

MCKEOWN
John
1884

MCKEOWN
John
1884

MCKEOWN
John
1884

MCKEOWN
John
1884

MCKEOWN
John
1884

2

MCKEOWN
John
1884

MCKEOWN
John
1884

MCKEOWN
John
1884

MCKEOWN
John
1886

MCKEOWN
John
1884

MCKEOWN
John
1884

MCKEOWN
John
1884

1

MCKEOWN
John
1884

MCKEOWN
John
1886

MCKEOWN
John
1884

10

MCKEOWN
John
1884

11

MCKEOWN
John
1884

MCKEOWN
John
1884

MCKEOWN
John
1886

MCKEOWN
John
1884

MCKEOWN
John
1886

JENKINS
Rodrick F
1893

MCKEOWN
John
1886

MCKEOWN
John
1886

MCKEOWN
John
1886

12

EASTERLING
Jefferson D
1897

CARPENTER
George W
1890

MCKEOWN
John
1886

EASTERLING
Jefferson D
1897

EASTERLING
Jefferson D
1897

MCKEOWN
John
1884

15

MCKEOWN
John
1884

MCKEOWN
John
1884

CARPENTER
George W
1890

CARPENTER
George W
1890

MCKEOWN
John
1884

14

DARRAH
Edward H
1886

MCKEOWN
John
1884

JENKINS
Rodrick F
1893

MCKEOWN
John
1884

JENKINS
Rodrick F
1893

MCKEOWN
John
1884

CARPENTER
George W
1890

CARPENTER
George W
1890

MCKEOWN
John
1884

13

JENKINS
Roderick
1891

JENKINS
Roderick
1891

MCKEOWN
John
1884

MCKEOWN
John
1884

22

MCKEOWN
John
1884

23

MCKEOWN
John
1884

MCKEOWN
John
1884

CARPENTER
George W
1890

24

CARPENTER
George W
1890

MCKEOWN
John
1884

27

WATSON
Amasa B
1884

WATSON
Amasa B
1884

WATSON
Amasa B
1884

WATSON
Amasa B
1884

WATSON
Amasa B
1884

CARPENTER
George W
1890

CARPENTER
George W
1890

WATSON
Amasa B
1884

26

WATSON
Amasa B
1884

KITCHENS
Sarah E
1911

WATSON
Amasa B
1884

WATSON
Amasa B
1884

CARPENTER
George W
1890

CARPENTER
George W
1890

KITCHENS
Marion Franklin
1914

WATSON
Amasa B
1884

25

CARPENTER
George W
1890

WATSON
Amasa B
1884

MCKEOWN
John
1884

WATSON
Amasa B
1884

WATSON
Amasa B
1884

GATTIS
James
1915

WATSON
Amasa B
1884

WATSON
Amasa B
1884

34

WATSON
Amasa B
1884

CARPENTER
George W
1890

WATSON
Amasa B
1884

WATSON
Amasa B
1884

WATSON
Amasa B
1884

CARPENTER
George W
1890

35

WATSON
Amasa B
1884

WATSON
Amasa B
1884

WATSON
Amasa B
1884

36

WATSON
Amasa B
1884

WATSON
Amasa B
1884

WATSON
Amasa B
1884

Helpful Hints

1. This Map's INDEX can be found on the preceding pages.

2. Refer to Map "C" to see where this Township lies within Jones County, Mississippi.

3. Numbers within square brackets [ ] denote a multi-patentee land parcel (multi-owner). Refer to Appendix "C" for a full list of members in this group.

4. Areas that look to be crowded with Patentees usually indicate multiple sales of the same parcel (Re-issues) or Overlapping parcels. See this Township's Index for an explanation of these and other circumstances that might explain "odd" groupings of Patentees on this map.

Legend

——— Patent Boundary

━━━ Section Boundary

No Patents Found
(or Outside County)

1., 2., 3., ... Lot Numbers
(when beside a name)

[ ] Group Number
(see Appendix "C")

Scale: Section = 1 mile X 1 mile
(generally, with some exceptions)

211

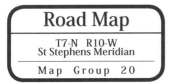

Road Map

T7-N R10-W
St Stephens Meridian

Map Group 20

Cities & Towns
None

Cemeteries
None

6

5

4

Road 201D

7

8

State Highway 536

9

18

17

16

Road 201-C1

Widow Landrum

Road 201-C

Road 213

Road
201-C2

19

20

21

30

29

Road
213E

28

Road 213F

Crowder

State Highway 15

Road 213A

Road 213F

Harmony
Will Young

31

32

Road 213-F1

33

Road 270

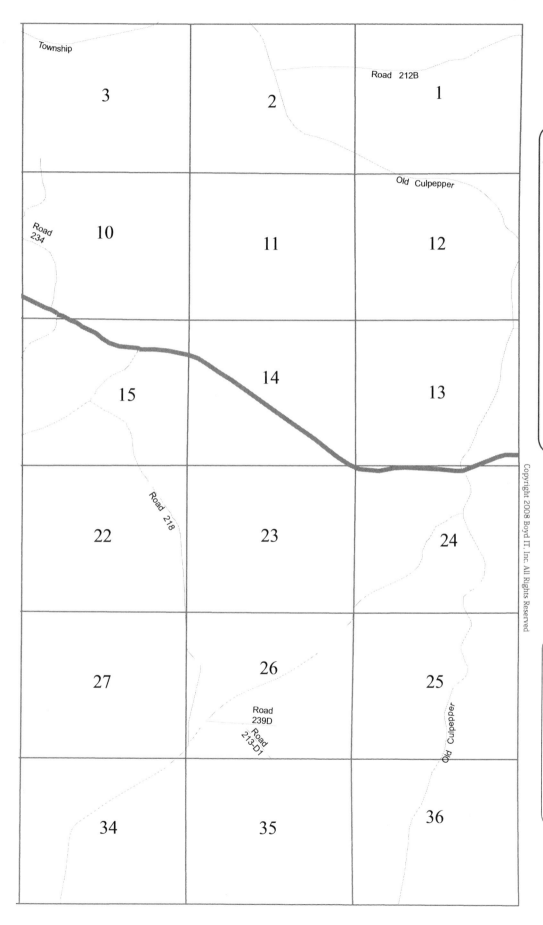

Township

Road 212B

3

2

1

Old Culpepper

Road
234

10

11

12

15

14

13

Road 218

22

23

24

27

26

25

Road
239D
Road
213-D1

Old Culpepper

34

35

36

Helpful Hints

1. This road map has a number of uses, but primarily it is to help you: a) find the present location of land owned by your ancestors (at least the general area), b) find cemeteries and city-centers, and c) estimate the route/roads used by Census-takers & tax-assessors.

2. If you plan to travel to Jones County to locate cemeteries or land parcels, please pick up a modern travel map for the area before you do. Mapping old land parcels on modern maps is not as exact a science as you might think. Just the slightest variations in public land survey coordinates, estimates of parcel boundaries, or road-map deviations can greatly alter a map's representation of how a road either does or doesn't cross a particular parcel of land.

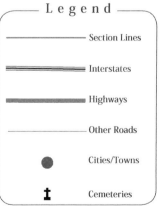

Legend

————— Section Lines

══════ Interstates

━━━━━ Highways

········· Other Roads

● Cities/Towns

✝ Cemeteries

Scale: Section = 1 mile X 1 mile
(generally, with some exceptions)

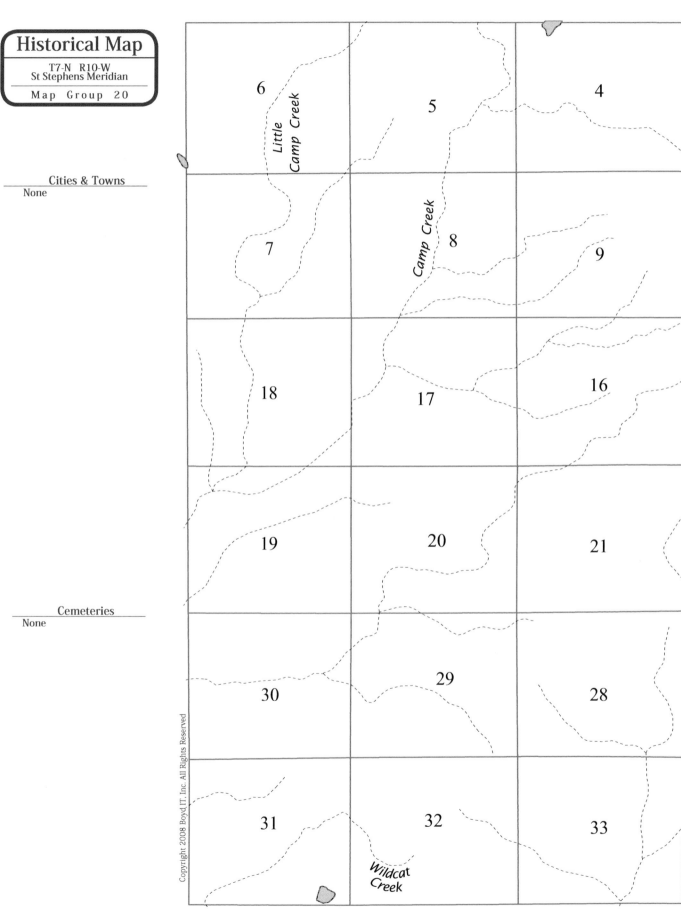

Historical Map

T7-N R10-W
St Stephens Meridian

Map Group 20

Cities & Towns
None

Cemeteries
None

6

5

4

Little Camp Creek

7

Camp Creek

8

9

18

17

16

19

20

21

30

29

28

31

32

33

Wildcat Creek

Copyright 2008 Boyd IT, Inc. All Rights Reserved

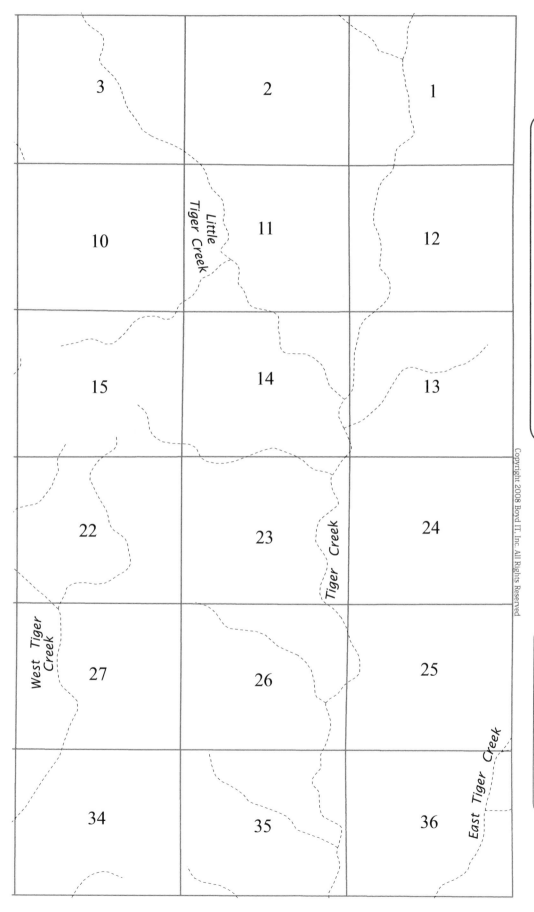

3

2

1

10

Little Tiger Creek

11

12

15

14

13

22

23

Tiger Creek

24

West Tiger Creek

27

26

25

34

35

36

East Tiger Creek

Helpful Hints

1. This Map takes a different look at the same Congressional Township displayed in the preceding two maps. It presents features that can help you better envision the historical development of the area: a) Water-bodies (lakes & ponds), b) Water-courses (rivers, streams, etc.), c) Railroads, d) City/town center-points (where they were oftentimes located when first settled), and e) Cemeteries.

2. Using this "Historical" map in tandem with this Township's Patent Map and Road Map, may lead you to some interesting discoveries. You will often find roads, towns, cemeteries, and waterways are named after nearby landowners: sometimes those names will be the ones you are researching. See how many of these research gems you can find here in Jones County.

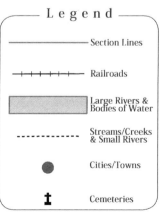

L e g e n d

———————— Section Lines

+++++++ Railroads

▓▓▓▓ Large Rivers & Bodies of Water

- - - - - - Streams/Creeks & Small Rivers

● Cities/Towns

✝ Cemeteries

Scale: Section = 1 mile X 1 mile
(there are some exceptions)

Map Group 21: Index to Land Patents

Township 6-North Range 14-West (St Stephens)

After you locate an individual in this Index, take note of the Section and Section Part then proceed to the Land Patent map on the pages immediately following. You should have no difficulty locating the corresponding parcel of land.

The "For More Info" Column will lead you to more information about the underlying Patents. See the *Legend* at right, and the "How to Use this Book" chapter, for more information.

```
                        LEGEND
              "For More Info . . . " column
A = Authority (Legislative Act, See Appendix "A")
B = Block or Lot (location in Section unknown)
C = Cancelled Patent
F = Fractional Section
G = Group (Multi-Patentee Patent, see Appendix "C")
V = Overlaps another Parcel
R = Re-Issued (Parcel patented more than once)

(A & G items require you to look in the Appendixes referred
to above. All other Letter-designations followed by a number
require you to locate line-items in this index that possess
the ID number found after the letter).
```

ID	Individual in Patent	Sec.	Sec. Part	Date Issued	Other Counties	For More Info . . .
3816	BOWEN, William S	24	NW	1894-03-15		A2
3687	BOYCE, Dan W	35	SWSW	1905-03-30		A3
3767	BROWN, Margarett J	24	N½SW	1905-03-30		A3
3768	" "	24	W½SE	1905-03-30		A3
3669	BRYANT, Abner A	22	E½NE	1898-03-15		A3
3670	" "	22	NESE	1898-03-15		A3
3684	BRYANT, Caroline	36	SW	1891-08-19		A3 G5
3705	BRYANT, Frances V	12	NW	1897-11-01		A3 G6
3738	BRYANT, John M	22	E½SW	1896-02-13		A3
3739	" "	22	NWSE	1896-02-13		A3
3740	" "	22	SWNE	1896-02-13		A3
3758	BRYANT, Joseph L	27	N½SW	1889-12-19		A3
3759	" "	27	NWSE	1889-12-19		A3
3760	" "	27	SWNW	1889-12-19		A3
3684	BRYANT, Lewis	36	SW	1891-08-19		A3 G5
3769	BRYANT, Mary D	27	NESE	1901-06-08		A3 G25
3770	" "	27	SWNE	1901-06-08		A3 G25
3778	BRYANT, Matthew N	22	S½SE	1890-02-21		A3
3779	" "	27	E½NE	1890-02-21		A3
3820	BRYANT, Willis A	22	S½NW	1896-02-13		A3
3821	" "	22	W½SW	1896-02-13		A3
3789	BULLARD, Samuel	25	S½NW	1898-02-24		A3
3790	" "	25	W½SW	1898-02-24		A3
3714	BYNUM, James	26	SE	1898-09-28		A3
3807	BYNUM, William	27	NWNE	1841-01-05		A2
3808	" "	27	SWSW	1841-01-05		A2 R3813
3782	CARTER, Redmond	23	NWSW	1859-06-01		A2
3783	" "	23	SWNW	1859-06-01		A2
3809	CRUMITY, William	25	E½SE	1901-03-23		A3
3810	" "	25	S½NE	1901-03-23		A3
3817	CULPEPPER, William T	12	SENE	1884-12-30		A3
3688	DELK, David	35	N½SW	1892-06-15		A3
3689	" "	35	S½NW	1892-06-15		A3
3721	DELK, James T	35	NENW	1895-10-09		A3
3722	" "	35	NWNE	1895-10-09		A3
3723	" "	35	S½NE	1895-10-09		A3
3734	DELK, John D	26	S½SW	1896-12-14		A3
3735	" "	27	SESE	1896-12-14		A3
3736	" "	35	NWNW	1896-12-14		A3
3811	DELK, William F	34	N½SE	1898-03-15		A3
3796	DENT, Peter	12	E½SW	1906-06-26		A3 G10
3797	" "	12	W½SE	1906-06-26		A3 G10
3796	DENT, Sarah	12	E½SW	1906-06-26		A3 G10
3797	" "	12	W½SE	1906-06-26		A3 G10
3671	DOSSETT, Absalom M	26	N½SW	1896-02-13		A3
3672	" "	26	S½NW	1896-02-13		A3

ID	Individual in Patent	Sec.	Sec. Part	Date Issued	Other Counties	For More Info . . .
3717	DOSSETT, James L	26	NE	1896-12-14		A3
3724	DOSSETTE, James W	35	NWSE	1889-01-05		A3
3725	" "	35	S½SE	1889-01-05		A3
3726	" "	35	SESW	1889-01-05		A3
3791	DYE, Samuel	14	N½SE	1899-06-28		A3
3792	" "	14	SWNE	1899-06-28		A3
3680	EASTERLING, Bennett	36	W½SE	1859-05-02		A2
3786	EASTERLING, Roderick D	27	E½NW	1896-01-10		A3
3787	" "	27	NWNW	1896-01-10		A3
3706	GLIDEWELL, Frank	24	E½SE	1918-04-11		A3
3743	GLOVER, David	34	NE	1907-12-09		A2 G31
3698	GRANBERRY, Ephraim	15	NESW	1892-04-29		A3
3699	" "	15	NWSE	1892-04-29		A3
3700	" "	15	W½SW	1892-04-29		A3
3776	GRANBERRY, Mathew S	34	N½SW	1890-06-25		A3
3777	" "	34	SWNW	1890-06-25		A3
3780	GRANBERRY, Moses H	34	S½SE	1891-06-30		A3
3781	" "	34	S½SW	1891-06-30		A3
3798	GRANBERRY, Thomas J	10	S½SW	1895-11-11		A3
3799	" "	15	NWNW	1895-11-11		A3
3678	GRAYSON, Augustus	14	S½SE	1892-07-20		A3
3679	" "	23	N½NE	1892-07-20		A3
3784	HADDOX, Robert A	14	W½SW	1897-02-15		A3
3727	HAIGLER, Frank	24	S½SW	1897-11-01		A3 G16
3728	" "	25	NWNW	1897-11-01		A3 G16
3727	HAIGLER, Jane	24	S½SW	1897-11-01		A3 G16
3728	" "	25	NWNW	1897-11-01		A3 G16
3813	HAMILTON, William J	27	SWSW	1896-08-26		A3 R3808
3814	" "	34	NWNW	1896-08-26		A3
3800	HARREL, Thomas J	15	SENE	1883-09-15		A2
3729	HARRELL, Jefferson	10	E½SE	1882-03-04		A3
3730	" "	15	N½NE	1882-03-04		A3
3763	HARRELL, Joseph W	11	W½SW	1897-01-12		A3
3764	" "	14	W½NW	1897-01-12		A3
3805	HOOD, W J	1	E½SW	1881-06-30		A3
3806	" "	1	W½SE	1881-06-30		A3
3676	JACKSON, Andrew	10	SWSE	1859-05-02		A2
3704	KELLEY, F M	13	E½SE	1901-12-30		A3
3823	KELLY, Wyatt H	23	SE	1897-02-15		A3
3696	LEE, Eliza M	23	S½NE	1899-05-31		A3
3752	LEE, John T	36	NWNE	1894-02-17		A3
3753	" "	36	S½NE	1894-02-17		A3
3754	" "	36	SENW	1894-02-17		A3
3677	LOTT, Asa C	3	NE	1895-12-14		A3
3681	LUMSEY, Bob	10	N½SW	1897-02-15		A3
3682	" "	10	NWSE	1897-02-15		A3
3683	" "	10	SWNE	1897-02-15		A3
3761	MASKEW, Joseph S	2	N½SW	1898-08-27		A3
3762	" "	2	S½NW	1898-08-27		A3
3769	MCCRANEY, Mary D	27	NESE	1901-06-08		A3 G25
3770	" "	27	SWNE	1901-06-08		A3 G25
3693	MCINNIS, Eli	13	NESW	1896-12-14		A3
3694	" "	13	SENW	1896-12-14		A3
3695	" "	13	W½SE	1896-12-14		A3
3822	MCLEMORE, Willis	36	E½SE	1898-12-27		A3
3765	MITCHELL, Joshua H	11	E½SE	1898-12-27		A3
3766	" "	12	W½SW	1898-12-27		A3
3812	MIXON, William F	35	NESE	1898-11-11		A3
3673	MORGAN, Anderson	15	NENW	1894-04-10		A3
3674	" "	15	S½NW	1894-04-10		A3
3675	" "	15	SWNE	1894-04-10		A3
3709	MORGAN, Henry	15	SESW	1891-03-16		A3
3710	" "	22	N½NW	1891-03-16		A3
3711	" "	22	NWNE	1891-03-16		A3
3741	MORGAN, John	25	E½SW	1890-08-16		A3
3742	" "	25	W½SE	1890-08-16		A3
3815	MORGAN, William	3	SE	1861-05-01		A2
3707	MOULDS, George M	2	N½NW	1901-03-23		A3
3715	MOULDS, James D	1	E½NE	1895-12-14		A3
3716	" "	1	E½SE	1895-12-14		A3
3743	MYRICK, John	34	NE	1907-12-09		A2 G31
3712	PAGE, Hezekiah W	12	NENE	1897-06-07		A3
3713	" "	12	W½NE	1897-06-07		A3

ID	Individual in Patent	Sec.	Sec. Part	Date Issued	Other Counties	For More Info . . .
3718	PATTERSON, James M	11	SENE	1901-03-23		A3
3708	PERRY, George S	12	E½SE	1901-08-12		A3
3719	PICKERING, James M	11	NESW	1901-04-22		A3
3720	" "	11	S½NW	1901-04-22		A3
3803	RAINEY, Thomas	2	E½NE	1859-05-02		A2
3804	" "	2	NESE	1859-05-02		A2
3801	" "	1	S½NW	1895-02-21		A3
3802	" "	1	W½NE	1895-02-21		A3
3818	RAINEY, William T	1	N½NW	1891-05-20		A3
3731	RIALS, Joel	3	SW	1895-10-09		A3
3745	RIALS, John	10	NENE	1859-11-10		A2
3747	" "	11	NWNW	1890-08-16		A3
3749	" "	2	SWSW	1890-08-16		A3
3746	" "	11	NENW	1894-08-14		A3
3748	" "	2	SESW	1894-08-14		A3
3750	RIELS, John	10	NWNE	1859-05-02		A2
3751	" "	10	SENE	1859-05-02		A2
3744	RIELS, John N	10	NW	1894-11-22		A3
3697	ROBERTS, Enos B	26	N½NW	1899-06-13		A3
3685	RODGERS, Columbus W	15	E½SE	1899-11-24		A3
3686	" "	15	SWSE	1899-11-24		A3
3755	RUSH, John W	35	NENE	1896-12-14		A3
3756	" "	36	NENW	1896-12-14		A3
3757	" "	36	W½NW	1896-12-14		A3
3785	RUSH, Robert T	36	NENE	1899-06-13		A3
3819	RUSH, William W	24	NE	1901-06-08		A3
3732	SELLERS, John A	25	N½NE	1859-05-02		A2
3733	" "	25	NENW	1859-05-02		A2
3690	SHOWS, Edward M	1	W½SW	1895-02-07		A2
3691	" "	11	NENE	1895-02-07		A2
3692	" "	2	SESE	1895-02-07		A2
3737	SMITH, John E	13	NE	1897-11-01		A3
3773	SMITH, Mary	11	SESW	1859-11-10		A2
3774	" "	11	SWSE	1859-11-10		A2
3775	" "	14	NENW	1859-11-10		A2
3788	THOMPSON, Sabra S	3	NW	1897-06-07		A3
3793	WAITES, Samuel M	13	NWSW	1897-11-01		A3
3794	" "	13	S½SW	1897-11-01		A3
3795	" "	13	SWNW	1897-11-01		A3
3701	WHEELER, Erastus	27	SESW	1890-02-21		A3
3702	" "	27	SWSE	1890-02-21		A3
3703	" "	34	E½NW	1890-02-21		A3
3705	WHEELER, Frances V	12	NW	1897-11-01		A3 G6
3771	WHITEHEAD, Mary J	13	N½NW	1895-02-21		A3
3772	" "	14	E½NE	1895-02-21		A3

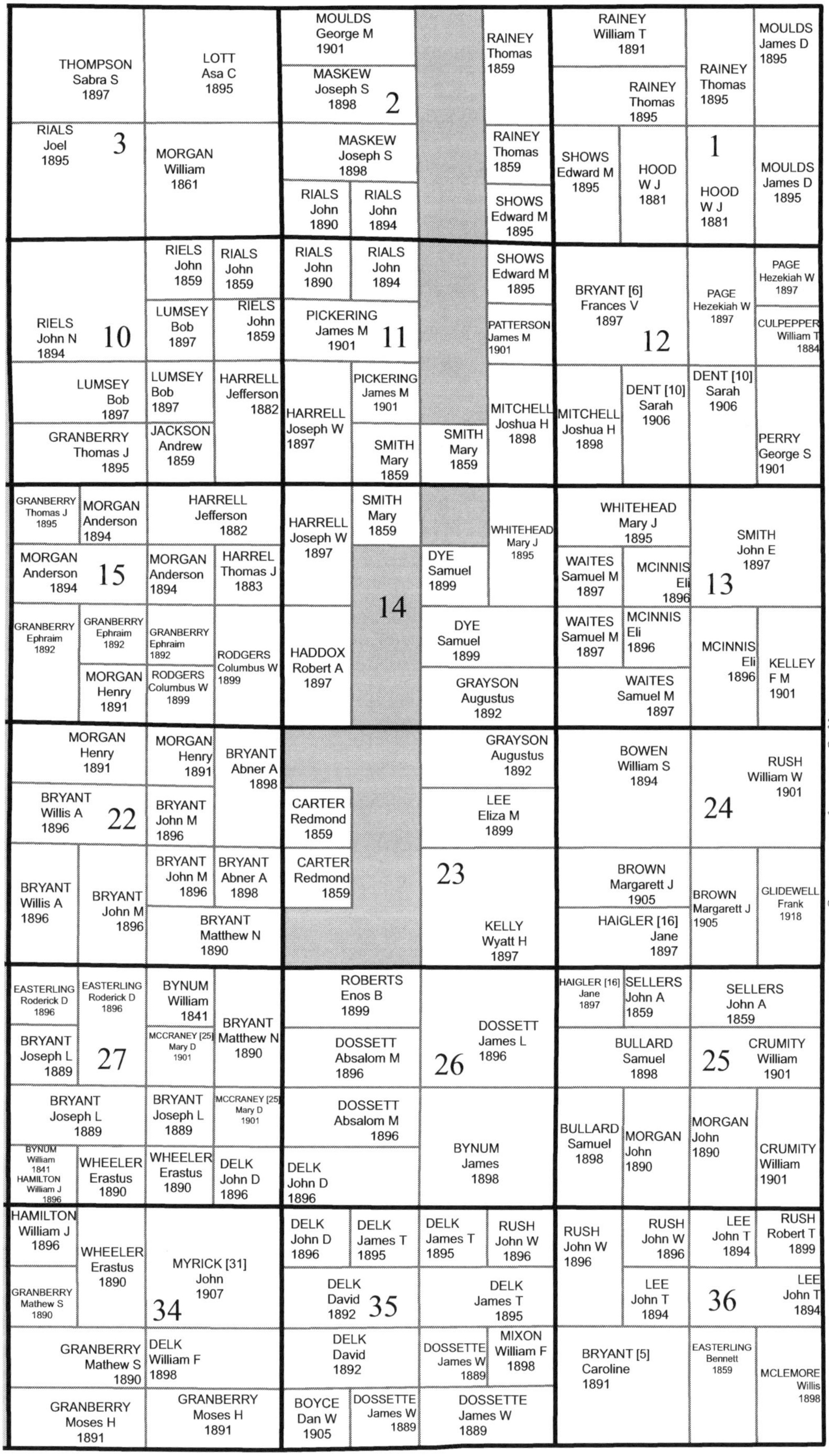

Map Grid (Sections)

Section 3
- THOMPSON Sabra S 1897
- LOTT Asa C 1895
- RIALS Joel 1895
- MORGAN William 1861

Section 2
- MOULDS George M 1901
- MASKEW Joseph S 1898
- MASKEW Joseph S 1898
- RIALS John 1890
- RIALS John 1894

(Section 1)
- RAINEY Thomas 1859
- RAINEY William T 1891
- RAINEY Thomas 1895
- RAINEY Thomas 1895
- MOULDS James D 1895
- RAINEY Thomas 1859
- SHOWS Edward M 1895
- SHOWS Edward M 1895
- HOOD W J 1881
- HOOD W J 1881
- MOULDS James D 1895

Section 10
- RIELS John 1859
- RIALS John 1859
- RIALS John 1890
- RIALS John 1894
- RIELS John N 1894
- LUMSEY Bob 1897
- RIELS John 1859
- PICKERING James M 1901

Section 11

Section 12
- SHOWS Edward M 1895
- BRYANT [6] Frances V 1897
- PAGE Hezekiah W 1897
- PAGE Hezekiah W 1897
- PATTERSON James M 1901
- CULPEPPER William T 1884
- DENT [10] Sarah 1906
- DENT [10] Sarah 1906
- PERRY George S 1901

- LUMSEY Bob 1897
- LUMSEY Bob 1897
- HARRELL Jefferson 1882
- PICKERING James M 1901
- HARRELL Joseph W 1897
- SMITH Mary 1859
- SMITH Mary 1859
- MITCHELL Joshua H 1898
- MITCHELL Joshua H 1898
- GRANBERRY Thomas J 1895
- JACKSON Andrew 1859

Section 15
- GRANBERRY Thomas J 1895
- MORGAN Anderson 1894
- HARRELL Jefferson 1882
- MORGAN Anderson 1894
- MORGAN Anderson 1894
- HARREL Thomas J 1883
- GRANBERRY Ephraim 1892
- GRANBERRY Ephraim 1892
- GRANBERRY Ephraim 1892
- RODGERS Columbus W 1899
- MORGAN Henry 1891
- RODGERS Columbus W 1899

Section 14
- HARRELL Joseph W 1897
- SMITH Mary 1859
- DYE Samuel 1899
- DYE Samuel 1899
- HADDOX Robert A 1897
- GRAYSON Augustus 1892

Section 13
- WHITEHEAD Mary J 1895
- WHITEHEAD Mary J 1895
- WAITES Samuel M 1897
- MCINNIS Eli 1896
- WAITES Samuel M 1897
- MCINNIS Eli 1896
- SMITH John E 1897
- MCINNIS Eli 1896
- KELLEY F M 1901
- WAITES Samuel M 1897

Section 22
- MORGAN Henry 1891
- MORGAN Henry 1891
- BRYANT Abner A 1898
- BRYANT Willis A 1896
- BRYANT John M 1896
- BRYANT Willis A 1896
- BRYANT John M 1896
- BRYANT John M 1896
- BRYANT Abner A 1898
- BRYANT Matthew N 1890

Section 23
- CARTER Redmond 1859
- CARTER Redmond 1859
- GRAYSON Augustus 1892
- LEE Eliza M 1899
- KELLY Wyatt H 1897

Section 24
- BOWEN William S 1894
- RUSH William W 1901
- BROWN Margarett J 1905
- BROWN Margarett J 1905
- HAIGLER [16] Jane 1897
- GLIDEWELL Frank 1918

Section 27
- EASTERLING Roderick D 1896
- EASTERLING Roderick D 1896
- BYNUM William 1841
- BRYANT Matthew N 1890
- BRYANT Joseph L 1889
- MCCRANEY [25] Mary D 1901
- BRYANT Joseph L 1889
- BRYANT Joseph L 1889
- MCCRANEY [25] Mary D 1901
- BYNUM William 1841
- HAMILTON William J 1896
- WHEELER Erastus 1890
- WHEELER Erastus 1890
- DELK John D 1896

Section 26
- ROBERTS Enos B 1899
- DOSSETT James L 1896
- DOSSETT Absalom M 1896
- DOSSETT Absalom M 1896
- DELK John D 1896
- BYNUM James 1898

Section 25
- HAIGLER [16] Jane 1897
- SELLERS John A 1859
- SELLERS John A 1859
- BULLARD Samuel 1898
- CRUMITY William 1901
- BULLARD Samuel 1898
- MORGAN John 1890
- MORGAN John 1890
- CRUMITY William 1901

Section 34
- HAMILTON William J 1896
- WHEELER Erastus 1890
- MYRICK [31] John 1907
- GRANBERRY Mathew S 1890
- GRANBERRY Mathew S 1890
- DELK William F 1898
- GRANBERRY Moses H 1891
- GRANBERRY Moses H 1891

Section 35
- DELK John D 1896
- DELK James T 1895
- DELK David 1892
- DELK David 1892
- BOYCE Dan W 1905
- DOSSETTE James W 1889
- DELK James T 1895
- RUSH John W 1896
- DELK James T 1895
- DOSSETTE James W 1889

Section 36
- RUSH John W 1896
- RUSH John W 1896
- LEE John T 1894
- RUSH Robert T 1899
- LEE John T 1894
- LEE John T 1894
- MIXON William F 1898
- BRYANT [5] Caroline 1891
- EASTERLING Bennett 1859
- MCLEMORE Willis 1898

Patent Map

T6-N R14-W
St Stephens Meridian

Map Group 21

Township Statistics

Parcels Mapped	:	155
Number of Patents	:	86
Number of Individuals	:	89
Patentees Identified	:	83
Number of Surnames	:	57
Multi-Patentee Parcels	:	9
Oldest Patent Date	:	1/5/1841
Most Recent Patent	:	4/11/1918
Block/Lot Parcels	:	0
Parcels Re - Issued	:	1
Parcels that Overlap	:	0
Cities and Towns	:	2
Cemeteries	:	1

Note: the area contained in this map amounts to far less than a full Township. Therefore, its contents are completely on this single page (instead of a "normal" 2-page spread).

Legend

——— Patent Boundary

▬▬▬ Section Boundary

▒▒▒ No Patents Found (or Outside County)

1., 2., 3., ... Lot Numbers (when beside a name)

[ ] Group Number (see Appendix "C")

Scale: Section = 1 mile X 1 mile (generally, with some exceptions)

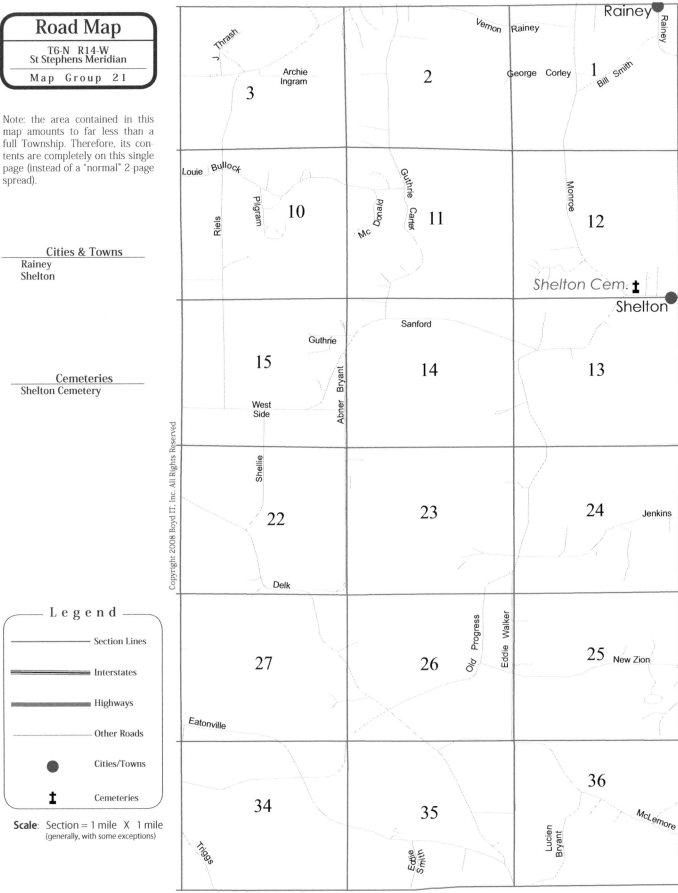

Road Map

T6-N R14-W
St Stephens Meridian

Map Group 21

Note: the area contained in this map amounts to far less than a full Township. Therefore, its contents are completely on this single page (instead of a "normal" 2-page spread).

Cities & Towns
Rainey
Shelton

Cemeteries
Shelton Cemetery

Legend
———— Section Lines
═════ Interstates
▬▬▬▬ Highways
———— Other Roads
● Cities/Towns
✝ Cemeteries

Scale: Section = 1 mile X 1 mile
(generally, with some exceptions)

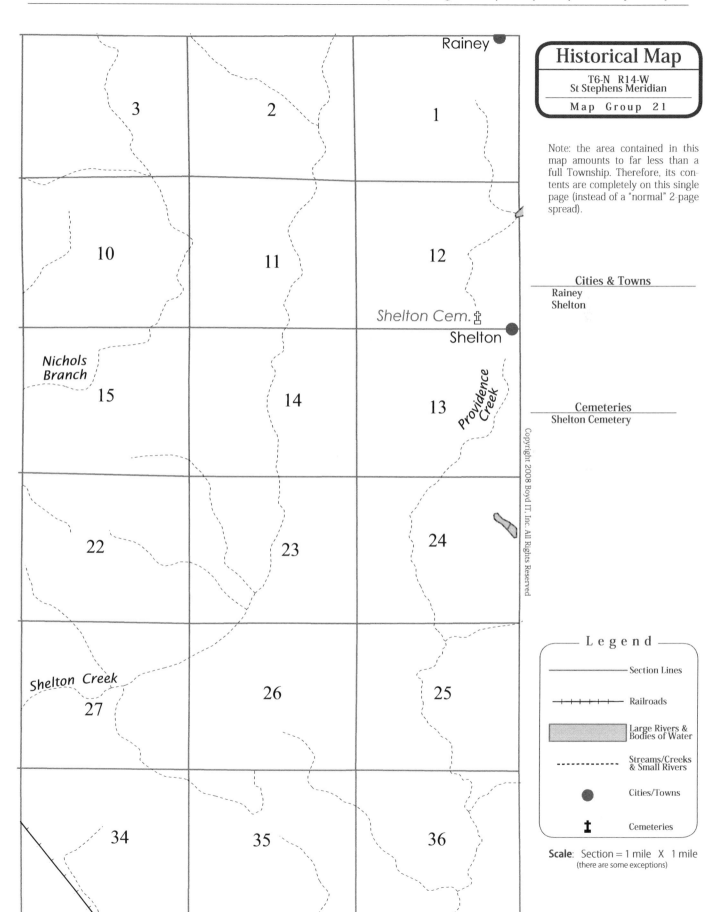

Rainey

3

2

1

10

11

12

Shelton Cem. ✝

Shelton

Nichols
Branch

15

14

13

Providence Creek

22

23

24

Shelton Creek

27

26

25

34

35

36

Historical Map

T6-N R14-W
St Stephens Meridian

Map Group 21

Note: the area contained in this map amounts to far less than a full Township. Therefore, its contents are completely on this single page (instead of a "normal" 2-page spread).

Cities & Towns
Rainey
Shelton

Cemeteries
Shelton Cemetery

Legend
——— Section Lines
+-+-+-+ Railroads
▨ Large Rivers & Bodies of Water
----- Streams/Creeks & Small Rivers
● Cities/Towns
✝ Cemeteries

Scale: Section = 1 mile X 1 mile
(there are some exceptions)

Map Group 22: Index to Land Patents

Township 6-North Range 13-West (St Stephens)

After you locate an individual in this Index, take note of the Section and Section Part then proceed to the Land Patent map on the pages immediately following. You should have no difficulty locating the corresponding parcel of land.

The "For More Info" Column will lead you to more information about the underlying Patents. See the *Legend* at right, and the "How to Use this Book" chapter, for more information.

ID	Individual in Patent	Sec.	Sec. Part	Date Issued	Other Counties	For More Info . . .
3850	ALLEN, Dave	32	W½NE	1897-02-23		A3
3879	ANDERSON, Jake	30	SE	1896-12-14		A3
3971	ARCHEY, William Jackson	17	SWNW	1931-07-16		A3
3946	ATWOOD, Sam Jones	13	SWSE	1913-12-02		A3
3881	BALFOUR, James	25	E½NW	1882-12-30		A2
3882	" "	25	SW	1882-12-30		A2
3883	" "	25	SWNW	1882-12-30		A2
3884	" "	26	SESE	1882-12-30		A2
3866	BAYLIS, George	32	NESW	1859-11-10		A2
3867	" "	32	SENE	1859-11-10		A2
3906	BAYLIS, John M	34	S½SE	1884-12-30		A3
3950	BAYLIS, Sarah A	32	S½SW	1890-02-21		A3
3984	BAYLIS, Wyatt L	24	S½SW	1898-11-11		A3
3985	" "	24	SWSE	1898-11-11		A3
3841	BEESLEY, Calvin H	7	SW	1898-03-15		A3
3934	BRADLEY, Oscar F	9	S½6	1914-05-28		A3
3864	CALLAHAM, Elizabeth	8	NWSW	1897-06-07		A3
3865	" "	8	SESW	1897-06-07		A3
3916	CALLAHAM, John W	17	NWNW	1894-11-22		A3
3917	" "	7	S½SE	1894-11-22		A3
3918	" "	8	SWSW	1894-11-22		A3
3967	CALLAHAM, William J	8	NENW	1896-12-14		A3
3968	" "	8	NWNE	1896-12-14		A3
3969	" "	8	NWSE	1896-12-14		A3
3869	CALLAHAN, George W	18	SE	1891-05-20		A3
3939	CAMPBELL, Robert	1	NE	1882-04-20		A2
3925	COPELAND, Moses	21	N½	1909-01-25		A2 G11 F
3927	CRAFT, Lewis	29	NW	1892-07-25		A3
3844	CREEL, Collin W	23	E½SE	1860-07-02		A2
3845	" "	24	NWSW	1860-07-02		A2
3891	CREEL, Jasper	25	NWSE	1861-05-01		A2
3976	CULPEPPER, William T	7	SENW	1884-12-30		A3
3977	" "	7	W½NW	1884-12-30		A3
3979	DICKENSON, Willis	3	SWNW	1859-05-02		A2
3980	" "	4	1	1859-05-02		A2
3824	DOSSETT, Abner	17	SW	1890-08-16		A3
3852	DOSSETT, Edward	18	E½NE	1896-02-13		A3
3853	" "	18	SENW	1896-02-13		A3
3854	" "	18	SWNE	1896-02-13		A3
3880	DOSSETT, James A	18	SW	1896-12-14		A3
3886	EASTERLING, James	21	SESE	1851-10-01		A2
3885	" "	21	NESE	1854-03-15		A2
3871	EATON, Handy	19	SENE	1911-10-09		A3
3925	EVANS, Josiah	21	N½	1909-01-25		A2 G11 F
3877	FOLKS, Isaac	9	10	1861-07-01		A2
3878	" "	9	S½9	1861-07-01		A2

ID	Individual in Patent	Sec.	Sec. Part	Date Issued	Other Counties	For More Info . . .
3951	GAINEY, Seaborn W	30	NE	1896-12-18		A3
3876	GILENDER, Hugh	27	SWSE	1859-11-10		A2
3897	GILENDER, John	26	SENW	1859-11-10		A2
3899	" "	35	NENW	1859-11-10		A2
3898	" "	27	NWSE	1860-07-02		A2
3900	GILLANDER, John	34	NWNW	1851-10-01		A2
3901	GILLENDER, John	27	NESW	1851-10-01		A2
3902	GILLINDER, John	27	SWSW	1848-09-01		A2
3960	GRAYSON, William D	3	NESW	1894-12-17		A3
3961	" "	3	SENW	1894-12-17		A3
3947	HOLLIMAN, Samuel	31	E½SW	1892-07-20		A3
3948	" "	31	SENW	1892-07-20		A3
3949	" "	31	SWSE	1892-07-20		A3
3826	HOOD, Allen	9	7	1859-05-02		A2
3962	HOOD, William	5	N½SW	1859-05-02		A2
3963	" "	5	NWSE	1859-05-02		A2
3964	" "	5	S½NW	1859-05-02		A2
3966	" "	5	SWSE	1882-04-20		A2
3965	" "	5	SESW	1887-05-27		A2
3970	HOOD, William J	6	S½NW	1884-12-30		A2
3919	HURST, John W	19	SW	1898-12-01		A3
3952	JACKSON, Silas A	19	N½NE	1893-09-08		A3
3953	" "	19	NENW	1893-09-08		A3
3954	" "	19	SWNE	1893-09-08		A3
3846	JOHNSON, Crawford	22	NWSE	1911-01-05		A3
3972	JOHNSON, William	29	W½NE	1891-03-16		A3
3973	" "	29	W½SE	1891-03-16		A3
3855	JONES, Edward K	26	NENW	1890-06-25		A3
3856	" "	26	W½NE	1890-06-25		A3
3974	JONES, William	22	SWSW	1851-10-01		A2
3978	JONES, Willie	3	NWSW	1859-05-02		A2
3838	KELLEY, Appleton P	20	S½SW	1895-11-11		A3
3839	" "	20	SWSE	1895-11-11		A3
3837	KELLY, Angus	32	NW	1895-11-11		A3
3842	KELLY, Clandy	20	SENE	1914-03-31		A3
3857	KELLY, Eli	31	E½SE	1890-08-16		A3
3858	" "	31	NWSE	1890-08-16		A3
3859	" "	31	SENE	1890-08-16		A3
3956	KELLY, Warren	36	NW	1889-11-21		A2
3931	KILGORE, Matthew T	26	SWSE	1860-04-02		A2
3932	" "	35	NWNE	1860-04-02		A2
3941	KNIGHT, Robert W	31	W½NW	1896-10-10		A3
3942	" "	31	W½SW	1896-10-10		A3
3873	LAMPORT, Henry	12	NENE	1884-12-30		A2
3874	" "	12	W½NE	1884-12-30		A2
3875	" "	12	W½SE	1884-12-30		A2
3926	LEE, Lena	29	SW	1895-12-14		A3
3863	LOCKHART, Eliel B	36	NESW	1918-04-11		A3
3924	LOFTON, Josephine	36	SWSE	1911-01-05		A3
3887	MCDONALD, James S	24	NESW	1892-06-30		A3
3888	" "	24	NWSE	1892-06-30		A3
3889	" "	24	W½NE	1892-06-30		A3
3955	MISSISSIPPI, State Of	21	4	1928-08-09		A4
3860	MOFFETT, Elias	31	N½NE	1896-01-10		A3
3861	" "	31	NENW	1896-01-10		A3
3862	" "	31	SWNE	1896-01-10		A3
3928	MOULDS, Marion W	6	E½NE	1899-06-13		A3
3929	" "	6	NENW	1899-06-13		A3
3930	" "	6	NWNE	1899-06-13		A3
3847	ODOM, Daniel Macon	6	N½SW	1910-01-20		A3
3848	" "	6	SWSW	1910-01-20		A3
3907	ODOM, John S	6	NESE	1912-06-20		A3
3908	" "	6	SWNE	1912-06-20		A3
3909	" "	6	W½SE	1912-06-20		A3
3940	PARKER, Robert J	8	S½NE	1859-11-10		A2
3872	PATTERSON, Henry H	30	NW	1895-02-21		A3
3935	PLOCK, Otto	13	SW	1882-04-20		A2
3936	" "	23	N½NW	1882-04-20		A2
3937	" "	23	NE	1882-04-20		A2
3938	" "	24	NW	1882-04-20		A2
3975	RICHARDSON, William P	1	S½	1882-05-10		A2
3890	RIDGWAY, James W P	3	SWSW	1910-03-17		A3
3957	RUSH, Wiley W	13	N½NE	1891-06-30		A3

ID	Individual in Patent	Sec.	Sec. Part	Date Issued	Other Counties	For More Info . . .
3958	RUSH, Wiley W (Cont'd)	13	NWSE	1891-06-30		A3
3959	" "	13	SWNE	1891-06-30		A3
3912	SELLERS, John	34	NWSW	1849-12-01		A2
3914	" "	34	SESW	1849-12-01		A2
3910	" "	27	NWSW	1851-10-01		A2
3911	" "	34	NESW	1851-10-01		A2
3913	" "	34	SENW	1851-10-01		A2
3915	" "	34	SWSW	1854-03-15		A2
3892	SELLERS, John A	23	E½SW	1890-06-25		A3
3893	" "	23	W½SE	1890-06-25		A3
3903	SELLERS, John H	18	N½NW	1896-02-19		A3
3904	" "	18	NWNE	1896-02-19		A3
3905	" "	18	SWNW	1896-02-19		A3
3943	SHARP, Rufus L	19	NWNW	1895-06-27		A3
3944	" "	19	S½NW	1895-06-27		A3
3849	SHOWS, Daniel T	3	N½NW	1892-03-07		A3
3840	SMITH, Benjamin W	5	SWSW	1910-06-02		A3
3851	SMITH, Edmon C	7	NENW	1899-04-01		A3
3870	SMITH, George W	6	SESW	1914-05-28		A3
3923	SMITH, Joseph H	6	NWNW	1915-03-22		A3
3825	THORNTON, Alfred	19	SE	1896-04-28		A3
3894	TISDALE, John A	26	SWNW	1859-05-02		A2
3895	" "	27	SENE	1859-05-02		A2
3896	" "	28	E½1	1859-11-10		A2
3868	TRAVIS, George	7	NESE	1882-08-03		A2
3843	VICK, Ada Lowry	9	5	1957-06-20		A1 G42
3843	VICK, Clyde H	9	5	1957-06-20		A1 G42
3827	WATSON, Amasa B	12	E½SE	1883-09-15		A2
3828	" "	12	SENE	1883-09-15		A2
3829	" "	13	E½SE	1883-09-15		A2
3830	" "	13	SENE	1883-09-15		A2
3831	" "	24	E½NE	1883-09-15		A2
3832	" "	24	E½SE	1883-09-15		A2
3833	" "	25	E½SE	1883-09-15		A2
3834	" "	25	NE	1883-09-15		A2
3835	" "	25	SWSE	1883-09-15		A2
3836	" "	36	N½NE	1883-09-15		A2
3945	WATTS, Sally	32	NWSW	1901-04-22		A3
3920	WILLIAMS, John	7	NWSE	1892-04-29		A3
3921	" "	7	SENE	1892-04-29		A3
3922	" "	7	W½NE	1892-04-29		A3
3933	WILSON, Munroe	30	SW	1897-02-15		A3
3982	WINDHAM, Willis	4	6	1848-09-01		A2 F
3983	" "	9	N½9	1854-03-15		A2 F
3981	" "	4	5	1859-05-02		A2

Patent Map

T6-N R13-W
St Stephens Meridian

Map Group 22

Township Statistics

Parcels Mapped	:	162
Number of Patents	:	101
Number of Individuals	:	89
Patentees Identified	:	87
Number of Surnames	:	65
Multi-Patentee Parcels	:	2
Oldest Patent Date	:	9/1/1848
Most Recent Patent	:	6/20/1957
Block/Lot Parcels	:	11
Parcels Re - Issued	:	0
Parcels that Overlap	:	0
Cities and Towns	:	2
Cemeteries	:	7

Section 6: SMITH Joseph H 1915; MOULDS Marion W 1899; MOULDS Marion W 1899; MOULDS Marion W 1899; HOOD William J 1884; ODOM John S 1912; ODOM Daniel Macon 1910; ODOM John S 1912; ODOM John S 1912; ODOM Daniel Macon 1910; SMITH George W 1914

Section 5: HOOD William 1859; HOOD William 1859; HOOD William 1859; SMITH Benjamin W 1910; HOOD William 1887; HOOD William 1882

Lots-Sec. 4
1	DICKENSON, Willis		1859
5	WINDHAM, Willis		1859
6	WINDHAM, Willis		1848

Section 4

Section 7: CULPEPPER William T 1884; SMITH Edmon C 1899; WILLIAMS John 1892; CULPEPPER William T 1884; WILLIAMS John 1892; WILLIAMS John 1892; TRAVIS George 1882; BEESLEY Calvin H 1898; CALLAHAM John W 1894

Section 8: CALLAHAM William J 1896; CALLAHAM William J 1896; PARKER Robert J 1859; CALLAHAM Elizabeth 1897; CALLAHAM William J 1896; CALLAHAM John W 1894; CALLAHAM Elizabeth 1897

Lots-Sec. 9
5	VICK, Clyde H	[42]	1957
7	FOLKS, Isaac		1861
7	BRADLEY, Oscar F		1914
7	WINDHAM, Willis		1854
7	HOOD, Allen		1859
10	FOLKS, Isaac		1861

Section 9

Section 18: SELLERS John H 1896; SELLERS John H 1896; SELLERS John H 1896; DOSSETT Edward 1896; DOSSETT Edward 1896; DOSSETT Edward 1896; CALLAHAM John W 1894; ARCHEY William Jackson 1931; DOSSETT James A 1896; CALLAHAN George W 1891; DOSSETT Abner 1890

Section 17

Section 16

Section 19: SHARP Rufus L 1895; JACKSON Silas A 1893; JACKSON Silas A 1893; SHARP Rufus L 1895; JACKSON Silas A 1893; EATON Handy 1911; HURST John W 1898; THORNTON Alfred 1896

Section 20: KELLEY Appleton P 1895; KELLEY Appleton P 1895

Lots-Sec. 21
4	MISSISSIPPI, State	O1928

KELLY Clandy 1914; EVANS [11] Josiah 1909; EASTERLING James 1854; EASTERLING James 1851

Section 21

Section 30: PATTERSON Henry H 1895; GAINEY Seaborn W 1896; WILSON Munroe 1897; ANDERSON Jake 1896

Section 29: CRAFT Lewis 1892; JOHNSON William 1891; LEE Lena 1895; JOHNSON William 1891

Lots-Sec. 28
4	TISDALE, John A	1859

Section 28

Section 31: KNIGHT Robert W 1896; MOFFETT Elias 1896; MOFFETT Elias 1896; HOLLIMAN Samuel 1892; MOFFETT Elias 1896; KELLY Eli 1890; KNIGHT Robert W 1896; KELLY Eli 1890; HOLLIMAN Samuel 1892; HOLLIMAN Samuel 1892

Section 32: KELLY Angus 1895; ALLEN Dave 1897; BAYLIS George 1859; WATTS Sally 1901; BAYLIS George 1859; KELLY Eli 1890; BAYLIS Sarah A 1890

Section 33

Section 3
SHOWS
Daniel T
1892

DICKENSON
Willis
1859

GRAYSON
William D
1894

JONES
Willie
1859

GRAYSON
William D
1894

RIDGWAY
James W P
1910

3

Section 2
2

Section 1
CAMPBELL
Robert
1882

RICHARDSON
William P
1882

1

Section 10
10

Section 11
11

Section 12
LAMPORT
Henry
1884

LAMPORT
Henry
1884

WATSON
Amasa B
1883

LAMPORT
Henry
1884

WATSON
Amasa B
1883

12

Section 15
15

Section 14
14

Section 13
RUSH
Wiley W
1891

RUSH
Wiley W
1891

WATSON
Amasa B
1883

PLOCK
Otto
1882

RUSH
Wiley W
1891

WATSON
Amasa B
1883

ATWOOD
Sam Jones
1913

13

Section 22
22

JOHNSON
Crawford
1911

JONES
William
1851

Section 23
PLOCK
Otto
1882

PLOCK
Otto
1882

23

SELLERS
John A
1890

SELLERS
John A
1890

CREEL
Collin W
1860

Section 24
PLOCK
Otto
1882

MCDONALD
James S
1892

WATSON
Amasa B
1883

24

CREEL
Collin W
1860

MCDONALD
James S
1892

MCDONALD
James S
1892

BAYLIS
Wyatt L
1898

BAYLIS
Wyatt L
1898

WATSON
Amasa B
1883

Section 27
27

TISDALE
John A
1859

SELLERS
John
1851

GILLENDER
John
1851

GILENDER
John
1860

GILLINDER
John
1848

GILENDER
Hugh
1859

Section 26
JONES
Edward K
1890

TISDALE
John A
1859

GILENDER
John
1859

JONES
Edward K
1890

26

KILGORE
Matthew T
1860

BALFOUR
James
1882

Section 25
BALFOUR
James
1882

BALFOUR
James
1882

WATSON
Amasa B
1883

25

BALFOUR
James
1882

CREEL
Jasper
1861

WATSON
Amasa B
1883

WATSON
Amasa B
1883

Section 34
GILLANDER
John
1851

SELLERS
John
1851

SELLERS
John
1849

SELLERS
John
1851

SELLERS
John
1854

SELLERS
John
1849

34

Section 35
GILENDER
John
1859

KILGORE
Matthew T
1860

35

BAYLIS
John M
1884

Section 36
WATSON
Amasa B
1883

KELLY
Warren
1889

36

LOCKHART
Eliel B
1918

LOFTON
Josephine
1911

Helpful Hints

1. This Map's INDEX can be found on the preceding pages.

2. Refer to Map "C" to see where this Township lies within Jones County, Mississippi.

3. Numbers within square brackets [ ] denote a multi-patentee land parcel (multi-owner). Refer to Appendix "C" for a full list of members in this group.

4. Areas that look to be crowded with Patentees usually indicate multiple sales of the same parcel (Re-issues) or Overlapping parcels. See this Township's Index for an explanation of these and other circumstances that might explain "odd" groupings of Patentees on this map.

Legend

————	Patent Boundary
▬▬▬▬	Section Boundary
(shaded)	No Patents Found (or Outside County)
1., 2., 3., ...	Lot Numbers (when beside a name)
[ ]	Group Number (see Appendix "C")

Scale: Section = 1 mile X 1 mile (generally, with some exceptions)

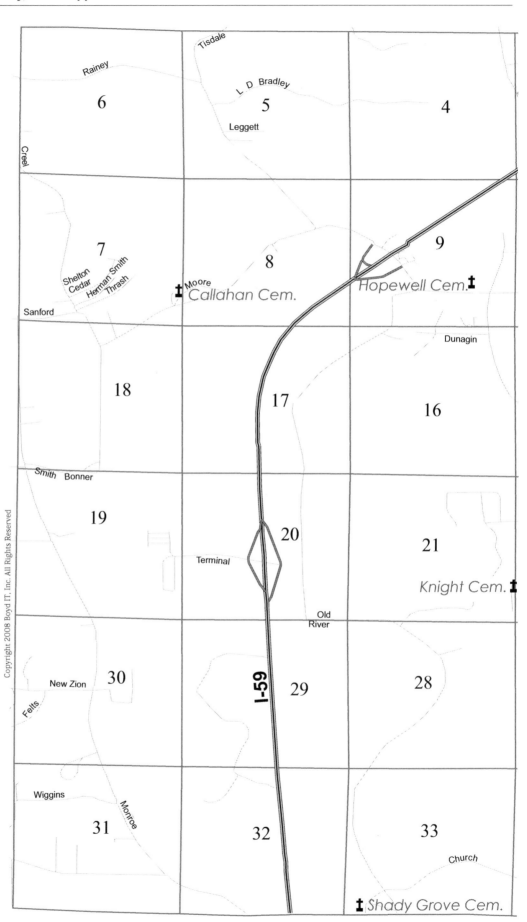

Road Map

T6-N R13-W
St Stephens Meridian

Map Group 22

Cities & Towns
Albeison
Moselle

Cemeteries
Callahan Cemetery
Eastabuchie Cemetery
Edmonson Cemetery
Fairchild Cemetery
Hopewell Cemetery
Knight Cemetery
Shady Grove Cemetery

Rainey

Tisdale

L D Bradley

Leggett

6

5

4

Creel

7

Shelton
Cedar
Herman Smith
Thrash

Sanford

Moore
Callahan Cem.

8

9

Hopewell Cem.

Dunagin

18

17

16

Smith   Bonner

19

20

21

Terminal

Knight Cem.

Old
River

New Zion

Felts

30

I-59

29

28

Wiggins

Monroe

31

32

33

Church

Shady Grove Cem.

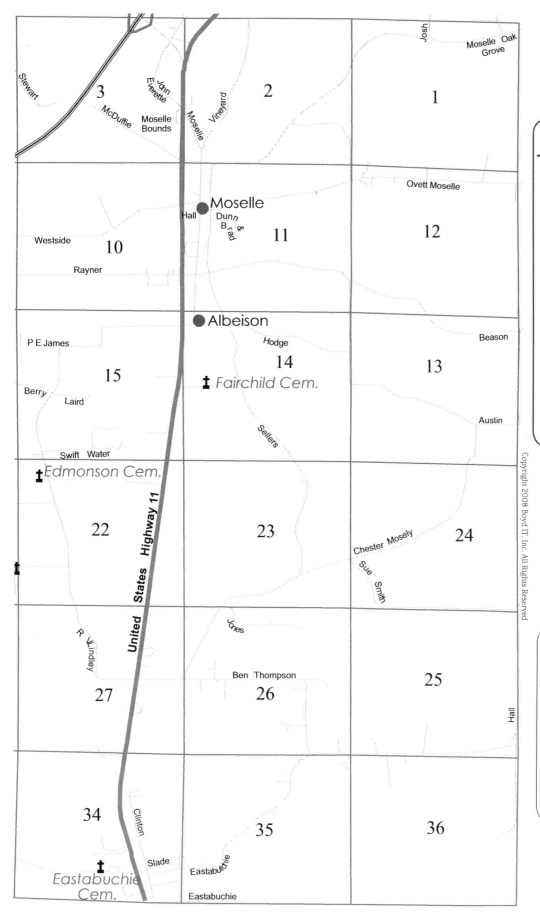

Helpful Hints

1. This road map has a number of uses, but primarily it is to help you: a) find the present location of land owned by your ancestors (at least the general area), b) find cemeteries and city-centers, and c) estimate the route/roads used by Census-takers & tax-assessors.

2. If you plan to travel to Jones County to locate cemeteries or land parcels, please pick up a modern travel map for the area before you do. Mapping old land parcels on modern maps is not as exact a science as you might think. Just the slightest variations in public land survey coordinates, estimates of parcel boundaries, or road-map deviations can greatly alter a map's representation of how a road either does or doesn't cross a particular parcel of land.

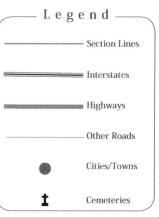

Legend

——	Section Lines
═══	Interstates
▬▬	Highways
——	Other Roads
●	Cities/Towns
✝	Cemeteries

Scale: Section = 1 mile X 1 mile
(generally, with some exceptions)

Historical Map

T6-N R13-W
St Stephens Meridian

Map Group 22

Cities & Towns
Albeison
Moselle

Cemeteries
Callahan Cemetery
Eastabuchie Cemetery
Edmonson Cemetery
Fairchild Cemetery
Hopewell Cemetery
Knight Cemetery
Shady Grove Cemetery

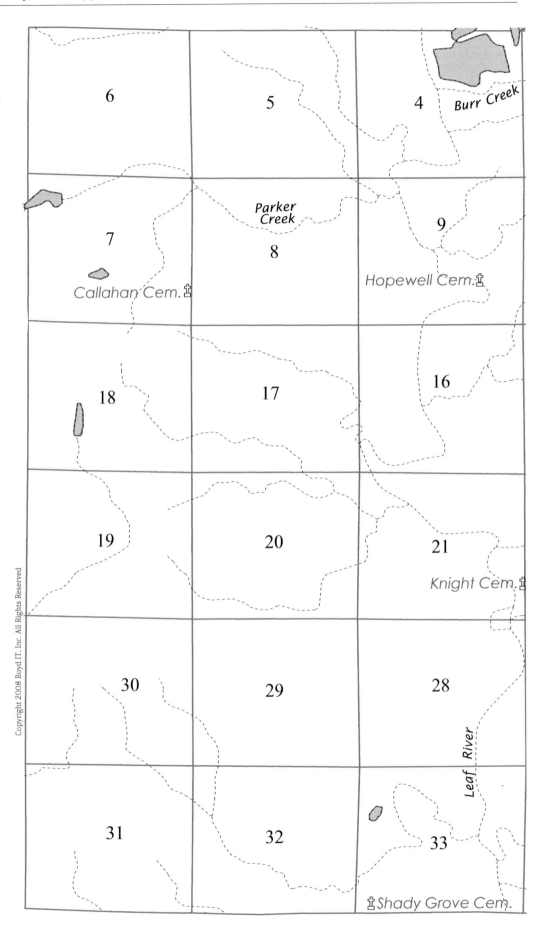

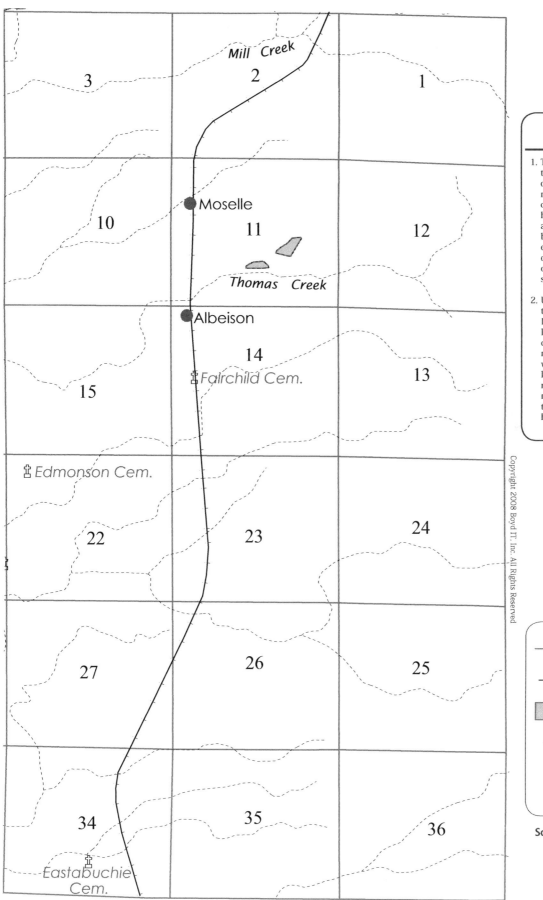

3

2

Mill Creek

1

Moselle

10

11

12

Thomas Creek

Albeison

15

14

13

✝ *Fairchild Cem.*

✝ *Edmonson Cem.*

22

23

24

27

26

25

34

35

36

✝ *Eastabuchie Cem.*

Helpful Hints

1. This Map takes a different look at the same Congressional Township displayed in the preceding two maps. It presents features that can help you better envision the historical development of the area: a) Water-bodies (lakes & ponds), b) Water-courses (rivers, streams, etc.), c) Railroads, d) City/town center-points (where they were oftentimes located when first settled), and e) Cemeteries.

2. Using this "Historical" map in tandem with this Township's Patent Map and Road Map, may lead you to some interesting discoveries. You will often find roads, towns, cemeteries, and waterways are named after nearby landowners: sometimes those names will be the ones you are researching. See how many of these research gems you can find here in Jones County.

Legend

————————	Section Lines
┼┼┼┼┼┼┼	Railroads
▨	Large Rivers & Bodies of Water
- - - - - - -	Streams/Creeks & Small Rivers
●	Cities/Towns
✝	Cemeteries

Scale: Section = 1 mile X 1 mile
(there are some exceptions)

Map Group 23: Index to Land Patents

Township 6-North Range 12-West (St Stephens)

After you locate an individual in this Index, take note of the Section and Section Part then proceed to the Land Patent map on the pages immediately following. You should have no difficulty locating the corresponding parcel of land.

The "For More Info" Column will lead you to more information about the underlying Patents. See the *Legend* at right, and the "How to Use this Book" chapter, for more information.

```
┌─────────────────────────────────────────────────────┐
│                    LEGEND                             │
│        "For More Info . . . " column                  │
│ ───────────────────────────────────────────────      │
│ A = Authority (Legislative Act, See Appendix "A")     │
│ B = Block or Lot (location in Section unknown)        │
│ C = Cancelled Patent                                  │
│ F = Fractional Section                                │
│ G = Group  (Multi-Patentee Patent, see Appendix "C")  │
│ V = Overlaps another Parcel                           │
│ R = Re-Issued (Parcel patented more than once)        │
│                                                       │
│ (A & G items require you to look in the Appendixes    │
│ referred to above. All other Letter-designations      │
│ followed by a number require you to locate line-items │
│ in this index that possess the ID number found after  │
│ the letter).                                          │
└─────────────────────────────────────────────────────┘
```

ID	Individual in Patent	Sec.	Sec. Part	Date Issued	Other Counties	For More Info . . .
4112	ANDERSON, Henry H	13	E½SW	1859-05-02		A2
4113	" "	13	W½SE	1859-05-02		A2
4114	" "	24	W½NW	1859-05-02		A2
4106	BARLOW, Henry	23	E½SW	1846-09-01		A2 G2
4107	" "	23	W½SE	1846-09-01		A2 G2
4104	" "	23	SESE	1854-03-15		A2
4105	" "	24	SWSW	1854-03-15		A2
4106	BARLOW, Norwell	23	E½SW	1846-09-01		A2 G2
4107	" "	23	W½SE	1846-09-01		A2 G2
4142	BEARD, John A	25	SESE	1905-02-13		A3
4201	BIRKETT, Thomas	31	S½SE	1884-12-30		A2 G3
4202	" "	31	SENW	1884-12-30		A2 G3
4203	" "	31	SWNE	1884-12-30		A2 G3
4204	" "	32	S½SE	1884-12-30		A2 G3
4205	" "	32	S½SW	1884-12-30		A2 G3
4131	BOUTWELL, James A	10	NENW	1884-12-30		A3
4132	" "	10	NWNE	1884-12-30		A3
4133	" "	3	SESW	1884-12-30		A3
4134	" "	3	SWSE	1884-12-30		A3
3991	BRADLEY, Alex W	2	NWNE	1911-10-09		A3
4137	BRADLEY, James M	1	W½NW	1897-04-02		A3
4032	CARTER, Asa G	3	NENW	1896-01-30		A2
4033	" "	3	W½NW	1896-01-30		A2
4034	" "	4	NENE	1896-01-30		A2
4222	CLARK, William C	34	NESW	1917-08-11		A3
4110	COLLINS, Henry C	9	SESE	1887-05-27		A2
4108	" "	8	NESE	1890-02-18		A3
4109	" "	9	N½SW	1890-02-18		A3
4111	" "	9	SWNW	1890-02-18		A3
4128	COLLINS, J J	15	NWSW	1881-09-17		A3
4129	" "	15	SWNW	1881-09-17		A3
4041	CREEL, Burton	31	NESW	1861-05-01		A2
4042	" "	31	NWSE	1861-05-01		A2
4209	CROMWELL, Thomas J	10	NWNW	1906-06-21		A3
4210	" "	4	SESE	1906-06-21		A3
4211	" "	9	N½NE	1906-06-21		A3
4164	DRAUGHN, Rufus T	34	SESW	1854-03-15		A2 G29
4072	EASTERLING, Elizabeth	20	NENE	1914-05-28		A3
4143	EASTERLING, John A	25	S½SW	1861-05-01		A2
4074	FERGUSON, Fergus	5	E½NW	1896-03-26		A2
4075	" "	5	NWNE	1896-03-26		A2
4076	" "	5	NWNW	1896-03-26		A2
4187	FERGUSON, Norman	7	N½NE	1892-04-29		A3
4188	" "	7	N½NW	1892-04-29		A3
4235	FERGUSON, Willis	5	S½SW	1896-12-14		A3
4236	" "	5	SWSE	1896-12-14		A3

ID	Individual in Patent	Sec.	Sec. Part	Date Issued	Other Counties	For More Info . . .
4237	FERGUSON, Willis (Cont'd)	8	NWNW	1896-12-14		A3
4146	FREEMAN, John	3	NWNE	1895-02-21		A3
4220	FURR, William B	5	NENE	1899-06-28		A3
4221	" "	5	SWNE	1899-06-28		A3
3990	GRANTHAM, Albert G	15	NESW	1884-12-30		A2
4039	GRANTHAM, Bryant	35	SWNW	1882-03-30		A3
4046	GRANTHAM, Charley U	24	N½SE	1901-03-23		A3
4047	" "	24	SENE	1901-03-23		A3
4048	" "	24	SESE	1901-03-23		A3
4053	GRANTHAM, Daniel	24	E½SW	1881-05-10		A3
4054	" "	24	NWSW	1881-05-10		A3
4055	" "	24	SWSE	1881-05-10		A3
4068	GRANTHAM, Elijah M	20	SESW	1911-11-20		A3
4147	GRANTHAM, John	25	N½SW	1861-05-01		A2
4148	" "	25	NESE	1895-12-14		A3
4149	" "	25	SENE	1895-12-14		A3
4150	" "	25	W½SE	1895-12-14		A3
4224	GRANTHAM, William	25	SWNW	1841-01-05		A2
4225	" "	26	E½NE	1846-09-01		A2
4223	" "	25	NWNW	1859-05-02		A2
4226	" "	26	SWNE	1859-05-02		A2
4185	GUNTER, Mary S	4	NWNE	1898-08-27		A3 G14
4186	GUNTER, Nathaniel	2	SE	1890-08-16		A3
4130	HALL, J Tom	5	SENE	1935-11-19		A3
4073	HARE, Elizabeth	26	SWSE	1851-10-01		A2
4044	HENSARLING, Catherine E	15	NENW	1893-04-12		A3 G18
4045	" "	15	W½NE	1893-04-12		A3 G18
4031	HERRING, Andrew J	28	NWSW	1918-04-11		A3
4040	HERRINGTON, Buford J	15	NESE	1905-05-02		A3
4118	HERRINGTON, Hubert	8	N½NE	1911-04-05		A3
4119	" "	8	SENE	1911-04-05		A3
4120	" "	9	NWNW	1911-04-05		A3
4165	HERRINGTON, Joseph	10	NESW	1890-08-16		A3
4166	" "	10	NWSE	1890-08-16		A3
4167	" "	10	SENW	1890-08-16		A3
4168	" "	10	SWNE	1890-08-16		A3
3992	HOLIFIELD, Alson	29	E½NW	1891-03-16		A3
3993	" "	29	NESW	1891-03-16		A3
3994	" "	29	NWSE	1891-03-16		A3
4155	JEFCOAT, John R	3	NESW	1894-02-17		A3
4156	" "	3	NWSE	1894-02-17		A3
4157	" "	3	SENW	1894-02-17		A3
4158	" "	3	SWNE	1894-02-17		A3
4197	JOHNSON, Samuel J	1	SENW	1889-04-23		A2
4067	JONES, Edward G	20	S½NW	1906-06-21		A3
4195	JONES, Rufus L	18	NESW	1896-12-14		A3
4196	" "	18	SENW	1896-12-14		A3
4229	JONES, William N	17	SE	1905-05-09		A3
4030	JORDAN, Amos T	17	NE	1895-02-21		A3
4049	JORDAN, Clark	33	N½SW	1892-07-25		A3
4050	" "	33	S½NW	1892-07-25		A3
4038	KIRKLAND, Benjamin L	34	W½SW	1892-05-16		A3
4069	KIRKLAND, Elijah T	27	E½NW	1889-01-12		A3
4070	" "	27	W½NE	1889-01-12		A3
4144	KIRKLAND, John Burruss	30	E½SE	1916-02-14		A3
4145	" "	30	SENE	1916-02-14		A3
4182	KIRKLAND, Martha	22	SESW	1896-12-14		A3
4183	" "	22	W½SW	1896-12-14		A3
4159	KNIGHT, John R	1	NESW	1897-02-15		A3
4160	" "	1	NWSE	1897-02-15		A3
4227	LANDRUM, William	36	W½NE	1890-08-16		A3
4228	" "	36	W½SE	1890-08-16		A3
4230	MCDONALD, William Perry	25	NENE	1912-10-11		A2
4185	MCGILL, Mary S	4	NWNE	1898-08-27		A3 G14
4043	MCKINLEY, Caroline	20	N½SE	1898-12-27		A3
4201	MCPHERSON, Alexander	31	S½SE	1884-12-30		A2 G3
4202	" "	31	SENW	1884-12-30		A2 G3
4203	" "	31	SWNE	1884-12-30		A2 G3
4204	" "	32	S½SE	1884-12-30		A2 G3
4205	" "	32	S½SW	1884-12-30		A2 G3
4201	MCPHERSON, Edward	31	S½SE	1884-12-30		A2 G3
4202	" "	31	SENW	1884-12-30		A2 G3
4203	" "	31	SWNE	1884-12-30		A2 G3

ID	Individual in Patent	Sec.	Sec. Part	Date Issued	Other Counties	For More Info . . .
4204	MCPHERSON, Edward (Cont'd)	32	S½SE	1884-12-30		A2 G3
4205	" "	32	S½SW	1884-12-30		A2 G3
4201	MCPHERSON, Martin	31	S½SE	1884-12-30		A2 G3
4202	" "	31	SENW	1884-12-30		A2 G3
4203	" "	31	SWNE	1884-12-30		A2 G3
4204	" "	32	S½SE	1884-12-30		A2 G3
4205	" "	32	S½SW	1884-12-30		A2 G3
4201	MCPHERSON, William	31	S½SE	1884-12-30		A2 G3
4202	" "	31	SENW	1884-12-30		A2 G3
4203	" "	31	SWNE	1884-12-30		A2 G3
4204	" "	32	S½SE	1884-12-30		A2 G3
4205	" "	32	S½SW	1884-12-30		A2 G3
4063	MELVIN, David	11	SESE	1875-08-20		A3
4066	" "	12	SWSW	1875-08-20		A3
4062	" "	11	NENE	1883-02-03		A2
4064	" "	12	NWSW	1897-11-22		A3
4065	" "	12	SWNW	1897-11-22		A3
4079	MELVIN, George W	2	E½NE	1889-12-19		A3
4080	" "	2	SWNE	1889-12-19		A3
4233	MELVIN, Willis C	1	W½SW	1892-04-29		A3
4234	" "	12	N½NW	1892-04-29		A3
4127	MERRITT, Isom A	29	NWSW	1916-11-09		A3
4140	MURFEY, James W	9	SESW	1895-12-14		A3
4141	" "	9	W½SE	1895-12-14		A3
4163	MURPHY, John W	22	SENW	1906-06-16		A3
4193	MURPHY, Ransy M	18	SWSE	1913-12-02		A3
4164	MYERS, John W	34	SESW	1854-03-15		A2 G29
4164	MYERS, Levi	34	SESW	1854-03-15		A2 G29
4198	NALL, David J	13	SESE	1905-08-05		A3 G32
4198	NALL, Sarah A	13	SESE	1905-08-05		A3 G32
4044	ODOM, Catherine E	15	NENW	1893-04-12		A3 G18
4045	" "	15	W½NE	1893-04-12		A3 G18
4180	ODOM, Margaret R	33	SESE	1885-05-09		A2
4077	PAGE, Franklin D	1	NENW	1889-11-29		A2
4170	PARKER, Little B	12	N½NE	1902-07-03		A3
4184	PARKER, Martin	11	W½NE	1883-05-25		A3
4190	PLOCK, Otto	6		1882-05-20		A2
4181	RAYNER, Margrett	5	NESE	1904-12-31		A3
4071	SCRIVNER, Elizabeth A	34	SE	1897-11-01		A3
4199	SHOLAR, Sherod H	24	E½NW	1890-02-21		A3
4200	" "	24	N½NE	1890-02-21		A3
3986	SHOWS, A G	12	SESW	1881-09-17		A3
3987	" "	12	SWSE	1881-09-17		A3
3988	SHOWS, Adam N	12	SESE	1895-02-21		A3
3989	" "	13	NENE	1895-02-21		A3
4052	SHOWS, Cornelius	13	E½NW	1844-09-27		A2
4059	SHOWS, Daniel J	12	N½SE	1890-03-28		A3
4060	" "	12	NESW	1890-03-28		A3
4061	" "	12	SENE	1890-03-28		A3
4101	SHOWS, Henry B	28	E½NE	1893-04-12		A3
4102	" "	28	NESE	1893-04-12		A3
4103	" "	28	SWNE	1893-04-12		A3
4115	SHOWS, Henry I	4	N½NW	1895-06-28		A3
4116	" "	4	NWSW	1895-06-28		A3
4117	" "	4	SWNW	1895-06-28		A3
4121	SHOWS, Isaac B	8	NENW	1891-06-30		A3
4122	" "	8	S½NW	1891-06-30		A3
4123	" "	8	SWSE	1891-06-30		A3 R4154
4124	SHOWS, Isaac Q	17	E½NW	1894-07-24		A2
4125	" "	17	NESW	1894-07-24		A2
4126	" "	17	NWNW	1894-07-24		A2
4135	SHOWS, James L	8	NESE	1883-05-25		A3
4136	" "	8	NWSE	1883-05-25		A3
4161	SHOWS, John	13	W½NW	1844-09-27		A2
4153	SHOWS, John M	8	SESW	1894-04-10		A3
4154	" "	8	SWSE	1894-04-10		A3 R4123
4174	SHOWS, Louisa	11	NESE	1889-12-19		A3
4175	" "	11	SENE	1889-12-19		A3
4176	" "	11	W½SE	1889-12-19		A3
4171	SHOWS, Louisa J	1	E½SE	1896-12-14		A3
4172	" "	1	SESW	1896-12-14		A3
4173	" "	1	SWSE	1896-12-14		A3
4191	SHOWS, Pleasant M	4	E½SW	1897-04-02		A3

ID	Individual in Patent	Sec.	Sec. Part	Date Issued	Other Counties	For More Info . . .
4192	SHOWS, Pleasant M (Cont'd)	4	W½SE	1897-04-02		A3
4231	SHOWS, William R	12	SENW	1899-07-15		A3
4232	"	12	SWNE	1899-07-15		A3
4164	STEVENS, William	34	SESW	1854-03-15		A2 G29
4056	STEVENSON, Daniel H	20	SESE	1891-05-20		A3
4057	" "	21	SWNW	1891-05-20		A3
4058	" "	21	W½SW	1891-05-20		A3
4138	STEVISON, James R	19	SESE	1896-10-31		A3
4139	" "	30	NENE	1896-10-31		A3
4035	STRICKLAND, Bedford S	17	NWSW	1906-01-30		A3
4036	" "	17	SWNW	1906-01-30		A3
4037	" "	18	SENE	1906-01-30		A3
4162	STRICKLAND, John T	1	NE	1895-02-21		A3
4189	STRINGER, Odius C	9	SENW	1939-02-06		A3
4078	SUMRALL, G B	10	S½SW	1881-09-17		A3
4151	SUMRALL, John H	15	S½SE	1892-04-29		A3
4152	" "	15	S½SW	1892-04-29		A3
4215	SUMRALL, Thomas V	27	E½NE	1861-05-01		A2
4212	" "	22	N½NE	1890-02-18		A3
4213	" "	22	NENW	1890-02-18		A3
4214	" "	22	SWNE	1890-02-18		A3
4083	TIPPIN, Guy	21	E½NW	1889-04-23		A2
4084	" "	21	NWNW	1889-04-23		A2
4085	" "	21	SE	1889-04-23		A2
4086	" "	21	SENE	1889-04-23		A2
4087	" "	21	SESW	1889-04-23		A2
4088	" "	21	W½NE	1889-04-23		A2
4089	" "	27	W½NW	1889-04-23		A2
4090	" "	29	NESE	1889-04-23		A2
4091	" "	29	SESW	1889-04-23		A2
4092	" "	29	W½NW	1889-04-23		A2
4093	" "	31	SESW	1889-04-23		A2
4094	" "	31	SWNW	1889-04-23		A2
4095	" "	31	W½SW	1889-04-23		A2
4096	" "	33	NESE	1889-04-23		A2
4097	" "	33	S½SW	1889-04-23		A2
4098	" "	33	SENE	1889-04-23		A2
4099	" "	33	W½NE	1889-04-23		A2
4100	" "	33	W½SE	1889-04-23		A2
4194	WALL, Robert W	27	SE	1906-06-16		A3
4081	WALTERS, George W	36	E½NW	1892-06-15		A3 R4169
4082	" "	36	E½SE	1892-06-15		A3
4177	WARD, Luther O	4	NESE	1897-09-09		A3
4178	" "	4	S½NE	1897-09-09		A3
4179	" "	4	SENW	1897-09-09		A3
3995	WATSON, Amasa B	18	N½NE	1883-09-15		A2
3996	" "	18	N½NW	1883-09-15		A2
3997	" "	18	N½SE	1883-09-15		A2
3998	" "	18	SESE	1883-09-15		A2
3999	" "	18	SESW	1883-09-15		A2
4000	" "	18	SWNE	1883-09-15		A2
4001	" "	18	SWNW	1883-09-15		A2
4002	" "	18	W½SW	1883-09-15		A2
4003	" "	19	NENE	1883-09-15		A2
4004	" "	19	NESE	1883-09-15		A2
4005	" "	19	W½	1883-09-15		A2
4006	" "	19	W½NE	1883-09-15		A2
4007	" "	19	W½SE	1883-09-15		A2
4008	" "	20	NWNW	1883-09-15		A2
4009	" "	20	SWSW	1883-09-15		A2
4010	" "	28	S½SW	1883-09-15		A2
4011	" "	29	S½SE	1883-09-15		A2
4012	" "	29	SWSW	1883-09-15		A2
4013	" "	30	W½	1883-09-15		A2
4014	" "	30	W½NE	1883-09-15		A2
4015	" "	30	W½SE	1883-09-15		A2
4016	" "	31	N½NE	1883-09-15		A2
4017	" "	31	N½NW	1883-09-15		A2
4018	" "	31	NESE	1883-09-15		A2
4019	" "	31	SENE	1883-09-15		A2
4020	" "	32	N½	1883-09-15		A2
4021	" "	32	N½SE	1883-09-15		A2
4022	" "	32	N½SW	1883-09-15		A2

ID	Individual in Patent	Sec.	Sec. Part	Date Issued	Other Counties	For More Info . . .
4023	WATSON, Amasa B (Cont'd)	33	N½NW	1883-09-15		A2
4024	" "	7	NWSE	1883-09-15		A2
4025	" "	7	S½NE	1883-09-15		A2
4026	" "	7	S½NW	1883-09-15		A2
4027	" "	7	S½SE	1883-09-15		A2
4028	" "	7	SW	1883-09-15		A2
4029	" "	8	W½SW	1883-09-15		A2
4219	WEEKS, Washington A	7	NESE	1898-12-27		A3
4169	WISE, Josiah	36	E½NW	1914-05-28		A3 R4081
4206	WOODARD, Thomas G	13	NESE	1891-03-16		A3
4207	" "	13	SENE	1891-03-16		A3
4208	" "	13	W½NE	1891-03-16		A3
4051	YAWN, Cornealous J	27	SW	1889-01-12		A3
4216	YAWN, Vincent C	28	E½NE	1896-12-14		A3
4217	" "	28	NWNE	1896-12-14		A3
4218	" "	28	NWNW	1896-12-14		A3

Patent Map

T6-N R12-W
St Stephens Meridian

Map Group 23

Township Statistics

Parcels Mapped	:	252
Number of Patents	:	117
Number of Individuals	:	113
Patentees Identified	:	103
Number of Surnames	:	64
Multi-Patentee Parcels	:	12
Oldest Patent Date	:	1/5/1841
Most Recent Patent	:	2/6/1939
Block/Lot Parcels	:	0
Parcels Re - Issued	:	2
Parcels that Overlap	:	0
Cities and Towns	:	1
Cemeteries	:	7

The map grid:

Section 6
PLOCK Otto 1882

Section 5
FERGUSON Fergus 1896 | FERGUSON Fergus 1896 | FERGUSON Fergus 1896 | FURR William B 1899
FURR William B 1899 | HALL J Tom 1935
RAYNER Margrett 1904
FERGUSON Willis 1896 | FERGUSON Willis 1896

Section 4
SHOWS Henry I 1895 | GUNTER [14] Mary S 1898 | CARTER Asa G 1896
SHOWS Henry I 1895 | WARD Luther O 1897 | WARD Luther O 1897
SHOWS Henry I 1895 | SHOWS Pleasant M 1897 | WARD Luther O 1897
SHOWS Pleasant M 1897 | CROMWELL Thomas J 1906

Section 7
FERGUSON Norman 1892 | FERGUSON Norman 1892
WATSON Amasa B 1883 | WATSON Amasa B 1883
WATSON Amasa B 1883 | WEEKS Washington A 1898
WATSON Amasa B 1883 | WATSON Amasa B 1883

Section 8
FERGUSON Willis 1896 | SHOWS Isaac B 1891 | HERRINGTON Hubert 1911
SHOWS Isaac B 1891 | HERRINGTON Hubert 1911
WATSON Amasa B 1883 | SHOWS James L 1883 | SHOWS John M 1894 | SHOWS Isaac B 1891

Section 9
HERRINGTON Hubert 1911 | CROMWELL Thomas J 1906
COLLINS Henry C 1890 | STRINGER Odius C 1939
SHOWS James L 1883 | COLLINS Henry C 1890 | COLLINS Henry C 1890 | MURFEY James W 1895
MURFEY James W 1895 | COLLINS Henry C 1887

Section 18
WATSON Amasa B 1883 | WATSON Amasa B 1883
WATSON Amasa B 1883 | JONES Rufus L 1896 | WATSON Amasa B 1883 | STRICKLAND Bedford S 1906
JONES Rufus L 1896 | WATSON Amasa B 1883 | STRICKLAND Bedford S 1906
WATSON Amasa B 1883 | WATSON Amasa B 1883 | MURPHY Ransy M 1913 | WATSON Amasa B 1883

Section 17
SHOWS Isaac Q 1894 | SHOWS Isaac Q 1894
STRICKLAND Bedford S 1906 | JORDAN Amos T 1895
SHOWS Isaac Q 1894 | JONES William N 1905

Section 16

Section 19
WATSON Amasa B 1883 | WATSON Amasa B 1883
WATSON Amasa B 1883

Section 20
WATSON Amasa B 1883 | WATSON Amasa B 1883
JONES Edward G 1906
WATSON Amasa B 1883 | STEVISON James R 1896 | WATSON Amasa B 1883 | GRANTHAM Elijah M 1911
MCKINLEY Caroline 1898 | STEVENSON Daniel H 1891

Section 21
EASTERLING Elizabeth 1914 | TIPPIN Guy 1889 | TIPPIN Guy 1889
TIPPIN Guy 1889 | TIPPIN Guy 1889
STEVENSON Daniel H 1891 | TIPPIN Guy 1889
STEVENSON Daniel H 1891 | TIPPIN Guy 1889

Section 30
WATSON Amasa B 1883 | WATSON Amasa B 1883 | STEVISON James R 1896
KIRKLAND John Burruss 1916
WATSON Amasa B 1883 | KIRKLAND John Burruss 1916

Section 29
TIPPIN Guy 1889 | HOLIFIELD Alson 1891
MERRITT Isom A 1916 | HOLIFIELD Alson 1891 | HOLIFIELD Alson 1891 | TIPPIN Guy 1889
WATSON Amasa B 1883 | TIPPIN Guy 1889 | WATSON Amasa B 1883

Section 28
YAWN Vincent C 1896 | YAWN Vincent C 1896 | SHOWS Henry B 1893
YAWN Vincent C 1896 | SHOWS Henry B 1893
HERRING Andrew J 1918 | SHOWS Henry B 1893
WATSON Amasa B 1883

Section 31
WATSON Amasa B 1883 | WATSON Amasa B 1883
TIPPIN Guy 1889 | BIRKETT [3] Thomas 1884 | BIRKETT [3] Thomas 1884 | WATSON Amasa B 1883
CREEL Burton 1861 | CREEL Burton 1861 | WATSON Amasa B 1883
TIPPIN Guy 1889 | TIPPIN Guy 1889 | BIRKETT [3] Thomas 1884

Section 32
WATSON Amasa B 1883
WATSON Amasa B 1883 | WATSON Amasa B 1883
BIRKETT [3] Thomas 1884 | BIRKETT [3] Thomas 1884

Section 33
WATSON Amasa B 1883 | TIPPIN Guy 1889
JORDAN Clark 1892 | TIPPIN Guy 1889
JORDAN Clark 1892 | TIPPIN Guy 1889
TIPPIN Guy 1889 | TIPPIN Guy 1889 | ODOM Margaret R 1885

CARTER Asa G 1896	CARTER Asa G 1896	FREEMAN John 1895			BRADLEY Alex W 1911		BRADLEY James M 1897	PAGE Franklin D 1889	STRICKLAND John T 1895

3 — JEFCOAT John R 1894 / JEFCOAT John R 1894 / JEFCOAT John R 1894 / JEFCOAT John R 1894 / BOUTWELL James A 1884 / BOUTWELL James A 1884

MELVIN George W 1889 / MELVIN George W 1889

2 — GUNTER Nathaniel 1890

1 — JOHNSON Samuel J 1889

MELVIN Willis C 1892 / KNIGHT John R 1897 / KNIGHT John R 1897 / SHOWS Louisa J 1896 / SHOWS Louisa J 1896 / SHOWS Louisa J 1896

CROMWELL Thomas J 1906 / BOUTWELL James A 1884 / BOUTWELL James A 1884

10 — HERRINGTON Joseph 1890 / HERRINGTON Joseph 1890 / HERRINGTON Joseph 1890 / HERRINGTON Joseph 1890 / SUMRALL G B 1881

11 — PARKER Martin 1883 / SHOWS Louisa 1889 / SHOWS Louisa 1889 / MELVIN David 1875

MELVIN David 1883

12 — MELVIN Willis C 1892 / PARKER Little B 1902 / MELVIN David 1897 / SHOWS William R 1899 / SHOWS William R 1899 / SHOWS Daniel J 1890 / MELVIN David 1897 / SHOWS Daniel J 1890 / SHOWS Daniel J 1890 / MELVIN David 1875 / SHOWS A G 1881 / SHOWS A G 1881 / SHOWS Adam N 1895

HENSARLING [18] Catherine E 1893 / HENSARLING [18] Catherine E 1893

COLLINS J J 1881 / COLLINS J J 1881 / GRANTHAM Albert G 1884

15 — HERRINGTON Buford J 1905 / SUMRALL John H 1892 / SUMRALL John H 1892

14

13 — SHOWS John 1844 / SHOWS Cornelius 1844 / WOODARD Thomas G 1891 / SHOWS Adam N 1895 / WOODARD Thomas G 1891 / WOODARD Thomas G 1891 / ANDERSON Henry H 1859 / ANDERSON Henry H 1859 / NALL [32] Sarah A 1905

SUMRALL Thomas V 1890 / SUMRALL Thomas V 1890 / MURPHY John W 1906 / SUMRALL Thomas V 1890

23

24 — ANDERSON Henry H 1859 / SHOLAR Sherod H 1890 / SHOLAR Sherod H 1890 / GRANTHAM Charley U 1901 / GRANTHAM Daniel 1881 / GRANTHAM Charley U 1901 / GRANTHAM Daniel 1881 / GRANTHAM Daniel 1881 / GRANTHAM Charley U 1901

22 — KIRKLAND Martha 1896 / KIRKLAND Martha 1896

BARLOW [2] Henry 1846 / BARLOW [2] Henry 1846 / BARLOW Henry 1854 / BARLOW Henry 1854

27 — TIPPIN Guy 1889 / KIRKLAND Elijah T 1889 / KIRKLAND Elijah T 1889 / SUMRALL Thomas V 1861 / YAWN Cornealous J 1889 / WALL Robert W 1906

26 — GRANTHAM William 1846 / GRANTHAM William 1859 / HARE Elizabeth 1851

25 — GRANTHAM William 1859 / GRANTHAM William 1841 / GRANTHAM John 1861 / GRANTHAM John 1895 / EASTERLING John A 1861 / MCDONALD William Perry 1912 / GRANTHAM John 1895 / GRANTHAM John 1895 / BEARD John A 1905

34

35 — GRANTHAM Bryant 1882

36 — WALTERS George W 1892 / WISE Josiah 1914 / LANDRUM William 1890 / LANDRUM William 1890 / WALTERS George W 1892

KIRKLAND Benjamin L 1892 / CLARK William C 1917 / MYERS [29] John W 1854 / SCRIVNER Elizabeth A 1897

Helpful Hints

1. This Map's INDEX can be found on the preceding pages.

2. Refer to Map "C" to see where this Township lies within Jones County, Mississippi.

3. Numbers within square brackets [ ] denote a multi-patentee land parcel (multi-owner). Refer to Appendix "C" for a full list of members in this group.

4. Areas that look to be crowded with Patentees usually indicate multiple sales of the same parcel (Re-issues) or Overlapping parcels. See this Township's Index for an explanation of these and other circumstances that might explain "odd" groupings of Patentees on this map.

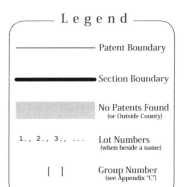

Legend

————	Patent Boundary
▬▬▬▬	Section Boundary
▒▒▒▒	No Patents Found (or Outside County)
1., 2., 3., ...	Lot Numbers (when beside a name)
[ ]	Group Number (see Appendix "C")

Scale: Section = 1 mile X 1 mile (generally, with some exceptions)

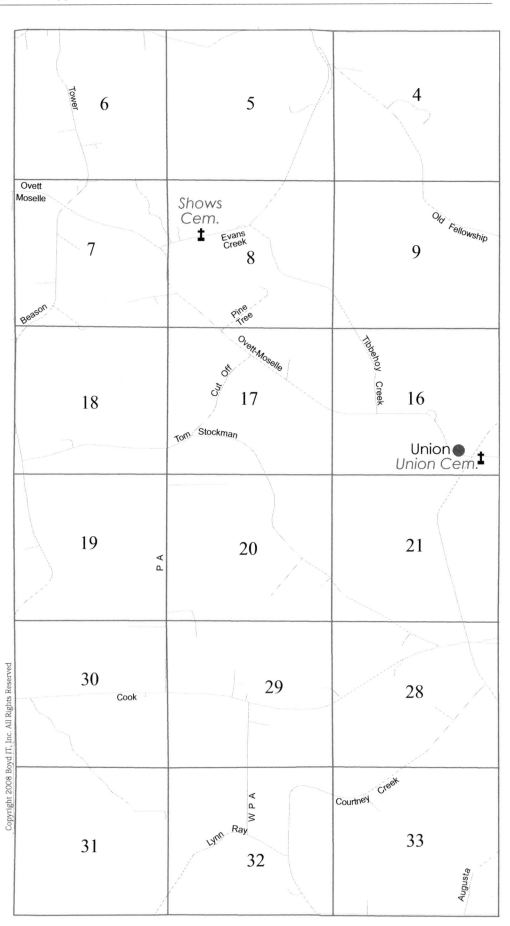

Road Map

T6-N R12-W
St Stephens Meridian

Map Group 23

Cities & Towns
Union

Cemeteries
Coltins Cemetery
Jordan Cemetery
Kirland Cemetery
Murphy Cemetery
Shows Cemetery
Union Cemetery
Walters Cemetery

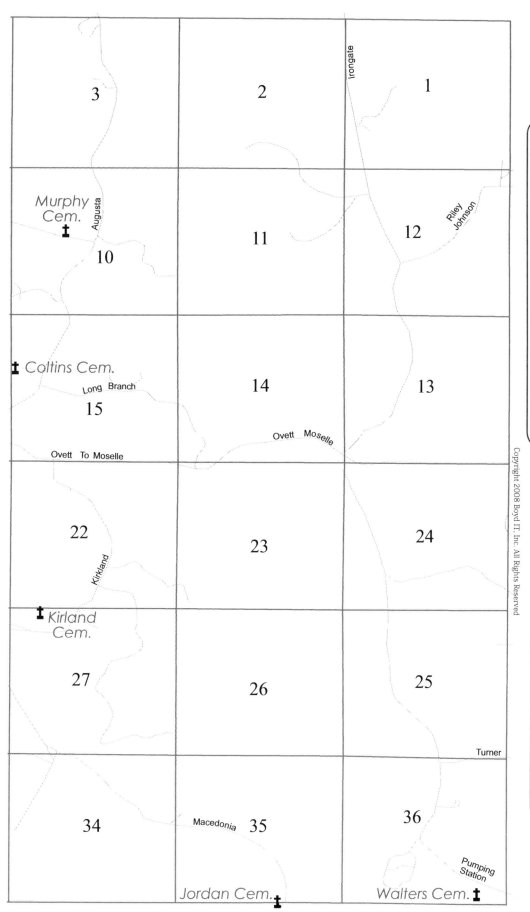

		Irongate
3	2	1

Murphy Cem. ♱ Augusta

Riley Johnson

10	11	12

♱ Coltins Cem.

Long Branch

15	14	13

Ovett Moselle

Ovett To Moselle

22	23	24

Kirkland

♱ Kirland Cem.

27	26	25

Turner

34	Macedonia 35	36

Jordan Cem. ♱

Walters Cem. ♱

Pumping Station

Helpful Hints

1. This road map has a number of uses, but primarily it is to help you: a) find the present location of land owned by your ancestors (at least the general area), b) find cemeteries and city-centers, and c) estimate the route/roads used by Census-takers & tax-assessors.

2. If you plan to travel to Jones County to locate cemeteries or land parcels, please pick up a modern travel map for the area before you do. Mapping old land parcels on modern maps is not as exact a science as you might think. Just the slightest variations in public land survey coordinates, estimates of parcel boundaries, or road-map deviations can greatly alter a map's representation of how a road either does or doesn't cross a particular parcel of land.

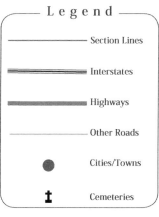

L e g e n d

———————	Section Lines
━━━━━━━	Interstates
▬▬▬▬▬▬	Highways
———————	Other Roads
●	Cities/Towns
♱	Cemeteries

Scale: Section = 1 mile X 1 mile
(generally, with some exceptions)

241

Historical Map

T6-N R12-W
St Stephens Meridian

Map Group 23

Cities & Towns
Union

Cemeteries
Coltins Cemetery
Jordan Cemetery
Kirland Cemetery
Murphy Cemetery
Shows Cemetery
Union Cemetery
Walters Cemetery

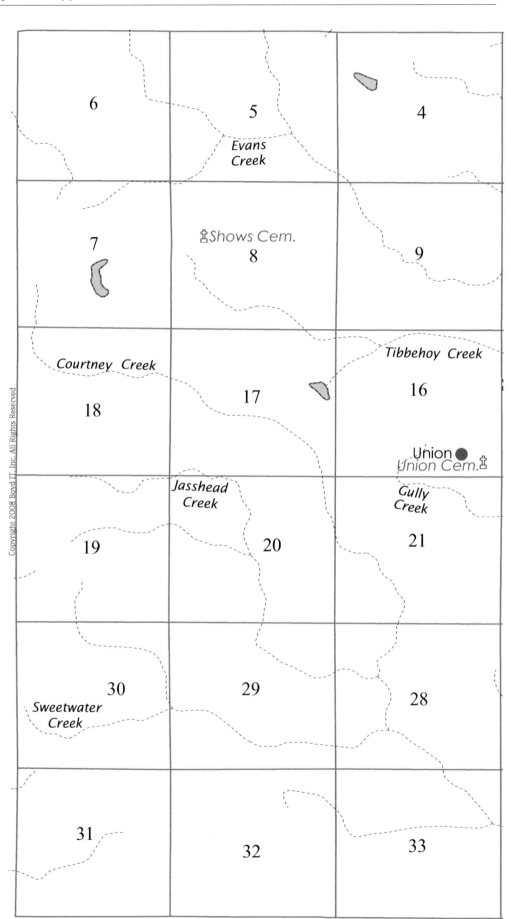

6

5

4

Evans
Creek

7

⚱Shows Cem.
8

9

Courtney Creek

Tibbehoy Creek

18

17

16

Union ●
Union Cem. ⚱

Jasshead
Creek

Gully
Creek

19

20

21

30

29

28

Sweetwater
Creek

31

32

33

Copyright 2008 Boyd IT, Inc. All Rights Reserved

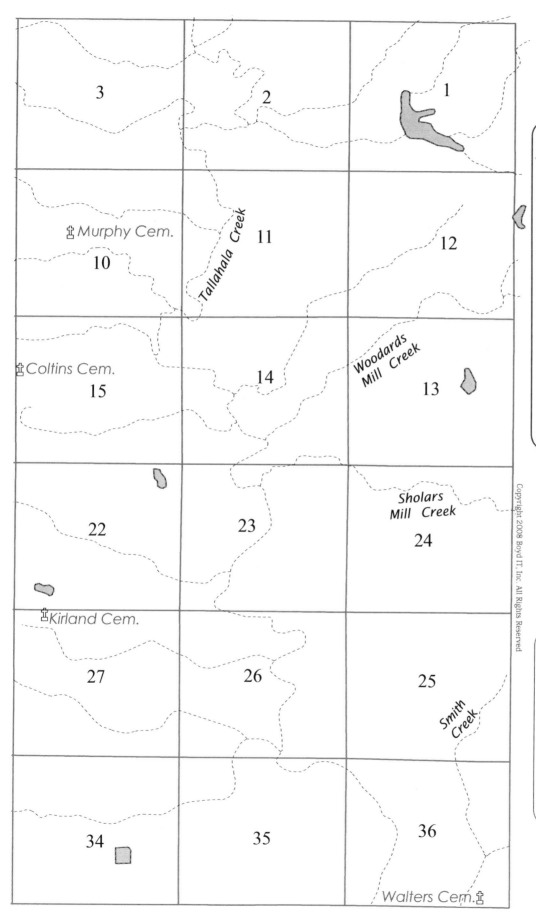

3

2

1

✝ Murphy Cem.

10

Tallahala Creek

11

12

✝ Coltins Cem.

15

14

Woodards Mill Creek

13

22

23

Sholars Mill Creek

24

✝ Kirland Cem.

27

26

25

Smith Creek

34

35

36

Walters Cem. ✝

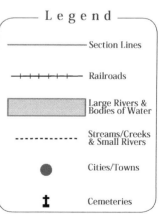

Legend

——————— Section Lines

++++++++ Railroads

�⬛ Large Rivers & Bodies of Water

- - - - - Streams/Creeks & Small Rivers

● Cities/Towns

✝ Cemeteries

Scale: Section = 1 mile X 1 mile
(there are some exceptions)

Map Group 24: Index to Land Patents

Township 6-North Range 11-West (St Stephens)

After you locate an individual in this Index, take note of the Section and Section Part then proceed to the Land Patent map on the pages immediately following. You should have no difficulty locating the corresponding parcel of land.

The "For More Info" Column will lead you to more information about the underlying Patents. See the *Legend* at right, and the "How to Use this Book" chapter, for more information.

```
┌─────────────────────────────────────────────────────┐
│                      LEGEND                            │
│            "For More Info . . . " column               │
│  A = Authority (Legislative Act, See Appendix "A")     │
│  B = Block or Lot (location in Section unknown)        │
│  C = Cancelled Patent                                  │
│  F = Fractional Section                                │
│  G = Group  (Multi-Patentee Patent, see Appendix "C")  │
│  V = Overlaps another Parcel                           │
│  R = Re-Issued (Parcel patented more than once)        │
│                                                        │
│  (A & G items require you to look in the Appendixes referred │
│  to above. All other Letter-designations followed by a number │
│  require you to locate line-items in this index that possess │
│  the ID number found after the letter).                │
└─────────────────────────────────────────────────────┘
```

ID	Individual in Patent	Sec.	Sec. Part	Date Issued	Other Counties	For More Info . . .
4352	AGNEW, George Samuel	24	NWSE	1926-02-27		A3
4400	BEECH, Joseph B	8	N½SE	1889-01-12		A3
4401	" "	8	NESW	1889-01-12		A3
4402	" "	8	SWNE	1889-01-12		A3
4430	BIRKETT, Thomas	17	SESW	1884-12-30		A2 G3
4431	" "	17	SWSE	1884-12-30		A2 G3
4432	" "	17	SWSW	1884-12-30		A2 G3
4433	" "	23	SESE	1884-12-30		A2 G3
4434	" "	24	NWSW	1884-12-30		A2 G3
4435	" "	24	SWSW	1884-12-30		A2 G3
4436	" "	25	NWNW	1884-12-30		A2 G3
4437	" "	26	N½NE	1884-12-30		A2 G3
4438	" "	26	W½NW	1884-12-30		A2 G3
4340	BROWN, Elias	11	SWSE	1859-05-02		A2
4341	" "	35	E½NW	1859-06-01		A2
4342	BROWN, Elihu	36	NESE	1859-05-02		A2
4343	" "	36	SENE	1859-05-02		A2
4345	BROWN, Elisha	14	N½NE	1859-06-01		A2
4399	BROWN, John W	36	SWNW	1905-02-13		A3
4415	BROWN, Mark	36	SWSE	1859-05-02		A2
4413	" "	36	E½SW	1861-05-01		A2
4414	" "	36	NWSE	1861-05-01		A2
4416	CAMPBELL, Mary	34	NESW	1904-12-31		A3
4417	" "	34	SENW	1904-12-31		A3
4373	CARLTON, James	22	NESE	1896-09-16		A3
4374	" "	23	NESW	1896-09-16		A3
4375	" "	23	W½SW	1896-09-16		A3
4239	CHAPMAN, Albert	29	NWSW	1902-07-03		A3
4403	CHAPMAN, Joseph C	20	SENE	1905-10-19		A3
4241	COOLEY, Albert S	35	N½SE	1896-02-13		A3
4242	" "	35	NESW	1896-02-13		A3
4243	" "	36	NWSW	1896-02-13		A3
4244	COOLEY, Allen	33	SWNE	1902-07-03		A3
4388	COOLEY, John	30	SWSE	1902-07-03		A3
4446	CURTIS, William	18	NWNE	1902-12-30		A3
4379	DONALD, James	36	NENE	1859-05-02		A2
4363	EASTERLING, Henry B	28	N½SE	1898-08-27		A3
4364	" "	28	SWNE	1898-08-27		A3
4387	EASTERLING, John A	33	SESE	1899-11-24		A3 .
4386	GRANISON, Joe	27	SWNW	1906-05-01		A2
4349	HERRINGTON, Francis M	34	NENE	1906-05-01		A3
4370	HERRINGTON, Houston	25	SESE	1915-03-22		A3
4245	HINTON, Alletha	5	NWNW	1889-01-12		A3
4246	" "	5	S½NW	1889-01-12		A3
4247	" "	6	NENE	1889-01-12		A3
4439	HOLLIMON, Thomas R	26	E½NW	1893-02-28		A3

ID	Individual in Patent	Sec.	Sec. Part	Date Issued	Other Counties	For More Info . . .
4440	HOLLIMON, Thomas R (Cont'd)	26	N½SW	1893-02-28		A3
4298	JOHNSON, William E	10	E½SW	1889-04-20		A2 G41
4299	" "	10	SE	1889-04-20		A2 G41
4300	" "	10	SWSW	1889-04-20		A2 G41
4301	" "	15	NENE	1889-04-20		A2 G41
4302	" "	15	W½	1889-04-20		A2 G41
4303	" "	15	W½NE	1889-04-20		A2 G41
4304	" "	15	W½SE	1889-04-20		A2 G41
4305	" "	22	E½SW	1889-04-20		A2 G41
4306	" "	22	N½	1889-04-20		A2 G41
4307	" "	22	SESE	1889-04-20		A2 G41
4308	" "	22	SWSW	1889-04-20		A2 G41
4309	" "	22	W½SE	1889-04-20		A2 G41
4310	" "	23	NW	1889-04-20		A2 G41
4311	" "	23	W½NE	1889-04-20		A2 G41
4312	" "	27	NWNW	1889-04-20		A2 G41
4313	" "	28	E½NE	1889-04-20		A2 G41
4314	" "	4	SESW	1889-04-20		A2 G41
4315	" "	4	W½SW	1889-04-20		A2 G41
4316	" "	5	NENW	1889-04-20		A2 G41
4317	" "	5	S½NE	1889-04-20		A2 G41
4318	" "	5	SE	1889-04-20		A2 G41
4319	" "	7	E½NE	1889-04-20		A2 G41 V4366, 4368
4320	" "	8	E½NE	1889-04-20		A2 G41
4321	" "	8	S½SE	1889-04-20		A2 G41
4322	" "	8	SENW	1889-04-20		A2 G41
4323	" "	8	SESW	1889-04-20		A2 G41
4324	" "	8	W½NW	1889-04-20		A2 G41
4325	" "	8	W½SW	1889-04-20		A2 G41
4326	" "	9	NENW	1889-04-20		A2 G41
4327	" "	9	S½SW	1889-04-20		A2 G41
4328	" "	9	SENE	1889-04-20		A2 G41
4329	" "	9	SESE	1889-04-20		A2 G41
4330	" "	9	W½NE	1889-04-20		A2 G41
4331	" "	9	W½SE	1889-04-20		A2 G41
4421	LANDRUM, Pinkney H	3	N½NE	1896-09-16		A3
4447	LAWSON, William H	19	S½NW	1906-04-14		A3
4448	" "	19	SWNE	1906-04-14		A3
4353	LOFTIN, George Washington	23	SENE	1915-05-18		A3
4405	MCADAMS, Larkin I	14	SWNE	1911-02-23		A2
4294	MCDONALD, Bryant L	11	SWNE	1912-09-05		A2
4450	MCGILBERRY, William	13	SW	1859-11-10		A2
4451	" "	14	NESE	1859-11-10		A2
4452	" "	24	NENW	1859-11-10		A2
4453	MCGILVERRY, William	14	SENE	1860-07-02		A2
4290	MCGILVRAY, Angus	24	NWNW	1895-02-21		A3
4291	" "	24	S½NW	1895-02-21		A3
4289	" "	24	NESW	1895-06-27		A3
4469	MCGILVRAY, William T	14	SESE	1898-11-11		A3
4470	" "	14	W½SE	1898-11-11		A3
4471	" "	23	NENE	1898-11-11		A3
4472	MCGILVRAY, William W	27	SWSW	1890-06-25		A3
4473	" "	28	S½SE	1890-06-25		A3
4474	" "	33	NWNE	1890-06-25		A3
4360	MCKAY, Henry A	23	N½SE	1898-12-01		A3
4361	" "	23	SESW	1898-12-01		A3
4362	" "	23	SWSE	1898-12-01		A3
4354	MCMANUS, Green	10	SENE	1907-07-13		A3
4430	MCPHERSON, Alexander	17	SESW	1884-12-30		A2 G3
4431	" "	17	SWSE	1884-12-30		A2 G3
4432	" "	17	SWSW	1884-12-30		A2 G3
4433	" "	23	SESE	1884-12-30		A2 G3
4434	" "	24	NWSW	1884-12-30		A2 G3
4435	" "	24	SWSW	1884-12-30		A2 G3
4436	" "	25	NWNW	1884-12-30		A2 G3
4437	" "	26	N½NE	1884-12-30		A2 G3
4438	" "	26	W½NE	1884-12-30		A2 G3
4454	" "	11	S½NW	1889-04-23		A2 G27
4455	" "	11	SW	1889-04-23		A2 G27
4456	" "	19	N½SW	1889-04-23		A2 G27
4457	" "	19	NESE	1889-04-23		A2 G27
4458	" "	3	NW	1889-04-23		A2 G27
4459	" "	3	S½NE	1889-04-23		A2 G27

ID	Individual in Patent	Sec.	Sec. Part	Date Issued	Other Counties	For More Info . . .
4460	MCPHERSON, Alexander (Cont'd)	33	NESE	1889-04-23		A2 G27
4461	"	33	SENE	1889-04-23		A2 G27
4462	"	34	SESW	1889-04-23		A2 G27
4463	"	34	SWNW	1889-04-23		A2 G27
4464	"	34	W½SW	1889-04-23		A2 G27
4465	"	4	NESW	1889-04-23		A2 G27
4466	"	4	S½NE	1889-04-23		A2 G27
4467	"	5	N½NE	1889-04-23		A2 G27
4468	"	9	NENE	1889-04-23		A2 G27
4430	MCPHERSON, Edward	17	SESW	1884-12-30		A2 G3
4431	"	17	SWSE	1884-12-30		A2 G3
4432	"	17	SWSW	1884-12-30		A2 G3
4433	"	23	SESE	1884-12-30		A2 G3
4434	"	24	NWSW	1884-12-30		A2 G3
4435	"	24	SWSW	1884-12-30		A2 G3
4436	"	25	NWNW	1884-12-30		A2 G3
4437	"	26	N½NE	1884-12-30		A2 G3
4438	"	26	W½NW	1884-12-30		A2 G3
4454	MCPHERSON, Edward G	11	S½NW	1889-04-23		A2 G27
4455	"	11	SW	1889-04-23		A2 G27
4456	"	19	N½SW	1889-04-23		A2 G27
4457	"	19	NESE	1889-04-23		A2 G27
4458	"	3	NW	1889-04-23		A2 G27
4459	"	3	S½NE	1889-04-23		A2 G27
4460	"	33	NESE	1889-04-23		A2 G27
4461	"	33	SENE	1889-04-23		A2 G27
4462	"	34	SESW	1889-04-23		A2 G27
4463	"	34	SWNW	1889-04-23		A2 G27
4464	"	34	W½SW	1889-04-23		A2 G27
4465	"	4	NESW	1889-04-23		A2 G27
4466	"	4	S½NE	1889-04-23		A2 G27
4467	"	5	N½NE	1889-04-23		A2 G27
4468	"	9	NENE	1889-04-23		A2 G27
4430	MCPHERSON, Martin	17	SESW	1884-12-30		A2 G3
4431	"	17	SWSE	1884-12-30		A2 G3
4432	"	17	SWSW	1884-12-30		A2 G3
4433	"	23	SESE	1884-12-30		A2 G3
4434	"	24	NWSW	1884-12-30		A2 G3
4435	"	24	SWSW	1884-12-30		A2 G3
4436	"	25	NWNW	1884-12-30		A2 G3
4437	"	26	N½NE	1884-12-30		A2 G3
4438	"	26	W½NW	1884-12-30		A2 G3
4454	MCPHERSON, Martin J	11	S½NW	1889-04-23		A2 G27
4455	"	11	SW	1889-04-23		A2 G27
4456	"	19	N½SW	1889-04-23		A2 G27
4457	"	19	NESE	1889-04-23		A2 G27
4458	"	3	NW	1889-04-23		A2 G27
4459	"	3	S½NE	1889-04-23		A2 G27
4460	"	33	NESE	1889-04-23		A2 G27
4461	"	33	SENE	1889-04-23		A2 G27
4462	"	34	SESW	1889-04-23		A2 G27
4463	"	34	SWNW	1889-04-23		A2 G27
4464	"	34	W½SW	1889-04-23		A2 G27
4465	"	4	NESW	1889-04-23		A2 G27
4466	"	4	S½NE	1889-04-23		A2 G27
4467	"	5	N½NE	1889-04-23		A2 G27
4468	"	9	NENE	1889-04-23		A2 G27
4430	MCPHERSON, William	17	SESW	1884-12-30		A2 G3
4431	"	17	SWSE	1884-12-30		A2 G3
4432	"	17	SWSW	1884-12-30		A2 G3
4433	"	23	SESE	1884-12-30		A2 G3
4434	"	24	NWSW	1884-12-30		A2 G3
4435	"	24	SWSW	1884-12-30		A2 G3
4436	"	25	NWNW	1884-12-30		A2 G3
4437	"	26	N½NE	1884-12-30		A2 G3
4438	"	26	W½NW	1884-12-30		A2 G3
4454	"	11	S½NW	1889-04-23		A2 G27
4455	"	11	SW	1889-04-23		A2 G27
4456	"	19	N½SW	1889-04-23		A2 G27
4457	"	19	NESE	1889-04-23		A2 G27
4458	"	3	NW	1889-04-23		A2 G27
4459	"	3	S½NE	1889-04-23		A2 G27
4460	"	33	NESE	1889-04-23		A2 G27

ID	Individual in Patent	Sec.	Sec. Part	Date Issued	Other Counties	For More Info . . .
4461	MCPHERSON, William (Cont'd)	33	SENE	1889-04-23		A2 G27
4462	" "	34	SESW	1889-04-23		A2 G27
4463	" "	34	SWNW	1889-04-23		A2 G27
4464	" "	34	W½SW	1889-04-23		A2 G27
4465	" "	4	NESW	1889-04-23		A2 G27
4466	" "	4	S½NE	1889-04-23		A2 G27
4467	" "	5	N½NE	1889-04-23		A2 G27
4468	" "	9	NENE	1889-04-23		A2 G27
4445	MORGAN, Walter	15	SENE	1909-07-06		A2
4337	NOBLES, Edmond A	17	E½SE	1892-09-09		A3
4338	" "	17	NWSE	1892-09-09		A3
4339	" "	17	SENE	1892-09-09		A3
4371	NOBLES, J E	20	SESE	1901-08-12		A3
4372	" "	29	NENE	1901-08-12		A3
4382	NOBLES, James M	30	SW	1899-11-24		A3
4385	NOBLES, Jasper J	32	NWNE	1906-05-01		A3
4389	NOBLES, John F	29	SESE	1899-05-31		A3
4390	" "	29	W½SE	1899-05-31		A3
4391	" "	32	NENE	1899-05-31		A3
4346	ODOM, Ezekiel C	6	E½NW	1895-02-21		A3
4347	" "	6	NESW	1895-02-21		A3
4348	" "	6	NWSE	1895-02-21		A3
4418	ODOM, Melton A	6	SESW	1899-04-28		A3
4419	" "	6	SWNW	1899-04-28		A3
4420	" "	6	W½SW	1899-04-28		A3
4350	OVERSTREET, George	2	E½NW	1895-02-21		A3
4351	" "	2	SWNW	1895-02-21		A3
4240	PARKER, Albert G	7	SWNE	1894-07-24		A2
4441	PARKER, Walden L	6	E½SE	1894-04-14		A3
4442	" "	6	SWSE	1894-04-14		A3
4443	" "	7	NWNE	1894-04-14		A3 V4366
4406	PRESCOTT, Lewis B	21	NESW	1860-10-01		A2
4407	" "	21	NWSE	1860-10-01		A2
4366	RAMSEY, Henry	7	N½NE	1904-08-30		A3 V4319, 4443
4367	" "	7	NENW	1904-08-30		A3 V4393
4368	" "	7	SENE	1904-08-30		A3 V4319
4404	REAVES, Joseph H	6	SWNE	1859-05-02		A2
4376	ROUNSAVILL, James D	29	E½SW	1898-12-27		A3
4377	" "	29	SENW	1898-12-27		A3
4378	" "	29	SWNE	1898-12-27		A3
4449	SCANLAN, William J	6	NWNW	1905-03-30		A3
4344	SHOEMAKE, Elijah L	34	SESE	1906-05-23		A3
4365	SHOEMAKE, Henry J	35	SWNW	1911-01-05		A3
4425	SHOEMAKE, Robert	34	NESE	1891-05-20		A3
4426	" "	34	SENE	1891-05-20		A3
4427	" "	34	W½NE	1891-05-20		A3
4238	SHOWS, Adam N	7	S½SW	1895-02-21		A3
4248	SHOWS, Almedia	17	NENE	1906-06-16		A3
4392	SHOWS, John F	21	NESE	1904-08-30		A3
4444	SHOWS, Walter C	36	SESE	1901-10-01		A3
4359	SMITH, Harvey J	33	NENE	1906-05-01		A3
4475	STEPHENS, Zack T	25	SWNW	1896-04-11		A2
4476	" "	26	NWSE	1896-04-11		A2
4477	" "	26	S½NE	1896-04-11		A2
4369	SUMRALL, Henry	12	S½NE	1859-06-01		A2
4393	SUMRALL, John F	7	NW	1890-08-16		A3 V4367
4394	THOMSON, John K	24	SESE	1902-01-17		A3
4395	" "	25	NENE	1902-01-17		A3
4396	" "	25	S½NE	1902-01-17		A3
4355	TIPPIN, Guy	31	NENE	1889-04-23		A2
4356	" "	31	NW	1889-04-23		A2
4357	" "	31	S½	1889-04-23		A2
4358	" "	31	W½NE	1889-04-23		A2
4292	TUCKER, Arthur	25	S½SW	1892-06-15		A3
4293	" "	26	S½SE	1892-06-15		A3
4295	TUCKER, Charles N	24	SESW	1892-04-29		A3
4296	" "	24	SWSE	1892-04-29		A3
4297	" "	25	E½NW	1892-04-29		A3
4333	TUCKER, Drayton N	25	N½SE	1897-02-15		A3
4334	" "	25	SWSE	1897-02-15		A3
4335	" "	36	NWNE	1897-02-15		A3
4384	TUCKER, James S	22	NWSW	1889-04-20		A2
4383	" "	21	NE	1892-06-15		A3

ID	Individual in Patent	Sec.	Sec. Part	Date Issued	Other Counties	For More Info . . .
4397	TUCKER, John M	25	N½SW	1905-02-13		A3
4398	" "	26	NESE	1905-02-13		A3
4408	TUCKER, Lewis B	11	NWNE	1895-06-28		A3
4409	" "	2	W½SE	1895-06-28		A3
4412	TUCKER, Louisa J	21	NW	1894-07-24		A2
4336	UPSHAW, Drury	6	NWNE	1891-05-20		A3
4410	VAN, Lewis	5	SW	1859-05-02		A2
4411	" "	6	SENE	1860-07-02		A2
4298	VAUGHAN, Coleman C	10	E½SW	1889-04-20		A2 G41
4299	" "	10	SE	1889-04-20		A2 G41
4300	" "	10	SWSW	1889-04-20		A2 C11
4301	" "	15	NENE	1889-04-20		A2 G41
4302	" "	15	W½	1889-04-20		A2 G41
4303	" "	15	W½NE	1889-04-20		A2 G41
4304	" "	15	W½SE	1889-04-20		A2 G41
4305	" "	22	E½SW	1889-04-20		A2 G41
4306	" "	22	N½	1889-04-20		A2 G41
4307	" "	22	SESE	1889-04-20		A2 G41
4308	" "	22	SWSW	1889-04-20		A2 G41
4309	" "	22	W½SE	1889-04-20		A2 G41
4310	" "	23	NW	1889-04-20		A2 G41
4311	" "	23	W½NE	1889-04-20		A2 G41
4312	" "	27	NWNW	1889-04-20		A2 G41
4313	" "	28	E½NE	1889-04-20		A2 G41
4314	" "	4	SESW	1889-04-20		A2 G41
4315	" "	4	W½SW	1889-04-20		A2 G41
4316	" "	5	NENW	1889-04-20		A2 G41
4317	" "	5	S½NE	1889-04-20		A2 G41
4318	" "	5	SE	1889-04-20		A2 G41
4319	" "	7	E½NE	1889-04-20		A2 G41 V4366, 4368
4320	" "	8	E½NE	1889-04-20		A2 G41
4321	" "	8	S½SE	1889-04-20		A2 G41
4322	" "	8	SENW	1889-04-20		A2 G41
4323	" "	8	SESW	1889-04-20		A2 G41
4324	" "	8	W½NW	1889-04-20		A2 G41
4325	" "	8	W½SW	1889-04-20		A2 G41
4326	" "	9	NENW	1889-04-20		A2 G41
4327	" "	9	S½SW	1889-04-20		A2 G41
4328	" "	9	SENE	1889-04-20		A2 G41
4329	" "	9	SESE	1889-04-20		A2 G41
4330	" "	9	W½NE	1889-04-20		A2 G41
4331	" "	9	W½SE	1889-04-20		A2 G41
4423	WALLEY, Richard H	26	SESW	1889-11-29		A2
4424	" "	35	NWNW	1889-11-29		A2
4332	WALTERS, Dicey J	9	SENW	1906-05-01		A2
4380	WALTERS, James E	9	N½SW	1893-04-12		A3
4381	" "	9	W½NW	1893-04-12		A3
4428	WALTERS, Sebastian	8	NENW	1897-06-07		A3
4429	" "	8	NWNE	1897-06-07		A3
4249	WATSON, Amasa B	17	NWNW	1883-02-03		A2
4250	" "	18	E½NE	1883-02-03		A2
4251	" "	18	NWSE	1883-02-03		A2
4252	" "	18	SWNE	1883-02-03		A2
4253	" "	18	W½	1883-02-03		A2
4254	" "	19	N½NW	1883-02-03		A2
4255	" "	19	S½SW	1883-02-03		A2
4256	" "	19	SENE	1883-02-03		A2
4257	" "	19	SESE	1883-02-03		A2
4258	" "	19	W½SE	1883-02-03		A2
4259	" "	20	NESE	1883-02-03		A2
4260	" "	20	S½NW	1883-02-03		A2
4261	" "	20	SW	1883-02-03		A2
4262	" "	20	SWNE	1883-02-03		A2
4263	" "	20	W½SE	1883-02-03		A2
4267	" "	29	NENW	1883-02-03		A2
4268	" "	29	NESE	1883-02-03		A2
4269	" "	29	NWNE	1883-02-03		A2
4270	" "	29	SENE	1883-02-03		A2
4271	" "	29	SWSW	1883-02-03		A2
4272	" "	29	W½NW	1883-02-03		A2
4273	" "	30	E½SE	1883-02-03		A2
4274	" "	30	N½	1883-02-03		A2
4275	" "	30	NWSE	1883-02-03		A2

ID	Individual in Patent		Sec.	Sec. Part	Date Issued	Other Counties	For More Info . . .
4276	WATSON, Amasa B (Cont'd)		31	SENE	1883-02-03		A2
4277	"	"	32	NW	1883-02-03		A2
4278	"	"	32	S½	1883-02-03		A2
4279	"	"	32	S½NE	1883-02-03		A2
4280	"	"	33	W½SW	1883-02-03		A2
4264	"	"	27	E½	1883-09-15		A2
4265	"	"	27	E½NW	1883-09-15		A2
4266	"	"	27	E½SW	1883-09-15		A2
4281	"	"	34	N½NW	1883-09-15		A2
4282	"	"	34	W½SE	1883-09-15		A2
4283	"	"	35	S½NE	1883-09-15		A2
4284	"	"	35	S½SE	1883-09-15		A2
4285	"	"	35	S½SW	1883-09-15		A2
4286	"	"	36	SWSW	1883-09-15		A2
4287	"	"	7	N½SW	1883-09-15		A2
4288	"	"	7	SE	1883-09-15		A2
4422	WILLIAMS, Redmon W		26	SWSW	1894-11-17		A2

Patent Map

T6-N R11-W
St Stephens Meridian

Map Group 24

Township Statistics

Parcels Mapped	:	240
Number of Patents	:	102
Number of Individuals	:	88
Patentees Identified	:	82
Number of Surnames	:	52
Multi-Patentee Parcels	:	58
Oldest Patent Date	:	5/2/1859
Most Recent Patent	:	2/27/1926
Block/Lot Parcels	:	0
Parcels Re - Issued	:	0
Parcels that Overlap	:	6
Cities and Towns	:	2
Cemeteries	:	4

Section 6
SCANLAN William J 1905 | ODOM Ezekiel C 1895 | UPSHAW Drury 1891 | HINTON Alletha 1889
ODOM Melton A 1899 | | REAVES Joseph H 1859 | VAN Lewis 1860
ODOM Melton A 1899 | ODOM Ezekiel C 1895 | ODOM Ezekiel C 1895 | PARKER Walden L 1894
| | ODOM Melton A 1899 | PARKER Walden L 1894

Section 5
HINTON Alletha 1889 | VAUGHAN [41] Coleman C 1889 | MCPHERSON [27] William 1889
HINTON Alletha 1889 | VAUGHAN [41] Coleman C 1889
VAN Lewis 1859 | VAUGHAN [41] Coleman C 1889

Section 4
| MCPHERSON [27] William 1889
VAUGHAN [41] Coleman C 1889 | MCPHERSON [27] William 1889
| VAUGHAN [41] Coleman C 1889

Section 7
RAMSEY Henry 1904 | PARKER Walden L 1894 | RAMSEY Henry 1904
SUMRALL John F 1890 | PARKER Albert G 1894 | RAMSEY Henry 1904
WATSON Amasa B 1883 | | WATSON Amasa B 1883
SHOWS Adam N 1895 | WATSON Amasa B 1883

Section 8
VAUGHAN [41] Coleman C 1889 | WALTERS Sebastian 1897 | WALTERS Sebastian 1897
VAUGHAN [41] Coleman C 1889 | BEECH Joseph B 1889 | VAUGHAN [41] Coleman C 1889
VAUGHAN [41] Coleman C 1889 | BEECH Joseph B 1889 | BEECH Joseph B 1889
VAUGHAN [41] Coleman C 1889 | VAUGHAN [41] Coleman C 1889

Section 9
WALTERS James E 1893 | VAUGHAN [41] Coleman C 1889 | MCPHERSON [27] William 1889
WALTERS Dicey J 1906 | VAUGHAN [41] Coleman C 1889 | VAUGHAN [41] Coleman C 1889
WALTERS James E 1893 | VAUGHAN [41] Coleman C 1889 | VAUGHAN [41] Coleman C 1889
VAUGHAN [41] Coleman C 1889

Section 18
CURTIS William 1902 | WATSON Amasa B 1883
WATSON Amasa B 1883 | WATSON Amasa B 1883
WATSON Amasa B 1883 | WATSON Amasa B 1883

Section 17
WATSON Amasa B 1883 | SHOWS Almedia 1906
| NOBLES Edmond A 1892
NOBLES Edmond A 1892 | NOBLES Edmond A 1892
BIRKETT [3] Thomas 1884 | BIRKETT [3] Thomas 1884 | BIRKETT [3] Thomas 1884

Section 16

Section 19
WATSON Amasa B 1883
LAWSON William H 1906 | LAWSON William H 1906 | WATSON Amasa B 1883
MCPHERSON [27] William 1889 | MCPHERSON [27] William 1889
| WATSON Amasa B 1883
WATSON Amasa B 1883 | WATSON Amasa B 1883

Section 20
WATSON Amasa B 1883 | WATSON Amasa B 1883 | CHAPMAN Joseph C 1905
WATSON Amasa B 1883 | WATSON Amasa B 1883 | WATSON Amasa B 1883
| NOBLES J E 1901

Section 21
TUCKER Louisa J 1894 | TUCKER James S 1892
PRESCOTT Lewis B 1860 | PRESCOTT Lewis B 1860 | SHOWS John F 1904

Section 30
WATSON Amasa B 1883
NOBLES James M 1899 | WATSON Amasa B 1883 | WATSON Amasa B 1883
| COOLEY John 1902

Section 29
WATSON Amasa B 1883 | WATSON Amasa B 1883 | WATSON Amasa B 1883 | NOBLES J E 1901
| ROUNSAVILL James D 1898 | ROUNSAVILL James D 1898 | WATSON Amasa B 1883
CHAPMAN Albert 1902 | ROUNSAVILL James D 1898 | NOBLES John F 1899 | WATSON Amasa B 1883
WATSON Amasa B 1883 | NOBLES John F 1899

Section 28
VAUGHAN [41] Coleman C 1889
EASTERLING Henry B 1898
EASTERLING Henry B 1898
MCGILVRAY William W 1890

Section 31
TIPPIN Guy 1889 | TIPPIN Guy 1889 | TIPPIN Guy 1889
| | WATSON Amasa B 1883
TIPPIN Guy 1889

Section 32
WATSON Amasa B 1883 | NOBLES Jasper J 1906 | NOBLES John F 1899
| WATSON Amasa B 1883
WATSON Amasa B 1883

Section 33
MCGILVRAY William W 1890 | SMITH Harvey J 1906
COOLEY Allen 1902 | MCPHERSON [27] William 1889
WATSON Amasa B 1883 | MCPHERSON [27] William 1889
| EASTERLING John A 1899

Map Grid (Sections)

Section 3
MCPHERSON [27] William 1889
MCPHERSON [27] William 1889

Section 2
LANDRUM Pinkney H 1896
OVERSTREET George 1895
OVERSTREET George 1895
TUCKER Lewis B 1895

Section 1

Section 10
MCMANUS Green 1907
VAUGHAN [41] Coleman C 1889
VAUGHAN [41] Coleman C 1889
VAUGHAN [41] Coleman C 1889

Section 11
TUCKER Lewis B 1895
MCPHERSON [27] William 1889
MCDONALD Bryant L 1912
MCPHERSON [27] William 1889
BROWN Elias 1859

Section 12
SUMRALL Henry 1859

Section 15
VAUGHAN [41] Coleman C 1889
VAUGHAN [41] Coleman C 1889
VAUGHAN [41] Coleman C 1889
MORGAN Walter 1909
VAUGHAN [41] Coleman C 1889

Section 14
BROWN Elisha 1859
MCADAMS Larkin I 1911
MCGILVERRY William 1860
MCGILBERRY William 1859
MCGILVRAY William T 1898
MCGILVRAY William T 1898

Section 13
MCGILBERRY William 1859

Section 22
VAUGHAN [41] Coleman C 1889
TUCKER James S 1889
VAUGHAN [41] Coleman C 1889
VAUGHAN [41] Coleman C 1889
VAUGHAN [41] Coleman C 1889
CARLTON James 1896
VAUGHAN [41] Coleman C 1889

Section 23
VAUGHAN [41] Coleman C 1889
VAUGHAN [41] Coleman C 1889
MCGILVRAY William T 1898
MCGILVRAY Angus 1895
MCGILBERRY William 1859
LOFTIN George Washington 1915
MCGILVRAY Angus 1895
CARLTON James 1896
CARLTON James 1896
MCKAY Henry A 1898
MCKAY Henry A 1898
MCKAY Henry A 1898
BIRKETT [3] Thomas 1884

Section 24
BIRKETT [3] Thomas 1884
MCGILVRAY Angus 1895
AGNEW George Samuel 1926
BIRKETT [3] Thomas 1884
TUCKER Charles N 1892
TUCKER Charles N 1892
THOMSON John K 1902

Section 27
VAUGHAN [41] Coleman C 1889
GRANISON Joe 1906
WATSON Amasa B 1883
WATSON Amasa B 1883
MCGILVRAY William W 1890
WATSON Amasa B 1883

Section 26
BIRKETT [3] Thomas 1884
HOLLIMON Thomas R 1893
BIRKETT [3] Thomas 1884
STEPHENS Zack T 1896
HOLLIMON Thomas R 1893
STEPHENS Zack T 1896
TUCKER John M 1905
WILLIAMS Redmon W 1894
WALLEY Richard H 1889
TUCKER Arthur 1892

Section 25
BIRKETT [3] Thomas 1884
TUCKER Charles N 1892
STEPHENS Zack T 1896
THOMSON John K 1902
THOMSON John K 1902
TUCKER John M 1905
TUCKER Arthur 1892
TUCKER Drayton N 1897
TUCKER Drayton N 1897
HERRINGTON Houston 1915

Section 34
WATSON Amasa B 1883
SHOEMAKE Robert 1891
HERRINGTON Francis M 1906
MCPHERSON [27] William 1889
CAMPBELL Mary 1904
CAMPBELL Mary 1904
MCPHERSON [27] William 1889
MCPHERSON [27] William 1889
WATSON Amasa B 1883
SHOEMAKE Robert 1891

Section 35
WALLEY Richard H 1889
BROWN Elias 1859
SHOEMAKE Henry J 1911
SHOEMAKE Robert 1891
WATSON Amasa B 1883
COOLEY Albert S 1896
COOLEY Albert S 1896
SHOEMAKE Elijah L 1906
WATSON Amasa B 1883
WATSON Amasa B 1883

Section 36
COOLEY Albert S 1896
WATSON Amasa B 1883
TUCKER Drayton N 1897
DONALD James 1859
BROWN John W 1905
BROWN Elihu 1859
BROWN Mark 1861
BROWN Elihu 1859
BROWN Mark 1861
BROWN Mark 1861
SHOWS Walter C 1901

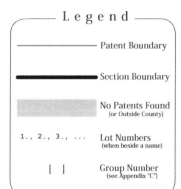

Helpful Hints

1. This Map's INDEX can be found on the preceding pages.

2. Refer to Map "C" to see where this Township lies within Jones County, Mississippi.

3. Numbers within square brackets [ ] denote a multi-patentee land parcel (multi-owner). Refer to Appendix "C" for a full list of members in this group.

4. Areas that look to be crowded with Patentees usually indicate multiple sales of the same parcel (Re-issues) or Overlapping parcels. See this Township's Index for an explanation of these and other circumstances that might explain "odd" groupings of Patentees on this map.

Legend

—————— Patent Boundary

━━━━━━ Section Boundary

No Patents Found (or Outside County)

1., 2., 3., ... Lot Numbers (when beside a name)

[ ] Group Number (see Appendix "C")

Scale: Section = 1 mile X 1 mile (generally, with some exceptions)

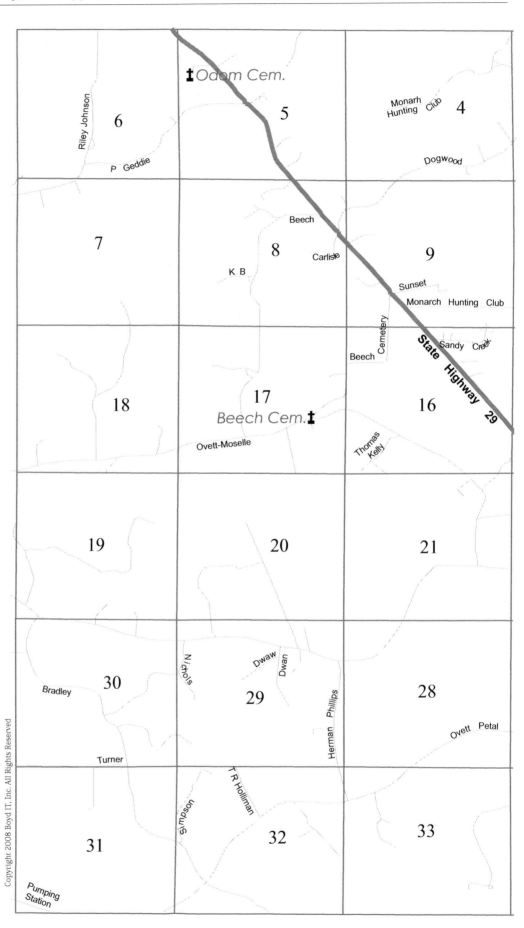

Road Map

T6-N R11-W
St Stephens Meridian

Map Group 24

Cities & Towns
Monarch
Whitfield

Cemeteries
Beech Cemetery
County Line Cemetery
Lancaster Cemetery
Odom Cemetery

‡ *Odom Cem.*

Riley Johnson

6

P Geddie

Monarh Hunting Club

4

Dogwood

5

7

Beech

8

K B

Carlisle

9

Sunset

Monarch Hunting Club

Beech Cemetery

Sandy Creek

State Highway 29

18

17

Beech Cem. ‡

Ovett-Moselle

16

Thomas Kelly

19

20

21

Bradley

30

Nichols

Dwaw

Dwan

29

Herman Phillips

28

Ovett Petal

Turner

Simpson

T R Holliman

32

33

31

Pumping Station

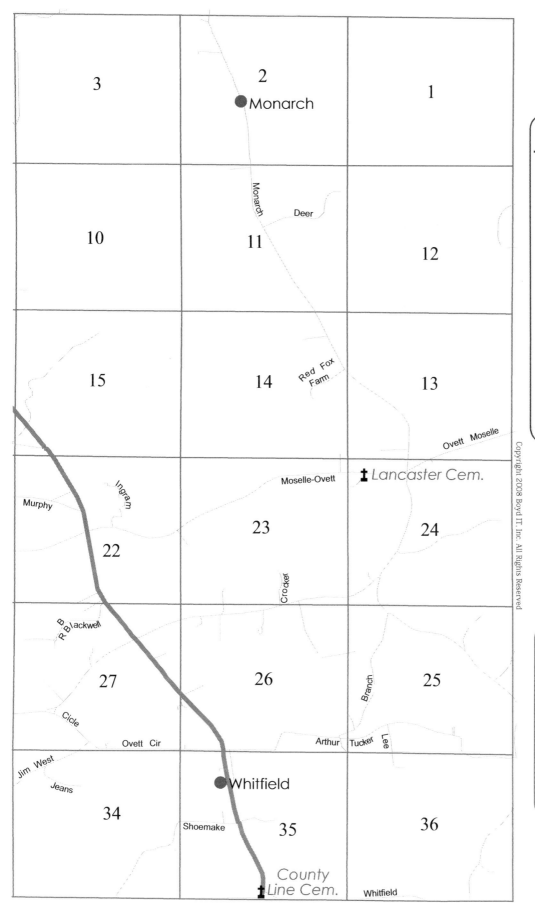

3

2
●Monarch

1

Monarch

Deer

10

11

12

15

14

Red Fox
Farm

13

Ovett Moselle

Murphy

Ingram

Moselle-Ovett

✝ Lancaster Cem.

23

24

22

Crocket

R Blackwell

27

26

Branch

25

Cicle

Ovett Cir

Arthur Tucker Lee

Jim West

Jeans

34

●Whitfield

Shoemake

35

36

County
Line Cem.

✝

Whitfield

Helpful Hints

1. This road map has a number of uses, but primarily it is to help you: a) find the present location of land owned by your ancestors (at least the general area), b) find cemeteries and city-centers, and c) estimate the route/roads used by Census-takers & tax-assessors.

2. If you plan to travel to Jones County to locate cemeteries or land parcels, please pick up a modern travel map for the area before you do. Mapping old land parcels on modern maps is not as exact a science as you might think. Just the slightest variations in public land survey coordinates, estimates of parcel boundaries, or road-map deviations can greatly alter a map's representation of how a road either does or doesn't cross a particular parcel of land.

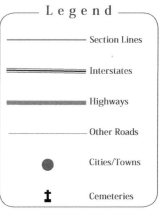

Legend

————————	Section Lines
════════	Interstates
▬▬▬▬▬▬	Highways
————————	Other Roads
●	Cities/Towns
✝	Cemeteries

Scale: Section = 1 mile X 1 mile
(generally, with some exceptions)

Historical Map

T6-N R11-W
St Stephens Meridian

Map Group 24

Cities & Towns
Monarch
Whitfield

Cemeteries
Beech Cemetery
County Line Cemetery
Lancaster Cemetery
Odom Cemetery

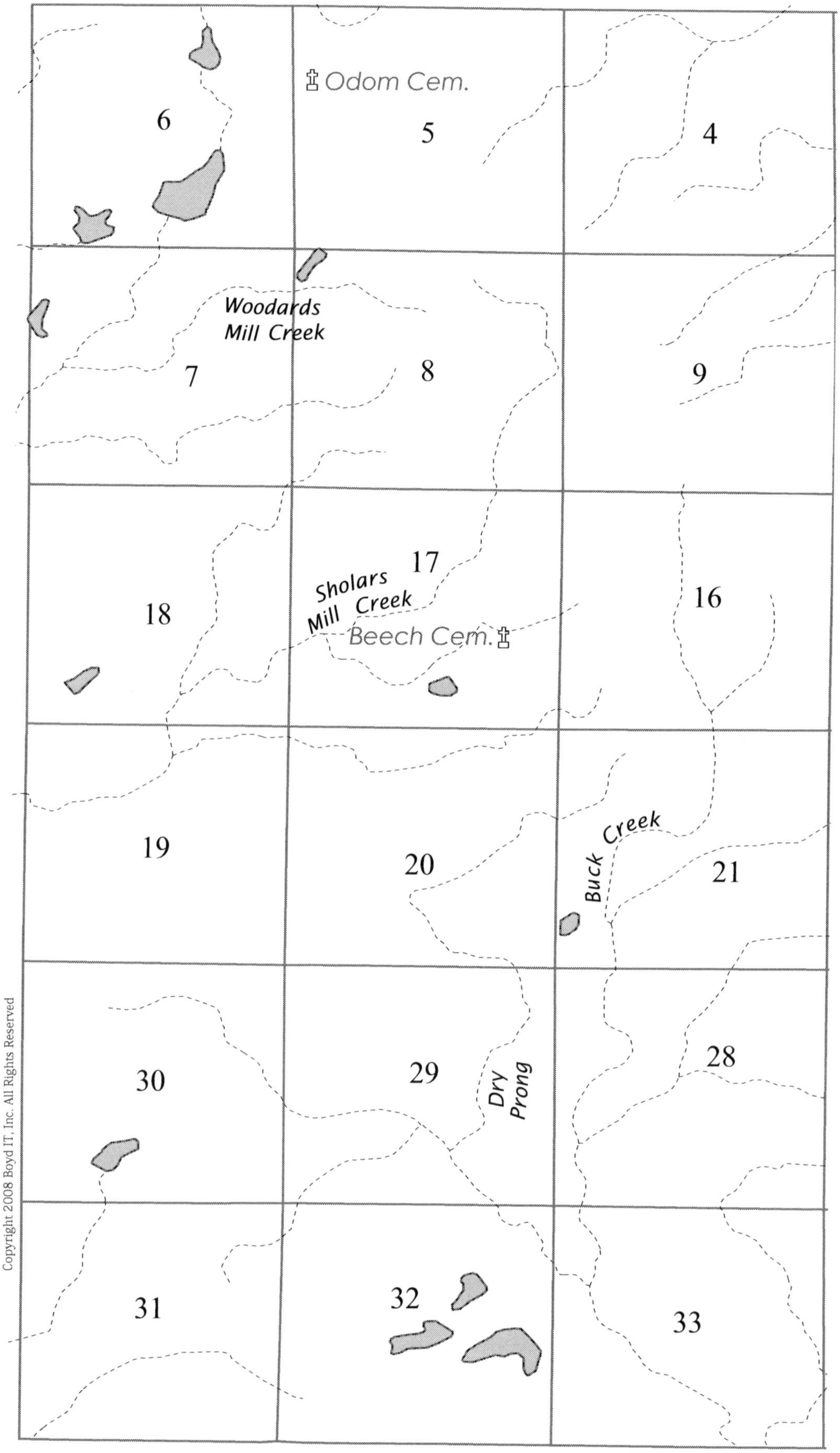

✝ Odom Cem.

6

5

4

Woodards
Mill Creek

7

8

9

Sholars
Mill Creek

18

17

16

Beech Cem. ✝

19

20

Buck Creek

21

30

29

Dry Prong

28

31

32

33

Copyright 2008 Boyd IT. Inc. All Rights Reserved

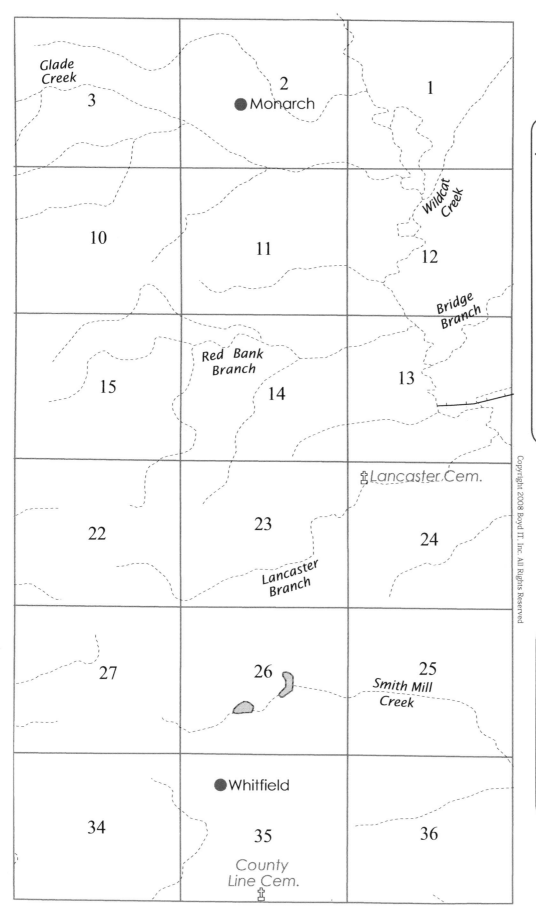

Glade
Creek

3

2
●Monarch

1

10

11

Wildcat
Creek

12

Bridge
Branch

15

Red Bank
Branch

14

13

22

✝Lancaster Cem.

23

24

Lancaster
Branch

27

26

25
Smith Mill
Creek

●Whitfield

34

35

36

County
Line Cem.
✝

Helpful Hints

1. This Map takes a different look at the same Congressional Township displayed in the preceding two maps. It presents features that can help you better envision the historical development of the area: a) Water-bodies (lakes & ponds), b) Water-courses (rivers, streams, etc.), c) Railroads, d) City/town center-points (where they were oftentimes located when first settled), and e) Cemeteries.

2. Using this "Historical" map in tandem with this Township's Patent Map and Road Map, may lead you to some interesting discoveries. You will often find roads, towns, cemeteries, and waterways are named after nearby landowners: sometimes those names will be the ones you are researching. See how many of these research gems you can find here in Jones County.

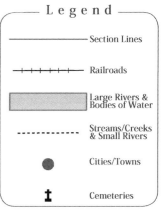

Legend

————————	Section Lines
┼┼┼┼┼┼	Railroads
�	Large Rivers & Bodies of Water
- - - - - - -	Streams/Creeks & Small Rivers
●	Cities/Towns
✝	Cemeteries

Scale: Section = 1 mile X 1 mile
(there are some exceptions)

Map Group 25: Index to Land Patents

Township 6-North Range 10-West (St Stephens)

After you locate an individual in this Index, take note of the Section and Section Part then proceed to the Land Patent map on the pages immediately following. You should have no difficulty locating the corresponding parcel of land.

The "For More Info" Column will lead you to more information about the underlying Patents. See the *Legend* at right, and the "How to Use this Book" chapter, for more information.

```
                    LEGEND
          "For More Info . . . " column

A = Authority (Legislative Act, See Appendix "A")
B = Block or Lot (location in Section unknown)
C = Cancelled Patent
F = Fractional Section
G = Group  (Multi-Patentee Patent, see Appendix "C")
V = Overlaps another Parcel
R = Re-Issued (Parcel patented more than once)

(A & G items require you to look in the Appendixes referred
to above. All other Letter-designations followed by a number
require you to locate line-items in this index that possess
the ID number found after the letter).
```

ID	Individual in Patent	Sec.	Sec. Part	Date Issued	Other Counties	For More Info . . .
4610	BAYLIS, George	19	W½SE	1826-07-25		A2
4564	BLODGETT, Delos A	26	W½SW	1889-11-21		A2
4567	" "	33	S½SE	1889-11-21		A2
4568	" "	34	N½SE	1889-11-21		A2
4569	" "	34	N½SW	1889-11-21		A2
4570	" "	34	NE	1889-11-21		A2
4571	" "	34	S½NW	1889-11-21		A2
4572	" "	35	E½SW	1889-11-21		A2
4573	" "	35	NESE	1889-11-21		A2
4574	" "	35	NW	1889-11-21		A2
4575	" "	35	NWSW	1889-11-21		A2
4576	" "	35	SENE	1889-11-21		A2
4577	" "	35	W½NE	1889-11-21		A2
4578	" "	35	W½SE	1889-11-21		A2
4579	" "	36	E½NW	1889-11-21		A2
4580	" "	36	E½SW	1889-11-21		A2
4581	" "	36	NWSW	1889-11-21		A2
4582	" "	36	SE	1889-11-21		A2
4583	" "	36	SENE	1889-11-21		A2
4584	" "	36	SWNW	1889-11-21		A2
4585	" "	36	W½NE	1889-11-21		A2
4557	" "	13	NWSE	1890-07-03		A2
4558	" "	13	S½NE	1890-07-03		A2
4559	" "	13	SENW	1890-07-03		A2
4560	" "	23	S½SE	1890-07-03		A2
4561	" "	23	SESW	1890-07-03		A2
4562	" "	26	NENE	1890-07-03		A2
4563	" "	26	W½SE	1890-07-03		A2
4565	" "	27	S½SE	1890-07-03		A2
4566	" "	33	N½SE	1890-07-03		A2
4642	BROWN, Mary C	25	E½SW	1929-01-09		A3
4646	BROWN, Millard W	25	SWSW	1892-05-26		A3
4647	" "	26	SESE	1892-05-26		A3
4648	" "	35	NENE	1892-05-26		A3
4649	" "	36	NWNW	1892-05-26		A3
4555	CARLISLE, David N	30	SENW	1841-01-05		A2
4556	" "	31	NWNW	1841-01-05		A2
4662	CARLISLE, Samuel P	28	SENW	1899-04-17		A3
4660	CHAMBLESS, Robert Andrew	6	NWSW	1932-11-02		A3
4665	COBB, Thomas	3	N½SW	1900-11-28		A3
4666	" "	3	SESW	1900-11-28		A3
4592	CRENSHAW, Ellen E	27	N½NW	1892-08-01		A3
4593	" "	27	SWNW	1892-08-01		A3
4594	" "	28	NENE	1892-08-01		A3
4637	DEMENT, John L	15	NE	1898-08-27		A3
4675	DEMENT, William	19	NESE	1859-11-10		A2

ID	Individual in Patent	Sec.	Sec. Part	Date Issued	Other Counties	For More Info . . .
4676	DEMENT, William (Cont'd)	19	SENE	1859-11-10		A2
4639	DRAUGHN, Rufus	31	SWNW	1854-03-15		A2 G30
4618	EASTERLING, Henry C	26	NENW	1896-12-14		A3
4619	" "	26	NWNE	1896-12-14		A3
4620	" "	26	S½NW	1896-12-14		A3
4627	EASTERLING, James Alfred	26	SESW	1940-03-06		A3
4641	EASTERLING, Margie Velma	21	E½SE	1931-11-19		A3
4553	GILLEY, David E	13	E½SE	1896-12-14		A3
4554	" "	13	SWSE	1896-12-14		A3
4544	GRAHAM, Charity E	34	S½SE	-12:00:00 AM-		A3
4545	" "	34	S½SW	-12:00:00 AM-		A3
4643	GRAHAM, Mathew B	21	SWSE	1898-01-19		A3
4644	" "	28	NWSE	1898-01-19		A3
4645	" "	28	W½NE	1898-01-19		A3
4677	GRAHAM, William G	24	NENW	1906-06-26		A3
4634	HOLLIMAN, John	30	SWNW	1859-05-02		A2
4635	" "	31	E½NW	1859-05-02		A2
4667	HOLLIMAN, Thomas	30	N½SW	1860-04-02		A2
4636	HOLLIMON, John	30	SESW	1859-11-10		A2
4668	HOLLIMON, Thomas	30	SWSW	1859-05-02		A2
4624	HUTTO, Jacob	31	SESE	1859-11-10		A2
4622	" "	31	E½SW	1860-04-02		A2
4623	" "	31	NWSW	1860-04-02		A2
4625	" "	31	W½NE	1860-04-02		A2
4626	" "	31	W½SE	1860-04-02		A2
4678	JOHNSON, William H	25	SENE	1912-06-27		A3
4540	KITCHENS, Andrew J	11	E½SE	1906-06-16		A3
4541	" "	11	SENE	1906-06-16		A3
4631	KITCHENS, James R	14	E½SW	1898-08-27		A3
4632	" "	23	NENW	1898-08-27		A3
4680	KITCHENS, William	23	NESE	1901-12-04		A3
4681	" "	23	SENE	1901-12-04		A3
4682	" "	24	SWNW	1901-12-04		A3
4589	LANDRUM, Dorkas	7	NENW	1895-06-22		A2
4633	LANDRUM, John Henry	15	NENW	1919-07-01		A3
4670	LANDRUM, Warren	14	NWNW	1917-08-11		A3
4661	LOPER, Samuel M	35	SWSW	1906-03-31		A3
4650	MCGILBERRY, Murdoc	18	NWNW	1859-06-01		A2
4652	" "	7	W½SW	1859-06-01		A2
4651	" "	20	W½NW	1859-11-10		A2
4653	MCGILBERRY, Murdock	17	W½SW	1860-04-02		A2
4664	MISSISSIPPI, State Of	19	SESE	1928-09-14		A4
4685	MORRIS, William M	33	W½SW	1907-07-13		A3
4639	MYERS, John W	31	SWNW	1854-03-15		A2 G30
4639	MYERS, Levi	31	SWNW	1854-03-15		A2 G30
4654	NICHOLES, Noah	18	NENW	1901-08-12		A3
4671	OVERSTREET, William A	7	NESW	1893-12-21		A3
4672	" "	7	SENW	1893-12-21		A3
4673	" "	7	W½NW	1893-12-21		A3
4679	OVERSTREET, William H	7	SESW	1890-04-25		A2
4616	PARKER, George Riley	22	NWNE	1916-06-10		A3
4655	PITTS, Henry	15	NWSE	1913-05-08		A3 G34
4655	PITTS, Polly	15	NWSE	1913-05-08		A3 G34
4663	SHOWS, Sarah	21	N½NW	1898-12-27		A3
4669	SHOWS, Walter C	31	SWSW	1901-10-01		A3
4542	SMITH, Buford F	1	SWSW	1901-08-12		A3
4543	" "	12	N½NW	1901-08-12		A3
4547	SMITH, Daniel	18	S½SE	1859-05-02		A2
4550	" "	19	N½NE	1859-05-02		A2
4546	" "	18	N½SE	1860-07-02		A2
4548	" "	18	SENW	1860-07-02		A2
4549	" "	18	SWNE	1860-07-02		A2
4551	SMITH, Daniel Y	2	E½NW	1892-04-29		A3
4552	" "	2	W½NE	1892-04-29		A3
4613	SMITH, George P	20	W½SE	1859-05-02		A2
4614	" "	29	SW	1859-05-02		A2
4615	" "	29	W½NE	1859-05-02		A2
4611	" "	15	N½SW	1888-04-05		A3
4612	" "	15	S½NW	1888-04-05		A3
4617	SMITH, Hamp	1	SWNE	1906-09-19		A3
4640	SMITH, Joseph	28	E½SW	1860-04-02		A2
4658	SMITH, Richard	6	E½NW	1890-03-28		A3
4659	" "	6	E½SW	1890-03-28		A3

ID	Individual in Patent	Sec.	Sec. Part	Date Issued	Other Counties	For More Info . . .
4639	STEVENS, William	31	SWNW	1854-03-15		A2 G30
4656	STINSON, Preston	35	SESE	1860-04-02		A2
4657	"	36	SWSW	1860-04-02		A2
4621	SUMRALL, Henry	6	SWSW	1860-04-02		A2
4638	SUMRALL, John	22	NWSW	1859-11-10		A2
4628	THOMSON, James E	20	E½SE	1901-06-25		A3
4629	"	20	SENE	1901-06-25		A3
4630	"	21	SWNW	1901-06-25		A3
4590	TUCKER, Drayton L	3	E½NW	1894-02-28		A3
4591	"	3	N½NE	1894-02-28		A3
4595	WARE, Emmor	17	E½	1882-12-30		A2
4596	"	17	E½SW	1882-12-30		A2
4597	"	17	NW	1882-12-30		A2
4598	"	18	E½NE	1882-12-30		A2
4599	"	18	NWNE	1882-12-30		A2
4600	"	20	E½NW	1882-12-30		A2
4601	"	20	NENE	1882-12-30		A2
4602	"	20	W½NE	1882-12-30		A2
4603	"	4	W½	1882-12-30		A2
4604	"	5		1882-12-30		A2
4605	"	6	E½	1882-12-30		A2
4606	"	7	E½	1882-12-30		A2
4607	"	8		1882-12-30		A2
4608	"	9	NW	1882-12-30		A2
4609	"	9	W½SW	1882-12-30		A2
4478	WATSON, Amasa B	1	E½NE	1884-12-30		A2
4479	"	1	N½NW	1884-12-30		A2
4480	"	1	NWNE	1884-12-30		A2
4481	"	1	NWSW	1884-12-30		A2
4482	"	1	SE	1884-12-30		A2
4483	"	1	SWNW	1884-12-30		A2
4484	"	10	E½	1884-12-30		A2
4485	"	10	N½SW	1884-12-30		A2
4486	"	10	NW	1884-12-30		A2
4487	"	10	SESW	1884-12-30		A2
4488	"	11	W½	1884-12-30		A2
4489	"	12	E½	1884-12-30		A2
4490	"	12	S½NW	1884-12-30		A2
4491	"	12	SW	1884-12-30		A2
4492	"	13	N½NE	1884-12-30		A2
4493	"	13	N½NW	1884-12-30		A2
4494	"	13	SW	1884-12-30		A2
4495	"	13	SWNW	1884-12-30		A2
4496	"	14	E½	1884-12-30		A2
4497	"	2	SW	1884-12-30		A2
4498	"	2	W½NW	1884-12-30		A2
4499	"	22	E½SW	1884-12-30		A2
4500	"	22	NENE	1884-12-30		A2
4501	"	22	S½NE	1884-12-30		A2
4502	"	22	S½NW	1884-12-30		A2
4503	"	22	SE	1884-12-30		A2
4504	"	22	SWSW	1884-12-30		A2
4505	"	23	N½NE	1884-12-30		A2
4506	"	23	N½SW	1884-12-30		A2
4507	"	23	NWSE	1884-12-30		A2
4508	"	23	SENW	1884-12-30		A2
4509	"	23	SWNE	1884-12-30		A2
4510	"	23	SWSW	1884-12-30		A2
4511	"	23	W½NW	1884-12-30		A2
4512	"	24	NE	1884-12-30		A2
4513	"	24	NWNW	1884-12-30		A2
4514	"	24	S½	1884-12-30		A2
4515	"	24	SENW	1884-12-30		A2
4516	"	25	N½NE	1884-12-30		A2
4517	"	25	NW	1884-12-30		A2
4518	"	25	NWSW	1884-12-30		A2
4519	"	25	SE	1884-12-30		A2
4520	"	25	SWNE	1884-12-30		A2
4521	"	26	NESE	1884-12-30		A2
4522	"	26	NWNW	1884-12-30		A2
4523	"	26	S½NE	1884-12-30		A2
4524	"	27	N½SE	1884-12-30		A2
4525	"	27	NE	1884-12-30		A2

ID	Individual in Patent	Sec.	Sec. Part	Date Issued	Other Counties	For More Info . . .
4526	WATSON, Amasa B (Cont'd)	27	SENW	1884-12-30		A2
4527	" "	27	SW	1884-12-30		A2
4528	" "	28	E½SE	1884-12-30		A2
4529	" "	28	SENE	1884-12-30		A2
4530	" "	3	S½NE	1884-12-30		A2
4531	" "	3	SE	1884-12-30		A2
4532	" "	3	SWSW	1884-12-30		A2
4533	" "	3	W½NW	1884-12-30		A2
4534	" "	33	NENE	1884-12-30		A2
4535	" "	34	N½NW	1884-12-30		A2
4536	" "	36	NENE	1884-12-30		A2
4537	" "	4	E½NE	1884-12-30		A2
4538	" "	4	W½SE	1884-12-30		A2
4539	" "	9	W½NE	1884-12-30		A2
4674	WATSON, William D	26	NESW	1930-12-13		A2
4586	WOODARD, Dicy	28	SWSE	1897-05-20		A3 G48
4587	" "	33	SENE	1897-05-20		A3 G48
4588	" "	33	W½NE	1897-05-20		A3 G48
4586	WOODARD, Ira	28	SWSE	1897-05-20		A3 G48
4587	" "	33	SENE	1897-05-20		A3 G48
4588	" "	33	W½NE	1897-05-20		A3 G48
4683	WOODDARD, William L	33	E½NW	1896-02-13		A3
4684	" "	33	E½SW	1896-02-13		A3

Patent Map

T6-N R10-W
St Stephens Meridian

Map Group 25

Township Statistics

Parcels Mapped	:	208
Number of Patents	:	81
Number of Individuals	:	65
Patentees Identified	:	60
Number of Surnames	:	38
Multi-Patentee Parcels	:	5
Oldest Patent Date	:	7/25/1826
Most Recent Patent	:	3/6/1940
Block/Lot Parcels	:	0
Parcels Re - Issued	:	0
Parcels that Overlap	:	0
Cities and Towns	:	2
Cemeteries	:	2

SMITH Richard 1890
WARE Emmor 1882

6

WARE Emmor 1882

5

WARE Emmor 1882

WATSON Amasa B 1884

4

CHAMBLESS Robert Andrew 1932

SMITH Richard 1890

WARE Emmor 1882

WATSON Amasa B 1884

SUMRALL Henry 1860

LANDRUM Dorkas 1895

OVERSTREET William A 1893

OVERSTREET William A 1893

WARE Emmor 1882

8

WATSON Amasa B 1884

WARE Emmor 1882

9

MCGILBERRY Murdoc 1859

OVERSTREET William A 1893

7

WARE Emmor 1882

WARE Emmor 1882

OVERSTREET William H 1890

MCGILBERRY Murdoc 1859

NICHOLES Noah 1901

WARE Emmor 1882

WARE Emmor 1882

WARE Emmor 1882

WARE Emmor 1882

SMITH Daniel 1860

SMITH Daniel 1860

18

SMITH Daniel 1860

MCGILBERRY Murdock 1860

17

16

WARE Emmor 1882

SMITH Daniel 1859

SMITH Daniel 1859

MCGILBERRY Murdoc 1859

WARE Emmor 1882

WARE Emmor 1882

WARE Emmor 1882

SHOWS Sarah 1898

DEMENT William 1859

THOMSON James E 1901

THOMSON James E 1901

21

19

BAYLIS George 1826

DEMENT William 1859

20

SMITH George P 1859

EASTERLING Margie Velma 1931

MISSISSIPPI State Of 1928

THOMSON James E 1901

GRAHAM Mathew B 1898

SMITH George P 1859

CRENSHAW Ellen E 1892

HOLLIMAN John 1859

CARLISLE David N 1841

30

CARLISLE Samuel P 1899

GRAHAM Mathew B 1898

WATSON Amasa B 1884

HOLLIMAN Thomas 1860

29

28

GRAHAM Mathew B 1898

HOLLIMON Thomas 1859

HOLLIMON John 1859

SMITH George P 1859

SMITH Joseph 1860

WATSON Amasa B 1884

WOODARD [48] Dicy 1897

CARLISLE David N 1841

HUTTO Jacob 1860

WOODARD [48] Dicy 1897

WATSON Amasa B 1884

MYERS [30] John W 1854

HOLLIMAN John 1859

31

WOODDARD William L 1896

33

WOODARD [48] Dicy 1897

HUTTO Jacob 1860

32

BLODGETT Delos A 1890

SHOWS Walter C 1901

HUTTO Jacob 1860

HUTTO Jacob 1860

HUTTO Jacob 1859

MORRIS William M 1907

WOODDARD William L 1896

BLODGETT Delos A 1889

Section 3
WATSON Amasa B 1884
TUCKER Drayton L 1894
COBB Thomas 1900
WATSON Amasa B 1884
COBB Thomas 1900
WATSON Amasa B 1884
3

Section 2
TUCKER Drayton L 1894
WATSON Amasa B 1884
WATSON Amasa B 1884
SMITH Daniel Y 1892
SMITH Daniel Y 1892
WATSON Amasa B 1884
2

Section 1
WATSON Amasa B 1884
WATSON Amasa B 1884
WATSON Amasa B 1884
SMITH Hamp 1906
WATSON Amasa B 1884
WATSON Amasa B 1884
SMITH Buford F 1901
WATSON Amasa B 1884
1

Section 10
WATSON Amasa B 1884
10
WATSON Amasa B 1884
WATSON Amasa B 1884

Section 11
WATSON Amasa B 1884
11
WATSON Amasa B 1884

Section 12
SMITH Buford F 1901
KITCHENS Andrew J 1906
WATSON Amasa B 1884
WATSON Amasa B 1884
KITCHENS Andrew J 1906
WATSON Amasa B 1884
12

Section 15
LANDRUM John Henry 1919
SMITH George P 1888
DEMENT John L 1898
SMITH George P 1888
15
PITTS [34] Polly 1913

Section 14
LANDRUM Warren 1917
14
KITCHENS James R 1898
WATSON Amasa B 1884

Section 13
WATSON Amasa B 1884
WATSON Amasa B 1884
WATSON Amasa B 1884
BLODGETT Delos A 1890
BLODGETT Delos A 1890
13
WATSON Amasa B 1884
BLODGETT Delos A 1890
GILLEY David E 1896
GILLEY David E 1896

Section 22
PARKER George Riley 1916
WATSON Amasa B 1884
WATSON Amasa B 1884
WATSON Amasa B 1884
SUMRALL John 1859
WATSON Amasa B 1884
22
WATSON Amasa B 1884
WATSON Amasa B 1884

Section 23
KITCHENS James R 1898
WATSON Amasa B 1884
WATSON Amasa B 1884
WATSON Amasa B 1884
KITCHENS William 1901
WATSON Amasa B 1884
23
WATSON Amasa B 1884
BLODGETT Delos A 1890
BLODGETT Delos A 1890

Section 24
WATSON Amasa B 1884
WATSON Amasa B 1884
GRAHAM William G 1906
KITCHENS William 1901
WATSON Amasa B 1884
WATSON Amasa B 1884
24
WATSON Amasa B 1884

Section 27
CRENSHAW Ellen E 1892
CRENSHAW Ellen E 1892
WATSON Amasa B 1884
WATSON Amasa B 1884
27
WATSON Amasa B 1884
WATSON Amasa B 1884
BLODGETT Delos A 1890

Section 26
WATSON Amasa B 1884
EASTERLING Henry C 1896
EASTERLING Henry C 1896
BLODGETT Delos A 1890
EASTERLING Henry C 1896
26
WATSON Amasa B 1884
WATSON William D 1930
BLODGETT Delos A 1889
EASTERLING James Alfred 1940
BLODGETT Delos A 1890

Section 25
WATSON Amasa B 1884
WATSON Amasa B 1884
25
WATSON Amasa B 1884
WATSON Amasa B 1884
JOHNSON William H 1912
WATSON Amasa B 1884
BROWN Mary C 1929
WATSON Amasa B 1884

Section 34
WATSON Amasa B 1884
BLODGETT Delos A 1889
BLODGETT Delos A 1889
34
BLODGETT Delos A 1889
GRAHAM Charity E -12:

Section 35
WATSON Amasa B 1884
BROWN Millard W 1892
BROWN Millard W 1892
BLODGETT Delos A 1889
BLODGETT Delos A 1889
35
BLODGETT Delos A 1889
GRAHAM Charity E -12:
BLODGETT Delos A 1889
LOPER Samuel M 1906
BLODGETT Delos A 1889
BLODGETT Delos A 1889

Section 36
BROWN Millard W 1892
BLODGETT Delos A 1889
WATSON Amasa B 1884
BLODGETT Delos A 1889
BLODGETT Delos A 1889
36
BLODGETT Delos A 1889
BLODGETT Delos A 1889
STINSON Preston 1860
STINSON Preston 1860
BLODGETT Delos A 1889

Legend

Patent Boundary

Section Boundary

No Patents Found (or Outside County)

1., 2., 3., ...   Lot Numbers (when beside a name)

[ ]   Group Number (see Appendix "C")

Scale: Section = 1 mile X 1 mile (generally, with some exceptions)

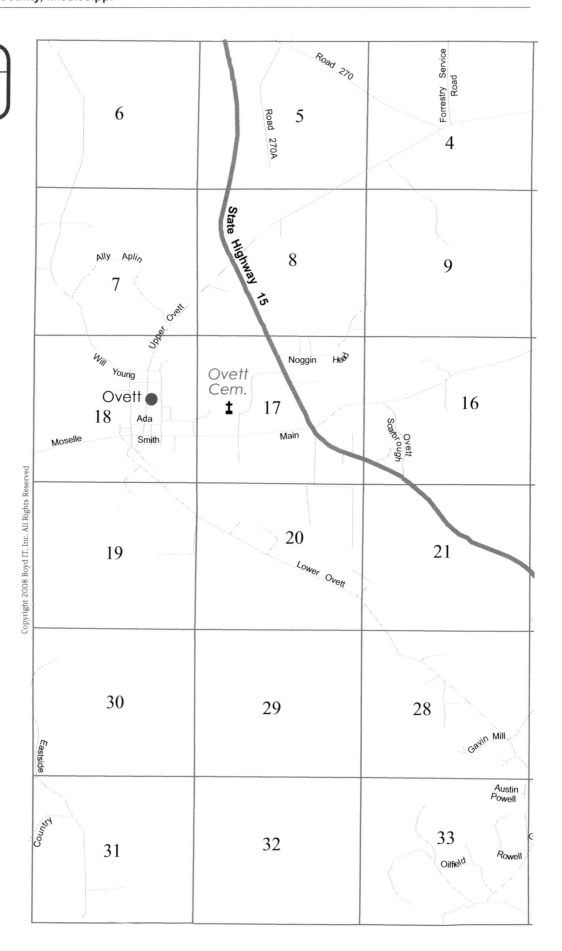

Road Map

T6-N R10-W
St Stephens Meridian

Map Group 25

Cities & Towns
Blodgett
Ovett

Cemeteries
Brown Cemetery
Ovett Cemetery

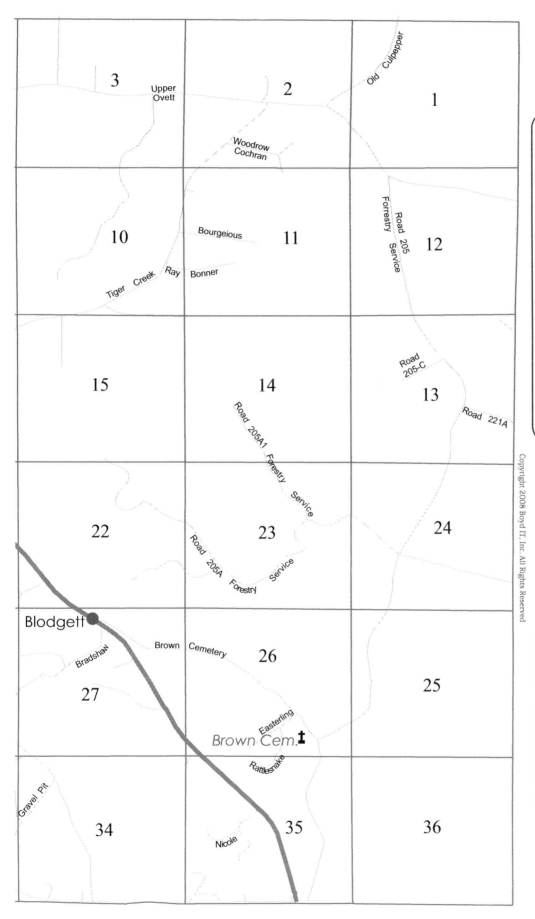

3

Upper
Ovett

2

Old Culpepper

1

Woodrow
Cochran

10

Bourgeious

11

Road 205 Forestry Service

12

Tiger Creek Ray Bonner

15

14

Road 205A1 Forestry Service

Road 205-C

13

Road 221A

22

Road 205A Forestry Service

23

24

Blodgett

Bradshaw

Brown Cemetery

26

Easterling

25

27

Brown Cem.

Rattlesnake

Gravel Pit

34

Nicole

35

36

Helpful Hints

1. This road map has a number of uses, but primarily it is to help you: a) find the present location of land owned by your ancestors (at least the general area), b) find cemeteries and city-centers, and c) estimate the route/roads used by Census-takers & tax-assessors.

2. If you plan to travel to Jones County to locate cemeteries or land parcels, please pick up a modern travel map for the area before you do. Mapping old land parcels on modern maps is not as exact a science as you might think. Just the slightest variations in public land survey coordinates, estimates of parcel boundaries, or road-map deviations can greatly alter a map's representation of how a road either does or doesn't cross a particular parcel of land.

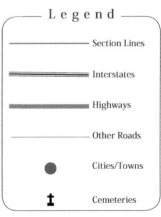

Legend

————————	Section Lines
═══════════	Interstates
━━━━━━━━━━	Highways
———————	Other Roads
●	Cities/Towns
☦	Cemeteries

Scale: Section = 1 mile X 1 mile
(generally, with some exceptions)

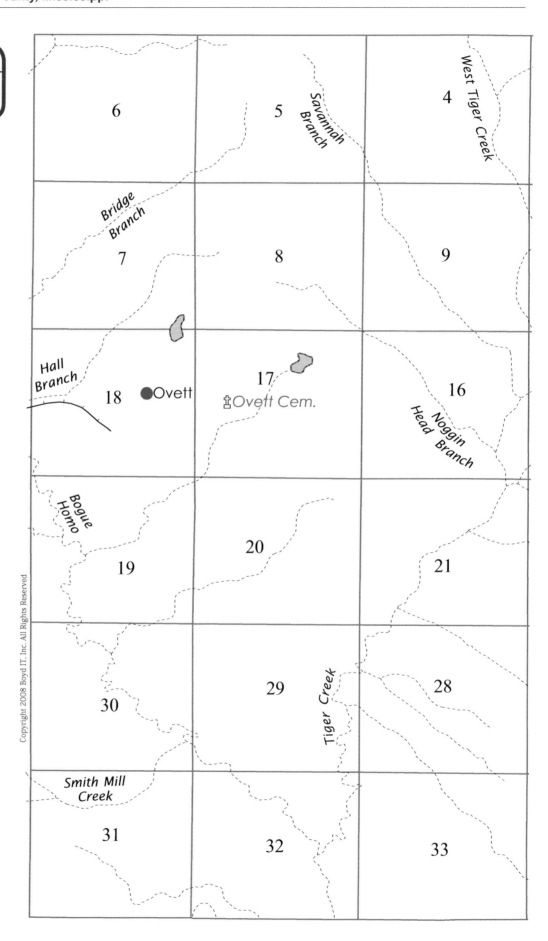

Historical Map

T6-N R10-W
St Stephens Meridian

Map Group 25

Cities & Towns
Blodgett
Ovett

Cemeteries
Brown Cemetery
Ovett Cemetery

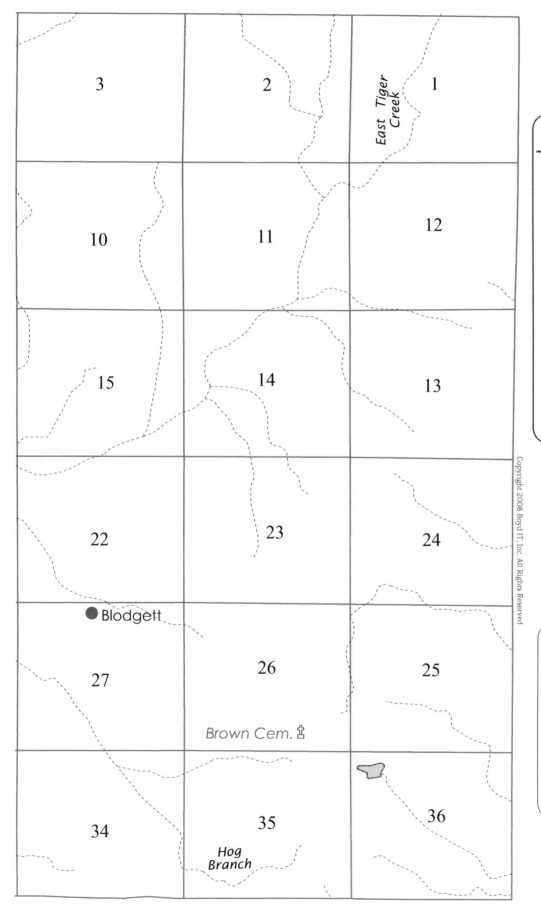

3

2

East Tiger Creek

1

10

11

12

15

14

13

22

23

24

● Blodgett

27

26

25

Brown Cem. ⚑

34

35

Hog Branch

36

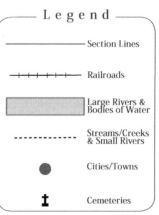

Copyright 2008 Boyd IT, Inc. All Rights Reserved

Helpful Hints

1. This Map takes a different look at the same Congressional Township displayed in the preceding two maps. It presents features that can help you better envision the historical development of the area: a) Water-bodies (lakes & ponds), b) Water-courses (rivers, streams, etc.), c) Railroads, d) City/town center-points (where they were oftentimes located when first settled), and e) Cemeteries.

2. Using this "Historical" map in tandem with this Township's Patent Map and Road Map, may lead you to some interesting discoveries. You will often find roads, towns, cemeteries, and waterways are named after nearby landowners: sometimes those names will be the ones you are researching. See how many of these research gems you can find here in Jones County.

L e g e n d

———————— Section Lines

+–+–+–+–+– Railroads

▭ Large Rivers & Bodies of Water

- - - - - - - Streams/Creeks & Small Rivers

● Cities/Towns

⚑ Cemeteries

Scale: Section = 1 mile X 1 mile
(there are some exceptions)

Appendices

Appendix A - Acts of Congress Authorizing the Patents Contained in this Book

The following Acts of Congress are referred to throughout the Indexes in this book. The text of the Federal Statutes referred to below can usually be found on the web. For more information on such laws, check out the publishers's web-site at *www.arphax.com*, go to the "Research" page, and click on the "Land-Law" link.

Ref. No.	Date and Act of Congress	Number of Parcels of Land
1	NA: Sale-Title 32 Chapter 7 (RS 2353 43 USC 672)	8
2	April 24, 1820: Sale-Cash Entry (3 Stat. 566)	2586
3	May 20, 1862: Homestead EntryOriginal (12 Stat. 392)	2089
4	September 28, 1850: Swamp Land Grant-Patent (9 Stat. 519)	2

Appendix B - Section Parts (Aliquot Parts)

The following represent the various abbreviations we have found thus far in describing the parts of a Public Land Section. Some of these are very obscure and rarely used, but we wanted to list them for just that reason. A full section is 1 square mile or 640 acres.

Section Part	Description	Acres
<none>	Full Acre (if no Section Part is listed, presumed a full Section)	640
<1-??>	A number represents a Lot Number and can be of various sizes	?
E½	East Half-Section	320
E½E½	East Half of East Half-Section	160
E½E½SE	East Half of East Half of Southeast Quarter-Section	40
E½N½	East Half of North Half-Section	160
E½NE	East Half of Northeast Quarter-Section	80
E½NENE	East Half of Northeast Quarter of Northeast Quarter-Section	20
E½NENW	East Half of Northeast Quarter of Northwest Quarter-Section	20
E½NESE	East Half of Northeast Quarter of Southeast Quarter-Section	20
E½NESW	East Half of Northeast Quarter of Southwest Quarter-Section	20
E½NW	East Half of Northwest Quarter-Section	80
E½NWNE	East Half of Northwest Quarter of Northeast Quarter-Section	20
E½NWNW	East Half of Northwest Quarter of Northwest Quarter-Section	20
E½NWSE	East Half of Northwest Quarter of Southeast Quarter-Section	20
E½NWSW	East Half of Northwest Quarter of Southwest Quarter-Section	20
E½S½	East Half of South Half-Section	160
E½SE	East Half of Southeast Quarter-Section	80
E½SENE	East Half of Southeast Quarter of Northeast Quarter-Section	20
E½SENW	East Half of Southeast Quarter of Northwest Quarter-Section	20
E½SESE	East Half of Southeast Quarter of Southeast Quarter-Section	20
E½SESW	East Half of Southeast Quarter of Southwest Quarter-Section	20
E½SW	East Half of Southwest Quarter-Section	80
E½SWNE	East Half of Southwest Quarter of Northeast Quarter-Section	20
E½SWNW	East Half of Southwest Quarter of Northwest Quarter-Section	20
E½SWSE	East Half of Southwest Quarter of Southeast Quarter-Section	20
E½SWSW	East Half of Southwest Quarter of Southwest Quarter-Section	20
E½W½	East Half of West Half-Section	160
N½	North Half-Section	320
N½E½NE	North Half of East Half of Northeast Quarter-Section	40
N½E½NW	North Half of East Half of Northwest Quarter-Section	40
N½E½SE	North Half of East Half of Southeast Quarter-Section	40
N½E½SW	North Half of East Half of Southwest Quarter-Section	40
N½N½	North Half of North Half-Section	160
N½NE	North Half of Northeast Quarter-Section	80
N½NENE	North Half of Northeast Quarter of Northeast Quarter-Section	20
N½NENW	North Half of Northeast Quarter of Northwest Quarter-Section	20
N½NESE	North Half of Northeast Quarter of Southeast Quarter-Section	20
N½NESW	North Half of Northeast Quarter of Southwest Quarter-Section	20
N½NW	North Half of Northwest Quarter-Section	80
N½NWNE	North Half of Northwest Quarter of Northeast Quarter-Section	20
N½NWNW	North Half of Northwest Quarter of Northwest Quarter-Section	20
N½NWSE	North Half of Northwest Quarter of Southeast Quarter-Section	20
N½NWSW	North Half of Northwest Quarter of Southwest Quarter-Section	20
N½S½	North Half of South Half-Section	160
N½SE	North Half of Southeast Quarter-Section	80
N½SENE	North Half of Southeast Quarter of Northeast Quarter-Section	20
N½SENW	North Half of Southeast Quarter of Northwest Quarter-Section	20
N½SESE	North Half of Southeast Quarter of Southeast Quarter-Section	20

Section Part	Description	Acres
N½SESW	North Half of Southeast Quarter of Southwest Quarter-Section	20
N½SESW	North Half of Southeast Quarter of Southwest Quarter-Section	20
N½SW	North Half of Southwest Quarter-Section	80
N½SWNE	North Half of Southwest Quarter of Northeast Quarter-Section	20
N½SWNW	North Half of Southwest Quarter of Northwest Quarter-Section	20
N½SWSE	North Half of Southwest Quarter of Southeast Quarter-Section	20
N½SWSE	North Half of Southwest Quarter of Southeast Quarter-Section	20
N½SWSW	North Half of Southwest Quarter of Southwest Quarter-Section	20
N½W½NW	North Half of West Half of Northwest Quarter-Section	40
N½W½SE	North Half of West Half of Southeast Quarter-Section	40
N½W½SW	North Half of West Half of Southwest Quarter-Section	40
NE	Northeast Quarter-Section	160
NEN½	Northeast Quarter of North Half-Section	80
NENE	Northeast Quarter of Northeast Quarter-Section	40
NENENE	Northeast Quarter of Northeast Quarter of Northeast Quarter	10
NENENW	Northeast Quarter of Northeast Quarter of Northwest Quarter	10
NENESE	Northeast Quarter of Northeast Quarter of Southeast Quarter	10
NENESW	Northeast Quarter of Northeast Quarter of Southwest Quarter	10
NENW	Northeast Quarter of Northwest Quarter-Section	40
NENWNE	Northeast Quarter of Northwest Quarter of Northeast Quarter	10
NENWNW	Northeast Quarter of Northwest Quarter of Northwest Quarter	10
NENWSE	Northeast Quarter of Northwest Quarter of Southeast Quarter	10
NENWSW	Northeast Quarter of Northwest Quarter of Southwest Quarter	10
NESE	Northeast Quarter of Southeast Quarter-Section	40
NESENE	Northeast Quarter of Southeast Quarter of Northeast Quarter	10
NESENW	Northeast Quarter of Southeast Quarter of Northwest Quarter	10
NESESE	Northeast Quarter of Southeast Quarter of Southeast Quarter	10
NESESW	Northeast Quarter of Southeast Quarter of Southwest Quarter	10
NESW	Northeast Quarter of Southwest Quarter-Section	40
NESWNE	Northeast Quarter of Southwest Quarter of Northeast Quarter	10
NESWNW	Northeast Quarter of Southwest Quarter of Northwest Quarter	10
NESWSE	Northeast Quarter of Southwest Quarter of Southeast Quarter	10
NESWSW	Northeast Quarter of Southwest Quarter of Southwest Quarter	10
NW	Northwest Quarter-Section	160
NWE½	Northwest Quarter of Eastern Half-Section	80
NWN½	Northwest Quarter of North Half-Section	80
NWNE	Northwest Quarter of Northeast Quarter-Section	40
NWNENE	Northwest Quarter of Northeast Quarter of Northeast Quarter	10
NWNENW	Northwest Quarter of Northeast Quarter of Northwest Quarter	10
NWNESE	Northwest Quarter of Northeast Quarter of Southeast Quarter	10
NWNESW	Northwest Quarter of Northeast Quarter of Southwest Quarter	10
NWNW	Northwest Quarter of Northwest Quarter-Section	40
NWNWNE	Northwest Quarter of Northwest Quarter of Northeast Quarter	10
NWNWNW	Northwest Quarter of Northwest Quarter of Northwest Quarter	10
NWNWSE	Northwest Quarter of Northwest Quarter of Southeast Quarter	10
NWNWSW	Northwest Quarter of Northwest Quarter of Southwest Quarter	10
NWSE	Northwest Quarter of Southeast Quarter-Section	40
NWSENE	Northwest Quarter of Southeast Quarter of Northeast Quarter	10
NWSENW	Northwest Quarter of Southeast Quarter of Northwest Quarter	10
NWSESE	Northwest Quarter of Southeast Quarter of Southeast Quarter	10
NWSESW	Northwest Quarter of Southeast Quarter of Southwest Quarter	10
NWSW	Northwest Quarter of Southwest Quarter-Section	40
NWSWNE	Northwest Quarter of Southwest Quarter of Northeast Quarter	10
NWSWNW	Northwest Quarter of Southwest Quarter of Northwest Quarter	10
NWSWSE	Northwest Quarter of Southwest Quarter of Southeast Quarter	10
NWSWSW	Northwest Quarter of Southwest Quarter of Southwest Quarter	10
S½	South Half-Section	320
S½E½NE	South Half of East Half of Northeast Quarter-Section	40
S½E½NW	South Half of East Half of Northwest Quarter-Section	40
S½E½SE	South Half of East Half of Southeast Quarter-Section	40

Section Part	Description	Acres
S½E½SW	South Half of East Half of Southwest Quarter-Section	40
S½N½	South Half of North Half-Section	160
S½NE	South Half of Northeast Quarter-Section	80
S½NENE	South Half of Northeast Quarter of Northeast Quarter-Section	20
S½NENW	South Half of Northeast Quarter of Northwest Quarter-Section	20
S½NESE	South Half of Northeast Quarter of Southeast Quarter-Section	20
S½NESW	South Half of Northeast Quarter of Southwest Quarter-Section	20
S½NW	South Half of Northwest Quarter-Section	80
S½NWNE	South Half of Northwest Quarter of Northeast Quarter-Section	20
S½NWNW	South Half of Northwest Quarter of Northwest Quarter-Section	20
S½NWSE	South Half of Northwest Quarter of Southeast Quarter-Section	20
S½NWSW	South Half of Northwest Quarter of Southwest Quarter-Section	20
S½S½	South Half of South Half-Section	160
S½SE	South Half of Southeast Quarter-Section	80
S½SENE	South Half of Southeast Quarter of Northeast Quarter-Section	20
S½SENW	South Half of Southeast Quarter of Northwest Quarter-Section	20
S½SESE	South Half of Southeast Quarter of Southeast Quarter-Section	20
S½SESW	South Half of Southeast Quarter of Southeast Quarter-Section	20
S½SESW	South Half of Southeast Quarter of Southwest Quarter-Section	20
S½SW	South Half of Southwest Quarter-Section	80
S½SWNE	South Half of Southwest Quarter of Northeast Quarter-Section	20
S½SWNW	South Half of Southwest Quarter of Northwest Quarter-Section	20
S½SWSE	South Half of Southwest Quarter of Southeast Quarter-Section	20
S½SWSE	South Half of Southwest Quarter of Southeast Quarter-Section	20
S½SWSW	South Half of Southwest Quarter of Southwest Quarter-Section	20
S½W½NE	South Half of West Half of Northeast Quarter-Section	40
S½W½NW	South Half of West Half of Northwest Quarter-Section	40
S½W½SE	South Half of West Half of Southeast Quarter-Section	40
S½W½SW	South Half of West Half of Southwest Quarter-Section	40
SE	Southeast Quarter Section	160
SEN½	Southeast Quarter of North Half-Section	80
SENE	Southeast Quarter of Northeast Quarter-Section	40
SENENE	Southeast Quarter of Northeast Quarter of Northeast Quarter	10
SENENW	Southeast Quarter of Northeast Quarter of Northwest Quarter	10
SENESE	Southeast Quarter of Northeast Quarter of Southeast Quarter	10
SENESW	Southeast Quarter of Northeast Quarter of Southwest Quarter	10
SENW	Southeast Quarter of Northwest Quarter-Section	40
SENWNE	Southeast Quarter of Northwest Quarter of Northeast Quarter	10
SENWNW	Southeast Quarter of Northwest Quarter of Northwest Quarter	10
SENWSE	Souteast Quarter of Northwest Quarter of Southeast Quarter	10
SENWSW	Southeast Quarter of Northwest Quarter of Southwest Quarter	10
SESE	Southeast Quarter of Southeast Quarter-Section	40
SESENE	SoutheastQuarter of Southeast Quarter of Northeast Quarter	10
SESENW	Southeast Quarter of Southeast Quarter of Northwest Quarter	10
SESESE	Southeast Quarter of Southeast Quarter of Southeast Quarter	10
SESESW	Southeast Quarter of Southeast Quarter of Southwest Quarter	10
SESW	Southeast Quarter of Southwest Quarter-Section	40
SESWNE	Southeast Quarter of Southwest Quarter of Northeast Quarter	10
SESWNW	Southeast Quarter of Southwest Quarter of Northwest Quarter	10
SESWSE	Southeast Quarter of Southwest Quarter of Southeast Quarter	10
SESWSW	Southeast Quarter of Southwest Quarter of Southwest Quarter	10
SW	Southwest Quarter-Section	160
SWNE	Southwest Quarter of Northeast Quarter-Section	40
SWNENE	Southwest Quarter of Northeast Quarter of Northeast Quarter	10
SWNENW	Southwest Quarter of Northeast Quarter of Northwest Quarter	10
SWNESE	Southwest Quarter of Northeast Quarter of Southeast Quarter	10
SWNESW	Southwest Quarter of Northeast Quarter of Southwest Quarter	10
SWNW	Southwest Quarter of Northwest Quarter-Section	40
SWNWNE	Southwest Quarter of Northwest Quarter of Northeast Quarter	10
SWNWNW	Southwest Quarter of Northwest Quarter of Northwest Quarter	10

Section Part	Description	Acres
SWNWSE	Southwest Quarter of Northwest Quarter of Southeast Quarter	10
SWNWSW	Southwest Quarter of Northwest Quarter of Southwest Quarter	10
SWSE	Southwest Quarter of Southeast Quarter-Section	40
SWSENE	Southwest Quarter of Southeast Quarter of Northeast Quarter	10
SWSENW	Southwest Quarter of Southeast Quarter of Northwest Quarter	10
SWSESE	Southwest Quarter of Southeast Quarter of Southeast Quarter	10
SWSESW	Southwest Quarter of Southeast Quarter of Southwest Quarter	10
SWSW	Southwest Quarter of Southwest Quarter-Section	40
SWSWNE	Southwest Quarter of Southwest Quarter of Northeast Quarter	10
SWSWNW	Southwest Quarter of Southwest Quarter of Northwest Quarter	10
SWSWSE	Southwest Quarter of Southwest Quarter of Southeast Quarter	10
SWSWSW	Southwest Quarter of Southwest Quarter of Southwest Quarter	10
W½	West Half-Section	320
W½E½	West Half of East Half-Section	160
W½N½	West Half of North Half-Section (same as NW)	160
W½NE	West Half of Northeast Quarter	80
W½NENE	West Half of Northeast Quarter of Northeast Quarter-Section	20
W½NENW	West Half of Northeast Quarter of Northwest Quarter-Section	20
W½NESE	West Half of Northeast Quarter of Southeast Quarter-Section	20
W½NESW	West Half of Northeast Quarter of Southwest Quarter-Section	20
W½NW	West Half of Northwest Quarter-Section	80
W½NWNE	West Half of Northwest Quarter of Northeast Quarter-Section	20
W½NWNW	West Half of Northwest Quarter of Northwest Quarter-Section	20
W½NWSE	West Half of Northwest Quarter of Southeast Quarter-Section	20
W½NWSW	West Half of Northwest Quarter of Southwest Quarter-Section	20
W½S½	West Half of South Half-Section	160
W½SE	West Half of Southeast Quarter-Section	80
W½SENE	West Half of Southeast Quarter of Northeast Quarter-Section	20
W½SENW	West Half of Southeast Quarter of Northwest Quarter-Section	20
W½SESE	West Half of Southeast Quarter of Southeast Quarter-Section	20
W½SESW	West Half of Southeast Quarter of Southwest Quarter-Section	20
W½SW	West Half of Southwest Quarter-Section	80
W½SWNE	West Half of Southwest Quarter of Northeast Quarter-Section	20
W½SWNW	West Half of Southwest Quarter of Northwest Quarter-Section	20
W½SWSE	West Half of Southwest Quarter of Southeast Quarter-Section	20
W½SWSW	West Half of Southwest Quarter of Southwest Quarter-Section	20
W½W½	West Half of West Half-Section	160

Appendix C - Multi-Patentee Groups

The following index presents groups of people who jointly received patents in Jones County, Mississippi. The Group Numbers are used in the Patent Maps and their Indexes so that you may then turn to this Appendix in order to identify all the members of the each buying group.

Group Number 1
ACKENHAUSEN, William; NORDMAN, John

Group Number 2
BARLOW, Henry; BARLOW, Norwell

Group Number 3
BIRKETT, Thomas; MCPHERSON, William;
MCPHERSON, Alexander; MCPHERSON, Martin;
MCPHERSON, Edward

Group Number 4
BOOTH, Matilda; HARRING, Matilda

Group Number 5
BRYANT, Caroline; BRYANT, Lewis

Group Number 6
BRYANT, Frances V; WHEELER, Frances V

Group Number 7
BYNUM, Benjamin; BYNUM, William

Group Number 8
COLLEY, Thomas S; WARNER, Leslie

Group Number 9
DEAVENPORT, Laura L; DEAVENPORT, Calvin A

Group Number 10
DENT, Sarah; DENT, Peter

Group Number 11
EVANS, Josiah; COPELAND, Moses

Group Number 12
FAIRCHILD, Sarah E; FAIRCHILD, Robert J

Group Number 13
GUNTER, Fannie F; DUCKWORTH, Fannie F;
DUCKWORTH, William B

Group Number 14
GUNTER, Mary S; MCGILL, Mary S

Group Number 15
GUNTER, Sarah R; GUNTER, Allen

Group Number 16
HAIGLER, Jane; HAIGLER, Frank

Group Number 17
HARGROVE, Hardy; FERGUSON, John

Group Number 18
HENSARLING, Catherine E; ODOM, Catherine E

Group Number 19
HERRINGTON, Jordan A; FAIRCHILD, William A

Group Number 20
HOLIFIELD, Mary T; HOLIFIELD, Mark

Group Number 21
KAMPER, John; SCOTT, Edward

Group Number 22
LARRE, Oscar Dugas; MATTREN, Joel

Group Number 23
LYNES, Sarah; LYNES, Albert G

Group Number 24
MCCALLUM, Matilda; MCCALLUM, March

Group Number 25
MCCRANEY, Mary D; BRYANT, Mary D

Group Number 26
MCGAHEY, Otto; EZELL, Hugh F; HOLT, Thomas B

Group Number 27
MCPHERSON, William; MCPHERSON, Alexander;
MCPHERSON, Martin J; MCPHERSON, Edward G

Group Number 28
MURRAY, Delpha M; MURRAY, W W

Group Number 29
MYERS, John W; MYERS, Levi; STEVENS, William;
DRAUGHN, Rufus T

Group Number 30
MYERS, John W; STEVENS, William; MYERS, Levi;
DRAUGHN, Rufus

Group Number 31
MYRICK, John; GLOVER, David

Group Number 32
NALL, Sarah A; NALL, David J

Group Number 33
PARKER, John; SCRIVENER, Jesse

Group Number 34
PITTS, Polly; PITTS, Henry

Group Number 35
QUANCE, Richard; QUANCE, Samuel H

Group Number 36
RAINEY, Sarah A; RAINEY, Appleton

Group Number 37
SMITH, Laura; SMITH, Abram

Group Number 38
STRICKLAND, Simeon; COLLINS, Stacy

Group Number 39
SYMES, James E; SYMES, George B; SYMES, Frank J

Group Number 40
THOMAS, John; BEAVERS, Martin

Group Number 41
VAUGHAN, Coleman C; JOHNSON, William E

Group Number 42
VICK, Clyde H; VICK, Ada Lowry

Group Number 43
WALLACE, Della; CRANFORD, Della; CRANFORD, John W

Group Number 44
WALTERS, Alafair; LOWE, Alafair

Group Number 45
WALTERS, Laura; MILLER, Laura

Group Number 46
WALTERS, Leacy; BUSH, Leacy

Group Number 47
WATSON, Sarah; ADCOX, Sarah

Group Number 48
WOODARD, Dicy; WOODARD, Ira

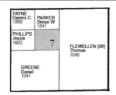

Extra! Extra! (about our Indexes)

We purposefully do not have an all-name index in the back of this volume so that our readers do not miss one of the best uses of this book: finding misspelled names among more specialized indexes.

Without repeating the text of our "How-to" chapter, we have nonetheless tried to assist our more anxious researchers by delivering a short-cut to the two county-wide Surname Indexes, the second of which will lead you to all-name indexes for each Congressional Township mapped in this volume :

Surname Index (whole county, with number of parcels mapped) ....page 18
Surname Index (township by township) ....just following

For your convenience, the "How To Use this Book" Chart on page 2 is repeated on the reverse of this page.

We should be releasing new titles every week for the foreseeable future. We urge you to write, fax, call, or email us any time for a current list of titles. Of course, our web-page will always have the most current information about current and upcoming books.

Arphax Publishing Co.
2210 Research Park Blvd.
Norman, Oklahoma 73069
(800) 681-5298 toll-free
(405) 366-6181 local
(405) 366-8184 fax
info@arphax.com

www.arphax.com

How to Use This Book - A Graphical Summary

Part I
"The Big Picture"

Map A ▸ *Counties in the State*
Map B ▸ *Surrounding Counties*
Map C ▸ *Congressional Townships (Map Groups) in the County*
Map D ▸ *Cities & Towns in the County*
Map E ▸ *Cemeteries in the County*
Surnames in the County ▸ *Number of Land-Parcels for Each Surname*
Surname/Township Index ▸ *Directs you to Township Map Groups in Part II*

The *Surname/Township Index* can direct you to any number of **Township Map Groups**

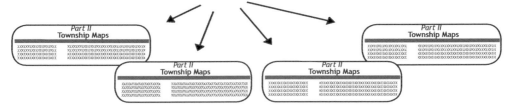

Part II
Township Map Groups
(1 for each Township in the County)

Each Township Map Group contains all four of of the following tools . . .

Land Patent Index ▸ *Every-name Index of Patents Mapped in this Township*
Land Patent Map ▸ *Map of Patents as listed in above Index*
Road Map ▸ *Map of Roads, City-centers, and Cemeteries in the Township*
Historical Map ▸ *Map of Railroads, Lakes, Rivers, Creeks, City-Centers, and Cemeteries*

Appendices

Appendix A ▸ *Congressional Authority enabling Patents within our Maps*
Appendix B ▸ *Section-Parts / Aliquot Parts (a comprehensive list)*
Appendix C ▸ *Multi-patentee Groups (Individuals within Buying Groups)*

Made in the USA
Lexington, KY
10 September 2016